Also by Steve Morgan

A Standard Religiously Irrelevant Version (S.R.I.V) Twist of Fate Edition
Wokeless Dictionary (A Wicked Wordbook)
Deconstructing Endtime Delusions (A study of Christian Endtimes)

Table of Contents

Deconstructing Endtime Delusions (A study of Christian Endtimes) ... 1

Front Pages: 12

Introduction: 36

Nail One: 74

Nail Two: 106

Nail Three: 118

Nail Four: 134

Nail Five: 175

Nail Six: 180

Nail Seven: 193

Vacating this blue marble: 208

Nail Eight: 219

Nail Nine: 249

Nail Ten: 354

Nail Eleven: 364

Nail Twelve: 381

Nail Thirteen: 398

Nail Fourteen: 436

Nail Fifteen: 462

Bibliography: 475

Appendix One: 499

Appendix Two: 517
Appendix Three: 526

STEVE MORGAN

DECONSTRUCTING ENDTIME DELUSIONS

A STUDY OF CHRISTIAN ENDTIMES

STEVE MORGAN

Deconstructing Endtime Delusions

A study of Christian Endtimes

Steve Morgan

DECONSTRUCTING ENDTIME DELUSIONS

ON ALL HANDS 'TIS ADMITTED that the Christian religion is a matter of most serious importance: it is so, if it be truth, because in that truth a law of faith and conduct, measuring out to us a propriety of sentiment and action, which would otherwise not be incumbent upon us, is propounded to our observance in this life; and eternal consequences of happiness or of misery, are at issue upon our observance or neglect of that law...

...to be in error one's self, is a misfortune; and if it be such an error as mightily affects our peace of mind, it is a very grievous misfortune; to be the cause of error to others... deceiving them ourselves, ...is a crime... a most barbarous wrong done to our brother man; it is the kind of wrong, which we should most justly, and keenly resent, could we be sensible of its being put upon ourselves.

Prolegomena: Reverend Robert Taylor, "The Diegesis"

STEVE MORGAN

"One story is good, until another is told"

Aesop's Fables.

"In matters of religion it is very easy to deceive a man, and very hard to undeceive him."

Pierre Bayle. Dictionary, 1697 - The Christ Scandal: Tony Bushby

---

"It is wrong always, everywhere, and for anyone, to believe anything upon insufficient evidence."

W. K. Clifford C. Grayling, The God Argument

"Truth is such a rare quality so seldom met in this civilization (sic) of fraud, that it is never received freely, but must fight its way into the world."

Professor Hilton Hotema - The Papal Billions

"Regardless of how many people may be disturbed, there is no religion superior to truth."

The Papal Billions

"All truth passes through three stages: first, it is ridiculed; second, it is violently opposed; and third, it is accepted as self-evident."

The lords of Avaris - David Rohl.

DECONSTRUCTING ENDTIME DELUSIONS

"A worshipper of Truth fears no destruction of false gods, nor any facts that may cause him to throw over treasured superstitions. He is willing to prove all things and hold fast to that which is true."

The Mistakes of Jesus

"It is part of your journey to encounter events that shatter your preconceptions of reality; were that not to occur, you could not expand your awareness..."

Kalika (Ancient Egyptian Mystic)

Cited in "Egyptian Mysticism..." - M. G. Hawkin

"If we cling to belief in God, we cannot likewise have faith, since faith is not clinging but letting go."

Wisdom of Insecurity

"When you listen to one person, you will gain opinion, when you listen to many you can form your own."

Paul Duncan - The God Myth

"Belief in Myths allows the comfort of opinion without the discomfort of thought."

John F. Kennedy

STEVE MORGAN

"To subscribe to any belief is to exclude all other possibilities. We should consider every possibility, avoid belief, and accept only hard facts."

John Keel

"...truth is a composite of different and complementary pieces of a puzzle"

Moustafa Gadalla. The Ancient Egyptian Roots of Christianity.

"Extraordinary claims require extraordinary Evidence"

Carl Sagan

"To be conscious that you are ignorant is a great step to knowledge."

Benjamin Disraeli, Sybil (1845)

"The real voyage of discovery consists not in seeking new landscapes, but in having new eyes."

Marcel Proust, cited by - Ziony Zevit.

"It is the Mark of an educated mind to entertain a thought without accepting it"

Aristotle

DECONSTRUCTING ENDTIME DELUSIONS

DEDICATED: - TO THE whip-smart.

Thank you for purchasing this book.

This compendia of essays are dedicated to all humanity. To the steadfast who are striving to enliven, and awaken our fellows to a higher state of consciousness. Whether the chosen path to this is through religion, scientific advance, esoteric practices, and ritual, brain entrainment, Stoicism or other: all must be practiced with pure benevolence of intent. For, there is already enough suffering in life that is fragmentary, schismatic, and ruction. Our goal therefore is to become a riant individual. Ensconced in the collective Universality of oneness. Humanity is most certainly a species capable, and yearning for the attainment of such a higher plane - of oneness. But, is at present wrestling with itself - in a state of fragmentary confusion and discord. Might the following pages assist, even so slightly, in this goal of Universal oneness becoming a piquant reality.

Though the journey may be rough, jagged, and often set on a narrow avenue. The author encourages all readers to stay the path. Knowing the journey is not the disturbance, but your perception and reactionary thoughts of the journey.

May the reading of the forthcoming material serve you well.

STEVE MORGAN

All Rights Reserved:

A catalogue record for this title is available

from the National Library of Australia.

ISBN: 9780645910544 (ebk)

ISBN: 9780645910551 (pbk)

Cover Image and design, [Dark Fantasy] Canvar free. (Artist unknown)

www.canvar.com.au[1]

Typeset and design by Draft2Digital

Published with assistance of Draft2Digital

www.draft2digital.com[2]

---

1. http://www.canvar.com.au
2. http://www.draft2digital.com

DECONSTRUCTING ENDTIME DELUSIONS

Copyright:

All Rights Reserved:

The text of this study may be quoted (in written, visual, or electronic form) provided those quotes are less than, and inclusive of ten per cent of the entire publication without express written permission of the publisher. Providing that the texts quoted, or used do not amount to a complete section of the book nor do the quoted text account for 50 percent or more of the total text of the work in which they are quoted.

Steve Morgan reserves the right to be named under the Copyright act of 1988, as the sole author and composer and owner of the intellectual rights of this study.

Copyright © 2012-2019; 2020-2023 Steve Morgan

Sacred' works consulted:

– LOGOS BIBLE SYSTEMS® (Standard and Reverse- Interlinear Bibles: electronic editions)

– The Judaeo-Christian Bible Fully Translated, by William Harwood. Ebook and hardcopy editions.

– The Original New Testament, by Hugh J. Schonfield.

– A NEW NEW TESTAMENT: A Bible for the Twenty-first Century Combining Traditional and Newly Discovered Texts. By Hal Taussig.

–Permission granted for quotations from The Christ Conspiracy, by Acharya S. (D M Murdock.)

Due care has been undertaken by the author of this book to not violate willingly any legalities surrounding the plagiarising of intellectual property and other written materials consulted. These were carefully noted and recorded. Never has it been a purpose to knowingly violate a cited author's work, or intellectual property. The intent has always been to knit a growing understanding with the materials from which has been learnt. Some citations are from works in the public domain. Logos sources may also be from the Public Domain.

DECONSTRUCTING ENDTIME DELUSIONS

deconstruct [diːk(ə)nˈstrʌkt]

: an analytical examination of a theory (or theories),

often in order to reveal its inadequacy

---

belief |biˈlēf|

:an acceptance that a statement is true or that something exists

- something one accepts as true or real; a firmly held opinion or conviction

[In the heart of belief is a 'lie']

Logos Bible Software 10 (basic) Copyright, 2000 - 2019 FaithLife Corporation

Licensed to: Steve Morgan

Front Pages:

BRITISH-AMERICAN HUMORIST, and anthropologist Ashley Montagu once quipped; "the Good Book, is one of the most remarkable euphemisms ever coined." It was the Free thinker, and apologist for agnosticism Robert G. Ingersoll who also insightfully commented: "Somebody should tell the truth about the Bible." I thought: as true as these statements are, such declarations might be expanded to include an articulation of apology for religious end times. These pages offer readers my testimony; enouncing a perspective of the standard religious view of End Times, my take on this Good Book – with a twist! Some readers may call this study a dysphemism, as it is intended to counteract the notion of the Bible being the 'Good book' by highlighting several deafening oddities; of doom and gloom scenarios so often voiced by all sides of society. Fed up with what seemed the brainwashing of nonsense I sat down to scribble my thoughts and study conclusions about the religiously, Christian concept of end time. Peering behind the veil; it seemed that our minds are scrambled. We have surely inverted reason and logic. There does not seem to be any room for dianoetic thought for the plethora of junk mail we see, read, and hear daily. Esp., the junk mail from religious doomsayers. Those inspired to write and publish their version of an apocalyptic end time. Doomsayers everywhere have hijacked our sensibilities. From the 'anthropogenic global warming' scaremonger shouting from the rooftop our apparent doom; shutting down viable industries while humiliating opposers of their cause. To the countless, religiously 'inspired' voices announcing a dire warning with the latest and most 'up-to-date' religious end time propaganda. No wonder our heads are stuck on the spin-cycle! The idea behind writing this tome was to inform readers with an apology of no regret following Christian friends and others who quickly withdrew precursory support; specifically when it was proposed there should be an investigation into why the believing community was so resolute regarding certain aniconic

DECONSTRUCTING ENDTIME DELUSIONS

ecclesiastical teachings. Explicitly, those that sprang from and played into an end time Apocalypse hypothesis. The continuing years spent in research, and writing meant that this investigation actively expanded the further practical, lucid answers were sought to the countless questions that study interests raised. Many conclusions surprised this author, and so are likely to gob-smack an audience also. It is not technically a monograph of what a reader might assume as a conventional study of the Christian religion, or various end-time presumptions. No apology. If you are hoping to read yet another end time tome from the usual speculative believing perspective, you may be disappointed. You may even be enraged at several conclusions drawn in the assorted studies conducted. Therefore feel justified in casting me a heretic. A label that would be welcomed. For, what is a recusant but one who refuses the party line; one who does not feel the need to submit to the idea that all studies must comply with the accepted ethos, and so, suffers the effects of discovering the acceptability – not the validity – of an unusual, or unexpected finding. There are plenty of the usual religiously indoctrinated books on the market from which to choose, if these are your leaning. This is not one of them, as there is no intent to tow the current religious zeitgeist and conventional procedures of religious enquiry. All which subjectively upholds the religious premise of the scriptures. Particularly those texts espousing an apocalyptic end time. If you are someone open to different ways of viewing Christian credenda; if you are open to perspectives that are unlikely taught by a believing institution; if you are curious about why humans believe, observe, and guess certain favoured end time practices; if you have ever wondered from where, or just how true certain beliefs are, then welcome aboard. Strap yourself in for an unconventional journey.

This investigation began by surveying the countless end–time dogmas and sacred cows of modern christianity. Disappointingly, a perusal of the current array of Christian end-time materials available in the marketplace, it was noticed most of those were simply unsatisfactory. Offering readers little else than the customary vapid and jejune spiritualised bias; that the world will soon witness deity-ordained extreme disaster. Or, there will in the not-too-distant-future be Apocalypse; a revealing of certain strange, mystical, and demonically inspired monsters. Apocalyptically inspired books on the marketplace focus their efforts primarily on fear-porn; that there are in the wings of history, demonically inspired chimeras waiting to burst upon the scene. These will likely wipe out most of the human race, not withstanding a climatic disaster beating them. Unless individuals comply and accept the invitation of 'preservation and deliverance' offered by a favoured God-man and some supreme deity figure. Such usual superordinate tomes, churned out by oxymoronic 'Christian' publishing houses are in essence only advocating more of that same hoary and weathered propaganda. Each year, the list and topics Christian end–time authors write seems to grow exponentially; Apocalypse and a looming end-time are big business. No one should be all too surprised to identify the growing plethora of books and 'teachings' that are available on platforms like several popular online media sources and retailers; online retailers for instance sports no less than four hundred pages of titles of Apocalypse, End of Days, End times. Few of the religious tomes written in this genre offer anything other than summations of a regurgitated theological position; an attitude the author has concocted from their own imagination or been taught in seminary, or by their churches. An example is offered by my brief descriptions below of a book by Derek Gilbert, and my study of Rob Skiba's book, "Babylon Rising" later in this investigation (Nail Nine). In likelihood, this study won't be so parochial or self-righteous as other publications focussed on Christian end-time topics. This is a journey of discovery, having attempted to attack this investigation from an ecumenical perspective. Readers will discover in these pages that the subjects of end-times, and other Christian/religious assumptions are not new to the Twentieth, or Twenty-first Century. Similar have been voiced for millennia during certain periods that populations felt were becoming extreme. It was decided then, a study of Christian end-times, Apocalypse, as with other relatable topics could be better understood by seeing these through an interconnected view of the whole. Instead of the usual symptomatic/Band-Aid approach of a dull Christian perspective that offered an audience little but a fearsome, and frankly depressing picture of the future. Marcel Proust once stated, "The real voyage of discovery consists not in seeking new landscapes, but in having new eyes." To have 'new eyes' into a topic is to fundamentally be politically incorrect. To see and understand our beliefs and understandings of certain topics, themes, and connected matters by "...looking outward to the world to gain understanding via the senses, concept formation, and logic." New eyes were sought through an outward peering. Not being satisfied with the explanations offered by christianity to the countless quandaries viewed in many religious explanations of end-time subjects. It was felt that there must be a turning to logic and reasoning. Specifically, by looking into the features and products of knowledge, reality, and existence. Having understood

> "[Such a] Philosophy is not so much about coming up with the answers to fundamental questions as it is about the process of trying to find these answers, using reasoning rather than accepting without question conventional views or traditional authority... [this type of] philosophy ...shapes everything we do. Our larger outlook on the world is usually the most interesting and important thing about us, expressing "our more or less dumb sense of what life honestly and deeply means," as William James wrote in Pragmatism."[i]

In this sense, the aim is to offer an analysis that although may not be all that new; rather is my meagre offering of answers to many questions that were raised. Questions that piqued an interest as the subject of end-times was explored. Using my understanding, knowledge, and life experiences of having been raised in the Christian faith. Confidently, these musings are seen as contributing to a reasoned hypothesis of the criticisms of Christian end-time ideas studied. "New ideas emerge through discussion and the examination, analysis, and criticism of other people's ideas."[ii] The following studies are the result of an attempt to engage, discuss, and introduce to readers. My examinations and analysis of questions met throughout this investigation. Instead of accepting the conventional views offered by the religious, the position was that we should always seek answers by an outward looking to the wider-world. To do this many subjects and fields of study was conducted. As a former Christian there is an understanding there are at least two types of believer. There are the spiritualists; who are largely anti-reason, and anti-reality when it comes to their sacred matters. Everything is viewed and interpreted through a sensationalist black and white spiritual prism. These are the fundamentalists. Second, there are those who assume spirituality, while at the same time do easily not so dismiss logic and reason. Many of whom fall into the category of Evangelical. Andy Clarkson in his treaties "The Impact Of Aristotle on Christian, Islamic, and Jewish Cultures," highlights this difference. Directing thoughts to a realisation there are the Augustinian and Aquinas types of christianity. The Augustinian Christian loves to peer upward, doesn't hold to an idea of 'reason or logic', but are the mentioned spiritualists who make a great song and dance about revelations from their deity. Clarkson calls this the 'Dark Ages.' Secondly, the Aquinas type believer is kind to more reserved, reasoning their way through their faith. "Scepticism is the first step to truth." Once commented French philosopher, and writer Denis Diderot. A truth that is worthy of acknowledging. As a novice of the Stoic philosophies, and skeptic, I was compelled to choose to diversify and broaden my foci in the hope of stumbling upon verifiable truth that offers readers something atypical; something that might allow or offer readers a chance to see Christian subjects and themes of end–times with 'new' eyes. I was not after disseminating any topic from the Augustinian 'upward/ultra-spiritualised' looking perspective. Rather, seeking to enhance something like an Aquinas version. Of reason, and logic in a way that I identify is not available today. Throughout this process, I pursued to understand end-time concepts from as near as possible to a potential original– zero point. That is, the origin, the Genesis if you like to an idea or theme. Often-times viewing something from or as close as possible to its origin affects interpretation and therefore perspective. Aesop's Fables summed this concept nicely: "One Story is good, Until another is told." Throughout, I endeavour to offer readers another story of the subjects examined. Hal Taussig enlightens us further to the closing remarks to his preliminary commentary to The Gospel of Thomas. In this gospel the alleged God-man Jesus illumines the importance of deciphering a beginning:

DECONSTRUCTING ENDTIME DELUSIONS

> **It is not the End of the World you need to Concentrate on. It's the Beginning:** Much of early Christian literature pays attention to the impending end of the world. Images of cataclysmic destruction are found in everything from the Gospel of Matthew to the Revelation to John. The Gospel of Thomas not only ignores all such images but explicitly challenges the notion of the end of the world. In Thomas 18, when Jesus is asked by his disciples when the end will come, he answers: Have you discovered the beginning that you ask about the end? For, in the place where the beginning is, there the end will be. Blessed is the one who takes a stand in the beginning. That one will know the end.[iii]

The plethora of books written by Christian authors should also follow suit. Many of these materials sadly however are attentive only to an impending and looming disaster, they call an end-time. Yet, in agreement to discover the end, you must ask regarding the beginning. In pursuit; therefore, to possible origins to any proposed end-time theory questioned in these studies, meant there had to be a broadening of efforts. Realising, that certain questions demanded and required exploration and research into numerous fields of pedagogic discipline. It was accepted early in this investigation there was a need to delve into areas many believers, and secular audiences likely presumed would not associate with an examination of religious proposals of end-time disaster; – the Cognitive Sciences and Evolution of Religion; The Anthropology of Religion, and a very broad spectrum of other scientific, academic, and non-religious disciplines. Including subjects that some would find quasi disciplines, like cryptozoology or, certain topics may seem too bookish. Including subjects of occult, and the very recent science of Humanology®.[iv]

Spiritual convictions vs. symbolism:

WHILE STUDYING FOR this project it was realised by quiddity, that all Christian sacred texts are symbolic. Intellectually we know this to be true. But, too often our feelings and having a certain 'faith' reinterprets and overrides intellectual rationality. It is then the feeling and 'faith' base that is relied upon. Regarding symbols, we habitually know from the earliest time we create allegories to represent what we see. These symbols do not however exactly define the information we either see or read. To this, Carl Purcell correctly highlights,

> "We create symbols for everything. [Which] is a method for compressing large amounts of information into smaller packages... The brain also creates symbols for the things we see, acting as shorthand versions. They are not meant to be a likeness of the item."[v]

The take-home point is that symbols represent likenesses; not actual items. This is an important fact to note. Just as the symbols of modern life, such as a road sign, clothing label, or even a graffito tag scrawled on a wall; we each know these are but representative. Yet, religious symbology is more highly regarded, and likely understood as not only a representation, but a reality. Comprehending this, it was soon realised it was important to delve into the topic of literary and religious Symbolism and Mythology. Surprisingly, studies in symbolism lead to my summation that there is much truth to be gained if we'd only choose, or be trained to view and understand religious myths and the countless ideologies that seem to spring from them. Not in a literal sense, as many religionists assume, but through the prism of symbol. As examples and representations of that which is written. A consequence of this. These studies have developed from many branches, from which many more questions have arisen and I guess, much <fruit> has potentially ripened.[vi] Many topics explored or mentioned may be seen as irreconcilable to my over–all concerns of Christian end–times. Given time it is hoped a correlation becomes evident. Though I have sought to attend to the topics and subjects commented upon from a vastly different angle than what countless others have. It is yet trusted this will prove enlightening to all readers. Just as it was for this author. As one finds with many books covering this same genre, "throughout these pages you will find fact, history, speculation, and theory."[vii] Broadening the scope of my research efforts into many academic fields and irreligious disciplines, and the questions and queries raised has ideally uncovered much that is lucid erroneous popular religious end–time matters. By

DECONSTRUCTING ENDTIME DELUSIONS

breaching the confines of theological parameters and including insights by many academic secular fields. This work offers readers a dissimilar appraisal of the subject(s) of end times than other publications of this genre would accept as proper; let alone have attempted. Therefore, this project is endeavouring in the following pages to weave my growing understanding of the evolution of human nature and religious thought and behaviour gleaned from the many fields consulted, into the over–all investigation. This has been and continued to be a fascinating journey of discovery. A journey hoped that readers find intriguing.

Jones and Flaxman offer readers this consideration: "Many of the greatest philosophers who ever existed believed that what lies within is mirrored without. As above, so below." Such, is an underlining premise for this investigation. A poignant testimonial by one other author also has surely been a driving catalyst as I submerged myself into the many areas and Sciences. It is perfectly specified by a former believer, Jonah David Conner. He effectively stated in his treaties on religion and the Bible; that religious apologists are not all that consistent when interpreting their 'sacred books'. On the one hand they all profess to care about the literalness of the text. But, as reality is faced, they only really care about a literal interpretation when and if it suits a specific purpose and preconceived ideology; otherwise, an interpretation becomes metaphorical.[viii] Christian authors and apologists writing on end time matters all-to-often also follow suit. Beginning with the premise the sacred text is a literal composition; that is, until it doesn't fit a particular narrative. Passages such as those that demand the slaughter of a dissident family, or clan member, see Exodus 21:17. The English plainly states that to 'curse' (essentially blaspheme) a mother, or father is to call upon the head a death penalty. Yet, modern society, Christian, and the Jewish religion most often largely ignore this command. Or, what about where in other places it is read that people suddenly became reanimated three and four days after death, or that suddenly numerous previously dead bodies were wandering about succeeding the demise of one particular individual. Then there is the notion that a 600year old built a ligneous bath tub, and it housed two or three pairs of the entire animal population. Clearly not enough room was left for human, as only eight people could fit afterward. This, because a deity awoke one day in a grumpy mood, and decided to throw not only the toys out, but deciding to also completely destroy the play room. Why are such verses, and tales reinterpreted? Diluted to be metaphorical? Or such tales are said to have been literal occurrences? Why are most calls to murder and other appalling acts now frowned upon? This is strange, for, moderns complain that the Islamic faith is barbaric, and murderous when Islamist extremists do take their holy texts as literal works. The world is aware that the Islamist texts call literally for the complete annihilation of the Jewish peoples. Statements Western religions (christianity in particular) find abhorrent. Yet, forgetting that their same texts also are often murderous, deceitful, and full of questionable rhetoric, and instruction. Which is it? Is the Bible text a literal or metaphorical composition? I wish christians would make their minds up! Readers I trust, might see this partial viewing and interpretation between the literal and metaphorical standard the further we traverse the mine-field that is end-times. Through these studies, the author has come to identify that religion as a whole, and christianity (particularly) is a fabulous make–believe Theory. A Theory that has plentiful underlying issues and propaganda that bounces between a literal and metaphorical understanding. Noticing this through the analysis and comprehension of many secular fields, coming to an understanding that religion and the Christian religion specifically are, as Cecil A. Poole confirms:

> "...based on feeling... the religious attitude [is], thought and reason are secondary, because religious experience involves recognition of a great mystery of life in the universe... religion needs both metaphysics and philosophy... [as these] free religion from fears, magic, superstition, worn-out cosmologies and anthropologies, and make it a reasonable and intelligent agent for man's spiritual and social progress."[ix]

My experience of religion is that it is very much feeling based. Many thoughts particular to an apocalyptic end-time studied in these pages all have a substructure of– feelings. Each Bible topic scrutinised have all derived from no thing but standard Church–ordained opinions and feelings. Church-goers of all types, the scholar, PhD recipient, and layman interpreter of the sacred books no matter the 'denomination' they adhere. They all certify feelings, opinions, and beliefs above most else, sensing that all these are categorically affirmed by their sacred texts and their deity. Mindsets, as I hope to show succinctly don't rely on much perceptive or logical thought. This is the major issue I hold with modern believers who insist on the sacred text of the Christian tradition particularly, is to be taken as a literal composition. Unapologetically, many religious readers will most likely then meet the content, commentaries and most conclusions with their own disturbing variances, as I do not recognise these texts as literal compositions. Fundamentalist believers will most likely mourn over some of the commentaries. For not adhering the usual religious zeitgeist. Disagreements being deduced from typical fears and superstitions, and the countless worn-out cosmologies that every Christian persistently avers. Nonetheless, an impartial judgement of the material, despite your own superstitions about what is presented in these commentaries is what the author wishes. Attending to an impartial judgement will neither cause harm, nor offence but rather nourish and widen one's insight into the subjects surveyed. Some viewpoints may insult a reader for not adhering to the rules of 'Political, or indeed religious Correctness'. But, as stated there was no attempt to follow the 'party-line,' the 'conventional and standard' Christian/religious view when it comes to any end-time topic under scrutiny. I won't whine and pule if certain readers become offended or disturbed by some of this material. To those people, I say: you have a right to be offended, but so what? It is not I that have to revise an opinion because of this. Rather, if offended, you are required to reassess the reasons and consider why the offence has arisen. Only then, after such assessment should any disagreement be appropriately dealt with.

It is the author's opinion that readers are free to critique and appraise the material commented upon to satiate any speculative reasoning that arouses. The author encourages all readers to engage in their own full research and reassessment; to show or invalidate for their own benefit the argumentation and conclusions. The author is of the opinion that all readers are free to their own opinions and are free to continue with their self-imposed immaturity through all manners of preferred pretend practices and beliefs of piety. He does not wish to compel through the following commentaries any reader to suddenly change in any way immature beliefs. That the believer intuitively considers correct and indispensable. That is, aside following their own full and proper reassessment of those beliefs and practices. In voicing this. There will not be any engagement in any written or spoken debate. Particularly of a religious nature with any reader or critic that holds a dissimilar outlook to what is proposed here; particularly, when those arguments are centred on a 'faith' presupposition alone. Faith, in every context –is subjective and is very personal and is no foundation for cognisance. Despite how some of the commentaries may read, be understood and scrutinised, the author holds no malice to any individual long–standing believer who is sincere in their convictions.

A brief word on religious terminology:

THE NOUNS 'BIBLE', God and 'Christian' and any number of other 'religious' words, though ordinarily and expected to be capitalised, are not necessarily so in this work. Although, because of the dictates of convention I was forced to capitalise those words that I sense do not or should not be. This was out of my control. This author notes the precondition to most texts upon publishing is that it is likely expected. Certain, and favoured religious terms were to be Capitalised. If any of these, or other words are not capitalised, there is no acceptance as correct or valid any 'special' quality is to be afforded to it. Recognising the capitalisation of certain religious, particular Christian words is a mere label created to give apparent 'importance' to the ideas they produce. Such importance is like the opinion of 'faith', subjective and personal. It is reasoned, there are few Christian/'religious' words deserving 'capitalisation.' Words like Christian, God, Jesus, or any number of other Demi–God sacred book appoint or terms; i.e., unless they are grammatically obligatory. Beginning a sentence or as part of an 'original' quotation is proper. Agreeably with the author of a brilliant little text, is an offering of the following statements in justification to quash any malice to this author for dismissing as right the capitalisation of certain favoured religious words. Including, the dismissal of the word 'God'. The believed being who represents an assumed supreme-deity figure of christianity. "I don't oppose the word God on a religious basis, but on a semantic one; ... I [would] encourage [... people] to use language with exactitude. Whenever I hear people utter the word "God," I wonder what they mean, to which of the myriad definitions they are referring."[x] A further note highlighting some facts regarding this 'God' being is offered by Barbara Walker in her brilliant study, "Man made God", where she unabashedly confirms that the deity many people assume is a supreme celestial being – is nobody but a man–made invention. Made in every image and likeness of mankind. Has every degraded behaviour; has every benevolent, and malevolent habit man has. The deity of the sacred books endorses and advocates sexism, rape, molestation of children, battery, bigotry, torture, theft, fraud, perjury, war, genocide. This deity wiped out and slaughtered whole nations and peoples. Destroying the entire Earth, but for a handful of slaves to a cause. This deity is described in the sacred texts as Creator of evil (isaiah 45:7), also the bringer of war (Matthew 10:34) – "...which Robert Ingersoll called the only biblical prophecy ever fulfilled."[xi] The deity espoused through the entire scripture is the epitome of passages often said as a warning to all generations, – specifically a generation that precedes an apocalyptic end time (1 Timothy 3:1–9). To square away any confusion I have chosen where applicable to use the more accurate, "Yahweh your God's" or, just plain deity for the alleged king of deities of Western Judaeo–Christian tradition. I have also chosen to dismiss with the usual religious word-Bible as much as possible as it technically only means book. Capitalised Bible holds I sense, too much religious weight for a work of fiction. Use of bible within the body of this book has little, or no religious connotation attached by this writer.

A word about the author:

THERE IS REALLY NOTHING of note about my life that warrants importance. A common male with an exceptionally common life. The product of our currant society. Holding the same memes as any other modern citizen. Like so many others, I was raised in a largely unadventurous, but religious Christian home. So, began this project as a conservative Christian. Children raised in religious homes inherit, through brainwashing great swathes of religious convictions, beliefs, and doctrines. Of all previous convictions then, it was never encouraged to find whether they were ever true, right, logical, or reasonable. It was rather like all believers, expected and encouraged that I just believe. Here, we have an issue: in their formative year's children are not given the choice whether the beliefs constantly drilled into them are actually worth the air expelled in explaining them. Rather, because the faculties of reason and common sense are lacking in a child's mind, the child becomes an easy prey for indoctrination. All indoctrinated beliefs about life and religious memes, are undoubtedly carried through to adulthood. Nineteenth century philosopher, Arthur Schopenhauer explosively expresses similar convictions in the opening comments to his title, "The Horrors and Absurdities of Religion":

> "The power of religious dogmas imprinted in early years is such that they are capable of stifling conscience and finally all pity and humanity... The only reason for this is that education is in the hands of the clergy, who take care so to imprint all the articles of faith in earliest youth that it produces a kind of partial paralysis of the brain, which then gives rise to that lifelong imbecile bigotry through which even people otherwise in the highest degree intelligent degrade themselves and make a quite misleading impression on the rest of the world..."[xii]

The short of it was perfectly summed by author Ivan Green: "Christians were all born atheists, and then had religion forced upon them."[xiii] This statement is true. Nobody on the Earth is born a Christian. Rather, Christian characteristics and religious ideologies are formed and nurtured through indoctrination by clergy, religious educators and not least, parents after birth. Continuing into adulthood until the adult steps aside and begins to seriously question their beliefs. Further, religious instruction whether via formal schooling or a specific religious institution has never taught its student in methods of thought and the debating of ideas; i.e., the indoctrinated are never taught to think critically about what is or not truth. It is just expected that these should be separate and are irrelevant when it comes to religious matters. Precisely, because the religious premises espoused are 'always' taught as unquestionably true. The goal of religion is to mould and shape a mind to a specific standard and view.

Like so many others, because of religious indoctrination all previous values and concepts were often expressed through the prism of religion. These lasted well into my adult life. The last fifteen or so years; however, becoming increasingly antagonistic to all religious formalities and those that peddle them. So, have wanted to make a formal study of what is considered contemptible. This manuscript offers the results of some of my findings. Therefore, as readers progress through these studies you are encouraged to form your own judgment through independent thought, considered analysis and personal insight by what you read in these pages.[xiv] In the words of R.G. Price, author of "Deciphering The Gospels", "... I am not qualified to write this book. I have no formal training in ancient history, ... textual criticism."[xv] I do not have any formal training in any of the sciences, or specialised fields consulted for this project. My only qualification of any importance (if it can be called that) for this project is the achievement of a Diploma in (1994). In six months', the equivalent to a second-year Bible college degree was successfully completed; a Diploma, which incorporated many theological and secular subjects. I have, and still use extensively what is generally considered the premier computer Bible platform for studies. The Logos Bible Systems® platform. Including video lessons of Hebrew and Greek interpretation methods offered by Dr. Michael Heiser, the scholar in residence for Logos Bible Systems. I do therefore have some sacred concept training, and a growing interest in other fields of academic and secular studies that aids our understanding and knowledge base of the human condition. Until recently, I attempted to keep abreast of many theological ideas and have found the tools and resources offered by Logos Bible Systems of great value and aid. Having now earnestly begun a journey through the Stoic philosophies, and mystic, occult topics. An emphasis on theological/Christian matters is only seen as periphery topics. At the beginning of this project then, I naturally thought to attempt to deny or confirm the subjects considered in this using the cognisance gained over the years. The shortfall, soon realising that the result of these studies would be no different to any other fundamentalist research. It would have offered only the regurgitation of what is most likely already offered. It would differ very little to any popular christianised study and other books that are easily bought in any oxymoronic 'Christian bookstore'. My research yet has instilled the confidence such works only ever seek to affirm the usual narrow-minded, indoctrinated and proselytised opinions of the purchaser. This book does not offer that! Imagined, is each chapter puts forward a very different slant to what may already be a familiar turf. Expecting this study challenges the usual religious postulations. Reason being, the more I invested in the subjects covered the more I realised there are schisms between what Christian theory preaches as truth. Compared to many other reputable fields of academic study that often imply the reassessment, invalidation or demolition of those claims successfully. The result: through reason and logic, and despite these not being immune from contempt christianity was seen as a theory that cannot be thought of as equitably true. Rather, is astoundingly wicked and feebleminded. Despite, such a conclusion there is throughout this research a desire to approach the following material from the perspective of one who understands modern Western Christian beliefs but who now stands at a position as near the sideline as possible. I can honestly say; thoughts about deities, not just those revered by christianity are like to the Greek philosopher –Xenophanes (around. 570 – 480 bc). He scolded the confidence in anthropomorphic gods. One of his more famous quips to the priests of Memphis (Egypt) reads "...if [anyone] thought Osiris a man they should not worship him, and if they thought him a God they need not talk of his death and sufferings."[xvi]

The same must apply to the God–man Jesus. Or any other believed holy-man, Prophet, or deity. It is a common requirement and belief for christians to instinctively imply that Jesus was (is) both, a man and a deity! Such a dichotomy is nonsensical. If he were a man, why then should anyone worship him? If a God - why conduct a yearly celebration of his birth and death?[xvii] If any extraordinary man-deity is assumed to have anthropomorphic qualities; i.e., he suffered the same envies or troubles, had the same cravings, faults, and characteristics as common individuals; what then is his distinguishing 'godly' attribute? The first recorded and initiator of criticism against the new and emerging belief-system of christianity; Celsus (around second century) was a learned Greek philosopher, and most likely the first to inspire many antagonists to the opinions christianity proposes.[xviii] He had much to say regarding the supposed death and resurrection of the God–man Jesus. Believers would be better informed about their deity, if, like Celsus and others they proposed to question everything they are taught. For instance, questioning the blood atonement Celsus poses the following to all believers: "What kind of ichör or blood dropped from his crucified body? Was it, such as from the blest immortals flows?"[xix] Being the ambrosia type fluid of many other mythic deities, or hero's. For christians to ponder: at the crucifixion of your God-man, Jesus, was it 'human blood', or, the rarefied 'golden' fluid said to course through the veins of any of the mythic gods of Egyptian and Greek mythology that flowed from his body? So, how did this make for atonement? Celsus further insinuates there is an air of reason among confessing believers that are contrary to all known reality. Has any deceased mortal, he asks, ever been raised from the dead. Surely, such postulating is the domain of mythic tradition! Further, if the intent of the deity-man Jesus had been to become immortal. Why was this hidden from public awareness? Why was his alleged immortality, and rising not visible to the wider population? Rather, was kept a secret but for a few women and close 'friends.'

> "This,... is to be considered, — whether any one (sic) who in reality died, ever rose again in the same body: unless you think that the narrations of others are fables, but that your catastrophe of the drama will be found to be either elegant or probable... If also Christ wished to be concealed, why was a voice heard from heaven, proclaiming him to be the son of God? Or, if he did not wish to be concealed, why did he suffer punishment, and why did, he [ignominiously] die?"[xx]

Eighteenth-century Frenchman, Baron Montesquieu succinctly summed the concept of a deity with the dictum: "If triangles had a God, he would have three sides." (Torrey, p. 175.) Another author bluntly wrote in "The Ultimate Guide to Cosmic Ordering" that "...you can't wish the dead back to life. While there may be an army of spiritualists who take an exception to this statement..." no formerly deceased individual has ever arisen.[xxi] The rising of any individual is a guessed premise of 'faith', which cannot be a platform for well-thought out information. In essence, all people, believer and nonbeliever must at some stage in their lives face their own nothingness/ending. German philosopher of the last century, Martin Heidegger (d. 1976.) termed this eventual ending, – das Nichts. "Everything has an end; only sausages have two! No matter how long our lives, the end is always unexpected. So, every "Man must accept that just as no one can die for him, no one can live for him. Without exception, each person is faced with his/her own eventual, das Nichts, – nothingness." (Great Thinkers, p.91–97.) Far too many religious people reading this, facing your own Nothingness, demise might be seen as a negative. Yet, 'Nothingness' is used here not as a negative. Just as the phrase of Nietzsche about God being dead.

> "Nothingness may sound negative [but] it is the exact opposite. The world of objects is limited, Nothingness is not... Absolute Nothingness, on the other hand, is limitless, pregnant with infinite potential. For this reason, we cannot truly say that Nothingness lacks 'anything', as it is utterly beyond the limitations of form. Nothingness is the very basis for reality itself, for

there are simply no 'things' that can exist without or outside of Nothingness. Nothingness makes 'being' and existence possible..."[xxii]

As confusing as this may first sound, your own Nothingness is the birth place to and of every something!

The birth of these studies:

IT WAS MOST CERTAINLY a new understanding of 'nothingness' that encouraged, and gave birth to the following variety of end time subjects in commentary. As I progressed, and questioned Christian end time topics. The more readily, and liberal were conclusions of those quoted sacred book passages, academic studies, and some well-respected theological giants of the past and present. Scripture references within the body and endnotes of this document readers are encouraged to refer to your own sacred book if owned. The use of reference works is not for confirmation to an argument, but as a possible example. Many Christian materials cited in this study are in my copy of Logos Bible Software. The vast majorities of other references consulted and quoted are in electronic format. Those Electronic editions (e-books) often do not provide specific page numbering (shown by 'Location numbers'). Several references are a hard copy. These can all be scanned in an extensive bibliography at the end of this book which is provided for further studies. Some data and statistics admittedly readers will be hard pressed to access without an electronic study platform. Or, without owning the reference cited. Readers of this work are encouraged to take advantage of the extensive endnotes, and references supplied to hasten their understanding and knowledge. Endnotes and other references cited are intended to assist only with the flow of argument, instead of detracting too much from the main presentation. I readily rely also upon a range of assorted sacred book materials for which I hope to have engaged meaningfully not only with the passage cited, but to also help readers in thinking about a theme, individual, or text seriously in ways they might not have considered. The citation of many works not specifically attuned to or collaborative of any religious inducement. Is to acknowledge that the believed sacred texts should not be understood in isolation to the wider community. A word of 'thanks' must be offered to the many authors of the literature consulted and learned. The current investigation then, would not have produced anything like that which is presented throughout the following pages without these commentators and authors. It is with great admiration for each that my sincerity and thanks is offered. Throughout this work were considered materials by many scholars and authors. Covering a diverse range of sacred, para-sacred, academic, pseudo academic, fringe history, occultist, and disciplines of gnosis. Including texts of both the new and old testaments, some gnostic writings, and commentators of these texts and other disciplines. Considered studies and materials in, Archaeology; Symbolism; Histories; Neurosciences; Cognitive Sciences; Biology; Mythology; Psychology; The Anthropology of Religion and Philosophy and others. Not all authors or texts hold to a religious persuasion. Exceptionally meticulous researchers who may or not be atheistic or religious in their approach, write many. The chosen approach should not deter readers. If this approach does dissuade some readers it only proves an unwillingness to self–regulate, self–criticise; and is a biased thought process that serves as a protective mechanism for uncertainties! Until staunch believers acknowledge and reconcile with this, they will unfortunately remain largely mind–blind.[xxiii]

Intention:

IT IS NOT THE PURPOSE to provide an exhaustive analysis of the subjects and personalities under scrutiny. There are plentiful possibilities and explanations on offer for the studious. Not all proposals offered here it is understood will be accepted. Although this would be a most pleasant and pleasurable experience for all if each of the following proposals met with approval. It is left to the diligent reader to scrutinise and search out the most probable and acceptable conclusions to any foreseen disagreement. In the hope of encouraging readers in thinking differently about a subject or theme in ways they might not have considered beforehand. I have endeavoured to supply even-handed thoughts for my reasoning. It should also be noted that although passages from the Judaeo–Christian sacred book are cited. Citations serve only as a highlight for the argument or opinion. I want made about the invented sacred cows of Christian belief. Particularly, those continually proclaimed or assumed to be factual and soon to be seen upon the face of the earth. Further, much end time christobabble is founded upon proclamations exclusively with patriarchal undertones. As taught to Westerners, the favoured deity is presumed to be of patriarchal descent. Here however, the endeavour is to introduce noteworthy efforts and the scholarship of various female authors of Feminist Theologies; as a matriarchal counterbalance. To this point, let a statement of Common Wisdom mull around your consciousness awhile. It states plainly:

"Only a fool or a man would believe that God is masculine. Fathers don't create anything; mothers do."[xxiv]

This is common biological knowledge. Although there is a disturbing trend in our modern day to 'acknowledge' as legitimate the fantasy of biological male gestation, and birthing. For a bazaar reason unknown to the author, societal trends wish to force such ideologies on the wider population. Maybe, such a concept was a reaction to a religious ideology that staunchly remains absolutely nonsensical. Continuing to insist there is a 'masculine' type deity busily somewhere 'creating'.[xxv] Or, that a masculine deity somehow 'created' in the distant past just because a dusty, worn-out, outdated parchments pronounced it so. Disregarding the history that will be hinted in the first Nail; the revered sibylline characteristics of women in the ancient past. As opposed to the current religious view of a masculine supreme deity-figure. Early religion, including that of the early Israelite/Jew seems to have been very much matriarchal by nature. It has been proved by many authors of early renown. Particularly by those writers of the late Nineteenth and Twentieth Centuries. Although these authors and scholars did not have the advantages of modern scholarship, many of their conclusions are once again becoming recognised as worthy of consideration. There are today many essays published on such subjects. Some of which are drawn upon in this study.

I have chosen to call each of my essays, a Nail. The purpose for doing so is to offer another perspective. Giving the impression of 'just as a wooden lid is nailed to seal a container'; so, might the Nails (essay) serve a similar purpose for end–time propositions and many Christian hypotheses examined. Within many of these essay topics, we might be seen to be playing leapfrog; as on more than one occasion it was unavoidable that 'other connected', or related topics attached to the initial belief/subject being examined; that these should be tackled then, and there. Again, there is no apology. These added subjects and topics just add further vitality to my over all summation; that Christian end-times are largely, built upon exaggerated and spiritualised innuendo. They may have an air of honesty, correctness, and precision; but, when scrutinised using reason and logic they fall astoundingly short of these aspirations. Geoffrey Ashe, a Fellow, since 1963 of the Royal Society of Literature essentially posits; the changing and revising of initial positions most likely is a sign that the researcher is engaging in an important way the chosen subject. In his book, he affirms:

> "When writing ... [many ideas] change as they go along and insist on being different from what [is] originally conceived... It's probably a sign of vitality."[xxvi]

Notwithstanding, debates about why there was a choice to explore certain unrelated topics, or the following consequences each source chosen highlights. I have throughout this inquiry sought to be diligent, but also offer readers a fair assessment of the topics explored. All sacred texts consulted are the usually familiar Standard English bibles from my Logos Bible Software library. These are mostly reverse-interlinear. Meaning the Greek and Hebrew information of English Bible's can be reviewed and studied without having to become a skilled sacred language scholar. I have sought to understand to the best of my competence the particular nuance behind the venerated language content and its overall context. There is no claim to any scholarship or scientific qualification.

DECONSTRUCTING ENDTIME DELUSIONS

Rather a reliance upon the precision of the scholarship that produced each sacred text and the other sources cited, and therefore, the sureness of my own comprehension of that material. Though not a scholar, but a passionate layman privileged to have access to an expansive variety of sources. One who is willing to put in the hard yards to 'flesh out' answers to a multitude of questions. A rare breed of person today who is unashamed to think, question, and chide what is and has been continually advocated as factually sound religious truth: despite reality, history, and many sciences continually disproving its veracity and binding genuineness. It is unfortunate that there is widespread ignorance in religious circles regarding the subjects I attempt to rationalise in these pages. An ignorance born mainly from a lack in curiosity. Unfortunately, too, a lack in curiosity is caused for the pitiful and unacceptable Christian fideism that is still prevalent among many believers; "God said it, I believe it, and that damn-well settles it!" What if a deity never said it? Why should anyone believe it? What if the figure labelled –God/deity, is as earlier hinted, really of our own intuit and making? What if traditional religion has subdued and labelled such as inherently evil and so must on all counts be irradiated from the human psyche. Face it, these matters are far from settled! Debates about this that, or the other will continue to rage long after I am done with any subject commented upon here. This book is just my Davidian (meagre) gift to the already Goliath publications available.

The importance of attempting the near proper intentio operis of a text; i.e., the aim, plan, or the conceptions formed by directing the mind to an object, or result of a passage; must also be borne in mind as we attempt to decipher any passage of the sacred works. Author, and Professor of Religious Studies at the University of North Carolina, Bart Ehrman wrote that readers should have the opportunity to view and interact with the reasons for all hypotheses presented by an author. Whether a book presents the life of someone famous, or ancient, or it presents many ideas surrounding a particular topic – the same applies – each reader has the right to know what proof, both for and doubtful are available and why the author's opinion matters. It is then on the shoulders of the reader to know which offers the greatest value in truthfulness (Reworded Preface: "Jesus: Apocalyptic Prophet of the new Millennium."). I have attempted to supply evidences for and against all subjects explored. All resources are duly shown and are hoped follow the requirements of Copyright law. Web addresses, and blog posts throughout this enquiry are also offered as a reference only and were valid at the time of writing and their inclusion. No responsibility shall be admitted if later some or all web posts are removed or changed without notice. As stated numerously already any reference cited is no way an outright endorsement of its full content. Rather, again, as a study aid. The interpretations, and conclusions drawn upon the few salient themes chosen for this disquisition; especially those in Part Two, will ruffle feathers. I have no doubt most of the views, and assertions offered throughout this book will also be new to some readers. Conclusions and assertions that follow will run counter to the accepted positions of many readers. Positions that will be difficult to defend without an acknowledgement of being situated firmly within your own indoctrinated belief-system. It is acknowledge that anything new, is often met first with reluctance and a healthy skepticism. Which is a given and bridge to growth in learning: a bridge that must be traversed if true, lasting, and significant growth is to emerge. Heather Lynn stresses the very same with the following remarks of one of her professors in her book, "Anthrotheology" writing:

> "...book[s are] to be used as general reference and is a great starting point but if at any time, we see something which does not resonate with us, we should explore it further through independent research and evaluation..."[xxvii]

As with all fields of scholarship and authorship each present a range of liberties, misnomers, and fallacies as well as strengths. It is felt though that each field and author consulted has a valid if not enormously interesting voice to add to the general project. It is therefore up to a reader's discretion and discernment of what is or not of ultimate worth. What is the most promising offering of truth? After-all, the overall objective of this project is to offer readers not only some of the weaknesses I have come across in my studies of Christian 'end-time' proposals; but to offer a possible Genesis to why, or from where an end time apocalyptic derived. For all purposes, every modern end-time proposal cannot defy scrutiny. Rather, "...it is essential to appreciate their weakness. The possibility of bias and of a misinterpretation of the limited information on which they are based should be borne in mind."[xxviii] It is the lies and willingness to accept as true or real of many convictions of Christian principles that I wish to expose, esp., those of end–times throughout this tome. Might this work then serve readers well among the many skeptical works already on offer. The final objective I hoped to have fulfilled is to examine and utilise various discoveries from whatever source, on merits, not whether a reader agrees or not. So please, for your own sanity, remember it's often the foundations and the screwball beliefs, doctrines, and practices under scrutiny. Not the individuals at large who may hold such views. As readers, you are therefore encouraged to abstain and distance yourself as much as possible from the biases we each bring to any table of enquiry. All conclusions hereafter drawn are my own (unless otherwise stated). Though I have consistently sought to comment upon all subjects in a fair, balanced, and harmless style I make no apology for what may be considered blunt, callous, or down right vitriolic. None of the perspectives that follow is material that was penned with malicious forethought. Rather, with the maxim best illustrated by:...a passage in the Zhuangzi, a proto-Daoist philosophical text, that says:

> "The fish trap exists because of the fish; once you've gotten the fish, you can forget the trap." I invite you to explore this book in that spirit. Use it like you'd use a fish trap, ever mindful of [its] purpose. Carry with you what you can use, so long as it continues to have use; discard the rest. and may your purpose serve you well."[xxix]

Steve Morgan, Australia, 11/12/2018.

Introduction:

HAS IT DAWNED ON THE reader to question why there are so many religions in the world? This is a very strange fact. Especially when we are all told by each individual religious creed that they alone hold the truth. This too is a very strange fact. Religions are supposed to allay fears, heighten hopes, and offer us all a sense of what a deity wants for us, and from us. Yet, why do all religions spruik countless doctrines of an apparent and looming apocalyptic end of time? Who the hell is right? Are any of the multitudes of 'predictions' actually true? Will any come to fruition– in our lifetime, or sometime soon? With the multitude branding of religion, which should be followed?[xxx] Author, entrepreneur, and radio personality Josh Tolley remarked:

> "It is not wrong to question things... the fact that you are asking questions shows that you are five levels of wisdom above the idiot who is objecting to you asking the questions."

Why then are so many people afraid of asking questions? Simply, because to ask questions is to expose the hearer to their own idiocy for not seeking to ask questions. Rather, happily going with the flow. Yet, without interrogation "Ideology makes people stupid. Employing ideology as the basis for policy [dogma, belief, or ardent hypothesis] is a recipe for disaster."[xxxi] This is what we can accept when reviewing the countless cataclysm improbabilities. Those proposed by Christian, and their secular counterpart ideologues who spruik catastrophe events they assume will be unleashed upon the earth in a not–too–distant– future epoch; the age labelled 'end–times.' A perilous period many religionists assume today is ludicrously velocious in its approach. So, we must all be vigilant. Those particular religious ideologies reviewed in these pages, are scrutinised in an effort to unearth reasonable answers to Why; not necessarily to questions of What? or Who? Or How or a When of an end-event that is of basic concern. Why, and from where does many

DECONSTRUCTING ENDTIME DELUSIONS

Christian presumptions arise? To what extent is religious opinions and conclusions factual? Are there any reasonable or frankly, better conclusions to draw from many sciences studied today for the many end-time personalities and topics. Those that have in recent years caught the imaginations of many believers?

Beginning March, through November 2010/2011, when this investigation was determined to diligently oppugn the validity of countless Christian, religious presupposed dogma of end time, Apocalypse, end of days. It was at the Genesis of these investigations. The author was still a believer in many of christianity's assumed spiritual truths, but these were increasingly becoming unbelievable. It was not until some years study into several academic fields that this analysis led me into, that my former religious opinions began to crumble at being deconstructed; eventually being understood on an anthropomorphic level. Many conclusions to why, and my intent in deconstructing sacred verses and proposed end-time ideologies assumed as spiritual certainties, no doubt will turn out some profoundly surprising conclusions for readers. A word of explanation to deconstruction is warranted here:

> "...deconstruction is an enterprise that exposes the inadequacies of texts, and shows how inexorably they undermine themselves."[xxxii]

It is my over-all aim throughout these pages to expose inadequacies of many Christian doctrines. Especially those we accept for an end-time hypothesis. Interestingly, there has throughout human history always been a fascination of Apocalypse and its varied subjects. Tina Pippin in the preface to her book "Apocalyptic Bodies" in a sense, highlights this point:

> "At the turn of the twentieth century apocalypseblob (sic) has almost completely taken over Christian evangelical television. Prophecy shows read for The End in every corner of the news. There is great ecstasy in describing the end time horrors. Still, only certain religious sensibilities indulge in these texts..."[xxxiii]

That is, the fundamentalist who is convinced that "it is the business of Christianity to conquer the whole universe to itself and not least the universe of thought."[xxxiv] We find this rumoured process rife throughout christianity as a whole; a believed process that began with the earliest inception of this institution (see Nail One.) Countless 'believers' see, read, and is taught today that their sacred texts are a literal composition, and that they are part of the elite 'saved'. So, it is their duty to pronounce the tidings of the 'good book' to all of creation. After all, such is a command given by their adored God-man.[xxxv] The themes, stories, actions throughout the text are 'known by faith' to have either happened sometime in history, or will happen.

> "Consulting the earliest Christian monuments, we find in every line the hope expressed, that Nature is to disappear and life die out— in a word, that the end of the world is at hand."[xxxvi]

Apocalyptic end-of-the-world scenarios are not new to the world stage. Such stories and thoughts can be seen throughout world mythology. Including that of the Norse, Aztecs, Sumerians, ancient Celts, and countless tribes, and peoples from all across the globe who have gloom-ridden prophecies and tales. All predicting a hellish time the earth and its inhabitance will eventually suffer. Not only are we witness to such prophecies and tales throughout world mythology, increasingly we are witness to the same thoughts in countless fictional works that also continue to inspire the imagination. Most mature believers would be aware that in the Christian tradition, the greatest attributed source of an apocalyptically inspired fiction. Is none other than the final text of their holey book: Revelation. In its pages, we read horrifying accounts of

> "...the wrath of God visited upon the Earth in a host of ways (fire, plague, hail, drought, earthquakes, flood, and much more), leading to the final judgment and the redemption of the righteous... apocalyptic visions are nearly universal in the religious literature of the world, and apparently always have been, [so] it is not surprising that they should figure largely in the fantasies of imaginative storytellers [also]. Even before the term "science fiction" had been coined, stories of universal or near-universal extinction

brought about not by the anger of the deities but by the innate hazards of existence were being written and achieving wide popularity. Nineteenth-century writers were particularly fond of them...."[xxxvii]

Authors the likes of H. G. Wells and Jules Vern and their contemporaries, all wrote fantastic and illecebrous stories and novels that incorporated elements of the Earth encountering destructive apocalyptic end-time themes. Such writing of fictitious novels continue unabated to the present. Christian/religious protagonists of such a genre; however, choose and seem to view and exploit an element of heightened fear when inspired to write their books regarding the apocalyptic scenarios that seem to occupy their sacred books. Choosing to continually pursue these as a literal probability, not just a possibility. Agreeing with Tina Pippin; however, I choose to not view the 'religious' texts cited in this investigation, and the presupposed end-of-the-world ideas arising from them as literal. Conversely, recognised is the benefit of being a secular hermeneut.[xxxviii] Therefore acknowledging:

> "A non-literal reading creates distance so that gender remains symbolic, not physical, and the gender-specific violence is tamed. A more literal reading which takes seriously the gendered images of Whore, Lamb, God, Beasts, and 144,000 could be seen as "low class"; literalistic readings should be left to the Christian fundamentalists. I choose to take the violence at face value and condemn it, but obviously in a different way than Christian fundamentalists." (ibid. Pippin.)

Undeniably today, religious factions generally seem to thrive on an end time period assumed impending. Periodically, various assumptions are posited and are often forced upon society by fundamental believers. Reaching fever pitch for several years before dying and eventually fading completely from the mind of its advocates when expected/predicted events do not materialise. These postulated dramas as earlier stated, are not new to any world scene, and will most likely continue ad infinitum. Most prevalent in our modern western society is the current "Climate Emergency" cult hoax, and those end–time horrors 'forewarned'; particularly by fundamentalist christians and their organisations. Each warning for instance posted by fundamentalist believer Thomas Horn and the band of authors that are usually promoted alongside his books; the likes of Derek P. Gilbert and Rob Skiba, and many others. All offer readers books containing a surprising smorgasbord of apparent new developments, new predictions, and a wealth of new and more accurate interpretation and accompanying theories of prophesy. All said, or inferred as a means of ushering in the end. Each 'new' publication printed offers its readers a motley array of predictions regarding whom, the how, and the when of the proposed sunset of life–as–we–know–it on Planet Earth. Countless publications either predict or offer readers never–before-noticed insight into our being 'one step closer' to the,

> "...hope that the utopian afterlife will make the earthly horrors worthwhile, but the complete trust given the supreme powers is full of cracks. Apocalypse is an uncertain certainty, a dreaded hope, an endless end. Apocalypse scares and scars; there are scars on the land (e.g. Babel, the old earth passing away) and on the human body (e.g. Jezebel's head, the absent space in the field, the Mark on the forehead). Is there a time before the scare? A prequel to the events of terror?" (Pippin.)

Yet, no new publication seems to be anything but another attempt to indoctrinate others with the author's own mythology. For, what is mythology but 'my-theology?' The same might be said for this publication. As any publication on any topic is truely only the my-theology of the author. Numerous secular commentators reason too many of these Christian postulations focus solely upon what 'scares' us. I for instance, have not come across one end-time themed book by a supposed Christian perspective that highlights an air of hope, fortitude, or fearless resolves. Unless, it is to manipulate the reader via a sense of guilt. Rather, most allude to a diabolical experience, one of inescapable gloom doom and destruction. The 'escape' route; the favoured mythology of 'salvation' offered by the favoured God-man, and deity. All modern 'Christian' studies of this type, it must be admitted have a predisposed mythology of the author. As stated, the theology of an adherent. Statements, and studies offered to fellow devotees to assist shape and mould their minds. Offering readers nothing but the usual subjective theocentric position. Voiced essentially to manipulate and indoctrinate the easily tricked. Contrariwise, proposed in the following are commentaries is the author's growing comprehension, my-theology of end time topics. Those assumptions taught to countless believers. The following studies are meant to challenge those usual doom and gloom religious postulations – and bring to the discussion an appreciative awareness of many an end–time subject. Derived from the stated multi–discipined, holistic approach. An approach that surely transports often mystical and scary ideas into the real world. All may not be as somber as is often portrayed by Christian authors.

Through this approach, the attempt is to remain as objectively open to accept religious views as much as humanly possible. Unlike many Christian authors stated throughout this investigation. It was continually wrestled with at how to best offer empirical reasons for any conclusion. I have endeavoured to not make arrogant statements, as if they are outright fact. Not without substantiating a claim; just as Rob Skiba, Derek Gilbert and others often seem to do. Gilbert for instance in the opening remarks to his publication; "Last Clash of the <Titans>" (2018) makes numerous nonsensical remarks set as truth narrative resembling the tone of the book. This 'new' end time publication of Gilbert's may be based on ideologies derived from programs like 'Ancient Aliens'. Which ran the narrative that ancient mythologies found throughout the world have their Genesis in extraterrestrial encounters with locals, including various well-known Greek and Roman myths of antiquity. Discounting every known myth possesses any valued lesson to teach, aside the favoured religious narrative. Readers of Gilbert's latest title notice in the opening pages the admonition and his belief that christians

> "... can ... gain a deeper understanding of the Bible by viewing the world through the eyes of the prophets and apostles, and they knew very well what their pagan neighbours believed. Much of what they wrote was directed at pagan gods."

This though, is the usual fundamental religious line. Which presupposed ideologies of ignorant christians with their 'holier than thou' attitude, assume the over–whelming veracity of the Judaeo-Christian book's apostles and prophets should be wholly believed, – because they are recorded to have said blah, blah blah blah in that book under the direct intervention of their deity, and that is the only valid or truthful source any believer needs! Bollocks! Just how is it expected that by digesting what is apparently recorded in some holey book, composed by numerous people, and for numerous reasons that any modern reader should discern anything other than realistically, their own presumptuous nonsense. Particularly when we know, those texts are far removed from our modern time! Gilbert goes on to proudly proclaim; also as if completely factual and authoritative he calls the God's of the Greeks and Romans: (1) real (2) he has a belief that the 'prophetic' utterances of the Hebrew prophets reveal 'startling' insights into what pagans God's were all about. As well as what lay ahead for the world, and (3) naming specific Greek deities; the mythic Zeus, Herakles, the Olympians, and Titans. All these are real. They each hate us (humanity), and they're all 'coming back'. So, we'd better get ready![xxxix] What tripe! These are not statements of fact. They are but statements of fancy. Clearly Gilbert has misread and misunderstood myth and the roles played in the world of the ancients. Including the myth of his sacred books. Such statements are the usual subjective, sensationalist postulating that is too often churned out by every oxymoronic Christian publishing house. As far as can be learned there is absolutely no empirical evidence made for any of Gilbert's assertions. The blurb for his publication as an electronic format reads similarly. Assuming the deities of the ancients weren't just mythical stories, Gilbert actually assumes to name certain of them. Linking them to believed real (and therefore true) characters found in the Judaeo-Christian mythic books. Accordingly, the Greek and Roman mythic tales are real but 'twisted' histories. The King of the Greek pantheon Zeus, is the dreaded evil entity 'Satan'; other Greek demi-deities; i.e., the Titans are the sons of Genesis 6:2 who mated with the daughters of man; while the mystical entities (nephilim), also of

DECONSTRUCTING ENDTIME DELUSIONS

Genesis fame (6:4), well, these are the heroes of the 'Golden Age'.[xl] To add further insult to the magnificence of Greek myth, Gilbert assumes his God (who is obviously Yahweh, the truer deity) who although has called the deities of the Greek pantheon real; he nonetheless has announced a death penalty on them for apparently rebelling. So, these mythical Greek 'deities' are now dyspeptic. Any day now, they're coming back! I Would like to know among other questions; from where are these 'deities' returning? The very same ideology is clearly seen in Nail Nine as a criticism of Rob Skiba's book, "Babylon Rising" and some of the more pressing issues that arose from that study. But, why are we prone to assuming such mythic tales as literal histories? Why don't more people rail against such obvious, unsubstantiated material offered by Christian authors? The most probable reason is that most of those books published today have a kind of 'silver bullet'. They are 'peer reviewed'. Through this process, they have been endorsed and validated by numerous 'other,' often scholarly believers. A brief word on the prevalent idea that nowadays that if any work; Christian book or article is 'peer reviewed' so that automatically heightened its validity and veracity, making it immune from dispute. To this, Robert John Langdon cites the editor of The Lancet:

> "The credibility of 'Peer Review' was perfectly summed up by Richard Horton, editor of the British medical journal The Lancet, who said that: "The mistake, of course, is to have thought that peer review was any more than a crude means of discovering the acceptability — not the validity — of a new finding. Editors and scientists alike insist on the pivotal importance of peer review. We portray peer review to the public as a quasi - sacred process that helps to make science [and religion] our most objective truth teller. But we know that the system of peer review is biased, unjust, unaccountable, incomplete, easily fixed, often insulting, usually ignorant, occasionally foolish, and frequently wrong - So much for peer review!"[xli]

Astounding remarks. Peer review is slated by countless academic institutions, most sciences, and definitely all current religious publications, as offering pinnacle reached; yet is nonetheless fraught with issues. Such a review system is clearly not a guarantee of authenticity free from error. So much of what is published today is reliant on a 'peer review' process – before publication is granted. Yet, the process as noted, is itself often flawed, seeking to establish whether the work is aligned to the believed consensus instead of objective truth. Alan Watts in "Wisdom of Insecurity" stated, "If we are open only to discoveries which will accord with what we know already, we may as well stay shut." (p.103.) Further, the tone of Gilbert seems to assert; some mythical entities hate and wish to obliterate humanity! This is often the case with a mythical fantastic story. Yet, surely to focus one's attention on these most human of emotions (hatred etc.), and to state it is of some super-spiritual, supernatural, and mystical mystery is to miss the mark of what the myth might be attempting to teach an audience about itself, and the wider–world. If the hatred of these entities is the premise; the sole focus of the entire book "Last Clash of the Titans", no wonder believers don't often marvel at scientific innovation, or technical, educational knowledge and prowess much in this life! Rather, more often are skeptical and fearful of these advances (unless they are needed. Medical sciences for example!) Fear, malice, hatred, and some conspiracy of total obliteration that we must be weary of are continually drilled into believers. This is apparently: 'the good news'! Why though do christians advocating an 'end-time' agendum seem to want to destroy the cake on the one hand, and then eat from that same cake with the other? Myth Gilbert states, have no relevance and any meaning to teach; after which he proceeds to use those same myths as the basis of his own postulating. As if they hold relevance– but, only because the myths he believe to hold merit– those of his sacred books are said to rebut those myths he dislikes, or likely misunderstands! You cannot have it both ways. Either all myths (religious or not) have lessons to teach, or they don't. One set of myths, because they are believed to be true (and therefore sacred), cannot demolish another set of myths one believes are irrelevant because they derive from something other than sacred tradition. Such illogical thinking is similar to the saying; 'Beatings will continue until morale improves!' Unfortunately, the sample text offered by Gilbert in the book itself doesn't provide much by way of anything astoundingly against the usual theological innuendo of myth–presenting and myth–bashing.

DECONSTRUCTING ENDTIME DELUSIONS

The impression is Gilbert asserts the conventional believer line when confronting anything mythological; the accepted Bible text, well that is factual. That mythology is excused. Other mythic tales might be real but must be re-interpreted through the 'reality' of the sacred text if anyone wishes to understand them correctly. Reiterating his previous assertions Gilbert states his beliefs regarding the myths presented by the ancient Romans and Greeks. Juxtaposing these with those Judaeo-Christian myths. Here, he adds a little more intrigue, a mix of other entities; Watchers, Rephaim, the Amorites, and a figure of Balaam. The Titans he says, are the (assumed wicked) entities– nephilim who in turn, are also the Rephaim. Now the spirits of these wicked entities (nephilim/Rephaim) were summoned through necromancy, by an ancient race of Mesopotamia, the Amorites. All which is nicely packaged and sent to the slaughterhouse, by a fellow named Balaam. In one of his 'prophecies' he announced the complete destruction of the evil nephilim by the alleged Messiah and deity-man. Confused yet? Talk about a convoluted scenario. This is unfortunately 'practice as usual' for religious authors. Whose goal it seems is to utterly confuse a reader into submission to their apocalyptic end game cause. In these studies is a reasonably extensive review into the episode of the nephilim of Genesis chapter 6. Those enigmatic entities mentioned in the Judaeo-Christian book of Genesis. These are enigmatic 'creatures' that have been given a life of their own as a type of monstrous 'giant'. A bit like the fairytale of Jack and the Beanstalk. As with these mystical beings, another strange entity <Rephaim>, are likewise reviewed in a later chapter, Nail Nine. This chapter looks at these entities of the Bible for they are often mentioned by authors wishing to make a mark on the Apocalypse scene. Conclusions are collected from the vast array of sacred and non–religious materials consulted. In the studies of Genesis chapter 6 and the numerous branching subjects arising from that study. Offered are several considerations sensed as more likely an offering of truth to those stories, than what readers will likely find in studies conducted by many religious authors and writers. Unlike religious writers, there were many questions of how and why such a story (as Genesis 6:1-4) became recorded in the Judaeo-Christian sacred book. All commentaries are trusted to have been a showing to not ignoring enigmatic queries for not aligning with a preconceived idea.

The appraisal study topics of the religious concept of an impending end-of-time scenario is purposefully divided into Two main Parts. Opening with these panoptic Front Pages and Introduction. These pages, before the seven Part One Nails cover quite broad but general thoughts of the Christian propaganda machine and numerous other related postulations. Many of the discussions throughout this Introduction, as well as the Part One essays do not necessarily relate to any specific end–time proposal. The intent is to 'break the mould' of conventional Christian/ religious piety. Which may turn out to be impossibly roseate; in a desiderate effort to induce readers with a diverse understanding of Christian topics and doctrines. These initial discussions might then go some way to set a stage, opening the reader to the difficulties of the sacred books and subsequent beliefs. Those that critics today identify as curious or flat out wrong, deceptive, or manipulative. At points, these early essays may read as if you are pushing a bolder up a mountainside; much as Sisyphus in the bowels of the Roman underworld. In that myth, he spent his days forcefully attempting to roll a stone uphill, only to have it defy his every effort by rolling back down again, leading to an endless cycle of struggle. The near same might be felt as readers traverse the subjects attended to throughout this investigation. There are numerous rabbit-holes and divergent enquiries. Some of which may seem irrelevant to the initial topic being discussed. An endeavour in these opening discussions is to also introduce readers to various concepts of a range of academic fields; that also, first may seem irrelevant and unrelated. But, by including them early in the discussion, the trust is these also further open a readers eyes to aspects of humanity that are often unacknowledged by the religious. The prime reason being. These concepts, ways of viewing the world are likely disregarded as potential tools to understand for a believing community.

As with the real notion that many believers simply are too invested in beliefs of nephology; with their heads in the clouds. Believers though,

DECONSTRUCTING ENDTIME DELUSIONS

would be well-equipped to make sound judgments of their sacred mythic story's if they gained the slightest empathy of the following. For instance, the philosophic term: *teleo-functional reasoning* is used to describe the preconceived thinking everything that exists – has a purpose. The ideology of purpose undoubtedly is an ingrained premise of all religious believers. The thought is, our lives born of God (of course) have a purpose. But do they? Does life really have a purpose? Does everything we encounter daily, have a set, functional purpose? Or, is 'purpose' only really applicable to the meaning we apply to something? Example: Is a rodent's purpose to be caught and killed by predator, trap, or poisoning? Is it the 'purpose' of annoying bugs, or deadly creatures we encounter to be slaughtered if we become threatened, harmed, or irritated by them? What of those animals and the countless other sources we slaughter and consume as part of our diet? Including plant-based foodstuffs. Is it their 'purpose' to become our foodstuff, or is it just that this is how we nowadays assume them? Does the notion of purpose only apply to humanity, or is it widespread? If by 'purpose', we only mean it to apply to fellow humans, what are we to conclude is the prime purpose of stubborn and obvious Terrorists. In regions of the known globe where terrorism is lauded as holy action. Are participants really to be thought of by victim and survivor, as truly or 'only' living within 'their' full and specified purpose? What of the millions of young men who were excited about the 'adventure' of the Great War, the 'war' to end all wars (World War One: 1914-1918), but were slaughtered and maimed for life if they survived this ordeal. What of the millions of Holocaust and other innocent victims of World-War Two? What about random murder and those killed by accidental means? Was or is it their purpose to be slaughtered, denigrated and die often times in a horrendous manner at the hands of people who are clearly deranged? If; however 'purpose' applies to all living things. Just as American poet Ogden Nash famously penned,

> "God in His wisdom made the fly/ and then forgot to tell us why." But to suggest that each individual horsefly is here for a special, unique reason— one different from that of every other horsefly that has ever lived or will

live— by using our theory of mind to reflect on God's intentions in crafting each its own destiny, may get us institutionalized (sic). (If horseflies don't do it for you, simply replace the nominal species with another nonhuman species of your choice; perhaps goats, elm trees, or wild boars may suit your imagination better.) Yet this is precisely what we do when it comes to reasoning about individual members of our own species; and, curiously, the concept of destiny doesn't strike most of us as being ridiculous, insane, or conceptually flawed at all."[xlii]

Bering is correct. Why do we not consider it theoretically impractical and flawed to insist that existence, esp. that of our own and human existence generally has a purpose? The underlining issue to be reckoned with a "made for a specific purpose" ideology christians tout as a valid philosophy. It is precisely a perception based solely on and supported by countless myth. Particularly, surrounding the myth that at some time in pre-history some deity assumed to mush some clay together and 'create' the first Nano/ Monocellular-entity that somehow 'evolved' enough to become sentient, and in time, learned to feed itself. Eventually allowing the birth and evolution of every other living organism. That evolved sentient 'Life,' - then mucked up, and so had to be saved from further disfunction. The 'saving' from that disfunction and regeneration of the 'proper', came through one particular man-deity. Further, if it is to be argued that all 'Life', with a capital 'L' has a purpose; pray tell, what could possibly be the purpose to Aids; Cancer; Smallpox; Anthrax or any other virus? Viruses and the raft of diseases we often encounter, or cause is after all alive! What about a Mosquito/ a parasite etc.? Do these irritants also have a set purpose? Mozzies, and other annoying and sometimes aggressive biting bugs and insects (wasps); why do they act the way they do? Further, why do they have wings? What is their sole purpose? Why did a specified altruistic deity craft such creatures and protrusions on some, but not all creatures? Every creature that has ever, and will ever live, has organs and body parts that have served an evolving multitude of functions. Some of which are definitely not in any way natural! To this historian, Yuval Harari wrote that the concepts known as 'natural, and unnatural', as related to 'purpose', does not come down to us from studies in biology, but from Christian theology. Meaning:

what we imagine as an 'original' purpose was given by the supreme deity figure. That deity 'created' the human body, then animal body with all its functions; each limb, and each appendage, and organ had one specific purpose. A 'naturally' deity-ordained purpose: "If we use our limbs and organs for the purpose envisioned by God, then it is a natural activity. To use them differently than God intends is unnatural. But evolution has no purpose." Harari further posits quite correctly that no thing 'evolved' with a specific purpose. They might have evolved for a particular function at one point in time, but they also adapted so they had multiple usages. His example is the mouth. Yes,

> "...it evolved so an organism could feed. But, feeding is not the only purpose (humans) use mouths for. Without a mouth how would you propose we speak; how could we kiss, laugh, smile? Wings of birds and insects evolved similarly; through a series of processes. They did not just magically naturally one day appear. They developed from organs that served another purpose. According to one theory, insect wings evolved millions of years ago from body protrusions on flightless bugs. Bugs with bumps had a larger surface area than those without bumps, and this enabled them to absorb more sunlight and thus stay warmer. In a slow evolutionary process, these solar heaters grew larger... Some insects started using the things to glide, and from there it was a small step to wings that could actually propel the bug through the air. Next time a mosquito buzzes in your ear, accuse her of unnatural behaviour. If she were well behaved and content with what God gave her, she'd use her wings only as solar panels."[xliii]

Here, is implied a purpose for and the evolution of wings. So too our bodily organ's. So, does a purpose only really apply to humanity? Now, apply a 'purpose' to an end-time. If such a scenario is to truly happen what is its purpose? What is the purpose of macabre end-time scenes depicted in any Christian text? Those weirdly fascinating scenes depicted in texts like revelation. A potential purpose I can learn that could be derived from apocalyptic, end-time books and other materials. Is these are supposed to instil a further sense of dread, fear, and guilt. That they must then adhere to some nemo-deity and its mandates. Which is very manipulative and oppressive. Moving from teleo-functional reasoning, is one other cognitive factor that warrants merit for the religiously inclined. This is termed by Developmental Psychologists, *Person Permanence*. Which seems a favourite of God-mythologists. Esp., those advocating a rapture, or resurrection. Jesse Bering explains this element of our being. That it embraces all mental processes via an awareness of things and people existing out of sight. For the religious– this is the believing that at death, people don't cease existing. But, somehow somewhere, at some point in time and space, – those who are known dead are engaging with the living; although in a semi-alive state. All of us are savvy to the fact that friends, family and other people are alive somewhere, doing something; even when we cannot physically see them. But, person permanence takes this idea further. Particularly for those who have a religious belief in an after–life. The idea extends to what is mentally represented or envisioned in the mind and in real time.

> "How to locate your loved ones in the afterlife isn't a problem we can solve here. But it's clear that when combined with the simulation constraints of our theory of mind, person permanence is another cognitive hurdle that gets in the way of our effectively realizing (sic) the dead as they truly are— infinitely in situ, inanimate carbon residue. Instead it's much more natural to imagine them as existing in some exotic, unobservable locale, very much living their dead lives."[xliv]

Person Permanence is undoubtedly a peculiarity of the religious. Who continue to affirm the idea that a sage/ deity-man figure who although apparently died some two millennia ago, still exists just as they? However, this God-man exists strangely in a realm that none have ever visited or lived to tell. Nonetheless, this special individual somehow still communes with certain people. Person permanence is a strange phenomenon indeed whereto each of us conforms; especially when a loved one dies. We do not appreciate that after death, all previous life becomes nothing. These and other cognitive components encountered in my studies have undoubtedly offered a more realistic base from which explanations of end-time matters could be placed. Specifically, to how and why certain beliefs and patterns of understanding for the religious could be considered. Readers may disagree – that is your prerogative, but it must surely be admitted the understanding of how or why we dream and concoct certain things, and what causes us to make all manners of weird religious philosophies shows some merit. One final, and kind of technical term to mention at the beginning of this investigation is an exegetical (interpretation) method often used by unskilled, fundamental believing authors. Where views, and proposals are offered as truths by fundamental 'Christian' authors like the few I investigate in these studies. Authors like Rob Skiba (Nail Nine) who has likely unwittingly committed the fallacy:

> "...termed *illegitimate totality transfer*." This is, supposing that the meaning of a word in one particular context expands to others in its semantic range in conflict with its context."[xlv]

Clear examples of *illegitimate totality transfer* can be found peppered throughout the whole of the Christian sacred text. One of the first occurrences is found and highlighted in Genesis, chapter three (Nail Four below). The same fallacy is played out in Derek Gilbert's assertions. Another, is mentioned in Part Two. Specifically, Nail Nine; in my study of nephilim/ giants and associated oddities. It is believed this fallacy is identified in the writing of Rob Skiba. Particularly, in his attestations surrounding nephilim of Genesis 6 and the ideas he proposes regarding a latter passage; Amos, chapter two, verse nine. Which he assumes to join to Genesis 6 and other passages. Such preliminary discussions, including the Nails of Part One are offered as a means that hopefully assists readers in considering the depth of knowledge and understanding we now possess. Especially the knowledge gained over the last 100 years of the Judaeo-Christian sacred texts; and the countless academic fields and sciences regarding the human species. What is beginning to emerge and be understood about how thoughts and feelings and opinions shape our actions and attitudes? Including theological attitudes. It is trusted that these precursory, Introductory statements open instead of occlude our view or understanding of Christian end–times.

Moving to the First Part: we take an excursion into often long-forgotten or conveniently understated Christian history and some reasons offered. The First Nail. Nails Two and Three, here are examined several Old

Testament story's; Nail Two examines the Exodus. In Nail Three we look at the destruction of Sodom et al. Reconsidering these for their historic authenticity alongside end–time thoughts. It will be realised in these first few Nails that much of what is assumed to be truth and Bible fact, really has no basis in reality. It will be stated for instance, there is absolutely no confirming evidence suggesting an Exodus happened just as is portrayed in the Judaeo-Christian tome, and that there is much disagreement also surrounding the Sodom et al episode. Nail Four, is a commentary that is pointedly altered in its view; specifically this Nail has a focus on the third chapter of Genesis. A perspective that is intended to challenge a readers' traditional religious explanation. I briefly dissect the chapter from the learned Hebrew perspective of a couple of scholars and authors. After which I begin looking at selected symbolism of Genesis three. Primarily seeking to learn what the symbolism of snakes and serpents could be representative in this Bible chapter. Undoubted, conclusions to what took place will either surprise or anger a reader. For the simple reason they dismiss completely the orthodox interpretation and so, conclusion. The story recorded in Genesis 3 does not infer some nefarious act committed. Rather, quite the opposite. Nail Four offers a conclusion and interpretation to the Genesis 3 narrative that yet is found by any other commentator! Nail Five looks briefly into the mythic tale of Gilgamesh (of Babylonian fame). The myth of Gilgamesh by modern Christian apocalyptic authors has become widely used as a supporting beam for their premise. Although an affirmed Babylonian King, Gilgamesh's status as a mortal being, transformed to become for many christians, one of the nephilim (see Genesis chapter 6). He has made an appearance in numerous Christian end-time materials. But, as fascinating as the story of Gilgamesh is, there is no discernible reason to assume he can be linked (even by theme) to nephilim. In Nail Five; it is submitted to readers a conclusion that might rattle the cage of those who advocate for immortality; the very ideology behind the mentioned earlier person permanence, or the Christian rapture theory. Although a major theme of Gilgamesh is his quest for immortality (i.e. person permanence), as with rapture theory are just invalidated. I show how (specifically) in the next Nail. Nail Six: I offer a compressed analysis of the modern 'Rapture' idea. Disputing it holds any validity as a proposal. Christians would be better served if they actually studied the texts instead of taking as gospel what some religious puppet master author dictates. Nail Seven, offers a small analysis of associated New Testament passages modern campaigners seem to attach and use in support for rapture theory. I conclude the First Part with satire based on Douglas Adams' 'Hitchhikers guide to the Galaxy'. After which is offered a quick reassessment and summary of the themes and study subjects confronted in the First Part.

The Second Part, comprises possibly the most extensive portion of this investigation. The Nails of this section is investigated a mere fraction of the assumptions and fantasies that surround modern end-time hypotheses. Assumed by millions of Christian and religious believers to be straightforward and soon unleashed upon the Earth. We explore in this section several specific Bible subjects. Reviewing these as directly as possible and drawing conclusions from what scholars, Bible helps such as dictionaries, theological studies, lexicons and other specialised texts have determined. During this process there will be numerous references, and Bible passages drawn upon. Where the process may seem illogical, and unnecessarily laborious. Yet, hopefully the leapfrogging to and fro of subjects and topics successfully draw for the reader a picture that no passage of the holy texts should in reality be read in isolation to another. Topics, and themes have a connecting point, and passages that were thought to have stated one thing, often do not. Or, that it is a far stretch of imagination to infer what is believed. Throughout this Part Two of investigations is reviewed also numerous Bible personalities and relatable themes. Such as, enoch, and the liquidation of Planet Earth. Both in Nail Eight. There is also a premise proposed by a Christian film-maker. I titled: "A Bad case of Christian Cryptozoology". Of the aforementioned author Rob Skiba. He authored a series of books with end-time themes. The first is basically thought by Skiba to be a 'Genesis Six Experiment'. This comprises the Ninth Nail. This is undoubtedly the longest Nail of this investigation. Here, I not only scrutinise the initial pages of the first chapter of Rob Skiba's book, "Babylon Rising" and the proposals from his 'studies' of the enigmatic beings – called nephilim/ giants of (Genesis 6:1–4). I also endeavour to flesh out several like issues to Skiba's chosen topic. For instance, countless Christian authors nowadays like Skiba, throw to their readership numerous postulations about what causes gigantism and other anomalies. There are also questions surrounding whether there were beings of huge proportions roaming the planet in prehistoric times. Further, what of skeletons with extra limbs and extra teeth? There seem to be numbers of detailed accounts of such skeletons being discovered around the planet. All these topics are often assumed by Christian authors and are used as 'proof' for their over all summations of an apocalyptic end-time scenario. Throughout my investigations into Rob's over all hypotheses, advanced are my own discoveries, which have lengthened greatly this Nail. Within this Nail also, the attempt was to offer lucid answers to other proposals that are closely linked by christians to nephilim; i.e., the numerous discoveries of elongated skulls; and the discoveries of various enigmatic, and strangely larger–than–average skeletal remains that have been unearthed in recent decades. We look at in Nail Ten briefly, the equally enigmatic subjects of angels/ angelology and demons/ demonology; Satan; Nails Eleven through Fifteen, seek to view objectively assumed end time subjects like; 'sons of God'; Apocalypse; the so-called blood moon, as a 'sign' announcing the imminent 'return' of a Messiah figure; the 7–year itch; gog and magog... including some further comments on the entity known as Satan. Part Two; therefore, tackles some of the pressing subjects and personalities of Christian end-time catastrophism. Those subjects that hold an interest to this author. It is not the intention throughout the investigation of any subject in this Second Part; however, to offer any predictions or timeline. Rather, as was stated in the Front Pages above my main objective is to arrive at a near zero point, – an origin; a potential, proposed or actual origin to end time apocalyptic topics. It is therefore assumed many conclusions and the materials utilised to reach and formulate illations, may offer readers a Damascus Road experience– just as is alleged to have happened to 'apostle paul' (acts 9:1–19). All subjects commented upon in this Second Part are anticipated and continue to form some basis of modern Western end–time theories. Wikipedia references later outlines just how prevalent apocalyptic ideas are and has been throughout documented human history. All subjects in this section are criticised and deconstructed for their value or lack of it. All having derived from contemptuous religious dreams; with only slight allusions to factuality. One commentator most interestingly offers insight into why Homo Sapiens have a proclivity to all kinds of religious insinuation. Ben Harrison Carter wrote:

> "...humans desire fantasy solutions to real life problems and are willing to sublimate facts to such fantasies, religions based on faith in nothing but old books and preaching representatives of the old ideas will continue to captivate people..."[xlvi]

Simply, all Sapiens have a liking of all sorts of 'make–believe' solutions to assist us in managing and surviving numerous difficulties faced daily. Driving us often to the perceived 'security' of religious solutions to many of those troubles. Though they may also be far–fetched and delusional. Deriving from nothing other than the imagination and rehearsing of outdated and often incorrect philosophies that offer a brief instant of comfort to the devotee. Jason Slone hit the nail perfectly in his earlier cited book stating a matter of factly the quandaries, asking; Why do people believe certain things when they shouldn't? It's not a matter of disliking what is believed. Rather, the greater issue is believing things according to one's own religious tenants. Certain of those beliefs are just stupid and do not align with those favoured texts. Sloan writes:

> "Why do religious people kill? Why do religious people philander? Why do Bible believers eat cheeseburgers when the rules in Leviticus say to not mix beef and dairy? Why are religious people racist? Why do religious people pray to win wars? And why do religious people pray to win football games (if God is at all like Christian theologians claim, then certainly he must not care about ... football, let alone favor (sic) one person's team over another)? Why is this problem important? It is important because, for one, it teaches us the lesson that theology doesn't determine people's actual thoughts and behaviours. In fact, the ideas that one learns in one's given culture, such as theological ideas, play only a partial role in what people actually think and do."[xlvii]

STEVE MORGAN

Despite sounding extensive, in no way is this compilation of select end-time topics an attempt to be all-embracing or exhaustive. Rather, each topic chosen for the Second Part of this investigation was so as they represent what is noticed as the most popular in recent years for Western christianity. These are then often inchoate developments. Instead of completely dilated. It was attempted; however, to expound upon all subjects as much as possible to offer a coherent examination. It cannot be stated categorically nonetheless, that every caprice examined is the same for different groups of religious believers. Diversity abounds. Accordingly, readers will not find in these pages an extensive commentary on various other subjects like U.F.O.'s. These are often phenomena not massively covered by most religious authors without an underlining 'evil' intent. Numerous more qualified writers often propose interesting and more reasonable commentaries on such subjects. No attempt in this work has been made to include subjects pertaining specifically to the other two—modern cosmic-world religions either; i.e., Judaism, and Islam and the connecting hypotheses each put forward to assist an arrival of an end–of–time–as–we–know–it. Readers will also not find any corresponding review or commentary on the subject of the building of a Jewish Third Temple; issues surrounding the birth of a red heifer, or its importance to both Judaism and Christian 'messianic'/end–time theology. The reinstating of a Sanhedrin, the Jewish religious governing body. Numerous accounts have been authored covering these themes already. Written from either an Islamic, the Christian or Judaic viewpoint, and so understandably, are rather prejudiced to an understanding from that religious perspective. Besides who can really discuss every avenue, every postulation, every ideology? Particular details of mystical angelic beings, labelled Watchers that feature in the religious Apocryphal books titled, 'Enoch', does not though averted to occasionally play a major role. These and numerous like subjects have been well represented and discussed by various authors. Especially by Dr. Anne Nyland. Dr. Nyland's material is highly recommended.

As an addendum there is offered at the back of this investigation several Appendices. In these essays, are briefly explored first the topic of

'Symbolism'; Appendix 1. Offering a very brief dictionary of those particular words <u>underlined</u> throughout this investigation. Also, offered to readers is a symbolic interpretation of Genesis 6:1-4 in this appendix to show how symbolism could be utilised as a means of understanding the sacred texts. In opposition to the usual ultra-spiritualised, literal passive Revelation conception that is prevalent today. If readers are interested, my interpretation of the symbolic nature of Genesis 6 (1-4) may assist in comprehending how much of their sacred books rely on symbolism; even the most mundane of words often has a symbolic meaning, and so, might best be understood as primarily emblematic, suggestive, and demonstrative; instead of purely literal when reading the sacred books.[xlviii] Appendix 2 offers interested readers a brief exposé on Religion as a whole. Exploring some elements surrounding the inception of religion; the 'gods;' Demi-gods and the countless monsters encountered in sacred texts. In Appendix 3, the following are discussed: 'myth', followed by Eschatology, Apocalypse and a few other subjects. Including the concept of 'belief'. Myth and legend are it may surprise, not illegitimate or corrupt statements of history. Myth and Legend are sources of often vital information of the history they espouse. But, as is too often the case with christians particularly, myth and legend are seen as a debased form of communication; that is, unless they seem to add a sense of validity to a favoured sacred topic (notable are those reviewed in the Second Part to this investigation.)

Apocalypse and End Time a modern obsession:

ANGLICAN BISHOP AND historian, Nicolas Wright in his book "The Millennium Myth" has a dig at the proliferation in modern times of apocalyptically themed materials widely available today. Noting that it is undeniably the Hollywood speak that sends minds into a whirling frenzy of fantasy. Numbers of people, believer and nonbeliever are convinced there will be soon any number of imminent cataclysmic events. All which they see as potentially devastating the planet. From the aforementioned anthropogenic global disaster, to 'space-alien invasion/ deliverance and everything between. Nicolas also states in a matter-of-factly-manner;

that in these first decades of the new millennium, Apocalypse has become an obsession. Yet, we have no idea of where any postulated disaster will lead us. To where, and what we will find there we have no clue. He affirms:

> "...the great political changes, particularly the collapse of the Berlin Wall and all that has followed from it; and the ecological changes of which we are now increasingly aware—all have contributed. Global warming didn't cause the end of the Cold War; that would have been taking a metaphor too literally, something which as we shall see intelligent readers of apocalyptic shouldn't do. But they just happen to have coincided, and together with lots of other factors they produce a sense of urgency, transformation, new possibilities and perhaps new dangers. All the stuff of which modern apocalyptic fantasies are made."[xlix]

Is this prognosis of Apocalypse as an imagined and fantasy world telling? Is he inferring that believers should view Apocalypse as little else than fantasy? Like any Hollywood blockbuster, subscribing to Apocalypse fantasies can and is often added the themes of any Christian/ religious end–time topic. Themes like rapture or resurrection; a cosmic alteration to consciousness; an invasion (by an E.T. who is usually misanthropic by nature), or we will witness some other projected frightful and looming cataclysmic event: that essentially wipes out most of life on our planet, plunging it again into a debased prehistoric/ preindustrial revolution era. Where the planet and its inhabitance are left as a fossilised silhouette of its former illustrious self. Recall the hype around the now defunct Mayan Calendar hypotheses surrounding the year 2012. For years preceding its believed eventuality a cataclysm was postulated. Vast tomes of literature and media focused on this one event was published. To what end?

Conspiracies abound:

MODERN LIFE IS AWASH with stories, tales, and legends. Most now classed as pseudoscientific and pseudo historical mythology of the ancient past. Some are humorous, many dark, and disturbing. For instance: how likely would events be as those described by the Mad Max movie franchise, the t.v. drama's Continuum, Fringe, and Roswell. Or,

DECONSTRUCTING ENDTIME DELUSIONS

indeed any other apocalyptically inspired drama? What might humanity learn from the multitude of tales, adventures and legends we continually tell each other through them? What might they be teaching? Are we headed for complete obliteration; an extirpation that is despicably pushed by those who should know better. Government personnel, some university academics through to school teachers are literally frightening the life out of children as young as 10 years of age; with catastrophic warnings of damaging and dire effects of the planet-wide global-warming meltdown! Is the world really going into great convulsions and finally end as many films, t.v. drama's, academicians and numerous media sources would have us postulate and guess? Honestly, there does seem to be a valid reason for a warning of sorts. Yet, the turmoil witnessed throughout the earth, is not necessarily a warning of an assumed physical catastrophic event; such as the insaneness of an elite class with their fear-porn postulating of a catastrophic Earthly boiling that will destroy humanity. Rather, the more the author witnesses such alarmism, the greater the need is for a 'conscious' transformation. A transformation of the human consciousness aligned to a Universal consciousness that rebalances all life forms; both flora, and fauna. But, this is another topic altogether. Might this compilation assist ever so slightly in its achievement.

There have increasingly been in recent decades numerous religious and secular accounts about our Planet in the ancient past being home to a long-lost advanced giant-race of hominid. Fearsome humans like creatures that possibly once terrorised ancient fauna. How much of this could be authentic? Might this just be clever manipulation of human hopes and fears, and a thriving imagination working overtime? How much is tangible? Considering there is an ever–increasing amount of information offered by various academics and researchers regarding what is newly established knowledge of our home planet – Earth – as well as other planetary systems and the workings of our Universe. Incipient are vast amounts of documented evidence suggesting that there are yet infinite amounts of undisclosed things that could go 'Thud' in the night. Documented intelligences that could very well parallel many world mythologies. What if the legends and mythic traditions of the world depict an unexpected truth – that is stranger than fiction? Conspiracies abound. There are literally millions of conspiracies insinuating that clandestine government agencies the world over possesses a vast array of alien/ extraterrestrial/ u.f.o. confirming documentation and evidence. Christian theorists are not immune to these ideologies, but have jump this same bandwagon also with a surprising array of end–time materials of u.f.o. invasions and alien-human hybridisation. Many of which are postulating sacred book links alongside some end-time ideology. Any Internet search displays astoundingly, over five billion results. Most comprising books, lectures, podcasts, sermons, Bible commentaries explaining the usual Christian side to the story. Countless non–religious and religious materials are flooding the Internet market. All which postulates various insights into countless mysteries. Many focus their attention on various U.F.O. phenomenon. Astoundingly, none of these however have yet, really 'for security reasons' been completely publicly disclosed. In the wake of the 'Roswell incident' in the late 1940's, and with the 'innovation' of the World-Wide-Web (Internet) published works of researchers into alternative, occulted history, surreptitious government operations, 'prophetic' oracles, and other secreted historic matters have flooded the marketplace. There are numerous 'documentary' programs. Search any media platform like Netflix, UTube, and television networks like the 'History' and 'Discovery Channel', and you will likely come across countless programs that espouse 'beliefs' of extraterrestrial infiltration of the Earth in the distant past. The discovery of skeletal remains with elongated skulls, hyperdontia and other anomaly's have lent themselves to many. Regards the u.f.o. phenomenon; The History channel released recently on dvd its documentary series; "Hangar 1: the UFO files", in which the mufon (Mutual UFO Network), a world respected u.f.o. investigative organisation (founded in 1969), made available its seventy thousand plus case files. Throughout this documentary series, a case is. It seems steadily built identifying there are very likely numerous surreptitious government u.f.o. operations. Mostly throughout the USA that seems to confirm the enigmatic u.f.o. phenomenon.

DECONSTRUCTING ENDTIME DELUSIONS

Swiss psychologist Carl Jung in one of his books, "Flying Saucers: A Modern Myth of things seen in the skies" (1958) weighed in on the emerging u.f.o. phenomenon. Jung was a skeptic of all such matters. Maybe because at the time the world had been in the grips of the 'Cold War' and, psychological unrest was uncontrolled in both the Western and Eastern hemispheres. His intrigue surrounding this marvel led him to conclude that the phenomenon was a myth making exercise. On the first page to his book, Jung calls U.F.O. apparitions a "visionary rumour." The current hype surrounding much of the u.f.o. phenomena for instance, could be understood as part of "Our Weltanschauung..." (Jung p. 13). That is: as part of individual and group views to life. Not necessarily hoax, but derived from unconscious group and individual thinking; the surfacing of "... symbols representing, in visual form, some thought that was not thought consciously, but is merely potentially present in the unconscious, in invisible form, and attains visibility only through the process of becoming conscious." (ibid. p. 14.) Much is probably the same in these first decades of the new Millennium; with the proliferation of Christian end time materials and the constant barrage of an apparent looming global-warming event. As is the ambition, is shown throughout this tome, Jung's perceptions sixty years ago is relevant to how many religious people today read, perceive, and interpret certain passages and 'themes' they recognise as solidly taught in those favourite sacred texts. They are to some however, no thing but another example of "Our Weltanschauung..." As this material is revised, 2023 there is a vast amount of 'evidences' coming to light that seems to verify the UFO phenomenon. Particular to the USA, there is a drip-feeding of materials for the awareness of a wider society about all manners of UFO confirming literature. Confirming biological, and 'other' worldly material recovery, and reverse engineering. UFO phenomena are also closely tied to the eerily spectacular radio play, "War of the Worlds" by Orson Wells (1938). The drama of the play had vast psychological impact as well, as looming upon the horizon, was World-War Two. In the not distant future, governments around the globe are preparing to announce with similar frightening psychological conjecture, a similar scenario to Wells' radio play. The American government has also recently launched a 'new' program, 'Space Force'. A largely military operation of intelligence gathering, as a means of thwarting nefarious operations from space. Intelligence has leaked that such a program was enacted, and launched as a way to 'safeguard' the Earth, and Space from an 'alien' attack. What a strange proposal this is?

Whether extraterrestrial beings exist, are nefarious, or benevolent is a topic best left to others. Let it be firmly stated however, aside the occasional meteor shower, and falling space debris from the space junk we have since the late 1960's littered in orbit. Has the earth ever been 'invaded' from a force/entity that is not terrestrial? If such has ever in the past taken place, surely records of it would exist; either as a chronicled written, or a pictorial form. The postulations by fringe authors are not true. That pictograms found in stone depict space aliens or the like. Besides, no doubt such an 'impending' attack would be initiated, and propagated by government; the sole purpose for controlling, manipulating, and subjugating the population. Dr. Steven Greer has come to acknowledge and warn the population that such an imminent 'attack' by an 'alien force' is a hoax; and will be widely broadcast for a nefarious purpose by governments. Rest assured that such an 'attack' if ever to materialise, such will be a complete hoax, a fabrication of government. Such will likely be initiated as a further and imminent means of 'saving' the planet, after efforts of climate scaremongers begins to fall upon deaf ears for the manipulative reasoning it too proposes. Jung's and the perceptions of Orson Wells sixty plus years ago surely seem to be more insightful today. Seems, a psychological battleground has been established. Government, using all known psychological manipulative tools, have their own best interests in mind. Not the interests of the governed population. Whether known, believed, understood countless Christian authors continue to publish various accounts that undoubtedly offer an attempt to direct attention to a growing intensity and an arrival of an alien type of disclosure. Tied somehow to an apocalyptic 'end–time' of biblical proportions.

DECONSTRUCTING ENDTIME DELUSIONS

In the 1970's it wasn't a U.F.O. invasion that weighed and frightened the minds of a generation, but a disaster caused by global-cooling. The planet should have frozen all life, and yet, we are fine and thriving! It seems though, the more technologically advanced humanity becomes, the more pea-brained we become. The more progressive society becomes; the more progressively unintelligent humanity is. We would nowadays rather rely on computers to think for us. Relying on a computer to compose, and 'spell-check' material that is then labelled ours. Not this author, who composed, and edited this work completely. We listen to and adhere information offered by crackpot 'elites' to direct our life movements. Then wonder why life gets difficult and not satisfying. It is a scarily strange and mysterious time, we are living in. The world, we are told is frankly, doomed. Apparently all ills are the fault of humanity. Either, there are too many of us populating the planet, depleting too many resources, too quickly. While destroying the planet, just by being! So, either we eradicate from our atmosphere all vital gasses (like the demonically inspired CO_2), there will be an announcement of an impending Space attack by aliens, or we're going to rely on these space-brothers for our deliverance. No wonder our children are fearful of the future. All they hear by society and are taught by the education system is that the world will soon melt away. Humanity has concocted all manners of super frightful events like the present 'global-extinction' scaremongering by elites; and funnily enough, humanity soldiers on. Is it not also strange there is nowadays a concerted effort to satiate our enthusiasm for anything mysterious, anything dire, and apocalyptic. Vast amounts of investigative 'intelligence' are published each year that focus on esoteric Earth Sciences and E.T.'s, and ancient not of this world and-subterranean archaeological remnant. Numerous books, articles, lectures, web-casts continue to surface explaining structures and monuments said to have been built not only on and under the surface of the Earth, but also 'out there' in Space. Built mysteriously and then suddenly abandoned on the surface of our near celestial neighbours. Mars and our own satellite – the moon.[1] An upsurge of information is now also coming to light explaining various mysterious ancient gigantic hominid skeletal remains found scattered across the globe. Which, for whatever reason have been related to various Judaeo-Christian sacred text themes and passages. Passages that are still very much not easily explained such as Genesis 6:1-4. The narrative regarding peculiar beings the sacred book calls – nephilim, or giants.[li]

Our Weltanschauung - Believing is seeing:

NONE OF THIS MATERIAL –biblical and secular – whether aimed at disclosing or exposing or not numerous enigmatic and mysterious events should ever prevent a healthy skepticism. A good deal of the information in the materials described as with those works quoted throughout the rest of this tome, in the end, may be proven to be little else than an exercise in cognitive bias. Or equally confirmation bias. As Jung above, Psychologists and Neuroscientists' research into human cognitive function confirms we are all plagued by these phenomena. Both prejudice mechanisms are part and parcel of our human makeup. Acting as a survival apparatus. It is essentially where data confirm what is already believed or is suspected to be genuine. Which then leads to what are seen and hence, confirming the belief it becomes true, and thus is believed. Ultimately, this is a closed loop. "Believing is seeing"; this is cognitive bias.[lii] Cognitive biases lead to false, or highly skewed reasoning. In turn this leads to decision making that confirms a belief. Our predilection to a cognitive bias seems to be increasingly spurred on and confirmed by emerging authors writing that our lives are a simulation. Which may or not be correct. Former 'footballer' (soccer) and sports broadcaster turned professional conspiracy theorist, David Icke in his book "Phantom Self", attempts to answer the question of whom or what is controlling the world. Quite directly a 'key premise' of Phantom Self is that we are really not who we think we are. We are rather the reflection seen in a mirror, – a simulated self: "What you believe you perceive and what you perceive you experience." (p. 42.) To a fair portion of the religious population the identically simulated believing and experience becomes unfaltering confirmed truth. This, should be likened to the single notion; 'faith'! For this then becomes the benchmark for everything. Through the simulated impulse of faith, certain 'things' are known to exist and be true, because this is the believed evident experience. Cognitive bias among other syndromes of the human condition, is also the "...stablemate of cognitive dissonance..." defined by psychiatrist and philosopher, Frantz Fanon who stated that all people hold core beliefs about numerous subjects. So when these are challenged by evidence that disputes a favoured or honoured belief, more often than not, we cannot conceptualise or accept that data. This is called, "...cognitive dissonance. And because it is so important to protect the core belief, [we] will rationalize (sic), ignore, and even deny anything that doesn't fit in with the core belief."[liii] The problem that many readers, specifically those holding loved and cherished beliefs about Bible and numerous concepts claimed to be derived from it will face. Is primarily that what you may read in these pages will butt against those ideologies, and may cause the stated cognitive dissonance. Readers are implored to note these, but persist through the commentary. In the following pages readers are introduced using the information and sources studied yet, to what is identified as the truth regarding religious concepts related to an apocalyptic end–times. Many of which, so it is believed are seen as mysterious and 'supernatural'. But with some difficult and often time-consuming investigation and research of a wide scope of data. Such mysteries are here revealed and exposed in all probabilities explainable. That many religious ideas of end–times are seen as mysterious and so have an element of supernaturalism added to them, led me to conclude that along with cognitive and confirming biases, there is another phenomenon plaguing religion. The author came to believe through these studies; there is a vast myopic psyche plaguing the religious. The religious population seems now, as ever, to be gripped by a stunting psychosis. A neurosis surrounding specifically the many 'Doctrines of Certainty'; to borrow from mathematician Christopher Essex and economist Ross McKitrick, that countless christians aver.[liv] I was surprised to realise that the doctrines of certainty championed by the Christian religion parallel and could more likely be easily explained by authors of some alternative, secular, and academic disciplines.

Nexus:

THE NEXUS OF THIS INVESTIGATION is concerned about the mass of popular thought and theistic arguments surrounding <u>Armageddon</u> and end–times. Those championed by the modern religious apologist. Those chaos theories of the apologist, hinting that the world will fall victim to a state of pandemonium, which never seems to quite acknowledge our own bitchiness to this planet and our fellow travellers. Catastrophism; one author says that humanity still suffers catasrophobia! Quite a fitting idea. Someone somewhere is always going to sit on either side of the fence; as a pessimist, or spiritualistic utopian sprouting the latest catastrophe theory and the means by which one can escape its devastations. Both lead to belligerence and intolerance, which is today heightened by those religious cataclysm theories. To the point, where there are multiple in-house and 'inter-religious' wars still waged around the World. These will only dissipate, or dissolve when all forms of religion are abandoned, or in the least, restrained to the point where people are not coerced through premonitions of guilt or noisy propaganda to connect some religious bandwagon. Through the time in study my awareness, attitude and comprehension to many areas of this enquiry were altered and keenly expanded into realms never before considered. Thoughts specifically about how and why we human beings sensationalise all manners of myth that surrounds 'calamity theories' supposedly derived from sacred sources. Has taken me on a journey not earlier considered. A journey of attempting to adequately divide facts from often believed fiction; a journey that has branched off into many fields of esoteric, academic, and occultist learning. I had once through my own ignorance 'believed' that certain unfounded theories and pronounced doctrines of sacred book supremacy; that these trumped natural sciences and 'secular' fields of study, because the text was presumed and widely presented to be infallibly the 'Word' of 'a' great deity who 'must' on all accounts be followed. Inviolability check: this sacred text is no more consecrated than any other work of literature. The 'sanctity' of the text is merely a designation. A label of men who wish to revere it; a marque that vast numbers of the unwary continue to respect. Employing the rhetoric of faith. A device lacking trustworthy merit as it relies upon argumentation independent of evidential truth. Lloyd Graham and Tony Bushby inscribe among many others; the whole concept of sacred text is a perversion by the priesthood. A claim that any studious study of its texts positively reveals.[lv] It is well known today that scholars recognise the early 'Christian' presbyter Eusebius as a liar, a cheat, and an encourager of 'cons'. Especially when an ecumenical benefit might be gained by the Church! He did after all at one point make the shocking comment: "It is an act of virtue to deceive and lie, when by such means the interests of the Church might be promoted."[lvi] Why believers still revere him as a 'Church Father' of renown is beyond explanation. Before 1907 Catholic encyclopaedias knew that their 'sacred' books were written by fraudsters and were not worthy of being regarded as historical: "The Church also admitted that the Gospel writers wrote what they liked: "It was the public character of a diviners (the glorified name given in modern times to early Church writers) to mould and blend... until they complied with their own fancy."[lvii]

Believers may now be getting quite despondent and agitated. Some may even be shouting obscenities, muttering/ grumbling and cursing me for these statements; that your sacred book is not at all of a 'sacred nature' but is just as un-sanctimonious as any other literature produced by man. Not accepting the fact, this 'holy book' is just the work of an ignorant and perverted priesthood who twisted and contorted what they liked for their own fancy. I am now inclined to believe alternate studies on Christian foundation(s). Authors Ahmed Osman, Moustafa Gadalla and several other writers who convincingly argue for a 'root' of Judaism and therefore, christianity in Egyptian Cultic Magic (Religion). See also Barry Ford's book in the bibliography who has found that both Old Testament and New Testament texts can be dated to 300B.C.E. Neither text can be categorically known as original. A blow no doubt to all those who contend the sacred texts is inspired. Then there are the works of other authors who make a convincing argument that the Old Testament is traceable to tales from Arabia; that the initial five 'books' of Bible are highlights and embellishments of tribal legends, religious myths, and cultic laws, and rites from all over the Mediterranean. Embellished to fit an Israeli/Jewish milieu. Also, are the countless contradictions that are within its texts. Many of which are not, or cannot easily be explained away. Let alone explained convincingly as truthful; a case in point is the two episodes I deconstruct in a couple of Nails below; the Exodus, and Sodom, and gomorrah story's. Nails two, and three respectfully. Jacques Berlinerblau highlights a few of the issues of contradiction for good measure that believers all too often ignore or are unaware. There are passages for instance that clearly state that the principal deity 'spoke' to Moses face to face, just as friends would. This is strange, as a few lines later, we also read nobody, no human can 'see' the face of the deity and live! (Exodus 33) There are also accounts where people are reported to have died in one passage, but then reappear as if alive, and not just a few people's names change, up to three times. All which can become confusing for the 'casual' reader. Besides, there are certain passages in the first five books of the sacred text that has according to scholars, been written by Four separate ancient authors. Two of these were ultra deists. Each using a different name for the principle deity (1) an elohist (his God was 'Elohim') (2) another used Yahweh as the principle focus (he's the 'Yahwist') (3) he was a 'priestly' author, and finally the author labelled the 'deuteronomist'. Scholars have found that certain passages have been blended and moulded by each of these separate redactors to make the sacred books a coherent whole. But by doing so: "Scads of biblical sentences...appear to be ungrammatical or without discernible meaning."[lviii] Aside such truths, when earnestly scrutinised one conclusion we can describe about this revered book is that its dialogue is absorbed and transfixed most often on the following four themes; fear, death, sin, and guilt. Page after page the authors are consumed with exposing some form of alleged sin and guilt, which ends in fear of death and eternal damnation if the prescribed antidote is not adhered. Not just a few such messages are of an apocalyptic end time genre. A crazy reckoning to say the least! Religious authorities however, still compel today's plebeian to 'accept as true' its message is ultimately positive, and that through it the Church, The 'House of Delusion', has sovereign authority over lives. Yet, line upon line of our sacred text is consumed with death, punishment, retribution, hell, violence, manipulation, rules, regulation, and all conduct of human vice. Some portions of its text read like a modern slasher flick. Others are subdued, reading like the movie, The Notebook.

It is bewildering that every human vice continually surfaces in every society. If so many of western populations supposedly guess in the 'integrity' and sanctity of this apparent sacred text as the pinnacle and moral apparatus, it is reasonable to imagine that at least after two thousand years of indoctrination, such vices would be near if not wholly extinct. Yet, they are very much alive and well. Why? One reason is that these scriptures are understood from the wrong perspective: the literalist's perspective. David Livingstone–Smith offers another. Positing that although we have a greater understanding of the many psychological processes that move and frame our day–to–day lives, we nonetheless frame our lives in a strange unverifiable manner:

> "Thanks to careful scientific research, we now know a good deal about the neurochemistry that makes brains run, the relationship between psychological processes and specific areas in the brain, and the mechanisms underpinning learning, memory, and perception. As a result, human beings are now at a crossroads in the way that they understand themselves. Faced with an impressive and rapidly developing scientific image of the human animal, it is difficult to avoid the conclusion that our mental states — the thoughts that we think, the passions that move us, and the decisions that mould our lives — are consequences of physiological processes occurring in our brains. But it is hard for many people to abandon the concept that human beings are angels imprisoned in earthly shells. According to this ancient, emotionally compelling vision, the core of a person is their nonphysical soul — a thing that is distinct from all that is flesh and blood, and immune from the causal laws that govern the behavior (sic) of merely physical things. It follows from this that human behavior is radically different from the behavior of nonhuman life forms because we, and we alone, possess free will. Lesser beings blindly, rigidly, and mechanically act out their biological programming, whereas we humans choose how to live.

This supposedly makes us the authors of our destiny, and this opens up a chasm between the human world and the realm of nature."[lix]

It is undoubtedly the concept of our being 'not of this earth' and a very literal agreement of the book that continues to feed, foster and consume many a religious believer. "Deconstructing End-time Delusions" is my attempt at offering a Davidian counterbalance to the Goliath of prose available that encourages the concept that human beings are angels imprisoned in earthly shells. A countervail that rather animates a stronger appreciation that we are not so immune from the causal laws that govern the behaviour of merely physical things, despite belief in and the rhetoric of religion. We must all admit that all of us must at some point in our learning, become familiar and mature enough in any sacred text. Even those of us who no longer hold any affinity with those sacred texts. Must learn to distinguish between what the text says, from what people have through the centuries claimed it says. Keep in mind also that these texts are nothing but a cento of old, dated revealation's of its original authors. No one in the twenty-first century is obliged to revere its content! These are but revealation's of the initial author. Everything we might glean from these texts then, are little else than hearsay. Yet, countless assumptions are made about the sacred text's relevance to modern society. It should go without voice that my objective to the best of my ability is to allow the Christian book as a body of literature to speak for itself. Pitting it against how many modern end-time apocalyptic scenarios are amply derived from its pages, or more correctly misused by theologians and the like in relation and light of other non-bible-based disciplines. I know enough of the following subjects to know. I don't know enough, and so I trust that all the proposals have drawn yet are found persuasive. In the least the trust is readers find some value in them. Even if they are not completely satisfactory, and despite its inherent limitations and my obvious own flaws – I am optimistic that these studies will prove candid and informative. Quoting Ernest Becker in his Preface:

DECONSTRUCTING ENDTIME DELUSIONS

> "... each honest thinker who is basically an empiricist has to have some truth in his position, no matter how extremely he has formulated it. The problem is to find the truth underneath the exaggeration, to cut away the excess elaboration or distortion and include that truth where it fits."[lx]

Through these presentations might readers be able to cut through possible exaggeration and keep a focus on the genuineness of what is delivered. In closing this somewhat panoptic Introduction, I couldn't agree with any more clarity than with the sentiments of William Floyd; a fellow seeker of truth, as with the wryly comments of Arthur Schopenhauer, the nineteenth century philosopher. First Floyd,

> "A worshipper of Truth fears no destruction of false gods, nor any facts that may cause him to throw over treasured superstitions. He is willing to prove all things and hold fast to that which is true."[lxi]

To which is added the insightful wisdom of Schopenhauer:

> "All truth passes through three stages: first, it is ridiculed; second, it is violently opposed; and third, it is accepted as self-evident."[lxii]

Readers are therefore encouraged to apply these three stages of truth finding as you continue in this journey and overthrow their own superstitious biases, to produce the birth and lasting growth of the third stage, – if possible. I propose readers attempt this for the reason that, as Jason Breshears concluded about neatly packaged

> "...facts that morph into mere supposition under scrutiny... [The religious] are condemned to exult infeigned• (sic) intelligence, to construct beliefs from wisps of phenomena, causes unknown."[lxiii]

In 1731 Benjamin Franklin once commented: "When men differ in opinion, both sides ought equally to have advantage of being heard by the public, and when truth and error have fair play, the former is always an overmatch for the latter." It is my intention in these pages to offer readers fair play. To submit commentaries of fair hearing to both a religious, and 'secular' humanistic views. Hippocrates – the father of medicine commented:

> "Leave nothing to chance. Overlook nothing. Combine contradictory observations. Allow yourself enough time."

Finally, readers should take to mind the once proud motto Nullius in Verba – take no man's word for it – as you journey through the rest of the book.[lxiv]

DECONSTRUCTING ENDTIME DELUSIONS

Part One

> It is worth noting that from the beginning there was a ruthless side to religion that had little regard for the lives of individuals.
>
> Richard Holloway - A Little History of Religion.

Nail One:

Christianity, an inauspicious history. Persecution at the behest of self-appointed narcissistic authorities.

PLOTINUS ONCE REMARKED "Mankind is poised midway between the gods and the beasts." Freud put it like this,

> "Men are not gentle, friendly creatures wishing for love, who simply defend themselves if they are attacked, but that a powerful measure of desire for aggression has to be reckoned as part of their instinctual endowment." Putting flesh on the bare bones of this idea, he added: "As a result their neighbor (sic) is for them not only a potential helper or sexual object, but also someone who tempts them to satisfy their aggressiveness on him, to exploit his capacity for work without compensation, to use him sexually without his consent, to seize his possessions, to humiliate him, to cause him pain, to torture and to kill him."[lxv]

Tina Pippin concurs:

> "Violence is never an end in itself. It is the extreme situation that best reveals what we are essentially... Violence is a force which can be used for good or evil, and among other things taken by it is the kingdom of heaven. But regardless of what can be taken by it, the man in the violent situation reveals those qualities least dispensable in his personality, those qualities which are all he will have to take into eternity with him."[lxvi]

Another, David Livingston-Smith again adds,

> "[Religion assists us to live in a world of Self-deception] Self-deception lubricates the psychological machinery of slaughter, providing balm for an aching conscience. By pulling the wool over our own eyes and colluding with our own deception, we can continue to think of ourselves as compassionate, moral, and pious people while endorsing or participating in the wholesale destruction of other human beings."[lxvii]

DECONSTRUCTING ENDTIME DELUSIONS

These are deeply alarming yet poignant observations. The human animal throughout time has been and is still inflicted with one of the most destructive and debilitating diseases known, - hatred! Modern mankind might assume it's sophisticated and enlightened, and yet we have not been coming in overcoming a basic history lesson; that our preoccupation with violence to each - other is centre-stage. Richard Holloway concurs:

> "It is obvious from our history that humans are good at hating each other. And it is usually those who differ from us in some way who become the objects of our hatred. In fact, religious hatred is probably the deadliest form of this human disease, because it gives human dislike divine justification. It is one thing to hate people because you don't like their opinions. It is another thing to say God hates them too and wants them exterminated. So it is worth noticing how intense religious conviction can add a dangerous element to human relationships..."[lxviii]

Modern society is increasingly awash with acts of violence and disdain to 'the other.' At the slightest of inconveniences we rage against other road users (road rage); we are all too familiar with our own distain to different races; to diverse 'religious' views; to 'no' religious view. We 'protest' as a rebuttal to long-held, beloved but ultimately outdated, and stultifying beliefs; we verbalise countless variances in political, economic, or social status and opinion. Simply,

> "[W]e are full of fears and anxieties over our position, which makes us doubly cruel and dangerous." Writes Yuval Harari (p.12).

In today's political and socially 'what's-in-it-for-me' climate this is most prevalently recognised by the rise of the Social Justice Warrior; those who take a principled stance against anything and everything they specifically see as morally bankrupt, about, and within Western culture. All backed by alternate fringe political 'party's' the likes of the 'Green Movement/ new–age religion,' and far-left 'action' groups like, 'Get–Up,' and the group Antifa: the apparent anti-fascist movement who expressly is fascist in the way they conduct themselves. We witness the consequences of such perspectives still today. There are in the News

Media a continuous barrage of reports; of dissent, 'protests', and flagrant propaganda rallies overflowing with 'hate' speech; of often violent opposition to lectures, the freedom of debate and speech; the boycotting of round table meetings or forums to combat civil unrest by certain societal factions. There are reports of continued murderous acts, surreptitious religious and political plotting. Omnipresent is theft, pyromania and any amount of violent and unlawful activity against our own kind. It is undoubtedly a very anthropological problem. Charles Darwin, "The Descent of Man", is quoted in the opening pages to Carl Sagan's little book, "The Dragons of Eden: Speculations on the Evolution of Human Intelligence", confirming that "...there can hardly be a doubt that we are descended from barbarians...[who]... were merciless to everyone not of their own small tribe." Yuval Noah Harari, "Sapiens: A Brief History of Humankind" again highlights a fact that intolerance and violence are not a modern particularity. Nor are they a modern quandary but most likely are a symptom of our being:

> "Tolerance is not a Sapiens trademark. In modern times, a small difference in skin colour, dialect or religion has been enough to prompt one group of Sapiens to set about exterminating another group. Would ancient Sapiens have been more tolerant towards an entirely different human species? It may well be that when Sapiens encountered Neanderthals, the result was the first and most significant ethnic-cleansing campaign in history."[lxix]

All over the World much of the witnessed violence and intolerant behaviour today is enflamed by religious conviction.[lxx] Vast tomes have been written recently documenting examples and highlighting past religious atrocities. While moderns continually berate and chastise one 'side' over another of an argument/ conflict. Solely based on prejudice. Nothing has changed since the historic accounts of past times. Skeptics, doubters, cynics, unbelievers and freethinkers of a bygone era, either educating themselves or critically analysing the sacred text. We read such persons were persecuted and most often executed by the self-appointed Church 'experts.' Authorities that viewed the actions of these heretics as worthy of such immolations. Unacknowledged, or most likely unknown by most Christian believers is the sheer brutality and mercilessness the

DECONSTRUCTING ENDTIME DELUSIONS

'new' faith inflicted upon those it saw as abhorrent and thoroughly demonic. In comprehensive contrast to the modern ideology that christianity's roots and spread throughout the world; that it were primarily one of temperance and considerate acknowledgement of other 'beliefs'; with gentle pleas to the 'outsider' to consider abolishing their 'false' God's and convert (whatever that meant at the time) to the 'one true' deity. The following disturbing commentary by Catherine Nixey is offered in evidence:

> "As one modern scholar has observed: 'The story of early Christian history has been told almost wholly on the basis of Christian sources.' But look for a moment at the spread of Christianity from the other side and what emerges is a far less easy picture. It is neither triumphant, nor joyful. It is a story of forced conversion and government persecution. It is a story in which great works of art are destroyed, buildings are defaced and liberties are removed. It is a story in which those who refused to convert were outlawed and, as the persecution deepened, were hounded and even executed by zealous authorities. The brief and sporadic Roman persecutions of Christians would pale in comparison to what the Christians inflicted on others – not to mention on their own heretics. If this seems implausible, then consider one simple fact. In the world today, there are over two billion Christians. There is not one single, true 'pagan'. Roman persecutions left a Christianity vigorous enough not only to survive but to thrive and to take control of an empire. By contrast, by the time the Christian persecutions had finally finished, an entire religious system had been all but wiped from the face of the earth...
>
> Christianity could have been tolerant: it was not preordained that it would take this path. There were Christians who voiced hopes for tolerance, even ecumenicalism. But those hopes were dashed. For those who wish to be intolerant, monotheism provides very powerful weapons. There was ample biblical justification for the persecution of non-believers. The Bible, as a generation of Christian authors declared, is very clear on the matter of idolatry. As the Christian author Firmicus Maternus reminded his rulers – perfectly correctly – there lay upon emperors an 'imperative necessity to castigate and punish this evil'. Their 'severity should be visited in every way on the crime'. And what precisely did God advise as a punishment for idolatry? Deuteronomy was clear: a person indulging in this should be stoned to death. And if an entire city fell into such sin? Again, the answer was clear: 'destruction is decreed'. The speed with which toleration slipped into intolerance and then downright suppression shocked non-Christian

observers. Not long after Constantine had gained control of the whole empire in AD 324, it is said that he forbade any governors who were still pagan from sacrificing or from worshipping idols, thus disbarring non-Christians from moving into the plum positions in the imperial government. Then he went still further, and passed two new laws against what he called these 'sanctuaries of falsehood'. One law 'restricted the pollutions of idolatry so that no one should presume to set up cult-objects, or practise divination or other occult arts, or even to sacrifice at all'. The second law, assuming the success of the first, ordered mass building and extension of churches: 'as if almost everybody would in the future belong to God, once the obstacle of polytheistic madness had been removed."[lxxi]

Many early believers were apparently ecstatically jubilant and proud of their efforts to eradicate from their slice of the world every edifice they saw as pagan; and so every demonically inspired ancient temple, deity, and remnant of early religious and worshipped practices was raised and exterminated. Does this sound familiar? The madness of the 'puritan, politically correct progressive' treats opponents in a similar fashion! The only difference. People are not 'literally', yet socially dismembered from the wider community; suffering debased slurs, a cancelling of financials, employment, and social standing for not adhering modern puritan wisdom. Such madness and outrageously restrictive and disrespectful wholesale destruction did not cease. At least people do not suffer the following madness where at one stage in London for instance, if anyone were caught merely reading the scriptures in English, as opposed to the 'sanctified' Latin tongue, or, if they happened to question or 'speak disrespectfully' of any early 'Church Father' they were sentenced to burn at the stake. The largely uneducated plebeian doubting and cynical population was especially vulnerable. Tony Bushby, in "The Christ Scandal" confirms.

> "After the Council of Trent (1545-1563) the Catholic Church declared: No person is permitted to read the scriptures in his native tongue without a written license from his bishop,... He that presumes to read or possess the Bible without such a license is punished by a penalty most terrible to a Romanist... and submits to other punishments at the will of his bishop." (p39.)

DECONSTRUCTING ENDTIME DELUSIONS

Whole tribes were slaughtered by command of a Catholic King or pope because of the presumed "bad disposition" they sustained in opposition to the emerging belief system; a wholesale slaughter for the crime of having no master saved their own will. What is more is that during these very early years, history dictates that the embryonic Church "...turned to a policy of Compelle intrare; i.e. 'make them come in.'" Force was truculently applied to build up congregations."[lxxii] Ordinary, illiterate peasants were involuntarily 'forced' into a belief agreeing with the newly emerging religion. The religious elite; accordingly, became far too headstrong and aggressive. Demanding allegiance of those they considered below them. So, rivers of blood have flowed throughout all regions of the world because of the Christian religion and its impending apocalyptic memes that apparently only the 'educated' cleric (Latinised) was authorised to disseminate.[lxxiii] That Apocalypse meme just happened to have been transferred to the 'uneducated' masses and those who were bold enough to voice their reservations regarding 'Church authority,' through "mass murder..." (Pippin, p. 28) Disgracefully, for millions of the peasantry "...salvation [came] through violence." (Pippin, p. 26). Shamefully for the new and emergent 'Church of christ', countless wars and insurrections dating to the earliest inception of the faith have decimated whole continents. European history specifically is replete with accounts of endless suffering. Heedlessly effected by the emergent Christian belief with its cantankerous clerics after the decline and collapse of the Roman Empire. Helen Ellerbe writes in her book, "The Dark side of Christian History" that when the emerging faith finally reached the pinnacle, becoming the dominant world power, it wasn't as 'gracious' or loving to those it conquered. Rather, in its strive for domination the Christian Church all but wiped out education, the sciences, medicine, history, commerce, and the arts. While the rest of the known world had languished in poverty, the Church collected huge stores of wealth that it fought tooth and nail to hold and continue to accumulate. The Church was so fearful of relinquishing power and wealth; it launch brutal attacks on every part of society. Instituting the Inquisition to ferret out and quash any dissent. Former 'pagan' beliefs and practices were all but destroyed by the cantankerous Church leadership who saw and 'preached' these were thoroughly demonic:

> "The common perception that the physical world was imbued with God's presence and with magic was replaced... with a new belief that divine assistance was no longer possible and that the physical world belonged only to the Devil. It was a three hundred year holocaust against all who dared believe in divine assistance and magic that finally secured the conversion of Europe to orthodox Christianity...edicts were far more than just words and it is disingenuous to suggest otherwise.[lxxiv] They gave carte blanche to Christians to cleanse the demons from the sinful pagans. Many were ready and waiting for the chance to do just that. Not always as mindful of Mark 12:31 as they might have been, many Christians declined to love their polytheist neighbours and instead agitated to reduce their temples to rubble. Bishops badgered their rulers for new laws then used their congregations as de facto troops to carry out demolitions."[lxxv]

Provoking an Apocalypse meme across the width and breadth of the European continent, Christian 'believers' (roused and urged on by the 'learned cleric') took upon themselves a charge of bringing heaven to the earth – often at the end of a sword. Tony Bushby again, piercingly writes

> "the true significance of records of such...military force in christianity nullifies the modern-day presentation of the 'sweetness and light' that the Church today says it brought to the world."[lxxvi]

True, the earliest periods from which this 'Christian faith' emerged was saturated with no 'sweetness or light' as is claimed often today; but was rather marinated in the most gruesome acts imaginable. English novelist and poet Thomas Hardy once remarked: "If a way to the better there be, it lies in taking a full look at the worst." (Becker, "Escape from Evil", Front pages.) So, we would benefit greatly if we took also to heart and mind while reading this chapter, and study the contemplative insight of 17th century philosopher, The Duc de La Rochefoucauld who we are informed "...relishes revelations of the debt that kindness owes to egoism...[insisting] we are never far from being vain, arrogant, selfish, and petty – and, never nearer than we trust in our own goodness."

DECONSTRUCTING ENDTIME DELUSIONS

Additionally, both religious and secular amongst us would be more the wiser by understanding:

> "[T]here [is] no evidence that religion makes people morally responsible, but history confronts us with a long, bloody record of wars, genocides, and other atrocities inspired by religious devotion and often executed by religious institutions... Believers in the One True God have [in fact] racked up an impressive record of atrocities over the centuries, including the attacks on the Pentagon and World Trade Center on September 11, 2001."[lxxvii]

The issue to be reckoned is just as, "Aldous Huxley in his book "The Olive Tree" observed that,

> "by suppressing and distorting the truth [about war and our propensity to violence against our own kind], we protect our sensibilities and preserve our self-esteem...The Enlightenment philosopher Voltaire explicated the problem succinctly: "Those who can make you believe absurdities; can make you commit atrocities."[lxxviii]
>
> One path (among many) to a more moral world is to get people to quit believing in absurdities."[lxxix]

It is hardly the outright intent in the following pages to make readers quit their absurdities. Like their devotion to a religious faith. Rather, that is achieved that highlights a sense of just how religion, and particularly the Christian theory has from its inception caused much harm to the psyche of many people.[lxxx] Aside those relevant quotes already cited, readers will be confronted with a brief history of christianity; one that unless actively searched for, you most likely will not come across. In these pages, it is not my intention to discourage anyone who holds a religious belief. Nor do I offer the following as a bigoted dissident; as someone who holds a grudge against his former beliefs. Rather, comments and statements offered should bring a sense of awareness to christianity that is most likely unknown. This side to Christian history is hardly spoken about or offered by pastors and ministers in weekly sermons or study sessions. Their focus is (understandably) rather an unbalanced and most surely biased perspective to their system of faith. Of an end-time scenario, it is fitting that this darker side to Christian beginnings is offered. It may be completely Panglossian that upon reading the rest of this first Nail, as a consumer of this material a grasp and sense of how, and from where a deathly obsession with end-time subjects fits into the over all scheme of the Christian theory.

Mene, Mene, Tekel, Parsin. The Christian apocalypse Meme:

THIS SUBTITLE COMES from Daniel, chapter five; the chapter in the sacred book that describes the mysterious ghostly writing that apparently appeared on the Babylonian palace walls before that Empire was completely razed by the Mede's and Persians. In many ways, the inscription and interpretation submitted in this sacred book's text parallels previous citations about the inception, as with the current Christian ideals surrounding the 'apocalyptic meme' expressed by believers:

> "This is the interpretation of the matter: Mene, God has numbered the days of your kingdom and brought it to an end; Tekel, you have been weighed on the scales and found wanting... Peres... your kingdom is divided and entrusted [now, to christianity.]"[lxxxi]

Listening with intent; Mene, Mene, Tekel, Peres can almost be heard through the actions of those 'believers' in the following descriptions. In chapter three: "Waiting for the Antichrist of Apocalypse: A History of the End of Time", John Michael Greer lists several atrocities committed by early 'Christian' believers. Particularly, the overreach of Pope John Twenty second who declared the Franciscan sect heretical. He started sending sect members who refused to renounce 'apostolic' poverty to the Inquisition which intimidated many 'moderate' believers. Prompting them "...to start asking hard questions about the Church – and plenty of these drew on the Apocalypse meme and spawned new predictions of imminent doom and deliverance." There was widespread violence against other faiths also. Anti-Semitism particularly, rose steeply. "God has numbered the days of your kingdom and brought it to an end..." Greer again: "From a medieval Christian perspective, it was a simple and logical step to claim that the Jews were waiting, not for the Messiah, but for his opposite, and Jewish traditions about the Messiah thus became a covert but central source for Christian ideas about the Antichrist." Much of documented 'Church' history is also awash with accounts of persecution of 'the other' Christian sects that Catholicism saw as heretical. For instance, the Ana-Baptists (Baptists) was one Christian sect that was continually brutalised. Chapter one of his book, "The Trail of Blood", J. M. Carroll documents the complete destructive history of the Anabaptists, saying it was written in blood. They were among the most brutalised sect of the 'Dark Ages'. No wonder at the time the then pope was fingered as the antichrist! He was the world's dictator, and he let it be known. One time:

> "At Zurich, after many disputations between Zuinglius (sic) and the Ana-Baptists, the Senate made an Act, that if any presume to rebaptize (sic) those who were baptized before (i.e. as infants) they should be drowned."[lxxxii]

Carroll further cites more atrocities committed by the same 'ruling' belief system. Countless nameless men, women and children were either burnt at the stake, drowned, or were tortured; had their garments shredded and were turned out to face the bitter environment; to die a lingering death through cold, heat and hunger. At their deaths, the religious world "looked on complacent, indifferent, or exulting." I wonder could the prediction of Thomas Horn (below) is an insight and warning precursor to similar action against fellow believers as these? Now, add the insightful words of Manly P. Hall's detailed account of the atmosphere after the Nicene Council.

> "Apology gave way to diatribe as the infant Church became surer of itself. It no longer spread its opinions with caution. It demanded allegiance, gradually shaping into a creed of total conformity. There was a 'quicker' eye for heresy... the Church eventually occupied 'key' positions of power, which influenced greatly the policies and policy makers of the period. It became a sovereign unto itself. Demanding allegiance from all sovereigns. It saw itself as the ultimate empire, reaching above and beyond all temporal empires. Kings

sat upon their thrones because of the favor (sic) of the Church, and at the dictates of the Great Mother, king and commoner alike must act. The Reformation brought to an end the Church's dream of temporal power. One after another the Protestant sects broke away. The Church thundered in vain. Men lost faith with their spiritual leaders because of the numerous occasions on which certain dogmas of theology had been proved fallible. The result is a Christendom divided against itself."[lxxxiii]

Erudite author D M Murdock (d. 2015) in her publications documents copious ancient and modern (19th and twentieth Century) denunciations of the historical authenticity of christianity. Noting the relentless and most disturbing tortures imaginable carried out under the Christian banner. Quoting American Lawyer Joseph Wheless in her book, "The Christ Conspiracy", the gravity as well as the hypocritical and murderous intent of the early Church is blatant:

"When the Christians were weak and powerless and subjected to occasional persecutions as "enemies of the human race," they were vocal and insistent advocates of liberty of conscience and freedom to worship whatever God one chose; the Christian "Apologies" to the Emperors abound in eloquent pleas for religious tolerance; and this was granted to them and to all by the Edict of Milan and other Imperial Decrees. But when by the favor (sic) of Constantine, they got into the saddle of the State, they at once grasped the sword, and began to murder and despoil all who would not pretend as the Catholic Priest commanded them to believe." (Preface)

What about the Inquisition? Let's not fool ourselves into believing the Inquisition was in reality, little but a mandated and authorised death squad. Its prime sanction being: to 'cleans Spain' from the thousands of Muslims and Jews. Unashamedly slaughtering millions with unimaginable brutality. It then turned its gaze upon those who declared themselves Protestant:

"One writer of the time declared the Inquisition to be a 'wild monster of such terrible mien that all Europe trembles at the mere mention of its name.'...When Columbus set out in his little boat he had red crusader crosses stitched to his sails. Columbus may have discovered the New World, but this was just a happy accident. He was actually looking for a way to sail around the world and attack the Muslim empire in the rear... Hundreds of

DECONSTRUCTING ENDTIME DELUSIONS

thousands, probably millions, of innocent indigenous [people] perished... They were burnt alive or tortured to death as a glorious testimony to the triumph of Christianity throughout the world."

Detailed Tim Freke in his book, "The Laughing Jesus": Religious lies and gnostic Wisdom, Chapter 2: A religious detox ([brackets mine]). Though an awareness is prevalent, the full weight of atrocities committed by the Inquisitors is lost to many believers today. Of the Inquisition, Professor of History in his new publication, Randall E. Floyd explosively narrated:

"The most famous victim of the French wing of the Inquisition was Joan of Arc, the so-called "Maid of Orleans," who was burned at the stake in 1431. A century earlier, in 1307, some 20,000 Knights Templar in France were tortured before being committed to the flames. According to a special Arts and Entertainment report, inquisitors would usually arrive in a town and make their presence known by announcements at either the Town Hall or on the steps of the local Church or cathedral. The purpose of this announcement was to offer citizens a last chance to admit to heresy. "Those who confessed received a punishment ranging from a pilgrimage to flogging," according to the A and E report. "Those accused of heresy were forced to testify. If the heretic did not confess, torture and execution were inescapable. Heretics weren't allowed to face accusers, received no counsel, and were often victims of false accusations." Unrepentant heretics were usually tried by a clerical court then, if found guilty, were handed over to secular authorities to be burned at the stake. Occasionally, however, especially in the smaller towns and villages, local clergymen took matters into their own hands and conducted punishments and executions.

The Inquisition in Spain was launched in 1480. At the time, the population of Jews and Muslims was quite large and figured prominently in the financial and commercial trades. However, in order to live and practice in Spain, most of these outsiders had converted to Christianity. As the shadow of the Inquisition spread, most of these sub-classes of "outsiders" deemed heretical were called in for questioning. At the heart of it all was their loyalty to the Catholic Church. Jews, Muslims and Protestants, for example, who could substantiate their faith were usually forced to pay a fine and released. Those accused of secretly continuing to practice their old religions, however, were forced to either confess or suffer the wrath of the inquisitors — which usually meant conversion, deportation or execution... It was not before 1834 that the Inquisition was declared defunct. In the year, 1826 a Spanish schoolmaster became the final victim of the inhumane and brutal blood–lust of the office of the Inquisition. He was hanged for the crime of alleged heresy. The Roman Inquisition ended quietly. In 1908, Pope Pius X renamed the old Inquisition the Congregation of the Holy Office. A few years later its duties were merged with those of the Congregation of the Index. In 1965, Pope Paul VI reorganized (sic) the Holy Office and changed its name to the Sacred Congregation for the Doctrine of the Faith. The following year he eliminated the Index altogether. "Hence," according to a report issued by the University of Notre Dame, "nothing of the original form of the inquisitions survives today, only their records, their memory and the potent myths which still surround them."[lxxxiv]

It should be astoundingly obtrude that inquisitors had a mandated right to slaughter those who did not conform to their particulars, and that upon arrival in any centre, it is implied that heretics had a 'last chance' to confessing to something no doubt, many were unaware and ignorant of for they were simply going about their lives as generations before them had done. Then there are the countless atrocious acts of enslavement, incarceration and massacres of particularly 'coloured' people groups committed by christians:

> "Of the many and various abuses and usurpations of humans by other humans, there is perhaps none so odious and oppressive as the ownership of one human being by another. This is slavery, and it has existed for as long as there have been those who, for the life of them, can't see the problem with having a bunch of people that they don't have to pay doing all of the soul-crushing grunt work for them. It is a custom that relies on an unspeakable lack of empathy, on the existence of a class- or caste-based, socially stratified society, and on a population and economy large enough to support it. Older than any written record, institutionalised slavery very possibly began at about the time of the agricultural revolution (with its accompanying ideas about ownership) approximately ten thousand years ago... Slavery has now been outlawed in every country, though amazingly enough it was only a little over thirty years ago, in 1981, that the last country to outlaw the custom— Mauritania— finally did so..."[lxxxv]

Long forgotten is the fact that generally, each of the major cosmic-religions recognised today have never really had an issue with the forced enslavement of countless people. Slavery, slaughter and the like is endorsed by their 'holy' books. According to many sacred texts of world religion, unnatural enslavement was seen as a virtue. A Christian/papal and Jewish context read:

> "Some religions, such as Catholicism, fully endorsed slavery, as Pope Nicholas V made clear when, in 1452, he issued the radically proslavery document Dum Diversas. This was a papal bull granting Catholic countries such as Spain and Portugal "full and free permission to invade, search out, capture, and subjugate the Saracens and pagans and any other unbelievers and enemies of Christ wherever they may be, as well as their kingdoms, duchies, counties, principalities, and other property ... and to reduce their persons into perpetual slavery." These last few words— to reduce their persons into perpetual slavery— sound not just sinister to us, but also psychotic. They make perfect sense, however, in a Christian context, given that the Bible is itself a heedlessly proslavery tome. It's hardly surprising then that it took almost two thousand years for Christians to twig to the fact that slavery is wrong.[lxxxvi] Slavery was bad only if it was Israel who was enslaved. Exodus 3:16,17; 12:44; 21:4; leviticus 25; deuteronomy 21; and deuteronomy 24:7."[lxxxvii]

William Harwood adds his own details in chapter nine, 'The Deuteronomist', in his book "Mythology's Last Gods". Describing the idea that slavery and the extermination of 'infidels' were acceptable, and even 'good' religious practice. He writes:

> "The Deuteronomist's philosophy, that killing the adherents of every mythology but one's own in order to protect believers from competing doctrines was a godly and laudable act, was in medieval times carried to its logical conclusion by the Christians who, over the course of several centuries, dutifully massacred between thirty and fifty million enemies of the various Christian gods... Among the[m]..was the extermination of possibly as many as seventy thousand Huguenots [Protestants] on St. Bartholomew's Day 1572, a purging of heretics that caused the jubilant Pope Gregory XIII to proclaim a year of celebration. (p.156.) See Deuteronomy 20:16-18. [brackets mine.]"

Enter the bastion and hero for many christians for the abolition of slavery: Wilberforce. However, it is most insightful that:

"Wilberforce's religious motives were complicated by his pushy and overzealous moralizing (sic) about virtually every aspect of life, and his great passion seemed to be to worry incessantly about what other people were doing, especially if what they were doing involved pleasure, excess, and "the torrent of profaneness that every day makes more rapid advances." Wilberforce founded the Society for the Suppression of Vice after King George III issued the "Proclamation for the Discouragement of Vice" (at Wilberforce's recommendation), which ordered the prosecution of those guilty of "excessive drinking, blasphemy, profane swearing and cursing, lewdness, profanation of the Lord's Day, and other dissolute, immoral, or disorderly practices." Wilberforce wasn't appeased with just this however. He cast his eyes and crusade to the colonies. He began insisting that 'Christian instruction' is taught to the citizens of these places too, boasting with brio: "Our religion is sublime, pure, beneficent; theirs is mean, licentious and cruel." In fact, Wilberforce's initial efforts were not concerned with the abolition of slavery but the ending of the slave trade (with existing slaveholders allowed to continue the practice that would presumably die out on its own in time without the outside source of slave replenishment). Slavery was not just an assault on the humanity of the slaves, Wilberforce argued, it was a blemish on the Christian religion that had for so long endorsed it. As he told the House of Commons on April 18, 1791, "Never, never will we desist till we have wiped away this scandal from the Christian name..."[lxxxviii]

Michael Paulkovich chimes in with some most damning and snide comments directed at christianity. He writes

"I have seen claims that in fact Christians led the fight to end slavery... It is true. Christians were largely responsible. Hooray for them? No, this is the logical fallacy post hoc ergo propter hoc: "after this, therefore because of this." Such causality is an artificial connection: of course, they were Christians. It was a crime, punishable by death, not to be Christian for the many centuries that came before. Almost 100% [of populations around the world] were Christian. Who else might have stepped up to end slavery, the [pagans]? The [witches]? [The 'coloured' races]? Or perhaps all those Jews, Hindus, Jains, and Buddhists... Wouldn't it have been ever so nice if Jesus-anywhere in his sermons- had said that slavery of fellow humans is immoral? Jesus might seem to have hinted at it in Mt 23:10, but this is merely a metaphor in view of the preceding verses..." (p.181-2. [brackets mine])

DECONSTRUCTING ENDTIME DELUSIONS

It would be foolish for anyone today to deny such well-documented homicidal, bloodthirsty antics of the Christian Church. There is an ever-growing quantity of documentation, literature, and other materials highlighting past and present atrocities committed by the Church and its laity.[lxxxix] Those that would argue against this are showing their great ignorance of that history. David Livingstone-smith again from his chapter three, informs us of more of the wicked, insufferable judgements of popes and those prepared to carry out their charges against the infidel. He writes that during the eight century pagan tribes were 'converted' to the 'true faith' of christianity at sword point. Reportedly, at Verden he is said to have slaughtered four and a half thousand 'rebel' Saxon noblemen. For the crime of 'deconversion'; for reverting to their previous practices. Hoping this would be a great disincentive to others. Thus:

> "... By the ninth century, the popes began to declare that butchering unbelievers was good for the souls of warriors. Every life taken in the service of the Church was supposed to expiate a bit of the knight's backlog of unexcused sin."[xc]

By these descriptions the opaque realism of the churches hypocrisy is astoundingly transparent. Is the 'Church' only concerned with 'expiating' apparent 'sins' of its patrons? What about the backlog of 'sins' of those they unashamedly murdered without rhyme nor reason? Much less known to moderns is the faith-based brutal and insane slaughter of 20 to 30 million Chinese people to begin to purge the planet of all forms of <demon> worship. The cause was the belief of one peasant in the mid-nineteenth-century China. This was the religiously provoked rebellion, The Taiping Rebellion. The instigator of this appalling atrocity believed he was the younger brother of christ. He then set about eradicating demon worship from the world. Preaching and slaughtering millions whom he found was not adhering his message; a message he called *The Era of Heavenly Peace*. He and his followers were likened to today's Jihadists; they did not fear death and fought with intensity and brutality of resolve, "... [they] banned the study of traditional Confucian texts and replaced it with mandatory biblical instruction... They looted, plundered, and slaughtered the inhabitance of entire cities who opposed their teachings...The Taiping gained control of large swaths of south and central China by the time of their final defeat in 1864. [The Taiping Rebellion is understood today as the] religious movement [which] had initiated the bloodiest civil war in history...[so] when the final curtain fell on the Era of Heavenly Peace, [this uprising of religious fervour] had taken 20 to 30 million lives."[xci] Closer to our recent history Acharya S. (D M Murdock) again insightfully adds,

> "...Hitler and the Church's behavior was not an aberration in the history of Christianity, as from its inception, the religion was intolerant, zealous and violent, with its adherents engaging in terrorism. For example, while blessing peacemakers and exhorting love and forgiveness of enemies and trespassers, the "gentle Jesus" also paradoxically declares: Do not think that I have come to bring peace on earth; I have not come to bring peace, but a sword. For I have come to set man against his father, and a daughter against her mother, and a daughter-in-law against her mother-in-law; and a man's foes will be those of his own household. (Mt. 10:34) Jesus further states that "nation will rise up against nation, and kingdom against kingdom"; thus, with a few sentences, Jesus has seeded extreme division, sedition and enmity wherever christianity is promulgated. In thus exhorting his followers to violence, however, Jesus himself was building on centuries-old Jewish thought that called for the "extermination" of non-Jews, i.e., "unbelievers," in Christian parlance. As an example of this Judaeo-Christian fanaticism, the apostle Paul was a violent zealot who as a Jew first persecuted the christians and as a Christian subsequently terrorized (sic) the Pagans. As Joseph Wheless says in "Forgery in Christianity": "And [Paul], the tergiversant*[xcii] slaughter-breathing persecutor-for-pay of the early Christians, now turned for profit their chief apostle of persecution, pronounces time and again the anathema of the new dispensation against all dissenters from his superstitious, tortuous doctrines and dogmas, all such "whom I have delivered unto Satan" (1 Tim. 1:20), as he writes to advise his adjutant [assistant] Timothy. He flings at the scoffing Hebrews this question: "He that despised Moses's law died without mercy..: Of how much sorer punishment, suppose ye, shall he be thought worthy, who bath trodden under foot the Son of God?" (Heb. 10:28, 29). All such "are set forth for an example, suffering the vengeance of eternal fire" (Jude 7); "that they might all be damned who believed not the truth" (2 Thess. 2:12); and even "he that doubteth (sic) is damned" (Rom. 14:23). This Paul, who with such

DECONSTRUCTING ENDTIME DELUSIONS

bigoted presumption "deals damnation ʻround the land on all he deems the foe" of his dogmas, is first seen "consenting to the death" of the first martyr Stephen (Acts 8:1); then he blusters through the country "breathing out threatenings and slaughter against the disciples of the Lord" (Acts 9:1), the new converts to the new faith. Then, when he suddenly professed miraculous "conversion" himself, his old masters turned on him and sought to kill him, and he fled to these same disciples for safety, to their great alarm (Acts 9:23-26), and straightway began to bully and threaten all who would not now believe his new preachments. To Elymas, who "withstood them," the doughty new dogmatist "set his eyes on him," and thus blasted him with inflated vituperation [criticism]: "O full of all subtly and all mischief, thou child of the Devil, thou enemy of all righteousness, wilt thou not cease to pervert the right ways of the Lord?" (Acts 13:8-10). Even the "meek and loving Jesus" is quoted as giving the fateful admonition: "Fear him which is able to destroy both soul and body in hell" (Matt. 10:28)-here first invented and threatened by Jesus the Christ himself, for added terror unto belief. Paul climaxes the terror: "it is a fearful thing to fall into the hands of the living God' (Heb. 10:31)."[xciii]

Readers are surely amazed, even repulsed to read of the shear brutality inflicted upon and to fellow humankind. It is incontestably a 'religious' oxymoron that in the early years of the emerging Christian 'faith'; that salvation were for countless men, women, and children earned by slavery, or sword-point, the hang-man's noose, maceration, torture and other gruesome acts; all to bring about an 'era of heavenly peace.' What was the trigger that urged such in-humaneness– esp., seeing these acts was committed by those who held to an obvious religious commitment? All these and more atrocities as those presented are undoubtedly, spontaneously triggered by our instinctive desire to be a hero. We each have a common disposition and a desire of supremacy, of power and domination. Essentially each of us is a narcissist – '...feel[ing] that practically everyone is expendable except ourselves.'[xciv] Effectively, Augustine called such 'feelings' a 'libido dominandi", – a desire to dominate! The instinctive desire of us all is to 'rule' another. In no matter what field of 'play' each of our own libido dominandi is the due cause of much violence, dissent and malice directed to someone else. The desire of domination we feel toward another is the reason opposing views, whether they are religious, political, economic, or another accepted and therefore recognised as wholly truthful opinion, are threatening. Primarily, because they pressure us to seriously question our own libido dominandi, –our own desire to dominate, which none of us can easily deny as existential, let alone forsake. Continually the 'pressure' to dominate is played out in our governments, on sporting fields, in corporate business; and is undoubtedly a telling scenario throughout all religious institutions. Why else would hardline religious factions– including christians –incite a brutal ideology of Jihad against a rival faction? Livingston-Smith highlighted our propensity toward a libido-dominandi similarly, writing:

> "The impressive record of atrocities racked up by the human race does not suggest that our conduct is guided by sympathy for others. Unfettered compassion would make saints of us all, but...compassion is not unfettered. It comes with strings attached. Our feelings of sympathy do not embrace all of humanity in equal measure. Some human beings matter to us. We care intensely about their well-being. Others do not matter very much, and still others do not matter at all. This is a hard saying, and may be difficult to accept but it is obviously and undeniably true." Scottish Enlightenment Philosopher, David Hume clearly recognised,

> "...our sympathies are skewed by three biases. The first is a bias toward similarity. We favor (sic) people who resemble us—who look like us, dress like us, speak our language, and share our beliefs and skin color (sic). Speaking bluntly, [as communities of people we feel that those] who resemble us are more valuable than those who do not... We [Westerners] do not care much about the fate of ...strange, foreign people. Their suffering elicits little sympathy. As Chris Hedges remarks: While we venerate and mourn our own dead we are curiously indifferent about those we kill. Thus killing is done in our name, killing that concerns us little, while those who kill our own are seen as having crawled out of the deepest recesses of the earth, lacking our own humanity and goodness. Our dead. Their dead. They are not the same."[xcv]

Secondly, we share a bias toward those who are near. We consider great care for those closest to us instead of the 'stranger' who might be across town, in the next suburb, or some other place on the other side of the world. An example of this bias can be seen in the Judaeo-Christian book, where the figure christ exhorts followers to 'love one's neighbour' (Matthew 12:31; 19:19; 22:39). Originating in an Old Testament passage (leviticus 19:19). Unfortunately, this was and still is taken literally. Thirdly, Hume demonstrated that by this bias, we are essentially all

> "... moral nepotists, favoring (sic) family members over people who are unrelated to us. The lives of our relatives are felt to be more valuable than the lives of others, and their sufferings seem to be of greater consequence."[xcvi]

No wonder the atrocities committed by the emerging Church were and in many ways still 'justified.' Do christians really have the absolute moral high-ground when it comes to those who today cause abhorrently malicious actions toward them? It may be considered also that the bellicosity described above and the thoughts that others, but not ourselves, are expendable; that this ideology is mainly kept to the 'male' species. That moral nepotism is not really part of the female makeup. Somehow females are immune. Yuval Harari posits however, the following interesting statements that clearly disagrees with such suggestions. "Women are often stereotyped as better manipulators and appeasers than men, and are famed for their superior ability to see things from the perspective of others. If there's any truth in these stereotypes, then women should have made excellent politicians and empire-builders, leaving the dirty work on the battlefields to testosterone-charged but simple-minded machos. Popular myths notwithstanding, this rarely happened in the real world. It is not at all clear why not."[xcvii] Most interesting and alarming are the findings of Joanna Bourke. She is a historian at the University of London. After conducting a study of the archival writings of wartime women, she concluded: "...women satisfied their aggressive urges by pestering their menfolk to act on their behalf and decimate the enemy."[xcviii] We see this in our day also. Western culture media sources continue to report that the wives and mothers of many Islamic fighters do laud and encourage their men to decimate the enemy! It doesn't only happen in times of war either. In "The Weekend Australian" newspaper (Saturday, September 29th, 2018, electronic edition), editor of the online magazine Spiked Brendan O'Neil, wrote a scathing article about the rising feminist trend of believing any accusation brought against a (white) male by any female. Increasingly we are witness to all women being assumed innocent of any wrong, and any accusation made against a male is to be seen (known) as factual before any due process or warrant; But, Women, Like men, Lie Too. Citing Margaret Atwood O'Neil wrote:

> "Women are human beings, with the full range of saintly and – demonic behaviours this entails. Women are not Angels, says Atwood. Indeed women lie, just like men do. Or they forget, like men do. Instant belief in women actually infantilises women. Worse, it is an invitation to lie..."

Undoubtedly, also repugnant or surprising to readers. Though women do not often physically show the same gesticulations of animosity of their male counterparts, they do however, encourage and urge their menfolk and each other to obliterate perceived enemies; recognised more through the '#MeToo' movement. Our current climate and the psychological push through all forms of media classically portray this ideology. The political left currently displays an agendum today focused on promoting an unbalanced, unbridled biased program. We see today:

> "The teaching of "Western civilisation" has come to be stigmatized (sic) as code for institutionalised sexism and racism... [social justice warriors] have demanded that entire realms of public policy be brought back into democratic politics. Their demands range from the economically unorthodox to the scientifically ignorant, from the implicitly discriminatory to the openly racist."[xcix]

Men of particularly high social and political status are often labeled misogynistic if they happen to question the current ideology. There are protests against Western values. Legislations are butchered and changed to suit or include the whims of a tiny proportion of society, the lists are seemingly endless. The point is; our twenty-first century culture has not moved on from any such narcissistic tendency. Instead of being focused on specific religious matters, the adjustment has been to a feminist and politically correct agenda that all-too-well parallel previous comments.

DECONSTRUCTING ENDTIME DELUSIONS

Twenty-first Century christianity is positively not immune. Misogynistic, and Feminist opinions and political correctness today undoubtedly influence religious policy also.[c] Astoundingly, the egotistical self-important attitudes and the homicidal actions described above, are predicted by some believers to be gearing up across the whole of western christianity. The agenda seems to wish to incorporate and parallel a desired end-time scenario. Example: Advertised on his organisations' website Thomas Horn published a 'new' apocalyptic meme (released July, 8th 2014).[ci] Titled, "Blood on the Altar: The Coming War between Christian vs. Christian." Here is yet another example of the sheer lunacy of bible scholarship that is increasingly prevalent throughout all christianity, but especially in North America at the present. A short promotional video clip that at this revision (2019) is no longer available; announced the thesis of his book. A resurgence of medieval Christian mysticism, announcing:

> "**A War Is Coming, and it will pit Religious Christians against truly BORN-AGAIN Believers in the bloodiest of battles. You don't believe? You will.**" (Last access 27/6/2014. Emphasis original).

From the perusal of a sample text (Introduction + chapter one) of the book, the text clearly seems very much an alarmist attempt to instil a sense of fear and dread that is typical of countless 'end time' themed books on the market today. Horn begins with a series of points 'outlining' the alleged increase in persecution of various 'christians' and their beliefs. Maybe, this is Fate revisiting christianity for the atrocious and deplorably wicked acts of persecution cited above. What goes around comes around! I must wonder also, from the brief preview can it be deduced by the proposals Horn outlines in his publication. Although not explicitly stated, fundamental end-time christianity with its destructive theories of world-wide mayhem (within and without its own belief systems) may be another offering to global society the recommendations of 18th century anti–humanism! Just as that first proposed by political economist Thomas Malthus (1766-1834). Thomas Malthus is undoubtedly the acclaimed 'Prophet' of anti-humanism. A 'political economist' Malthus argued that human reproduction always outstripped the production of resources. Which, was used to give licence for the brutal oppression of certain people groups. Namely, the poor and disenfranchised. He produced in 1798 a pamphlet advocating that over population growth could be restrained, suppressed and contained by raising the death rate. Specifically, by visiting frequently <famine>, disease, plague, and destruction by any means. Including, insisting the building of villages near disease infested swamps and marshlands and all manners of unwholesome places:

> "But above all, we should reprobate specific remedies for ravaging diseases; and those benevolent, but much mistaken men, who have thought they were doing a service to mankind by projecting schemes for the total extirpation of particular disorders. In short, Malthus argued that we should do whatever we can to encourage disease, and we should condemn doctors who try to find cures. In addition, everything should be done to keep the wages of working people as low as possible."[cii]

It must then be concluded, this ideology is resurfacing! Only wrapped in the guise of a 'planet-saving' green/environmental movement! Is the continued misinterpretation of America's "Second Amendment" also, a rehashing of Malthusian ethics and population controls outlined also part of this ideology? Is the belief of countless American citizens; that they have a mandated Right to Bear Arms, essentially just another policy of the elite to keep population down by raising the death rate? How much influence will America's belief that each citizen has a right to own a gun/ weapon have on a Christian versus Christian 'war' scenario? We are already witnessing the tragic and senseless loss of lives by crazed gunmen (in and outside churches). Surely, America's NRA (National Rifle Association) and its staunch supporters are no more than the world's most Malthusian 'power–brokers'. They neither support nor ensure firearm 'control' legislation becomes law for American citizens. Such proposed 'laws' are assumed to encroach upon a misguided interpretation of the Second Amendment of the Constitution - "...to bear Arms." Although in the last forty-years, more than Three Hundred and Sixty thousand innocent lives have been lost through senseless

DECONSTRUCTING ENDTIME DELUSIONS

slaughter by a crazed gunman.[ciii] Surely, the NRA are acutely aware of this statistic. But, the revenue raised and the buying of Congressional votes to veto legislative alteration runs deeply in the veins of Congressmen/women. Bluntly stated by Albert Jack, most American citizens do not realise that the Amendment in question does not in essence categorically mean that every citizen (without cause or due care) has an absolute 'right' to a firearm for their own discretional use. The Amendment is conditional and is very precise regarding why it was initially inscribed in the Constitutional Document. After 'Independence' had been wrestled from British regulation, America was very much still at risk of invasion by counter British and other invading forces! This is the reason such. An outdated 'law' must now be revised; to reflect the twenty-first century. It is no longer germane. An antiquated mindset of puerile belief about certain 'rights' and liberties of citizens, and no doubt christianity has never been completely evicted. Rather has been this time reborn in North America, and Europe. Particularly through astoundingly powerful organisations like the NRA, the WEF, and countless modern politicians, and self-proclaimed elites who openly support means to halt, or drastically diminish world populations. Under the guise of 'saving the planet from overcrowding", which, is said to further the likelihood of a planet boiling point, leading to an unliveable status for the world. Does the world really need to witness and succumb again to the selfsame futile idiocy of the emerging Church and its authorities? The presumed impression is that citizens the world over considers themselves 'greatly enlightened.' Could this be a mistaken assumption? Today, we do observe there are pockets of such ill treatment and troublesome acts occurring around the world, and not only in the Mid-Eastern Bloc. America faces the risks of daily school shootings... and other 'crimes against humanity' because of the Malthusian refusal and unwillingness of its government to sweep the power-base of the NRA from its congressional halls. 'Death' penalties and so-called honour killings are carried and apportioned for some believed 'religious offence' right around the globe, –i.e. for a presumed 'blasphemy' of family name and religion. Or, for the depictions in cartoon form of various highly regarded religious icons long since deceased. Radicals of non-occidental religious orders not only commit such crimes against humanity. Though it is these who today are given the limelight by the Western media. The documented medieval history above of many Christian sects is responsible for similar Malthusian doctrines and crimes to this very day, are still carried out under the 'Christian' and religious banner. What screwed up, narcissistic mind justifies killing someone for not converting, or resisting the overbearing advances of any religion? How is it that it is somehow able to be justified - by invoking an out-of-date statute when some deranged individual decided they'd 'like to kill' innocents. Primarily because they do not agree with the others' policy, belief, or actions. How frequently has it been witnessed in the media that an abortion clinician was targeted, murdered, or severely maimed because a religious brain–donor believed them to be an abomination? How much further must we travel into the twenty-first century before governments and law makers twig to the idea that new forms of violence are fast becoming the 'norm', and so legislate accordingly; without encroaching upon a citizen liberties: free speech, freedom of worship etc. You'd must have been residing under a rock or on another planet to not know that increasingly today:

> "... new forms of violence have emerged, in which states are attacked by non-state groups, interstate conflicts are fought using non-military means (such as cyberwarfare (sic)), and the distinction between policing and military intervention becomes blurred... individuals and governments living in a state of constant and heightened alertness, rely increasingly on feeling rather than fact."[civ]

Another author opens our eyes further:

> "The whole of the Middle East is caught up in murderous conflicts that are articulated and fought not in economic but in religious terms. The politics of Pakistan and Israel, both founded as explicitly secular states, are increasingly confessional. In Indonesia and Nigeria, Myanmar and Egypt, communities are attacked and individuals killed on the pretext that the practice of their faith makes them aliens in their own country. India, whose constitution enshrines the state's equidistance from all religions, is convulsed by calls

for the government to assert an explicitly Hindu identity, with grave consequences for Indians who are Muslims or Christians. In many countries, not least the United States, immigration policy – effectively the case against immigrants – is often framed in the language of religion. Even in largely agnostic Europe, the Bavarian Prime Minister urges the presence of the cross in official buildings as the marker of a Catholic Bavarian identity, and the French government bans the public wearing of the full-face burqa. In Switzerland a referendum is held to ban the building of minarets, while thousands march regularly in Dresden to protest against alleged 'Islamization' (sic). The most populous state on earth, China, claims that its national interests, the very integrity of the state, are threatened by the exiled spiritual leader of Tibetan Buddhists, the Dalai Lama, a man whose only power is the faith he embodies."[cv]

Have followers of many world's religions, and that of the Christian belief system, esp. those who might be gearing up for a last-ditch effort and all-consuming end–time war. Have these people everywhere conveniently forgotten one of their 'founders' supposed 'words of wisdom'? Plainly stated, "...you will know them by their fruits." (Matthew 7:20).

Tekel:

Religion, you have been weighed on the scales and found wanting

Has the Church and its sacred books, added a useful sum of knowledge to the world–stage?

MUCH DISSENT AND A shear useless loss-of-life the Church has and continues to cause, is disregarded, or worse, denied to have even happened. Being written off as unrelated to the 'true Church' of today. Religion's literalist might well argue that the religious institution they adhere, despite the above brief macabre history is still most beneficial for societal progress and harmony. Those that would argue for this are also showing their ignorance of that history. Chapter two, "Christianity is not Great", John Loftus highlights my argument with the words of Robert G Ingersoll who wrote a paper entitled, "A Thanksgiving Sermon." Throughout he asks poignantly:

> "During the centuries what good has the Church done? Did Christ or any of his apostles add to the sum of useful knowledge? Did they say one word in favor (sic) of any science, of any art? Did they teach their fellow-men how to make a living, how to overcome the destructions of nature, how to prevent sickness- how to protect themselves from pain, from famine, from misery and rags?"

Rather, countless generations of believers are still taught on a sunday morning/ evening at a 'service' that material wealth and all earthly pleasures are essentially an abomination. Sermons spruiking such heartless messages are justified as a 'plan' the deity has for mankind. The dullard believer is coerced into forfeiting huge sums of money, which seems to be squandered by the elitist hierarchy of the 'faith'. Furthermore,

> "What illustrious deed did Jesus accomplish worthy of a God who beholds from on high with contempt [the trifling pursuits of] men, and derides, and considers as sport terrestrial events?[cvi]

> "...(speak-ing (sic) to Jesus), "What beautiful or admirable thing have you said or done, though you were called upon in the temple to give some manifest sign that you were the son of God?"[cvii]

DECONSTRUCTING ENDTIME DELUSIONS

Any thoughtful person alive today would be completely uninformed of the facts, if, an answer to the questions of Ingersoll, and those of Celsus are positive in light and recognition of previous statements. With a similar appraisal, Ingersoll confirms:

> "From the very first... [the Church] taught the vanity – the worthlessness of all earthly things. It taught the wickedness of wealth, the blessedness of poverty. It taught that the business of this life was to prepare for death. It insisted that a certain belief was necessary to ensure salvation, and that all who failed to believe, or doubted in the least would suffer eternal pain. According to the Church natural desires, ambitions and passions of man were all wicked and depraved... [Asking further], did the Church find the medicinal virtue that dwells in any weed or flower?"[cviii]

The mini tv-drama adaptations of Ken Follett's books, 'The Pillars of the Earth', and sequel, 'World without End' illustrates graphically the corruption, deceit, lust for power, and ignorance of the emerging 'Church' throughout the Middle-Ages. The opening scenes of World without End depict a character who has a nasty arrow wound. The recommendation for healing his wound by the churches' official surgeon was to dress it with fresh dung; i.e., human or animal <excrement>. This, as opposed to the healing properties of herbs and ointments. The pope and every clergyman and those of elite municipal rank, labelled all practitioners of natural healing who studied meticulously the beneficial properties of herbs and ointments, and who favoured understanding the body through dissection of the dead; witches. These poor souls were immured, tried, and sent to the faggot pile or the hangman's noose. A Netflix series, "Witches: A Century of Murder", focuses on the eradication of presumed witches across the U.K. during the witch-craze of the 16th-17th Centuries. That the accused were most often the poor and disenfranchised is disheartening. False accusations and hearsay spread about disliked persons of any community could also evoke a charge of witchcraft. Not only were the marginalised (particularly women) accused of such 'crimes'; there are cases of disliked clergy accused, tortured, tried, and executed for the alleged crime of witchcraft also. No one was immune. The elderly, disabled, poor, bad-tempered were all particularly targeted. The tersely authored and earlier cited title, "Witches, Midwives, and Nurses: A History of Women Healers" (2nd Edition.) offer the following brief for why such persons (particularly elderly women, middle-aged women, and young girls) were targeted as deserving the faggot pile, drowning, or hangman's noose:

> "Witches represented a political, religious, and sexual threat to the Protestant and Catholic churches alike, as well as to the State... [furthermore it was decreed] Anyone failing to report a witch faced both excommunication and a long list of temporal punishments... The point is obvious: the witch craze did not arise spontaneously in the peasantry. It was a calculated ruling class campaign of terrorization (sic)." (Ch.1. Under the subtitle: The Witch Craze. [brackets mine]).

Additionally, one of the most bazaar indictments the Church charged witches with was the astoundingly unbelievable crime of *helping* and *healing*. As far as any witch hunter of the period had been concerned; and despite the equally fantastic and false charges surrounding all manners of dissent, those witches deemed as good, un-harmful, and practitioners of health and wellbeing, it was said that – "It were a thousand times better for the land if all Witches, but especially the blessing Witch, might suffer death." (ibid.) These and Ingersoll's poignant indictment cannot be understated; that the early Church displayed and carried out with complete brutality its neurosis to those it was threatened by and considered of lesser standing. Every natural desire and any attempt at empathy (esp., by women) to better the lives of fellow citizens through healing herbs and ointments were all believed to be abhorrent and against the will of deity. Despite the fact also that:

> "...as medicine-man, astrologer or Prophet, necromancer, priest, physician...in these earliest day's woman is all, in all and plays every part... For thousands of years. The people had one healer and only one, – the Sorceress." But what a price she paid for her fidelity!... Magian queens of Persia, enchanting Circé, sublime Sibyl, alas! how are you fallen, how barbarous the transformation...suffered!... She who from the throne of the Orient, taught mankind the virtues of plants and the motions of the stars, she who... gave oracles to a kneeling world, is the same that, a thousand years later, is hunted like a wild beast, chased from street to street, reviled,

DECONSTRUCTING ENDTIME DELUSIONS

buffeted, stoned, scorched with red-hot embers!... The Priest realises clearly where the danger lies, that an enemy, a menacing rival, is to be feared in this High-priestess of Nature..."[cix]

Astoundingly, the medieval Church also recommended bloodletting as a cure for numerous sicknesses, fevers, and mental disorders as it insisted on these maladies were caused by demons and devils. Sent by deity as a punishment because the inflicted had grievously 'sinned' against deity. Instead of offering any comfort or empathy to the sorely inflicted, the (peasant esp.) was ordered they must: Thank and 'praise' deity, endure the suffering and if so, die. The literalness of the following Matthew chapter five passages must have weighed in on many a decision:

> "If your right eye causes you to sin, tear it out and throw it from you! For it is better for you that one of your members be destroyed than your whole body be thrown into hell. And if your right hand causes you to sin, cut it off and throw it from you! For it is better for you that one of your limbs be destroyed than your whole body go into hell."[cx]

Like Oedipus in Sophocles', of the famous play the grievous 'sinner' was to 'prove' their remorse and despair; not only to the Church authorities, but to deity by removing either the eye (like Oedipus) or the offending body part. Anyhow, sacrifice was required! If that happened to coincide with death, all the better (so it was assumed). Even today in our 'enlightened–ness,' the same conviction is prevailing. Either through unbridled ignorance, religious bigotry or an unwillingness to understand and acknowledge scientific evidences of natural causes and restorative benefits of medical knowledge; ubiquitous beliefs still flourish. Many literal beliefs and practices; either via blood–letting, or the literal maiming of individuals for some 'religious' offence lead to the demise (and, salvation via death; Hooray for them?) of many citizens. The author of "Man Made Gods" further emphasises such idiocy:

> "For the last three thousand years, mankind suffered various maladies but people had no scientific efforts to find out the causes and remedies of these illnesses. What was the reason? Priests informed people to read only religious texts. They discouraged writing and reading of scientific books.

Since new inventions were considered against gods, several scientists were convicted and punished in the last two thousand years. Thus, priests and their books delayed scientific progress for nearly two millennia."

The problem the world faced then, as now, was that the Church largely claimed a superior knowledge through the ingestion of its holy books of what lay beyond the grave, but absolutely nothing about the world in which lives are lived. Recall my previous statements regarding the book, "Last Clash of the Titans", by Derek Gilbert! In essence

> "those interested in eliminating Indians, Irish, Jews, Slavs, Africans, or any other race [or people following a different creed] has argued [as the Church continues to do so today] that their policies [doctrines and end-time scenarios] while harsh, are simply necessary to "make the world a better place.""[cxi]

The same ignorance and denials are prevalent to this day. It is these claims that feed and fuels an end–time hypothesis. Fundamental/ literalist christians promoting numerous websites; what these ultimately reveal – with their elaborate productions, is the same incitement and pandemonium of a superimposed supernatural worldview sweeping the planet. The worldview that only christianity has the 'keys' to correct doctrine and so, 'save' the planet from a looming cataclysm; that there are also clandestine demonic forces behind every scientific experiment, or 'strange' occurrence conspiring the annihilation of Planet Earth. Postulating ideas as these reveal for me at least, the true difference of character and idea of a supposed 'supreme' deity that governs the thoughts and actions of its admirers – void! Readers may wince, groan, and become incensed at these statements. You may also be questioning what has any of this to do with an end-time? Every statement made in this Nail has any amount of links to an end-time scenario. Although humankind is plagued with narcissist disposition, undoubtedly the sheer bullishness of the emerging 'new' faith of christianity did little to quash that tendency; rather, seems to have only heightened it. Aren't these emerging world-views only revealing mankind's evil intent though? That typically seems the indoctrinated 'Christian' conclusion. Except: if mankind is reportedly created in the image of a supreme deity who display's like actions and it does. Glancing through the Old Testament reveals this very character. The one cannot cancel the other! There is a very high probability that believed 'facts' about the bible and other 'sacredly' held writings, including the countless passages in sacred texts, those seen as apocalyptically inspired; with the many characters, entities, deities, 'prophecies' and doctrines. All are not so elucidate-cut and certain as one would assume, or as some would have us believe. As I now propose to highlight in the remainder of Part One.

Nail Two:

Old Testament query one - we should get out of this place. Exodus stage right:

THE DISASTROUS EXODUS legend or astoundingly related events that are recorded in the Judaic-Christian books occurred. Very much is validated, so it appears according to numerous authors.[cxii] In the Introduction to his book, "Egypt knew no Pharaohs nor Israelites", Ashraf Ezzat writes: "The Exodus really took place but in a much humbler way and on a much narrower scale in an obscure little village in ancient South Arabia." Other records offer various appealing explanations. For instance, Jewish historian Josephus in, "Against Apion" offers a few explanations for an Exodus out of the lands of Egypt. First, an Exodus, by an attempted military campaign, is mentioned by Manetho, an Egyptian historian and priest who wrote in the third Century B.C. The result of the peoples of Hyksos (later explained, Part Two), being driven from Egypt. T.W. Doane offers the second reason, also from Josephus' treaties 'Against Apion'. In the sixth chapter, 'The Exodus from Egypt' of his book "Bible Myths", Doane writes:

> "We find, from other sources, what is evidently nearer the truth. It is related to the historian Choeremon, that, at one time, the land of Egypt was infested with disease, and through the advice of the sacred scribe Phritiphantes, the king caused the infected people (who were non-other than the brick making slaves, known as the children of Israel), to be collected, and driven out of the country. Lysimachus relates that: "A filthy disease broke out in Egypt, and the Oracle... being consulted... commanded the king to purify the land by driving out the Jews (who were infected with leprosy...), a race of men who were hateful to the Gods." The whole multitude of the people were accordingly collected and driven out into the wilderness." Diodorus Siculus, referring to this event, says: "In ancient times Egypt was afflicted with a great plague, which was attributed to the anger of God, on account of the multitude of foreigners in Egypt: by whom the rites of the native religion were neglected..."[cxiii]

DECONSTRUCTING ENDTIME DELUSIONS

Zechariah Sitchin's book, "End of Days", chapter three, 'Egyptian Prophecies, Human Destiny' seems to confirm these statements. Adding the event was a cause of some 'religious' changes that happened throughout the land. Using as evidence, a papyrus often linked to the bible Exodus event. "The Ipwuer Papyrus": "It was indeed a religious change that caused the political and societal breakdown, the unidentified Ip-Wer (sic) wrote;

> "...we believe that the change was Ra's becoming Amon. The upheaval began with a collapse of religious observances and manifested itself in the defiling and abandonment of temples, where "the Place of Secrets has been laid bare, the writings of the august enclosure have been scattered, common men tear them up in the streets magic is exposed, it is in the sight of him who knows it not." The sacred symbol of the gods worn on the king's crown, the Uraeus (the Divine Serpent), "is rebelled against religious dates are disturbed priests are carried off wrongfully." After calling on the people to repent, "to offer incense in the temples to keep the offerings to the gods," the papyrus called on the repenters to be baptized—to "remember to immerse." Then the words of the papyrus turn prophetic: in a passage that even Egyptologists call "truly messianic," the Admonitions speak of "a time that shall come" when an unnamed Savior (sic)—a "God-king"—shall appear... It is astounding to find such messianic prophecies of apocalyptic times and the end of Wrongdoing that will be followed by the coming—the return—of peace and justice, in papyrus texts written some 4,200 years ago; it is chilling to find in them terminology that is familiar from the New Testament, about an Unknown, the Triumphant Savior, the "Son-Man."[cxiv]

That the Exodus really happened but in a much humbler way and on a much narrower scale seems to bear witness in the above quotations. Adding more colour and possible realism to the story of the texts. Albeit the above statements offered are not exactly alike, and that Sitchin as a reputable scholarly author are groundless, it cannot be denied that the same points are made. Which are to the effect, ancient Egypt was at some point in its ancient history, sorely inflicted with disease. Such affliction was blamed upon the residing foreigners. Chosen as either the Hyksos, or the 'children of Israel'. These people were believed by the Egyptian to be an unclean people. Egypt's priesthood esp. was very careful to avoid anything that could putrefy. Avoiding wearing garments tailored from animals, they also "...circumcised themselves, and shaved their whole bodies, even to their eyebrows, lest they should unknowingly harbour any filth... We know from the laws set down in Leviticus that the Hebrews were not a remarkably clean race." Wrote T.W. Doane in studies comparing the Judaeo-Christian texts with other mythic tales.

It does seem that the Exodus event of the bible never happened exactly as recorded but is a montage of various source materials and similar events. There seems to be convincing evidence from various extra-biblical sources, especially one particular Egyptian text, the Ipwuer papyrus which indicates numerous cataclysms occurred around the presumed time of the bible migration. Leading to numbers of people fleeing Egypt's lands. Moreover, these are still according to some researchers, extant. However, can this source be reliable? Are the records in this one Egyptian poetic papyrus convincing? Parallels have for decades been drawn by scholars and the average believer between the Exodus account of the bible and this Egyptian text.[cxv] The impression and widespread acknowledgment that the Egyptian poem, the Ipwuer papyrus may allude to an Exodus comparable to the recorded events of the bible is extensive. Riaan Booysen and archaeologist David Rohl in their titles, "Thera and the Exodus" and "The lords of Avaris"; however, both offer us some interesting comments; noting first that our expectations regarding the validity of such an event as the Exodus from the land of ancient Egypt are dashed. Booysen for instance writes there are no specific Egyptian records illustrating Exodus events occurring. Confirmed again later. David Rohl quotes the doyen of Israeli archaeology –Professor Israel Finkelstein –of Tel Aviv University who says phenomenally:

> "There was no Exodus from Egypt. There was no violent conquest of Canaan. Most of the people who formed early Israel were local people – the same people whom we see in the highlands throughout the Bronze and Iron Ages. The early Israelites were – irony of ironies – themselves originally Canaanites!...Something clearly doesn't add up when the biblical account, the archaeological evidence, and the Egyptian records are placed side by side." (The Lords of Avaris, Ch. One: The Walls came tumbling down.)

DECONSTRUCTING ENDTIME DELUSIONS

Similarly, in the chapter 'Did the Exodus Happen?' of "The Bible Unearthed", Finkelstein and Silberman inform that there is not one shred of evidence to indicate any ancient Israelite people group was ever near Egypt. There is nothing physical; no inscriptions, no tombs, no written records that would indicate an Israelite presence in Ancient Egypt; either as friend, foe, or enslaved nation! More so Finkelstein and Silberman write:

> "Putting aside the possibility of divinely inspired miracles, one can hardly accept the idea of a large group of slaves from Egypt [travelling un-molested] through the heavily guarded border fortifications [which were present all along the desert regions of northern Sinai between the delta and Gaza], into the desert and then into Canaan in the time of such a formidable Egyptian presence. Any group escaping the will of the Pharaoh would have easily been tracked down not only by an Egyptian army chasing it from the delta but also by the Egyptian soldiers in the forts in northern Sinai and in Canaan." (pp. 27, 30-31. [brackets my addition.])

Reiterating with confirmation to these comments, Professor Ze'ev Herzog in a 1999 article titled, 'Deconstructing the walls of Jericho,' in the Israeli magazine Haaretz made this surprising commentary (as retold by Ashraf Ezzat):

> "Following 70years of intensive excavations in the land of Israel, archaeologists have found out: The patriarchs' acts are legendary stories, we did not sojourn in Egypt or make an Exodus, we did not conquer the land. Neither is there any mention of the empire of David and Solomon... This is what archaeologists have learned from their excavations in the land of Israel: the Israelites were never in Egypt, did not wander in the desert, did not conquer the land in a military campaign and did not pass it on to the 12 tribes of Israel...and that the early Israelite religion adopted monotheism only in the waning period of the monarchy and not at Mount Sinai..."

What made Herzog's testimony so poignant is the fact he was the professional eyewitness, with firsthand access to all the archaeological evidence from all over Palestine in the final three decades of the twentieth century. Which calls into question the true validity of the current intra-Phoenician conflict; between modern Israel and the Arab states. Have not Christian and Israeli arguments about deity-ordained land ownership through an ancient command and subsequent conquest; just really bought into another lie? Much like the nativity narratives in the New Testament, we would expect the historicity of such momentous events; and yet there are none found anywhere in documented history records of the ancients. Even the Exodus and Canaan's sacking by hordes of Israelite soldiers commanded by joshua, has not been recorded by any secular sources of the time. These events we might think should have made front-line 'news' up and down the Egyptian delta and throughout surrounding nations. Alas, the Exodus episode and its 'miraculous events', as it becomes visible in the Judaeo-Christian books appear rather of a papier-mâché construction; the fabrication and manipulation of similar true regional events. Ezzat further enlightens us with the following poignant statements:

> "Try and imagine yourself amongst ancient Egyptians who had survived the devastation of the ten plagues. You had witnessed firsthand the might of the God of the Israelites ...Yahweh had forcefully shown to the Egyptians the utter impotence of their gods and demonstrated beyond reasonable doubt his power over them... what would your reaction be? Humbled by the might and Revelation...certainly you would have gotten down on your knees... (to renounce your 'old' gods – imploring the protection and forgiveness of Yahweh – the Israelite deity) ...If Egypt was the land of the Israelites' bondage and Exodus, the whole ancient Egyptians would have converted to Judaism around 1400 – 1200bc...but that...never happened..." (Ch. 1: Tale of two Egypt's.)[cxvi]

All that we have outside the bible account is a few fragmented scraps of an Egyptians' poetic papyrus (and possibly other pieces from other lands similarly), and the 'histories' and several apologies of both Egyptian and Jewish writers indicating there were some terrifying disturbances throughout Egypt. These disturbances forced people to flee Egyptian territories. That these people were ancient Israelites seems to be based upon the guessed and doctored readings of the quotations cited. Besides, it is most unlikely that any Israelites entered Egypt for any length of time. Arabic/Lebanese author and historian of note, Kamal Salibi, "Secrets of the Bible People" confers: "...no one has yet found the slightest trace of an ancient Hebrew or Israelite presence in Egypt, and scholars remain in disagreement as to when, and by what route, the Israelites made their Exodus out of Egypt, ultimately to reach Palestine."[cxvii] Whether readers 'believe', the Ipwuer papyrus or some other ancient document source is a legitimate and comparable picture of the Exodus narrative is irrelevant, also most unlikely if Booysen's comments also ring true:

> "One would expect that such a significant event in Egyptian history would have been recorded by the Egyptians themselves as well as historians from other nations. [But] there are practically no extant Egyptian records to confirm the Exodus story. What we have comes largely from Josephus, who repeated accounts from other historians verbatim for the purpose of refuting their 'false' interpretations. Scraps of information also survive in the records of various other ancient historians including Diodorus, Artapanus and Africanus."[cxviii]

Equivalent comments have attracted frequent remarks by detractors. Some imply that a lack in Egyptian records explicitly referring to such an event as the Exodus, is really of no historical import given such an event would most likely have been seen as 'placing a spotlight of unfavourable disposition' upon the land and its government. It would most likely then not be recorded. According to Moustafa Gadalla (Historical Deception) however, the ancient Egyptians were meticulous record keepers of everything. Government and business transactions were recorded on papyri. Letters too, communicated everyday life. Still, extant records for instance detail the invasion of Egypt by the 'Sea Peoples' who eventually, was defeated, according to archaeologist Eric H Cline in the opening remarks of his book, "1,177 B.C.: The Year Civilization Collapsed." Ancient Egyptians remained consistent in describing attention to how grand the land, its people, and Nesut or Nesu (Queens and Kings) were. They were a very patriotic people. Negative accounts (including defeats) were we are told through mainstream historians' textbooks, distinctly anathema. But, as above, some negative accounts are still extant. Other commentators make equally valid assertions that, 'words were to the ancient Egyptians far too powerful' to be trifled with. Despite the letters communicated by the population daily! Egypt recording any great event was essentially to remind 'the gods' of Pharaoh's faithfulness to secure safe passage in the afterlife. He was after all the God's doyen; their true, bodily, physical representative on the terrestrial plane. Records of their exploits therefore were often inscribed on temple walls; where the very performance of writing was a powerful act. Writing, the ancient Egyptians believed was a sacred discharge of duty. It was seen as the "counterpart of the words of the God's" themselves, and thus shared their magical power. To the ancient Egyptians, words were creative. They saw in them the template for bringing" life, reality, and being to what was represented. Words had a magical power –over life and death. They could magically bring both chaos (death) or (life) order. That is – they could cause chaos out of and order out of chaos. Hence the numerous spells, charms, and depictions of food and everyday items that are scrawled on walls. Recording a negative event like the Exodus might have been believed to be able to reignite its devastating effect. Provided such an event actually happened, which no one with absolute surety knows; for as stated above archaeological evidence does not exist indicating an Israelite Exodus occurred from Egyptian soil![cxix]

The belief of the ancient Egyptian that secular practice and belief that 'words' are magical in a religious/mythic sense; that they can induce a deity to action, protect the human speaker, or bring animation to the inanimate is not lost to modern religious practice. The transubstantiation of the communal elements; the belief that both wafers/ bread, and wine/ grape juice; the 'sacraments' of any Church 'communion' become/ came the living deity. These are but two instances that come to immediate mind where, although undoubtedly unrecognised by believers the same 'magical import' is assumed. The modern response of 'bless you' after a sneeze is another. Many reasons and explanations are offered for these superstitious practices. Probably the most commonly known for a 'bless you' are the mythic belief that somehow, the gesture of offering a 'Blessing' is a magically potent formula; to protect the sneezer from evil spirits or the <Devil>. Pure superstition. Other magical 'power' words have not been lost to modern religion. The same Egyptian formulas have filtered into Christian dogma. Consider these brief but in no way extensive highlights: "Genesis opens with the creation of things by the spoken word. Which parallel Egyptian and Babylonian creation myths, i.e. the Hermopolis, Enuma Elish Creation Myths." There is an underlying belief in Christian sects that 'prayer' has a 'power' to move the deity to action. Which stems from passages like, Matthew 21:22. Similar beliefs are identified in texts like 'The Egyptian Book of the Dead'; which is filled with incantations and spells to be prayed over the dead. Also, spell 125 in this ancient Egyptian text, was the very foundation of the bible's Ten Commandments. See Tony Bushby's "The Christ Scandal". Jesus, the believed doyen of the new testament is likened to the word. He has the power over life and death. Then, the final book in the Christian cannon – Revelation, is full of commands, curses, and blessings... which in many ways are believed to be of 'magical' import, closing with the pseudo-magical exhortation, beckoning the literal return of the Jesus figure. These comments and especially those of Finkelstein, Ezzat, Gadalla, Osman, and Riaan Booysen should cause much sober reflection upon such narratives as an Exodus by a certain ethnic group portrayed in the Judaeo-Christian texts. There is obviously a vast array of opinion to wade through.[cxx] One or the other proposal; however (that Exodus is or not factual and relevant) must be correct. Either that, or these and other revered bible stories are greatly biased fabrications –with a hint of historicity. An account verifying the veracity of the Exodus as recorded in the Judaeo-Christian book remains elusive. Readers and believers alike should therefore be guided by the premise testus unus, testus nullus: the expression that a single witness is not enough to corroborate a story. Testus unus, testus nullus applies equally to any bible story; hard evidences cannot affirm many. In the Exodus this is puzzling. The simple reason, as Booysen confirmed above, the ancient Egyptians are known to be meticulous record keepers –especially of the history of the whole of the Mediterranean. Knowledge that the Egyptians were extremely diligent record-keepers dates to ancient times indeed. John Burrow informs us that Herodotus, the specified 'father of history' in his most famous work - Histories –

"...paid tribute to the Egyptians for their preservation of knowledge of the past: "by their practice of keeping records of the past, [they] have made themselves much the most learned of any nation." He follows a brief discussion on Herodotus with: "...the records so preserved go back more than two thousand years before Herodotus' own time, the mid fifth century b.c.. The Egyptians were indeed then the world's premier record-keepers..." (Burrow, A History of Histories.)

Think of the legendary Royal Alexandrian library of ancient Alexander - Egypt. Which most unfortunately was destroyed by fire. A sacking that was some say roused by christianity. No one knows for sure whom. The culprit was. However, and most; unfortunately; incalculable ancient knowledge, history, and learning was destroyed forever. It is said the library housed upwards of 200,000 (some researcher's intimate there were possibly 700,000) rare works and scrolls of literature gleaned from all corners of the ancient world. Works pertaining to pre- and ancient history, science, astrology, cosmogony, literature, the arts, and general knowledge are now thought to be lost. Could this once world-famous depository of knowledge actually have housed an ancient Egyptian scroll detailing an Exodus event, and records of other now-lost civilisations; i.e., Atlantis? Sadly, we are most likely now never to know. Whatever the case, the record of the Exodus seems likely to have been birthed if through anything, the occurrence of multiple local terrestrial catastrophes, sparked by a possible extraterrestrial collision (as explained shortly).[cxxi] How then do we determine the veracity of any record? A principal that assists scholars, researchers, and writers in the verification of events is called Multiple Attestations. Used mainly in sacred studies, it is the understanding that the more independently references to an event; the more likely a conclusion can be drawn verifying its reliability. Yet, few if any significant references are available detailing an Exodus event – let alone any other mildly significant sacred book personality/ event. Confidently, if readers were present during the described plagues of the sacred text's Exodus account, thoughts of the world's end; of an Apocalypse would be at the forefront of the mind. Considering the vast and fantastical events ascribed in the Exodus account. Survivors and contemporary eyewitnesses would have made some type of record or written historic testimony afterward – like Ipuwer. Similarly, historians of surrounding nations would have made sufficient and detailed attestations also; alas, there is none extant. As referred to the only record of such an event is in the pages of the sacred book of the Jews and Christian believers. We can be assured then that to dismiss this episode, as sheer fabrication will not cause a striking blow from 'above,' rather, is justified. A lack in Multiple Attestations simply they mean it did not occur (as recorded and taught to believers!)

Miracles?

ABOUT THE MIRACULOUS nature ascribed by the author to the Exodus event. An affirmative No! Numerous past, and current researchers provide more possible explanations to these events. Including Ralph Ellis and Booysen who propose that the (Ten plagues) of the recorded Exodus events was more correctly the result of a massive eruption of Thera, Santorini. Another is the 'rogue' heretical publication of independent scholar Immanuel Velikovsky in his (1950) title: "Worlds In Collision". What though is a 'Miracle?' "The Holman Illustrated Bible Dictionary" offers a standard Christian perspective.

> "A deity created everything, including what we call 'Spiritual, or Supernatural' things. Natural events to believers are just that, natural. Things. But, they also allow their deity 'intervening', and 'interacting' with nature. This, is claimed 'A Miracle'. Because the deity is believed to be able to interact, at will outside the parameters of the natural world. Despite, such a premise must be "...Based on [one's] belief that God intervenes in the natural order to do the miraculous. One's view of the miraculous is related to one's view of the universe. A Mechanistic Perspective Believes the world is controlled by unalterable natural laws, and cannot allow for the possibility of miracles..." T. R. Mcneal[cxxii]

The "Maverick Philosopher" counters with the 17th Century philosopher, Spinoza's argument:

> "...any event happening in nature which contravened nature's universal laws, would necessarily also contravene the Divine decree,.. [and] he, ipso facto, would be compelled to assert that God acted against His own nature—an

evident absurdity... Further, as nothing happens in nature which does not follow from her laws, and as her laws embrace everything conceived by the Divine intellect, and lastly, as nature preserves a fixed and immutable order; it most clearly follows that miracles are only intelligible as in relation to human opinions, and merely mean events of which the natural cause cannot be explained by a reference to any ordinary occurrence, either by us, or at any rate, by the writer and narrator of the miracle. (p. 84) In sum, since the course of nature, being ordained by God, cannot be contravened, miracles ontically construed are impossible. Talk of miracles, therefore, is simply talk of events we cannot explain. Miracles are thus parasitic upon our ignorance. They are natural events that simply surpass our limited human comprehension..."[cxxiii]

Simply Stated in the easy to digest book "Great Thinkers", is outlined Spinoza's challenging rebuttal of not only his native Judaism, but also religion generally. In sum:

- God is not a person who stands outside nature.

- there is no one to hear our prayers.

- or to create miracles.

- there is no afterlife.

- man is not God's chosen creature.

- the Bible was only written by ordinary people.

- God is not a craftsman or an architect. Nor is he a king or a military strategist who calls for believers to take up the holy sword. God does not see anything nor does he expect anything. He does not judge. He does not even reward the virtuous person with a life after death. Every representation of God as a person is a projection of the imagination.

- everything in the traditional liturgical calendar is pure superstition and mumbo-jumbo.[cxxiv]

Not to dwell too much on it, Spinoza surely hit-the-nail-on-the-head. Clearly, these eight points deserve more consideration, particularly by the religious apologist. Those who would insist that it is 'by some faith' that the above is demolished. Sorry this doesn't wash; because 'faith' is a letting go! Once let go where does this leave the advocate? Very close to Spinoza's latter conception: atheism! One answer regarding why the events of the Exodus should not be construed as miraculous seems obvious. To assert deity violates, his/her own nature and any universal parameters already governing our planet and the universe generally are simply unreasonable. It affixes only confusion and leads to more questions regarding that deity. Whether a deity is actually capable (purposefully or mistakenly) of such a thing without violating one other divine or natural 'law'; of omnipotence, omnipresence, or the 'laws' of the cosmos. Miracles simply do not happen. They cannot completely without disturbing or destroying a set of known universal 'regulations,' or without destroying the deity's own governing factors.

Nail Three:

Old Testament query two: An almighty napalming; Sodom it – That blasted hedonistic population - God.

FOR SODOM, GOMORRAH and the five other towns the sacred book asserts as bearing the brunt of a carbonisation cataclysm caused by the Judaeo-Christian 'God' through the sulphuric burning and melting effects of 'brimstone and fire' from heaven. Where "... the Almighty napalmed [carbonised] every man, woman, and child... subjecting them to an extremely agonising death,"[cxxv] is attested by many believers as happening sometime in 'biblical history'. However, a likely scientific explanatory scenario is specified below postulated by independent researcher Immanuel Velikovsky. Not only do these cities generally and regionally lay along the same Rift Valley as another famous city also 'conjectured' by christians to have been obliterated with the assistance of divine intervention, - Jericho. They are also prone to devastating earthquakes and volcanic eruptions.[cxxvi] The narratives of the destruction of these towns may parallel the proposals offered below, or equally they are simply meant to be understood as mere literary metaphor that is to teach a moral principal, – not unlike the most famous and widely read of dialogues; Plato's Republic. Seeking answers to 'what is justice', and 'whether an unprejudiced and morally ethical person is 'happier' than he that is not ethically honourable.' It may be of a surprise to know the town of Jericho in the time of its supposed destruction was little more than a hamlet. According to scholar Peter Brancazio "...in Joshua's time Jericho was at best a small poor unfortified village." So its destruction by joshua and the Israelite army is relegated to nothing more than folk legend.[cxxvii] Should we not also consider Sodom et al similarly. Further, the expanse occupied by this township and Sodom and gomorrah is potholed with tar/asphalt pits. The

DECONSTRUCTING ENDTIME DELUSIONS

"Lexham Bible Dictionary" interestingly seems to confirm these opening thoughts.

> "A large number of scholars believe that Sodom and the Cities of the Plain never existed at all but comprise only a moralistic metaphor. They consider "the world of the patriarchs as a fiction, not reality" (Lemche, Prelude to Israel's Past, p39).

For such scholars, Sodom is an example of God's wrath set within the context of Israel's metanarrative. However, if the Sodom tales identify a location for the Cities of the Kikkar that was, in fact, populated by the ruins of significant Bronze Age cities dating to the time of Abraham, it would be difficult to dismiss such a correlation between text and ground as mere coincidence. Further, if archaeology should confirm [Velikovsky and others seem to have offered something worthy of our consideration toward this] that a violent conflagration destroyed those cities and towns during the time of the biblical patriarchs, then perhaps serious consideration should be given to the history behind the Sodom narratives.[cxxviii] Thoughtful consideration must be extended to the assertion above – that the episode of the destruction of these cities is nothing other than moralistic metaphor. To this, Staks Rosch on Nov 19, 2013 posted an article asking should God, and the Bible be thought of as mere metaphor?[cxxix] Why not: if certain narratives of the texts are proposed to be mere works of moralistic fiction, what evidence is there to say its prime characters should not occupy the same realm? How can any narrative be thought of as metaphor, and not also the characters within that narrative? "Doomsday Chronicle" author Anthony Souza offers a possible, scientifically provable natural disaster as an explanation for the destruction of these cities if it is insisted these are real places. But, we continue to have much difficulty surrounding the pinpointing of their location. In section [c] 'Vertical Distortion' he writes,

> "According to Strabo, a Greek geographer (circa 63 bce – 24 ce), the cities of Sodom and Gomorrah in that region [the Dead Sea] disappeared "in the ancient past" when the ground beneath them was overturned and separated from the Mediterranean, giving rise to a lake of salt." He continues with the

opinion of a geologist who believes that the crust under the Dead Sea is cause of their destruction: that it was literally flipped over. "If Sodom and Gomorrah were located as Strabo professed, they were rowdy waterfront cities that in a drastic shift of the earth were buried instantly beneath tons of rock and dirt." (Doomsday Chronicle, Ch. Anatomy of a Catastrophe (free).

Such a scenario seriously undermines the projected Christian ideal that the supreme deity had a hand in the devastation; but offers an enormous reason for why the remains of Sodom and gomorrah have not yet been discovered under any territory so far excavated. They are not to be found in surface archaeological digs under tons of soil. Maybe geologists, theologians and others interested in finding these cities to authenticate or discredit their place in history might need to do extensive surveys below the watery surface and coastline of the Dead Sea. Should there not be more studies using geophysics and like disciplines?[cxxx] Credibly: another natural and scientifically sound conclusion explaining the destruction of the region Sodom et al are purported to belong. Is that the expanse suffered the devastating effects of unheard-of celestial upheavals. Such as, a meteoroid shower causing widespread destruction and volcanic/earthquake eruptions? Combine this with deadly suffocating plumes and showers of Sulphur dioxide.[cxxxi] Here, the cause was likely the result of comet Venus' close encounter with our home (see Velikovsky). I consider that what writers and researchers like Souza and Velikovsky and others cited in this work have offered the wider population reasonable explanations. That is probably worthy of more open-minded examination. The mainstream academic and Christian community may well label many of these works and the hypotheses they espouse as pseudoscientific. Should that be reason enough to disregard any reasonable proposal without further investigation? Confirmation of meteoroid showers occurring in recent history is offered by author's John Chambers and Jacqueline Mitton in their book "From Dust to Life", writing: "...on April 26, 1803, ...Following three loud bangs some 2000 to 3000 stones rained down on the fields [in France] ...prompting a full scientific investigation..."

DECONSTRUCTING ENDTIME DELUSIONS

Recent history also adds confirmation to the frequency of these destructive anomalies. In Russia for instance, (2013) many captured on film and witnessed a large meteor light up the darkened sky as it entered our atmosphere causing widespread and costly damage and injuring 1,500 people. Indisputably, any meteoroid shower has the potential to wreak devastation on regional fauna and flora. Whether they are the result of debris from the tail of a nearby passing comet, or a lone meteor. Such events were witnessed in antiquity as verification of a disastrous heavenly and very unpleasant incident caused and ordained by one's ruling deity. In the sacred book the controlling deity of the author of the Sodom et al episode and not the least, a principle figure of the account, Abraham. Was Yahweh who many are now connecting to the planetary deity – Jupiter. We will get to the planetary deity summation shortly. First, let us ponder a few thoughts about this deity. Trusting most readers is somewhat familiar with the episodes under discussion. Why is it nowadays not 'politically correct' to call the supreme deity or cosmic bastard - to account? Why did Jób and his family not rail bitterly against their being forcefully evicted from their home? It is recorded that abraham might have pleaded a bargain with his deity (Genesis 18:22-33); regarding its veracity the episode of this petitioning is inconclusive. We only have what is recorded in the sacred book. If people of high ranking (specifically) did petition their deity regarding such destructive events where is the archaeological evidence? Indeed, such a devastating experience warrants widespread confirmation written in official archives (like those of the Egyptians earlier referred and below). Which immense cataclysmic or disastrous incident around the world would nowadays not become a headline 'news' event?[cxxxii] Why do moderns not think that the acumen of the ancients was anywhere as astute as we consider ourselves today? Assuredly I would assume that any life-impacting event, or act was known to countless people groups; no matter their actual station in life! If this deity as many guess was an all-encompassing celestial being of 'Love' (transcending a planet-deity) who then condones and 'causes' earthquakes and meteoroid showers and other celestial or terrestrial calamities to rain down upon those it deems as disobedient – or through other cataclysmic phenomena - it is pitiless! Any reasonable individual using their own intelligence would not hesitate to question 'this deity's' validity. What insensitive deity is this? Furthermore, why is this deity never in the minds of today's believer brought to account for the millions of bloodthirsty genocidal acts it is reported in the sacred text to have committed? Even in our modern day, are those that are supposed to 'represent' it to the wider community not committed to an insane asylum? Why don't we bring such a deity to account for the crimes of sexual infidelity recently exposed? Maybe 'believers' have been duped. Maybe the reason we as a society don't bring charges against and sue the ass off this deity is. Primarily because deep down in our subconscious self, such a deity is of our own imaginative making and therefore, does not exist and we know it! So, to bring charges against a nonexistent entity is sheer madness. A concept we don't want to take ownership.

It is most intriguing also that this same deity is not still today held to account for any and every devastating modern natural occurrence (fires, floods, earthquakes, tsunamis, cyclones, heat waves, drought, cold snaps, disfigurement, and disease etc.,) that strike's individuals and civilisations all over the world.[cxxxiii] If this was to happen surely all churches would become bankrupt very soon and they'd have to deny any deity's existence outright. They'd have to disband and shut-up shop! The (2001) movie "The Man Who Sued God" classically portrays this concept quite perfectly. We can conceptualise a supreme deity figure making quaint arguments fitting personal presumptions all we like, but facts don't change...if God (or some other supreme entity) is the instigator of disasters that wipe out whole cities and devastate regions – because of some 'religious or other offence' – this entity is nothing less than narcissistic. No wonder humanity – especially many religious factions claiming to be followers of a benevolent deity - are plagued with the same qualities. Besides, it has always intrigued me that 'christians' buy into insurance schemes similar to the rest of us. Schemes that more often than not – we subconsciously understand - do not have an ounce of integrity behind them when disasters not in our control or making strike.

DECONSTRUCTING ENDTIME DELUSIONS

These are labelled ridiculously 'acts of God.' To insist that a supreme deity is in governance and then sign up for insurance of any kind seems nonsensical. Isn't 'faith' in the protection of deity enough? Why does 'faith' not transfer through to the rest of one's lifestyle – regardless? The irony of apparent active faith is the famous pope mobile – with its three-inch protective (bullet proof) plexiglass enclosure – 'protecting' the pope. Protecting him from what exactly?[cxxxiv] Alternatively, are such insurances 'just in case' there really is not a benevolent deity who looks out for your welfare? With more research such a deity any deity is primarily a fabrication of the mind; an entity of the imagination and our own making. It (or whatever concept is held) is birthed and given existence only in our heads and wild eccentric imaginations which are not at all dissimilar to the ancient concept of deity after all. It could be said then we still are plagued with the mind of an outdated rudimentary man. Little has changed since the initial inception of religious conviction and its trimmings. All that has been altered refined or dismissed are the arguments and rhetoric of defenders and his antagonist. On the celestial planet-deity Jupiter/Yahweh/Zeus/Thor...having caused the cataclysm that befell Sodom et al, via celestial anomalies and destructive sources author IR. Jim K K Wong "The Evolution of the God Illusion" interestingly narrates:

> "Jupiter was indeed a great planet, and a mighty God. Abram found this glorious planet exciting. Imagine he, the illusionist or magician, could use Jupiter-Yahweh to performs great wonders. Jupiter-Yahweh was indeed his living and active God!.. Jupiter-Yahweh seems to be easily provoked and is most of the time angry. Why? Briefly, the poets and mythologists or God-makers derived the characteristics of their gods from the behaviour of planets. Jupiter is known to be a rumbling and grumbling planet, due to its agitated planet's electrical and radio noises. The Giant Red Spot of Jupiter emits noisy radio waves; legends have Jupiter shooting out fierce interplanetary thunderbolts; the God is depicted as holding bolts of lightning or hammer." (Chapter 3, Astounding birth of Venus...p.29-31.)

Another author confirms the belief of the ancients that the Planets of the solar system were regarded as gods. Writing, "... the ancients regarded all solar system heavenly bodies as gods, Gods of Heaven especially because of their effect for better or for worse on a person's future."[cxxxv] It was thus thought by the ancients, that the 'heavenly' deities showed their distain for the population. By either threatening a disaster from the skies above, or some other 'naturally' occurring event; like a drought! We witness this often throughout the Judaeo-Christian sacred books. The 'prophets' often rail against the wider populous with rantings from the alleged deity, that a calamity will befall them unless they 'repent' of some assumed misdemeanour. This will become more evident in Nail Nine of this investigation where I supply further evidence from the book of Amos and isaiah.

Besides the above expressions, what of the many other marvels bible readers assume as also patent fact solely because it is recorded in their sacred text: like a worldwide cataclysm; a disaster that engulfed the entire Earth sometime in prehistory (which as will be seen in Part two did happen; around 10,000 to 13,000 years ago); also, apparently a cause of a fed-up merciless deity. These and numerous other disastrous bible phenomena can be won lost or better explained using outside historical corroboration and modern archaeological scientific evidence. But for many believers attesting the veracity of the texts they read and studies only ever subjectively; such 'miraculous' events and supernatural phenomena are particularly reliant upon one's 'faith;' who's ultimate motto is "God said it; therefore, believe it, and that settles it." Shame on those who are so thoughtless. Checking out their brain at the door every time, they rehearse bible reading or study! Maybe it's just that too many people who enter the Christian covenant, those same people read way too many Marvel comic books or watch their modern movie adaptations? They would then see the world through this filter. Note: I wonder if the inhabitants of each city destroyed and other catastrophe renditions recorded in the Judaeo-Christian books; i.e., the devastating plagues recorded in the Exodus event, considered it was the fin de siècle–or better, fin de world; world's end! If found to possess a glimpse of facts at some later stage, in many respects, we can then say with confidence these napalm incidents were indeed, fin de world. Thousands, if not millions of the flora and fauna never saw another day afterward,

DECONSTRUCTING ENDTIME DELUSIONS

but potentially lay entombed – somewhere, awaiting their disclosure by archaeologists and similar scientific disciplines. Still, when it comes to an end-time catastrophe theory of 'biblical' proportions not just a few hopes "...a religious claim somehow has a unique status which is immune from disproof. This will really not do, as it merely opens the door to gullibility. In practice, no one talks of religious truth generally, but 'my religious truth', which is limited to the speaker's own religion, thus falling foul of the principle of universalism." Today, apocalyptic books, lectures, and videos and contemporary subjects are still flooding the Internet and marketplace. An amazing amount of Christian material is prevalent chiefly focused on the subjects – end-times 'rapture', or a perceptible and 'looming' heavenly sanctioned catastrophe. These publications seem to attempt to capture an air of verisimilitude. Without doubt, all are heavily biased and very objectionable. However, should 'christians' let alone anyone else be so intently focused and often worried about such issues? Is there any true credibility in what is produced in religious literature and preached from pulpits today? End-times are after all one of the many periodic themes of both secular and religious society; as was acknowledged through the hype surrounding the twenty-first day of December 2012, and the Mayan Long-count calendar. Recent intense fires and the unusually extreme weather patterns buffeting Eastern Australia and other regions around the world, including the destructive tornados and tsunamis in the Philippines (2013) have been by some, nonsensically and ridiculously pinned by climate change scaremongers as evidence of events that must be seriously addressed. As if by fulfilling any so-called climate change 'strategy' devised by experts and government officials, will or can reverse or slow such events occurring! From this perspective, the embryonic religion of climate change is a favourite of many catastrophe theorists.

> "[Bruno] Latour uses the example of ecological fear, comparing it to the stories of Chicken Little. Now "we too are afraid that the sky is falling. We too associate the tiny gesture of releasing an aerosol spray with taboos pertaining to the heavens." "The sky is falling; the sky is falling!"[cxxxvi]

For this writer and, countless others a sacredly ordained end time or disastrous hype is essentially no different to any of the major themes encountered in a study or cursory glancing at the world that brought us Ancient mythology. The very same themes of the classical Greek and Roman myths and legends and their predecessors dovetail the present as they did antiquity. They dovetail precisely because more than several anecdotes and stories in the pages of the Judaeo-Christian books were filched; manipulated to fit a certain demographic from surrounding cultural myths and legends. Humanity as a whole has not changed all that much. We all have a tendency on occasion to pilfer what resonates well with us at certain times. Obviously, as we have seen and will see further the sacred book contains many scenarios that could easily fit a catastrophe theory. Yet, religious believers seem to be unaware of their frequency. Preferring instead to add a supernatural explanation. Explanations that when exposed to the natural ebb and flow of our violent planet don't seem so super, but rather natural in the end. Because the discussions yet and the exposure of some of what I recognise as 'conceivably' areas of real concern; of those ideologies and beliefs; of both end-time and not that believers should be at least aware, instead of ascribing a status of fact where no fact is warranted. One author ascribes a phrase of note to this immediate concept: the earlier cited book of Jason Slone, "Theological Incorrectness". He insightfully writes:

> "Most of us are well aware of the existence of theological incorrectness. We might simply dismiss it as an unfortunate but harmless bit of folk religion. In fact, because it is so common most people don't consider it to be weird at all. Upon second glance, however, theological incorrectness challenges every bit of conventional wisdom, and a great deal of the scholarship, that we have about what religion is and how it works... plenty of other evidence confirms, we do not simply learn religion from our culture or society. Rather, we actively generate and transform religious ideas. We might even say, with fashionable jargon from the humanities, that religion is performative."

Religion is performative in three ways: (1) we generate religious representations in our minds (an internal performance); (2) we communicate (in stories, rituals, etc.) some of those representations publicly; and (3) the latter process results in a transformation of religious ideas—sometimes slight, other times considerable—because when others see and hear (experience) those representations, they internalize (sic) them. The internalisation of public representations starts the whole process over again. This is how cultural ideas spread." (Sperber 1996). Though common, the generation and transformation of religious representations by individuals is not always harmless. Consider religious violence of those atrocious, cruel, rancorous acts of murder previously described at the beginning, the First Nail. [Or more recently] The terrorists who hijacked four jet planes and crashed three of them into the World Trade Center and the U.S. Pentagon on September 11, 2001, killing thousands of innocent global citizens, professed to be Muslims, probably shouting "Alla'u'akbhar" (God is great!) at the moment of impact. Afterward, many asked how could it be that the religion of Islam justified (caused) such violence? Or, given that Islam is a "religion of peace," how could these particular individuals twist their religion's teachings to such horrific ends? Religion, we assume, isn't supposed to work that way. So why does it? These are undoubtedly,

> "... the right kinds of questions to be asking about the role of religion in our world. But these questions require scientific answers, for ironically the best answers come from neither the religions themselves nor from simple folk psychology the natural way humans "theorize" (sic) about each other's intentions, beliefs, and desires. "Insider" religious answers don't suffice in this case, for obvious reasons: religious answers to questions about religious behavior (sic) tend to reflect the beliefs of the person answering the question more than the actual cause(s) of the behavior. Yet folk psychology doesn't get us very far either, because we cannot simply presume that we know instinctively why people do what they do no matter how emotionally satisfying that may be, because humans are often generally unaware of the reasons for their thoughts and actions in the first place."[cxxxvii]

Men and Lions:

RAPTURE – AS TAUGHT in fundamental believer circles most people I assume, know is instinctively fallacious, and is in fact one mainstay example of 'Theological Incorrectness' across much of christianity. Protestant, Catholic, and Fundamentalist fraternities. I hope to show specifically how this ideology of rapture is fallacious later in this section; in later Nails. Somehow, this predisposition is overwhelmingly trounced in many minds by the scores of Old Testament and New Testament passages used by rapture proponents; passages noticed to be similar in theme to Genesis 5:23-24. We explore and elaborate later (Nail Eight below) this passage for it concerns the evidently sudden disappearance of the first recorded prophetic/shamanic voice of the Judaeo-Christian scriptures, –enoch. He, as recorded in the bible, suddenly was no more but was taken by deity. Yet why? What caused him to be singled out for this treatment, if indeed this is what the author envisages his readership to understand? What is meant by taken anyway? Curiously somehow this episode for countless believers is about rapture theory. Where enoch suddenly disappeared, assuming by-passing the sting of death! But do such phrases or instances substantially advocate for such preconceived ideas? Did such passages of bible mean then, what is taught today? What is meant by the word Rapture. Does, or can it represent what many fundamentalists determine? Is it a bible word? Such questions are likely, or are rarely considered by believers. Yet, I will endeavour to offer an answer in the coming pages.

There must be recognition by now, any passage claimed as the word of deity can be and is all-too-often assimilated to fit a personal hypothesis. One's personal 'my-theology'. There is simply no way anyone can really approach any piece of literature, be that a sacred or secular text totally dispassionately. Any that way we assume to approach a text is bound to his or her particular receptivity. This summation is poignantly made all the clearer by the ancient fable offered by Aesop, entitled 'The Man and the Lion'. This wonderful tale narrates,

> "A Man and a lion traveled together through the forest. They soon began to boast of their respective superiority to each other in strength and prowess. As they were disputing, they passed a statue carved in stone, which represented "a lion strangled by a Man." The traveler pointed to it and said: "see there! How strong we are, and how we prevail over even the king of beasts." The lion replied: "This statue was made by one of you men. If we Lions knew how

DECONSTRUCTING ENDTIME DELUSIONS

to erect statues, you would see the Man placed under the paw of the lion. One story is good, until another is told." (Aesop's Fables.)

Readers of any sacred text subconsciously perform a delicate balancing act. A balancing and weighing between understanding how their particular and chosen deity speaks through the sacred text and the conclusions drawn, which often come from our own presuppositions. Professor Dunn offers a timely warning for christians. Reminding that the way they hear their God speaking:

> "...can easily become self-deceptive. Individual presuppositions can easily bracket out what one doesn't want to hear. Or a meaning can be heard in a text, which is quite divorced from its original or scriptural sense. A text can become a pretext. Or strange teachings and actions can be justified by a selective hearing of Scripture."[cxxxviii]

Some of these misapplications and interpretations are criticised and specifically addressed in section two of this study. Parenthetical sacred book references offered, as stated beforehand also, are presented in the understanding that a potential thought or converse parallel exists, and are therefore, potentially illustrative and suggestive of a point made. Instead of being exhaustive or determinative. Which are how many religious people abuse especially, sacred texts. Example: If it is written, one's understanding of an English Bible passage specifically stands infallibly true and should not be questioned. A further example of this is offered at my brief dissection of a misunderstood, misinterpreted passage; 1 thessalonians 4:17. A favourite passage many assume to speak of a literal vanishing of believers. On such a premise, is there any wonder there is copious strife among the three most acrimonious religions. Fundamental Islam considers itself as universally true and correct and so all men 'must' adhere. The alternative, –forfeiture to the right to life! That 'choice' is interpreted solely to be at the behest of the Muslim believers Cleric/Imam. Conversely, in the main and despite the obvious factions within their own walls, christianity and Judaism consider Islam and all competing 'religions' as counterfeit. Neither side of the arguments put forward though seem to understand. Maybe, humanity has it all wrong considering: "The tragic irony of the current intra-Phoenician cold war is that the Jews, and many christians, who call their state Israel but do not worship the Israelite God, Allah, are at war with the Arabs, who do worship the God of Israel but mistakenly imagine themselves to be descended from a Jew." Undoubtedly divisive doctrines, particularly of any of the above three 'monotheistic' religions have led to what we witness today. Widespread mass slaughter and the bigoted insanity, especially in the Middle-Eastern bloc. Acharya S. (D M Murdock) rightly shared similar judgments, writing:

> "Religion, in fact, is dependent on division, because it requires an enemy, whether it be earthly or in another dimension. Religion dictates that some people are special or chosen while others are immoral and evil, and it too often insists that it is the duty of the "chosen" to destroy the others. And organized religion puts a face on the divine itself that is sectarian, sexist and racist, portraying a male God of a particular ethnicity, for example. The result is that, over the centuries, humankind has become utterly divided among itself and disconnected from nature and life around it, such that it stands on the verge of chaos."[cxxxix]

Society today not only stands on the verge of chaos; it is fully immersed in a chaotic and vice-like grip. All media is witness to this insanity. Chaos, often symbolically represents several things; the initial state of creative force; absence of love; and my favourite description, of being the human spirit becoming overawed with a sense of unshakeable ludiosis; the sense that everything is inane, and you are just 'making it all up' anyway. If anyone asked why you do what you do, no reasonable answer would become available.[cxl] Despite much of this early written exposé sounding or pointing in a particular direction already, let me remind readers that yes there is a sense that the religious proposals of end times are likely inane; and just the ludiosis expressions of a chaotic state of humanity. It should be understood by readers that I have not purposefully set planning to dispense with as a complete mythological fantasy any notion of an end-event occurring.[cxli] An 'end' will occur. First, on an individual scale; humanity will die out. Our encephalon and every neural activity will terminate. Our every chemo-electrical activity

DECONSTRUCTING ENDTIME DELUSIONS

and sentience will assuredly become void, and we will all cease to be! We each deeply know and understand this truth, although, mainly through religion we deny, or more so wish to subvert its eventuality. After our own personal demise, undoubtedly cosmologically our known universe will become supernova; an exploding star-system. Which in some instances causes a 'black-hole'! Scientists and physicists once believed it that 'black holes' only engulfed surrounding matter, including light particles (hence the difficulty of spotting them) into oblivion within its reach. This is now likely an understood misnomer. The opposite occurs. There is a vast probable train of evidence and proof today showing that these celestial oddities actually spew forth the 'seeds' of creation. They are "...the source of infinite light and are the creative forces in the cosmos." Says one author.[cxlii] Black holes not only consume surrounding matter, if two in nearness happen to collide, they emit the seeds of life. Space, time, and the cosmos as we currently know it will still at some stage disintegrate, becoming the stated supernova. But, the remnants of this event for our particular Universe will not have the necessary gravitational force needed to transform it into a black hole. Our Sun is just too small. However, current entropic forces are evident of this phenomenon even now seen by watching through a telescope, the remote past exploding and collapse of our distant star system neighbours. That the Cosmos will in the far-far future expire is poignantly confirmed by one of today's foremost Physicists. Prof. Brian Cox whom, along with Andrew Cohen authored the booklet, "How the Universe will End." They explain,

> "The Cosmos will die; every single one of the billions of stars in the hundreds of billions of galaxies in the Universe will expire, and with them any possibility of life will be extinguished...life in the Universe will only exist for a fleeting, dazzling instant in infinite time, because life, just like the stars, is a temporary structure on the long road from order to disorder." (pp.39-40)

These comments should offer the reader insight into what we currently understand about life, the Universe, and everything, ... it does not equal forty-two as Douglas Adams humorously quipped in his 'Hitchhiker's Guide to the Universe'. But, many religionists hold a certain level of denial and conspiracy of silence of such well-documented and new scientific facts. Preferring instead to instil fanciful whims that does not require the extensive use of common sense. Rather, those ensnared by fundamental and in some respects, conservative religion, still believe blindly what they are 'taught' during sunday services. Proponents see their sacred texts as portraying life as not so temporary: postulating life from a state of order to disorder, and back to order. There is an hourglass effect; first, apparently all terrestrial life was ordered, serene, and in every way perfect; i.e., a reading of Genesis chapters, 1-3. Then, mankind came along and from ignorance nicely stuffed it up... everything then became sour. Chaos reigned whereby a supreme deity had to make a choice; wipe it all out and begin again (which was regretted after the recorded 'flood episode', in a later study). But not to worry, a wonderful deity-man rectified this somehow. Offering the rest of humanity the sure path that effectively disregards the reality of death.[cxliii] At the apparent end we all find ourselves again at perfection. Evidence, and much of the arguments mentioned above however disputes this portrayal. I do reinforce there is nothing in the perceived holy writ to indicate modern proposals of rapture for instance, by which countless people suddenly disappear or any other modern accompanying end time scenario is accurate or even vital knowledge. I have found these suppositions are no more scriptural or useful benefactors to humankind than bar codes or a microchip insert is the dreaded mark of the beast (Revelation 13:17-18). As has been proposed by numerous authors of the 1970's through the 1990's! Mostly because although most modern ideas seem to come from texts of the New Testament, the roots of the New Testament passages are somewhat grounded in the Old Testament. Therefore, they possess context! That bible context itself has a context from which many a Genesis to its myths can be assumed and revealed. Though admittedly often inconclusively. But that should not deter honest seekers. One of the most fascinating studies that describes the context of the first book of the sacred text, Genesis, is the publication, "Hebrew Myths: The Book of Genesis", by Robert Graves, and Raphael Patai. This text alone is well worth the attention of many modern believers. Patai, quite extensively

DECONSTRUCTING ENDTIME DELUSIONS

explains from where the myths of Genesis have originated. Hebrew Myths and another text will be of assistance in the following Nail, as I delve into Genesis, chapter three. Which I now attend.

Nail Four:

Go up as he came down:

THERE IS ACCORDING to the religionist an end time secret aptly illustrated by an analogy of one of Charles Spurgeon's students. He went into the pulpit with every expression of confidence, but he had an extremely difficult time. He came down distressed, almost broken-hearted, so he went to Spurgeon about it. The words of Spurgeon to him were these, "If you had gone up as you came down, you would have come down as you went up."[cxliv] As recorded earlier, Robert Ingersoll beautifully in his outlined 'Thanksgiving Sermon' captured practically all that the Church is 'fixated upon'. A believer, according to Church doctrine essentially is to live as if the worthlessness of all earthly things is best policy. Knowing the wickedness of wealth, espousing the blessedness of poverty: with the understanding that the business of this life was to prepare for death, so they at least, could be ushered into the utopian promised mansion in the heavens (john 14:1-4.) Such beliefs are advanced still generally as one of the rewards of redemption. For many believers little else needs to be said, except maybe to elaborate minimally on one other of the favoured texts of Christian catastrophism. As it is also widely believed that increasingly in

> "...the final days, a troublesome time is going to be on hand. There are going to be humans, self-promoters, money-grubbers, boasters, arrogant, abusers, disobedient to parents, thankless, disrespectful, callous, inflexible, slanderers, undisciplined, uncontrollable, haters of the orthodox, betrayers, reckless, self-opinionated, pleasure-lovers instead of God-lovers, displaying a kind of religiosity while repudiating its authority. Avoid them..."[cxlv]

These verses are from the 2 Timothy epistle. Describing nothing exceedingly new concerning the behavioural patterns of any man, woman, or child. Whether alive or now departed. All the above described behaviours are common to every human being. Each archetype behaviour described above is undoubtedly continually displayed all through life. So, what exactly is it that is so 'enlightening' about these being exhibited to a so-called religiously inspired end-time period? As if we must believe that these personality peculiarities will somehow become more malignant the 'closer', an end time period peaks above a horizon. That these are not what we each today continually display to each-other. Besides, according to the 'feel' of these verses I am most likely such a person. In the Old Testament it is stated that my parents should have me executed, – for being so headstrong against them. For now ceasing to be one of the communities of faith! See the instruction that: "Israel was to execute those who cursed their parents or were obstinate. Exodus. 21:17..."[cxlvi] According to the doctrine of the second Timothy passage above I should not have anything to do with any believer either. I should have been executed when I forsook my Christian background. Period! If, indeed christians should continue to view their text as a literal composition and believe they have a right to supplant Israel as a metaphor for the 'Church'. Furthermore, "Avoid them..." In the quoted passage above seems to be a most astoundingly bazaar statement. That essentially believers are instructed to not have any contact with such persons as those described. Sounds very 'cultish'. So, believers should have nothing to do with any of the populations that is not part of their particular religious society. We witness countless groups of people following this 'message' quite literally already. There continues to be countless religious cults and sects secluding themselves and its 'members' away, forbidding contact with 'outsiders.' What happened to those cult members? Recall, or review: Waco Texas; Jones Town; The 'Heaven's Gate' cult members; Scientologists! Members are often forcibly prohibited from contact with outside 'family members', and pretty much any other member of society who the cult views as seditious. The list goes on... But, 2 Timothy above cannot possibly be hinting of the exact same cultish mindset... Really? We were awakened throughout the Introduction and Nail One to the fact that we live in an age of increased narcissism to each other. Much of the world's population has become mad with envy, jealousy, theft, hatred... there are gossips, deniers of all types of good and astoundingly, not just a few are religious. Today's socialist counterculture of 'political correctness' has waged war on Western civilisation. It's aiming to destroy or in the least maim severely, the values and democratic processes of Western life. Wars of detestation over who's deity is supreme, has not as far as I am aware, hit the limelight; although we witness in the News-media daily a growing intensity of Anti-Semitism and other religiously roused hatred raging across the planet. There is also the proposed 'expectation' by some fundamentalists that soon enough the world will succumb to a religiously angered war between religious sects and their citizens. Undoubted, societal beliefs are awash with concepts borne upon the outstretched wings of distorted logic! No modern individual can escape the influences of advertisers and marketing gurus who propagate this dysmorphism; believers call them pastors and prophets. These men and women have mastered its genius, taking full advantage of our insatiable appetites - by tapping this unrecognised, often subconscious activity and obsession with myths and myth-making that we all engage with daily. That, "I'm right, and you are wrong" because your views and lifestyle are different from mine, and frankly, I don't like that; despite the ideology that such and such a deity reigns supreme. All others are but dust. We seem to be hard-wired with such distorted logic. Such activity and ideologies must feed and nourish the attributes of discontent within us all discussed so far. Those driving our narcissistic tendencies. What though is distorted logic? Author Richard Wetherill coined this startling concept, saying; it is the acceptance of a wrong idea. Alternatively, we could also call it a prosthetic memory. A memory or idea fallaciously held to be true. Ideas falsely expressed as truth that when emotionally attached to individuals, have the tendency to operate under compulsion.[cxlvii] Freud similarly called attention to this mental process coining the term – neurosis in his book, "Moses, and Monotheism". One other author similarly calls our attention to this ideology, phrasing it differently. Humanity is evidently plagued with

> "...the existence of an invisible mind virus (the hapiym (sic)), which functions in a hive structure, that is hierarchal in nature, and that all

DECONSTRUCTING ENDTIME DELUSIONS

humanity has been infected with this virus. The presence of this virus inside us all is the basis for beliefs in the soul, the afterlife, and the false persona referred to as the ego..."[cxlviii]

Scripturally, I see we're introduced to a distortion of logical activity at creation, in the early chapters of the bible. Precisely the saga I wish to focus my attention on to demonstrate this awareness, is the third chapter of Genesis. The yarn that we have been led to believe where a woman (Eve) was compelled by the lust of her eyes; from which desire was quickened, ending with the birth of humanity's apparent disobedience. A defiance that if you accept it, we need to somehow avert. Does 'salvation', whatever that means really change anyone? Has 'salvation' truly rehabilitated; transformed any claimant? Are those who accept this difference any more of an 'enhanced' population demographic regarding their acceptance of the 'claims' of their sacred texts? Are 'Christian' communities astutely more moral, and ethical than the irreligious or those who choose alternate practices?

Let us now take the detour into the third chapter of the bible; where we see the long-held distorted logical, and misogynistic assumption surrounding Eve's encounter with a devilish serpent/ snake. The chapter that for countless devotees of christianity informs them of why and how 'evil' entered the world-stage. Samuel Langhorne Clemens, better known by his pen name Mark Twain wrote several humorous renditions of this chapter of Genesis. Below, are a couple of his musings on this episode of bible lore. First, from his posthumously published work: "Letters from the Earth". This brilliant, beautifully crafted satirical title was only published posthumously as it was considered too blasphemous for printing beforehand. Let us take a sneak-preview into a little-imagined background to the <serpent/ snake> episode of which we see the acknowledgment of knowledge filtration. From the wickedly satirical pen of Mark Twain, we read a humorous accounting of events leading to and afterward of Eve's encounter with that sinuous crafty little bugger. In his book, "The Diary of Adam and Eve" Twain offers the following rendition of the days leading to the encounter:

> Tuesday: she has taken up with the snake now. The other animals are glad, for she was always experimenting with them and bothering them; and I am glad, because the snakes talk, and this enables me to get a rest.
>
> Friday: she says the snake advises her to try the fruit of that tree and says the result will be great and fine and noble education. I told her there would be another result, too - it would introduce death into the world. That was a mistake. It had been better to keep the remark to myself; it only gave her an idea, - she could save the sick buzzard and furnish fresh meat to the despondent lions and tigers. I advised her to keep away from the tree. She said she would not. I foresee trouble. Will emigrate.

Emigrate poor Adam does attempt before his predicted calamity results. He is forced to ride away as fast as he can to a distant land. Only to be caught in the midst of the outbreak. His horse being eaten by tigers, and he only escaping being consumed by "going away in much haste" to a place outside the 'Park'. Continuing the story:

> Wednesday:... but she found me... in fact, I was not sorry she came, for there are but meagre pickings here, and she brought some of those apples. I was obliged to eat them; I was so hungry. It was against my principles, but I find principles have no real force except when one is well fed... (Adam's Diary)

So, the apparent 'fall' into wickedness and all manners of 'evils' has occurred. All because someone couldn't resist the 'influences' and 'charms' of a beguiling creature, they had in a sense 'shacked-up-with.' Twain's rendition of this very episode with the serpent in "Letters from the Earth", is the shortened version. Still, an evident allusion to the events of Genesis, chapter three:

> "The Serpent said the forbidden fruit would store their vacant minds with knowledge. So they ate it, which was quite natural, for man is so made that he eagerly wants to know; whereas the priest, like God, whose imitator and representative he is, has made it his business from the beginning to keep him from knowing any useful thing." (Letter Three.)

The 'serpent' offered to store the vacant mind with useful understanding, but it is the 'priesthood' that discourages such education. Statements from Philip Gardiner's book "Secrets of the Serpent" concur: "In truth, there is one definite thing we all know about the religions of the world, they have all, at one time or another, been used as tools of manipulating mankind into action indeed inaction. They have all been used to maintain and grow massive power bases that today appear unbreakable. They have all been used to increase the coffers of those in positions of authority."

Genesis chapter three:

I FORMERLY OPEN THIS study of this Genesis investigation with the following poignant statements of the late D. M. Murdock who bluntly agrees with many other reputable scholars:"Like other major biblical characters and tales, the fable of Adam, Eve and the Garden of Eden is based on much older versions found in numerous cultures around the globe. The Hindu version of the first couple was of Adima and Heva, hundreds if not thousands of years before the Hebraic version, as has been firmly pointed out by Hindus to Christian missionaries for centuries... these myths "seemed to have originated in Africa, but they were told all over the world in ancient times..."

Obviously, we will not find any historical Adam and Eve in Mesopotamia. In the Sumerian and Babylonian versions of the Garden of Eden myth, from which the Hebrew one is also derived, the original couple were created equal in stature by the great Goddess. When the fervent patriarchy took over the story. The tale/ myth was altered to make women not only inferior but also guilty of the downfall of all mankind. Of this demotion, Stone says:

> "Woman, as sagacious advisor or wise counselor, (sic) human interpreter of the divine will of the Goddess, was no longer to be respected, but to be hated, feared or at best doubted or ignored.... Women were to be regarded as mindless, carnal creatures, both attitudes justified and "proved" by the Paradise myth... Statements carefully designed to suppress the earlier social structure continually presented the myth of Adam and Eve as divine proof that man must hold the ultimate authority."[cxlix]

The issue that modern readers and their interpretations of the currently available sacred texts, is the coming to grips with the fact that what we read in these ancient texts are but snippets. They are, but tiny parts of those stories mentioned that were much wider and known to its original audiences. All the favoured stories, of not only Genesis, are but fragmentary hints to the ancient and long-lost mythological richness from which they originally derived.[cl] This is no less factual for the current book under scrutiny; Genesis. When studied through the prism of mythology and symbol, we come to a realisation that the entire text is based, and was pilfered and doctored from surrounding ancient myths; the stories of countless ancient God's, and various monsters. Raphael Patai fascinatingly in his extensive research and examination completely concur:

> "Genesis nevertheless still harbours vestigial accounts of ancient gods and goddesses—disguised as men, women, angels, monsters, or demons. Eve, described in Genesis as Adam's wife, is identified by historians with the Goddess Heba, wife of a Hittite Storm-God, who rode naked on a lion's back and, among the Greeks, became the Goddess Hebe, Heracles's bride..."[cli] "Genesis, [he writes], is more closely linked to the ancient myths of the Greeks, Phoenicians, Hittite, Ugaritic, Sumerian. Their myths greatly influencing the original author(s) of the Genesis tales, for moralistic ends. The Ham myth was once identical with that of the conspiracy against the shameless God Cronus by his sons Zeus, Poseidon and Hades: Zeus, the youngest, alone dared castrate him, and as a result became King of Heaven. But Ham's (or Canaan's) castration of Noah has been excised from Genesis just before the line: 'Noah awoke from his wine, and knew what his little son had done unto him.' The revised version, a moral lesson in filial respect, sentences Ham to perpetual servitude under his elder brothers for no worse a crime than accidentally seeing his father's nakedness..."[clii]

Relevant to the current investigation, Patai enlightens the modern reader with insight that might go some ways in dispelling the modern ideology surrounding the entity; Satan. The one figure in the sacred text that modern believers love to hate, and have a somewhat obsessive fear and dread. Although this comment may initially seem to contradict my own findings and explanation that is stated in later essays. I would not be so quick to conclude these statements of Patai are irrevocably and mutually exclusive; and so, are not reconcilable. Patai insightfully informs:

> "There are pre-Biblical references to the angel Samael, alias 'Satan'. He first appears in history as the patron God of Samal, a small Hittite-Aramaic kingdom lying to the east of Harran... Another faded God of Hebrew myth is Rahab, the Prince of the Sea, who unsuccessfully defied Jehovah ('Yahweh'), the God of Israel—much as the Greek God Poseidon defied his brother, Almighty Zeus. Jehovah, according to Isaiah, killed Rahab with a sword... A Ugaritic deity worshipped as Baal-Zebub, or Zebul, at Ekron was consulted by King Ahaziah (2 Kings 1.2ff) and centuries later the Galileans accused Jesus of traffic with this 'Prince of the Demons.'"[cliii]

Aside having little or no awareness of the surrounding myths from which these sacred stories were filched; most unfortunate for modern bible readers and interpreters of those texts is that in our times a transference has occurred. No longer are many people interested or encouraged to attempt to view these stories as the ancients once did. No longer is it common to attempt to grasp the intentio operis of a passage. Greatly neglected is the reading and study of certain passages from an earlier, and maybe esoteric conception and meaning. In essence, the sensus spiritualis (spiritual/allegorical sense) was trampled by sensus literalis (literal interpretation.) As attempted to show in the previous commentary throughout the previous Nails an appreciation of ancient wisdom and acumen and modern academic findings is all-too-often forsaken by countless modern interpreters of sacred passages; which leads to perplexing issues surrounding modern, but typically Church ordained perspectives and interpretations. Modern interpreters may from time to time mention a little something of what scholars know of the intentio operis of a passage/ story. But, most often this is done in passing. This will be most notably identified in Part Two – "The Genesis Six" explanation and succeeding sub-sections. There are numerous studies available to assist readers in their attempt to claw back at the esoteric and symbolic perspective; i.e., the study of Raphael Patai; the analysis, "Hidden Truths from Eden: Esoteric Readings of Genesis 1–3." The compilations of "Apocryphal new and Old Testament's"; and "The

Pre-Nicene New Testament", and the "Holy Fable" series compiled by Robert M Price; various Nag Hammadi translations, and the book, "What Really Happened in the Garden of Eden?" by Ziony Zevit. (Yale University Press.) All these studies offer for the interested student of religion contrasting observations on familiar Church-sponsored bible stories. How though can a student of bible show themselves as deity-approved; by reviewing and the study of only familiar, recommended manuscripts? Where is the fun in that? Where is the challenge? The personal growth in experience and appreciation for the acumen of the ancients and bible milieu? Numerous parallel inferences to Genesis three could be drawn for instance, in reading and the study of manuscripts the likes of: "Acts of Andrew", and the "Apocryphon of John". I will however leave this to the readers discretion. These two esoteric texts are interestingly studied by two authors of "Hidden Truths from Eden". I will not regurgitate those studies. The summations below were developed not so much by the study of such texts. But, appeared through my research into the symbolic meanings of certain characters and objects encountered in this story. Throughout the coming pages, Ziony Zevit's title will be utilised. His study scrutinises the Hebrew text, which undoubtedly, will open and is focused on what the text actually says. While, earlier was offered a satirical rendering of the Genesis three story by Mark Twain. Via his pen he comically recited the story of how human's apparently fell into wickedness, coming through an encounter. The Eve had with that sneaky bugger, -the serpent. Told through the imagined daily diary entries of the first man, – Adam. What if there is a dissimilar yet just as polemic interpretation to this story? What if this dissimilar interpretation; esp., regarding whom 'serpents' could be representative, made more sense to an overall understanding of the Genesis three episodes than our traditional comprehension? To grasp in a contextual sense this prevalent chapter of Genesis, let a few comments of Zevit be cited.

DECONSTRUCTING ENDTIME DELUSIONS

Genesis chapter three. A context:

IT IS NOTEWORTHY TO understand that this chapter is by believers often only "... concerned with surface phenomena, with what the eye sees and the ear hears when reading the story through once."[cliv] Primarily, any Christian study/ sermon is focused on this passage in Genesis on the accidental; the peripheral elements of the chapter. The focus is on the presumed satanic ophidian, and the waywardness/ 'fall' of mankind from perfection after its encounter with Eve. So, where might this ideology that a satanic ophidian beguiled the female human into a sinful act have come from? Precisely, not in the pages of the bible itself, but a much recent piece of literature. Dr. Nyland explains:

> "The Hebrew Bible / Old Testament does not say that Adam and Eve ate an apple – the identity of the fruit is not mentioned – this is a myth based on John Milton's Paradise Lost. In the same way, the snake is not named in the Bible, although Paradise Lost does name the snake as "Satan." In the Bible, the snake is not identified with any evil entity but is described as an animal of the field that God had made. Revelation does call the adversary an ancient snake, but this is not evidence that this ancient snake appeared in the Garden of Eden. And even if the two are one and the same, we still do not have the name of the snake."[clv]

A perusal of Zevit's sound and detailed analysis further shows there is more complexity to the Genesis three stories than modern fundamental believers care to admit. A diligent and studious revision causes numerous disturbing questions and comments that fundamental christians particularly, would be wise to consider further. For instance, as pointed out by Zevit - (1) nowhere, absolutely nowhere in the Old Testament is an idea of a 'fall' of humanity ever mentioned. It simply is not anywhere to be found in the text (Location 337) (2) any serious reader of the bible text must conclude that their 'self-apparent' and obvious considerations are actually not self-apparent, or obvious. Rather, are the wishful interjections of the indoctrinated mind (location 342), and (3) the idea that an 'Eve' personality is 'to blame' as an explanation of a 'fall', is again sheer guess, and only becomes apparent in the Jewish apocryphal book of

'Ecclesiasticus.' This idea of the female discretion that caused humanity's waywardness, is nothing but a hoax (location 485. p.10.) Therefore,

> "...it is difficult to argue that the author of the story considered events in the Garden paradigmatic for humankind's subsequent behavior (sic). Similarly, it is difficult to maintain that this story betrays the author's generally negative assessment of humanity or the physical world outside the Garden, the world that he, his family, and his audience inhabited." (location 639-40. p19.)[clvi]

That the myth of this Genesis chapter portrays any negative assessment of the human condition, caused by some 'satanically' inspired serpent, is pure and simply a very modern misogynistic projection. Misogynistic for it betrays womankind as weak and of inferior character when confronted by the assumed Devil-serpent. A premise that Zevit plainly asserts, "Only in medieval interpretation was the devious fused with the evil, creating a Devil. Thus, a serpent in the Garden was transformed into Satan who rules in Hell." (pp.163-164). Such a negative assessment more than likely was meant to instil a sense of 'fear' for the control of congregants, and/or alongside the 'lesser' population. The women of a society. We clearly see that Church-sponsored sacred texts have assumed a misogynistic morality, derived from the apocryphal writings noted by Zevit. Even in our modern times there is an assumption that humanity fell-from-grace at the waywardness of a female. Yet, this is an outright alien concept. A concept birthed through an insidiously venal reading of apocryphal texts. Nowhere in the (Hebrew) bible is such a concept even hinted! Zevit again writes of the 'prophetic' literature; that it originated in public harangues. Which is a great indicator of shared–common knowledge. Casual readers and believers should therefore be astute enough to understand what those texts likely infer. There is nothing really astoundingly 'spiritual', or mystical in their dialogues. Zevit notes:

> "It is strange, then, that the common twenty-first-century understanding of the Garden story as the Fall, which would have been rhetorically powerful when Solomon's temple stood, is not reflected at all in prophetic texts. Neither Adam nor Hawwa [Eve] is ever singled out in the prophetic literature as a source for Israel's misfortunes or for the miscreant actions of

DECONSTRUCTING ENDTIME DELUSIONS

any other people. Even Ecclesiastes, a composition of the Late Persian – ...reserves its misogyny for a certain type of woman:...(Eccles 7: 26). Despite his sour attitude, the crotchety author of this verse does not consider the wiles and deceit of the type that he condemns due to inherited nature."

The same can be inferred for both testaments, and all recorded writings of the bible text. In the New Testament, the garden episode was known to be myth that had theological authority. There are absolutely no references to a 'Fall' in any of the psalms. There are no indications that the events described in Genesis three had any bearing on any suffering. It is astoundingly strange that,

> "No negative confession of wrongdoings alludes to some inherent guilt or flaw in human nature connected to antediluvian ancestors. Even in the negative confessions in Nehemiah 9:16–31 ...and in Psalm 78, no association with the Garden story is found. Psalm 78 lists sins and rebellions from the time of the Exodus through the period of the Judges until the establishment of the Temple during Solomon's reign... mea culpa lists are anchored firmly in what the Iron Age psalmist and the later Persian official perceived as historical time. Every sin that they listed was a unique act committed at a particular time and place. Each was unrelated to and not symptomatic of, any underlying human pathology. The composite lists reflected bad decisions by rational people. Both lists overtly indicate that the people of Israel suffered collectively only because of wrongs they perpetrated wilfully and not because of some flaw inherent in their humanness as descendants of Adam and Hawwa - (Eve). It is as if this primal story about what transpired in the Garden had no implications for ancient Israelites and no application to their situation."[clvii]

Despite the best efforts of near-on all known Church-sponsored bible commentaries, attempting to offer their readers a succinct explanation of chapter three of Genesis, they are grossly mistaken to drag the usual Church sponsored misogynistic eisegesis, – a reading and interpretation implanted into the text of what is not within the text itself. The view that Genesis three describes humanity's inherited bad disposition. This is a common error of all believers, of every denomination whether known or not consistently does. Minister/ pastors/ lay-believer alike need to seriously redress this delusion. There is absolutely no textual or other evidence in any of the surrounding materials bible scholars use for the ideology of an apparent flawed humanity. See also the citation and comments about Korpel and de Moor below. No wonder society is awash with confused, deluded imprudent, and wrong interpretations that only serve to further oppress and deceive believers and others in society. Affirming these statements is Robert Price, "Holy Fables" in his commentary on this chapter of Genesis. He reiterates that Genesis three tales are pure myth:

> "...it is a myth that attempts to explain the author's perspective of what he/they saw as development tales; of why we dislike snakes, why we wear clothing, why all humanity must labor throughout our days, why we die. "If the Priestly account is implicitly polytheistic, the Garden of Eden story is explicitly so. The order of events... is significantly different, and the harmonizations (sic) offered to reconcile them are ad hoc contrivances that would never look good to anyone not looking to get out of a tight spot...The Garden of Eden story has nothing to do with Original Sin. Nor is the serpent supposed to be an incarnation or puppet of Satan...on the rare occasions when Satan does appear in the Old Testament he is an agent, not an enemy, of God."[clviii]

Zevit additionally reiterates: "Moral evil," "sin," and other vinegary words in ...characterization (sic) of the Bible's presentation of women emerge from the thought-world of Greco-Roman civilization (sic) and Hellenistic biblical interpretation. They are not in the text of the Hebrew Bible itself and are found only in post-biblical exegesis."[clix] Noticeably, modern Christian scholars commenting on this chapter of Genesis have not understood or been made aware to acknowledge that the concept of 'sin, and moral evil' is fundamentally flawed and is actually not in any way supported by the story's text itself. Numerous well-intentioned believers have then fallen headlong into that trap; by that inciting others to the same disfigured interpretation. Seen and heard from the pulpits of countless churches.

Sacred trees and Serpents:

WE NOW DELVE INTO SOME of the more symbolic nature of this story. Though no attempt is made to be exhaustive there is much to be gleaned from the imagery in this one chapter. For a mythological conception of the Genesis pericope, readers are encouraged to study the earlier cited study offered above, of Raphael Patai. Others have also successfully attended to the symbolic nature, and have done so in a more exhaustive manner than is attempted here. In this section of our Genesis study I will only be able to briefly explore two symbols of interest. There are plenty from which to choose. But for my purposes, and interests we'll take a glancing view of one prominent symbol; the sacred tree. Secondly, we'll meet with the snake; particularly seeking to understand more regarding this (un)scrupulous entity. Principally, we will seek an answer to just who, or what such an entity could be representative. As is commonly taught by Christian clergy to believers, the snake represents the Devil who seduced the woman...and so, causing all hell to break loose and spread throughout the world. Though as stated by Price and Zevit above and other reputable scholars, and thinkers the serpent cannot and does not represent the 'assumed Devil/ Satan.' This is simply illogical if the reader has any understanding of what Satan represents throughout sacred works. Explained later: Part Two. But first, a brief excursion into the sacred tree. The following ideas and concepts of sacred trees are primarily gleaned from several texts. The authors, Arthur and Elena George's study, "The Mythology of Eden"; the "Women's Bible Commentary": Third edition.

It is an unfortunate fact that unless believers are prepared to exercise their minds and view sacred stories from a perspective outside the set theological parameters. More of the same mechanical innuendo will prevail and they will most likely not come to understand certain Bible stories from anything other than the usual bland, unenlightened perspective. The challenge is readers join me and explore Genesis three from a contrasting perspective to the typical, established rendering. First looking briefly at sacred trees. The sacredness of certain trees is a prominent and well-known feature in the iconography of all world-mythology. Here as expected, we focus our efforts on the regions where the Genesis story is reported to have been composed. So, "...in Mesopotamian and Egyptian iconography two trees, pillars or mountains commonly frame a deity...thus rendering the pair of trees as a visible gateway to the divine." (Arthur and Elena George, 'The Mythology of Eden", Location 5520.) They further inform that mythically, sacred trees can be viewed as either 'two aspects of the same tree', or, as an emphasis of a life-giving regenerative force. That is, as a tree that affords one the essence of the divine life; or, of knowledge and wisdom. Thus,

> "When having an oracular [a Delphic, or prophetic] function to communicate divine information and knowledge, it may be called a tree of knowledge or wisdom." (ibid. [brackets mine] Location 5529.)

Clearly the architect of this Genesis story was acquainted with an understanding of the sacredness of certain trees and so chose to also accentuate each. Highlighting a tree of wisdom, and of 'life.' Whether these are two separate trees or each attribute is combined into the one tree, is difficult to determine from the text, and may just be the way these have been separated by scholars and interpreters. I happen to suspect a singular tree. The redactor of this Genesis episode employs a figure of speech; a hendiadys. Where the expression of one idea is conveyed by two words (Genesis 2:9). The same figure of speech is used for the Adam and Eve. However, trees throughout antiquity have always held a special place in the minds and 'spirituality' of man. From the beginning of human 'spirituality', they were revered, being thought to have been:

> "...charged with the divine... They are the largest and tallest living things on the earth. Their branches rise through the air toward the heavens, while their roots reach into the earth towards the underworld... they outlive humans and seem eternal, wise, and venerable. In step with the seasons, they wither in the colder months... but eternally renew themselves..." (ibid. Location beginning 4987.) In the Genesis three stories, we see the first reference to a couple of sacred trees; one of which mankind is prohibited to partake.[clx]

DECONSTRUCTING ENDTIME DELUSIONS

Why – if such a tree is noted by deity, as being part of the creation that was very good, considering deity apparently stated quite clearly, "Behold, I have given you every plant yielding seed which is upon the face of all the earth, and every tree with seed in its fruit; you shall have them for food." - Genesis 1:29-31.[clxi] Commentary on this issue by Robert Price is informative. Stating there was only one type of 'fruit' mankind was barred from consuming/touching:

> "...Though a natural inference, it is probably incorrect to assume that the fruit somehow provides him who eats it with moral judgment or conscience. If this were the case, how could one be blamed for committing the "sin" of deciding to disobey his creator by eating the fruit? "It was wrong? What's a 'wrong'?" No, "good and evil" is more likely a figure of speech: a hendiadys, in this case the indication of the whole range of things, "from A to Z." Yahweh does not want the man to become too smart. It is just like Pierre Boule's novel, The Planet of the Apes (the loose inspiration for all those movies): People train chimps and gorillas to act as domestic servants. They are docile and obedient– until somebody gets the bright idea of enabling them to speak. It takes only a simple operation on the vocal apparatus. The power of speech fuels a rapid rush to full intelligence, and the newly self-confident apes rebel. That is pretty much what happens in the Garden of Eden myth. The trigger is eating the forbidden fruit."

Adding further, "Please note that throughout the narrative it is Yahweh who deceives the man and the woman, while the serpent tells them the truth."[clxii] Arthur and Elena George further inform us regards a sacred tree that we might recognise:

> "Sacred trees were not merely infused with the divine like the rest of nature but had a special transcendental status: They were regarded as more highly and permanently charged with divinity. The ideas that trees connect with the divine and that humans and the deity can communicate (both ways) through trees were often taken a step further, such that the sacred tree (or equivalent symbol) was regarded as the abode (momentarily or permanently) of an indwelling deity. This idea also makes the tree an ideal medium for a theophany... (Gen 18:33). Trees were also thought to draw on the divine through their roots, which connected to the underworld where departed spirits resided and wisdom and knowledge of the future were vested... Indeed, given that trees embodied and symbolized (sic) divinity and were

oracles for communication with the divine, naturally they were associated with wisdom and were looked upon as a means for enlightenment and Revelation." (ibid. George.)

The sacredness of trees and parallel symbolism extends throughout the world. Arthur and Elena George again mention one of the most interesting parallels, adding their summation to the symbolically representative divine energy centre of the human body; known as Kundalini. Derived from Indian thought. These are the chakras that spiral through the spine, with the pinnacle at the crown of the head. There are believed to be seven of these energy centres; each stage having a different emphasis for different body parts/ function. The connection to trees is the concept that,

> "Sacred trees or pillars are sometimes depicted in the form of the spinal column, the most famous ancient example being the djed pillar symbolizing (sic) Osiris, who was encased in a wooden pillar/tree before being reborn. In other myths, worthy mortals who underwent a special experience were actually transformed into trees..." (ibid. Location 5062).

Undoubtedly not often appreciated by the modern viewer, is the fact countless mythic tales surrounding sacred trees are still prevalent. For example, there are many hints of a sacred tree in numerous modern films. One depiction is a particular 'sacred tree' in the Game of Thrones saga. Though one of the story's characters does not essentially become the sacred tree, he is endowed with certain 'divinatory insight' closely linked to it. Another instance of modern myth encapsulating the sacred tree theme, illustrating a 'special mortal' who is transformed into the dying sacred tree to revive its power. Is encountered in the fantasy production, "The Shannarah Chronicles". The opening scenes depict after several mesmerising insights, one of the King's daughters must become the sacred tree to assist the heroic figure to defeat and overcome, and so 'save' the kingdom from a looming cosmic–disaster of evil. It was commonly believed in all sacred tree myths that:

> "To partake of the fruit of a sacred tree, or the milk of the Goddess within it, was to imbibe and thereby acquire some qualities of divinity... In the ancient

DECONSTRUCTING ENDTIME DELUSIONS

Near East, being divine (like a God) consists of having two classic attributes: immortality and wisdom (or knowledge)." (ibid. George.)

Accordingly, a strong connection to the serpent coiled about the tree in many 'religious' depictions in paintings, and trees generally of this Genesis three pericope can be easily extracted. Not understanding or knowing the significance of 'trees' as described above however, allows our minds to concoct any amount of fanciful ideologies. Such as those explored throughout this compendium of End time studies. Which, I believe has occurred in modern Christian thought as described briefly below. There are numerous subjects to explore from this one chapter, but time, and space do not allow any extensive investigation. It must be confirmed; however, that a truth of this chapter in the words of Lloyd Graham, "Deceptions and Myth in the Bible", is that the Genesis three stories as with all creation myths: "...whatever happens in it, happens to the Creator, not man." A fascinatingly insightful statement. Recall Price above who stated also the principal deity is the deceiver, not the serpent! Much could, and likely should be commented on regards this thought as undoubted such statements may cause more remonstrance with readers. Particularly in the knowledge that for centuries beliefs and religious thoughts have been shaped by the current Genesis chapter. Genesis 3:1 introduces an excuse of 'evil'. At some time; the myth in this chapter became a story that presents apparent 'literal facts' that have plagued humankind; an embellished believed truth never originally intended. It is undoubted that it is from this chapter that believers have arrived at the 'idea' of; (one) 'mankind sinned' (two) there was an 'origin to our sinning' (three) 'mankind needs salvation from the lost-ness that resulted, and (four) the cause, the origin of all our frailties came from an encounter of the female of our species, with a spiteful presence that had taken the form of a 'snake/ serpent.' Statements and beliefs of utter Taurus excretio! None are factual statements, but are embellishments of the plain text. No man, woman, child alive, or departed; past, future, or present is 'sinful.' The concept of sin is just another unfortunate myth that religionists have fallen headlong; a persistent myth that is still peddled by the elite of religious orders. The goal, subjugation, fear-peddling, manipulation. Just as was witnessed in (Nail One). Rather, it appears that every knavery that results in living as a mere common entity of our species has been relabelled 'sin'. Yet, no such thing as sin exists in, or outside the dusty old Judaeo-Christian parchments. These parchments do however encourage an earnest attempt at stifling, curtailing all adverse attributes, and characteristics common to each of our personalities. The same the Ancient Stoic surely had eyes for at saying,

> "You must know that it is no easy thing for a principle to become a man's own, unless each day he maintain it, and hear it maintained as well as work it out in life." (Golden Sayings of Epictetus)

It seems also that unbeknown to great portions of believers is the fact that exact parallel themes of this chapter are known to exist in other ancient stories. Without exception, all themes of this chapter are not unique to the sacred book of the Judaeo-Christian tradition. They are extant in many older cultural myths. As was stated above at the beginning of this investigation; those found in ancient Greece, India, Persia, Babylon, Assyria, and as far reaching as the America's, Mexico, China, and throughout European lands. Including myths, legends, and poetry of Norse and Viking hero's. The myth in question (Genesis 3) however can be elucidated using a parallel tale that many readers most likely will be familiar; the Grecian myth of Prometheus, Zeus, Pandora, and Epimetheus. About how the world's ills came to afflict and be among mortal men. It was through Pandora's inquisitiveness and incurable curiosity regarding the 'box' gifted to her by Zeus, the father of gods. He had expressed to her upon presenting this box as a 'wedding gift' that under no circumstance was she to open it and peer at its content. We know however that her inquisitiveness had the better of her. A host of evils escapes... and so Pandora (like Eve) is blamed for the diseases and misery that are visited upon all humanity. Some scholars believe

> "[this story] is based on the need to maintain the secrets of the mystery religions. The box contains the sacred instruments of the cult. The story is a warning to young initiates (especially young females) not to pry too closely into the mysteries... in care of the elders... Similar boxes, baskets, and other containers for sacred objects were common in Greek and Roman

DECONSTRUCTING ENDTIME DELUSIONS

religions for centuries, and their images are easily found in many pieces of surviving artwork. Serpents were often represented as the guardians of these boxes."[clxiii]

Just as is identified in cultural myths of surrounding regions (all from which the Genesis three myths likely derives), the serpent is present, and most probably placed in this position of the myth to be the guardian of the sacred tree(s). Ponder a moment: assuming for argument sake that the instruction to Pandora and it's parallel in Genesis three is meant as a warning and test by deity of humanity's obedience (as is often taught in Christian parlance); is this test not also such a terrible misguided mistake! To demand that something inquisitive and secret, is to remain so. Every adult alive knows through experience and the recollection of their own childhood: that this type of order only ever invites stubborn action. It is no different to modern parents expressing to a child they should stay their hands from doing something. Which consistently invites inquisitive defiance? Pandora's incessant inquisitiveness so the tale goes, led her to 'open the box', and by that unwittingly unleashes disease, misery, death, poverty, sadness, and every other 'evil' imaginable...[clxiv] Similar to Adam and Eve partaking of the 'fruit.' Other equivalent themes throughout many more world tales to the Genesis 3-bible account is exquisite. Only varying in the detail. In certainty. All extant ancient myths similar to Pandora's box pre-date the sacred text. Kersey Graves in "The World's Crucified Saviors" (sic), confers alerting,

> "...the reader to the important fact that three out of four of the cardinal doctrines of the Christian faith are taught in [no less than] two heathen mythological stories of creation..., [namely]: Original sin; The fall of man caused by a serpent; and The consequent corruption and depravity of the human race. These doctrines, then, it must be admitted, are of heathen origin, and not, as Christians claim, "important truths revealed from heaven."[clxv]

Interest and added mystery surrounding this myth, is the possible and most probable understanding of this and many of Genesis' stories, having roots in early Persian, Egyptian, Mayan cultic creation stories also. Gary Greenberg, in his book "101 Myths of the Bible", highlights an Egyptian connection:

> "Initially, events in the Garden of Eden were about the children of Geb and Nut and the conflicts among them. The Garden of Eden lay along the Nile. The Tree of Knowledge of Good and Evil and the Tree of Life were derived from symbols associated with the Egyptian deities Shu and Tefnut."[clxvi]

Bible authors he further says, replaced two Egyptian gods and their myth with what people today know as the forebears to humanity. 'Adam' and 'Eve.' We must assume this act of 'replacing' these deities were done to make an acceptable 'Hebrew' version of the Egyptian creation myth: making it more palatable. Added emphasis come from comments of (Myth 21) in the same text: "The purpose of this story is to condemn the Egyptian idea that knowledge of moral order, would lead to Eternal Life, which conflicted with Hebrew monotheistic teachings." T. W. Doane, "Bible Myths..." offers a Persian twist:

> "According to Persian legend, Arimanes, the Evil Spirit, by eating a certain kind of fruit, transformed himself into a serpent, and went gliding about on the earth to tempt human beings. His Devs [demons] entered the bodies of men and produced all manner of diseases. They entered into their minds, and incited them to sensuality, falsehood, slander, and revenge. Into every department of the world they introduced discord and death." (Footnote 2. Seventh [brackets mine])

Snakes. Why Snakes?

THE MORE PRESSING SUBJECT in this narrative of Genesis three concerns the serpent/ snake. To this, we now attend. Intrigue surrounds the theme and symbolism of serpents and snakes throughout world mythology and religion. A short lesson is to be learnt here. In most popular Church-sponsored sacred books, the translators have made up the minds for the reader, – that this reptile is to be known as a completely odious, satanic/ evil entity, and therefore is the ultimate cause of humanity's 'fall–from–grace'. This description of the serpent is a distorted position of logic that believers are happy to think is true; that the 'serpent' in this chapter is in the guise of a Satan; bipedal and conscious; enabled with 'speech' and 'calculated guile'.[clxvii] Although this reptile clearly slithers today, there is evidence that it did at some time in ancient history sport some sort of protrusion, hind legs. "Snakes slither, but the skeletal remnants of hind legs are found in primitive snakes." Wrote Donna Hart, "Man the Hunted: Primates, Predators, and Human Evolution".[clxviii] Clearly advocates of the satanic ophidian idea are not all that familiar with myth: or any mythic, symbolic or religious meaning given to snakes and serpents. Or, indeed to what snakes may refer. I do not accept that there is much if any hint that Adam or Eve actually did partake of the 'fruit' of the forbidden plant. Rather, something else most likely triggered the deity to expel them from the garden. The ophidian of the story happened to play a role in that decision. But, before delving into the mythic symbolism of these reptiles, it must also be brought to a readers attention that although most modern 'Church-sponsored' translations render the Genesis snake/ serpent as either 'crafty', 'subtle', or 'shrewd'; all these carry a basic biased thought. Today, we automatically 'think' a shrewd or crafty person in a morally negative sense. Why? There is one other word used, found in the Septuagint (Greek Old Testament): wise. The "Oxford Dictionary" definitions of both wise, and subtle tell another story!

- Wise: showing experience, knowledge, and good judgement.

- Subtle: capable of making fine decisions, delicately complex and understated.

The 'archaic' meaning often preached by christians, being somehow nefarious and deceitful does not figure. Neither does subtle coincide with any negative sense: crafty; cunning. "Merriam-Webster's Collegiate Dictionary" confers. Offering five categories of meaning, the final of which is: 'operating insidiously subtle poisons'. In addition, Zevit provides several arresting statements regarding the serpent of this Genesis three episode. He writes the 'serpent' is cast as a generic figure, not identified by any other specific animal of the sacred books. Also of the specific Hebrew word for serpent Zevit writes,

> "the word nāḥāš did not evoke anything sinister in Israelite culture. It was even a personal name in Israel (2 Samuel 17: 25) and among Israel's neighbors (sic), the Ammonites (1 Samuel 11: 1 – 2)."

As opposed to the Hebrew word that would denote a wicked, evil entity, which the serpent is never called. Rather, as with sacred book characters, the word used to describe the serpent in Genesis 3, means essentially a concealing of 'what is known.' Not in the sense of wickedness or deception, but in careful calculation, or assessment of situations. Signifying very much what was stated above by the dictionary definitions;

> "[being] shrewd and calculating, willing to bend and torture the limits of acceptable behavior but not to cross the line into illegalities. Nowhere in the Hebrew Bible is the serpent referred to as a rāša', a wicked or evil creature. By describing the serpent as 'ārūwm, the Iron Age author signalled, Caveat lector! Caveat auditor! Reader, beware! Listener, beware! Attend carefully to the use and misuse of language in the story that is about to follow. Scrutinize closely what is said and what is omitted... the serpent's words are goal-oriented, measured, and hardly random... The serpent said nothing of substance. His grammatically incomplete sentence lacks content, but it shapes the following dialogue. Israelites sensitive to such ploys would have understood that the serpent purposely inverted the permitted and the forbidden—had gotten it all backwards—a point that the woman corrected impatiently, breaking into the serpent's incomplete sentence in Genesis 3:2..."[clxix]

A completely different picture must now be emerging for readers. That despite translators having chosen any of the above four usual words to describe the serpent, does not necessarily confer the negative sense. The serpent in these passages could and should probably be noticed as a positive entity of the text. One that is fixed through understanding the above quote from Zevit. Nowhere in the text is this serpent called wicked or deceitful. The plainest of readings just calls it either 'crafty', 'subtle', or 'shrewd'. To indict this entity as anything remotely 'evil', is to have

DECONSTRUCTING ENDTIME DELUSIONS

concluded such from complete silence; which in Nail Nine, is explained as a complete fallacious and unwarranted misunderstanding. You cannot make a text say what it never does! Which is unfortunately, how numerous believers are taught to read their sacred books. What though is the mythical and symbolic nature of snakes and serpents? On this, we are introduced to a wide and varied array of 'meanings.' Which are warranted in this story? Nadia Julien's description in the mammoth book of symbols – "A Dictionary of the hidden language of Symbolism", offers the following comment to assist our emerging comprehension:

> "The snake symbolizes (sic) the unconscious where all the rejected, hidden, unknown or misunderstood factors accumulate, as well as the possibilities latent within us." Another encyclopaedia informs readers that the serpent symbol is highly complex and universal. It is often interchangeable with 'dragons'. With no clear difference between them in far Eastern mythology. It is often polyvalent: "The serpent was also believed to be androgynous and is the emblem of all self-creative divinities and represents the generative power of the earth... Serpents, or dragons, are the guardians of the threshold, temples, treasures, esoteric knowledge and all lunar deities. They are producers of storms, controllers of the powers of the waters, encircling the waters, and are both water-confining and water-bringing. They are invoked in all incantations of the dead who cross the waters of death. As moving without legs or wings, the serpent symbolizes (sic) the all-pervading spirit; as penetrating crevices it is the inner nature of man, and conscience..."[clxx]

Living underground, serpents were also believed to be a conduit for the powers of the 'underworld'. To this, we add explanations given in the compendium and essential guide to symbolic imagery: "The Book of Symbols". In its essay, 'The Archetypal Symbolism and imaginal forms' of snakes and their intrinsic qualities evoke' are explained.

> "They symbolise the: ... primordial life force...[an] elemental spirit. Emerging with S-shaped movements from primal waters, spiraling (sic) or coiling up on itself (like the dna in every living cell) ... the snake enters our mythologies as cosmic creator, progenitor, destroyer and sacred being... The snake is the theriomorphic form of countless deities... the snake has always conveyed power over life and death, making it everywhere, a form of the ancestral spirit, guiding to the land of the Dead and mediator of hidden processes of transformation and return."(pp.194-96. [brackets mine.])

Clearly, the symbolism of serpents and snakes evoke more than what pastors, ministers, bible scholars, and religious teachers care to admit. Or, have known for that matter. An issue is that modern interpreters seem to have jumbled and transferred a meaning of serpents, adding it to the eating of the fruit; essentially, that such 'disobedience' "provide[d] him who eats it with moral judgment or conscience." As will be shortly outlined, I have come to believe this episode of Genesis three profiles the sentients of our early hominid ancestors. Although deities in all mythological story's do not want humans to bear any sentient consciousness, and so any likeness to them. As the "Enuma Elish", the Babylonian creation tale has it,

> "...mankind was created as the deities slave and groundkeeper of a Paradise, the express oasis of the gods, where the trees, and fruits of that place were the sole property of and food for the gods. The fruit trees are first and foremost the food of the gods, even the Tree of Life, from which the gods eat to renew their immortality. This sounds outrageously strange when we read the story through the lenses of Christian theology, but it all makes perfect sense when viewed against the background of ancient mythology. The Greek gods ate ambrosia and were nourished on the smoke of sacrifices (as God is in Genesis 8: 21), as were the Vedic gods. Yahweh allows the man to eat from most of the trees, just as the Torah provides for the poor, ordering farmers to leave the edges of their grain fields unharvested for the indigent to glean (Deut. 23:25; cf., Deut. 25:4, "You shall not muzzle the ox as it treads out the corn."). Only one type of fruit is off limits. It is, of course, that of the Tree of the Knowledge of Good and Evil."[clxxi]

In "Secrets of the Serpents", Philip Gardiner adds his voice to unravelling this mystery. Specifically regards who, or what a serpent may be representative:

> "Christianity has 'borrowed' extensively from the numerous, but singular, serpent cults and pagan beliefs of the ages. The relation of Chrishna in his various forms as a serpent deity, and being hung upon a cross, has remarkable similarities to the 'Brazen Serpent' of Moses, which according to the Christian writer Barnabas, was set up on a cross, and... was a simple sign of salvation..." (p.49)

DECONSTRUCTING ENDTIME DELUSIONS

Further intimating that the Sanskrit (the ancient and religious language of India), term for Serpent, Naga is wise-ones...adding,

> "...but there is yet a more revealing element of the names given to Jesus, which in the light...is most revealing. Jesus is called the carpenter, but what is the root of this word and why was it used for a man that plainly did not have the inclination or time to sit and carve out wood? The word carpenter contemporaneously was 'naggar' meaning wise man and serpent. Mark 6:3 "Is this the carpenter?" now reads "Is not this the serpent?" (ibid. p.57.)[clxxii]

Wise-ones, adds a very interesting postulation to what very possibly occurred, and should and could legitimately be taught about the Genesis three stories. It is true that early Jewish commentators saw such a correlation as proposed by Gardiner. Therefore, if Nadia Julien's description, the above dictionary definitions, the comments of the Book of Symbols above; if all these comments and those of Zevit, Price and Gardiner are taken into serious consideration. Surely a completely different story emerges? It was not the serpent that deceived the human species. The human species then did not commit some heinous crime against some nemo-deity, rather acted as children often do (explained later). Most unfortunate for the modern reader; however, is that as stated above, translators 'seem' to have made readers minds up by 'how' certain words are translated without offering a brief examination, highlighting the history, the mythology of these reptiles. Who in their right mind today really automatically 'believes' this reptile could converse meaningfully with anyone? Do they still 'talk' with any of us today? Or, that it actually were a personification of the dreaded Devil? Why is it accepted that a 'snake' coerced Eve to commit some 'forbidden' command? Or, that the 'knowledge' gained afterward was unbefitting and grievously harmful to one's wellbeing. Snakes/ Serpents somehow; however, came to symbolise an 'evil' and devilish entity: eliciting fear and unrest. Instead of healer, wise-one, and the many other 'good' and beneficial archetypes these reptiles continually convey throughout world mythologies. There is a continuing phobia surrounding this creature and its assumed connection to the Genesis three passages. The serpent throughout world mythology and the earliest 'religious' practices and worship known was also regarded as a phallic symbol of male virility; a symbol of fertility. Robert Price again, in his wonderfully titled "The Politically Correct Bible" adds the following insightful 'twist' to this Genesis three narrative:

> "Now the serpent, an obvious phallic symbol, was craftier than any other creature God had made. One day it reared its ugly head and whispered unto Eve, "Hath God said ye shall in no wise partake of the fruit of carnal knowledge?" And Eve said to the serpent, "We may indulge freely, but God said, of the fruit of monogamous heterosexuality ye shall not eat, lest on the day you eat of it you become homophobic."

Homophobic many the 'religious', and a heterosexual world has become! Based upon 'certain' and undoubtedly influenced readings of religious texts. Populations the world over has succumbed to heartily believing modern misogynistic, masochistic translations as factual and beyond reproach. Popular translations as earlier stated that read as if 'blame' for the insanity of humans; of every hurt and deceitful act/ion and presumed sinful state, should be squarely placed at the feet of the 'female' species. As an entity of deceit, malice and trickery the Genesis of the idea that the reptile represented in this creation passage came through the modern reading of scholars again 'back into' the Genesis three episodes. Particularly of various apocalyptic ideas that had canvassed the region. It is in the Apocryphal "Book of Wisdom" that the 'Devil/ Satan' can be equated to the Genesis three passages: "But by the envy of the Devil, death came into the world."[clxxiii] Notice a particular likeness to Apocalypse 12:9 which reads:

> "And the gigantic dragon, the snake, the archaic, the one called Slanderer (diabolos) and the Enemy (ho satanos), the deceiver of the whole inhabited place, was tossed out to the land, and his messengers were tossed out with him."[clxxiv]

It is here also. We identify the mentioned earlier fallacy, "Illegitimate Totality Transfer". The transference of the meaning (presumed I must add) of one personality mentioned in one passage into another. Scholars and modern believers continue to do so with the passages mentioned, and our study concern of Genesis chapter three. This passage of Revelation however cannot I believe to be tied directly to the Genesis three passages in question. Not without 'possibly' acknowledging its representational gesture regarding both <dragons> and serpents. One interesting proposal (noted by the author of the mentioned earlier article, "The Serpent in the Garden" is the proposal of authors, Marjo Korpel and Johannes de Moor in their book, "Adam, Eve, and the Devil: A New Beginning." Suggesting that the first 'sinner' was an evil God, instead of humankind. Again confirming similar statements noted above. A highly scholarly yet readable work, from the back-cover of the book we read:

> "A number of clay tablets from Ugarit, dating from the late thirteenth century b.c.e, throw new light, Korpel and De Moor argue, on the background of the first chapters of Genesis and the myth of Adam. in these tablets, el, the creator deity, and his wife Asherah lived in a vineyard or garden on the slopes of mt. <Ararat>, known in the Bible as the mountain where Noah's ark came to rest. the first sinner was not a human being, but an evil God called Horon who wanted to depose el. Horon was thrown down from the mountain of the gods, and in revenge he transformed the tree of life in the garden into a tree of death and envelope the whole world in a poisonous fog. Adam was sent down to restore life on earth, but failed because Horon in the form of a huge serpent bit him. As a result Adam and his wife lost immortality. this myth found its way into the Bible, the apocrypha and the pseudepigraphical literature, though it was often transformed or treated critically. Adam and Eve and the Devil traces the reception of the myth in its many forms, and also presents the oldest pictures of Adam and Eve ever identified."[clxxv]

Many proposals have been offered by various scholars as to the origin of the serpent in Genesis 3. No consensus has been reached, however. "The epic of Gilgamesh" also has a serpent that deceives the hero of the 'plant' that affords everlasting life. Nonetheless, the scholarly suggestion of Korpel and de Moor is I believe on the Mark; on where the Genesis account of a twisted humanity derives. Could a mystic's viewpoint shed any light, if we were to liken dragons/serpents in a similar category as they are in the Apocalypse text above? Jack McKeever, "Mystic's Bible" offers:

> "In mystic circles, dragons are the oldest of physical races known, and the serpent is a sign of change, of awakening to newer awareness and understanding. It is not bad, nor is death, for we are made in his likeness; death becomes but a new beginning." (Mystic's Bible: Axiom 21.)

Noticeably snakes, serpents and dragons comprise similar meanings as earlier revealed in "A Dictionary of the hidden language of Symbolism". As has been shown as inherently 'evil,' neither of these entities (snakes or dragons) can be factual. They do not represent anything devilish. As something abhorrent and decidedly pernicious, un–friendly or ill–natured came very late to the scene (explained further in Part two in the discussions on Satan, fallen angels, demons.) Dragons and serpents were often interchangeable. Having very similar symbolic meanings. Interesting, is the fact that dragons only became demonised after christianity developed as a world religion. Theresa Bane in her latest book, "Encyclopaedia of Beasts and Monsters in Myth, Legend and Folklore", in the entry Dragon, Occidental ("Western") she interestingly infers:

> "Found in the myths of cultures from all over the world, the dragon is perhaps the best known and most recognized (sic) of all mythological creatures. Man-made artefacts depicting the dragon date back as far as the fourth millennium, BC. The most ancient known traditions about vanquishing dragons go back to the Sumerian, Akkadian, and Egyptian mythologies of the first three millennia BC... In the pre-Christian traditions of Western Europe, the dragon had a largely ambivalent relationship with mankind... After the introduction of Christianity the dragon was demonized (sic) and became the symbol of evil and the Devil..." (p.105-106.)

To assume the 'snake' of Genesis three is in essence, the rebellious 'fallen' angel – a Satan who apparently appears also in the Revelation text, as a dragon offers far more incongruities than we can examine here.[clxxvi] Simply, it is not legitimate to guess these passages are even speaking of the same entity, despite popular Christian opinion. Snakes we have seen are symbolically more than this narrow-mindedness. So too are dragons. Could the serpent and his beguiling speech in the story of Genesis 3, not just as easily symbolically refer to the voice of 'living waters' of a river system-deity, or, a wise-one? Which through time was transmuted into a speaking reptile, or demigod of wickedness for the Israelite/Hebrew, and now, Christian audience? Immanuel Velikovsky wrote such a scenario may not be all that far-fetched. Writing this is "...a perfect setting for hearing words in the voice of nature..."[clxxvii] One other interesting development that could assist in explaining Genesis three reflects on prehistoric serpentine mythology and the great goddess. We will touch upon this theme later in section two when we delve into the myth of the believed demi-deity, Satan. Nadia above confirmed, we must assume that what the 'Eve' type did was to think and question life, the universe, and everything. Adam and Eve consulted a wise-man (serpent). Recall Mark Twain earlier stated: "The Serpent (wise-one) said the forbidden fruit would store their vacant minds with knowledge": the unconscious psyche. Those latent possibilities that are brought to bear on life. A new awareness awakened. Reviewing their surrounds, she, and her helpmate made the conscious decision to partake that which simplifies and offered wisdom. Thus, signifying a 'change' taking place on all planes we inhabit; spiritual, mental, physical. All which happened to take place in the surrounds of a 'sacred tree(s)'. The serpent just happened to be the guardian of that grove as was the custom of such mythology. Lloyd Graham in the same chapter mentioned toward the opening salvo of this Genesis three discussions reminds Christian readers with these poignant remarks:

> "Be ye wise as serpents," said Christ. It was in the knowledge of this the ancient Midianites called themselves "sons of the snake." The Egyptian hierophant said, "I am a serpent, I am a snake," and the Druid, "I am a serpent," meaning "I am a student and exemplar of the wisdom-knowledge." Our proto-Hominid ancestors partook of the polymorphous tree: of the knowledge of good and evil. And was thus, endowed with "wisdom-knowledge."

Provided the Adam and Eve are not hendiadys, symbolically representing Androgyne.

The newer more English version:

AN UNQUENCHABLE CURIOSITY of our proto-ancestors like Pandora's got the upper hand. This then led to 'self-awareness.' The rest we say is history! A concept I was to later stumble across when out of curiosity I purchased a fascinating version of the first five books of the bible. "The Newer, More English version", by Tom Carver. The usual rendering of Genesis three isn't entirely dismissed in the text, but rather followed, and cleverly conveyed. It is as the title represents. A more palatable, realistic, and fashionable read: fit for twenty-first Century minds. Here, we discover:

> "...the hominid learned to shape his world, so the world shaped the hominid, and it came to pass that one day the female named Eve felt compelled to taste fruit of the tree of the knowledge of good and evil, and to open her eyes to know of good and of evil, ... Adam and Eve's eyes were not poisoned, and Adam and Eve's minds were not rendered void, and Adam and Eve saw visions and opened their eyes, and their minds, and knew they were alive and naked. And Adam and Eve enjoyed the fruit of the tree of the knowledge of good and evil and thenceforth they partook of it on occasion with great ceremony and great joy. And the ceremony and joy gave unity to the man and woman and their brethren and in unity they prospered. And with prosperity and ceremony came wise men and rituals also..."[clxxviii]

Thus, at the enlightenment via the consuming of the tree of knowledge came great pomp and circumstance; the unity of mankind, wisdom, joy, ceremony, and ritual... Instead of perpetuating an irrational fear and dread of the ophidian known today as the personification of 'evil'. Of 'being' a Devil "... we should probably be thanking the snake..." it is a primary reason that we higher primates have superior vision and larger brains.

"Snakes... made us smarter." Narrates Seth Andrews in his book, "Sacred Cows".[clxxix]

DECONSTRUCTING ENDTIME DELUSIONS

Serpent as wise one. Awakening to self-awareness:

THE EVE CONSULTED A wise-one! The serpent in this story undoubtedly symbolises a wise-one; whereto Eve consulted regarding 'knowledge of good and evil'. Thus, instead of 'sinning' this act made us smarter![clxxx] We find the tree of latent Knowledge, offered by any wise-one is most beneficial. We 'grew' as a species. Acquiring skills to control and domesticate the Earth. Essentially, I see in the story of Genesis chapter three how humanity achieved ethical discernment. Much likened to the 'classic' we study briefly - the Epic of Gilgamesh in the next Nail. Following the subjugation of a friend of Gilgamesh, Enkidu by the exalted harlot Shamhut, whose ultimate role was to soothe and temper the not-so-proverbial beastly savage, we are told:

> "Enkidu was now capable of thought, of higher reasoning. He was now no longer merely a wild man. He was a man."[clxxxi]

After which, Enkidu, a representative of primordial man in the Gilgamesh tale, forsook his previous animalistic demeanour. His unruly lifestyle; frolicking about and satiating his thirst and hunger as an animal vanished. He no longer lapped at water-holes or "ate grass." He thus, happened upon a 'new' civilised lifestyle. Shamhut, the bringer and architect of this mighty change to a primal species. If it essentially were an action of a female in the Gilgamesh epic who was the instigator to a civil demeanour, why can Eve not be acting in a similar fashion in the Genesis three episodes? The repercussions of a 'cultivated and sophisticated' demeanour most positively plunged humankind headlong into the laborious and difficult life we now accept as our lot. Yet, is this death? It is however, a fact of life. It is hard, sometimes fraught with danger. Nothing happens without effort. All animals now hold a fear and dread of this upright bipedal entity, - humankind. Ultimately, we are offered the choice to follow; either, deal with it via a superior, advanced disposition, or with a contemptible, sordid character. Large-scale ignorance by consistent suppression by contrast, through a lack in curiosity; however, "...as numerously pointed out is sheer madness and flightless to good lasting growth and wellbeing. Which in a sense does equal death! Our self-awareness and civility born from our hominid ancestors' self-awareness have generally enhanced 'life'; and is what truly differentiates all sentients from non-sentient life. Scientists studying all manners of animals and insects, understand that they though not consciously sentient. They do display socially an incredible 'collective and 'emergent' intelligence! This is quite a remarkable achievement." Say authors Kevin Grazier and Patrick Di Justo in confirmation of our ability of self-awareness. They state:

> "...self-awareness is one of the foundations of human intelligence. Without it, humans would be non-thinking brutes, unable to plan, to remember, or relate to other people.[clxxxii]

'Self-awareness' qualities are likely what set hominids aside from other life forms. But what is 'self-awareness'?" In chapter 2 of the book, "Evolving Brains, Emerging Gods", E. Fuller Torrey concluded that:

> "...self-awareness..is not dependent on achieving a specific chronological age but rather on achieving a critical level of brain development ..." Then asking the specific question: "What precisely is self-awareness? Bud Craig, a neuroanatomist at Arizona State University, defined self-awareness as "...knowing that I exist and the feeling that 'I am." Others called it "the sense of one's own being," "the ability to become the object of your own attention," "the material me," and "the sentient self." Craig also noted that "an organism must be able to experience its own existence as a sentient being before it can experience the existence and salience of anything else in the environment. Evolutionarily, self-awareness probably developed to provide "updated maps of the body state... necessary for the brain to regulate life, and it would have been advantageous insofar as it allowed hominids to integrate their physical and mental states. Self-awareness is also a prerequisite for most higher thought processes; without an "I" there can be no "you." As Gordon Gallup, a psychologist at the University of Albany, correctly noted, "Descartes's dictum should be revised from "I think, therefore, I am" to "I am, therefore, I think." (p.41.)

Another clarification: "The first "breathings of the human soul" were manifested under the sacred tree or grove, whose refreshing shade is so highly valued in the East."[clxxxiii] Thus, as previously stated the legendary figures of Adam and Eve's eyes were not poisoned, and Adam and Eve's minds were not rendered void, and Adam and Eve saw visions and opened their eyes, and their minds, and knew they were alive and <naked>. Being and knowing one's own 'nakedness' is rather curious. In the previous bible chapter (Genesis 2:25), we read that although 'naked', they were not ashamed! Man was ignorant, not self-aware. The Adam and Eve did not hold to a concept of their own existence as a sentient being. Thus, it must be assumed they neither experienced the existence and salience of anything else in the environment! Now; however, according to popular Christian belief and teaching; (Genesis 3:7-10) onward this same nakedness (sentients) = ignominy. It is unfortunate that from this point onward, the sacred text according to modern interpretation equates 'nakedness' with all associated themes of indignation, humiliation, and disgrace. Which calls for countless modern believers to shun sex and 'out-of-wedlock' progeny as abhorrent, evil, and soul destroying. Countless believers in all ages, have been taught to abhor that unless certain parameters are adhered, what is a natural desiring of all humans; our sentients and (most of all) our desiring of sexual and commonplace intimacy with other Homo Sapiens. Interesting, about the point of awareness and sexuality. Because clearly in this Genesis incident it was not until after the tasting of the so-called 'forbidden fruit', that 'nakedness/ sexuality' were viewed as a debased desire. Recall in the first Nail above described the acts, and beliefs of the early Church. Many clergy despised the female form, encouraging mankind, and believers in general to adhere to their theology. The modern 'Church' and its proponents are squarely blamed for this distorted logical stance. Is there a lack in any forthright understanding of the mythic/ symbolic themes in these early chapters of the bible? Or, is this an illustration of knowledge filtration? Mircea Eliade, in the Foreword to his book, "Images and Symbols: Studies in Religious Symbols", rightly states:

> "... sexuality has everywhere and always been a hierophany, [the manifestation of or bringing to light the sacred] and the sexual act an

integral action (therefore also a means to knowledge.)" (p.14. [square brackets my inclusion])

Clarifying further these thoughts in the Introduction to another of his books, "The Sacred and the Profane: the nature of Religion", Eliade again writes,

> "For modern consciousness, a physiological act - eating, sex, and so on - is in sum only an organic phenomenon, however much it may still be encumbered by tabus (sic) (imposing, for example, particular rules for "eating properly" or forbidding some sexual behavior disapproved by social morality). But for the primitive, such an act is never simply physiological; it is, or can become, a sacrament, that is, a communion with the sacred." (p.14.)

Accordingly, the decision was made at some point in history to partake of what the 'serpent' (wise-one) 'suggested'; whatever that possibly was who knows. One thing we do know from this Genesis myth, is early hominid reality most assuredly shifted; our primal ancestors undoubtedly took a massive step in evolution. Like Enkidu, the Adam and Eve, a hendiadys for the human species became capable of thought, of higher reasoning. The result: they were now no longer merely like the other animals of the field; no longer conducting their lives like any wild man. They were Homo Sapien (Latin: 'wise man'!) A conception expanded upon in my study of Genesis chapter six, and the nephilim of Nail Nine. Leading from this early step in our evolution, our hominid ancestors developed over time the skill of empathy; which is labeled by psychologists as the "Theory of Mind." Meaning: it is gaining "...an understanding that the behavior (sic) of others is motivated by internal states such as thoughts, emotions, and beliefs." (Torrey, p.55.) Theory of Mind is the ability to get inside the minds of others. Understanding and empathising with their situations. It seems rather likely that the development of an empathetic mind would not have been possible if as is stated in Genesis three, the Eve had not had the temerity to forsake the Adam's, and the deity's misinformation; instead, she chose to check out the statement of the wise-one. In short, yes- she shacked up with the wise-one! Imagine if Eve hadn't regarded the serpent's words as well-intentioned; surely humanity would still be unthinking brutes! Are

DECONSTRUCTING ENDTIME DELUSIONS

we today regressing to this state of sheer brutality, the animalistic? Considering the social atmosphere of people prevalent around the world. Example: the mentioned earlier 'Social Justice Warrior' with their ill-natured views and demands of those they continue to degrade! Torrey also posits that "a theory of mind is a necessary precondition for a belief in gods." In "The Belief Instinct", Jesse Bering detailed how theory of mind leads to assumptions about gods. Summarising: "God was born of theory of mind." (Torrey, p65.) As Theory of Mind had evolved so evolved brain function and so, an 'awareness' of 'God', or 'gods.' The evolution of the limbic system, the amygdala specifically caused great leaps in proto-hominid experiences of the world around them:

> "...the amygdala, [is] the part of the brain responsible for strong emotional processing, and fear in particular. The amygdala doesn't do subtlety; it senses something might be amiss and initiates a red alert straight away, a response far faster than the more complex analysis in the cortex could ever hope to be. This is why a scary sensation, like a balloon popping unexpectedly, produces a fear response almost instantly, before you can process it enough to realise it's harmless. In fact, the amygdala (in conjunction with the hippocampus and overlying temporal lobe) [also] contributes in large part to the production of very bazaar, un-usual and fearful mental phenomenon including dissociation states, feelings of depersonalisation, and hallucinogenic and dream-like recollections involving threatening men, naked women, the experience of God, as well as demons and ghosts and pigs walking upright dressed as people..."[clxxxiv]

However,

> "When humans first became aware of a 'God' or 'gods' cannot be determined. Nevertheless, the antiquity of religious and spiritual belief extends backwards in time to over 100,000 years. It is well established that Neanderthals and other Homo Sapiens of the Middle Palaeolithic (e.g. 150,000 to 35,000 B.P. [before the present.]) and Upper Palaeolithic... engaged in complex ritualistic behaviour. These rituals are evident from the manner in which they decorated their caves and the symbolism associated with death..."[clxxxv]

Thus, our self-awareness resulting in the concept of 'theory of mind'; our ability to show empathy for and of another's situation; and thus, the evolutionary accoutrements of brain function this effected, is most probably the whim behind the bible's inception that humans were created in the likeness; the image of deity figures. Hence, birthing the totem as a representative. The oldest known is the 'Lion Man'. Ideas and fears of malevolent entities and various unpleasant other hallucinations; of ghosts, or demons; and the transmigration of a soul, into another 'world' that lay beyond the grave:

> "The appearance of new ways of thinking and communicating, between 70,000 and 30,000 years ago, constitutes the Cognitive Revolution. What caused it? We're not sure. The most commonly believed theory argues that accidental genetic mutations changed the inner wiring of the brains of Sapiens, enabling them to think in unprecedented ways and to communicate using an altogether new type of language. We might call it the Tree of Knowledge mutation. Why did it occur in Sapiens DNA rather than in that of Neanderthals? It was a matter of pure chance, as far as we can tell. But it's more important to understand the consequences of the Tree of Knowledge mutation than its causes. What was so special about the new Sapiens language that it enabled us to conquer the world?" And, "As far as we know, only Sapiens can talk about entire kinds of entities that they have never seen, touched or smelled. Legends, myths, gods and religions appeared for the first time with the Cognitive Revolution. Many animals and human species could previously say, 'Careful! A lion!' Thanks to the Cognitive Revolution, Homo sapiens acquired the ability to say, 'The lion is the guardian spirit of our tribe.' This ability to speak about fictions is the most unique feature of Sapiens language. It's relatively easy to agree that only Homo sapiens can speak about things that don't really exist, and believe six impossible things before breakfast..."[clxxxvi]

Another author confirms: "Natural selection is the sole workable scientific explanation for the variety and design of all life—plant, animal, and every other form—on this earth. It is also the only workable explanation for the design and function of the human mind, which is the real birthplace of gods."[clxxxvii] However, if it is true that our inception of gods is 'without ourselves' and such an entity is therefore divorced from any human thought process, as is attested by countless believers; why would such an active all-knowing, intelligent, benevolent 'deity' feel the need to restrict, suppress, or snuff-out our growth and maturity?

DECONSTRUCTING ENDTIME DELUSIONS

Our 'enlightenment!'[clxxxviii] One other idea that may have lead to the Genesis three myth being recorded is the idea that humankind in the distant past encountered a type of extraterrestrial entity who manipulated the DNA of our species. This concept is but one other fringe ideology that is in some respects becoming widely accepted, and disseminated through video, and other media sources. Such will not be commented upon further in this study. As Genesis three stories are interpreted, it is continuously taught that mankind's forbears were not removed from the garden because of an act of disobedience. The proto-ancestor's were removed as an act of compassion. Should they, now in a 'fallen state' consume from the <tree of life> afterward![clxxxix] How compassionate though is it to flatly deny someone, whether one 'believes' they are 'fallen' or not life? Who made the binding choice that bundles the whole of humanity in whatever ages, into the same basket? The dissenters' basket; those who deserve punishment to the third or fourth generation (Exodus 34:6-7 et al.) Yet, can a deity truly be trusted or 'worshipped,' after realising what actually is recorded in the first few pages of an apparent biography. After all, in the opening pages of Genesis several limits that are placed upon humanity after its 'creation'. Eat whatever you like, – but for the obviously sustaining and nutritious manna of the tree of the knowledge of good and evil. Which seems perfectly reasonable – until – annoying and critical Why questions are asked? Was this deity jealous? Undoubted the recorded Judaeo-Christian principal deity is jealous. Not only so, but also intolerant. Concepts pilfered from other ancient sources. From similar tales like the Babylonian ancient tale "When God's were human" (see Nail Nine.)

Throughout the sacred text, readers are warned. This deity is jealous and intolerant, and will punish insubordinates. Therefore, did it only really want pre-programmable beings that did as they were told unquestionably! Much like an A.I. or Terminator. Was the presumed deity afraid that if the hendiadys of humankind, represented by Adam and Eve, and later progeny did eat of the specified 'forbidden' plant of 'knowledge' that all would then be set free to travel the path of total liberation? Which obviously is contrary to what 'the gods of Genesis' desired? Besides, if the tree of 'Life' were also part of creation that was initially viewed as 'very good', why forbid any fruit to be consumed at all? Apparently, this component of creation was not all that great after all! What ill-natured creator creates something so 'perfectly untouchable'? Was this 'deity' spoiling for a fight? Do readers now see in the least why it was stated earlier in this investigation that the whole of the so-called sacred text is nothing but a human product; a product set in the guise of some spirituality. The sole purpose for which is nothing but to coerce, and manipulate an unweary, unthinking society. A product of control that was authored and is upheld by an elite class to this very day! What is read in these texts are but outdated, unsubstantial, inconsequential 'revealations' of the ignorant! This deity obviously made more than a few unforeseen mistakes, considering. It is supposed to be omniscient – infinitely wise! Yet, just in these opening chapters of the Judaeo-Christian books we clearly see its ignorance and arrogance to those it apparently created. It obviously suffers amnesia and dementia. Below are several questions such a deity must be held accountable:

- Why allow a test he knew mankind was going to fail?

- Why the outburst of rage, and subsequent punishment?

- Why was he determined to keep the Adam and the Eve in a state of childlike stupidity and ignorance?

- Why the short fall in education? A state carried through into the New Testament also. We are all 'supposed' to be in a perpetual state of 'childlike' lack of common sense. See: Luke 18:17.

What happened to the 'slowness to anger' as portrayed in the Exodus passage above? When, and why did the knowledge of bad and good; i.e., wisdom, become intolerable for any but the deity to possess; and so it is only its pre-ordained pre-sanctioned cleric/Imam/Prophet/shaman/religious teacher who is allowed to disseminate and explains to us plebs any meaning? Never mind also the verity that Psychologists know for a fact that every person is born with an innate ability to decipher good from bad: from birth, and possibly earlier! Each of us can tell 'right' from 'wrong' from the earliest stages of our lives. So, what could possibly be the problem of honing this skill by another naturally occurring law of nature, –cause, and effect; i.e., all actions have consequences and outcomes, which stem from the value of curiosity. Charles E. Brown in his book, "The Apostolic Church", succinctly summed in a way what I perceive as a modern trouble faced by many in christianity. He recognised in 1947 that a loss of

> "...historical perspective is a great evil in our modern Christian world. It leaves millions of thoughtless Christians open to the changing winds of sensational religious doctrine which blows them here and there like autumn leaves in a storm."

There, we have it; a brief study of some of the issues I have thought was strange, and often not thoughtfully considered by any Christian study of Genesis chapter 3. I trust that the above has stirred the juices of inquiry and deeper thought. Though I have attempted to be succinct, the aim was to also offer readers a totally 'new' way of reviewing this early chapter. The hope was this analysis readers have come away with a sense of 'new eyes' regarding this chapter of the Judaeo-Christian sacred text. That (1) nowhere in this chapter is there even a hint of something sinister (sinful); (2) the serpent tells the truth whereas the principle deity is the one that tells the 'porky'; (3) there are very good reasons why this story takes place in a 'grove' that just happened to be guarded by a serpent; tree(s) having been thought as divine 'go-betweens' and the serpent being the guardian of such places to the ancients; (4) to this writer, whether correct or not is irrelevant, but it seems clear that this story of Genesis three depicts a complete 'overhaul' of the prehistoric hominid brain, birthing sentients, empathy, and an acknowledgement and appreciation of his wider world scene; and therefore also acquiring the necessary skills to domesticate and better his world. In short - he became man. Mankind became capable of thought, of higher reasoning. Self-awareness was born! Readers may still not be able to bring themselves to accept such a proposal. That is your prerogative. But know this: to dismiss the above purely on religious grounds is your unwillingness to disregard presupposed assumptions and the old, dated, and biased thoughts attached to them. It is most unfortunate that this chapter of Genesis mythic folklore seems to be or is very close to the Genesis of a debased outlook on life generally. Blame the female Homo Sapien for the apparent ills of the world and our very nature. As brief as this has been I yet hope to have at least offered readers something interesting and thought-provoking. Something that although may be frowned upon as complete nonsense, has instilled an air of intrigue in the mind of each reader.

Nail Five:

Gilgamesh - light on mortality:

THE BABYLONIAN EPIC of Gilgamesh is one of the most ancient of texts known. Pre-dating the Judaeo-Christian sacred books and the classic tales of the Greeks and Romans. The epic is a resplendent story of the king of Uruk. For an ancient story, its popularity was astoundingly widespread, having influenced far-flung regions beyond Sumerian city-states. Countless ancient cultures preserved this story, adapting it for their own milieu. This folklore was told, and retold, learnt, and relearnt. Its influence is not confined to ancient times, however. Its messages have reached down through the ages into our sphere and milieu. The most intriguing aspect of the story is not that it is one of the oldest documents discovered. But, the fact that scholars praise it as being one of the first pieces of high art, of high literature composed:

> "Gilgamesh was a stepping stone in world literature, insofar as being the first real literary work that we know... Indeed, it wasn't the oldest written document, not even the oldest written creative literary piece. But it was the first piece of high art, of high literature, the first true instant classic."[cxc]

To this day, it is a fascinating story. This myth continues to bewitch and lure countless people of the modern era. The epic tale is a story of the journey; a quest of Gilgamesh and his drive for immortality. Thus, from the earliest time of the invention of the written prose, humankind has been dogged by quests and questions about the eternity of life. In today's parlance, particularly in Christian religious circles such a quest refers to a 'Rapture of the saints', or 'resurrection' status of 'believers'. Does such an ideology hold any merit? Is Gilgamesh's quest for immortality really the point of the epic? So, we now come to explore a little of this story. The

> "... subject was the Legend of Gilgamesh, a composite story made up probably of different myths which had grown up at various times around

the hero's name. He was one of the earliest Kings of Erech in the South of Babylonia, and his name is found written on a tablet giving the rulers of Erech, following in order after that of Tammuz (the God of vegetation and one of the husbands of Ishtar), who, in his turn, follows Lugalbanda, the tutelary God of the House of Gilgamesh... Expressed in a language which has perhaps the simplicity, not devoid of cumbrousness, of Hebrew, rather than the flexibility of Greek, it can nevertheless describe the whole range of human emotions in the aptest language, from the love of a mother for her son, to the fear of death in the primitive mind of one who has just seen his friend die, to the anger of a woman scorned."[cxci]

A disturbing realisation in modern times is that the story of Gilgamesh has been hijacked by numerous christians who have attempted to use the tale as one of their diabolical 'nephilim' creatures of Genesis 6:4 fame for their apocalyptic, end-time scenario. The story in the plainest of readings, does in no way lend itself to such postulating. To attempt to squeeze and mould Gilgamesh into any end-time scenario is crazy; and shows the complete ineptness of the commentator attempting to do so. There seems to be several triggers prompting the guessing that Gilgamesh was one of the Genesis 6:1-4 'nephilim'. First, he is described as a 'towering figure'. Taller than others of his generation. Secondly, he is described as being two-thirds a deity, and one third man. Thus, the mind of the inept assumes to link this fellow with Genesis 6:1-4 as such descriptions seem to parallel the Genesis verses.

> "Surpassing all Kings, renowned for his stature, Gilgamesh towered over all others... Gilgamesh was the son of King Lugalbanda and suckling child of the Great Wild Cow Goddess, Ninsun. Gilgamesh was unsurpassed in strength. Taller than all others, he was majestic and fearsome. Mountain passes did he open, and wells did he dig upon the slopes of the mountains... Two-thirds of him was a God, one-third of him was a Man. The Great Goddess Aruru, Mother of All Birth, designed the form of his body. Ea, the God of Wisdom, endowed him with perfection. He was perfect in face, perfect in form, perfect in mind."[cxcii]

Those who insist on a connection between Gilgamesh and the Genesis story, ignore the fact, Gilgamesh, in his own tale is clearly written as living after the disaster of a flood narrative. Not before as some people

DECONSTRUCTING ENDTIME DELUSIONS

assume. Primarily, it would seem because they believe the account of their sacred stories are an older composition than the epic! Wrong again! On all accounts, christians who assume to use this story for their own end-time scenario, are barking mad and have no clue of what they speak! Never mind also the question: what does a two-thirds God and one third man individual actually look like? Can any Christian proponent attempting to use this story for a crackpot end time scenario explain this concept? Which two-thirds was the deity; which third the man? How does one differentiate either from the other? Later, in the study of nephilim in Nail Nine, readers will become aware that such a description of people likened to a deity, or persons of huge proportions and feats were not unusual for the time. Such descriptions were used in a specific manner, and for a pointillistic reason when describing certain people of renown. See Korpel and de Moor. Besides, as others of greater skill have mentioned, nephilim are never mentioned in the Gilgamesh tale. So again it is pure and simple, a misapplication and abuse of the tale by dullard and inept believers who don't know what they are talking about. To insist on this fellow has any connection to the nephilim of the Genesis story. All books or other sources that advocate for this idea should simply be burnt as the heretical nonsense they are! What then is one lesson we can legitimately derive from the story of Gilgamesh? Professor Oden, in one of his lecture series describes the Revelation of Gilgamesh. Gilgamesh considers life upon his return home from his quest: when he suddenly becomes conscious of the fact that,

> "...life is with people. He understands we are mortal.[cxciii] That we're all going to die. But, the right response to that is not to wander off into the wilderness, not to make a party of every day, not to see if one cannot be the one exception who is granted immortality. But rather, to work with his fellow human beings; for their betterment, and the betterment of the world in the days he has remaining..."

Oden narrates further that Gilgamesh "...has [had] to find out that the lesson of maturity is the lesson of accommodating himself to mortality saying ...we are being dishonest with ourselves and each other if we con ourselves into thinking that any of us have a chance to become a God, which means; to be immortal [essentially what rapturists I deduce are really, deep down in their subconscious grasping at.] So, Gilgamesh grows up, acknowledges that we are so very mortal. But that doesn't come as a stunning bit of pessimism... the ultimate answer to the myth is not, oh good gosh, what am I going to do, we're all going to die. It is given the fact that I'm going to die, given the fact that my life is a narrative I can shape, and I know it's going to end...the answer is to be socially responsible, to recognise that in the time left what I can do with and for my fellow human being, is as much and importantly, is as anything I can do..."[cxciv]

Ernest Becker in his book "Denial of Death" adds: "Our task for the future is exploring what it means for each individual to be a member of earth's household, a commonwealth of kindred beings."[cxcv] Surely, lessons we can all learn. Death is a natural phenomenon. No-one can escape, be it through the wishful thinking of some rapture or resurrection event after death. Another lecture series adds weight to these thoughts. Professor Robert Garland (PhD.) cites an ancient Egyptian poem. Dated to approximately, 2,100 B.C.E. entitled: "Song of the Harper" which was found in a tomb of the pharaohs. This deeply moving inscription captures beautifully the previous Revelation of Gilgamesh. It is undoubtedly a quintessential peering into the realities and enjoyment of existence, and the inevitability of fatality. It reads:

> "Be of good cheer, forgetfulness is advantageous to you. Follow your heart's desire all your life. Anoint your head with myrrh, clothe yourself in fine linen. Do things while you are here on earth. Do not grieve until the day of lamentation overtakes you. Enjoy life and do not grow weary of it. No one takes his possessions [out of this life] and no one who has departed returns."[cxcvi]

If the above comments seem to be not quite acceptable to believers, for it is drilled into them that "the main task of human life is to transcend death through the complex symbolic system that is covertly religious." (Becker). That is, a resurrection or rapture event! Maybe those christians who earnestly champion the illogical vacation of rapture/ resurrection, are really only espousing their fear of death and a predisposed view and Christian ideal of a salvation promise as a Covenant of grant; that their God/ nemo-deity is somehow obligated now to 'protect' them unconditionally. All because one day they accepted the presumed deity-figure Jesus as their personal saviour! Those that rejected his ideal are from now on a 'caste' of the damned! But, what did him/Jesus argue explicitly regarding such a self-deluding impulse; not everyone will be afforded the fullness of the gift of redemption, despite his or her rhetoric; that is (Matthew 7:21; luke 6:46.) Besides, the Jesus figure is also described in the gospels as rejecting personal salvation in the scenes of the crucifixion. It seems likely the emphasis of personal salvation is rather irrelevant. Plenty of believers will however still insist there is to be 'rapture', a catching away into the heavens of a select group, at a specific time period, sometime later. Let us now turn our attention awhile to the concept of rapture.

Nail Six:

Rapture - a very (brief) look at 1 Thessalonians 4:14-18:

AS THE ASSERTIONS MADE surrounding the reality of life using the Epic of Gilgamesh and an ancient Egyptian poem, contemporary impressions of rapture are proven to be invalidated. In case further Nails need to be applied to seal the 'rapture of the saints' coffin, making it airtight; come explore this belief a little further. Despite copious books and other media sources from 'believers' who insist on a rapture /Apocalypse scenario is clearly described in their sacred books. Many materials cited by believers are founded upon history past. From past believers who held the same ideology. Using these poses a potential unforeseen problem. Michael Baigent insightfully adds to this inference with, "The unfortunate truth we need to confront is that history can be rather like statistics: anything can be proved; a fraudulent story of the past can be maintained so long as all unwelcome data are excluded."[cxcvii] Such exclusion of relevant data that assist comprehension of meaning when reading certain sacred texts are widespread. Most readers would subconsciously be aware their sacred books were not written in English. They are reading a translation. The issue is, English translations do not alert the English only reader to the different nuances and expressions of the originating languages that a native audience most likely would have been aware. Lay interpreters, readers, and non-diligent (non-specialist) authors attempting to explain any notion of 'rapture', would likely be prone to concocting all manners of meanings that just are not valid. Esp., if the only source relied upon were an English Bible. We English only readers are prone to seeing in a text, and emphasising what is invalid. Countless people have fallen into this trap, and so, have been led astray. This is exactly what is witnessed with the current thessalonian passages. Specifically, with several issues surrounding the words chosen for (1 thessalonians 4:17.) Just as modern writers, authors, commentators use certain tools to emphasise what they wish to highlight. So did the ancient Greek authors according to skilled Greek lexicographers. But, English readers of the Greek texts, from which all New Testament books derive, until recently were left to their own devises. What the English translation of a text meant to the reader, was what it is believed to have meant. To redress this issue and assist English only readers (like myself) Logos Bible Systems ingeniously came up with what they have endeared: "The Lexham Discourse", and "High Definition Greek new testaments". Reading or studying a passage using these resources enhanced comprehension of what a Greek author emphasised in the passage. Knowing 1 thessalonians 4:17 is a favoured text of a disappearing 'rapturist', I made an effort to either verify, or discredit this assumption using this Logos resource. Turns out the actual emphasis in Greek do not conform to what English readers assume. It was very different. Accordingly, the "High Definition" translation reads:

> "(17) Then we who are alive, who are left, will be caught up **together with them** in the clouds to meet the Lord in the air, and so we will **always** be **with the Lord**."[cxcviii]

Was it noticed? The Greek (bold) text. The words and phrases that are emphasised are clearly: 'together with them'... 'always' and, 'with the Lord.'[cxcix] Most readers I suspect would disagree. Preferring rather the seemingly more obvious English phrases of 'caught up and... meet the Lord in the air.' Which frankly, to an English reader seems the more obvious focus and emphasis. According to the High Definition New Testament, the former phrases (in bold) are those that are emphasised in the Greek text. Yet, because of our own dictating theological predilections, which are habitually formative of all views we are likely to choose to emphasise 'caught up, and meet the Lord in the air'! We'd be wrong, however. Basing an interpretation on what we'd prefer leads to misinterpretation and fanciful whims; hence, wrong beliefs. It should be recognised that maybe contemporary theories surrounding a text, and especially regarding a rapture that is based upon what we would emphasise (i.e. caught up...meet in the air). Today, we are inclined to emphasise these two phrases, but would be extremely misled. Showing invariably our predisposition, liking, and the biases of our own devising. Instead of the original author's intent. To 'grasp,' the 'intentio operis' we'd need to look at the Greek. Most I assume will not have such a resource as a "High Definition" text, let alone be proficient in this ancient language. This is where a resource like Logos Bible Systems most likely would become handy. If readers are unwilling or unable to utilise such sacred book helps. There is another resource that is most likely already in their possession; an ordinary dictionary. Dictionary definitions of rapture are stated below. As with many other verses, many people 'feel' confident that 1 thessalonians 4:17 teaches, or in the least hints at 'rapture' being solidly founded upon the scriptures. Yet no scholar, bible authority, or author of difference will announce it so. Consider briefly the 'standard' definitions of rapture offered in English Dictionaries. If a reader were wondering about whether this thessalonian passage does have leanings toward a 'rapture of the saints', as is likely the explanation offered by numerous believers. To verify, or allow the curious to dismiss the rapture theory outright. All one needs is review the definitions offered by standard English Dictionaries. Both the "Oxford" and "Merriam-Webster's Collegiate Dictionary" (Eleventh edition) for instance have in their Rapture entry the following major explanations, in this order:

> (1) an expression or manifestation of ecstasy or passion; (2) a: a state or experience of being carried away by emotion, b: a mystical experience in which the spirit is exulted to a knowledge of Divine things...

It is only after these definitions that the usual third option. The Christian ideal of believers being whisked away, is referred. Accordingly, might that alone indicate that the final explanation should not receive, nor does it deserve the initial or favoured emphasis and consideration that it has currently acquired in many Christian circles. Such an idealistic theorem continually proposed by many contemporary theologians, as rapture of the saints is most difficult to find within and outside scripture. Aside from showing a preconceived bias. Further evidence is, it would suddenly rather seem 'christians' or the true 'Church' vanishing, is very loosely based upon those word and phrase associations of the verse under discussion. Of those very English phrases stated above which allows us to make a vanishing type rapture of believers a persistent doctrine. Read once more the above verse of 1 thessalonians 4: 14-18. Some readers may protest with a loud remonstrance at this point; hang on, it is impossible to know the original intent, and, the author is no longer available! Or, I really don't want to spend the money to purchase some fancy computer program or the particular resources highlighted above from Logos Bible Systems. Isn't that a 'pastor/ minister's job? Undoubtedly, Logos' sacred resources have become a widespread resource for many professional religionists. But, even if a pastor or minister does have access to this and like resources, does that then mean the 'original' intent will come out in a sermon – No! Sermons today are not there to actually 'teach' anything of the intention. They are to give the hearers a 'pleasant feeling' and little else! Theologian Walter Kaiser implies the importance of knowing or in the least attempting to find intention, commenting, "Often it is possible to infer from the context what an author meant, even when he or she has failed to express that intention clearly."[cc] Bruce Chilton and Deirdre Good in their book, "Starting New Testament Study: Learning and Doing" (2009) note also:

> "Historical distance does not reduce the effectiveness of a text: it can encourage the production of meaning that enables moderns to overcome their own thought system and broaden their reality."[cci]

To what then do we owe the pleasures of gainsay? Is it just our own preconceptions, the influence of others, or a combination of several factors? Often, our distortions of logic, as shown above by 1 thessalonians 4:17 is affected by remembrances as well. As was noted in previous chapters we often experience a prosthetic memory; that is, there is a familiarity with and comprehension of what often actually did not happen or was not said. Rather it is a rehearsing over and again what elders, or the community dictum teaches. Cast your mind to the favoured religious festivals that are still loved dearly; those of christmas and the equally mythic and cock-and-bull easter story. These two are terrific examples of how a prosthetic memory affects motivation and beliefs; those coinciding with these two yearly practices and rituals. Regarding modern convictions surrounding a vanishing rapture event. Much of this belief is derived from a mish-mash of random, often unrelated ideas. It would be wise to acknowledge:

> "...when we remember bits and pieces at random, we sometimes can get the wrong end of the stick! Take the notion, very common among some churches ... that suddenly, sometime soon, some Christians are going to be whisked away into the clouds to be with Jesus—this is referred to as 'the rapture' and presented as Paul's teaching in 1 Thessalonians 4:14–18. But this bit of remembering also forgets that Paul later abandoned this notion; and so it just remained in the memory as a curiosity..."[ccii]

Prosthetic memories create an alternate reality. Which is then adopted as an authentic experience. It then passes unquestionably into community lore. Such has happened to the proposed rapture theory and indeed with the other subjects we tackle throughout the rest of this investigation. Others of note are the conceptions of an evil identity labeled, Satan, the Devil, lucifer...and subordinates. Bonus: The Greek of the text of (1 thessalonians 4:17) does NOT support the usual and modern believer concept; that there is to be a 'catching up into the air', a 'rapture' = a disappearance/ vanishing act of believers. Rather, the actual emphasis implied is completely different. The words the Greek emphasises are specifically those words and phrases translated into English as, 'with them'... 'always' and, 'with the Lord.' This must mean believers are required to recalibrate their thoughts and beliefs. A completely different understanding of what the author of this apparent (rapture/ end-time) passage means must be noticed. Rapture, according to the emphasis of the Greek text cannot be a disappearing act. Rather, must be understood to mean the believer would become exceedingly joyous. Or similarly, some other kind of exceptional mental paroxysm. "The Dictionary of the Apostolic Church" confirms:

> "The English word 'rapture' is derived from Lat. raptus, the act of seizing and carrying away, hence transport of mind or ecstasy (ἔκστασις). In classic Greek ἔκστασις means frenzy; in the NT it rarely expresses this high degree

of emotion, but may include distraction of mind, caused by wonder and astonishment, or exceptional joy and rapture..."[cciii]

Hence, the 'carrying away' of those spoken about in the 1 thessalonian passage has more to do with an exuberance, and energetic transformation of the believers mind. Any recollection to what apparently took place in some blokes man-cave, in the loft of his residence? We look at this episode in Part Two. In acts chapter two a bunch of hide-a-way fugitives were suddenly struck on the head. Accordingly, they were 'raptured'. Rapture has absolutely no thing to do with physical, magical, supernatural disappearing/ vanishing act is erroneously taught by countless Fundamental religious 'teachers' and authors. Anyone espousing such rubbish in reality, are only pushing this ideology to influence and mould the vulnerable and weak. According to the proposed original Greek of this passage. A disappearing act is void. You will not, by a rapture be suddenly whisked into some other mystical, supernatural realm. To clarify this, below is my interpretation using symbolic expressions of this text. The translation of 1 thessalonians 4:17, as offered by William Harwood reads:

(4:17)"Then we the living who remain are going to be caught up together with them in the clouds to meet with the Master in the air so that we will always be with the Master."[cciv]

My symbolic interpretation, after noting the symbolism, and nature of the passage reads:

(4:17)"The living who still live amongst us will also have their minds energetically transformed [caught up] [in clouds] with divine protection. Their minds being on the same mental plane [in the air] as the Master, they too, will show the same exuberance of mind as he [always with the Master]..."[ccv]

In short: the essence of what the author was attempting to engage the reader was knowing that the status of the believer, whether physically dead or not, really doesn't matter. Rather, believers should take comfort in the ideology and knowledge that if they live and die under apparent (if you believe it) divine protection! To render a better and fuller symbolic interpretation, would require more thought than I am willing to use in this brief look at this thessalonian passage. But, I trust that with just this most tiny of snippets, readers are in the least able to grasp something of what this writer perceives as the actual meaning of the original Greek author of 1 thessalonians 4:17. That believers should take comfort that (according to their own premise of faith and beliefs), death has no sting, so what the hell are you 'worried' about? The thessalonian author wasn't saying, or even hinting that believers somehow are one day magically floating through the sky to absurdly meet up with some presumed man-deity figure. Too often though, this is the false futuristic 'teaching' and belief of many of the religious.

Quick synopsis of the rapture theory:

WHAT ABOUT THE BEGINNINGS of the crazy enactment - rapture? Much documentation is available to the diligent student for research into the beginnings and history of 'rapture' theory. The modern usage of which incidentally, seems to really have only emerged on the scene fully in the 1800's. But, this is not the sole approximate date. Another premise states a Jesuit priest proposed this theory in the late sixteenth Century. One scholar writes rapture was an invention "...to take pressure off the Roman Catholic Church system that was being fingered as the Anti-Christ, the Beast, and the Whore of Revelation."[ccvi] It is needless however, to regurgitate such findings when they can be easily sourced through a search on the Internet and in any amount of scholarly historical accounts and records. A free booklet to download in pdf format called, 'RAPTURE of the Saints', outlining some rapture beginnings offered a short history. Interested parties should search the Internet for 'rapture histories'. All 'Rapture theories' to this day teach that 'every worthy Christian saint' alive on the earth will miraculously disappear, flying up to the heaven: either, before, during, or after a time of Great Tribulation on Earth. Few however realise that (1) the modern notion of 'rapture' is very recent to the world stage in history, –becoming prevalent only in the 1800's. (2), there are advocates that class it as an invention of a sixteenth century Catholic Jesuit Theologian to counter the then widespread Reformation argument. Neither date makes a great disagreement. Despite being seemingly contradictory, rapture theory is a totally false futurist development: one that has the potential to captivate any believer. Directing his future path to an ever-increasing apathy for the welfare of neighbours. Every religion without exception, is a witness to this being the case. Muslims, christians, and Jews generally all despise and put down the other, and any that do not view the world as they. Each proposes that others will be forever damned. For christians, it's as if the thought is as one fundamentalist pastor stated bluntly:

> "A few politically-correct pastors, New Age Church members, and secular humanist religious leaders will remain, and they will be hard-pressed to explain why they didn't vanish with the true saints of God."[ccvii]

Insensitive words from a 'Christian' pastor! With 'pastors', sprouting such sadistic palaver like this who really is the enemy? I thought one set of pillars christianity espouses was (Matthew 5:3-11)? Imagine for a moment holding the view of this pastor. How would you honestly feel if such an event does not materialise as expected? Would you be more disgruntled and bitter? Would you somehow console and justify it to yourself that maybe this was God's plan (will) and, he decided you should learn something else before the thousand year Reich? Others may well postulate there is "...nothing particularly bad with picturing oneself flying through the clouds. But, how far do Christians think they need to fly to get to their travel destination? Besides, 'Heaven' is not up; it is 'in.' It should also be noted that the "rapture theory" never penetrated the Church of the East (Aramaic); it is of Western origin."[ccviii] There are numerous reasons, and articles posted online that advocate both for and against 'rapture' as will be shown by any simple Internet pursuit. The point here is that most advocates for such a theory do not take into serious account its origins or any of the original emphases. Another proposed entrée to muse: albeit still largely inconclusive. Might we suppose the occurrence and transformation of particular and popular

Judaeo-Christian characters into the heavens, like: enoch, elijah, and the Messiah, as no more or less than the "quick 'translation' from "physical to spiritual flesh while alive..."[ccix] Then again what the hell pray tell is 'spiritual flesh?' Spirit, the bible says does not consist of 'flesh!' It cannot. It is an amalgam that can neither be physically felt nor seen; it is ethereal. Like the wind which also neither is physically grasped or has seen? Some may argue that we can. Yet, what we see and feel are the effects and results of rushing air molecules! Esteeming the verdict of Welker and others no doubt to some extent seems to be paul's commendation:

> "Listen, I will tell you a mystery! We will not all die, but we will all be changed, in a moment, in the twinkling of an eye, at the last trumpet. For the trumpet will sound, and the dead will be raised imperishable, and we will be changed. For this perishable body must put on imperishability, and this mortal body must put on immortality."[ccx]

The challenge to readers is to link these verses with the summation offered above regarding rapture. Is the corinthians passage really stating what was pointed out above? Rapture is NOT a mystical and magical flying lesson. Rather, is a complete change of mind and conscious![ccxi] If 'rapture' somehow did occur as countless christians wrongly assume most surely it will not happen the way many today hope it would. That despite being dead and buried, and decayed, resting in their eternity box. A select few will magically resume animation, with all the trimmings previously acquired. What nonsense. Let it be stated and understood that paul in the corinthian passage is not advocating any remote or otherwise, 'flying tour' theory. Death is still present, despite his assertion that some may not succumb to it. A false assertion for no doubt for all humanity as earlier stated, dies! Also, the changing paul mentions is essentially an alteration, an amendment to one's character; the imperishableness has also, the sense of becoming incorruptible through the association and working of deity. Meaning that maybe believers become completely enveloped like enoch of old: so much so that there is no room for anything else![ccxii] Alternatively, he may also be recognising what many

DECONSTRUCTING ENDTIME DELUSIONS

Eastern religions aver: that of the journey of reincarnation. After-which we become fully a part of the cosmos itself. Hypothetically, if the theory of a 'rapture of the saints' as proposed by its many dispensational crackpot's was to be a biblically sound doctrine. Readers are encouraged to muse further over the following questions and statements.

- Ok, you disappeared suddenly; what does that mean for those left behind?

- Maybe other believer's, some of your friends 'don't make the grade' and are left behind! What then?

- How does the 'Church/believer' then fulfil the supposed calling, to be a 'light to the nations'? If indeed that is what it is supposed to be? Which it isn't.

- What about the many scripture references stating, 'trial and tribulations' is 'part and parcel' of a believer's life?

- How does this God Save or even 'offer' salvation to the populations that 'missed the boat' when you are gone? Is he such a callous deity to forsake people, after he states elsewhere he desires that none should perish?

- Again, what if you were one of those that 'thought' you had-it-in-the-bag, but it did not materialise as you'd hoped? What I wonder would that do to your 'Faith'?

What's more, what is to be made of the many other crazy notions that high profile well-respected rapturists fastidiously propose? For instance, many promote and assume (Revelation 4:1-3); that an assumed apostle john was somehow 'raptured', though temporarily into the Heavens, the throne room of Yahweh (of the gods)! Of this crazy notion, one commentator writes this is one of famed Christian author, Grant Jeffrey's ludicrous theories:

"John's being directed to "Come up here" is a depiction of the rapture in the same way that the Church will be "caught up" at the time of the pre-tribulational rapture. Jeffrey writes, "When John was 'in the Spirit' ... he was 'Raptured up' to Heaven...."[ccxiii]

This is absurd exegesis to be sure, but it is standard dispensational teaching.[ccxiv] If the opine as Grant Jeffrey's writes, is that when john was in the spirit it was his being raptured into the heaven: how is this whim maintained for other texts with similar phraseology? Do we then consider a similar or same result to happen to believers when they are exhorted in other passages of their sacred texts. Such as Ephesians 6:18: which calls believers to 'pray in the spirit?' If being in the spirit is akin to a disappearing by 'rapture' experience there would be few or none left I should imagine. Does such a concept have ties to the practices of many a Shaman who enter an asc (Altered State of Consciousness) in search of 'specific' answers? It would seem likely that these two 'practices' are comparable. The sacred account, to a large degree has subdued any relation to the latter and has essentially condemned it as an otherworldly and iniquitous practice. Grant Jeffrey, Hal Lindsay and others espousing such a crazy theory as that proposed above, is surely offering illogical madness! Clearly, this opens the door for more speculation. Is this a partial rapture event? What's a partial rapture anyway? Is it truly plausible and possible? The questions this poses are endless. Yet, as stated later christians might want to rethink and take the word to (titus 3:9-10) more seriously:

> (3:9) "But avoid pointless arguments.. For they are unprofitable and useless... (3:10) As for a human who is a sectarian (*hairetikon-heretic*), after admonishing him once or twice, avoid him..."[ccxv]

It is exactly these types of people that Jeffery's and Co are. Instead of esteemed scholars, I view them as any number of a very long line inept amateurs who have no clue about what they preach/ teach. Such people persistently offer the dullard believer, pseudo-theological guesses that cause more harm than they explain. Avoid them! A john was not raptured in the 'modern' sense, but as the chosen vessel to relay a message of his deity, Yahweh, he was probably the final privileged Jewish 'astro-Prophet' to write his visions in the vernacular he and his original audience understood: that of the connection between signs and visions of the celestial/cosmological variety.[ccxvi] At a risk of sounding more cynical, I wonder how many proponents of any 'rapture theory', or indeed any other modern 'man ordained supposition' (trinity, or tongues: as a type of senseless 'babbling' for instance), have honestly sat down with their sacred texts and searched such questions out without bias (john 15:26; 16:5-15)? Instead, it is true, many even more so today in our technologically advanced society, "...accumulate for themselves teachers to suit their own passions [teachers that] turn them away from listening to the truth, making them to wonder off into myths."[ccxvii] Rapture is one such escapist and absolutely false myth and is a dreamy way of viewing the world. I am not the first to say so. To harbour such a viewpoint as proposed by any rapturist is an immature belief that we are all tempted to fall headlong. Such beliefs show invariably an immaturity we only really see in early childhood. That is, the willingness to follow and believe blindly almost anything they are taught. Andrew Roth in one of his appendices notes to the AENT (the Aramaic English New Testament) sums up the present 'rapture theory' rather pithily:

> "The goal..is not Rapture (or religion) but Spiritual Regeneration, because the time of Ya'akov's (Jacob) trouble is coming for the benefit of the "Church..." Ya'akov represents Christians who are deceived and cheating themselves and others by not entering into the protection of the Kingdom of Elohim...[by adhering to Torah, the Old Testament].., so as the One World Government continues to rape and pillage the Earth of Righteousness, one can expect even more false prophets to advertise cheap religious travel packages into the clouds."[ccxviii]

Such a 'regeneration' comes through a calming down of the mind that believes silly things. Things that cannot be atoned. Therefore, cease believing in silly conjecturing that rapture is a floating away into clouds. A thought that is little but the wishful thoughts of a misplaced nephology study. Rapture theory and what it proposes is even more beautifully summed with Suetonius' words. It is a '... pernicious superstition....'[ccxix] A superstition that has the odour and hallmark of Aristotelian ethics by which there is only a select few, morally virtuous, and elite (males only according to Aristotle) who qualifies. There are when you search, and think of it many passages that seem to offer bible readers 'end–times,' rapture or associated subjects. We here cannot however, review all of them in any depth. There are numerous others that have included many of these passages in their treaties against christianity. Audacious Christian readers are directed to texts like; **Jesus Lied: He was only Human**, and **God hates you, hate him back**, by C.J. Werleman; **Miraclescam**, by Frank Goodwilie. There is also the book **Lies have ruined the world**, by Dennis Richard Proux. As well as **The Christian Delusion: Why faith fails**, edited by John F. Loftus. Some sacred texts worth rethinking closely about follow. Though some may not be essentially regarding our main topic. These show Jesus and the gospel writers as liars and manipulators of those who claim to follow the sacred texts. Clearly, Jesus didn't return before many of his own generation died. A promise he positively made. Plainly, seeking anything through prayer, as another instance, in the name of Jesus is farfetched. Why is it only through this son, that the 'Father' is glorified? If we are all made in the image of God, well why is this deity not glorified except for this deity-man? Readers will undoubtedly get the point when a critical eye is cast upon the following:

- Matt 6:25-27; 10:23; 13:38-42; 24:3.

- Luke 21:32.

- John 14:13-14.

- Acts 10:34 – 35.

Nail Seven:

Some of Gods outstanding New Testament end-time mistakes:

"But of that day and of that hour, knoweth no man, nor even the angels of heaven, but the Father only."[ccxx]

CONDUCTING AN EXPERIMENT for interest sake, I typed into the search engine of Google; Matthew 24:36. Not surprisingly over 1million results display. Most of the 'hits' generated that were quickly reviewed carried the usual end–time, second coming explanation, esp. if commentary were supplied. Some 'hits' commentated on the textual differences within the Greek text that this and the markan parallel story throw to a discerning reader. Why for instance, does the author of mark include the phrase –not the son, but Matthew deletes it? It would be a disservice if I were to regurgitate the arguments surrounding the Greek text. For; frankly, those interested can research competent Greek scholars. Besides, few 'common' English readers of the sacred book are remotely interested in such material. Here; therefore, we concentrate on the English. If in conversation with you were asked to focus attention on the words of this verse, what would be your immediate response? What thoughts might begin to race through your mind? How would you react if it were asked that this verse is explained?

If readers were raised in a Christian family we have all heard, read, or been taught a little of the above verse at some stage in our years of religious indoctrination. Or is that initiation? Most commentators of this verse have concentrated their efforts on the first half and particularly highlighting that no man knows... and mostly regarding an end–time, second coming hypothesis. But, the way religionist's use it seems to be playing into the idea that we humans are forever subjected to ignorance. Whether that's unawareness at the hands of some 'elitist' class; i.e., the priesthood who expect you to 'believe' what they would have you knows, because 'they' said a certain subject is taught clearly in 'the sacred texts', or it is through your own lack of knowledge because you have not bothered to verify certain so-called religious ideas. The result is the same. Many 'christians' remain blissfully dull and inconsistent regarding copious 'faith claims.' A case in point is this verse: Why is it that believers especially affirm such stupidity? That no one 'knows' anything, because that's what that text seems to affirm. Especially when some so often amuse themselves milling over catastrophe possibilities! However, at the first sign of illness, the same people all too happily rush off to a pillbox and medical professional in the hope of an explanation and amelioration for whatever ails them? Are we not taught humans were all made in the perfect image of a perfect intelligent deity? Something is amiss. Yes, forsooth, such intelligence is a fallacious ideal to place all one's hope in. Humans, believer and nonbeliever alike get ill regularly. Is this one other side of our makeup deity over looked? Neither of us knows when illness occurs, so what's the distinction? None of us know when, or the hour that sickness, or death visits, and no one apparently 'knows' what this verse is talking about. We might have a general idea nowadays of seasonal afflictions like Hay fever, or the Influenza virus, and so we prepare. Yet, none of us know when or if more destructive diseases will strike us. Nor are we privy to their severity. Medical Professionals to a large degree also are just as ignorant. Though I hold these men and women in high esteem (being the son of a General Medical Practitioner), we nonetheless must also come to accept, as Harriet hall M.D. in her article for "Skeptic magazine" highlights,

> "Doctors are not scientists; they are practical users of sciences who apply scientific evidence to patient care. Medicine deals in probabilities and informed guesses, not certainties."[ccxxi]

It would seem this too is relevant to a deity and religion as a whole. Maybe your deity does also; deals in probabilities and guesswork, not certainties? If so I find it difficult to comprehend his/her supremacy. I also gather the same afflictions we suffer dog this supreme deity!

DECONSTRUCTING ENDTIME DELUSIONS

Obviously, the supreme deity must suffer colds/ influenza. Does it not also endure cancer, loss of eyesight, deafness, polio, or any other clement or severe affliction common to mankind: those which creep up on it without foreknowledge? The 'bible' does inform and affirm humanity is made in deity's image and likeness after all in Genesis 1:26. Image and likeness in Hebrew at this verse are both interesting: Accordingly,

- Strongs 6754; image, likeness, i.e., that which is a pattern, model, or example of something, note: the exact reference of whether this is moral, ethical, physical, nature, etc. is not clear...[ccxxii]

- Strongs 1819; likeness, resemblance; concr. model, shape; adv. like: —fashion, like (-ness, as), manner, similitude.[ccxxiii]

If we therefore suffer numerous complications regularly and without forewarning, –reason and logic informs me that so does any proposed deity! Otherwise, as stated earlier one must submit to and conclude such a deity is imaginary! As in my case, does deity suffer the complications of a Neuropathy? Does he/she similarly don daily a pair of spiritual ankle and foot orthopaedics, and mechanical braces so mobility is more achievable? If a deity labeled 'Father', played a role in forming bible passages such as the current passage of Matthew, it seems that it has a lot to answer for. It's biased and inconsistent! But we digress. The above passage seems pretty outspoken, and I may be accused of taking this passage out of context. But was I really? No human knows the day or hour. Of what, I ask? Yet, as 'believers' so often do they merrily and unquestionably surrender and attempt no doubts to justify or rationalise that regular tipple! I once did! It just seemed naturally obvious. Despite our supposed creation by an intelligent deity in its image, that characteristic weren't passed on to any of us: but remains of his or her exclusive domain. Recall similar sentiments highlighted above in the study of Genesis chapter 3. Deities in all mythologies simply do not want humans to become too intelligent! We are quite the persistent dullards then! I now pose statements that altogether might initially sound stupid, irrational, and again vitriolic. Yet really aren't if we are honest with the rest and ourselves. Besides who's being vitriolic, the bible or me for questioning the validity of its statements?

The New Testament in numerous places clearly states believers (should) have the mind of christ. Right? (see 1 corinthians 2:16) So how does one reconcile the concept that no man knows the day or hour, with the idea that believers are supposed to as is plainly contended, be not only like-minded as 'christ,' but also be possessed by his mind. This, for the simple fact also. The 'gospel' of john clearly asserts compliant believers are no longer slaves but are his friends. Slaves aren't told anything significant by their masters but are rather required to obedience in what is obligatory of them. Not so with friends. As 'friends' of christ it therefore stands to reason that believers should possess some privileges of peace and knowledge (john 15:15)? The very same understanding and knowledge the christ figure supposedly possessed. Deep calls unto deep so the saying is (psalm 42:7). Despite the arguments surrounding the christ figure's humanity, which annuls any notion of deity status. If this christ figure is to be likened to the all-knowing father which in other places of the sacred books is also affirmed, then it's not rational. Nor is it impartial to declare believers is friends: possessing his mind, which, coincidently is the mind of the nemo-deity, because somehow these two are one. Further, if the deity-man Jesus was likened to Gilgamesh, being of deity- and - man. Does this mean that the human 'side', for lack in better terminology was somehow barred from the divine knowledge, the knowledge the deity characteristic of the Jesus figure is supposed to also have possessed. It cannot be both ways. Neither can any then turn about and declare that still no man has any knowledge of what is to come. That whole concept unravels upon deeper thought. To be exposed as a tome of pedagogical abuses and oppression. 'Free Will,' a common enough fallacy explained later, accounts for nothing.

Cognisance, accord and Wisdom herself accounts for nothing! Does this again not remind you of the previous discussion surrounding Genesis three? Fairly, the above calls into question the veracity and validity of certain loved practices many believers insist are worthy. Like the burdens

DECONSTRUCTING ENDTIME DELUSIONS

of daily prayer, bible reading and prophecies! If an act of prayer is vital, how is it determined and discerned that the wee still 'voice,' said to be in answer by the deity, is not actually of our own self-deluding making? It is after all widely acknowledged in many scientific fields of academia, and we know it on a personal level also. When we read there is a wee small voice articulating in our minds almost audibly; the words, phrases, and sentences as the eye scans the page? This is a fact. Try concentrating on listening to it while reading these sentences for a moment. It's just as a full-blown commentary assisting our brain with comprehension. So who is to say the same isn't occurring in these beloved religious practices? The answer most believers I suspect would reply with the usual indoctrinated 'faith/confidence' ideal. But, faith does not adequately explain. Nor can it answer the question. Though not immediately questionable; faith is not objective, something that offers discernibly empirical and repeatable data. Rather, as stated often already, faith is a very subjective and personal viewpoint. It is primarily a 'get out of jail – free' card. Working like the 'roll-of-the-dice' to get double figures, or two of the same number in a game of monopoly, before being released from the 'jail'. Besides, why pray or offer anything of the sort if there is a supreme source who knows our every waking and sleeping thought? If an act of prayer is required or sought after by the deity, does that not trounce the deity's all-knowingness and omnipotence? I, as we all, still have similar 'confidence' to that which believers cling: that which they label –faith. It is just not directed to a mythical cosmic fraudster. Example: Each of us confidently 'knows' there will be another dawning of the sun on the morrow (although this too is a known lie). Such assurance arises from the universal and empiric knowledge that no one alive would be unintelligent enough to deny. That being; it is not the sun that rises and sets, but the course of the earth's rotation giving the impression so. It might surprise more than a few readers to be told that human consciousness has known and understood this; that the earth rotates, and so, it is perceived that the sun rises and sets for no fewer than 10,000 years! What? Prehistoric mankind wasn't as dull-headed as might be believed or at least written of in most history texts? This is another fact. Author of "Celestial Key to the Vedas: Discovering the origins of the world's oldest civilization", B. G. Sidharth affirms it through the existence and remarkable advanced concepts and knowledge of the authors of the ancient Indian sacred texts "The Rig Vedas". Offering an example derived from the Aitareya Brahmana (3.44), which declares:

> "...the sun never sets nor does it rise. This is apposed to the common belief of people that at night, the sun sets, and at daybreak the sun arose. In actuality, the sun produces two opposing effects; day in one place, and night in the opposite. It never sets." (Introduction).

A deeply profound text. We all know and understand this concept today. Yet, all of us have been duped into thinking and believing ridiculous notions that such insight, as the Earth's rotation, was only brought to 'light' (pun intended) during the 'Enlightenment' years (1650 – 1800), or because of the marvels of technology and space exploration. Clearly; the case is brought to your attention. Mankind has understood such phenomena for a very long time.

This diversion serves to highlight several anomalies with the passage under review. Someone is lying! Either all-empirical, calculated knowledge is a farce, and the above Indian text has been falsified and dated incorrectly and deceptively, or the penmanship of this passage in Matthew 24, an attributed announcement of the God-man Jesus, is inaccurate, manipulative, and self-serving in what is recorded! Ok, time to breathe. I am not beating up on believers. Nor have I confused this with knowledge that we can't 'predict' accurately the future. A dilemma with this Matthew text lay in the fact that the whole verse and chapter did in no way make reference to any modern 'end-time' apocalyptic scenario just as it is often assumed. One of the unforeseen disadvantages of popular modern bibles (NJKV, ESV, NIV) is that they segregate certain verses and passages within so-called themes. Translators for some reason seem to be willing to categorise the texts. For whatever reason bible scholars, men and women feel the need to make slight alterations or additions to the text by entitling those passages; which altogether does not constitute adding to the text. Apparently explicitly forbidden, proverbs 30:5-6; Matthew 5:17-20. True, many of these titles are most

DECONSTRUCTING ENDTIME DELUSIONS

likely meant as nothing more than helpful 'guides' to certain themes. Even so, too many believers have sought out such 'headings' to assist them in their study pursuits. Not really cognisant of the fact they don't exist in the text (like the endnotes of passages). Which are then taken too often as gospel. Though these also are unconsciously recognised as nothing but possible helpful insights to assist the studier. Upon finding a desired heading, the student in a sense is obligated to read only the chunks immediately within the vicinity of the heading, and so believe that what they read does indeed pertain to such passages, because: (1) that's what it has been labeled, and (2) that's what is also continually reinforced by pastoral leaders and religious teachers. That, we can label – is blatant conditioning! Again, as referred to we are dulled into passive routines of mindlessness. Many headings are misleading and dare it is suggested, damaging to the reader's mind and understanding. Leading he or she through a convoluted contorted mismatching of ideas that often are not present within the text itself. The likelihood of greater confusion thus is exemplified. Again, Genesis chapter three is a prime example. This chapter of Genesis has in numerous modern sacred books been 'titled' – "The Fall". This is one such example where readers are prone to only read a text within the bounds of the alleged title, and so, come to a text with a preconceived idea of what a passage 'probably' according to scholars and translators means or talks about. A subconscious act brought about by the alleged 'title' of chapter three of Genesis. In that study, I hope to have assisted readers in realising that this is fallacious. A lie imposed by religious elites; NOWHERE in the whole of the sacred text is any type of 'fall from 'grace" actually intimated. It is pure fantasy and a manipulative tool used by those who want to control and manipulate. Back to Matthew 24.

Above was stated many commentators project ideas on the first part of the verse, 'that no man knows...' Which I hope readers might even minimally, grasp is utter nonsense. The greater concern I have with this Matthew verse pertains to the meaning of the second half of the verse. Particularly who or what are the angels of heaven that the writer mentions? Assuming so, some believing readers would jump to a conclusion this phrase is speaking of the ethereal, otherworldly superhuman beings that are said to surround the throne of the deity. Maybe in some minds they are the archangel's Gabriel or Michael. These were after all, the sacred texts say were sent to apparent dignitaries: Daniel, zechariah, joseph, and miriam (mary) with a special announcement. However, I do not accept as true it is to these that this writer refers. Besides, if I were incorrect, why would these 'angels' need to know anyway? Did they know about the cataclysm of Genesis; what difference would that have made? Later in the second section below are tackled the question of angels, which might startle a few readers. So who are the 'angels of heaven' recorded by the author of Matthew in this verse? Is he referring to a 'heavenly' host as said; or maybe it's a reference to some astrological anomaly? Or shamans? There is no reason to disbelieve the possibility; "...Jewish attitudes to astrology generally are typically tolerant and are based on the assumption that its practice is acceptable as long as it does not challenge one's devotion to God." Wrote Nicolas Campion, in his book "Astrology, and Cosmology in the world's religions."[ccxxiv] Throughout antiquity mankind deified planetary and star systems. Any study into the origins of Zodiac and its use throughout the world informs as much. So what's going on in Matthew here? Simply, I think the matthean writer could possibly be referring to 'prophets/shaman's'; the adepts in interpretation of sky and other celestial anomalies, as the angels in this verse. They could also be other 'apparent' godly persons, – maybe a caste of the elect. Which may include the assumed gospel disciples? Why? Repeatedly, these are the messengers that the deity has, according to the sacred books, always used to transmit a message. There is no hint within the text to any other figure. Though admittedly this is my own pontification; Louw-Nida Greek lexicon seems to affirm this suspicion. The contrast, between 'angel,' and 'Prophet' are attributed below:

> "In many languages, a term for 'angels' is borrowed from another dominant language, but in other instances a somewhat descriptive phrase may be employed. The most common expressions for the 'angels of God' are 'messengers' and 'messengers from heaven.' Sometimes these angels are called

> 'spirit messengers' and even 'flying messengers.' In some instances, they have been called 'the holy servants of God,' but an expression such as 'servants of God' or even 'messengers of God' tends to overlap in meaning with expressions used to characterize (sic) the role and function of the prophets who were sent as messengers from God. In some languages, a term for 'angels' is contrasted with that for 'prophets' by calling angels 'messengers from heaven' and prophets 'messengers from God.' The 'angels of the Devil' are often called 'the Devil's servants...'"[ccxxv]

The matthean author then likely is referencing persons with the skill and ability to decipher, or interpret sky visions and dreams– being the 'Prophet', or skilled disciple. These are the angels referred– according to the matthean author. They are the men, and women possessed of the skill and knowledge of celestial expression. Bruce Malina whom we have already cited has interestingly concluded that the final sacred book of the Judaeo-Christian books, Revelation, is the account, and expression of a sky journey. Put another way, of visions shown expressly to a john. He witnessed the activities of the Celestial places. Mostly, of past events to assist in dealing with and explain any real and present situation his Christian addressees faced. The book, Revelation is thus more of an astrological than apocalyptic or eschatological text, than most modern commentators assume. Which would go a fair way to disqualifying it as the 'end-time' book that sketches modern encounters and lexis? That is, Revelation does not speak with and through our current situations and vernacular. It has no bearing on modern society. Rather, just as the opening 'book' of Genesis, the final book also speaks very probably as a refined astrological guide of events and myths past! This matthean chapter (24): as apostle paul is recorded to have announced in places, seems to be teaching the believer to wait in holy expectation (1 corinthians 13:9; 1 thessalonians 1:9-10.) Read, and understand the 'signs.' Just as you know when a fig tree will blossom, also just as a fellow by the name of Amos had earlier seen!' (Amos 8:9-10.) This is also verified by the following verses (Matthew 24:37f). Disputably the assumed God-man Jesus knew such an event of his demise was inevitable and was very close nearby. Which is also apparently a theme of Matthew 24. The God-man just did not know precisely when that was to happen.

Aside that very human quality of the alleged deity-man, how much influence did he (Jesus) have on bringing these events to pass? See Michael Baigent, "The Jesus papers: Exposing the greatest cover up in History." It would seem this fellow was indeed an antagonist, egging and aping the audiences and authorities on. As if sticking two fingers up!

> "So watch out, for you do not know on what day the master will be coming." (Matthew 24:42) One will be taken and one will be left (Matthew 24:41)

One other example from the writer of Matthew. Upon consideration regarding the 'meaning' of these two verses of Matthew 24:41-42. I do not perceive these as advocating a doctrine of divine election resulting in some disappearing 'rapture'. It does not advocate a 'flying/ or disappearing act. Where one of two people will miraculously vanish suddenly. Leaving the other to flounder about in some state of distress of not knowing what the hell just happened! I suspect most religious readers would themselves perceive Matthew 24:41–42 eludes to a similar scenario. It has been heard preached and taught that these verses of Matthew are hinting and warning 'believers' that this might be the case; they'll be blissfully going about their days, when suddenly, they, or someone else– vanishes without warning. Maybe in a blink of an eye. Nonsense! Even at a cursory glance at the Greek meaning of 'taken' does not allow such guessing. Provided the reader has the temerity to question what might be going on, while also not assuming an idea from the head is valid! The Greek work translated into English, taken, is (paralambano –Strong's 3880). A word that explicitly means something is 'accepted, learnt from another person, or essentially 'buddied' with.' Bit like how toddlers are buddied with a classmate. The equivalent Hebrew term seems to confirm. Adding further light on passages like (john 14:1-3) and what has been earlier stated; that not everyone will receive the 'kingdom' despite what rhetoric they use. See also (Matthew 7:21-23.) Accordingly, two or more readers, might be taken (will accept, almost what is written here) with this book, while others will not. The reality of life however appears that it really doesn't matter what 'language,' as in good or bad, religious, or not anyone uses. Nobody will know this side of death. Funny, but death seems to be the great leveller of human clans. Being a worldwide phenomenon no one escapes!

Rapture theories:

EACH COMMUNITY, OF each society in each country has its own brand of Christian belief. Each has a certain doctrinal stance, which in many respects differs greatly to the next. In the middle of the mix is our subject of 'rapture'. Spread liberally across the denominational divide lie the pre-millennial; post-millennial, and the Amillennialist, rapturists. Coinciding to the equally confusing and nonsensical ground of, pre-tribulation rapture; mid-tribulation rapture; post-tribulation rapture; pre-wrath rapture; and partial rapture theories. Confused yet? You should be. For, this as far as can be seen, rapture is not a theory derived from the plain understanding of the scripture! The sacred text forthrightly teaches clearly that the principal deity is not the Elohim (gods) of confusion (1 corinthians 14:33). One other commentator, confirming these conclusions makes the same point:

> "Because of the steady barrage of fanciful speculations by millennial teachers, many devout Christians are greatly confused. I do not blame them. We have today the Post-Mil, Pre-Mil, A-Mil, Pre-Trib, Mid-Trib, Post-Trib, Ultra-Dispensational schools of interpretation. Recently we have heard of the "Pan-Millennial" idea, which says, "it isn't really important what you believe. If you are saved, everything will PAN OUT all right in the end anyway.""[ccxxvi]

So who or which modern 'rapture' theory is correct? Simply; accordingly, to believe in any has no baring anyway. One could it is supposed, just as well believe a nineteen eyed Startle Blupleguer is a deity, and saviour who might, or not give a damn about your life. Besides, maybe it all matters whether there is a Starship with an Improbability Drive? It does not truely matter. Hinted more than once throughout this writing. Now categorically, absolutely none are correct! Neither is correct; because they are all cleverly devised 'doctrines of man,' and is not supported even minimally by any sacred text. Support can neither be found in the Old Testament, nor the New Testament'. The prime misconception surrounding any 'rapture theory,' as with Climate Change, is that we forget it is only another theory! Theory, according to Oxford is

> "a supposition or a system of ideas intended to explain something, especially one based on general principles independent of the thing to be explained."[ccxxvii]

This is scarcely a substantial launching pad! If christians, or other believers in rapture were to honestly view this concept, and many other so-called 'sacred parchment' doctrines. They would surely realise it does not serve any purpose other than to vilify and subject adherents to unruly control. Nor do these seem to magnify their Messiah, or the prime deity either, which these types of doctrines are supposed to do, right? But, each derives from a mixed bag of unrelated hypothetical guesses simplified to fit an already-accepted whim. A. W. Tozer once wrote: 'Any doctrine, any experience that serves to magnify Him is likely to be inspired by Him.' Rapture theory; let alone the other subjects explored later; however, are not recognised as aspiring from either. Think about it: Rapture, as christians like to think about it is centred on the experience of the 'believer.' Not as Tozer states: on magnifying the presumed deities –Jesus or Yahweh. So, how can any professed believer honestly ascribe to such absurdity with any clear conscious? In all respects, even the best and world-renowned supporters of these theories are misleading. There are many theologians and laity deceived into believing what their sacred books neither report nor support. How can I assert this is truth? Because of one other ingredient: such 'rapture' theories and interpretations of the so-called 'rapture verses' are based solely upon a 'Western- Greek', and Catholic understanding. It does not consider, generally, the Semitic mindset of the authors whose passages they distil these theories from. Advocates do not view favoured verses alongside their rightful historical or contextual environment. Bishop Wright seems to be in agreement. Highlighting a connection many westerners seem to for whatever reason, make today; that the 'Lords Prayer' is somehow millennial; the proposed thousand-year reign/Reich of the returned Messiah. Specifically: "the belief and hope that God's kingdom will come, and God's will be done, on earth as it is in heaven." Note well how many people you may know who holds the belief of being removed from the earth to heaven –as that supposedly is where 'the Kingdom of God is.' You yourself may still be dogged, and insisted such a 'belief' is correct. But, we should not be fooled into such a confidence. Such thinking is unJewish and absurd myth making to say the least. On this, Bruce Chilton offers an interesting observation,

> "What most of all struck scholars at the end of the last century was that in early Judaism "the kingdom of God" was used neither of an individual's life after death in heaven nor of a movement of social improvement on earth. Those had been dominant understandings of the kingdom, deeply embedded in the theology and preaching of the period."[ccxxviii]

Further, noting the work of two scholars of the period he continues to say they "demonstrated that the kingdom of God in early Judaism and in Jesus' preaching involved God's final judgment of the world; the concept of the kingdom was part and parcel of expectation of the last things."[ccxxix] The kingdom of God is not specifically a 'place.' A destination to be reached. Andrew Roth above confirmed this. Rather the kingdom manifests explicitly, so the bible asserts, the absolute authoritative dictum of the deity and its apparent holy servant, Jesus. This I vouch was most likely the intent behind paul's as well as the other New Testament writings. Including the so-called apocalyptic or end-time portions. We have glimpsed this idea in passing above. See also the word of advice attributed to paul, re: the kingdom of God that is apparently governed by righteousness, peace, and joy in the holy spirit (romans 14:17.) But how much peace and joy in the spirit does the wider world witness regularly? More often the platitudes of religious 'believers' are amiable, until their truth towers are shaken, and begin to topple. Christianity over the centuries has built for itself a vast multiplex library of doctrines. Does the tower of babel ring any bells? Shake an apple tree laden with fruit enough and eventually that fruit will fall. Recall the fable of Aesop! In sum, Hebrew scholar Dr. Michael Heiser, in his 14-part study on obsessing over Eschatology poignantly adds:

> "Are you a splitter or a joiner? Any view of a rapture is heavily dependent on splitting up passages that speak of the return of Jesus into two categories (one of which = a rapture). The splitting is done along the lines of slight "discrepancies" between all the "return of Jesus" passages, assuming that they describe two events, not one. But why split these when we join such passages everywhere else in the gospels (we harmonize (sic) so as to remove disagreement rather than highlighting disagreements)? Who made up the rule that the return passages should be split to produce a rapture? Why not harmonize? Maybe the answer is because then the rapture disappears. Ultimately, splitting or joining is our guess."[ccxxx]

Heiser is on the correct path with these statements. Yet, christianity seems to also want to play both sides equally. It wants to 'split' numerous passages that suit a purpose, while also insisting on 'joining others' to make a case 'seem' more inviting, truthful, and historical. Finally, "The Dictionary of the Apostolic Church", confirms again the complete arguments placed before readers yet. That 'rapture' as insisted today by many promoting the latest end time scenario is unwarranted and is counterfeit to what the New Testament actually teaches:

> "The English word 'rapture' is derived from Lat. raptus, the act of seizing and carrying away, hence transport of mind or ecstasy (ἔκστασις– ekstasis?) In classic Greek ἔκστασις means frenzy; in the NT it rarely expresses this high degree of emotion, but may include distraction of mind, caused by wonder and astonishment, or exceptional joy and rapture... the verb ἐξίσταμαι is used, also in reference to the effects upon the multitude of the bestowal of the 'gift of tongues' (Acts 2:7, 12), and further of the preaching of St. Paul in the synagogues immediately after his conversion (9:21). The stronger sense of the word, translated in English as 'trance,' is found in the description of St. Peter's vision of the vessel full of unclean beasts (Acts 10:10, 11:5)."[ccxxxi]

So, we have reached the full circle of our brief foray into the Christian idea of a 'rapture of the saints'. This dictionary entry reaffirms my proposed statements above; that rapture is not a floating away into some sky realm by believers. Rather, is more the point of having a mind regeneration, of emotion. Likely of extreme joy. It is nonsensical therefore to listen to advocates proposing a whisking away of believers into a cloud region to be with a deity.

Vacating this blue marble:

IN THE CASE THAT YOU are persistent in rapture and other Christian delusional beliefs, and you still wish to take an early and permanent vacation, sidestepping that apparent boogyman death from the blue marble we call home. The following guide may be of assistance. It is recommendable that like any life or funeral insurance, the logistics of your desired departure, must be fully funded, agreed on and most importantly, officially signed off by your Government's: Births, deaths, and Marriages Department anterior to your mass departure. Failure to fully comply with all regulations, leads to forfeiture of all Tithe's paid. Affordable weekly payment plans, and packages for both Family and Singles are offered. Check with your chosen religious rapture-ready Department. No medicals. No paperwork. Instant cover– works similarly to the absurd proposal of clergy; that after confessional ritual, they have the means and power to absolve permanently one's nonexistent 'sins.' An oxymoron for sure! Some rapture packages may include or offer special rates and insurances for beloved pets to join you. Be sure to read the fine print and get legal advice before signing contracts. Also, highly advisable: Read, reread, and intimately understand all books in their proper sequence of "The Hitchhiker's Guide to the Galaxy" saga by that brilliant satirist, the late Douglas Adams. The information there may prove vital to your continued existence! If your chosen rapture sector proves to be unsuccessful, initiate Adams' recommendations for leaving the planet; i.e., he recommends concerned people should first: Phone NASA... explain to them that it's very important that you get away promptly. Or, soon, at the earliest convenience. Alternately, try contacting the few billionaire's who today are striving to build the world's first commercial space-craft. Mr. Elon Musk, or Sir Richard Branson to name but two.

DECONSTRUCTING ENDTIME DELUSIONS

- If they do not cooperate, phone any friend you may have in the White House or your national Government – ask them to have a word for you to the guys at NASA or the suitable billionaire.

- If you don't have any friends in the Government, phone the Kremlin, the South Koreans, or the Chinese government or Isis - Syria (ask the overseas operator for -0107-095-295-905). They don't have any friends either (at least none to speak of), but they do seem to have a little influence, so you may as well try.

- If that also fails, phone the Pope...I gather his switchboard is flawless (a direct line) so no charges will be incurred.

- If all these attempts fail, flag down a passing flying saucer and explain that it's vitally important you get away before your phone bill arrives.

- If the recommended steps above also fail, for God's sake DON'T PANIC! Persist and don't abandon hope so bloody easily. You have the rest of your life to sort it out.

However, act quickly – according to many Christian postulations – Time is a luxury you probably don't have. But, you can purchase the dvd blockbusters – 'In Time' + 'I Am Number Four', formerly titled 'I'm Mortal' for a good price! The last trumpet call, may, yet most probably not, be announced through all wireless broadcasters in the very near future. Act now - buy the dvd! Only minutes could remain for your lasting security. Incidentally, an Inter-Galactic Construction Fleet fast approaches to annihilate the earth to make way for a proposed Inter-Galactic Expressway. So also find yourself a – Mr. Maurice Minor - and hitch a ride. You have less than twelve minutes now! For further assistance on locating the specified Mr. Maurice Minor, there are many space agencies established throughout the world. Someone is bound to know where he's at and take you seriously – eventually! For World Wide Space Agency information and further contacts, any Space agency. Search the Internet, and maybe make their site your Homepage. This site offers links to official Space Agency information. There are also numerous other linked information pages to getting your space/rapture adventure off 'the ground', with Start-Up Ventures, Launch sites/

providers, and other vitals. Maybe we'll all meet again at the Restaurant at the End of the Universe!

FAIRWELL,

AND GOOD LUCK!

...YOU'LL NEED IT

DECONSTRUCTING ENDTIME DELUSIONS

Summarising investigations:

THE FRONT PAGES, INTRODUCTION and the Nails of the First Part readers might have found vitriolic and unnecessarily tedious. If only for the prime reason; the subjects commented upon are not ordinarily considered as having anything remotely adjacent with an end time or apocalyptic hypothesis. Trusted however is readers have made it this far into this study, I have successfully offered you 'new eyes'. New ways of seeing, studying, or just reading a sacred book. There will undoubtedly be those who hold the view that such a panoptic scope is that I (1) have 'breeched my britches' over my former beliefs and the myriad decent Church-folk who still hold weird religious beliefs. So, set as my goal the debunking of all religious teachings. Or (2) that I were attempting to cram and overwhelm readers with irrelevant information or convoluted discussion. In a hope to fortify my intelligence. Not at all. Rather the wish was to attempt to engage and open readers to the idea that despite religious institutions and hierarchy having a monopoly on the meanings of their sacred texts; it's best policy to engage and use one's own intelligence. Best policy is with the mentioned earlier motto, Nullius in Verba – take no man's word for it! It is therefore, most beneficial to utilise as many tools, and your own intelligence that is always available, instead of glibly accepting everything some 'ordained' Ph.D personality tells you when they explain in a book or sermon, what a certain belief, custom, or religious idea likely means. As is the custom. Most of the time they will be flat out wrong unless the author/ preacher has done the required assessments, and not just come to a conclusion from their own preconceived ideologies. For serious sacred book studies there are numbers of helpful resources. Logos Bible Systems are but one among the many. If a skeptical and circumspect attitude to an understanding of your loved sacred texts were employed every time you entered a sacred space or joined with others to peruse and discuss sacred texts; you might identify more and more just how many are the numerous difficulties in those works that you cherish. Believers, having made it this far, can no longer be confident regarding anything heard in a sunday sermon or read in a community/private 'bible' study. It did therefore, and is trusted these have served to lay an authentic foundation for the arguments upon the table to the numerous modern ideas and questions that a subject of 'end-times' conjured. Those we will embark upon. According to conclusions; the copious attestations heard and churned out by various publishing houses are little else than the result of myopic illusions and emotional blackmailing.

Introduced in the opening comments were several academic theories; teleo-functional reasoning: the notion or basic premise of which is: everything has a basic meaning and reason/ purpose behind it. Person Permanence, the idea and subsequent belief that things and/ or people still exist despite not being able to see them. Although we acknowledge the dead as dead, we still want (the comfort if you like) to believe. They are in a state of semi-aliveness, living out their deadness in some Utopia or dystopia, called heaven/ hell. Readers were introduced also to Theory of Mind; which is: the ability to attribute mental states–beliefs, intents, desired emotions, knowledge, –to oneself, and to others. As well as understanding that others have beliefs, desires, intentions and perspectives that are different from one's own. Religionists apply these to a deity figure. All three theories are philosophical ways psychology studies brain function. Offering these and other theories as reasons behind why and how we operate and determine our lives. In short: how we tick! Nail One focused attention on offering readers. An overview of long–forgot Christian history. Much of that history no doubt was an amazing revelation; to realise the extent which the Church and its governing bodies were prepared to use brutality to secure its place as a complete powerhouse among world religion. We saw a reason for the destructive nature at the inception of the Christian religion. Tying it succinctly to how human nature actually is. We each are essentially narcissistic. We each have an innate desire to dominate. We also were made aware that numerous scholars and writers have advanced another little conscious truth; that there is widespread filtration of knowledge. Reviewed very briefly were several favourite bible stories that don't necessarily pop–out as, or relate to a catastrophe hypothesis; primarily for the express purpose of highlighting areas of disagreement that believers may wish to follow up for themselves regarding the veracity of their sacred texts as literal compositions. Finding that multiple attestations or their lack, either confirm or deny the validity of sacred stories. Thus, these tales as they are preached and taught to modern believers, might not have happened the way preachers and religious authorities assume. A slim number of bible words of one particular passage; 1 thessalonians 4:14-17, often associated with end-time material were also briefly glanced. Attempted in discussion was offering a succinct explanation, noticing that, with the resources available today to anyone. Any layperson can find what the original author most probably intended his/her readership to emphasise. It is a poor excuse to not tempt fate and source a variety of resources when the intention is to study the sacred works. A helpful resource available that offers assumed opinions of 'original' intention according to Lexham: The High Definition Old, and New testament texts offered by Logos Bible Systems. Noted was that many believers understanding of certain verses and passages of their sacred books are more often than not, derived from a Distortion of Logic; i.e., readers conclude an understanding or a knowledge of something is again, often from the wrong perspective. Nail Two, ventured into the Exodus story. Finding there is absolutely no evidence of its veracity! The Third Nail, looked into the Sodom and gomorrah episode. Finding also modern summations is fallacious. Next was offered a study of Genesis three, Nail Four, looking purposely to highlight some of the myths from which this story derived. Also, looking at the symbols of trees in myth, and more expressly at what snakes and serpents could symbolically represent in this bible chapter. Postulating, with the assistance of several secular fields of study that gods and spirituality were birthed through the evolution of the early hominid brain. As Bering postulates, deity was born through theory of mind. The 'birthing' of an empathetic mind; through what are known now in studies of belief and the roles the mind has in that process. Which the whole Genesis three episode seen is a story of how ancient mankind gained an understanding of not only himself and neighbour, but of the wider world he inhabited. He no longer thought and acted as his primitive self once did; primal instincts for survival were changed. Provided the reader chooses to view these and other sacred book stories through the prism of symbol. Not as a literal composition. A literal understanding does lead to death, and comes from the usual, unenlightened teaching of Genesis chapter three! We also chanced upon in Nail Five; a surprising comparable conclusion to a tale from antiquity, that was suggested as dispelling a rapture theory completely. Coming to this conclusion upon using statements of a few scholars' studies regarding the Epic of Gilgamesh. Which most probably would have been well known to the penmanship of several stories of the Old Testament. Reason: sacred scripture was not written in isolation. They never just miraculously emerged – presumably out of thin air, in a 'puff' of some Holy Ghost incense and imagination. Taken for granted is that many religious people would presume 2 Timothy 3:16-17 means. Sacred writings rather had a context, and that context was an ancient milieu filled with a religious as well as secular atmosphere; among the mix there were myths and legends, used 'primarily' as the educational textbooks of the ancients.

Moving to a synopsis of the history of rapture theory in Nails Six and Seven. Which sought in these Nails to briefly analyse a couple of New Testament passages. Highlighting what rapture proponents add to this whimsical ideology. To assist readers who have neither the money, time, nor will purchase bible computer programs, a simple and likely resource most people would own; a modern dictionary. The meanings of rapture as found in two standard dictionaries. From this, it was observed that modern assertions of the pious; i.e., the 'Church' being whisked out of harm's way at or close to an end-of-time, is complete bonkers. This ideology, as preached by countless religious people. Is nothing but a fallacious, futuristic invention; (possible as) a rebuttal to the emerging reformation of the sixteenth Century at least. Modern opinions and assertions of a rapture-of-the-saint are quite recent, dating to nineteenth and twentieth Century history. Rapture is not a biblical term. The whole idea of vanishing 'statesmen' is lunacy; as with many other favoured theological/ 'churchy' terms, like Eschatology. These are not found in the sacred books anywhere. Apocalypse too is a very modern invention. An invention that is often twisted to suit one's own purpose (see Appendix 3). We then concluded this First Part with lighthearted musings for those who insist on Rapture theory is yet a biblically mandated and truthful ideology. Basing these thoughts on the satirical pen of Douglas Adams - The Hitchhikers Guide to the Galaxy.

Where to from here?

THE NEXT SECTION IS where we encounter the meat of the subject matter for this book. The whole of this Second Part examines specific end-time personalities and themes and places. This often takes us into some of the more maybe unfamiliar texts and modern suppositions even more closely linked to a catastrophe theme. We read at least one apocryphal and extra-biblical text from which today several startling theories have emerged. Many are believed to have lent themselves to the confusion and hype surrounding the modern end-time articulation. There is a gluttony of hypotheses emerging in many circles. Not just among laymen, but also academically, of non-religious and religious persuasions. Some of the more and seemingly bazaar focus on what some highly acclaimed ethologists and evolutionary biologists like Richard Dawkins, and Physicist Brian Cox is now stating; that the evolution of humankind were made possible only really by the generosity of an exploding supernova: a dying star! This idea is humans are little else than stardust. The basic premise assumes: "From stardust, we came – to stardust. We return. The thought is, forget the death and resurrection of Jesus, he is after all, a mere mythic being – rather, thank your lucky exploding star(s)...as it were, as they by their deaths, made life possible." Human anatomy after all contains every element, and mineral known to be present also in stardust. Therefore, "Mankind is made and will return to the same dust. Joining the cosmic apparatus again at death, to only begin the cycle anew." Which are all factual. One example will suffice. In their book The "Cycle of Cosmic Catastrophes: How a Stone-age Comet Changed the Course of World Culture" Alan West, Richard Firestone, and Simon Warwick-Smith plainly affirm the above three points:

"...Supernovae influence our everyday lives far more than most people know. For example, as you are reading this, you are looking at the book's paper and ink, and, most likely; you are holding the book with one or two hands (the same applies to an electronic format, adjust accordingly). All the things involved – the paper, the ink, your hands, your eyes, and your brain – contain atoms that formed in the distant past in a supernovae explosion." (The Cycle of Cosmic Catastrophes...)

To propose such takes us directly into cosmology. Most interestingly Nicholas Campion, author of the recent publication "Astrology and Cosmology in the World's Religions", affirms through his studies that our world and all life emerged through a sequence of steps, not in some 'poof' of instantaneous materialisation as is often declared to have occurred, i.e., a reading of Genesis 1–2. Everything is characteristically relational: Mankind is related to the stars, stars to animals, and animals to the land.[ccxxxii] Another author also concludes: better knowledge of the Earth is connected directly to knowledge of the stars; both having have been forged from the same elements of earlier generations of stars: "The stars call to us and exert a power on us, perhaps since we are formed from them as all the atoms in our bodies come from inside a long-lost star."[ccxxxiii] We explore somewhat the connections between cosmogony, physics, and creation science to see whether any parallels are uncovered. Along the way, there will be a need to stopover in more (assumed) esoteric, mystical phenomenon; angelology, evil, Satan, and armageddon. Every modern catastrophe belief system seems to have these, and more subjects tucked away within it. Regards to Angelology, the focus is on one religious proposal, "The Genesis Six Experiment". The basic premise is, 'Fallen' angelic type beings cohabitated with human women who gave birth to a mystical creature - the nephilim of the books, Genesis and numbers. We will explore the legitimacy of this ultra-weird, Genesis six hypothesis by Rob Skiba II in Nail Nine. Especially to the accepted and reasoned meanings offered for these and other verses by today's Old Testament and extra-biblical/apocryphal scholars. Is such a thing as a giant humanoid terrorising the planet even possible? How large were they? Were they ever angels or demons? What about the difficult meaning of that Hebrew word; nephilim?

The rest of the Nails in this second Part to my investigations, from Nail Ten onward, I take a look at subjects like; sons of God, angels, armageddon, 'blood–moons', the seven–year itch (tribulation), Satan, and sub–subjects that may arise during these. Some readers may be surprised at what is proposed in the following material and the conclusions that are drawn through this analysis. Some readers may also again not agree with any conclusion or methodology employed. But, agreement is not the objective for their presentation. It is to further help determine and better learn where modern end-time ideas might have derived and so fit in today's world. If at all they have a place. Let us now take a tour in the apocryphal/pseudepigraphical work – enoch to open the second section to this investigation. Noting how some modern commentator's and writers have attempted to reconcile its multitude of themes with their assumptions of events that are assumed will occur in the very present, and not-too-distant future. Note: readers are encouraged to keep in mindful touch with the following statement by Frank Gelett Burgess as you progress through the following material. Much of it is suspected a challenge to established ideologies:

"If in the last few years you haven't discarded a major opinion or acquired a new one – please check your pulse, you may be dead" (1866-1951)

STEVE MORGAN

Part Two:

Convictions are most difficult to tame, let alone change. Tell a man with a conviction that you disagree, and he will question your integrity. Show empirical facts, he will question their legitimacy. Appeal to logic and reason, he'll likely miss your point.

Author

Nail Eight:

Reigning in distorted logic:

JOHN F. KENNEDY ONCE commented: "The great enemy of truth is very often not the lie, deliberate, contrived, and dishonest, but the myth, persistent, persuasive, and unrealistic." Rapture, - we know for sure is one of countless persistent unrealistic religious myths people cling to although it's nowhere found in scripture. Historical records, the Greek text with its emphasis of certain words, and standard definitions in modern English, as well as well-respected theological dictionaries invalidate it as a 'doctrine' of any difference as well. It is proven to be nothing other than a mere abstraction, an effort of myopic logic! This is definitely accurate despite probable objections from some christians who will vehemently defend it, and no doubts in the process expostulate with my previous statements. Modern proposals for rapture however simply do not align scripturally. Nor do they have any foundation upon reason. Let us now turn our attention awhile to the many other end-time proposals. Those often proposed in sermons and much Christian literature that are alleged to have an end time theme. There is a multitude of ideas and theories proposed by various factions, religious and secular that essentially pertain to catastrophism and a looming end to Planet Earth. Many are fanciful whims concocted by superstitious religious minds. Some; however, may offer a little credence. This part of the investigation focuses on those numerous Christian themes associated with the end-time meme. First, we will examine an often-enigmatic figure of the Christian scriptures. A figure that is consistently thought to unequivocally validate a rapture of a deity's elect. It is taken primarily from an ancient Jewish text; the book of enoch.

Enoch, a vanishing shamanic voice:

ACCORDING TO THE "METAPHYSICAL Bible dictionary", Enoch carries the meaning: an entrance into, and instruction in 'new' thought and understanding. An interesting concept. For, this fellow we are told 'walked in the new instruction of deity.' Which deity this refers is indeterminate as the title of the deity given Genesis 5:24 is Elohim. A 'plural' designation– thus, any of the then known or worshipped deities of the region might be in reference. Nonetheless, a fellow named enoch apparently 'walked with deities, doing so very perfectly that he simply vanished. That is, until some Qumran sect and New Testament author decided to resurrect him. Of the titled books of enoch in one lecture series on the "Dead Sea Scrolls", Professor Gary Rendsburg clarifies:

> "At Qumran, it seems that the books of Enoch and Jubilees were seen as canonical. The "Book of Enoch": Eleven copies of the book of Enoch, all in Aramaic, were found at Qumran in Cave 4, all fragmentary...Enoch is based on the statement in Genesis 5:24 that Enoch did not die per se but God simply took him... The book of Enoch dates to the 3rd Century B.C.E. and thus predates the Qumran sect...The book was only canonized (sic) by the Ethiopian Church...The Qumran manuscripts afford us four of the five parts of the book in the original Aramaic...[ccxxxiv] the Qumran sect placed a high value on the Enoch literature, which profoundly influenced their conceptions of God, creation, salvation, sin, and the coming judgment."[ccxxxv]

An influence that has also filtered through to christianity. Few people interested in the figure enoch; however, seem to understand there are 'up to-seven distinct parts' that make up the anthology, 'Book of Enoch'. There is simply not 'one'; singular text called– the book of enoch. Titled sections are: similitude's; dream visions; 'apocalypses'; a 'book of Watchers'; and, 'Birth of Noah'; an Appendix (also known as another book of enoch); and 'A book of the heavens'... all titles make up the actual 'book of enoch'. Besides giving his age (365 years), the book of Genesis says of him only that he "walked with God," and afterwards "he was not, because God had taken him" (5:24). This exalted way of life and mysterious demise made Enoch into a figure of considerable fascination, and a cycle of legends grew up around him.[ccxxxvi] The 'book' though has no real end time scenario. Despite one section of its texts carrying the designation, – apocalyptic by scholars. An Apocalypse is simply a 'revealing'. Not necessarily in reference to some ghastly end time scenario. Such ideologies only arise through a preconceived process of the readers' mind that attempts to link certain of its themes with the latest end time postulating. Which is vastly popular among religious writers. Of enoch, and the book(s) bearing that name, Tony Bushby, in "The Christ Scandal" interestingly presents the following corroboration:

> "The book of Enoch contains secret coded information by deliberate design, preserving in symbolic manner evidence concerning the true nature of the Bible. The very word 'Enoch' means 'initiated', and its mystic meaning is also revealed in the years of life given to Enoch in the Bible... being exactly equal to a solar revolution, and the prominent number of ancient rites. The priests of ancient Egypt preserved a hidden system of high Wisdom that was subsequently secreted into the Bible and the book of Enoch when they were written and then guarded with utmost secrecy. For the first time in history it was unveiled in another of [Tony Bushby's] books. The Secret in the Bible."[ccxxxvii]

Reputable scholars of enoch tradition have also repeatedly undermined an enochic Apocalypse 'apple-cart' announcing: "In Judaism the name Enoch comprehends a whole group of ideas which are often very different from one another. Thus, the title "Book of Enoch" usually refers neither to a book by enoch nor to a book about him, but to the kind of material found in the work. This material is naturally linked with the ideas gathered up in the name enoch. It is rather as though we might use the title "Book of Darwin" for any presentations of the theory of evolution."[ccxxxviii] Enoch then does not embody 'one' singular theme. But, a multitude of ideas associated with the namesake– enoch. Not one of the texts carrying the title enoch is explicitly 'about' nor was it written by him. Traditions found in the 'books' of enoch include "a legend of fallen 'angels', or otherwise, 'Watchers'/Nephilim."

It undoubtedly is this theme that doomsayer religious writers focus their effort on when they attempt to espouse the latest end time script. I will tackle one such proposal, – in the preceding Nail Nine below; which purportedly uses extensively the section, book of Watchers (chapters 1–36) of the 'enochic' texts. 1 Enoch, and Ethiopic or Slavic Enoch – comprise the complete anthology of texts known. The most important and most focussed on is 1 Enoch. This text and those themes mentioned above, are thrown around today like a rag-doll by those who love to focus their energies on describing the latest rapture, end–time scenario. It would seem in some minds that such works lend credence to these treaties. Unlike the many who assume today the individual mentioned in the bible, the figure of (Genesis 5:24-25) is not accepted as a justifiable source that explains the ideas that had emerged in these non-canonical books. Rather the individual at the center of these writings provides:

> "the occasion for linking these ideas with the person of Enoch. Indeed, the record itself gives evidence of the fact that for the priestly author the name already stood at the centre of definite speculations. We may assume that at the time of writing various traditions in Judaism were already united with the name Enoch. We can only guess at the character and content of these traditions."[ccxxxix]

Though numerous parallels can be drawn between the texts of enoch and both old and New Testament passages, it is a stretch of the imagination to make vigorous doctrinal conclusions from each. Especially it would seem if they attend to an 'end-time.' Some have also suggested Enoch is a figure with some connection to the sun and sun myths.'[ccxl] Enoch, like so many other of the world's mythical figures and gods of high stature is also said to be associated with the Egyptian God –Thoth. Who at some stage in history, like any other demigods had a name change; from the Egyptian - Thoth, to the biblical Hebrew, –enoch. Primarily to suit the region in which he was now revered! Similarities between the histories and occupations of both Thoth and enoch are amazing. Which adds the aplomb necessary to the understanding that the Genesis of Judaism and therefore by association, christianity is plagiaristic of particularly ancient Egyptian magical rites. Yet, still a mystery surrounds the figure of enoch

DECONSTRUCTING ENDTIME DELUSIONS

for many believers. Was Enoch actually an individual? One question rarely earmarked for a satisfactory answer by the religious is: Was Enoch actually an individual. Was he a real person? Lebanese author, Kamal Salibi, in chapter 2 of his book "Secrets of the Bible People", under the subtitle: The Noah People, writes: "...Enoch [is] historically attested as [one] of three tribes of the... region of...Yemen." (p48). Undoubted, this announcement throws a cat among the pigeons. If enoch represents an Arabic tribe, I assume this also launches questions about the validity of any and every Christian hypothesis that has emerged to date surrounding this figure. It must surely change the whole complexity of meaning. Whether this information is known to end–time pundits it obviously has not deterred the emergence of numerous philosophies being projected. Unfortunately, most people are not interested in the Genesis of whom, how, or from where the Bible personalities emerged. Rather, Christian and the generally religious are only concerned about what is assumed to be factual sacred works; those that acknowledge and confirm to the reader presupposed beliefs. In the following pages, I will attend to surveying very briefly only a few passages from both the Old Testament and new testaments, to see whether modern convictions are confirmed. Before we do so, it is also important to grasp the idea that 'enoch' does not belong solely to Judaism, christianity or the dead sea scrolls either. Rather, as another author writes enoch is potentially a construct of Mandaean mythology, which had obviously been poached by Judaism and now also the Christian fundamental religion. Andrew Collins in his book "Ashes to Angels" explains:

> "Mandaean mythology is a confusing mixture of Babylonian, Persian, Judaic and Gnostic Christian traditions, meaning that the origin of specific stories is often impossible to place in a definite time-frame or geographical context. Despite these difficulties...it was from the Mountains of the Madai that their 'first priest', Anush, or Enoch, had originated. Yes, this Enoch was indeed the same antediluvian patriarch found in Judaic tradition...he was venerated in Iraq more than he ever was in Palestine. Yet, to the Arabs, he was known by the name Edris, or Idris – a great Prophet and teacher who had once lived in Iraq...Enoch was very important, for in Azerbaijani tradition [he] was said to have been the teacher of ...the first legendary king of Iran and all the world." (p.148-149, Among the Angels).

The Mandaean sect however claims to this day no kinship with christianity, or the Jewish religion. So where did they originate? D. M. Murdoch offers a learned opinion. In her book "Suns of God", she highlights the hypothesis that this people group: "It appears that this sect migrated from Egypt, through Palestine, and eventually became fused with Indo-Babylonian Oannes-worshippers, demoting the local water God under their own 'demiurge,' Ptahil (Ptah)." (Murdoch, The Mandaeans and Nazoreans.) As stated it appears there is another connection to Egyptian religion. Enoch, and his famed exploits –documented in the so-called books of enoch - which seem to have originated in the lands and mountains of Iraq/Iran/or the Afghan highlands; the lands of ancient Egypt. Not in Palestine as many Jewish and Christian dead sea scroll apologists would assert. From where and why do countless believers today insist that the figure of enoch, has some claim to an end time/ Apocalypse, rapture scenario? Does the modern bible actually claim this, or is it again another prosthetic memory? Our survey begins with the New Testament. In the New Testament texts we find there are only three occurrences mentioning enoch; one in each; luke 3:37; hebrews 11:5; and jude 14. The Old Testament meanwhile has only 14 occurrences in 13 verses in its entirety. All occurrences but one (1 chronicles 1:3) are found in Genesis 4:17 – 5:24! Of the New Testament verses mentioned, only the latter two give the impression or resemble the man that disappeared. As is often thought about Genesis 5:24. Yet, Genesis 5:24 does not hint of any disappearing. The English Standard Version plainly states: "Enoch walked with God, and he was not, for God took him."[ccxli] We will get to this verse shortly. Luke's enoch is connected somehow to the genealogy of the nemo-deity man, Jesus. Yet, as the TDNTA explains below this seems likely to be in opposition to any tradition of ascension, as that would announce him (enoch) as an exalted 'son of man.'[ccxlii] But, what could be a problem with enoch being an exulted son of man? Christianity itself reveres the apparent male Jesus as an exulted 'son'. But, this only occurred three hundred or so years after the apparent death of this individual. Jesus was only deified in the 'fourth Century C.E.'. That is precisely 325 years after the supposed fact. Before the Nicene council convened in 325C.E. believers would have found it anathema to even entertain Jesus being a God-man, – provided he existed! It is amazing that the 'holy' Roman Catholic Church to this day presumes to wield the 'power' to deify mortals. Pope John Paul II who has only been deceased for a decade or so (at this writing), is well on the way of receiving a saintly knighthood! He is on the way to be deified as saint! Ridiculous to say the least. But this is another story. Paul, alleged author of the epistle to the 'hebrews' mentions enoch to the tradition of 'faith'; while jude seats him as adversative to the emergence of all blasphemous

> "...persons [who] blaspheme all that they do not understand, and all that they understand by instinct like the irrational animals, by these things they are being destroyed. Woe to them! For they have traveled in the way of Cain and have given themselves up to the error of Balaam for gain and have perished in the rebellion of Korah."[ccxliii]

He further warns, "These people are grumblers, discontented, proceeding according to their desires, and their mouths speaking pompous words, [showing partiality to gain an advantage]."[ccxliv] Undoubtedly, jude's thoughts closely resemble how some today insist on exploiting various enoch ideas. Particularly his anomalous departure. What can only be described also as blaspheming what is unknown so as to show partiality for gain? Many enoch traditions are also recognised in various other extra-biblical texts. For instance, in Ecclesiasticus or The Wisdom of Jesus Son of Sirach. Sirach for short. Below we see a slight discrepancy when compared with (Genesis 5:24 as translated by the ESV):

> "Enoch pleased the Lord and was taken up, an example of repentance to all generations."[ccxlv]

Compare this esv translation with this NRSV verse from the Apocryphal book of Sirach. Scholars as on the most important of the apocryphal texts affirm Sirach. A text originally they concur, was penned in Hebrew in 180 B.C.E., but unfortunately now only survives as a Greek translation (circa 132 B.C.E.). Sirach is attested as a work of wisdom and proverb that many scholars also suppose on occasion, approaches the high level of gospel. It is also essentially celebrated as a primitive form of Sadduceeism. If while reading Sirach and coming across this reference to an enoch figure, would you wonder what the author may be alluding to in this verse? Particularly that enoch here too is apparently 'taken up'! Could it be similar, or is it different to what was outlined earlier: when we briefly looked at (matthew 24:41f) above, where we found the matthean author describing one person being taken, and the other evidently left behind? To assist English only readers with understanding the Greek language that lay behind the English of this apocryphal book, is the powerful electronic resource again offered by Logos Bible Systems; Logos' powerful reverse-interlinear capabilities of the nrsv Apocryphal texts are now also available to interested students of the sacred books.[ccxlvi] Readers may recall the specific Greek word earlier reviewed as 'taken' was paralambano. Paralambano, we found out essentially meant to be accepted into the kingdom; that's the meaning we found in (matthew 24:41.) Using the reverse-interlinear capabilities of Sirach, readers can see however that the author of Sirach uses a totally different Greek term; a term we find not only in the Septuagint. The author of Sirach uses metatithemi to denote enoch being 'taken up' by Yahweh.[ccxlvii] I wonder if 'Up' here could or is misconstrued to mean disappear, as into the heavens (the Sky – the realm of the gods). Yet, neither a new nor any Old Testament 'enochic' text actually supplies readers with unmitigated confirmation that any type of disappearing rapture/ carrying away happened! The closest we get to that idea comes from a biased arcane reading into another favoured New Testament passage (hebrews 11:5); thus, those predisposed to this ideology all too happily subscribe to the conviction that enoch's not 'seeing/or experiencing' death; meant he was raptured. That this fellow disappeared in to the sky realm. Again I draw readers' attention to the previous Nail where it was discovered that such an idea of a sky realm disappearance 'rapture' is totally unfounded in the sacred books. To insist on such an idea simply opens a wider range of other study opportunities. What does it mean to not experience or see death? What is meant by death, and how might the two relate? Furthermore, what does the author of the Sirach passage mean when he says that enoch is an example of repentance for all generations? I'll leave such questions for the reader to muse in their own time. Each no doubt could require a separate book itself. Returning however to our task at hand. We found out with the assistance of the reverse-interlinear capabilities of Logos, that the word Sirach used, translated as 'taken [up]' is: Metatithemi. Metatithemi: is the Greek word behind our English term 'taken [up]' in the above passage of Sirach. Interestingly, the verb form in this passage is found in the nrsv (14x) fourteen times. Mainly in the other apocryphal passages, but not only so. Six of the fourteen we find it variously translated throughout the New Testament across all popular English Bible translations. But what does it mean? To assist us let us draw on the entry in the "Theological Dictionary", little kittel (TDNTA):

metatíthēmi, metáthesis.

- In secular Greek the verb means to bring to, or set in, another place, to alter, and middle, to change over. The noun means change of place, alteration, or change of mind.

- The LXX removing boundaries, transplanting peoples, or translating from the earth, as well as for convincing or talking around. The noun denotes transition to Greek custom in 2 Macc. 11:24.

- a. In the NT the verb means to carry to in Acts 7:16, to take up in Heb. 11:5 (Enoch), to transform in Jude 4, to be done away in Heb. 7:12, to fall away in Gal. 1:6. b. The noun is used for Enoch's translation in Heb. 11:5, the alteration of the law in 7:12, and the metamorphosis of shaken creation in 12:27.

- The apostolic fathers use only the verb (cf. the local sense in Barn. 13:5, Enoch's translation in 1 Clem. 9.3, and changing one's mind in Mart. Pol. 11.1.)[ccxlviii]

Unless mistaken, point two, or possibly point four are of most interest. Either being probably the viable explanation for this verb in context. We find also that it may go some way to explaining what happened to this highly regarded fellow of Old Testament myth. It appears to carry a similar meaning and sense to what was discovered in Matthew above. Pending one's understanding of translate, would possibly render a different reason also. Word meanings of sacred texts are difficult to attain. Especially when the English translations are, the only one read. As stated earlier, we have a tendency to concoct meanings from a modern perspective. Most likely then, the meanings we ascribe to certain themes and passages do not align with possibly what was an originating meaning. As today, we know instinctively that words they cannot be derived solely in isolation. The surrounding phrases and individual words and greater context must also be somehow accounted. The broader context surrounding the verse of Sirach is. It is the first of a hymn; a hymn in honour of six Hebrew ancestors; enoch, abraham, Moses, noah, and isaac and jacob. Sirach (44:1) begins:

> "Let us now praise famous men, and our fathers in their generations..."[ccxlix]

So the over arching context of this chapter of Sirach is to remind readers of the patriarchs and those held in high esteem. An interpretation then of the rest of the chapter, should then need the fame or esteem of those people. Let us now look briefly at the words 'translate and repentance.' A simple clarification to translate is either: to grasp, to convert, or to transform. Yet, this hardly explains sufficiently what might have happened to the fellow enoch. These also do not explain to where, or even why he is thought to have suddenly vanished and was neither seen or heard any longer. Provided that is what the writer is attempting to convey to his readership. Ultimate, and satisfactory answers however may never be found. All the same, whatever assumption is made I am not convinced enoch's 'taking up' complies with the whimsical notion that he vanished. That is. He disappeared into some ethereal realm, the realm of some sky deity! Surely not as modern dispensationalists would have many believe. Why? Briefly, the meaning behind another term: metanoia (repentance) as it is used in the Sirach 44:16 passage. Relative to enoch,

DECONSTRUCTING ENDTIME DELUSIONS

the Old Testament corpus and its New Testament idiom, metanoia essentially holds a

> "...basic meaning, [to] "change opinions, regret, be grieved about something," but [is] used almost exclusively for the attitude of unbelievers and sinners returning to God,♦[ccl] and they are laden with a new theological density; they form an essential part of the kerygma♦[ccli] lexicon, urging "conversion" to Christianity. There is no longer any question of distinguishing between change of thoughts, of heart, of actions. The change is that of the soul, of the whole person (the new creature), who is purified of stains and whose life is transformed, metamorphosed."[cclii]

Enoch, if an actual and real person I assume then, maybe had an epiphany; maybe it was conversion, or even a deconversion experience. The hint from the text is plain enough- the bloke enoch was known by the author of Sirach for instance of repentance to all generations! Maybe he reverted to a former belief system- and it was that which afforded him; the prestige of being known as the example of repentance for all generations? This would I think to fit with the metaphysical meaning offered at the beginning of this Nail. Nonetheless, to what the epiphany was we can only guess. Enoch texts seem to hint. It was epiphany of God. But which God? Modern scholarship and study have opened the ancient world, making it accessible to all who would desire knowledge. The regions of all bible stories, including those of apocryphal books were peppered with any amount of religious fervour. We know now the Greeks had their Pantheon of deities and the Romans theirs. Egypt also had a massive pantheon, and no doubts did the peoples of ancient Arabia, Iran, and the whole of the Mediterranean. Which is to say, it would be difficult to think surrounding regions and their religions and mythic tales didn't at least have a minor acquaintance and influence upon the Jewish writers of the books of enoch. Further, readers might be surprised to know the passage under scrutiny adds intrigue to my question about which deity. The Hebrew word translated God in the English text is again, Elohim. As earlier attributed, Elohim is the generic plural form of God. Thus, is more accurately gods. So, the gods took enoch. It was not as many presume. That Yahweh, the assumed singular supreme deity of Israel who took this action! Unfortunately, still, not even this explains where enoch is said to have disappeared. Again, it seems to me. The whole passage of Sirach does not remotely explain a 'rapture/ disappearance' incident. Rather, we can deduce that the fellow this myth is based upon had some 'changing of former opinions.' After which one can only speculate, he took leave and was no longer seen nor heard from again. Enoch –if he actually existed – as far as I am concerned, cannot logically be thought of as a 'disappearing rapture' figure. This is a completely crazy musing offered by an indoctrinated mind with a prosthetic memory of something that quite probably and logically did not, will not, and cannot happen. Only those who have not done at least some minor work to test a predisposed theory when it comes to certain personalities of their sacred books could conclude otherwise. This then is a very brief excursion into one passage citing the personality enoch. Delving any deeper would further require additional investigation; of book length itself so we will not attend such. Though, the above detour allows readers to see and think a little differently about a passage often presumed to be absolute. No enoch passage; whether it is Genesis 5, Sirach 44, or any of the New Testament passages often cited, allows the accepted rapture hypothesis legitimate or enduring life. Many enoch traditions as with copious other sacred myths and legends however recount moral stories. They often are moral metaphors that the originating audience most likely understood. Besides, the books of enoch exploit are with the wider community of people. Not with a single fella called enoch. It's how they reacted to his 'preaching' of righteousness, and how his transformation into myth occurred. We find themes like this in many other works; like the 'Legends of the Jews' that I feel add to modern guesses surrounding this fellow. We read that:

"On a certain day, while Enoch was giving audience to his followers, an angel appeared and made known unto him that God had resolved to install him as king over the angels in heaven, as until then he had reigned over men. He called together all the inhabitants of the earth and addressed them thus: "I have been summoned to ascend into heaven, and I know not on what day I shall go thither. Therefore, I will

DECONSTRUCTING ENDTIME DELUSIONS

teach you wisdom and righteousness before I go hence." A few days yet Enoch spent among men, and all the time left to him he gave instruction in wisdom, knowledge, God-fearing conduct, and piety, and established law and order, for the regulation of the affairs of men. Then those gathered near him saw a gigantic steed descend from the skies, and they told Enoch of it, who said, "The steed is for me, for the time has come and the day when I leave you, never to be seen again." So, it was. The steed approached Enoch, and he mounted upon its back, all the time instructing the people, exhorting them, enjoining them to serve God and walk in His ways."[cccliii]

Briefly, this passage speaks with enoch preparing for and announcing his departure. We are told throngs of people flocked still to hear him. He taught wisdom, righteousness, piety, and God-fearing conduct... Then a gigantic steed approached and he apparently disappeared into the heavens while still exhorting listeners to heed the deity's instruction. How many horses do we know that fly? How many are of gigantic proportions? I propose this is undoubted hyperbole: an exaggeration. The only steeds/ horses that remotely fit this idea, are mythic:

· The ancient Pegasus is a mythological winged horse.

· The Valkyrie rode winged horses from Asgard to choose souls among the slain in battle to go with them to Valhalla.

· Al-Buraq is a steed who carried Prophet Muhammad.

· Tianma was a winged 'celestial' horse in Chinese folklore.

· A Chollima is a mythical winged horse which originates from the Chinese classics.

· In Islamic tradition, Haizum is the horse of the archangel Gabriel.

· Tulpar is a winged or swift horse in Turkic mythology.

· Ucchisravas is the white winged horse, who comes from the churning of ocean of milk story, in Indian origin, along with the four tusked white color elephant Airavatam, wishing cow Kamadhenu and many more.[ccliv]

The instance of a gigantic steed arriving and whisking the fellow enoch from the crowds is hyperbole. Meant to instil a sense of wonder in the reader no less! In the 'gospels' of the New Testament, the personality Jesus seems to mirror at least some of the thoughts of enoch above for its writers: specifically, at the close of the New Testament 'gospel' writings and at the beginning of the acts of the apostles? While in the text of Revelation a Prophet named john, seems to see the reversal as he watches a related unfolding from within a Sky vision. Where the Jesus figure allegedly descends to earth on the back of another steed. Such descriptions are in my mind another example of christianity's plagiarism and embellishment of much older beliefs and practices. Maybe some of those outlined in Wikipedia above. The texts of enoch and its predecessors are clearly of older composition than the New Testament at least. The written text and modern composition of scripture are clearly an example of the obvious expression of a christianity determined to control what was believed to be subversive pagan/occultist practices; for the sole purpose of incorporating such themes into its believed higher God-given cause. Aside the acknowledgement in an earlier Nail that christianity pilfered and destroyed much of paganism (Nail One); it did also convert numerous other beliefs it saw as profitable. Copious other extra-sacred and historic writings also play on enoch ideas. He is even said to have been the discoverer of Astrology in one text. There is a manuscript called the Wisdom of Solomon, a text that as Sirach above, accepts the idea that enoch was an exceptionally righteous teacher who espoused this virtue to his audience. We also have writings from the Hellenised Jewish historians; Philo, and Josephus. In the early Christian writings of the apostolic fathers, we witness several enoch ideas established. 1 Clement 9:2-3 mentioned by Kittel above records:

DECONSTRUCTING ENDTIME DELUSIONS

"Let us fix our eyes on them that ministered perfectly unto His excellent glory. Let us set before us Enoch, who being found righteous in obedience was translated, and his death was not found."[cclv]

A 'plain' comprehension of this passage might as well have meant that seeing the subject wasn't found in death, why does this specifically have to mean some sort of vanishing act? That he miraculously floated away makes little actual sense. Could the meaning of... 'his death was not found' after dying somewhere. The body of the deceased enoch was not long afterward buried; without markings who was buried and where that burial took place; hence, he wasn't for death! I guess though that is an explanation that isn't 'spiritual' enough. Being too mundane, too human, and too realistic. When digging into a subject like the Bible character enoch we clearly sees there are numerous illusions found in both very early Christian and ancient Jewish manuscripts that come from the pre-and post first Century. Enoch traditions then are nothing new. There are no 'new' ideas postulated by religious writers when they have an end time agendum to fulfil, and so employ the character of enoch to bolster their premise. Not considered often by the religious, is also the fact their scriptures mention more than one personality named enoch. Unfortunately, only a handful of occurrences in the Judaeo-christ books relate specifically to the man who is assumed to have vanished! Still, it is normally only in the vacuum of the vanishing statesman that those selling their wares of rapture and an end time, where enoch becomes the focus. Whoever this story was based on he most surely is not a vanishing statesman. Throughout this Nail so far, I have only shown a few sources that mention enoch. What about the book enoch itself? What does that say? Does the text of the actual book confirm a disappearing vanishing statesman theory? The opening statements of the text of enoch 1:1-9 I anticipate, another wonderfully clear foundation from which to muse further. It reads:

> "The words of the blessing of Enoch, wherewith he blessed the elect and righteous, who will be living in the day of tribulation, when all the wicked and godless are to be removed."

Adding,

> "...not for this generation, but for a remote one which is for to come. Concerning the elect I said and took up my parable concerning them: The Holy Great One will come forth from His dwelling, And the eternal God will tread upon the earth, (even) on Mount Sinai, [And appear from His camp] And appear in the strength of His might from the heaven of heavens. And all shall be smitten with fear, and the Watchers shall quake, And great fear and trembling shall seize them unto the ends of the earth. And the high mountains shall be shaken. And the high hills shall be made low and shall melt like wax before the flame and the earth shall be wholly rent in sunder, And all that is upon the earth shall perish, And there shall be a judgment upon all (men). But with the righteous He will make peace, and will protect the elect, and mercy shall be upon them. And they shall all belong to God, and they shall be prospered, and they shall all be blessed. And He will help them all, And light shall appear unto them, And He will make peace with them. And behold! He cometh with ten thousands of His holy ones. To execute judgment upon all, And to destroy all the ungodly: And to convict all flesh Of all the works of their ungodliness which they have ungodly committed And of all the hard things which ungodly sinners have spoken against Him."[cclvi]

It is interesting that clearly the understanding of the original author(s) to the 'book' of enoch is some presumed future tribulation period. But, notice whom the tribulation affects; it is stated clearly the wicked and godless are removed. None of the 'elect'. The elect is said to be 'blessed' during this time. But, the blessing does not seem to be as a disappearing act— a 'rapture'. Rather, the deity will apparently somehow assist, or 'support' them. Might modern ideas surrounding a 'tribulation' and rapture derive from a complete misunderstanding, misinterpretation and misapplication of these first verses of enoch 'chapter 1'? We might also deduce from the spattering of texts of the 'Church Fathers' that translation, removal, or protection of the godly is very much dependent upon 'righteousness;' a prominent theme I have stated that is in many enoch traditions. Besides the above texts, the enoch writers seem to also display a great hatred of anyone who doesn't follow a particular brand of religion. That's familiar ground. What has changed in our day? Christianity often threatens the mythical 'eternal damnation of hell' upon those that refuse to comply with its doctrines and beliefs. But, who the hell is the wicked. Those who apparently are removed. Why does it also seem that despite what religionists, the principal deity is partial in the treatment of certain peoples! The elect, according to enoch, are the one's who will be somehow supernaturally protected. Maybe in similar fashion to another Old Testament personality. I refer your thinking to the tribe of cain (Genesis 4:15). In that story, we are told cain had a protective (but indeterminate) seal placed upon his forehead. If such an indeterminate 'protective seal' were placed upon the forehead, –how the hell did anyone know about it? Especially to mention it in the text? Indeterminate = vague, unspecified, unstated! It is illogical to assume an ability to mention an unmentionable indeterminate thing. That is a non-sequitur. Also, notice carefully that in other apocryphal accounts, those from accepted canonised scripture; that there are in many enoch traditions several similarities with them. The elect is said to be sealed, sanctified and assuredly mystically protected. Stevie Wonder once wrote a tune to this effect; signed, sealed, and delivered! I wonder if he had any of these passages in mind when he wrote that song? What's more, if enoch represents a 'rapture' that is surely to occur during, before, or sometime after a tribulation period, why then does the Revelation read and other similar passages the supposed command of the deity: "Do not damage the earth or the sea or the trees, until we have marked the servants of our God with a seal on their heads."[cclvii] Corresponding to (Revelation 6:6; 9:4; 14:1; 22:4; ezekiel 3:8,9; 9:4). Such ideas and statements seem to run completely counter to the modern Christian ideal of rapture at some stage during devastating tribulations! Unless, readers are prepared to view these as all symbolic, not literal! Still, as already mentioned numerous times, many Christian teachers, and preachers today insist there is a secreted removal of God's elects (which obviously includes them) sometime prior, during, or after the immediate return of the Messiah. A sure prosthetic memory taught through the ages. Think on this a moment: If there was to be rapture as is so often proposed by fundamental believers, and the enoch of Genesis 5 accounts for it, one that takes place as an act has done in complete secrecy (for, he was 'taken' mysteriously. Nobody knew to where he'd gone (Genesis 5:24); why would there be reappearing at a later stage in Earth history? What would be such a disappearing, or reappearance act? Would those who reappeared be returning to hostile ground? The whole disappearing of certain people, and then a miraculous reappearance is unconscionable. An idea that makes no sense. But back to the book of enoch.

From the opening verses of the account of the book, we can clearly deduce that the principal figure looks to be a compassionate, and prophetic voice of reason for repentance. Astoundingly, this is often overlooked or ignored by many contemporary writers with leanings to explaining the validity of 'rapture'. I accept Alexander Whyte however. His summations below are blisteringly correct in his estimation about the importance of this esoteric, extra-sacred literature - The Book of Enoch. In that –it isn't! For the ordinary lay-believer, such a work holds no worth in study. For the religious scholar, he says it may be argued there is some minor merit. Yet, the unearthing of such merit is a most arduous task. Indisputably Whyte's musings are worthy of anyone's attention: esp., for those who would assume or wish to concentrate their efforts on using these materials for an end-time scenario. I can only hope such persons come to one day realise they have imposed upon the rest of us disappointments, and all have employed deception. Whyte writes that no one who has ever seen or comes across this esoteric text can deny that the personality it espouses, 'ever saw' the actual book itself. If there were an individual who went by the name enoch, he could not have penned a single word, phrase, or any of the one hundred other pages (chapters) of this composition. Rather, the 'book of enoch' is an inflated text of pure fantasy. So,

> "...unless you are a Bible scholar, and are able to get good out of a book that returns but a far-off echo of your Bible, you will spend your time and your money far better than by spending either on The Book of Enoch..."[cclviii]

A contemporary scholar seems to confirm.

DECONSTRUCTING ENDTIME DELUSIONS

> "The remarkable development of Enoch was carried out during the Second Temple period by a group of faithful oppressed Jews. Like their predecessors...they did not belong to the orthodox wing of Judaism, a negative correlation that should probably be seen as fundamental to the development of their only specific identity factor. They found him in scripture, and implied by a longstanding and widespread tradition. This led them to put him forward as the agent of their imminent vindication by God, a change of perception primarily due to the needs of a grievously oppressed community."[cclix]

It would seem the very same sentiments play upon the minds of modern writers who assume to use this material to bolster their end time predictions. Whyte again elegantly summarises the message that he believed at the time; the message the deity would have all people come away with after reading those explosive words - Enoch walked with God - and was no more, because God took him. The gist and lie are that this fellow never died, which cannot be factual as reality states all people die. Everyone we know will eventually die- that is a fact, whether acknowledged or not. Hence, the failure of this revered text is perfectly summarised again by Whyte. When he finally sat to read the text, he realised the book of enoch did not offer any of the supposed wonders attributed to this ancient book. Rather, within its pages was found a plethora of 'mystical' and strangely frightening entities. Whyte writes that

> "...when I made an effort and got the book, what was I in every chapter introduced to and made to walk with, but cherubim and seraphim, principalities and powers, angels and devils, seven holy ones, and four holy ones, and three holy ones; behemoth and leviathan; wild camels, wild boars, wild dogs; eagles and elephants and foxes; giant men and siren women—till I rose up and put Enoch in my shelf and took down William Law..."[cclx]

William Law was an English devotional writer, controversialist and mystic (1686-1761). He wrote works on practical piety that is considered among the classics of English theology. Whyte believed that more gain would be had if people 'devoted' themselves to a digestion of the works of William Law instead of postulating over the texts of enoch! I tend to agree.

Possibly however are connections to the fellow enoch and a few statements allegedly authored by another fellow, paul. Seeing not just a few people revere enoch, might a similar message be anticipated and desired in a similar fashion for readers and hearers to heed? With vigour and understanding such might have driven paul to urge his readers to attain a full measure–like enoch of old. Walk as children of the Light... he admonished (ephesians 5:8). But alas, few dare to subscribe completely to such an attainment. Surely partly, this could also be his reasoning behind a philippians passage. Where the alleged author, paul clearly shows a problem forming in his mind in this passage. He's in two minds. For him questions whether it is of any real benefit to remain alive, or whether death is the more advantageous? On the one hand he apparently believes death is better; person permanence has kicked in here. Believing his deity-man is somewhere, doing something. Carrying out a semi-aliveness in another realm. Then, we see a hesitation. Life though is eventually, what he recommends (philippians 1:20-24). Are these the musing of one suffering schizophrenia? No wonder christians have a weird concept of rapture. Being but the psychological outgrowth and effect of Person Permanence. How much reasonable sense does these sentiments really offer readers? Think a moment: How does one walk as 'light'? Just as is admonished in the ephesian passage. How do you walk as something intangible like light? Further, why are these and other like verses taught as metaphor, when others are clearly taught as happening? According to paul's passages, believers should represent their God ('walk as light') to the wider community. Does that then mean they too display the qualities of that deity? Seen in the Judaeo-Christian books: who is surely not much else than a Stalinistic-Hitlerian deity, preferring to fulfil his own whim, – i.e., to frighten others into a life of "purity" – over behaving humanely? Seems many nefarious qualities come quite naturally to all people. You don't necessarily need to 'be' an enthusiastic religious person to harbour any nefarious quality (See Nail One).

Knowing I have only drawn upon a tiny fraction of 'enochic' material the point was not to assess or evaluate fully any of it. Rather, the hope was to direct thoughts to the many enoch traditions with the credenda proposed by early theologians. Those that lay-believers in the Judaeo-Christian tradition likely are aware. The enoch of Genesis 5 who is among a list of antediluvian 'patriarchs' is unfortunately, a source for many whom advocate him experiencing 'rapture' vacation. Based solely on very whimsical and rash decisions regarding an interpretation of the phrase: 'God took him, and he was no more.' Leading a reader, as if by rote, to automatically assume this myth is solid ground for a disappearance act, a 'rapture (vanishing into thin air) of the saints.' Not so. If indeed previous Nails, Five, Six and Seven above, are accounted as correct and more sensible. Namely, 'rapture' does not mean, and never has meant a mysterious flying escape for an elite class of people. Rather, is again a very earthly and emotional change in one's demeanour. No more, no less.

A cataclysmic liquidation:

THE OPENING CHAPTERS of Genesis describe a major disaster. One that occurred in pre-history. An incredibly devastating global flood which wiped all but a handful lives out. This episode; incidentally, parallels many more and earlier creation compositions; i.e., The Enuma Elish– The Babylonian Creation Epic is one example. Irving Finkle's study, "The Ark before Noah" is a fascinating work that opens readers to the fact such disastrous occurrences were widely known and disseminated throughout ancient cultures. Such a cataclysmic instance may also share life with one other tale that to this day, still draws the attention of numerous writers and investigators of mysteries. A place called <Atlantis>. Recent scientific and scholarly sources propose a land mass named Atlantis may have been a factual island. British writer and journalist Graham Hancock, specialises in unconventional theories involving ancient civilisations, confirms this idea in the opening statements of one email posting: quoting a senior Indonesian geologist he wrote:

"Everything we've been taught about the origins of civilization may be wrong," says Danny Natawidjaja, PhD, senior geologist with the Research Centre for Geotechnology at the Indonesian Institute of Sciences. "Old stories about Atlantis and other great lost civilizations (sic) of prehistory, long dismissed as myths by archaeologists, look set to be proved true."[cclxi]

That Atlantis may be proved an island that distantly was destroyed by a massive catastrophe causing widespread flooding, could have been three times the size of Cuba according to some.[cclxii] Other researchers postulate that such a landmass existed in the prediluvian world, and Atlantean descendants were still present during the Holocene epoch.[cclxiii] If indeed true, a cataclysmic occurrence, an inundation of flooding waters must have caused this landmass to sink into the ocean around the time of the closing of the last 'ice-age.' In prehistory, "The Earth cracked, and undulated, and groaned when an intense paroxysm ended the Golden Age."[cclxiv] The magnitude of this devastation (estimated 12,000 – 10,000 years ago) caused a tsunami of massive proportions; there were probably 2-3-mile-high water walls. Possibly higher still. One commentator of this phenomenon offers a possible scenario: "Such a wave would race around the entire water areas of this planet and far up rivers and deep into the lower areas of the surface of the Earth. Only very high mountain areas might be immune. Every single community along every river delta would have been destroyed, setting civilization (sic) back thousands of years."[cclxv] Accordingly, Atlantis suffered a seismic disaster and thus, was engulfed by the ocean which 'controversially' swallowed up the earth, and wiping out all of that civilisation. As was intimated earlier with the controversies surrounding the where of Sodom and gomorrah, there are proposals that if Atlantis is to be found, more extensive analysis needs to be conducted under oceanic waters in regions likely to have been dismissed by established science and 'histories,' or those not considered earlier. According to Walter Parks, Plato, who many believe initially concocted the Atlantis myth, was not the first to document musings about it. Parks writes, "We have found a very much earlier document. It was written in 9619B.C.

DECONSTRUCTING ENDTIME DELUSIONS

approximately 9,250 years before Plato's writing. This ancient document is believed to be the oldest document that has survived almost intact down through the ages." (Parks, "Atlantis the Eyewitnesses", book 1, Chapter 1, Introduction.). Theories abound whether Atlantis is, or not, real. Every theory proposed however is contrary to another. Even if not a real, stone and earth city-state of antiquity, why can this story not be read and understood as a warning to the ancients, of the devastating effects of moral disintegration? Just as Plato most surely formulated it for his audiences. Plato's inference to Atlantis is a moralistic story. As with his former title –The Republic, in which he does appeal to the forming of a moralistic society. "Fad's and Fallacies" author, Martin Gardiner hits back at the raft of literature that continues to proliferate on this subject:

> "Although geologists agree that in remote ages the arrangements of the land and sea were quite different from [today], there is unanimous agreement that no great continental sinking's have occurred within the relatively brief time man has been on the scene. There is in fact, not a shred of evidence, geological or archaeological, to support the... myth of Atlantis..." Following with the conclusion that, "... it is safe to say that speculations about Atlantis...will occupy the minds of pseudo-archaeologists for many decades to come. Until the last square mile of the oceans' depths is fully explored..." (Chapter 14: Atlantis and Lemuria.)

Atlantis aside, the Judaeo-Christian flood narrative account undoubtedly derives from ancient Sumerian/ Akkadian accounts of a regional destructive flooding of the Tigris and Euphrates River systems, about 3,200 B.C and covered 40thousand square mile of Sumerian villages with eight feet of clay and rubble. Causing widespread death, and a collapse of that civilisation. The book Hebrew Myth offers a potential zero-point. A 'potential' beginning to how and from where such a deluge tale emerged. To find its way into Judaeo-Christian lore: "Two ancient myths parallel the Genesis Deluge: one Greek, one Akkadian. The Akkadian, found in the Gilgamesh Epic, was current also among the Sumerians, the Hurrians and the Hittites. In it the hero Utnapishtim is warned by Ea, God of Wisdom, that the other gods led by Enlil, the Creator, have planned a universal deluge, and that he must build an ark. Enlil's reason for wiping out mankind seems to have been their omission of his New Year sacrifices. Utnapishtim builds a six-decked ark in the shape of an exact cube, with sides of one hundred and twenty cubits, and uses bitumen to caulk it. The ark is completed in seven days,

Utnapishtim having meanwhile given his workmen 'wine to drink, like rain, so that they might feast in the style of New Year's day.' When a blighting rain begins to fall, he, his family, craftsmen and attendants bearing his treasures, besides numerous beasts and birds, enter the ark. Utnapishtim's boatman then batten down the hatches..."

Further,

"The Genesis [flood] myth is composed, it seems, of at least three distinct elements. First, historical memory of a cloudburst in the Armenian mountains which, according to Woolley's Ur of the Chaldees, flooded the Tigris and Euphrates about 3200 B.C.—covering Sumerian villages over an area of 40thousand square miles with eight feet of clay and rubble. Only a few cities perched high on their mounds, and protected by brick walls, escaped destruction."

A second element is the autumnal New Year vintage feast of Babylonia, Syria and Palestine, where the ark was a crescent-shaped moon-ship containing sacrificial animals. This feast was celebrated at the New Moon nearest the autumnal equinox with libations of new wine to encourage the winter rains...[cclxvi] While the third surrounds numerous accounts of 'the Ark' being discovered on Mount Ararat – "Mount Judi near Lake Van'–are mentioned by Josephus who quotes Berossus and other historians; Berossus had written that the local Kurds still chipped pieces of bitumen from it for use as amulets." (ibid. p 117.) Realistically, the flood narrative of Genesis is noway unique. It cannot be a narrative dictated to an elderly fellow by an ethereal entity. It is one of many such narratives from the surrounding region as one of countless flood narratives around the world. In the title "Forbidden History" (Edited by Douglas Kenyon) the authors of the essay 'Cataclysm! Compelling Evidence of a Cosmic Catastrophe in 9500B.C'. D. S. Allan and J. B. Delair are said to have collected a "...formidable quantity of known evidence corroborating the flood/conflagration legends stored in the world's mythological record..." (Forbidden History, Chapter 10: The Enigma of India's Origins.) That there is extensive evidence of a disastrous flood event occurring in prehistory does not necessarily warrant a belief that all/ or most details as recorded in the

DECONSTRUCTING ENDTIME DELUSIONS

Judaeo-Christian sacred book, are not significantly circumstantial. There are simply numerous 'massive flood' accounts found throughout the world. Most important of all the flood stories is the Babylonian account. Interest in it rises because it comes from the same Semitic context and the same geographical area as the Genesis narrative, and because it is similar to the Genesis account in so many ways. The Babylonian flood story was part of the library of King Ashurbanipal of Assyria (in 1853 and 1873. The story was on the eleventh tablet of a twelve-tablet piece entitled the Gilgamesh Epic, an account of Gilgamesh's search for immortality. In the eleventh tablet Gilgamesh (king of Uruk, biblical Erech) interviewed Utnapishtim, the "Babylonian Noah," and learned from him the story of the flood and his securing of immortality. Fragment of Tablet XI of the Gilgamesh Epic (the Babylonian flood account) written in Assyrian cuneiform.[cclxvii] This tablet details the building of the ship, the storm, and the landing on Mt. Niir (Trustees of the British Museum).

Of all sacred stories, the Judaeo-Christian 'flood' is undoubtedly one of the most popular. Trumping the early mentioned Akkadian story of the flood, written in Mesopotamia about 1,600 B.C. and known as the Atra-asis Epic, and the Sumerian version of the Babylonian flood story in its popularity.[cclxviii] Although a literal occurrence in ancient history T. D. Alexander reminds us: "If we are to properly understand sacred stories we must be willing to step beyond the literal interpretation and embrace the allegorical interpretation, for the literal interpretation is but the uppermost layer of truth, the milk. The allegorical interpretations are the meat of Scripture and myth." (Ancient Secrets, Ch. Three). Unfortunately, countless christians still unashamedly believe in the literalness of the sacred flood myth. They are only partaking of the 'milk' – the weakest of all interpretations. The meat of the flood narrative of the Judaeo-Christian books is yet to be discovered. Any of which could be one or all the following:

"...as a physical event; as a symbol of the cycle of destruction and regeneration; as baptism of the world; as a physiological process; as a psychological process; or, as a celestial occurrence, or a veil."[cclxix]

I do think that the sacred flood story is pure and simple allegory and should not be assumed to be literal. Despite, numerous accounts of devastating floods wreaking havoc in ancient times in the regions where bible narrative is assumed to have been written. The elect of the Bible tale (Moses, and family) also, may or not have been real people. Likely not, but represent symbolically tribes who 'survived' a massive flooding event. The biblical record being doctored accounts derived from story's of the devastation and survival of persons, invented for posterity sake! Much like a biography of a famous personality or history text today. Surviving characters went through tribulations and turbulences of floods and a host of other cataclysms along with everyone else, – the only difference is their legends and stories survived to our day as the myths of the Judaeo-Christian books. However, if the 'flood account' recorded in the sacred book transmits a factual occurrence as is still believed by many, how did noah and family save 2 or 7 of each 'animal' life? Considering the depictions of the ark to the modern equivalent! Modern civilisation has and continues to build vessels that would dwarf the assumed ark of the Bible. The ark depicted in any typical Christian graphic is completely incorrect. According to the research of the curator of the largest collection of Ancient Cuneiform Tablets at the British Museum in London, Dr. Irving Finkel. The christianised depiction of 'the ark'. Is undoubtedly an ill-informed illustration compiled by modern believers.[cclxx] Not as one ancient cuneiform tablet depicts where; on a 4000-year-old Tablet text describing another Babylonian deluge sequence, the principal character of the story is instructed by the gods to construct an Ark that was to be circular.[cclxxi] Aside not being circular, as it is portrayed in similar ancient texts there is several other oddities in the illustration. The vessel portrayed is for instance, an incredibly small vessel I would have thought to accommodate a pair of every living creature on Planet earth: with appropriate supplies and provision for over 6months floating around the globe. Even if the animals had gathered were essentially directly, and of the immediate localised region. It is rather like a very large dingy. Or, at the most, an oversized 'life raft' of the QE2! If the flood story as depicted in Church-sponsored books is literal, as many believers seem to understand, here are some questions and comments that every Christian should ponder: "The Ark's Biblical dimensions contravene the principles of shipbuilding: a wholly wooden three-decker 450 feet long would have broken up in even a slight swell. The timber used by Noah was not necessarily cedar, as most scholars hold, 'gopher-wood' being elsewhere unknown. It may have been acacia, the timber of Osiris's funeral boat." (Graves, p.118.) It is also worth considering:

- It is interesting to see that when the birth narrative of noah in the Bible and the parallel narrative in the book of Enoch (Noah Apocalypse) is read consecutively, there seems to emerge a startling enigma. There is a whim that noah was conceived of a 'Watcher.' Born in the likeness of a nephilim. See (Genesis 5:28-31) and parallel expansion to the birth of noah, enoch 106:1-2. Clearly the newborn noah - does not have the same form as any of his direct relatives. As Andrew Collins narrates, "His appearance is entirely unlike other 'human beings', for his skin is white and ruddy, his long curly hair is white and beautiful, while his eyes mysteriously enable the whole house to 'glow like the sun.'" (Ch. 1, p1: "From the Ashes of Angels"). Lamech, afraid of this crazy event fled to his father, Methuselah: "And he said unto him: 'I have begotten a strange son, diverse from and unlike man, and resembling the sons of the God of heaven; and his nature is different, and he is not like us, and his eyes are as the rays of the sun, and his countenance is glorious. And it seems to me that he is not sprung from me but from the angels, and I fear that in his days a wonder may be wrought on the earth." Albeit, this fragment is recognised as falsely attributed, if noah is ascribed as being in appearance of a nephilim who develops in the very next chapter of the Bible. Why did the deity choose to save this individual nephilim? This doesn't make reasonable sense. How could noah find favour in the sight of the Lord if he were one of the nephilim whom, many postulate, were the offspring of the cause to human wickedness (the Watchers/nephilim) and so, the Cataclysm.

- Furthermore, why doesn't noah complain bitterly with his deity, that 'he' has the wrong priority, saving only eight persons and hordes of animals – all 1.5 million species, including I imagine, the 400 or so known to kill humans? What were God's reasoning here - that animals are more commendable of salvation than humans? Though the sacred book seems to affirm that the apex of creation were humans! No wonder today there is organisations like p.e.t.a. Who, though I agree every creature must be treated ethically; p.e.t.a. goes one step further, discouraging animal products as a valid food and clothing source. p.e.t.a.' s website banner for instance reads: "Animals are not ours to eat, wear, experiment on, use for entertainment, or abuse in any other way." I wonder how grass/flax overalls, underwear, socks, shoes, shirts etc. would fair in frigid or extremely hot and humid regions. Surely, to wear such materials would become a health risk, of say, severe chaffing, fire, or frostbite? Further, readers of this story must recognise that in the entire flood narrative neither noah, his wife, nor the other six persons on board the vessel ever speaks! There are no conversations between the assumed deity and those it chose to save. The silence is deafening.

- So, a God called for the salvation of a multitude of animal's - what does this say to our continued assumption that humanity is the pinnacle of the deity's creative prowess? Humans make up <1% of created life on planet Earth! (Not to mention, humans are responsible for no less than 85% of the extinction of other life forms on Earth). Further, what does one do with all the waste products generated by those on the ark? How was sanitation accommodated? Surely, there was a 'poupe' deck and animals were trained to use it (no relation to the French - la poupe – the original meaning and usage.) Surely two, or even seven pairs of dung beetle would struggle too to adequately clean up waste we all generate. What about stale and fresh foodstuffs?

- Why in the hell did deity suddenly not approve of its creation? The same created entity made in its own image, the image that deity was all too happy to declare (it is assumed) as good also, or even very good. If deity is very good, it wouldn't fail to create anything in its own image as also very good! Thus, the conundrum: didn't the all-knowing deity know in advance that the creature made in its very own image, would one day become corrupt. A side the deity must also possess.

- What of seasickness pills? Did noah suddenly have to run off to a prototype of the "Chemist Warehouse' before it too was liquidated? (pun intended.) Seasickness would have been a prominent feature. The Levant population of this time period is described as living in a dry and desolate landscape and so; I doubt they would have experienced much via seafaring adventure.

DECONSTRUCTING ENDTIME DELUSIONS

- Like the statement above, why did this so-called benevolent deity order noah to 'save' animals only? I am aware the text says all humanity was corrupt, but it seems as though this deity is a spoilt child with an extremely bad attitude – who if he doesn't get his own way, deliberately destroys everything. Calls into question again the opinion that humanity was the pinnacle of his creative prowess, and again, doesn't the deity also possess a corrupt nature? After all, to be made in deity's very likeness is to also have its counter intuitiveness.

- Where was the storage of fresh water, exercise yard/pens, etc. and how did noah and Co segregate animal species so they did not devour each other, or themselves and become extinct? 'Live Animal Exportation' regulators would have a field day! This is after all; the first mentioned 'Live Animal Exportation' Pty. Ltd. the world had ever seen, is it not? What about the entertainment? How did crew and animal alike curb boredom, or the temptation to 'eat' each-other? Did they have a couple of ancient talking-wise-cracking Parrots (Galah's) who could not only tell roaring jokes, but also recite loved ancient stories.

- There is much evidence of a major cataclysmic 'worldwide' flood event. But, why does the alleged ark come to rest upon the top of Mt. Ararat –in Turkey? As some propose there seems to be photographic evidence of an "anomaly...located along an unstable precipice near the edge of the permanent glacial icecap atop Mt. Ararat." This is according to the U.S., defence agency (1995)[cclxxii] Surely though the oceanic currents drift, wind direction would have been fiercely strong to push the vessel a greater distance from where it allegedly began. The story's account is surely 'regional'. Further, presuming the Ark is found atop Ararat, are there any fossil remains present around, or on the mountain itself? Without doubt some, if not all the occupants of the ark found it terribly foreboding and dangerous to descend the mount when they finally disembarked. Nothing died in the stampede to descend? I find this difficult to comprehend. The world's best mountaineers would find this mount a most difficult and torturous task to climb and descend.

- Lastly, but noway the least, how come the deity doesn't seem to have any ethical humane regulations already drawn up, or legally binding guidelines in place before he decided to wipe the slate clean?

To those who insist on such sacred stories as noah and his animal playpen, cruising around the globe for 6months, believing this story is fact and therefore must have occurred as recorded in the text of our modern sacred books, are terribly shortsighted. Sadly, there is much explaining to do. The logistics were surely epic! The scaffolding upon which the Bible narrative and other worldwide 'flood narratives' stand, however, are possibly related to the yet proven accurate: 'Earth crust displacement theory' which; numerous writers are beginning to see as a reason for many of Earth's prehistoric birth pangs and cataclysms.

Nail Nine:

A bad case of cryptozoology - Skiba's Genesis Six experiment:

> Note to readers: This (Nail) chapter traverses numerous subjects. Some of which may seem irrelevant to the topic of end-times. Though it may seem to certain readers, I do not intend this critique to be a chide of Rob Skiba's, or another author's character. Rather, I do reprove numerous postulations; those that were seen to have been birthed through little actual research. This Nail began by critiquing one particular end–time publication that arrived on the scene around 2008. The title; "Babylon Rising: and the first will be last", by Rob Skiba.[cclxxiii]

IT WAS ALVIN KHUN WHO once said: "When we throw away the myth-key we cannot read the history!"[cclxxiv] This is what is observed when scrutinising a new book (2008) by Rob Skiba II. Where Rob has clearly thrown away the 'myth-key' of the assumed Bible chapter he has used as the platform for his book: "Babylon Rising: and the first will be last." Alvin Khun again, illumines best practice of research and study, noting: "...competent research and study has a way of dissolving most of the encrustations that harden in the naive mind." (Shadow... Location 852.) Several ideas Rob proposed I am at pains to verify as remotely scriptural. They just do not offer a reader any enlightening statements. Many of his proposals are simply ideas. They are ideas born from pure guess! Which seems only to again offer readers a bent interpretation of an enigmatic passage of the sacred text; Genesis 6:1–4. Attempting to call it somehow a Bible truth. Skiba's "Genesis Six Experiment (Babylon Rising)" offers us a table set upon the typical fundamentalist believer intrigues and numerous hypothetical inquiries. It must be stated at the beginning that I find Rob disturbingly churns-out some most erroneous, unreasonable, and unstable, and absurd misapplied research. Attacking his subject matter from a predisposed angle that the Judaeo-Christian texts; its stories, anecdotes and fables should be taken as literally as possible. Most unfortunately for Rob and any other author scrutinised in this Nail, is that he and they do noway consider any useful material outside the usual predisposed theological parameter that could have been utilised to inform a perspective. Which then would have also undoubtedly, diminished speculative interjections and offered a readership a well-balanced evaluation. Yet, I do suppose this would have been difficult as any material outside the noted parameter. To do so would have offered an evaluation that opened wide all predispositions to criticism; which undoubtedly would have destroyed any credibility to those initial thoughts and evaluations; specifically, of the favoured passages from which they have drawn their comments. Unfortunately, by the narrowing of material consulted to that which is the usual and accepted 'christianised' baggage. Rob and those who have endorsed his project fall foul to several usual fallacies, aside those mentioned earlier in this study. Every one of us at times falls foul to misapply interpretation. But, this cannot be an excuse for sloppy irrationality. As was stated in the opening pages to this investigation, I am not so much seeking a 'new' and therefore profoundly accurate understanding of any subject studied. Rather, I seek to offer readers 'new eyes'; possible novel/ unusual ideas that will likely open readers to a different way of seeing and reading their favoured texts with underlying symbolic nuances. To assist in this, I have utilised numerous academic studies and fields of enquiry. The focus of Rob Skiba's book is the nephilim of Genesis, chapter 6, verses one through four. From the start clearly Rob has an agendum and specific bias; that nephilim are of an evil and corrupt lineage and temperament. Are these assumptions in any way justified? Let us find out. In the following pages, the focus will primarily be on critiquing the initial chapter of Robs book. Highlighting just a few of the blaring issues that arose out of examining his statements as I trudged through the book.

> "In Chapter One [Rob writes], we will examine Genesis 6, which is the foundation Scripture... This particular chapter tells us what was going on in the days of Noah and sets the stage for helping us to understand what may happen in the not too distant future..."[cclxxv]

DECONSTRUCTING ENDTIME DELUSIONS

Rob also clearly states his over-arching objective in one of his related blog posts:

> "I seek to understand the times we are living in, to become educated, and to not fall prey to the Coming Great Deception (which is already well underway)..."[cclxxvi]

Clearly Rob has bought into the sense of fear the Church unashamedly peddles. The idea that something is terribly wrong with the world. A doom and gloom outlook of the present and future state of world populations. That there will shortly be a clear and present division of peoples across the globe; some will fall foul to deception; but the elect (Church members primarily), will largely escape this tragic state. Part of his urge to understand the times we are living in. Undoubtedly lead to his writing of the present book under scrutiny, "Babylon Rising: The First will be Last". Openly admitting in the Preface, Rob confesses he is

> "...not a theologian, historian, scientist, or scholar. [Rather, he is] simply a filmmaker who is a Christian that has a passion for research. That said, [he writes] I do not claim to have the corner on truth. I do, however, confess that I have strong, and what I consider to be well-informed opinions. But that's all it is..."[cclxxvii]

Undoubtedly passionate, indeed the case is verified. Unfortunately, Rob is not a very perceptive researcher. Below I show why, and how this is a true statement. Directing attention to where he has made several imprudent, unplanned mistakes. The opinions he draws from his studies, are clearly not all that well informed, or well-thought out. They are rather weak and aqueous and not all that different to any other Christian study. His assertions and arguments lack permanency and do not stray from the 'close-loop' spiritualising of favoured topics. The methodology and his conclusions show a lack in awareness of the variety and depth of scholarly and other materials available. If Rob had consulted a variety of sources (outside the conventional Christian grab) surely hints of them would be present in his work. This would have shown discerned readers Rob did have a well-informed assessment. Alas, no well-informed presentation is offered to readers. One of the major issues that surround his chosen subject matter. Genesis 6:1-4 is a known telling of much older currents; a relaying of more ancient mythic beliefs. This becomes ever more evident by digesting books like "Hebrew Myths". Through this and like books, discerning readers are confronted with the numerous allegories that influenced the redactor of the Genesis 6:1-4 passages. Throughout antiquity this passage and others linked to it; like 1 enoch, Jubilees, or Jasher is still the cause of some of the most diverse, obscure, bazaar and erroneous interpretations. However, I propose and present readers with several different hypotheses in explanation for this episode of Genesis: postulating that the Genesis six account most probably is an interpretation and ingrained memory of ancient/pre-history survival tales surrounding likely; predators, Neanderthals, Cro-Magnon's, Denisovans or another early ancient hominoid, or other people group yet to be discovered. The interactions and tales surrounding violent, menacing and very large (not necessarily large in height) people groups who displayed actions similar to the famed Greek Spartans. The Spartans were recognised as the war-society of Greek antiquity. Not ill-disciplined, but vigorously and well-trained fierce people in battle. The tales of some like people group and their interactions with the early residents; the skhul-quafez (Israel) and later descendants of the Levant that occurred thousands of years ago, circa. 40 – 50k in pre-history, right up to the time of this myths' written record. Hebrew Myth seems to corroborate this in a later commentary. There are numerous books, and scholarly articles currently in the marketplace on this subject matter. Primarily because these verses are considered to be some of the most confusing passages for Old Testament scholarship. No article, or paper, book/ study so far; however, as can be determined, have ever remotely attempted to intertwine the subjects of Genesis 6:1-4 with the fields of study discipline I have sought to utilise. The hope therefore, is despite its length, this is a fascinating journey for all readers.

DECONSTRUCTING ENDTIME DELUSIONS

Babylon Rising - and the first will be last:

AROUND THE PUBLICATION of Skiba's book, there was an increasing cacophony of voices and opinions to the Mayan Calendar, and predictions of the 'end-of-the-world'. It seemed, nearly every Christian author and scholar had a belief and could not wait to announce their latest 'finding.' Rob Skiba seems to be among this crowd. So, because of the interest in Genesis 6 and the surrounding theme of nephilim, and their use as a 'prop' for any end-time scenario by countless Christian authors, I chose to zero in on more than one of Robs assertions. Those I felt begged for attention, particularly those of his first chapter. Reasoning, if this first chapter were to withstand scrutiny, the rest of his book would follow suit. What struck me as I read his treaties was I did not have to venture too far into the book before blaring curiosities and obvious fallacies lured my focus. It was clear that Rob relied heavily on much of the usual and well-worn Christian 'fringe history' surrounding the verses of Genesis 6:1-4. Jason Colavito explains fringe history:

> "Fringe history can be difficult to define but generally refers to the writings of non-specialists that advocate supernatural, extraterrestrial, or conspiratorial explanations for history. These tend to rely on selective evidence and a broad generalization (sic) from a narrow range of evidence to make sweeping claims. These works frequently claim that mainstream historians, archaeologists, or the government are purposely hiding particular historical truths that only the fringe historian is able to discover, usually through appeal to obsolete literature, unusual interpretations of historical documents, or wide-ranging conspiracies. Ronald H. Fritze noted the challenge of defining fringe history, which he calls pseudo-history, and offered this explanation: Objective scholars with an honest agenda view evidence without bias or preconceptions—or at least they try hard to guard against them as far as it is humanly possible. Pseudo-historians usually approach their subjects with preconceptions or a hidden agenda. As a result, often one would find a pseudo-historian picking and choosing their evidence—to bolster their case.[4]"[cclxxviii]

Skiba and countless other Christian writers are now seen by this author as pseudo-scholars/ religious authors who parrot the fringe history of an end-time that christianity has proposed for the longest time. Picking and choosing assumed 'evidences' from not only their sacred traditions, but also from sources they 'claim' as related to their favoured topic. With only the very slightest differences between them. The primary being Rob clearly shows his own preconceived guesses of select evidence he uses. As a commentator, Rob is clearly not objective in the way he projects his summations. He has, it seems not attempted to guard against his own preconceived ideologies. In the following pages, are examined several of Rob's preconceived ideologies and his unrealistic projections, conjectures. Highlighting their waywardness with provided evidence of reason and logic before stepping into my own research and the results of those efforts that follow. For instance, Rob Skiba curiously opens his title attempting to explain some of the usual ideas concocted by sacred passages that seem to announce a connection between 'the apparent "days of noah", and an end-time scenario. One many hope will apparently be filled with nephilim.[cclxxix] 'As in the Days of noah' is a loved curio that many end-time authors use to support their postulating. So, like countless others Rob has desired to add his voice to the cacophony of Christian end-time authors already present. Presenting his thesis as one of many in a long line of apparent truths. The conclusions he draws however; prove to me they are nothing but simple, untested fanciful musings! In the opening pages to his book for instance, it takes very little effort to notice numerous flaws. This first chapter of Robs is riddled with error. The prime being the earlier mentioned, illegitimate totality transfer. One of the first blaring instances of illegitimate totality transfer Rob commits comes through an idea that 'giants' were described by one Old Testament Prophet: Amos. He writes,

> "And these weren't "short" giants either. The biblical giants were huge! Yet destroyed I the Amorite before them, whose height was like the height of the cedars, and he was strong as the oaks; yet I destroyed his fruit from above, and his roots from beneath. (Amos 2:9) Yes, there were real, literal giants that walked this earth. In fact, the further back in the biblical record you go, the taller they were."[cclxxx]

Right off-the-bat it is noticed that Rob as a non-specialist, advocates a supernatural and conspiratorial explanation for the history that the

DECONSTRUCTING ENDTIME DELUSIONS

'Prophet' Amos is assumed to have written his text about; that literal giants - in the guise of the ancient Amorite - roamed the ancient world and that these were of huge stature. Rob seems to come to this idea through transferring our modern knowledge and understanding of Cedar and Oak trees, as if this is what the Amos passage envisages readers understand.[cclxxxi] He then proceeds to further intimate (without substantiating the claim) that apparently the further back in the biblical record, the taller giants were. What? Has he begun to speculate that giants are somehow mentioned in the five previous chapters of Genesis? Maybe there is a belief giants are mentioned cryptically in these early chapters of Genesis? Maybe, assuming somehow the hyperbolic ages of the antediluvians mentioned in (Genesis 5), are cryptically, really hinting these people were of gigantic proportions? So very disturbing and sad if that is the case. The plainest of readings of the texts in no way leads anyone to such a conclusion. Rob unfortunately has not considered, or thought to consider just what 'a giant' in mythology (including the mythology of his sacred texts) actually is. Although I take a look at 'giants' later in this Nail, comments of Gerald Massey should suffice to get the juices of intrigue flowing. The following are in no way meant to be irreconcilable with my later comments, but are offered to whet appetites to open one's eyes to the esoteric/ symbolism of the many figures of their sacred works. No figure is literal. Massey insightfully states:

> "In the most primitive phase Mythology is a mode of representing certain elemental powers by means of living types that were superhuman like the natural phenomena. The foundations of Mythology and other forms of the ancient wisdom were laid in this pre-anthropomorphic mode of primitive representation... One of the most universal of the Folk-Tales which are the débris of Mythology is that of the Giant who had no heart (or spark of soul) in his body. The Apap-Dragon, in Africa, was the first of all the Giants who has no heart in his body, no root in reality, being as he is only the representation of non-existence, drought, darkness, death and negation. To have no heart in the body is an Egyptian expression for lack of understanding and want of nous..."[cclxxxii]

Here, readers are informed clearly as to 'what' expression is given to the figures of 'giants'; what these 'beings' were originally conceived to be; that they were heartless, not part of reality, basically, being representative of none-existence, or darkness etc. I find it extremely poignant that Massey highlights exactly what these entities were known by the ancients to represent. Specifically, that for the Ancient Egyptian (from which all Bible mythology derived) a 'giant' was one who possessed no nous, or understanding. Such is borne out again in what I further discovered in my brief look into 'Giants', later in the investigation of this Nail. Wrong and fallacious interpretation methods are clearly employed by Rob at the beginning of his study. Which leads me to consider the rest of the book will be the same. Unfortunately, he clearly has used what seem to be parallel statements about a group of people from the Amos passage and mingled (actually mangled) that Amos passage. Assuming to link the themes (he) sees as relevant, with another favoured Old Testament passage (numbers 13:33). The number passage mentions that the observers of the land saw 'giants' and felt they were 'grasshoppers'. Thus, to Rob and countless other Christian readers, these three passages; Amos 2:9; numbers 13:33; and Genesis 6:4 have a common denominator (nephilim/giants) and therefore they are legitimately and intimately entwined. Utter Taurus excretio! Unfortunately, for Rob and his readership, his conclusion regarding these passages is nothing short of the usual spiritualised, sensationalist claptrap that is too often proposed by Christian writers. Rob clearly has not attempted to check his assumptions. Or, seek what a probable meaning of the numbers passage is, in relation to Moses, and the grasshoppers statement. Readers are therefore encouraged to reconsider this idea from the following brief interjection:

> Number 13:33 and the saying, "...we were as grasshoppers [interchangeable with locusts]..." to 'giants' could, or most likely be symbolically announcing: "Good, prosperous times are afoot. If we choose to continue..."

As opposed to the usual Christian interpretation of fear and dread. Which, is exactly how Rob Skiba and most Christian interpreters view this numbers passage to mean. An interpretation that can ONLY be derived at when viewing this story as literally happening. But, this is a mythic tale. Mythic tales should be interpreted as symbol. Connotatively; therefore 'Grasshoppers' offers readers several interesting things to consider. These insects do not carry a specific meaning of fear, little (small in stature), dread... anywhere in mythology, nor in a Bible passage for that matter. Despite the impression of their mention in the Exodus tale, and this Numbers passage. To the religious punter who has not considered what is a moral of the numbers passage, grasshoppers often can ONLY be in reference to the people being hesitant because of fear. A little further investigation into these insects and their role in Mythology, we realise a most interesting fact is:

> Grasshoppers can only jump forward..... not backward, or sideways... This is why grasshopper is the symbol of good luck all over the world. Grasshopper's ability to connect and understand sound vibrations is why he is also a symbol of your inner voice. he could be telling you to trust yours.

Take fair note of this injunction. Those assuming the number 13 passage denote a negative view, are not very astute. Having not completed any thought and assessment of a symbolic, esoteric meaning to these tiny insects in relation to the Bible tale. In this particular number passage, grasshoppers yes, most certainly are metaphor. But, believers have chosen the wrong outcome attached to this metaphor. Numbers 13:33 in no way is meant to be recognised, or read as a negative. Rather, as a positive (stated below). If clearly recognised, there is a belief that the majority, if not the entirety of the Judaeo-Christian texts derives from Ancient Egyptian texts and Myths. What then, did/do these insects mean to ancient Egypt? Did these insects feature in Egyptian texts and myths? Astoundingly, the answer is a resounding,– yes! Grasshoppers do feature predominantly in Egyptian myth and texts. According to, "Nile Magazine" issue (#23, Jan-Feb 2020. pp 41-50) there are a number of fascinating insights regarding these insects and the Ancient Egyptians. In Egyptian texts Grasshoppers often metaphorically denote 'Large Numbers and/ or weakness'. Primarily for the sheer numbers of them that swarm and the 'occasional' would-be invaders, who were defeated in battle. For instance, in a text of Rameses' son, King Merenptah documented with great pride the aftermath of a victory he'd had over an invading force; likening the defeated warriors to grasshoppers. It reads:

> "You (Merenptah) have made them to be like grasshoppers, for every road is scattered with their [bodies]" (p45.)

While, secondly: It is also pertinent, and very interesting that the Egyptian word for these insects can, according to the article's author Jan Koek, be literally translated as, – "son of plundering." Further, the author makes an astounding comparison between how the Egyptians used these insects metaphorically, as compared to how they are used in the Judaeo-Christian texts. Writing:

> "In the early 20th century, Canadian archaeologist W. E. Staples considered [Egyptian inscriptions] "... declare their enemies to be like locusts [because of large numbers and their weakness in battle]... the idea of [these insects being] a dangerous foe ... is not considered... On the other hand, "The authors of the Old Testament, for the most part, speak of locusts literally. They are mentioned as food and as a destroying multitude, frequently as agents of God's vengeance." ([my inclusion] p 45. Electronic edition)

Assuming Rob had not thought to review any grasshopper passage, we find in a simple search, that the other passages where 'grasshoppers/locusts' are mentioned. That is, it is true these insects are most likely ONLY mentioned as a foodstuff, or a destroying multitude. Review Exodus 10; leviticus 11, and Joel 1:4 to name but three instances. It might have been advantageous if Rob had consulted a decent Theological Dictionary that had a full discussion outlining these insects and their uses by Bible authors. The likes of; "The Anchor Yale", or "The International Standard Bible Encyclopaedia". Some serious reflection must occur from now on, if the Christian community is to declare, or propose only one literal meaning to passages like numbers 13:33. Much reflection and a sincere searching for context and meaning must occur prior to any assumption of an 'accurate' position is deduced, regarding the spies of this numbers passage. A little digging undoubtedly widens, and 'changes' completely one's preconceived understanding. I implore readers to conduct more extensive research of such passages, and not just glibly accept the mundane, conventional interpretation. Clearly, several lessons could very well be learnt from the passage of numbers 13:33. Combining the symbolism of grasshoppers with what was stated above regarding 'giants', I would hope readers at least begin to notice that another valid interpretation could be present. Being, although Moses sent 'spies' to scope out the land ahead of them, and despite thinking they were but insignificant to the flora and fauna (which was claimed to be 'gigantic'), the inhabitance (being giants) were seen, as the Ancient Egyptian would have stated: "Having NO heart in his body." Either deceased, metaphorically, or recognised as weak. So, having no 'heart' as the Egyptian would have stated. Moses, after all was raised an Egyptian according to the Bible. Why then would this character not be familiar with such statements?

The 'spies' of the number 13 Bible passage should have thought of the inhabitance of the 'new' land as 'weak' and easily defeated (considering the shear numbers of Israelites that were purported to have 'escaped' Egypt). In itself, if true, the Israelites should have thought to themselves in similar vein as the cited passage of Rameses' son above. Which, most surely changes the entire complexion of the number passage. The standard Christian interpretation is self-defeating. Showing an ineptness in interpretation; being really only oppressive and manipulative. How is this the 'good news'? Where is the hope offered to people facing vast challenges today? Such an alternate 'interpretation', of hope, and fortitude is confirmed through the reaction of both the deity and the figure Moses. That none of that weak, feebleminded generation will proceed. They will all perish in the 'wilderness' of that place for they 'grumbled against their own 'reality', being vast in number (as a plague of locusts) able to devour the faced 'giant' who is really of no consequence. The only personality of the story, who recognised this was caleb: "Let us go up at once and occupy it, for we are well able to overcome it." Caleb here is clearly the only one who saw the 'bones' of the story. The rest only saw the 'flesh' of what was reported, and so, miserably failed in the objective. What the spies viewed were but the none-reality of the giants of the land. Readers are encouraged to scope out a symbolic meaning to Grasshoppers and test this hypothesis and draw your own conclusion whether the above rings veridical or not. There are throughout antiquity countless stories with similar lessons to draw. The word zeroed in on is nephilim. Mentioned twice in this passage. Thus, to Rob and countless other Christian readers, these three passages; Amos 2:9; numbers 13:33; and Genesis 6:4 have a common denominator (nephilim/giants) and therefore they are legitimately and intimately entwined. Once more this conjecture is utter Taurus excretio! Unfortunately, for Rob and his readership, his conclusion regarding these passages is nothing short of the usual spiritualised, sensationalist claptrap that is too often proposed by Christian writers. Rob, and others 'studying' these passages and making connections, where no connection truly exists clearly have not attempted to check assumptions, or initial preconceived thoughts. But, have usually come to such passages with a preconceived idea. Any conclusion therefore that might disprove, or butt against that idea will surely cause the aforementioned statements regarding cognitive dissonance, and cognitive biases. The fable surrounding the numbers 13:33 episode in the sacred text narrative, might just have well-been one pilfered from tales with similar themes; like the poem of the 1 or 2 century Greek Poet: Babrius' "We are Ants to the Gods".[cclxxxiii]

We are ants to the Gods:

> Once upon a time a ship sank with its crew. Someone watching said that the gods made unjust decisions. For, because a single impious man had been aboard, many who had done no wrong died along with him. At the same time he was saying this, as it happens, a great swarm of ants came up to him, hurrying to make a meal of the chaff of some wheat. When he was bitten by one, he stomped on lots of them. Hermes appeared next to him and, hitting him with his rod, said, "And so you won't suffer the gods to be the same sort of judges of mortals as you are of ants?" (ibid. Anthology of Classical Myth (p.62)

THIS POEM HAS SIMILARITIES in theme to the jonah myth and various New Testament fables based also on the Great Flood and jonah tales. There could possibly be links in theme here also to the myth of numbers 13:33. Like so many Christian authors writing on their pet themes, Rob Skiba clearly opens himself to further criticism for several other misguided interpretations. In other opening statements he is seen as totally confused. Presenting the discerning reader with an air of his ineptness as an interpreter/ researcher. Believing,

> "Short of a literal reading of Genesis 6:1-4, how are giants produced? I don't care how much spinach you feed a normal human being, kissing cousins do not give birth to 12- and 30-foot giants! The only explanation that makes any sense is that something supernatural must have caused those creatures to exist."[cclxxxiv]

The only explanation is supernatural. Really? Of course, there are other explanations. Just as a coin doesn't have one side only, there are two sides to every story. One story is good, until another is told! Clearly the favoured, and therefore the only one Rob is willing to entertain has to be 'supernatural'. Otherwise, the premise of the entire book disintegrates into typical fantasy. Which is exactly what happens from this point forward? With a little digging and further investigation of materials outside the usual parameters of theological preferences. It can be found that such phenomena as gigantism and associated oddities, that these could be explained. That is, provided such passages as Amos 2:9, and Genesis 6:1-4, and other sacred book passages that 'show traces' of believed gigantism; that these ARE to be taken in a literal sense. That the Judaeo-Christian book tells of some sort of giant humanoid being terrorising the Earth. However, as I have attempted to point out all through this study, the sacred texts ARE NOT literal compositions; but are infused with metaphor (symbol); being myths describing the wider world stage. These were to teach audiences what the original author wished to make known! They are infused with life lessons. One other example of 'illegitimate totality transfer' is seen in Robs assertions regarding the Judaeo-Christian patriarch, noah. Astoundingly, Rob attempts to make this figure sound as if he were somehow genetically superior to the rest of the planet! It was this that piqued the nemo-deities interest, singling him out for the building of the ark. Rob states:

> "Scripture says that Noah was "perfect in his generations," which literally meant genetically pure. We know this because the word used there is "tamim" (Strong's 8549). It is the same word used when the Lord referred to a red heifer that had to be physically pure, without spot or blemish:..." (p.27).

Objection! Recall previous comments that noah was believed by some early Jewish commentators to have been born nephilim! If true, what does this mean for Rob's assertions? Do we have a major problem here? Linking the Hebrew term tamim with genetic purity is sheer nonsense! Though tamim is the same word used for the heifer of numbers 19:2, does not mean genetically pure! Tamim does have the meaning of being 'blameless, righteous'. Which is to say, is completely different to being pure in a genetic, DNA sense![cclxxxv] Besides, how the hell did anyone at the time of this passage's composition know with absolute certainty who, or what was genetically pure? The science of genetics is very recent, and we are only now beginning to unlock some of its mysteries. Was someone acutely aware and practiced this science in the ancient past? If so, we should have been aware of genetics long before it was discovered in the nineteenth century![cclxxxvi] Think on this a moment: If noah is of a genetically pure stock, and he was born a nephilim, as hinted in the previous Nail, would that not then mean according to Rob's logic, nephilim were also - genetically pure? Here is another example trampling on Robs parade. So, noah is genetically pure because he is called tamim; then that must also mean the believed Satan was as well. Yes, I do mean that despised and feared nasty devilish entity, for this 'personality' too was tamim from its apparent creation also... (see ezekiel 28:13-15.). To highlight my point verse 15 for instance reads:

> "You were blameless in your ways from the day you were created..."
> (ezekiel 28:15 (ESV)).

The word blameless in this passage in Hebrew just happens to be tamim also! According to Rob's logic, the Satan must also be genetically pure. Isn't that a kicker! Even the Septuagint, the Greek translation of this same passage concurs having translated (amomos) as blameless also! A reasonable explanation I can see is that Rob must not really have carried out any important study on the word tamim in context. He does not seem to have consulted any Lexicon/ Wordbook, or vocabulary lists, to check his reasoning and conclusion that would have assisted with the meaning of this Hebrew word tamim. Rather, he either concluded the genetic purity from his own head; or maybe he concluded this reasoning from another author's work that he consulted. The other author's work then seemed to Rob to lend credence to a DNA corruption assumption. Finding that explanation, because it fits with his preconceived assumption, was then chosen without any fact-checking. This is simply very bad theology, and bad research.[cclxxxvii] Using the same incorrect 'logic' as Rob, christians must also assume that their God-man (Jesus) was also genetically pure- and so by association, so too was the alleged mother, mary! After-all, was this Jesus figure not also said to be without spot (to use the same english term used to describe the heifer of numbers 19.); blameless and righteous! Surely, readers must be able to see that this illogical thinking is nothing other than an illogical totality transfer of unrelated ideas and concepts cherry-picked to fit an assumption. Where does it stop? Rob and those who hold such ideas as a genetic purity, from my understanding is so very wrong! Committing this usual untruth that fundamental believers touting the literalness of their favoured passages consistently perpetuate. Reading the noah text plainly, he is said to be 'blameless' tamim; above reproach. NOT genetically pure in all the earth! To talk of pure DNA strands peppered throughout the sacred text, and to insinuate the writer of the sacred texts knew and understood perfectly genetics, is complete rubbish! The Science of Genetics has ONLY been around since it was discovered in the nineteenth century A.D.! Good luck 'proving' some extraordinary fellow(s) knew and understood the molecular structure of things and some of the mutations etc. that happen; that these people deciphered genes before Gregor Mendel.

Moving on. Throughout, Rob has also fallen into the trap of insisting 1 enoch and two other ancient manuscripts; the Apocryphal books of Jasher and Jubilees are a worthy addition to his cause. That somehow these ancient Jewish texts add a sense of validation to the select subject matter of nephilim. I guess, substantial evidence really isn't a factor of consideration for many believers. Manuscripts like Jasher and Jubilees are often thought by those that use them, as factual (and historically accurate) accounts of past life-experiences.[cclxxxviii] So, their prime use is as offering an ancient sense of 'proof' and validity to the particular sacred myth being commented on. Here that of the subject of nephilim of Genesis 6. The impression is that the stories told, and the accounts gleaned from these para-sacred texts offer a valid source of verification and are therefore, just as historically accurate as any presumed sacred source. In short, the thought seems to be that if an ancient (most often religious by nature) text, or story 'outside' the corpus of scripture seems to be validating a preconceived ideology of a specific sacred story, then, that source must offer a sense of confirmation for the proposed ideology. But does it? It might be very disturbing to Rob and his readers to know reputable scholars will assert that the text of Jasher (particularly) is not really extant today. If this manuscript is available it cannot be in its original format, but is a copy of a copy of a copy. If the texts of these are but known copies of copies of copies, there is little reason to believe in their accuracy, let alone validity. They are most likely just as unreliable and historically inaccurate as any new and Old Testament text for we simply do not possess any 'original'. Besides, it is rightly stated by Dr. Nyland:

> "Despite some wild claims on the internet, the Book of Jasher does not mention Nephilim or Watchers at all..."[cclxxxix]

Nonetheless, Jasher, and Jubilees specifically, along with the book of 1 enoch are erroneously used by numerous Christian authors today as scaffold support for their favoured end–time scenario. Question: Which version of Jubilees does Rob claim to have used for his book? Dr. Nyland in her study, "The book of Jubilees" offers again her learned opine:

> "There are twenty seven Ethiopic texts of the Book of Jubilees, and manuscripts in Greek, a Latin translation of the Greek, and Syriac. Fifteen Jubilees scrolls written in Hebrew were discovered at Qumran... Scholars have suggested it was originally written in Hebrew..."[ccxc]

DECONSTRUCTING ENDTIME DELUSIONS

So, which version of Jubilees does Rob favour? Surely, each of the twenty-seven in circulation is not exactly alike. Back to the scaffold, which is to assist in the retelling of the threatening rise again of the ancient figures labelled giants, or nephilim. In defence to his use of these non-canonical Jewish texts, Skiba plainly shares his belief in their benefits:

> "Regarding extra-biblical texts, I do read and often quote from such books; primarily the books of 1 Enoch, Jubilees and Jasher. I do not consider these books to be canon, but I do consider them to be valuable sources of information, which can serve as ancient commentaries that both elaborate on the canonized (sic) Scriptures as well as provide added insight into the beliefs of those who wrote the books we now consider canon. I look at those and other similar books much the same way I view any commentary on the Scriptures. I believe there is added value in using these ancient texts in that way because they were written around the same time as the canonised Scriptures were written. Thus, it shows the mind-set and beliefs the Biblical writers had as well as the audiences to whom they were writing. As such, many of the extra-biblical texts that are now available to us provide a window into both the beliefs and the cultures of the ancient world, and serve to provide added insights and perspectives we may lack today in our modern world."[ccxci]

Aside Dr. Nyland, I have some other legitimate reservations with any use of these three texts (Jubilees, Jasher, as with 1 enoch) as 'proofing' for any end-time hypothesis. It seems the only probable connection of each book (possibly) noticed is the theme of righteousness. Yet, this theme seems to be completely ignored by those who assume each of the above three 'apocryphal' texts can legitimately be called upon as supporting evidence and commentary on a specific end-time hypothesis. Many Christian authors are gravely mistaken and short-sighted. For they are too busy moulding these texts into some end–time configuration to notice the overall contexts of righteousness. Skiba's objective clearly was to utilise these non-canonical Jewish texts as sources of valid commentary to assist his comprehension and understanding of the enigmatic Genesis 6 passage; but he has clearly taken their observation at a distance from any original intention. Either forgetting, or not grasping the fact all texts; 1 enoch, Jubilees, and Jasher are concerned about a sense of righteousness. Sure, there are elements and themes and certain passages of each text that seems to support his hypothesis; but only so through a misuse and disregard for their over-arching contexts. In the remainder of this, and the sub-essays confronted throughout this Nail I will attend to the guess offered by Rob Skiba to support his own ideology and end-time hypothesis. Most unfortunately for his Christian readers. The tone of the work is from the perspective that some genetically modified (corrupted) entity is spoken of in Genesis 6 and the other sources; particularly select passages from 1 enoch, jasher, and jubilees. Again, I query the validity of such a reckless perspective. Where is the evidence that the ancient authors of these texts specifically meant a corruption of DNA (i.e., they had a science of genetics akin to modern studies in this field!) Ancient Jewish authors and commentators share a vast array of similar interpretations; but from a modern perspective why should these be noteworthy? Rob's concepts throughout his book contend to be from a 'Christian perspective,' and is endeared as...

The Genesis six experiment:

IT IS A PRETTY DIFFICULT task to take Rob and every assertion he makes at face value. Rather his, and others' assertions derive simply from and are little else than pure speculation. For starters, Rob offers nothing by way of an actual bibliography of probable/ possible substantiating material! Rather, his consists of links to his own 'blogs', and various subjective sacred book passages, as well as those passages of the favoured para-sacred books mentioned above. This should alert readers with a red light! Issues abound. Aside the above conjectures, Rob also asserts that the mentioned Canaan, grandson of the noah figure, was possibly of the nephilim ilk, and that was very, very bad! Nephilim are nowadays said after all, to be wicked, depraved, and evil. Clearly, there is no idea that noah was thought to be nephilim! He acknowledges:

> "I have a theory about Canaan based on the strange situation described in Genesis 9:20-25. In that passage of Scripture, Ham finds his father naked, and Noah curses his grandson, Canaan. Why? Scripture is silent, but I

suspect it was because there was something obviously wrong with him. First of all, the narrative implies that Canaan had to have been present for Noah to have cursed him. That means he was either born on the ark or shortly thereafter. My belief is that he may have been born with six fingers and six toes, which is a notable characteristic of the Nephilim giants. If this is true, then when Canaan was born, Noah must have looked at his grandson and said, "Oh boy, here we go again!" Canaan's lineage settled the land that was named after him, and we know from Scripture that Canaan was full of giants. Remember Numbers 13:33? After the Exodus, the spies went into the land and saw themselves as grasshoppers by comparison. These giants were all the "ites" (as in the Hittites, Jebusites, Amorites, etc.) that Joshua and his men and later David and his men had to wipe out in the Old Testament."[ccxcii]

This hunch is audacious! Simply stated, a passage cannot be made to say what it does not say. Thus, as other christians Rob has fallen for another fallacy: that of the fallacy of silence! The fallacy of silence states: To make an argument from silence (Latin: argumentum ex silentio) is to express a conclusion that is based on the absence of statements in historical documents, instead of their presence. Christians and religious authors and commentators, as we all continually fall foul to this fallacy, relying on their own preconceived ideology. To combat this, it is on good authority that I indulge the reader with the myth from which the Canaan passages are likely derived. Unfortunately Rob, it seems has not attempted to find out the remotest of original intentions of the originating author to the Canaan episode before finalising his thoughts. Rather has again let his imagination run wild with very little concern for any actual contextual comprehension. It seems because this most favourably suited his purpose and the writing of his book. Robert Graves and Raphael Patai, "Hebrew Myths", narrate and offer the context of the Canaan myth:

> "...The Genesis version of this myth has been carelessly edited. Ham could not be blamed, in justice, for noticing his father's nakedness; and Noah could never have laid such a grave curse upon Ham's innocent son Canaan, even if this involuntary act had been Ham's only fault. The text: 'And Noah awoke from his wine, and knew what his little son had done unto him,' points to a gap in the narrative, plausibly filled by the midrashic account of his castration. Noah's curse shows that the sinner was little Canaan, not

Ham. 'Ham, father of' is clearly an editorial insertion... The myth is told to justify Hebrew enslavement of Canaanites—Canaan was Chnas for the Phoenicians, and Agenor for the Greeks. In one midrashic passage, sodomy has been added to Ham's crimes. A long list of Canaanite sexual offences is contained in Leviticus XVIII; and King Rehoboam's subjects are reproached in 1 Kings XIV:24 for practising 'all the abominations of the nations whom the Lord drove out before the Children of Israel.'

The sexual modesty of Shem's Hebrews is emphasized (sic) in this midrash, and God's blessing extended to all sons of Japheth who have now joined them." Further, "...The myth of Shem, Ham and Japheth is related to the Greek myth of how five brothers, Coeus, Crius, Hyperion, Iapetus and Cronus successfully conspired against their father Uranus. Not only did Cronus castrate and supplant Uranus but, according to the Byzantine mythographer Tzetzes, Zeus followed his example in both particulars, with the help of Poseidon and Hades. In the Hittite myth, based on a Human original, the Supreme God Anu's genitals were bitten off by his rebel son and cup-bearer Kumarbi, who afterwards rejoiced and laughed (as Ham is said to have done) until Anu cursed him. The God El himself, according to Philo of Byblus's quotation from Sanchuniathon, castrated his father Uranus. The notion that any son could behave in this unfilial manner so horrified the editors of Genesis that they suppressed Ham's castration of Noah altogether as the Greeks suppressed the myth of Cronus's castration until Christian times; Plato in his Republic and Euthyphro repudiated even Uranus's castration. Nevertheless, the myth of Noah's castration and consequent supersession as God's priest because of his injury, was preserved by the Jews. Canaan's use of a cord for the operation does not ring true; a pruning-knife from Noah's vineyard is likely to have been the original instrument."[ccxciii]

Here, there seems to be a fair stack of skullduggery, and censoring of mythic tales. Why? Simply, to suit the purposes of both audience, and storyteller alike. Just as we all still do in our day. We each censor what we find repulsive, and not suited to a cause. So, we have read here in the Canaan episode, as preserved in the Judaeo-Christian sacred book. That it resembled, and was likely pilfered and doctored from a Hittite and Greek tale with similar themes. That Rob is likely unaware of these myths and their close likeness; is directly related to the fact of Christian 'research' and thinking. Research from a 'Christian perspective' only seeks that which is presumed to be clearly favourable to a predisposed ideology. Still, how is this a legitimate excuse? Disturbingly, there is one unsubstantiated guess after another made throughout this first chapter of Rob's book, Babylon Rising! Thankfully, the final disturbing quote of the chapter of Rob's follows. After which I delve into actual evidences and scientific reasons for possible answers to this enigmatic creature; nephilim; as with analogous themes and topics of giants, elongated skulls and others. It is clear to me, Rob has a clear and present God/supernatural virus hampering his objective sane self! He concludes his first chapter proposing:

> "The mythology of the infamous Greek gods can literally be traced back to sometime just after the Great Flood of Noah. These gods came from Crete. Furthermore, if you study the history of Crete, you will find that most of what we now call "Europe" used to have to pay tribute to this tiny island in the Aegean Sea. They had to send young virgin men and women to the Minotaur of the Labyrinth as tribute to King Minos. How so much of Europe could have been held in subjugation to such a tiny island doesn't really make sense, unless you realize (sic) that the gods of antiquity likely really did exist. These gods were always described as giants with "superpowers." Thus, they were definitely something more than merely famous humans. The Bible tells us exactly who/what they really were and where they came from. These are the post-Flood Nephilim who sprung up through the lineage of Ham."[ccxciv]

Oops! This is clearly another skewed and mangled reading; this time of ancient history and its inherent mythology. To assert as Rob has done, is a complete bastardisation of the beauty of ancient stories to fit a certain modern agendum! Did you catch it too? Those nasty nefarious appalling deities of the ancient Greeks apparently appeared literally sometime after the flood episode of the Judaeo-Christian book Genesis. What a load of absolute Taurus excretio! To believe this tripe is to have no clue of any of the subjects you claim from a Judaeo-Christian perspective. Sorry Rob, this is all wrong. As far as I am concerned there needs to be more homework done on the effects of ancient mythology. Particularly regards to these narratives and their mythic deity figures; why were these created in the first place. It is absurd to state that there is some nephilim/giant connection. The connections Rob and other religious authors propose anyway! Throughout the rest of this Nail, I will offer readers substantial reasons that can be verified through scientific and medical documentation and analysis. I encourage readers to take note of the evidences employed for my arguments, which incidentally, none of the authors mentioned and rebutted in this Nail, ever mention or hint of having knowledge. They are instead, too busy filling their pages with sensational and supernatural 'proofs' to bolster their own opinion!

Blatant but usual Christian posturing:

A NOT TOO DISSIMILAR secular account of what Rob is attempting to establish as sacred end-time truth; that surrounding nephilim and giants are the equally absurd – Astronaut-Angel hypothesis. This hypothesis has been proposed by the late Zechariah Sitchin, and other speculative fringe authors. Sitchin has by numerous reputable scholars been discredited as a scholar of renown. He often misread/misinterpreted the Sumerian, Hebrew, and Aramaic languages. Yet, this has not stopped numerous people believing and championing his theories, or variations of it. The most speculative and absurdly are the so-called American History Channel, Ancient Aliens program (2010). Sitchin's assertion of nephilim as 'fallen ones', Dr. Nyland again plainly debunks the claims:

> "Author Zechariah Sitchin incorrectly said that the word Nephilim meant fallen ones: "those who came down from above," "those who descended to earth," but Nephilim does not come from the word naphal, to "fall." Besides, it was the Watchers, not the Nephilim, who came down to earth. All accounts tell us that the Nephilim were born on earth. Rather, the word Nephilim is from the Aramaic word naphil, "giant." ...Put it this way - we have no evidence that the Nephilim were not ancient astronauts. We do, however, have evidence that the word did not mean "fallen ones" or "people from the fiery rockets." ...Sitchin also identifies the Nephilim with the Sumerian deities, claiming that the Sumerians knew of their existence and that they came from a planet called Nibiru. This is all wrong."[ccxcv]

It is not the intention here to evaluate either the Ancient Alien, astronaut, nor any other theory made popular by television. But, readers are urged to let Dr. Nyland's assessment stand. Many others have debunked these hypotheses also. By the earlier cited Dr. Heiser.[ccxcvi] A probable explanation seen as valid for any of Rob's, and other author's assertions about the Genesis 6 episode, or any links to an alien/ astronaut is. They are sheer and obvious theory. They only really promote guesswork and shoddy investigation. These should not be taken as serious scholarship and research. It is pretty easy to explain and call into serious question near-on every assertion made if one has the temerity of a curious mind. Interestingly, the (April, 2018) edition of Skeptic Magazine, volume 23 Number 1, has an informative article by Osteologist Elizabeth Weiss: I am Not an Alien: Understanding Human Skeletal Variation, in which she outlines some of the issues of fact. Those facts that have either been over-looked, or completely dismissed by proponents of the Alien-Astronaut hypothesis regarding giant skeletal remains unearthed around the globe. The finding of countless giant skeletal remains, weirdly elongated skulls, and other oddities from around the globe have set ablaze the wild imaginations of numbers of christians. But, how legitimate are their verdicts? A discussion of what Rob Skiba with his Genesis Six Experiment proposes regarding nephilim and these analogous subjects, might yet prove useful and interesting. Going some ways to answering whether many specific end-time conjectures of supernatural/ malevolent entities aren't just a modern attempt by the Church in heightening a fear factor; much as the Hydra of Hamburg (below). If only to show readers some of the typical Christian guessing and absurd misapplication of certain stories and legends of sacred and para–sacred texts. Those that are still ubiquitous and accessible to any interested party. Rob's hypothesis as numerously mentioned, follows pretty much the same believed proposals as other giant/nephilim believers of those in the above Skeptic Magazine article. Author Scott Alan Roberts in his book "The rise and fall of the Nephilim: the untold story of fallen angels, giants on the earth, and their extraterrestrial origins", claims to have written the truth surrounding the mystical nephilim of the scriptures. As does Fred Harding. Writer of: "Nephilim skeleton's found". There are also the writings of acclaimed screenwriter Brian Godawa. Brian has authored numerous books and novels; a series of saga novels; "Chronicles of the Nephilim"; "Chronicles of the Apocalypse", and "Chronicles of the Watchers". Most noteworthy is the fact that these titles have made "the Top 10 of Biblical Fiction, and lauded as imaginative retelling of Biblical stories.[ccxcvii] I wonder how many readers of these stories actually realise they are classed as Bible fiction? Does that even matter? Besides, Brian's book from which the quote below was taken, is endorsed by a prominent scholar; Michael Heiser. He wrote the Forward. Thus, why wouldn't an unassuming believer presuppose that Brian's work: "When Giants Were Upon the Earth" was anything other than a factually, and biblically sound theological treaties. This is where I, even as a non-specialist, non-scholar disagree with Heiser's praise of Godawa's book. I do in a sense agree however with Heiser when he says, "Fiction and fantasy are tried-and-true vehicles for transmitting theological truths and biblical concepts." That much I can agree. As for the rest, not many else rings the veridical bell. Dr. Heiser in the following quotation presents Brian's treaties in a 'glowing' fashion:

> "Brian Godawa offers a remedy to [a] crisis. The Chronicles of the Nephilim does the impossible—it turns serious academic scholarship in ancient primary sources into engaging entertainment. Fiction and fantasy are tried-and-true vehicles for transmitting theological truths and biblical concepts. This is what reaches the masses... Each volume of The Chronicles of the Nephilim contains resources and commentary for exploring the biblical text in its own context. When Giants Were Upon the Earth collects all that information and expands on it. It's a biblical-theological feast. But don't mistake the feast for smorgasbord theology. As someone Brian has tapped as a resource, I can tell you his focus is on peer-reviewed biblical scholarship. His sources are not his own opinions. He's not grinding axes and "solving" conspiracies. He's not pretending questions are answers. He knows the difference between supernatural possibilities grounded in the biblical text and sanctified speculation."[ccxcviii]

Having Brian's title 'peer-reviewed' by Dr. Heiser (as a respected scholar of renown) is supposed to quash and allays any suspicions. A reader might have when reading Brian's text. Readers should just take what

DECONSTRUCTING ENDTIME DELUSIONS

Brian has written as factually sound just because a respected Bible 'scholar' confirms it as much? Further, in each of the mentioned books, are we to believe all authors are factually accurate? Painfully trudging through these volumes, I find them offering their readership nothing else than among a long line of the usual Christian psychobabble; here we have authors who pack their work with a cascade of 'proof texting' and insinuation, but little else. The evidential verification for support of opinions was garnered via the usual theological parameters; despite (Brian's specifically) being focused on some peer-reviewed scholarship. Recall previous statements regarding peer–reviewed materials; that such can often be just as wrong. As with Rob Skiba; Roberts, and Harding's opinions seem to be garnered solely from their understanding of what a sacred text says and means, i.e., each opinion is harvested from a very modern perspective of Bible and the other texts consulted. Each author relies heavily on texts like 1 enoch and what is apparently written in it about the 'Watchers'. Many modern Christian authors commentating on the 'Watchers' show a belief that they are, or closely linked to alien greys. Or, as was mentioned in the brief of Derek Gilbert's new publication, "Last Clash of the Titans", that The Titans, the old gods of the Greeks, are the biblical Watchers. Confused yet? For God's sake why can't christians make their minds up on what or who represents The 'Watchers'. It is also stated by various Christian writers that The Watchers are called giants and are thus linked to nephilim within the enochic tome. The opinions of various skeptics or materials that do necessarily not 'comply' with these preconceptions are often over–looked or cherry-picked in support, or most often, shown in a discouraging light. Dr. Nyland again though may disappoint a number of readers. The following should render Gilbert's and indeed Skiba's assertions moot! "Greek mythology tells us that the Giants were the brothers of the Titans. Remember the movie, Clash of the Titans? There were in fact no clashing Titans in it, so best not to rely on any information from that! ...[To] summarize (sic) the account of the Giants in Greek mythology. The Giants were the children of Gaia (Earth), their father being her son, Ouranos. Gaia gave birth to 18 children..." (3 giants; 3 cyclopes; 12 Titans.)[ccxcix] Noticed anything strange? If Dr. Nyland's assessment is accurate; Gaia gave only birth to a grand total of three giants and they are not the Titans, or cyclopes. These are totally separate entities. Someone has surely misplaced and misread certain things. Are the 'Watchers' of 1 enoch these Titans? What then of the 'giants'? Who or what are they? There most surely is a cross-interpretation of both myths; of the Genesis 6 tale, and of the Greek tale. It seems to me authors who have attempted to make a 'biblically' sound case for the Genesis 6 tale by inserting entities from the Greeks, have done so through misleading means.

All these volumes that of Godawa, Roberts, Harding, Gilbert and Skiba, as with countless others are as far as can be determined, nothing but accounts that the authors 'claim' to have studied and concluded from a Christian point of view. They are therefore in their minds completely truthful and accurate. Yet, as I have stated above when peering at Rob Skiba's first chapter, we can only conclude such 'studies' use the usual christianeze and indoctrinated opinions; opinions that attempt to mask their obvious use of supernatural, extraterrestrial, or conspiratorial explanations for history. Proving again the veracity of my earlier statements: – that christianity breeds members with a dangerous and debilitating psychosis. A debilitating neurosis of mind–blindness. If an author begins a project with the 'closed loop' premise that every word, act, being, story of the Judaeo-Christian book, and that extra/para-sacred works are also probably factual accounts; then necessarily, research of any kind must be seen to concur and stay within that specific boundary. For an accurate and scholarly dissection of Watchers and the para-sacred texts consulted and utilised by Skiba, and the mentioned earlier authors, I remind readers of the book: "Fallen Angels, Watchers, Giants, Nephilim, and Evil", and the other cited materials of Dr. Nyland. She is a well-respected author, ancient language scholar, and lexicographer. She is well qualified to write and offer an informed judgement. If the authors under scrutiny had in the least consulted such treaties as Dr. Nyland's range of books on these, and analogous esoteric subjects, their summations would surely have shown that evidence. Although Rob Skiba assumes to have done an amount of valid research, this is simply not the case. The issue is. He and other like authors only consider what was and what is the typical, when it comes to any subject of christianity. Readers all too often seek out only those materials that affirm a predisposed ideology. Only those that are seen as attesting a 'spiritual' perspective. That however, is not the full gamut of what necessitates research. "Research," used as either a verb or noun indicate a searching for knowledge; a systematic inquiry, enquiry, and investigation that seek to establish (often in a scientific manner) facts. Unfortunately, what Skiba and countless other Christian authors fail to understand is that faith, and the subjective selection of study materials does not constitute facts. Facts are: verifiable, and provable beyond reasonable doubt. All facts are shown to have either existed, or they did not. Facts, show that events and circumstances occurred, or that the truth to a cause, circumstance, inference is actually, – true. This is why we call them facts! Facts cannot be born from subjective 'faith' reasoning. Faith, demands we give something away. It is not a dogged clinging to but a 'letting go'! To claim 'faith' but refuse to let go of a predisposed ideology is nonsensical; only proving one's indoctrinated parameters are busily at work constricting the boundaries to enquiry. One of the most favoured and related explanations of this is a saying of Aristotle, as cited in quotation in the first few pages of this book: It is the Mark of an educated mind to entertain a thought without accepting it! Substituting faith with credulity in the famous faith passages of the new testament book of hebrews (chapter 11) offers the reader the same opinion. Credulity and faith are interchangeable blood–brothers.

Moving on: one of the most bazaar doctrines to have been drawn up by the Roman Catholic Church specifically and wholly derived from a skewed understanding of the Genesis 6 tale, is the doctrine that humanity in its prehistoric past was infiltrated and interfered with by 'demonic'/Watcher/alien forces. A whim circulated from integrating Genesis 6:1-4 with the 1 enoch, and Jubilees, Jasher tales. Scott Roberts, as with countless other modern commentators of the Genesis 6 episode clearly believes this is a truth. Seeing within it an avenue for the largely unexplainable premise of, – 'Original Sin'; otherwise, he would not have felt the need to include the following statement without due rebuttal and verifiable reference. Rather readers are expected to take his word as gospel truth. Regurgitating this Catholic doctrine, he intimates that demonic influence upon humanity:

> "...stems from the very first impregnation of Eve in the Garden, by the character known as the 'Serpent.' It was he who fathered Cain, the first of the Nephilim. This act was repeated throughout all of antediluvian humanity until God had had enough, and there was judgment." (Chapter 10: Where are they Now?)

More Bollocks! Where in the ...is the doctrine of 'original sin' actually intimated in the sacred works. Provoking this doctrine (of original sin) is pretty well established across the ecclesiastical board. A quick Internet search substantiates this. But does widespread belief of the "original sin" doctrine make it an absolute truth? Witnessed above (Nail Four) in the discussion of Genesis three. Recall it was specifically stated by at least two scholars that there was no concept of an 'original sin'! Neither, any so-assumed agent of some deity (angels), or, any human 'falling from 'grace" can be supported by any sacred text. Such ideas are complete theory by the wider Church, and authors mentioned. Robert's, as does Skiba and most other Bible commentators are regurgitating a 'prosthetic memory'. A thought that is clearly a desired false assertion.

Skiba's apparent Genesis 6 Revealtion:

ROB SKIBA IMPLIES THAT the creatures (nephilim) are not 'fallen aliens', as the popularised television program 'ancient aliens' asserts; but they are the offspring of the unholy union of human women and 'fallen angels.' Clawing at evidence he cites (2 Peter 1:21) as his New Testament confirmation that Moses is allegedly to have written. A worthier passage I'd assume though is (2 Peter 2:4-14.) These verses contextually attempt to warn believers against false teachers. The mention of the 'fallen angels' in Peter and Jude, is apparently set as a strong warning of a similar destiny to such teachers of those peddling a 'false' gospel. Thus, contextually the passage of 2 Peter 2 seems to use 'angels' as a metaphor for human

DECONSTRUCTING ENDTIME DELUSIONS

'teachers'. Not as Rob, and his supporters; that the author of second Peter chapter 2 is referencing supernatural entities. These very angels are, or can be cited by association, as verification for a belief in the creatures of Genesis 6 being angels. Do supernatural entities specifically 'teach' the gospel anywhere in the sacred books? Believers might assume so, but as far as I am aware nowhere in the whole sacred book does any such being remotely hint at doing so. Maybe Rob unwittingly falls near such a description; as described by the 2 Peter 2 passages? For, he seems to further intimate that the creatures, the nephilim, forced deity's hand. As it is attested by countless others that when the fallen angelic beings interbred with human women, it resulted in the birth of nephilim. The worldwide flood was the means by which the deity sought to rectify. By nonsensically wiping the slate clean of all life. Just as a child throws toys about when things do not work out as they like. As if not being able to differentiate between the evil hearts and intent of humanity, or the other that had corrupted the earth because of them. But, I have to wonder; (1) how strong is this principal deity if it can be swayed to wipe out life on Planet Earth because of the actions of some 'corrupt' beings that were themselves 'apparently' created by the selfsame deity? As hinted above - the nephilim might have been genetically pure also. (According to the logic and reasoning Rob employed earlier). Not to mention that (2) clearly there is no change to the demeanour of mankind across the board; hearts are still as corrupt. Humanity is very much still plagued with a propensity to war, to rape; to maim, and deride and show disdain and malice to each-other. Traits easily witnessed in greater capacity in our modern day. This I trust was made all the clearer in my very first essay, Nail One above. Therefore, the 'flood' failed in its purpose! Furthermore, there is also absolutely no indication in the text that the 'daughters of men' had a choice in the matter. Were they essentially coerced into union that resulted in rape? Maybe. To wear this indictment by reason of faith is bizarre. It exposes one's total ineptness and ignorance. To support his premise like so many others, Rob obtusely pushes upon his readers a further ridiculous notion writing:

> "In Genesis, Moses wrote that some of the angels of God left their prior estate [Skiba's footnote to Jude 6] and came down to earth and mated with women, which produced a race of super-human hybrids known as the Nephilim. Moses went on to write that these creatures corrupted the whole earth, and in verses 11-13, we learn that this was the reason why God decided to destroy the earth with the Flood."[ccc]

Has it been noticed? Nowhere in Genesis does the author, be that either Moses, or more likely a redactor, assume to propose that angels of a deity left their prior estate... came down to earth and mated with women, and that produced a race of super human hybrids known as the nephilim. One can argue black and blue on this, but you cannot make a text say what it never does. Clearly Rob has made a transference of a New Testament passage (jude 6) that is built upon the same assumption! Is such a transference warranted? Just because a New Testament passage intimates that some beings forsook their former post, does not give license to guess. Context, as I have earlier attempted to state clearly always trumps guesswork. A further result of Robs distorted logic is to call upon a latter text; i.e. (2 Peter 1). Calling it as 'evidence' for his nonsense. There are numerous difficulties and blunders (some mentioned at the beginning of this Nail) with Rob's assertions and the assertions of 'other Christian' authors.[ccci] Too many to outline here. Scanning the pages of "Babylon Rising..." it is disturbing to take note that near on every statement made and reference offered, shows a complete lack in aptness as a researcher. This is truly surprising and sad for it reminds me of the words of Reverend Robert Taylor, cited in the first pages of this document, of "The Diegesis" that: "...to be in error one's self, is a misfortune; and if it be such an error as mightily affects our peace of mind, it is a very grievous misfortune; to be the cause of error to others... deceiving them ourselves, ... is a crime... a most barbarous wrong done to our brother man..." The very warning that the author of 2 Peter was supposedly attempting to avert!

Though there are countless recognised blunders I can mention but a few that I sense are more pertinent for this project. First, nowhere does the Genesis, or anywhere else in the Judaeo-christian books account state nephilim were the result of a union between bad 'angelic-type' beings and human women. Nowhere in the text does it assume any 'angelic' type procreating. It is pure and simple, theory on behalf of Skiba and others who project such announcements. This clearly shows a skewed and predisposed reading of these sacred texts. Obviously, this is the injection of one's own ideas and the ideas gleaned from other seemingly 'analogous' works influencing the meaning of that text. Underscoring the 'closed loop' reasoning mentioned numerously. The first four verses of Genesis 6 can noway be read as some supernatural procreating episode. It clearly begins by stating people began to naturally multiply, and that daughters were born to them, and some folks liked the daughters, taking them as wives (Genesis 6:1-2). It seems clear that some other group of mankind known to the author as the sons of the gods (plural). It was this collective, known as sons of the deities that were attracted to the daughters. Another disagreement with the usual Christian interpretation is there is absolutely also no mention that this second group specifically had any carnal desire; just that they found the daughters attractive. Bursting the bubble of these 'people' having a lustful disposition to the daughters; is that absolutely nowhere in the rest of the Old Testament does the Hebrew word translated as either 'attractive', 'fair', 'good' or another close derivative indicates any lustful character. I defy anyone to actually see anything sexual spoken in the verses where the same Hebrew word is found; see ESV: Genesis 24:16; 41:26 (two times); 41:35; deuteronomy 6:10; and 23:6; judges 7:22; esther 2:16. No lust. But attractive, that's it! A carnal interpretation was imported from some other source. That being 1 enoch and other similar stories. Besides, logically it disturbs the flow of the message too much if the guess of some supernatural entity arrived (out of the blue) on the scene; only to again vanish in the next instant! The very next verse (verse three) is astoundingly confusing. Why is this arbitrarily placed in the middle of the current established scene? Where did this ideology originate? Why bring up some arbitrary standard to 'life' now; shouldn't this have been mentioned sometime earlier. Considering the hyperbolic extreme ages of the antediluvians of the previous chapter! Following immediately is the equally confusing and most unfortunate interjection of a strange

Hebrew word: nephilim or, as is often translated; giants. Verse (4) only states that these mighty men were around the time when the choosing and marrying of fair daughters of men unfolded; at the multiplying of mankind on the earth. So, I must ask the religious punter, where is the clear mention of angels? Or, the equally clear mention that nephilim or the 'sons of deities' are angels? Or anything explicitly had carnal thoughts regarding the daughters! This quick outline of the Genesis 6, verses one through four, is the Literal yet plainest understanding of what is read in this chapter of Genesis! Isn't it that we are prone to conjecture and linking what should not be, only because it is in proximity, and we have already come to a segment with a predisposed idea. Below is the text of the Genesis passages from one of the most popular bibles published to date. The "English Standard Version" (ESV). I challenge a reader to see any mention of angels or some supernatural procreating going on:

> (6:1)"When man began to multiply on the face of the land (6:2) and daughters were born to them, the sons of God [Elohim] saw that the daughters of man were attractive. And they took as their wives any they chose. (6:3) Then the Lord said, "My Spirit shall not abide in man forever, for he is flesh: his days shall be 120 years." (6:4) The Nephilim were on the earth in those days, and also afterward, when the sons of God came in to the daughters of man and they bore children to them. These were the mighty men who were of old, the men of renown."[cccii]

For a potential symbolic rendering of these verses, I refer readers to Appendix 1. Which offers (I think) a better understanding. Let us now deconstruct these verses a little, for frankly, as stated these verses make little actual sense to think an angelic/alien type being had a conjugal union with humans. Resulting in a demonically inspired progeny. Verse one for instance; it must be agreed upon that here it is clearly deduced that the subject of this fable is mankind. No mention of any 'supernatural' entity should enter the mind at the plainest of readings. Contextually; therefore, the fable must follow suit. It makes no logical or reasonable sense to suddenly assume some supernatural entity burst on the scene. Verse (2), to assume that the sons of deities are angel-type being is no thing but pure unfounded, unmitigated insinuation on behalf of the commentator! To suggest an angel type entity (that mated with human women) as is the custom of countless 'christians' and early Jewish commentators writing on these verses, as will be shown shortly; is nonsense. To continue with this summation is to make known to any discerned reader that the author has come to interpret this scene from an ancient, yet still predisposed ideology. The third verse, as it reads in English, is nonsensical too. One must ask where did this come from. Why is it here? To what is it related? Also with verse four; there seems to be much information missing. There seems to be a gaping hole where the redactor has either misplaced purposely, or completely obliterated a great portion of the tale. He/ they have nonetheless, tacked onto the remarks of verse two, verses three, and four that do not seem to equate with the premise of the opening two verses. Scholar and translator, William Harwood's "Pre–Pentateuch Torah's: before they were interwoven" is insightful and may go some ways in filling in some of the gaps. Instead of the usual biased endnotes of what Church-sponsored sacred books offer, he adds his own challenging commentary within the body of the text. His (unbiased and coherent) translation + historic commentary (in bold) reads as follows. Harwood's interpretation of Genesis 6:1-4 reads:

(6:1) The time came when humans had begun to proliferate on the land and daughters had been born to them, (6:2) that the sons of the gods saw that the daughters of humankind were attractive, and they coupled with as many as they chose. [**The "sons of the gods" were the seven planetary gods. In post-Captivity Judaism they became Yahweh's messengers, and in Christianity the archangels Mercury/Gabriel, Jupiter/Raphael, Venus/Satan, Mars/Michael, Saturn/Uriel, Sol/Galgaliel, and luna/Ophaniel.**] (6:3) Yahweh then said, "Humankind must not retain forever the breath that is mine, since he is mere protoplasm. Henceforth his life is to be limited to 120 years. [**The redactor failed to delete this verse, even though his final Torah showed most of the Jewish patriarchs living beyond 120 years. In 1997 a woman died in France at the age of 122. What are readers to think of the veracity of this verse then?**][ccciii] (6:4) There were giants in the land in those days, when the sons of the gods were getting into the daughters of humankind and they were bearing their offspring. They were powerful in the old days, and won great reputations. [**Much later Jewish mythology viewed the offspring of those God/mortal couplings as giants with mortal bodies inherited from their mothers and immortal spirits inherited from their fathers. (This was long before Judaism had any "afterlife" concept.) When the giants' mortal bodies drowned in Noah's flood, their immortal spirits, needing bodies to satisfy their lusts, began "possessing" humans, creating a lucrative market for exorcists like Jesus.**][ccciv]

There are more than just a few very interesting points arising from this translation and Harwood's accompanying commentary. Rightly, as I have stated above the passage begins as a commentary on the population multiplying. For some reason, the redactor then inserts, as correctly pointed out by Harwood that potentially a (mythic/symbolic) bunch of 'planetary deities' are introduced; all of whom apparently had a 'thing' for the daughters. How and why this was, or became evident to the originating author is unknown and remains completely cryptic. For, the Genesis author has supposedly chosen to not divulge the reason for why the 'sons of deities' became attracted to them. However, what if these 'planetary' Archangels (as Harwood notes) are a suggestion or, indication of women's role in the community as powerful Sibylline oracles? Providing a sense of jealousy, hubris (although veiled); that the 'son's of 'God" desired. Could it be that the 'attractiveness' of the daughters is attributed to their Sibylline status? Added confusion is noticed by the addition of (verse three). There is a sudden and abrupt interjection with the subject of life spans. See Harwood's explanation and my above commentary. Evidently, the deity of the Genesis (6:1-4) author got it very wrong! Several further quandaries arise here. Should verse (6:3) not be more at home in the preceding chapters of Genesis? After all, the redactor does intimate hugely hyperbolic ages of people. That is, unless these should also be reconciled with symbolic meanings. The patriarchs being deities of old also. Finally, it is interesting that Harwood chose to translate the Hebrew word used in verse four, as giants also. The commentary he offers on this verse in addition is compelling, aligning somewhat closely with my later commentary on the meaning of another Hebrew word, translated as Shades. See the sub–section Hell of a giant factory below. In confirmation to not only my understanding but also that offered by Harwood, despite some obvious differences is the following commentary offered by Graves and Patai, from chapter 18: The Sons of God and the Daughters of Men, in "Hebrew Myth":

> "The explanation of this myth, which has been a stumbling block to theologians, may be the arrival in Palestine of tall, barbarous Hebrew herdsmen early in the second millennium B.C., and their exposure, by marriage, to an Asianic (sic) civilization. 'Sons of El' in this sense would mean the 'cattle-owning worshippers of the Semite Bull-God El'; 'Daughters of Adam' would mean 'women of the soil' (adama), namely the Goddess-worshipping Canaanite agriculturists, notorious for their orgies and premarital prostitution. If so, this historical event has been tangled with the Ugaritic myth of how El seduced two mortal women and fathered divine sons on them, namely Shahar ('Dawn') and Shalem ('Perfect'). Shahar appears as a winged deity in Psalm [139:9]; and his son, according to Isaiah 14:12, was the fallen angel Helel. Unions between gods and mortals, that is to say between kings or queens and commoners, occur frequently in Mediterranean and Middle Eastern myth. Since later Judaism rejected all deities but its own transcendental God, and since He never married or consorted with any female whatsoever, Rabbi Shimon ben Yohai in Genesis Rabba felt obliged to curse all who read 'Sons of God' in the Ugaritic sense. Clearly, such an interpretation was still current in the second century A.D., and lapsed only when the Bene Elohim were re-interpreted as 'sons of judges'. Elohim meant both 'God' and 'judge', the theory being that when a duly appointed magistrate tried a case, the Spirit of El possessed him: 'I have said, ye are gods.' (Psalm 82:6). This myth is constantly quoted in the Apocrypha, the New Testament, the Church Fathers, and midrashim."[cccv]

True. An angel-type interpretation is prolific throughout early Jewish and Christian commentary.[cccvi] Interesting also is one other point made by another author, Steve McRoberts. In questioning the sons of God assertion made by countless Christian authors like Rob and those already mentioned. In his book, "A cure for Fundamentalism: Why the

Bible cannot be the word of God", McRoberts adds the following comments related to the verse (Genesis 6:2). The following thoughts are worth more consideration, being relevant to our overall discussion in this section. He writes:

> "Elsewhere we are told that Jesus is the "only" begotten son of God. (1 john 4:9) so how can there be sons (plural) of God as related here? At least one of these scriptures must be wrong."

Confirming this reference and the question directed at (1 john) the Greek word translated as 'only' in English is monogenes. A word used to denote Jesus' strictly unique (without equal) status as deity's son. This, according to (Strongs 3439) Thus, yes, just how many 'sons' does the deity have?[cccvii] Furthermore, can we really honestly assert that such a conjugal union between the 'sons of gods' and 'daughters of men' was taboo in the creators' mind? Maybe such thinking comes about because of the equally indoctrinated ideology that 'procreating, i.e., nakedness is now taboo unless by wedded coupling (see prior comments in Nail Four: the study of Genesis chapter three). Is not this just another example of our indoctrinated prosthetic memory at work? A critical look at this verse highlights the fact that nowhere in the verse (Genesis 6:2), or the preceding verses does the deity strictly forbid such unions. As McRoberts points out also, neither does the deity offer counsel for those who were planning this 'apparent' abhorrent act. Something is skew-whiff. Which verse, or verses are then correct? Which are we to believe? Is Jesus the only (singular-without equal) son, or are there others that sit upon that throne and status? Is any coupling that produces a progeny outside marriage really taboo? Surely, countless other and similar questions arise when attempting to look at such verses with a more critical eye. A careful analysis of both the Old Testament and New Testament reveal clear paradoxical statements. Confirming my assertions, Jewish folklore is also not immune to such ideas as those proposed by Skiba and other religious theorists. Surely, Rob sourced the following text for his ideas, and possibly failed to note it as his resource? Chapter 4: Noah; "The Punishment of the Fallen Angels" in "Legends of the Jews", is where we read an accounting of the events and the ideas championed by those who insist 'fallen angel' types are spoken of here in our Genesis 6 passage. Legends of the Jews reads in part:

> "Chiefly the fallen angels and their giant posterity caused the depravity of mankind. The blood spilled by the giants cried unto heaven from the ground, and the four archangels accused the fallen angels and their sons before God, ...Gabriel was charged to proceed against the bastards and the reprobates, the sons of the angels begotten with the daughters of men and plunge them into deadly conflicts with one another....[cccviii] When the angels came to earth, and beheld the daughters of men in all their grace and beauty, they could not restrain their passion. Shemḥazai saw a maiden named Istehar, and he lost his heart to her. She promised to surrender herself to him, if first he taught her the Ineffable Name, by means of which he raised himself to heaven. He assented to her condition. But once she knew it, she pronounced the Name, and herself ascended to heaven, without fulfilling her promise to the angel. God said, "Because she kept herself aloof from sin, we will place her among the seven stars, that men may never forget her," and she was put in the constellation of the Pleiades... Azazel began to devise the finery and the ornaments by means of which women allure men. Thereupon God sent Metatron to tell Shemḥazai that He had resolved to destroy the world and bring on a deluge..."[cccix]

Undoubted the whole idea of 'fallen' angelic beings mating with human women and corrupting the earth is pilfered directly from this Jewish folk-legend as well as Rabbinic tradition. Even if Rob used only the 1 enoch passage (which describes this episode in a similar fashion) he surely had taken either source out of context. That is the only way I see, he could have such story's confirming his presumptions. Respected scholar Wayne Grudem does not agree. Rob Skiba and the rest of Christian fundamentalists who favour a sinful angel-type entity would be all-the-wiser for taking heed of a little wisdom. In Commentary on 1 Peter, Grudem writes plainly:

> "Jewish literature frequently mentions human, not angelic sin, as the reason why God brought the flood on the earth. The texts are too numerous to cite here but it is sufficient to give the references: Targums Onkelos, Pseudo-Jonathan, Neofiti, and the Fragmentary Targum on Genesis ... And the phrase 'the generation of the flood' is used frequently in Rabbinic

writings as a paradigm of extreme human wickedness... All... texts (forty-five [in total], from every strand of Jewish tradition) must be seen in contrast to the slight evidence of a tradition of angelic sin at this time: one text (Jubilee 10:4–5) which mentions angelic sin in Noah's day and two... which say angels were punished at the flood (one of which, T. Naph. 3:5, also says the earth was made 'without dweller or produce' because of angels' sin). Not one text from any strand of Jewish tradition mentions angels disobeying 'during the building of the ark'. The overwhelming weight of extra-biblical tradition—as well as the biblical evidence itself—emphasizes (sic) human sinners, not angels..."[cccx]

As relevant these words are to the point I desire to have made. I again remind readers that although Grudem is correct; there is no Jewish tradition confirming any 'angelic-type' misdemeanour, there is also the issue alerted to in my previous Nail (Four above). Neither does the Bible assume any man, woman, or child committing any sin. Period! Thus, both men have come to their topic with an already distorted view. Both seem incorrect on the point of sin. Nonetheless, Rob and others are extremely off the mark. Effectively any author postulating a fallen angel-type reason for the birth of 'giants'/ nephilim as a cause for the flood that follows the narrative; all such authors and commentators stating this have lost the plot. Ideologies as these aren't worthy of anyone's time. They were birthed through a misguided and preconceived ideology. One that has been peddled for eons. If Rob Skiba used the texts cited above as a source and came to the text with a belief that some angel-type entity mating with women. From where might the myths recorded in 1 enoch and "Legends of the Jews" have originated? Obviously, we would be required to search outside sources and disciplines; like archaeology. There are sources available today for the studious who is unwilling to take the projections by religious authors as complete gospel. Aside "Hebrew Myths", there seems to be a title that closely resembles, and so has offered readers probable mythic traditions from which these stories derived. I sought however to go back further. Asking from what or where might the myths Rob uses have derived. Finding that most likely such myths like 1 enoch, and "Legends of the Jews"...were pilfered, doctored and revisioned from a more ancient source. One such source could very well be an ancient Babylonian tale; titled "When the Gods were Human". In relevant part, noticeably regarding the rebellion of the angelic types of the 'Legends tale' it offers a rebellion: (The rebellion of the Igigu●).[cccxi] It reads:

> "For 2,500 years in excess the gods bore the hardship day and night. (Then) they sat down and began to berate (each other); [they] muttered in the pits: 'Come, we will apply to the throne-bearer so that he takes away our great hardship from us! The God, the advisor of the gods, the hero – come, we will lift (him) from his seat! Enlil, the advisor of the gods, the hero, come, we will lift (him) from his seat!' We opened his mouth and spoke to the gods, his brothers: 'Let us beat the throne - bearer of old times; ... will appoint Enlil! ... another he will appoint, ... before us ...' (We incite the gods further) 'The advisor of the gods, the hero – come, we will lift (him) from his seat! Enlil, the advisor of the gods, the hero – come, we will lift (him) from his seat! Now call out for the fight, we will stage a battle!' The gods listened at his behest, they put fire to their tools, They set fire to their shovels, put their hampers to the torch. They clasped each other when they approached the gate of the sanctuary of the hero Enlil. It was night at half-watch, the house was surrounded, the God does not know [it]. It was night at half-watch, the Ekur was surrounded, Enlil does not know [it]. Yet then Kalkal took note (and) let all be locked, he seized the bolt, checked the gate. Then Kalkal awakened Nusku, they heard the clamour of the Igigu. And Nusku awakened his master, let him rise from the sleeping berth: 'My Lord, surrounded is your house, the fight is fast approaching your gate. Enlil, surrounded is your house, the fight is fast approaching your gate.' (Thereupon) Enlil let weapons be brought into his apartment. Enlil opened his mouth and spoke to the vizier Nusku: 'Nusku, bolt your gate, take your weapons (and) step before me!' Nusku bolted his gate, took his weapons, stepped before Enlil."[cccxii]

Although very fragmentary, I postulate there is relevance with this text and 1 enoch and Legends of the Jews. The title is the ultimate dead giveaway! The mindset of the ancient author and his community is on full display. The story is of an ancient mythical period before a time recorded by humankind. Much the same as that which is recognised in the Legends of the Jew's story above, which is also a telling of a long–since–past time? A rebellion of sorts took place! Maybe, just before or just after the creation of mankind in pre–history. The title of this Babylonian tale proclaims; this myth is titled, "When the Gods were

Human". The story is of an ancient and mythical period, a time set long before humankind. When the gods had to toil and do chores themselves (a common theme in numerous mythic tales) and being fed up with work and the noise of the created human, they rebelled! The gods' toil soon became unbearable, and so mankind was created as their slaves/ servants. Mankind, then begins to procreate and become so numerous clamour of their incessant noise (the drum (heart) beat was heard) and this begins to irritate the gods (Enlil- the supreme Babylonian deity specifically) who then threatens to eradicate them with a flood.

> "The land was loud as (roaring) bulls, through (their clamour) the God became restless. Enlil had to listen to their racket, (and) he spoke to the great gods: 'Troublesome has become to me the Racket of mankind, resulting from their rowdiness I lack sleep..."

When the Gods were Human undoubtedly shares some interesting parallels (if not explicitly, they may be implied) with the Genesis 6 and subsequent tales we read in the Judaeo-Christian sacred books; the flood narrative and Legends of the Jews. That this text, like any ancient work is fragmentary, and so assumptions of parallels are only theory at best. Still, such texts as this Babylonian story surely offer us a possible if not wholly probable zero–point; a potential beginning to the Genesis 6 myth. It may be the source of the 1 enoch text and indeed the Legends of the Jews text cited above. Aside Legends and the text of 1 enoch, both clearly having some parallels to the Genesis 6:1-4 story in certain of its passages.[cccxiii] Tales of angels, giants, and other mythic entities that hate, wish to eat, copulate with or who are hell bent on destroying human life is part and parcel of all myths right around the world. Christians need to wake up and realise for once their particular 'brand' of religious myths are not 'new' revelations about some entity or deity. Christians would be the wiser by jettisoning the ideology that their beloved sacred stories are truthful and all others are false, abhorrent, and demonically inspired. I remind readers again with the words of Wilberforce. To all others, Wilberforce bluntly admonished his belief about christianity, that "Our religion is sublime, pure, beneficent; theirs is mean, licentious, and cruel." With such an ideology, spreading there is no wonder why many Christian 'writers' and end-time commentators are gearing up for a last ditch battle! Religion demands an enemy that must on all accounts be destroyed completely. Did anyone happen to catch the cosmological reference in the above 'Legends of the Jews' commentary? That the maiden "...was put in the constellation of the Pleiades." Where or what is the <Pleiades>? We have an amazing amount of information today regarding this star-cluster. Interestingly it sits in the constellation of <Taurus>.[cccxiv] To the ancients:

> "The Pleiades were associated with rain because their rising and setting marked the limits of the Mediterranean sailing season. One of them (not two) appears from Greek myth to have become extinct in the late second millennium B.C."[cccxv]

Just as intimated earlier, many legendary allegories of the ancients were specifically attempting to reconcile or explain anomalous cosmic characteristics roundabout. Some of that folklore made it into the corpuses of what we now call scripture. A major problem with attempting to use numerous ancient tales and like texts as support for a particular idea such as some end-time phenomena, is the failure by modern commentators to truly recognise their type: as complete cultural folklore. As noted, there is a vast array of Jewish literature that is legend. As with enoch, 'Legends of the Jews' is a collection of folklore; these are mere fictional stories. The title even admits that the stories found within are, but Legends, being literary devises of the imagination that is often deliberately false offerings of the improbable. What is to be made of the countless other known para–sacred works in circulation now being studied? Ancient tales and pseudo-religious texts like the various Apocalypses; the numerous Gnostic Gospels; Dead Sea scrolls; the various Visionary Wisdom Texts; the Christian Apocrypha; the Jewish Pseudepigraphal works, and Jewish Kabbalah texts and the countless other highly regarded spiritual teachings from around the Mediterranean. First Century Jewish historian Josephus equally put forward a comparable theory to the fallen angels in his (Antiquities

1.3.1.) No doubt Josephus was offering his interpretation (with embellishments) of the Jewish commentary he received:

> "For many angels of God had sex with women, and fathered wanton children who disdained everything that was nice, due to the confidence they had in their own power. The tradition handed down is that that these dared to do similar acts to those called Giants by the Greeks. Noah was unable to endure their accomplishments and wanted to persuade them to change their minds and do better, However, as he could not change their minds, and seeing that they would not yield to him, but were stubborn and enjoyed being powerful, he was afraid they would kill him, along with his wife and children, and those with whom they were living, so he emigrated from that land."[cccxvi]

To say the least, assuming there is any connection between Genesis 6:1-4, with an angelic/human hybrid frankly speaks with a long-lost misogynistic mythology apparent at the time of its composition. Undoubted, the Genesis 6 tale of nephilim as the cause for the Bible's 'Flood' narrative was pilfered, doctored and embellished by generations of interpreters. Possibly, those stories mentioned above like the Babylonian and later Greek tales that assumed 'God's' were originally human. That the ancients revered some highly esteemed individuals as deities is not new. Recall the Judaeo-christian psalms (82:6) states as much. Such tales of human/hybrid type gods are still prevalent. Recall, Korpel and De Moor's insights, mentioned in Nail Four. It is truely absurd to read the tales in the Judaeo–Christian books, and those extra-para-sacred books as literal. They were never meant to be read from a literal perspective. Ancient audiences and the original authors knew the narratives they penned weren't literal. But were tales explaining the ancient world in which they lived.

There is a surprising array of material to assist us today with myth. Explaining, Why and how they were understood and used by the ancients. Thanks to scholars like Joseph Campbell the world of myth was reborn. Yet, Christian interpreters and commentators largely ignore studies in mythology. Unless the myth assists with a preconceived hypothesis. In the 17th - 18th Century a tale arose to instil in a generation great fear and trembling; the greatly feared and legendary creature: The "Hydra" of Hamburg.[cccxvii] A ghastly creature said to have been killed in the late 17th Century C.E. It was completely fictitious (like the angel hypothesis of Genesis 6). It was a man-made <u>beast</u>; a composite being made of 'clay' and various animal heads and other parts spliced ever so meticulously. The separate parts being cleverly fitted together to represent a most hideous and fearsome entity: the unsightly multi-headed monster portrayed in the book of 'Revelation'. The individual who finally uncovered this hoax believed with good reason, it was nothing but a sharp manipulative tool of medieval monks. (1) to keep potential wayfarers from wondering from the 'faith', and (2) to illustrate the veracity of the 'Christian message.' Carl Linnaeus, the discoverer of this most bazaar forgery, also believed that the creature's initial invention (by various skilled Christian monks, including a taxidermist) was to literally augment the fear-factor and utterly terrify the believing community. So they believed the end-of-the-world-was-neigh.[cccxviii] The Hydra is an undeniable historic example of Christian myth making. A manipulative and deceptive tool of clergy who knew no bounds to propagate viral beliefs for no other purpose than control of their 'flocks'. Thus, Genesis 6:1-4 is still an enigmatic tale to attempt to explain. Having several branches that seem to be tangled among others. Leaving all this aside. As stated numerously. What of the strange entity nephilim. Who or what were they? Were they real, and why do some bibles translate this Hebrew word giant; others leave this Hebrew term effectively a transliteration only? It is a perplexing Hebrew word if ever there was!

Nephilim giants:

MANY 'CHRISTIAN' WRITERS like Rob leave readers with the impression that the meaning of nephilim is 'Giants.' It is after all one translation of this enigmatic Hebrew word in many Church-sponsored sacred books. A brief understanding from a scholarly perspective though may be of assistance. The "Theological Dictionary of the Old Testament", entry Nephilim explains in a little more depth than Dr. Nyland's brief explanation above.[cccxix] Stating,

> "While some scholars attempt to relate this term etymologically• to nāpal via the noun nēpel "untimely birth" or "miscarriage" (as productive of superhuman monstrosities), a more likely reconstruction is the proposal of a root nāpal, akin to other weak verbs, pûl "be wonderful, strong, mighty," pālā' "be wonderful," and even pālâ "separate, distinguish," pālal "discriminate." This pattern of semantically related groups of weak verbs with two strong consonants in common is a notably recurrent phenomenon in Hebrew lexicography. Actually, the translation "giants" is supported mainly by the [Septuagint] and may be quite misleading. The word may be of unknown origin and mean "heroes" or "fierce warriors" etc. The RSV and NIV transliteration "Nephilim" is safer and may be correct in referring the noun of a race or nation."[cccxx]

Despite a recommendation that the Hebrew word nephilim may be a 'safer' option, there are many English Bible translations where the translator chose 'giant'. Reasons for doing so are just as enigmatic to ferret out as the word nephilim itself. Bible dictionaries and theological lexicons are all not that helpful either. Unless they provide a decent discussion. One or two sentence entries offered by some popular Bible dictionary's are terrible guides. Not just a few begin an entry arguing for an affiliation with the English word, giant. The popular "New American Standard Hebrew-Aramaic and Greek Dictionary", and the standard Bible lexicons -"Strongs" are really only useless guides. Only supplying a small 'gloss' of words, and very minimal, nonexistent discussion from which to draw an informed conclusion. Example:

> "Nephilim (658c); from [Strongs] 5307; "giants," name of two peoples, one before the flood and one after the flood:—Nephilim"[cccxxi]

To state the obvious: this is a useless reference to make any kind of informed judgment and formulate an interpretation. There is absolutely no reasonable information. No reader needs such a short 'explanation.' Is this not just parroting the verses of Genesis 6:1-4? No wonder Rob and others commenting on Genesis 6:4 have assumed a 'giant' interpretation.

DECONSTRUCTING ENDTIME DELUSIONS

Standard Bible 'helps' like 'Strongs lexicon' or the 'NASB dictionary' make our minds up. Offering very little but to sanction our automatic assumptions that nephilim are enormous; that they were a by-product of superhuman hybrid monstrosities – because they 'fell'. Fell from what? "The Lexham Bible Dictionary" entry of nephilim is a much better guide; however, as it offers commentary instead of a few word glosses. But, why are we likely to hold a predisposition that giant means enormously in height? Because this is how 'giants' are portrayed across all forms of media in the modern era. Fairy-tails, folk stories and favoured myths on television, including blockbuster movie adaptations; all portray a 'giant' as enormous in size and strength. Many are a "grotesque" ('fallen') and fearsome. Few have a kindly disposition.[cccxxii] There are story's of egotistical (malevolent) races of giant deities who fought battles against the (benevolent) Greek pantheon of Zeus – the King of deities. The Titans. In Greek fables, near all 'giants' are known today as fearsome creatures that would have easily towered over even the tallest man alive today. Giants of countless myth and tales from around the world depict persons of huge stature– this much is true. Such persons are said to have built cities, temples, and other mammoth structures of antiquity. For example:

> "...the Mexican city of the gods Teotihuacan. It is located near Mekiho (Mexico). It is much more ancient than even the Aztec civilization. There is a version that the city was built in order to turn people into gods. The layout of the "city of gods" is similar to the model of the solar system. If the Temple of Quetzalkratl (Quetzalcoatl) can be represented as the Sun, then the rest of the planets, including even Uranus and Pluto, can be found to match on the plan of the city. Consequently, even then the inhabitants of the city knew about the structure of the solar system! But, probably, after the departure of the giants, the city fell into neglect and gradually began to collapse. Perhaps, if...these cyclopean structures (were not built), no one would have suggested that there was a race of giants. And so, a legend was created about powerful, rational, strong giants ...[who] built on earth a kingdom of harmony and justice. An interesting fact is that every nation that inhabits Earth today has legends about giants."[cccxxiii]

Further,

"It is also easy to find in the Koran the story of how Noah built the ark, and the giants living on Earth at that time said to him: "The Flood will not harm us. We are too tall. Our feet are so big that we can block the rivers with them." But the Great Flood swallowed up self-confident giants. There are such records in the Babylonian books of sacred information: "Noah saved the giant Og by allowing him to fit behind the lattice door of the ark. Through this lattice, Noah served him food every day." The rescued giant, in consequence, had offspring– the giants began to live on Earth again. The largest colony of giants settled in Palestine. When Moses led the Jews away from Egypt, he sent intelligence agents to Palestine and this is what they said: "... There we also saw giants..., from a gigantic family; and we were in our eyes before them like locusts, so were we in their eyes." Residents of Sparta wore military campaigns instead of the banner of the skeleton of a giant warrior named Orest (height 3.5 meters) ... Numerous finds of skeletons of giants in the Caucasus can confirm the assumption that the region of the Caucasus Mountains became another place of concentration of the settlements of giants. Perhaps this is not by chance. After all, it was in the mountains that the giants, whom Noah did not take into his ark, tried to escape from the Flood. Two residents of Georgia, who were looking for adventures in mountain caves, discovered the skeleton of a four-meter giant, near which there was a weapon in the form of an ancient sword from some unknown metal."[cccxxiv]

From these descriptions, readers must surely be able to glimpse numerous parallels between the story of Genesis 6 and its apparent giants, with contemporaneous ancient writings and stories. Surely, by now the author of the Genesis 6 episode is known to have recorded – a 'take on' or re-telling of stories known and in wide circulation. Must this Genesis episode be of some divine revealation? Surely not! As with most Christian commentators the assumed enormity of the nephilim is these entities were fallen. From what exactly did these creatures 'Fall'? What does it mean to 'fall' anyway? Do Christian advocates use 'fall' as described by any dictionary; as a move from a higher to lower level, often rapidly without control. The Hebrew term often translated giant or left as nephilim: scholars affirm both terms are as legitimate as the other. 'Giant,' being an apt descriptive of the Septuagint – the Greek translation of the Old Testament. But, does not mean 'to fall.' This was identified earlier. Just as the "Theological dictionary" entry above stipulates.

DECONSTRUCTING ENDTIME DELUSIONS

Unfortunate for the modern Bible reader both terms nephilim and giant, are extremely unclear and are not easily understood. Translators have to admit. They have been rather inconsistent and sloppy in their translating, using this term. According to Strongs lexicon, nephilim also carries the meaning – to fall, apostates, or rebels. By which those accustomed to this interpretation add the meaning as Rob to a 'race' of angels (Watchers or other) who at some stage in antiquity became rebels and apostate and 'fell' from the heaven to mate with human daughters. The Hebrew English Bible, the ESV and the NKJV; however, correctly I believe call attention to the identity of the mysterious beings– nephilim. These standard sacred books assist readers in determining what these might represent. Assisting the average reader by italicising English words that do not appear in the actual Hebrew Manuscripts. Aramaic scholar Andrew Roth also contributes with the standard messianic/ Jewish study to shore up the difficulty of this Hebrew term:

- Calling Nephilim angels is a bit of a pagan and/or later rabbinic incursion on the pshat (plain meaning) of Genesis 6. These ideas were given greater currency in some Jewish pre-rabbinic sources also, such as the apocryphal book of Enoch and the works of Phil Judaeus.

- I would caution people in strongest possible terms on this matter: any doctrine solely based on this term and without further context is dangerous and overly simplistic! Also "sons of Elohim" don't necessarily HAVE to be the nephilim but could be another group - the text is only saying that nephilim were around the same time the sons of Elohim went into the daughters of Cain. Saying they are the same is an assumption, not proof. The Hebrew kind of goes roundabout like this, from A to B and back to A, so there is no way to know for certain.

- The Nephilim as a word is best translated as "mighty men"; it is a synonym for gowrim (warriors). In ancient literature, great men in strength and heart were often depicted as giants in stature as well. But there is no way to know how the real Nephilim's stature matched their prowess in war. I do think though their appearance with respect to Joshua's spies shows both a tendency to exaggerate when afraid, but also that there may have been a kernel of truth that they looked more powerful than the average man, somehow. Maybe their armor (sic) was just really cool and they had platform sandals, who really knows?

- So who were the sons of Elohim if not the Nephilim? No one knows for sure! I do know that the whole angels debate is useless as real angels don't commit fornication, which is a sin against YHWH, whether or not they can "do it". (I personally think they cannot.) But on this point, I do believe that the sons of Elohim could have represented a separate ancient group of men.

- It is interesting that their name Nephilim gets translated directly in effect - maybe it comes from an archaic tongue? See Genesis 6:4b.[cccxxv]

Andrew has above confirms previous thoughts that (1) calling these creatures nephilim angels is unwarranted, (2) to do so based on a simplistic understanding is wrong, and outrageous, (3) a better interpretation of the enigmatic Hebrew word is 'mighty men', (4) nobody knows who, or what these 'entities' (for lack of better term) were, so it is silly to assume as Rob, and countless others continue, they were some type of supernatural composite, and finally, (5) nephilim is likely a direct translation of an archaic tongue lost to time. Also disturbing while perusing this first chapter of Rob's book is that he insists the 'Sons of God' is referent to these 'fallen angels.' A school of thought that postulates these 'sons' are the fathers of the human-angelic hybrid 'giant' – nephilim. This is again complete fiction; such an interpretation is fallacious and completely wrong. It is however, likely the oldest and most worn-out interpretation known! Cassuto concurs:

> "The oldest interpretation, so far as we know, is: the angels. This view serves as the basis of a complete narrative in the Book of Enoch (The Ethiopic Version, ch. vi ff.); it is also reflected in many passages of the Pseudepigrapha and in the Zadokite Document... and was accepted by Philo, Josephus and by many of the Church Fathers and ecclesiastical writers. Consonant with this is the reading found in several MSS of the Septuagint, ἄγγελοι τοῦ θεοῦ, that is, 'angels of God'. The legends based on this interpretation have been incorporated in a number of Midrashim, for example, in Pirqe Rabbi Eliezer xxii, in the Yalqut xliv (which undoubtedly drew upon an ancient source), and also in other books."[cccxxvi]

An angelic type 'fall' is simply the consensual interpretation. So, is nothing new. Yet, just because it is the oldest, long standing interpretation does not necessarily affirm its validity. Those like Rob

DECONSTRUCTING ENDTIME DELUSIONS

Skiba who affirm the angel hypothesis often also employ a visual aid. Any Internet search of presumed 'giant sizes' results in numerous charts of apparent sizes. From an average human, of 6ft, through to the possible and massive sizes of the famed nephilim/ giant in hopes to bolster their opinion and give it credence.[cccxxvii] Another favourite to confirm 'nephilim giants, are claims assuming the Old Testament passage of (Amos 2:9) provides a present connection to his summation of Genesis 6. It is postulated that what this Old Testament 'Prophet' means is what he (Skiba) clearly hopes and wishes this passage to mean. That the description of the Amorite in reference to Cedar and Oak trees is therefore confirmation that there were then, enormous giants. This is little else than the fallacy: illegitimate totality transfer (I show why below in the section Amos 2:9). Questions surrounding the strangeness of nephilim/ giants eventually lead me to wonder what we are beginning to understand and discover of the world's ancient creatures. Are there any that could substitute for the nephilim/ giant entity? Soon, these questions are attended. Images of the sizes of the mentioned earlier chart of the presumed but totally subjective sizes offered for nephilim. Although there are various reports of skeletal remains being unearthed, just as portrayed in many charts found online. I take a study tour at and offer scientific and medical answers that explain gigantic sizes below. See also "Forbidden Archeology", (Ch. 6.) Though it would be foolish to subscribe to the fallen or otherwise 'angel/hybrid' hypothesis as an explanation of the 'nephilim' episode. It would seem there is some consensus to an angelology throughout the scripture. Most modern ideas and assertions on this subject despite our own presumptions, have also been drawn from many prevailing myths and tales that surrounded the sacred book's composition. Interestingly too is that there are numerous comments written by various others to Genesis 6:1-4, and another 'prophetic' book; isaiah 14:12-23, which for some is also said to speak of a 'fallen' angelic type. However, the context does not allow this interpretation as it speaks of the king of Babylon. Affirming that there are some Bible materials that contain a myth of rebel angels is stated by the author of "Fallen Angels: Soldiers of Satan's Realm". Bamberger writes:

> "The Bible contains some of the materials of which the myth of the rebel angels was fashioned. But the story itself and the ideas it expresses are found neither in the Bible nor in the heathen sources which Scripture occasionally echoes."[cccxxviii]

Statements as this however should cause researchers and advocates of an angelic type rebel alliance pause and further reflection. If there are any stories of a rebel angelic contingent, it, like the ideology of 'Original Sin' cannot be found, and is not expressed explicitly in or outside the sacred books. Aside those folklore texts already cited, where was the concept of a rebellious angel contingent originally geminated? Simply, in someone's own cognitive processes: a concept confirmed by Neuroscientists studying the effects of belief and faith on human brain function. This is expressed at a later stage. Brain function and its influences on belief and faith, and conversely is a new but fascinating science, and it is yielding some absorbing results. Readers would be well informed to source. The resources cited. Leaving aside the nephilim and 'sons of God' angel hypothesis, researchers of other disciplines have concluded that there is a vast amount of evidence globally that larger-than-the-average-human beings existed in antiquity. I am confident that such beings however were not in any way angelic or demonic types as is postulated. This is rather the designation attributed to them. Coming about through (oral) embellishment by those they encountered, and so, the audiences and storytellers proliferated the same messages in time. So, what can we know about giants?

Giants:

THE DEFENCE OF THE prospect of larger-than-today's-average human beings (giants) roaming the earth seems to be the object of many texts published today. Jason Breshears in his book "Giants on Ancient Earth: An In-Depth Study on the Nephilim" opens his study outlining the magnitude of larger–than–average skeletal remains currently unearthed throughout the world, from ancient times, through to the present day (I have already mentioned some of these). Unfortunately, as with the other authors who write on these subjects, Breshears then follows the usual sacred book, para–sacred train of thought regarding these beings; which I think, is stale and over–emphasised when attempting to explain these presences. The sacred book is the main source that researchers and authors use. Stepping outside this typical theological parameter, and casting one's net into the wider ocean of scholarly material, proves to be a worthy exercise; as I now hope to show. Though, for many, the emphasis of the 'giant' subject focusses on whether sometime in Earth–history there was giants roaming around; my emphasis in this sub–section asks why, and how these persons developed. Some of the following material therefore might be unfamiliar and 'new' to readers. In (2013) a Netflix documentary program titled, 'Forbidden History' dedicated one of its episodes to the mystery of giants. Particularly, much of the episode focused on giant stone (tomb-like) structures and various 'eye-witness' accounts of skeletal remains found throughout Sardinia– Italy. Interestingly, nephilim are mentioned on numerous occasions throughout the program. Jason Colavito, essay (29) Who were the Nephilim in his book "Faking History" interestingly narrates:

> "I'm going to admit here that what follows is mostly speculation, though I hope based on fact. I find Genesis 6: 4 interesting, but I think it belongs in the broader context of early Near Eastern myth. Literally, the phrase translated as "sons of God" says in Hebrew "sons of the gods" in the plural. This has been rationalized as something akin to the Royal We, but many have suggested it is a remnant of a pre-Judaic polytheistic pantheon. We know that in other Near Eastern cultures, the gods had sons and these sons were considered superhuman beings. The most famous is Gilgamesh, two-thirds God and one-third man, the hero who built the high walls of Uruk. Another is Humbaba, the terrifying, radiant giant who was the child of Hanbi and the ward of the sun God. The Greeks, too, imagined that the race of heroes that preceded their own— mostly the sons of the gods— were of gigantic stature, which they "confirmed" by claiming the bones of prehistoric elephants to be the remains of the giant heroes. But here is where it gets interesting. By 100 BCE, the writers of the Jewish apocryphal text called the Book of

Giants— a sort of sequel to the Book of Enoch— included both Gilgamesh and Humbaba as two of the antediluvian giants. This in and of itself is not conclusive, since it is centuries after Genesis, but it suggests that there was a tradition that the giants of Genesis reflected a Jewish interpretation of the widespread Near Eastern claim that the giants of old were the sons of the pagan gods. Since we know that other widespread Near Eastern myths had Biblical versions, including the Near Eastern Flood myth and the battle between the storm God and the chaos monster, it seems to me that the origins of Genesis 6:4 are to be found in Near Eastern hero stories that would have been the common folk culture of the region. I'm not the only one to see such a connection; unfortunately, though, most of the alternative writers who see the same connection claim that Gilgamesh is one of the Nephilim and therefore is an alien hybrid! It comes down to the key assumption one makes in thinking about ancient myth: are these stories to be taken as literature, or as fact? Until some skeletons of these giants show up— and no, the elephant bones don't count— it is terribly dangerous to take literally stories that have been told and retold in countless forms across time and space. Bonus: Alternative theorists like to take ancient texts literally, but for those paying attention, this poses a problem. In the Epic of Gilgamesh, Gilgamesh lives after the Flood, but in the Book of Giants, he lives before the Flood. Clearly, both ancient texts can't be right, and if one is wrong, this calls into question the practice of using ancient texts uncritically as literal reports of mythic events."[cccxxix]

Though I do not recommend outright the assertions made, particularly by religious authors regarding sizes, it is very interesting to note:

"...many of the Late Carboniferous and Early Permian arthropod species had body sizes that were five to seven times larger than their modern-day counterparts, and an overall size range from three to as much as 12 times larger. What type of an Earth could have produced such [megafauna/ mega-flora including huge humanoids]?..."[cccxxx]

Further, gigantism 'could' and is most likely explained by the assertion of several scientists of other scientific fields who have projected some interesting suggestions; one theory advances new findings surrounding the 'apparently' demonically inspired, Devil gas, – CO_2 (Carbon Dioxide) –according to devoted gw (global warming) scaremongers. Ignored today by elite politicians pushing for a decarbonisation strategy, is the factually prevalent and vital atmospheric gas that all life exhale as a waste product. CO_2 is scientifically proven to be not as damaging to our planet as we are told by ignorant politicians, and global warming activists. Nor, is it detrimental to carbon-based lifeforms (unless maybe purposefully ingested in considerably high quantities); despite what global-warming fatalists insist. Rather CO_2 seems to be most unexpectedly beneficial: promoting better growth, and superior nutritional value of crops, vegetation, and those that consume them. Directly from the web-store page, the new publication, "The Many Benefits of Atmospheric CO_2 Emissions", outlines fifty-five benefits of this gas. The blurb for this publication in part reads:

> "Global warming alarmists tell us the horrors of increasing atmospheric CO_2 concentration. Skeptics tell us that it's not all that bad. Finally, there is a non-apologetic treatise that tells us of the benefits of atmospheric CO_2 enrichment in an alphabetical format. This extensively referenced 360-page color (sic) book by [father and son] Drs. Idso... tells us of fifty-five benefits of atmospheric CO_2 enrichment, and belongs in the library of all who study CO_2 and climate. That's 55 benefits. Fifty-five! The benefits are not squeezed out of computer models, but are based on real data. CO_2, after all, is plant food, absolutely necessary for all of the biosphere."[cccxxxi]

In the opening pages, the many benefits to increase CO_2 levels are succinctly summarised and are offered for quick perusal. I draw your attention to the following for further consideration because the current topic– giants. Some headings read:

- **Avoiding Human Starvation and Plant and Animal Extinctions** – Unless the air's CO_2 content continues its upward trajectory, humans will experience mass starvation, and untold numbers of plants and animals will face extinction over the last half of the current century.

- **Biogenic Volatile Organic Compounds** (BVOC's) – Real-world evidence indicates that (1) both rising air temperature and CO_2 concentrations significantly increase desirable vegetative BVOC emissions, particularly from trees, which constitute the most prominent photosynthetic force on the planet, and that (2) this phenomenon has a large number of extremely important and highly beneficial biospheric consequences.

- **Herbivory** – As the air's CO2 content continues to rise, more productive and profuse terrestrial and aquatic vegetation will likely support a proportional increase in plant herbivores, with both "the eaten and the eaters" benefitting alike.

- **Human Longevity** – The last 150 to 200 years has seen a significant degree in global-warming...Simultaneously the planet has experienced a rise in atmospheric CO2 concentration that has...had no discernible negative influence on human health, as represented by... [the] human lifespan. In fact, they may have actually helped to lengthen human lifespan. (Bold original.)

These are just a few of the fifty-five astoundingly poignant conclusions that the Idso scientists were able to determine about the influences, benefits of this vital trace element CO2. The authors have determined in their extensive research of (55) studies into CO2 and what effects it has on a planetary scale. Herbivory statements are of interest. Going some-ways to a reasoned explanation for known megafauna and mega-flora. Has it arisen to ponder questions of how and why many <dinosaurs> were so large? Surviving rainforests are still full of ancient massive plant species (esp. ferns). Other publications confirm that in prehistoric times our home had a much greater concentration of these vital gasses– particularly O2– Oxygen. Steve Preston in his title, "Incredible Titans" offer the following interesting comments also:

"A massive hole somehow appeared where our modern Pacific Ocean is today. Almost immediately after this event, animals began to get huge. Hundreds of modern human footprints have been found comingled (sic) with dinosaur prints. Many of these footprints are huge and they have been found around the world. Ancient and massive stone and metal tools and axes have been found around the world as if large people lived around the world... [The antithesis is] Immediately following the Cretaceous Extinction, animals became much smaller... Three hundred samples of oxygen levels in captured air inside amber shows we had a much higher percentage of Oxygen when the Amber was sap coming out of prehistoric trees... The air captured in sap, hundreds of thousands of years ago, had a much higher concentration of oxygen... the Earth's atmosphere was getting less and less during the Mesozoic Era. While the Oxygen content may have been 50% or more in the ancient atmosphere, by the Cretaceous Age, the T-Rex would get winded more quickly and things were getting problematic until something happened 120 thousand years ago... Analysis of the gases in these bubbles showed that the earth's atmosphere, during the last portion of the Mesozoic, contained about 35 percent oxygen compared to present levels of 21 percent. Results are based upon more than 300 analyses by U.S. Geological Survey scientists of Cretaceous, Tertiary, and recent-age amber from 16 world sites. The oldest amber in this study was "early Cretaceous."[cccxxxii]

These and the statements on human longevity above are definitely one that will be of some interest to believers; it would seem to offer empirical data supporting the mystery of extended (hyperbolic) lifespans the Genesis text infers. Without much by way of empirical data, the Christian community assumes the total veracity of all the bibles' mythic assertions. As earlier hinted, believers nowadays just don't seem to think outside their presumed boxes of made-up 'truth'. One Christian commentator in his interpretation confirms, writing:

> "Here is a mystery: The life span of Methuselah, who died at the age of 969 years, was shorter than that of his father, Enoch, who lived on this Earth for only 365 years. After 365 years of what was apparently an exceptionally righteous life, Enoch disappeared—without dying.[cccxxxiii] This incident suggests mankind is immortal—that there is actually life beyond death. Living forever was God's original plan and purpose for mankind from the beginning. If God can cause a person to live forever, then for Him to allow some to live 1,000 years is nothing in comparison. Genesis 1:31 and Gen 5:1–32 suggest that in the pre-Flood world climatic conditions were favorable (sic) and food was abundant. Still, other factors must have contributed to giantism and greater longevity."[cccxxxiv]

He further tells,

> "I recently heard an interesting story. A resident of Los Angeles, California, passed out while visiting our campus in Dallas. His friend, who was accompanying him, quickly inserted an exhaust pipe of a car into his friend's mouth. After several gulps of exhaust fumes, the man recovered. Upon reviving, the man exclaimed he wasn't accustomed to the Texas fresh air.... As humorous as this may sound and as miserable as smog may be, the exhaust from factories and automobiles does contain a by-product valuable to mankind: carbon dioxide (CO_2), the same gas that humans exhale... In other words, the great amounts of fossil fuels—such as coal, oil and

gasoline—being burned for industry and automobiles are, in some ways, an advantage. We hear about all the negative effects of CO2 on our environment, but some advantages do exist: greater plant growth and less human brain deterioration."[cccxxxv]

The recorded but undoubted greatly inflated lifespans are only a mystery because religious adherents attempting to offer a reasonable interpretation, do not consider any of the findings of modern Earth Sciences. Many would not imagine that assessing data from scientists like Drs. Idso, and McGhee, could be of benefit. Rather, as is common the window of research and therefore interpretation is extraordinarily narrow. Much else could be said regarding the benefits of CO2 and the effects of a world with a hyperoxic atmosphere.•[cccxxxvi] Studies show there were gargantuan vertebra and invertebrate species; both of herbivore and carnivore "genera (genera are groupings of related species, e.g. the genus Homo includes the species Homo sapiens and Homo neanderthalensis)"[cccxxxvii] roaming the landmasses, and swimming the waters of our world in pre-history. We are talking about the world of the <dinosaur>. Fascinatingly,

> "Dinosaurs are no longer the green or grey, dim-witted, lizard-like creatures we thought they were before the 1980s, nor the scaly, reptilian predators we remember best from Jurassic Park. Today we know they were fleet-footed and often feathery, with sharp intellects and also strange behaviours, physical attributes and adaptations... As more sauropod discoveries come to light in many regions, from Egypt to Australia, experts are better able to answer questions about how they grew so huge, and why an evolutionary trend for gigantism existed in the first place. While the herbivorous sauropods were rapidly growing ever larger during the Late Jurassic and the Early Cretaceous, feathered theropod carnivores were quickly evolving in the opposite direction... We can now piece together a remarkable evolutionary sequence through the 50 or so species of feathered dinosaur found as fossils. We now know that a number of very weird experiments in flight were going on at this time, too, as revealed by species such as the four-winged gliders Changyuraptor and Microraptor, and one of the weirdest dinosaurs ever discovered, Yi qi ('ee-chee'). This species, revealed in 2015, had both feathers and leathery gliding membranes like those of a bat. Even the experts who discovered it could barely believe this species had existed."[cccxxxviii]

It should be distressing to religious readers, that very few are willing to consider a scientific explanation. Specifically, for what is noticeably enigmatic when reading their favoured sacred stories. Broadening the scope of research into seemingly unrelated, because they are largely dispassionate about 'spiritual matters', streams of data collection is not damaging. Scientists are now able to at least piece together answers explaining how and why certain prehistoric creatures became so gigantic. While other species were de-evolving, becoming smaller. George R. McGhee Jr. further confirms below in the section 'Hell of a Giant Factory'.

Acromegaly:

TRACKING DIFFERENTLY, and just as likely as massive CO_2 levels producing 'giants' is another, and most possible suggestion that science is now able to show conclusive evidence and reasoning behind giants. There are still today phenomenal people who in all respects are normal humans, but grew to be 'giants.'[cccxxxix] Steve Jones, author of "The Serpents Promise:The Bible retold as science", concludes gigantism is cause of a dna anomaly. Specifically, such exceedingly great growth is caused by a tumour on the pituitary gland at the base of the brain. Called an acromegaly: a mutation causing hyper-production of growth hormones, resulting in enlargement of bones, feet, hands, and face; often also accompanied by headaches, muscle pain, and various emotional disturbances. Recall Skiba's absurd statement that the only explanation for the Bible's account for giants was 'spiritual'. Absolute rubbish. Like most Christian commentators of such 'mystical' and religious material as certain sacred book passages, do not remotely attempt any potential truth. Rather, automatically assume everything must have some mystical, spiritual cause! When are Christian writers actually going to use the grey matter between their ears? Gigantism is still a remarkable phenomenon. André René Roussimoff (May 19, 1946 – died, January 27, 1993) was best known in the 1980's till his death as the wwf wrestler, André the Giant. He had larger-than-average dimensions that were attributed to the acromegaly anomaly. There are also several cases here in Australia;

but of the animal type: (1) of an enormous bovine - named Big Moo! The 'product' of the same mutation as Andre, causing hyper-production of growth hormones. Big Moo is Australia's largest cow. She weighs over a ton and measures an amazing 14 ft long and 190cm tall. She literally dwarfs cattle companions in Glencoe, South Australia. (2) Meet 'Knickers' (who may take the title of Australia's Largest bovine now); He's a massive Holstein Friesian steer standing at a height of 194 centimetres in Western Australia.[cccxl] Various other modern cases of this genetic glitch are still prevalent right around the world. Gigantism as an anomaly does not only inflict Homo Sapiens. The same condition can be found in animal species, even today. All without the positive effects CO_2 has on the environment. It rather seems that particularly Christian, religious authors are at best, lazy. At worst, ignorant. To assume only a 'supernatural' explanation for an assumed 'giant' in their scripture affirms they have not thought, or been encouraged to research anything outside their predisposed theological, Bible parameters.

Neanderthal, Cro-magnon, Denisovans, predator. A violent species, race of people's as 'sons of Elohim' and Nephilim:

A HYPOTHESIS OF EARLY hominid's, such as our Neanderthal or other proto-ancestor, as the nephilim is nothing new. However, through these studies I have come to think that Neanderthal peoples actually represent the class of people known as sons of God/Elohim (gods), while Cro-Magnon peoples more likely became known as nephilim. To many audiences of this sacred text. This assumption may be new; as in Neanderthal = sons of the gods, while Cro-Magnon peoples represent in the sacred text possibly, nephilim. I have yet to become aware of anybody who assumes so. Nonetheless, though the Neanderthal/nephilim assumption linking Neanderthal mankind to the Genesis 6 episode, is nothing new, this is still a fascinating idea to outline and adds my Cro–Magnon assumption into the fray. Let me begin with what is understood about Neanderthals, Cro-Magnon, and other early humanlike species. In his interesting book, "Them+Us: How Neanderthal Predation Created Modern Humans", Australian author

DECONSTRUCTING ENDTIME DELUSIONS

Danny Vendramini quotes various anthropologists' findings and conclusions surrounding the physique and possessed knowledge regarding Neanderthals and other early humanlike ancestors.[cccxli] To set the scene, he piques our attention with:

> "Neanderthal bones which, when compared to human dna, shows conclusively that although Neanderthals were members of the same genus as us – homo – they weren't human." (Ch. 3: The Perfect Predator.)

Reading this I took pause and began to think a little more about our passage under scrutiny (Genesis 6:4) –that maybe there can be found a reasonable connection between Neanderthals and the mythic creatures of this Genesis passage. I was unaware of Fred Harding's, or Andrew Collins' books and research: "Nephilim skeletons found", and "From the ashes of Angels" at the time. I hadn't yet also come across the text of Pat Chouinard: "Lost Race of the Giants". All folklore, myth, and legend including those of the christians sacred texts, derives from some natural source that at the time of its original composition or telling was largely unexplainable. The impression of the creatures described in this passage surely seems to fit these genres. Hominoid beings we assume were not entirely human –though extending undoubtedly also from the same genus as we, - homo. Several realised facts about Neanderthals (particularly) may throw the sons of deity/ Neanderthal hypothesis into the limelight as the prime candidate for the Bible account myth. Interesting are the following comments from Steven Mithen regarding what is now understood about our pre-history ancestors; Neanderthals. Life was not easy– with 70–80% of Neanderthals dying close to 40 years of age. Because they were a very physical race,

> "...A very high proportion of Neanderthals suffered from stress fractures, and degenerative diseases. In fact they show a very similar pattern of physical injuries to rodeo riders today... Neanderthals were hunters...[and] were habitually engaged in prolonged periods of locomotion involving strength and endurance. Their large nasal apertures and projecting noses are likely to have been partly to get rid of excess body heat during prolonged bouts of activity... In summary: it was undoubtedly a reliance on a natural history intelligence; the concept that behaviours co-evolved with the environment

in response to the changing circumstances, conditions, and surroundings of the Natural world. Understanding natural intelligence requires an understanding all these influence on behaviour and their interactions, which allowed Neanderthal survival throughout the world. But, when the environment became too taxing, too difficult, Neanderthals employed another tactic of survival, – they left! Densely wooded forests seem to have been regions Neanderthals could not cope well with. Particularly in regions … of climatic warmth squeezed in between two periods of cold tundra environments and expanded ice sheets… So as with the manufacture of tools, in some ways Early Humans appear to be very modern, and in others they seem to be very distant human ancestors."[cccxlii]

Neanderthal man most surely interbred with proto-human females. So, the offspring must have been a fashioned humanlike hybrid? No divine entity needs are present! Danny Vendramini describes further some fascinating insights of early hominids. Neanderthals (and later Cro-Magnon) we now know roamed, migrated, invaded, and lived in the Levant –the Mediterranean; in the very areas where the Judaeo-Christian sacred book is believed to have been composed. Robert John Langdon in his mini–e-book, "Giant Skeleton" adds further intrigue surrounding the genus Cro–Magnon (early-man) although technically Cro–Magnon refers to a rock shelter structure of France.) He writes the Cro-Magnon were over a foot taller, were twice as strong, and had lived much longer than those who discovered their bones. We have an idea of our two million year old distant cousins– the blue–eyed, large brained relative; the mentioned earlier Homo Neanderthal. The discovery that the genus Cro-Magnon shares similar features with Neanderthal man is compelling for this study. In regions of the world where 24,000 year old fossils have been found, it was discovered that the remains studied suggested an admixture of Cro–Magnon and Neanderthal populations. Genetic evidence published in 2010 suggests that Neanderthals contribute to the DNA of anatomically modern humans, probably through interbreeding between 80thousand and 50thousand years ago with the population of modern humans who had recently migrated from Africa. Neanderthals had larger brains, were stronger and 3 % of our DNA comes from their genes and had similar

DECONSTRUCTING ENDTIME DELUSIONS

'traits' to Cro-Magnons - but that's not all, what wiki failed to disclose is that they also had blue eyes and ginger /blond hair! So is it possible that Cro-Magnons are the product from Homo Sapien / Neanderthal cross breeding and if so, when did this happen? To find out exactly when such crossbreeding began, or when the first Cro–Magnon child was born is impossible to determine. No history text, no scientist, no anthropologist, or specialist in our proto–hominid ancestors could ever determine this. Nonetheless, it is most compelling to come across such data as a choice that two of our proto–ancestors crossbred with each-other, esp., to the study concerns of this Nail: – such discoveries seem to correspond with the passages of Genesis 6:1–2; where we are told the daughters of man interbred with another similar, but unrelated genus of our family.

> "The stature of Cro-Magnon is very tall on average well over six feet. Their longevity was exceptional for a prehistoric Society as some skeletons are found to be over 50 years-old – this should be set in context to other ancient civilisations. The average age of a Neolithic (farmers) man was 25 and a Roman only 30. You can see why the Victorians, with an average height of 5' 2" and an average age of death at 34 (44 for the academic classes and 25 for the working class) saw Cro-Magnon man as a sub-species as far apart from themselves as the Neanderthal... Cro-Magnons were the result of cross-breed between migrating sapiens from Africa and Neanderthals...Apologies to Frank Sinatra, but the real Ol' Blue Eyes has been found — a 7,000-year-old Spaniard whose fossil genes reveal that early Europeans sported blue eyes and dark skin... The origin of blue eyes was traced for the first time in 2008; by a group of researchers from Copenhagen University who claimed that just one person was responsible for the blue coloured eyes of millions of people living on the planet. This means all blue-eyed people have a single common ancestor... Blue eye colour is ... common among Israeli Jews ... So what have 'blue eyes' got to do with the Cro-Magnon Giants? Langdon's research, the successful interbreeding of Neanderthal man and another Homo Species thrived for over 100,000 years during fluctuating climatic changes of the period. Then – as if 'over–night', archaeological evidence disappeared, i.e., these people became extinct. Nobody knows the actual cause. But, it has been suggested that extinction was hastened for several simple reasons: the ratio, female to male being too great or, too small to support. It's been suggested also that an introduction of a disease, deadly to Neanderthal, and possibly Cro–Magnon potentially wiped them out... So why was there crossbreeding? Males of any species [tend to] 'mate' at random without

emotional or family connection for self-fulfilment and so the pairing would leave a Neanderthal 'single mother' and a Cro-Magnon child who shared the positive aspects of both species. Alternatively, if the species was disappearing due to the lack of males or a selective disease, the Neanderthals may have no other option but to pair with Sapiens for pure survival... Cro-Magnons are the 'mutational' group of the crossbreeding of humans and Neanderthals; this sub-species possessed blond haired and blue eyes. They were the prehistoric giants of Victorian's archaeology are alive and well in our 'modern world' and we see them nearly every day of our lives..."[cccxliii]

We have in these statements very poignant descriptions of Neanderthal and Cro-Magnon people groups. Could the above descriptions go some ways in deciphering whom the nephilim peoples were; those described as mighty men of Genesis 6 fame! Taken at face-value can it not be just as valid an assumption to relate both these early species of hominid at least, as a passing interest, to the Genesis 6 passages under review? We have read that Neanderthals are believed to have mated with another Sapien species. A coupling that was in essence indiscriminate, and possibly out of necessity. I do not see any logical reason to assume only a spiritual, intangible meaning is to be attached to this enigmatic Genesis tale; just because it is in 'the Bible', and a reader of that book, more often than not assumes everything in it must be of some mystical intangible manner. The offspring of the pairing described have been determined to be the Cro-Magnon peoples. Further ancestors of modern peoples. I implore readers to now compare these thoughts again with Genesis 6:1-2! (6:1) states clearly men began to multiply, and (6:2) it were another Sapien-like (as in genus - Homo) that chose, for whatever the actual reason, certain females they found attractive to interbreed with. The author of this Genesis 6 story may have deliberately chosen to dismiss any known reason; like disease, or there was no foreseen choice other than to interbreed- for survival of the Species!

It turns out, and it seems very likely that Cro–Magnon fit a slightly better profile of nephilim peoples we read in the scenario of Genesis 6, then Neanderthal people. Being just as well–built as Neanderthal, they were on average a foot taller than the average human (therefore most probably recognised as a giant); they had piercingly unexpected 'blue–eyes' and were polydactyl (six–fingers/toes) and so, might have been seen as divine; they were long–headed, they lived in houses; they were the result of a cross–breeding between sapiens from Africa and Neanderthal peoples. Finally, I assume all who came across the path of Cro–Magnon must have had an impression of them as mighty men (women) of renown. After all:

> "Cro-Magnons were [also] accomplished artists, musicians, craftsmen, sorcerers, and extremely talented hunters, fishermen, and highly efficient gatherers and herbalists. When they emerged upon the scene over 35,000 years ago, they carried and fashioned tools and weapons that had never been seen before. They had the know how to make and bake pottery to construct clay figurines as well as baking bread by constructing kilns and burn coal to fire and mould their mind's creations."[cccxliv]

Could parallels not then be drawn between the nephilim of Genesis 6; as mighty men (women), people of great renown, as with the description cited above? The author of the previously cited book, "Near Death..." most interestingly offers some further insight into what researchers believe of the Cro-Magnon attributes. The following description may also possibly tie with the opening verses of our Genesis 6 passage. Parallel the following description of Cro-Magnon/ Neanderthal peoples with Genesis 6:2: "... the sons of God saw that the daughters of men (Neanderthal and hence, likewise Cro–Magnon) were attractive; and they took wives for themselves, whomever they chose."[cccxlv] R. Joseph writes,

> "Neanderthals died out as a species around 30,000 years ago; but for at least 10,000 years they shared the planet with the Cro-Magnon people. The Cro-Magnon men stood 6ft tall on average and the males and females were handsome and beautiful, with thin hips, aquiline noses, prominent chins, small even perfect teeth, and high rounded foreheads. There was nothing ape-like or Neanderthal about these people."

A strikingly similar depiction to how the Genesis story portrays the daughters! Coincidence? Of the Cro-Magnon Wikipedia informs:

"...[they] were anatomically modern, straight limbed, and tall compared to the contemporaneous Neanderthals. They are thought to have been on average 176.2 centimetres (about 5' 7" to 5' 9") tall, though large males might have stood as tall as 195 cm (6' 5") and taller. They differ from modern-day humans in having a more robust physique and a slightly larger cranial capacity..."

Interestingly, a further note regarding Neanderthals Danny says:

"...in the 1960's a near complete skeleton of a Neanderthal adult male was excavated in a cave in the region of Mount Carmel, – Israel. What was extraordinary about this adult male (known as Amud 1) was that he was almost six feet tall – an exceptional height in those days – and ostensibly a giant who would have towered over early humans of the period." (They are believed to have had) Slit-shaped pupils are better suited to the eyes of nocturnal primates because they can close down tighter, preventing damage to their super-sensitive eyes from strong sunlight. NP theory argues that, like modern nocturnal predators, Neanderthals had slit-shaped pupils to protect them from snow blindness.[cccxlvi]

"Despite usually being slightly shorter, the average Neanderthal was much stockier, weighing about 25 percent more than a human. They were heavily muscled, their skeletons had to develop extra thick bones and attachment points to take the strain. With massive barrel chests, arms like Arnold Schwarzenegger and legs like telegraph posts, it has been estimated Neanderthals were about six times stronger than modern humans." ..."One of the most characteristic features of the Neanderthals", writes paleoanthropologist Erik Trinkaus, "is the exaggerated massiveness of their trunk and limb bones. All of the preserved bones suggest a strength seldom attained by modern humans... It wasn't just the Neanderthal adults who were bigger, stronger, and burlier than modern humans. Their children were too. "You should see some of the skeletons for these individuals," anthropologist John Shea told Discovery News. "The females were big and strong, while a 10-year old kid must have had muscles comparable to today's weight lifters."[cccxlvii]

From these above descriptions and impressions many research scientists and writers are now confident. We know what Neanderthals and their Cro-Magnon relatives/ progeny, likely would have looked and acted like. Instead of the anthropomorphised description often found in

DECONSTRUCTING ENDTIME DELUSIONS

educational texts –that they were much like a primitive version of modern mankind. Neanderthals for instance says Vendramini, were much burlier, and more muscle-bound than the average human today. Numerous anthropologists agree. One other interesting aspect might also be the Neanderthal brain seems to have been greater in size than ours, as was the cranium of the Cro-Magnon. Brain researcher, David Linden confirms in his book, "The Accidental Mind":

> "...estimates derived from skull volumes indicate that Neanderthals had brains that were, on average, somewhat larger than ours today." (Ch. one: The inelegant design of the brain.)

A larger brain however does not necessarily equate to superior intelligence. Skeletal remains hint that unlike popular belief Neanderthals were not knuckle-grazing idiots either. These fearsome hominids were potentially rather analogous to an oversized, extremely robust Silverback Gorilla. Beings who were most likely apex-predators by nature. Night-time predators possessing incredible vision well adapted to darkness and low light (with slit-shaped pupils), and nasal receptors to boot; thus, being able to 'sniff' out and see their prey from miles away. It is not too difficult for our minds to ponder, or even make a connection between Neanderthals, Cro-Magnon, sons of the gods and nephilim, as described in the myth of (Genesis 6:1-4). Stumbling across the previously mentioned supernatural adventure novel titled, "The Ninth Generation: surviving the giants of pre-flood Earth", in which the author, John Owens imaginatively also describes nephilim as:

> "...look[ing] similar to an ape with a wide face and angular forehead, and its size stretched beyond every normal human dimension..." Following with "there was a mystery behind the Nephilim. They were not a variation of any known earthly kind. Something other than giant size was evident. There had been something in the eyes that...had been seen –something other than human –chilling and repulsive."[cccxlviii]

Eyes depicted on Danny's website, Them+Us look also to be eerily 'slit-shaped' (similar to a cat, but showing red pigmentation) are like another sacred symbol, - the Vesica Piscis (search Internet for Vesica

Piscis). Neanderthal/ Cro-Magnon, sons of the gods/ nephilim hypothesis is somewhat 'new.' It may be an innovative ideology used as an explanation to the baffling story of Genesis, but that is all it really is; quaint. Why though do we consistently feel the need to issue such postulations when we find things frustratingly unexplainable? The reason we concoct such hypotheticals in the first place is that we each have what psychologists call; an innate explanatory drive. Which is an inner drive and searching for answers or an explanation to what otherwise is often mystical and unexplainable? Just as children have a drive to seek answers to interesting, yet perplexing things. This drive is especially prevalent in childhood and is part of the development process. It's the drive to gather as much information and facts about the wider world as possible. All toddlers do it, – they explore the sandbox; kitty–litter box; or ask an unexpected question about our anatomy, or why there is hair in certain regions on our bodies, but not others? Adults also engage in similar explorative questioning. In defiance to an order, we see as irrelevant, harsh, or inconsequential. We are all more than likely to do something when explicitly commanded we shouldn't. We go explore that, – just 'cause we can! Jesse Bering again:

> "The thing is, ... explanation(s) (don't) actually need to be correct to give you that satisfying bolus of orgasmic pleasure driving your search for answers..." Likewise, when it comes to the innate explanatory drive, you've just got to believe you've solved the problem to derive the pleasure: "This may help resolve the otherwise puzzling question of whether having a bad explanation or a pseudo-explanation is the same as having no explanation at all ... Genuine explanation might take place, and yet the outcome might be [incorrect] much of the time. This is perfectly consistent with the view that the system evolved because, in general, and over the course of the long run, and especially in childhood, it gives us veridical information about the causal structure of the world. In other words, although our explanations are scattershot, questionable, and often flat-out wrong, they're also occasionally right— especially when we're working from within a scientific framework. And getting it right some of the time is a lot better than never attempting to solve problems to begin with."[cccxlix]

DECONSTRUCTING ENDTIME DELUSIONS

So, it is with the explanations of numerous modern and past Christian authors regarding these enigmatic verses of Genesis chapter 6. Though each has packaged their summations ever so slightly differently than a contemporary, or previous author. They essentially have reached the same conclusion as they have used the same line of enquiry and consubstantial parameters as a guide to their investigations. I am however, not saying the explanations of these authors are wholly wrong. They may well be; as might the postulations above. But, each of us possesses the innate desire for an explanation to what is seen as puzzling. Above are but the result of some of my-theology after attempting to determine from outside the usual theological parameter, who or what the nephilim of Genesis chapter six could represent. If; however, readers cannot accept for whatever reason that Neanderthals or Cro-Magnon peoples might have resembled the figures portrayed in this Genesis six episode (sons of the gods–Neanderthal; Cro–magnon, as the famed nephilim, the mighty men of renown). Maybe the following description will settle the mind. Mind you, no one, whether hardened 'creationist' or 'evolution' advocate really knows what these ancestor-hominies of ours actually looked like; they could well have been hideously apelike (hairy) people. Every representation and hypothesis presented is based on individual theory! These are all just impressions, based solely upon what information is available and utilised by the researcher. Therefore, Vendramini, Skiba and Harding are likely just as misinformed as the other. By extension, so might the above, and later postulations. Numerous Christian/ religious authors question the validity that Neanderthals were similar in many ways to a primate yet was also descended from the Homo genus! Equally the same skepticism must be applied to him resembling a 'primitive-type' of modern human –largely hairless! What if the Genesis story is somehow a basic retelling by the redactor/author of Genesis, of known or experienced confrontations with numerous war-mongering/ hunter/gatherer tribes of Neanderthal or Cro-Magnon peoples. As stated above– analogous to the Spartans of Greek antiquity. Their prowess and discipline in battle and war is just as well-known today as any commentary on the atrocities committed by the Nazi regime, against humanity. Largely thanks to the silver screen, and the books and articles one can easily find with an Internet search. We also have some very interesting thoughts of another author, Susan Mendez. To the closing remarks of the Introduction to her book, she lists and comments briefly on five early races of proto-man. In order: First race, Asu; Second race, Ihin; Third race, Druk; Fourth race, Ihuan; Fifth race, Ghan.

- Of the Asu the most poignant is that they were the 'Adam' of the Homo genus. 'He' was rather a simpleton dwelling on land and in trees and without speech and meagre consciousness. Since su (she writes) means "spirit," Asu means "man without spirit..." – (recall Genesis 3 and my conclusions about Adam/Eve, Enkidu.)

- The Ihin man: "... (was only three feet tall) ...like biblical Abel...able to think, understand, and commune spiritually..."

- Druk man: "a cross (though forbidden) between Asu and Ihin; equivalent...to H. erectus and also to the biblical Cain... [they were] (pit dwellers); omnivorous, long-armed, curved back, often quite large ("giants") ...Known also as the barbarian hordes..."

- Ihuan man: "... [were anatomically modern humans, like the Ihin] ...tall, strong, and copper-colored (sic) "mighty men"; the last of the Ihuans to survive into the modern era were the American Paleo-Indians."

- Ghan man: "a cross between Ihin and Ihuan; fully modern in type; ...Stately but willful souls with all the arts and sciences of man. Kings and born conquerors. Masters of the sun kingdoms in the Mesolithic. They tamed the earth.[cccl]

It is not difficult to draw several parallels and startling conclusions regarding these early races of man. Each 'age' of early men described here by Mendez could very well also be thought to describe the eight known Homo proto-ancestor classifications attributed by modern anthropologists and palaeontologists. It seems the above classifications also coincide with at least some part of the descriptions of nephilim found in modern Christian sacred books. Druk man is most foreboding! Here, we have a forbidden interbred race of 'giants' described as a barbarous horde. A concept that is familiar with Genesis six. The overall point however of this exercise was to not consider what Neanderthals or any of the other early 'races' of man looked like. We may never know. It was direct attention to the fact that quite possibly the mythic anecdote we read in passages like (Genesis 6:1-4) and Neanderthals and the early hominoid species; Cro-Magnon, or known recent historically known warlike races, the Spartan's. All these genus/species might well be related. There is no logical reason to dismiss it outright. There is also no logical reason to assume as Rob Skiba has done so (quite wrongly and deceptively (from ignorance) I believe; that nephilim can only be explained supernaturally. This is simply showing that he chose to not attempt to do any real research into the matter. He has either dismissed any validity of other modern studies into the Ancient past, or he simply didn't actually think in any depth about this episode. Rather chose to follow the well-worn theological path, - which, has also been overridden by various scholars (as stated above). With more diligent research, I began reading the earlier cited fascinating book, "Deadly Powers..." In this text Paul Trout outlines some very interesting facts and mythological stories that have become known and understood through studies in Anthropology. Trout's premise is that instead of the assumed hypothesis that our Proto-ancestors were hunter-gathers, they were first scavengers and were themselves part of the food-chain of numerous predators; long before Homo-Sapiens Sapiens: modern Humans climbed the food-chain ladder to become the predator themselves. Pondering this one can begin to understand how such complex mythology might have germinated and been birthed, to eventually have a life of its own: a life that many conspiracy theorists, Christian and secular, continue to propose as some newfound divine Revelation. This however need not be the case. Studies in anthropology and like disciplines into the earliest stages of our species clearly and surely offer greater, and believable understandings into the many anecdotes found in sacred texts; like enoch's narrative regarding 'Watchers.' The statements of Neanderthals and the descriptions offered by Susan Mendez for sure act as an addendum for this study and should not be dismissed because of one's religious predilection. But warrant more serious consideration. The Genesis 6:4 account could be describing the long-lost stories of Neanderthal, Cro-Magnon and the inter-bred progeny of these two early races of hominid interactions, with each-other, and various predatory species. We know for instance that Neanderthals interbred with another homo-sapient species. Resulting in the birth of Cro-Magnon. Robert John Langdon again affirms.

> "This interbreeding of the thin and nimble dark skinned Homo Sapiens and the large and muscular Neanderthals, with their red hair and green eyes, created several offspring of mixed colouration, who interbred together to create the blonde/red hair and blue/green eyed variations we see today through our even more extensive interbreeding with indigenous sapiens..."[cccli]

Their progeny is nicely named by Robert John Langdon, Homo Superior– i.e., Cro–Magnon! It was possibly the mythic stories told orally around the camp fire that evolved, surrounding their interactions with locals. The Skhul-Quafez of the Levant; which became morphed and were embellished over the centuries into what we recognise now as part of Judaeo-Christian sacred lore; Genesis 6:1-4.

> "Almost by accident something wonderful happened on the shores of the Caspian Sea thirty-thousand years ago. This evolutionary event changed the course of humanity in which we live and experience its benefits today. But the most amazing aspect of this 'true history' is the people and the civilisation it created. These blue-eyed blonde 'Gods' lived a life of 'self-sufficiency' living on the land and creating a society so very different from today. In reflection they lived an idyllic life of sailing houseboats through warm calm waters that flooded our landscape long ago...so very different from now that if you were to travel back in time, to be aboard one of those boats, the views you would behold would be totally alien and bewildering... What I find interesting is the timing of the 'monumental event' in the Homo Superior time-line for it seems to be linked with the destruction of their homeland – Atlantis falling to the North Sea in 4200 BCE. Was this the catalyst that split the civilisation in two, as they needed to find new lands to settle, which we find surrounding Doggerland in the North Sea. Did some decide at this point to relocate to warmer climates of the Mediterranean and live in a place where the population was less developed and could be subdued for the pleasure of the 'master race'? We now know that the Egyptian Pharaohs and priests thousands of years later were of 'Celtic Blood' with red and blonde hair and blue green eyes, who bred only within their own 'blueblood' genetic line. The influence of these

DECONSTRUCTING ENDTIME DELUSIONS

> Homo Superiors is almost impossible to accurately calculate. But without doubt, these unique men that have almost disappeared into the multicultural societies we see today took Stone Age man to rocket man at a speed never seen before, and maybe because of the erosion of their blood line, will never see again in the future."[ccclii]

The Genesis 6 narrative might also have been derived from stories analogous and parallel theories. One other is growing in acceptance. That is, as the book, "Mystery We Universe" has it, – the ABIT (Advanced Being Intervention Theory) - which, "postulates the involvement of beings much more advanced than human physical, technological, social, and psychological levels of development." Similar to Sitchin's alien hypothesis. As may be suspected, this writer does not subscribe to Sitchin's theory. That an advanced 'alien' race from somewhere out there in space infiltrated humanity in our distant past; rather, an understanding is a belief that if abit proves truthful; it would seem more likely these beings were very fearsome and a beefier species. So were thought of as a 'giant' race of our 'earth-bound' ancestors– Cro–Magnon. Or, simply Genesis 6:1-4 retells now long–lost real, and probably most often frightening recollections of (hominids living around the Levant regions); their survival tales of attacks by fierce predators and other hominid ancestor warrior type civilisations. Like, again, the famed Spartans. Spartan society was based on war. They were one of, if not the greatest warrior class/ race in Greek antiquity. At this juncture, it might prove more than useful to add the insight of the Lebanese historian Kamal Salibi. Salibi is a historian of note, whose findings should not be totally dismissed without due and reasoned contrary conclusions. His comments surrounding these passages follow:

> "In Genesis 6:1-4, it is made quite clear that Yahweh was one God among many. So far, translators of this passage have been thrown off course by the Hebrew ydwn (6:3a), which is only attested in Biblical Hebrew in this context. The word must be translated 'approach, come near'... Instead, as in the Revised Standard Version translation (RSV), it has been taken to mean 'abide, dwell', which in Hebrew would be ylwn, not ydwn. Some translators were also confused by the expression b-sgm (6:3b), which simply means 'in weakness', in the sense of 'weak' (said of mankind.) The word sgm, instead,

was taken to be essentially ...'go astray', ...allegedly meaning 'the going astray of them', i.e. 'their going astray'. I would translate the passage in question as follows, leaving it to the reader to compare it with existing translations: Mankind began to multiply on the face of the earth, and daughters were born to them. The sons of the gods...saw that the daughters of man were fair, and they took wives for themselves from all the ones they chose. Yahweh said: 'My spirit shall never approach man...; he is weak..., flesh ...and his days are a hundred and twenty years... The Nephilim... were on the earth in those days. Again, after that, the sons of the gods came in to the daughters of man, and they bore children; those are the Gebor folk (h-gbrym) who have always been the people of Hashem... Here it must be noted that the 'Nephilim' (...'handsome young man') must have been the ancient inhabitance of the present twin villages of Nawafil and Nawafilah ..., near the border of North Yemen. The 'Gebor folk' (...usually translated 'mighty men') are an ancient tribe of North Yemen called the Jabr, still found there to this day. 'Hashem' (...misread as... 'the name' and taken to mean 'renown') is today the oasis Al Hashim in nearby Wadi Najran...actual geography validates the new translation of the Biblical Hebrew."[cccliii]

There are numerous paths and subjects that arise from further study of his findings. Salibi in his extensive research found some glaring misreading of the Hebrew text (he ignored the Masorete renderings of the words he highlights), saying earlier in the book, these were largely (but not always) insufficient and could well be rendered any number of different ways. His conclusions in this passage alone open yet another Pandora's box of possibility. Gebor folk (nephilim) as native peoples from Yemen and the other points made. There is no real conflict with his understanding and my previous posturing – nephilim could possibly = Neanderthal/Cro-Magnon hybrid race. Or indeed, as the mentioned earlier Netflix program Forbade History interestingly also postulates. The nephilim of Bible lore could be an ancient Semitic tribe of larger-than-the-then-average warriors that were encountered by those they conquered. It is these accounts that made it into sacred lore. The difference being, they were morphed into the terrifying, merciless, sex-crazed angels/demons of the other texts we read; of enoch, jasher, jubilees, and other esoteric works. "Forbidden History" also interestingly suggests that certain Pharaoh's, and members of the Egyptian royalty; i.e., King Akhenaten, might have had ancestral links to nephilim/giants.

DECONSTRUCTING ENDTIME DELUSIONS

The Egyptian Kingdom it is also postulated, once hired as mercenaries these beings. The deduction that Akhenaten might have had ancestral links to nephilim is unsurprising. Any quick Internet search for statues and stone relief depictions of him and other members of his family. Is that this king as somewhat very feminine. Feminine facial features, and body type; wide hips and feminine lips. Representations of one of his daughters are depicted as sporting an elongated head. Discovered stone reliefs show similar features. However, before jumping to unwarranted conclusions, we should take note that:

> "...in Mesopotamia and Egypt artists used [disproportionate features] to express the greatness of the deities or kings as compared to normal human beings. Famous kings and heroes became ancestral deities after their death and acquired corresponding tallness." (de Moor, and Korpel. p.71.)

Recall that in the brief study of Gilgamesh (Nail Five), it was stated the descriptions of him were astoundingly similar and not anything new for those regions. Here, de Moor and Korpel affirm this with the above description. The famed peoples of the ancients were more often than not. Described in such a fashion; as gods; as huge in stature; as 'mighty' in battle. Just as the description of the nephilim in this Genesis 6 passage. The footnote accompanying the above citation offers us further insight explaining the 'tallness' of one Ugaritic deity; Ba'lu depicted on a stele. Stating:

> "The tallness of their spirits is implied in [a Ugaritic text that states] ...'There towered the Saviors of Ba'lu, ... In Palestine folklore the ...'Rebel' was a giant evil spirit whose head reached the clouds." (ibid. de Moor, and Korpel. footnote, 284.)

Amazing! A particular deity understood to be a 'rebel' in Ugaritic folklore, had a head that reached the clouds. That's tall! Some would say even gigantic, – and (let me burst the bubble) of no doubt, utter hyperbole. But, christians seem to be lost in the magnification, the embellishment of such statements when a text or particular folklore story is read. They themselves have their heads in the clouds no doubt in their attempts to make something fit a complete guessed hypothesis. It should not be that much of a surprise that christians writing on the latest, or offering their own hypotheses on giants/ nephilim and a Genesis 6 connection, have absolutely no clue, or any interest in what scholars the likes of Marjo Korpel and Johannes de Moor have made available to any reader. It just never seems to enter the minds of christians to actually seek out a possible understanding from what other reputable fields of scholarly work are concluding about the vast array of materials now being studied. It is assumed a reason for this is much of this 'alternate' material doesn't seem to hold any parallels to a favoured topic. Or, simply the various Christian authors are unaware of this material; if so, another case of knowledge filtration. However, I do not see how this could be an excuse today. If I can source these scholarly materials, why do they not consider these also? All the same, if the prolific publications of alternate history texts – Michael Cremo's "Forbidden Archaeology", or the previously mentioned book, "Mystery Us Universe", and other cited authors continue with their aim; current understanding and knowledge of history is bound to be changed. History, and sacred texts may then be required to be completely rewritten; for the suppression of knowledge that does not fit the establishment cannot be totally ignored, shelved, shunned, or ridiculed forever. Recall the wisdom of Schopenhauer: "All truth passes through three stages: first, it is ridiculed; second, it is violently opposed; and third, it is accepted as self-evident." (Introduction, The lords of Avaris, by David Rohl.)

Mini summation:

SO FAR, WE HAVE COVERED quite a bit of ground. We have also traversed several rabbit-trails that have caused us to take a few detours from the initial subject. I cannot apologise, as these had to be dealt with when they arose. Introduced were several findings from my research that more than likely have grated upon the usual religious rendering and accepted hypotheses about whom, or what, and from where this sacred story Genesis 6:1-4, potentially derived. The evidence provided above seems to correlate with my summation that; (1) the sons of the gods were/ are Neanderthal peoples who mated with local women of the Levant (or anywhere that Neanderthals settled) and (2) the progeny of this coupling resulted in another, nonetheless hybrid proto-ancestor, the Cro–Magnon species (the Homo–Superior). It was these, homo–superiors that in the Genesis myth became known as the nephilim. Potentially, as Silibi attests nephilim are a tribe of North Yemen– those described in Western Church–sponsored sacred books as mighty men. Does this seem not a reasonable if not wholly probable testimony; other than the usual spiritualised and sensational Christian summations that are placed before the believing community? In relation to 'giant'; yes, this is a reasonable transliteration, but only of the Septuagint. Other sacred versions rightly have chosen nephilim. In the immediate context of Genesis 6, giant does not make any reference to an astoundingly large person; other than either, Cro–Magnon or Neanderthal peoples. Both of who were, we saw, of a higher stature than the average population. Despite the acknowledgement that nowadays there are countless huge skeletal remains being discovered (any searching of Internet for giant skeletons affirms). They were not resembling any deity/ demi-deity/ person of mythic proportions in the numerous mythic tales we still possess; those of the gods/ titans. Most likely, their sizes could be owed to Earth's early pre-diluvial atmosphere. A much greater concentration of CO_2 and hyper-toxicity (Oxygen levels). Including the scientific causes of the large growth pattern of the acromegaly. If however, it is argued these cannot possibly be a realistic or valid explanation to the Genesis 6 story, as it is by faith that a Christian must understand the odd entities as fallen angelic types (i.e. enoch's 'Watcher' class). Why can't the same faith be legitimately applied to the above or any of the following explanations? We already know the books of enoch are fictions, and Bible story's are also fictitious compositions. Reminiscent of numerous fragmented memories of tales of early–hominids in proximity to the Levant such as - Iran![cccliv]

Hell of a 'giant' factory:

ANCIENT HISTORY WE now know tells a story of a vast array of gargantuan creatures. In the new publication, "Carboniferous giants and mass extinction: the late Paleozoic Ice Age world" by George R. McGhee Jr. outlines the fascinating, scientifically dense world of times past. In chapter four, "Giants in the Earth", McGhee interestingly highlights:

> "In actual fact, [despite the oft 6,000yr timeframe proposed by the religionist as to when giants roamed the earth] the first giant land animals on the Earth existed in the Carboniferous, some 345 million years ago... in summary, many of the Late Carboniferous and Early Permian arthropod species had body sizes that were five to seven times larger than their modern-day counterparts, and an overall size range from three to as much as 12 times larger. What type of an Earth could have produced such huge arthropods? How could ...gigantic scorpions, millipedes, spiders, silverfish, mayflies, griffenflies (sic), and cicada-like sap-suckers have existed? Gigantism convergently evolved in multiple phylogenetic lineages of arthropods in the Carboniferous... To make matters even more mysterious, there were other giant animals on the Earth in this interval of geologic time..."[ccclv]

Aside gargantuan insects, vertebrates/ invertebrates and all manners of animal and mammal, ancient sources and countless writings of the Egyptians, Romans, Greeks, Aztecs, Hindu's, and other ethnic groups confirm the earth was once also teeming with behemoth tribes. Most all continents and Islands of the world have at least several ancient mythologies. Telling of 'often' unruly, boisterous 'giant' hominids roaming the landscape. These were the 'antediluvians' of old. The legends surrounding them were often said to have constructed countless temples and immense structures that defied the imagination. On the expansive giant mythology Randall Floyd writes:

> "Some legends suggest these ferocious, over-sized beings were descended from star-gods who walked the Earth countless eons ago. They were said to have built handsome stone temples and walled cities and were capable of incredible feats, such as flying, walking on water, even turning lead into gold. Nobody knows what happened to these legendary "supermen" of old. Some say they returned to the stars. Others say they simply died off, leaving nothing behind but their bones and scattered legends. But stories about giants and ogres and larger-than-life humans live on in the oral traditions of a variety of cultures around the world. Goliath, the Titans, the Cyclops—even the giant in Jack and the Beanstalk, one of England's most enduring myths, are as popular in the twentieth century as they were in days of old. To be sure,

modern giants can be found today—the Watuzi tribe in Africa, for example, who average between seven and eight feet in height. The American Robert Pershing Wadlow is on record as the tallest human known in modern times. He stood just shy of nine feet and weighed 490 pounds before his death in 1940 at the age of 22. In Roman times, the emperor Maxiumus, who reportedly stood nine feet-six-inches in height, was said to be the tallest man in his day. An equally imposing figure was Goliath, the famous Philistine who supposedly measured an inch taller than Maximum before his head was removed by the diminutive David..."[ccclvi]

Further,

"According to Josephus, a Jew named Eleazar the Giant, stood over ten feet high and was among the hostages the king of Persia sent to Rome to insure a peace. Pliny, the historian, wrote that during the reign of Claudius (A.D. 41-54), a ten-foot giant named Gabbaras was brought to Rome from Arabia and put in command of the famed Adiutrix legions. The giant so awed his troops that some worshipped him as a God...[ccclvii] Other larger-than-life humanoids included the Tritons, a race of giant gods spawned by Poseidon which supposedly fled Atlantis when it sank; the Titans, a race of equally big Greek gods; the Ari, the "shining ones" in Sumeran mythology; the Ellu, another race of Mesopotamian kings synonymous with the Nephilim of Genesis; the one-eyed Cyclops in Greek mythology, said to have built the ancient city of Mycenae; and the Cimbri, Celtic giants with long, blond manes, also known as the Cimmerians. Numerous other individual giants are found in theologies and literary traditions around the world, notably Hercules, Albion, Quetzalcoatl, Atlas, and Votan. Some accounts claim that King Arthur, the "once and future king," was in reality a giant. In his reputed grave at Glastonbury, archaeologists found the bones of a man that measured just over nine feet tall. The bones have long since disappeared. If giants were real, the question has to be asked, what happened to them? Where are their bones?..."

Likewise, we must ask:

"Hoaxes and fables aside, what is modern science to make of the old stories about giants? Could one or more races of larger-than-normal human beings have flourished long ago, their presence now a distant memory shrouded in myth and legend."[ccclviii]

Well-versed people of 'the book' of the Jews and christians would undoubtedly acknowledge – their sacred book is full of giants. There are several texts aside the Genesis 6:4 passage that alludes to giants. One other text (1 chronicle 20:6), is pointed to in hopes of likely proof that enormous human-angelic hybrid monster/nephilim existed. Though English translations of the text of 1 chronicle often reads the 'man of great stature'. Was a descendant of 'giants', meaning, 'giant' in this passage means that he was born of a tribe known as the Rephaim – who were descendants of a Transjordan tribe, maybe – Yemen? We'd be hard-pressed to find in the text evidence that 'giant' is a referent to size or an angelic type. Though an Amos passage discussed shortly, likens giants to the known mammoth size and strength of Cedar trees. This Transjordan tribe (1 chronicle 20:6), scholar's note was exceedingly wicked in the eyes of the principal deity. Many tales of these 'giants' tell of these hominids sporting strange features; the likes of double-rows of teeth, and six <fingers> and <six> <toes>. Are these phenomenal features? Or, is there are reasonable and scientific explanation to these persons sporting such odd additions? Through careful study, we find that the reference to the six fingers and toes in the 1 chronicles passage, in all probabilities was a real abnormality. The website Medicinenet.com clearly states what is known about this medical abnormality:

> "Six fingers or toes: The presence of an extra sixth finger or toe, a very common congenital malformation (birth defect). This condition is called hexadactyly. The word hexadactyly literally means six digits. In medical usage, hexadactyly does not specify whether the six digits are fingers or toes (although in Greek "dactylos" is without equivocation a finger).. Hexadactyly is the most frequent form of polydactyly, a diagnosis that encompasses all cases of extra digits, irrespective of the number of extra digits in a particular case.".[ccclix]

Robert Langdon again,

> "This rare inherited anatomical variation affects 1 in 500 humans, in which the individual has more than the usual number of digits; this is known as polydactyly. It is caused by a dominant allele of a gene. This means it can be passed on by just one parent if they have the disorder. Extra fingers can

be functional. One individual with seven fingers not only used them but claimed that they "gave him some advantages in playing the piano". The countless mythology of this birth 'defect' can be seen throughout history, but [here is] a tantalising extract from the Bible that hopefully will whet your appetite for we read that David's nephew Jonathan (not Saul's son Jonathan) slew a "giant" who taunted Israel. The episode resembles the story of David himself with Goliath, except that this giant had six fingers and six toes: "There was a giant of a man, who had six fingers on each hand and six toes on each foot, twenty-four in all; he too was descended from the Raphah (plural: Rephaim). When he taunted Israel, Jonathan, the son of David's brother Shimei, killed him" (2 Samuel 21:20–21). In the Levant, polydactylism—an excess of fingers or toes—was considered to be a Mark of the Rephaim, a race of giants, or as we now know them Homo Superior (CroMagnons)."[ccclx]

There are people alive today who have this same anomaly. Any quick Internet search uncovers thousands of details and photos of people living with this anomaly. So, although an unusual and congenital malformation. It is essentially just another of the wonders of life that doesn't require a supernatural cause. Some people are born with this malformation. To the sacred book writers, this phenomenon figuratively speaks of an individual's wickedness. However, a modern example of the anomaly of people born with extra digits has the following written about a Cuban man, stating there:

> "...is really nothing new about 6 fingered humans either. Ancient cultures origins from Africa have been found to have 6 fingers and 6 toes. The man with 12 fingers and 12 toes. Yoandri Hernandez Garrido is a 30-year-old Cuban who has 6 fingers on each hand and six toes on each foot and ensures that it never was an impediment to a normal life. In his village located in the Toa river basin in the province of Guantanamo, the easternmost tip of Cuba, Yoandri is called by his acquaintances as "Twenty-four."[ccclxi]

Undoubted, in premodern times, all anomalies (as having been born with six fingers and six toes), and persons somewhat of a much larger stature then the average person; such persons would most likely have been seen as maybe of divine or demonic origin, according to their actions. Those seen as divine, were kindly, while the tyrannical would most likely be known as 'demonic.' Is the Cuban fellow described a modern nephilim? Through the advances of many sciences, we now have a greater understanding of causes and countless oddities. For instance, Humans are born every day with extra fingers or toes, perfectly formed and functional. If having twelve fingers had conferred a big advantage some time in our evolutionary past, you can bet that everyone would have twelve fingers now. Genes important for embryonic development have far-reaching effects and so mutations in just the right spot can make large anatomical rearrangements. These rearrangements are random and therefore usually result in harmful birth defects, but when we're talking about evolutionary timescales, events that seem unimaginably rare are possible... The mutation-driven tweaks and tugs of evolution can sometimes be undone, with dramatic results. Because we are constantly reminded of the slow and steady pace of evolution, we don't normally think of it as dramatic.[ccclxii] What of the double–rows of teeth? This too, doesn't seem so supernatural or demonic. Despite numerous wild declarations by the usual religious author who postulates that weird skeletons with extra digits, often also sporting skulls with extra teeth; these are not alien, angelic, or of the famed nephilim of Genesis and other Bible passages. After researching a little about hyperdontia we come to identify this anomaly too is quite a natural occurrence; though rare, it still presents in modern people:

> "Hyperdontia is a condition that causes too many teeth to grow in your mouth. These extra teeth are sometimes called supernumerary teeth. They can grow anywhere in the curved areas where teeth attach to your jaw... The 32 adult teeth that replace them are called permanent teeth."[ccclxiii]

Thus, the sacred texts without a predisposed hypothesis as to the meanings ascribed to various mythic tales, are wholly a product of human invention; completely comprising very human dna! The supplied web address is informative as to possible causes and diagnoses of this quite naturally, but unusual condition. The issue then is not so much that these natural oddities occur. Rather, that believers are all-too quick to assume the most mystical and bazaar interpretations (dreams); that as something odd is recorded in a sacred text, it must therefore only have a 'spiritual' meaning/ explanation. How short-sighted are the religious to not consider alternative understandings? Believers are only willing to seek answers that fit neatly with their predisposed conclusion; which are very rarely objective by nature. "The Theological Wordbook of the Old Testament" confirms my assertion above, regarding the Rephaim. By interestingly highlighting his propensity for idolatry:

> "... finger(s)" refer to work artfully produced, especially in regard to God. They refer to the handiwork of his creative power, e.g. the heavens, the plagues, and the Law on the stone tablets. In regard to man, it often deals with his artistic work which is contrary to God, as the making of idols and cultic objects. These and other sins defile the finger; this expression means man is separated from approaching God, especially cultically. Rather, the fingers should have the instructions of the wise teacher bound to them (Proverbs 7:3)."[ccclxiv]

Not only were the handiwork and creative prowess of the Rephaim deemed by the author of sacred texts as totally contrary to that which the religious elite obviously regarded as worthy of the principal deity, the famed deity Yahweh; but their 'mission,' and ultimate 'life-goal' if you will. Was set to wickedness in every action. Also, see a converse sampling of warnings scattered throughout the Judaeo-Christian book, psalms 119:101, 105; psalms 140:4; proverbs 4:26, 19:2; hebrews 12:13. Do readers realise this same attitude was pointed out in my first Nail; that just as the author of this passage in Western sacred books, assumes that his principal deity is supreme, above all others, especially above reproach to what the Rephaim were doing and how they were conducting themselves. Need a refresher, revisit the final pages of Nail One above. These descriptions fit rather neatly with a metaphysical understanding of giants also. In his little book, "The Revealing Word – a dictionary of metaphysical terms." C. Fillmore wrote:

> "(regarding the OT races deemed giants) ...represent the untrained or undeveloped states of mind in the sub consciousness that Truth is to subdue and to discipline. When they become obedient to the law of Being they will be man's servants..."

Accordingly, until subdued into obedience metaphysically such people remained 'giants' – simply meaning amateur in all their endeavours. Cast your minds again to Enkidu of Gilgamesh fame. Recall he was the fellow of the Gilgamesh myth who was animalistic, i.e., amateur in all he did prior to his 'enlightenment'! Revisit my Genesis 3 studies above for a refresher if required. It may be of further interest to some readers that Rephaim in other places in the Hebrew books gives the impression of them called 'shades'; that is, spirits of the dead. A concept undoubtedly linking them to nephilim. A brief article in the revised and updated "HarperCollins Bible Dictionary" reads,

> "The Hebrew word repha'im is translated "shades" in a number of passages where it seems to refer to the spirits of people who have died."[ccclxv]

'Shades' in the Bible is thus linked to Sheol, the Old Testament biblical place of the netherworld/underworld, also known as the place of the dead. HarperCollins again,

> "Sheol usually refers to a place (Genesis 37:35), namely, the underworld where departed spirits go (Prov. 9:18). The dead in Sheol are referred to as "shades," pale reflections of the men and women they had once been (Isaiah 14:10; Ecclesiastes 9:10). Existence in Sheol is characterized (sic) by forgetfulness and inactivity (Psalms. 88:12; Ecclesiastes 9:10), but Sheol is not a place of punishment in the Bible."[ccclxvi]

Contrary to current Christian belief and teaching. The underworld is not, and never has been seen or thought of as a place of severe and everlasting punishment; let alone somewhere where deity purposefully sends all unbelievers and the 'wicked' believers upon their death. But simply refers to where the dead lay! It is the place where every dead body, whether cremated or simply buried, eventually finishes – in the ground. This should open a whole new paradigm for study. It should also for believer's cause pause again. Regarding their beliefs on hell, and the damnation of unbelievers and the 'wicked.' If Sheol, the place of the dead in your sacred book doesn't confer with the popular teaching of the abode hell. Today, serious reflection must then be undertaken.

DECONSTRUCTING ENDTIME DELUSIONS

Somewhat obscure passages like isaiah 26:14a, clearly confirms. This verse also puts a dampener on rapture – as the disappearance of the 'saints' hypothesis. Clearly the writer says "The dead do not live; shades do not rise." Taken at face value this verse could not be any clearer. Those who continually spruik a doctrine of 'rapture' of the true christians/Church; do not account for this verse, nor would I add, do they understand what shades mean or what Hebrew word it describes. Shades – this verse = repha'im. The new paradigm of study then I assume also. Must encourage a review of the sacred and extra-sacred concepts of Sheol; hell, Hades, Tartarus, and other cognates. How were these terms used in other ancient mythologies? Even more interesting would be to 'flesh' out the relationships between these explanations and the Rephaim. There will most probably be found a close connection between the sacred account of nephilim in Genesis 6:4, numbers 13:33 and such peoples appointed Rephaim (Shades). It is a case of the writer of both accounts that by referring, or rather using the greatly unclear term nephilim, in Genesis 6:4 he is recounting a cultural understanding of this Hebrew word: as another evocative and ancient tantamount term for Rephaim: who is now - a Shade – one of the giant (untrained/ill-disciplined) dead! Rephaim also seems to have close ties/links with other ancestrally analogous people groups found in the sacred text. The mentioned Anakim, Emim, and Zamzummim who are also referred as either nephilim or giants. No, there should not be a belief these people groups have a connection to the famed Greek pantheon of gods and demi-gods; as some believers and religious authors have already guessed. Not without evidence! My reasoning: according to the "Eerdmans Bible Dictionary", article:

> "Rephaim and Ugarit texts, states clearly scholarly agreement. The consensus is that these texts refer to the Rephaim... as epitomising the powerful, Canaanite, royal dead on behalf of whom an ancestor or death cult emerged at Ugarit.[ccclxvii] Accordingly, "the texts indicate that they were once a living collective reality, then a mythologized, heroic group, long before they became inhabitants of the netherworld as the powerful dead. This reconstruction of the Ugaritic traditions is routinely cited in support of the notion that a similar set of circumstances underlies what must have been the

original connection between the Rephaim as gigantic [etymologically, sons of Gaia, or the Earth] autochthons [native inhabitants] and the Rephaim as the powerful dead in Hebrew tradition."[ccclxviii]

Was it noticed? Rephaim are 'sons of Gaia', – very much earthbound; autochthons! "The Anchor Yale Bible Dictionary" affirms in the opening statements of its article on Rephaim:

"... the Hebrew Bible ...uses fall generally into two categories: (1) descriptions of the dead in the underworld, or (2) references to a group or nation of giants or warriors."[ccclxix]

Accordingly, the powerful dead, the praised 'warrior' mighty men. The nephilim are likely symbolically representative of the mentioned earlier Cro–Magnon as nephilim; those who are now deceased, the fallen.

Earthen giant factory:

A BURNING QUESTION therefore is, were larger-than-average disfigured persons (giants) roaming the earth? Was prehistoric Earth a giant factory? Probably. Published works of archaeology, and numerous other available studies confirm some truly amazing discoveries that affirm a 'giant-humanoid' reality![ccclxx] It is a known fact also because of scientific investigation that such larger-than-average humans still roam and are present on the earth. The websites cited in the endnotes conclusively confirm that there are and were large atypical individuals still roaming all global regions. Sightings are prevalent according to various authors who have published their research. Specifically, confirmed in the work by Steve Jones, one 'hot-spot', so-to-speak where birth irregularities, causing gigantism, are prevalent is Ireland. Irish genealogical records admit quite as much also candidly. What's more widely reported around the globe are skeletal remains of exceptionally great sizes. Much like the depictions portrayed and the former charts mentioned earlier. There are countless articles to be found in any Internet search explaining (speculating) or highlighting skeletal remains of unknown origin, like the following that states:

DECONSTRUCTING ENDTIME DELUSIONS

> "February 01, 2013 - UNITED STATES - Scientists are remaining stubbornly silent about a lost race of giants found in burial mounds near Lake Delavan, Wisconsin, in May 1912. Apparently, there are nine-foot skeletons with huge heads and strange facial features that have really shocked scientists when they were uncovered 100 Years Ago. The dig site at Lake Delavan was overseen by Beloit College and it included more than 200 effigy mounds that proved to be classic examples of 8th century Woodland Culture. But the enormous size of the skeletons and elongated skulls found in May 1912 did not fit very neatly into anyone's concept of a textbook standard. They were enormous. These were not average human beings."[ccclxxi]

A larger-than-average skeleton photo are likely pictures circulated on the Internet as either (1) an entry to a photo shopping competition, or (2) as somehow offering empirical 'proof' to beings of (gigantic) proportions; of persons reaching 4+ meters in height. There are indeed numerous reports of countless such huge skeletal remains being discovered right around the planet. As the website from which one photo is noticed: "The images were assembled from various individual hoaxes that presented them with varying back stories sourcing them to recent archeological discoveries in the Mediterranean, e.g., Greece. The Middle East, e.g., Iran, Saudi Arabia, or India, and tying them to Biblical accounts of giants." Further, many skeletons in photos have been noted to sport larger-than-average skulls, and housing another quandary; double-rows of teeth! Again, we read:

> "One of the Skhul skulls [in Israel] was reported to have had hyperdontia, or a double row of teeth. This dental anomaly has been reported in populations that have been of legendary great height. "The Babylonian Talmud" claimed that the Biblical giants, (Amorites) had in some cases, a double row of teeth. In The British Isles the legendary Fomorians (Muru or Amorites) also had double rows of teeth. This anomaly also occurs with some frequency in North America within the Shell Mound Culture, the Glacial Kame, and the later Allegewi Hopewell mound builders. All of these North American populations also display archaic facial features along with their great height. Stephen Coons, reports in "The Neanderthaloid Hybrids of Palestine" that "The Neanderthal group was extremely variable, and showed within its ranks clear evidence of evolutionary change in a human direction." He sites (sic) the discoveries found in Palestine within the Mount Carmel caves where,

"the skeleton of a small woman, fully Neanderthal and associated with it was a male mandible equal in size to that of [homo] Heidelberg, but possessed of that human feature, a chin."[ccclxxii]

At some point in time, scientists and field researchers seeking answers to such phenomena as the claimed findings of gigantic hominoid skeletons. Skeletons with extra digits, and a second row of teeth; they may choose to formally disclose their findings and their conclusions to their research. Until such a time as this occurring, maybe Michael Cremo, author of the mentioned earlier "Forbidden Archaeology", insightfully adds a valid warning to all readers and interested people. In another of his publications, "Human Devolution", he writes:

"...the picture of newly discovered early hominids is quite confusing and contradictory. In all these cases, scientists are speculating about fragmentary fossil remains, seeing in them human ancestors, when they most likely are simply varieties of apes with some few features in common with modern humans..."[ccclxxiii]

With such discoveries however, it is, as intimated already not only professional scientists and amateur archaeologists who offer speculation of such skeletal remains. There does also seem to be mounting documented evidence that gargantuan people most surely roamed the earth, alongside many gargantuan animal species. Clearly many religious researchers among others, by adding their particular 'religious' twists, do also. Christian authors and researchers like Rob Skiba, Scott Roberts, Fred Harding, Derek Gilbert, L. A. Marzulli and their supporters. Even with discoveries of huge skeletal remains of an obvious larger-than-average hominid-like being. We cannot contend that photos of 'dead bodies' are the remains of Bible story creatures, i.e. of Genesis 6:4 and other sacred book stories. Which is in itself, has been attempted to be shown above is pure speculative reasoning? It is not possible to know or verify these things with any actual surety. Besides, it would prove mightily helpful to remain somewhat skeptical with some of the information readily available on the Internet, and in books produced en–masse these days. An advance in our technology allows that any

DECONSTRUCTING ENDTIME DELUSIONS

number of photos, and other material can easily be 'photo-shopped' and doctored to resemble something true, when actually it may not be so. Not everything seen is to be believed!

The struggle faced while perusing Rob Skiba's text is he and supporters and other Christian researchers interested in this topic. Do not seem to have carried out much, if any, valid research before attempting to formalise a hypothesis regarding the nephilim. Moreover, the above valid hypotheses that could possibly go to some way to explaining the Genesis 6 episode. I wonder if religious authors are aware, as most people undoubtedly are not; that it appears to be that there was a giant Apelike creature called –Gigantopithicus Blackii - roaming the earth with our ancestor hominids the focus of the former noted title, "True Giants". It is estimated. The Gigantopithicus 'ape' stood to a staggering 3 meters tall. To place this in perspective, think of viewing a blue whale carcass; or better yet, a bear in a museum. They are both great creatures. Bears are massive in size on all fours, as was the gigantopithicus, but when viewed standing bipedal, their size often doubles, towering over a 6ft, or even a 7ft adult. Now, in the least double this height again. This would give some perspective how enormous these apes were. Menacing, to say the least! There is then no reason to believe some photo's of huge skeletons possibly aren't the skeletal remains of a Gigantopithicus Blackii.[ccclxxiv] If so this would also go to some lengths in explaining why the author to the article above seems a little-dumbfounded, writing:

> "...the enormous size of the skeletons and elongated skulls found in May 1912 did not fit very neatly into anyone's concept of a textbook standard. They were enormous. These were not averaged human beings."

The reason I deduce is the remains is not necessarily of human origin, rather are maybe, likely of the prehistoric apelike creature or a creature of close kin. In 1912 nobody had discovered gigantopithicus. He wasn't discovered until 23 years later! Though one feature that disputes this hypothesis is the teeth and jaw structure of the skeleton above which does not resemble that of apes. These remains may be the remains of a yet unnamed prehistoric hominid, as those described by: "When Giants

Ruled the World." Despite, these skeletal remains as possibly those of the Gigantopithicus family. There is one other hypothesis worth mentioning for it adds to the intrigue. Such remains may also belong to various 'giant' persons who well-credentialed researcher's state has now passed into legend and myth. Such people are attributed to have existed up to and including the sixteenth and seventeenth centuries of the current era. They are again mentioned in ancient writings of the ancient Egyptians, texts –like the Edfu (Horus) Building Texts. In "True Giants" we read:

> "Giants have been interpreted as personifications of natural phenomena, as older gods in conflict with newer ones, and as demons from a realm of the dead. ...mythologist John A. MacCulloch has this to say: They have been regarded as an earlier and wilder race of men, with stone weapons, opposed to the more cultured race which uses the plough... The stature of giants is explained by their identity as a different genus of primate Gigantopithecus. The "universal" nature of giants could be explained by the following hypothesis. The distribution of "giant men" is nearly coincident with the dispersal of human beings around the globe. Our hypothesis to explain the success of True Giants would be that they were good at mimicking the cultures of human beings. In clothing, language, and subsistence patterns they may have done well by copying the models they observed in neighbouring humans. The brains of these giants combined with their physical skills give them the capacity to live like human beings, communicate with humans, and adapt to the world's varied climates ...The surviving knowledge of True Giants suggests to us three phases of their interaction with human beings. The first, is a time where in ancient times giants and men lived in shared cooperation: of culture and language. The second phase emphasises a schism between the two species: caused by the menacing feats and height of giant peoples. They might have been too competitive for their smaller kin, having greater appetites, apparently, also being notorious for resorting to cannibalism– which always involved the consumption of humans, not their own kin. And so, maybe numbers of giants grew and overwhelmed the populations of their smaller neighbours. Another cause to the second phase schism: "True Giants may have lacked the capacity to advance culturally along with human beings. Now, in ancient times, the lives of our ancestors were rough and crude in comparison to the world we see today. The cultures of Europe, for example, were not models of gentility. They sometimes rated the label of barbaric. John Grant refers to a "disgusting age" when he compares the sports of Viking and Scottish warriors centuries ago. Mankind's greater tolerance for crudeness and earthiness was probably

universal in ancient times. Our ancestors shared a primitive and harsh world with True Giants. Cultural change may have exaggerated the primitive and unattractive traits of the giants as viewed by humans. The advances that humans were bound to make would have increased the differences between the two groups. The consequence of the falling out in phase two is the deaths of many giants at the hands of human giant-killers. The third phase of relations is the removal of True Giants to a reclusive life in remote locations. Today's giants may be regarded as primitive in contrast to their own ancestors. They might be said to have degenerated because cultural borrowing is now denied them. However, they also may be smarter than their ancestors because they have come to avoid confronting humans."[ccclxxv]

In "Atlantis Rising's" anthology library: "Lost Ancient Wisdom", Freddy Silva, one of the world's leading researchers of sacred sites, ancient systems of knowledge and the interaction between temples and consciousness; has written about these numerous ancient beings that have been largely lost to human consciousness.[ccclxxvi] Andrew Collins has also researched and documented his findings of this and similar material to the Edfu Building Texts in his books, "From the ashes of angels" and "God's of Eden". Both researchers reach an astounding conclusion. According to Silva:

> "The initiates at the temple of Edfu were instructed to "stand up with the Ahau" who measured nine cubits tall.[ccclxxvii] There is evidence that such beings not only existed but their descendants survived well into historic times. In the Pacific Ocean, the first European explorer to reach the island of Te Pito o Te Henua ("Navel of the World') was Jacob Roggeveen, who did so on Easter Sunday, 1722, hence its recent, anglicized (sic) name of Easter Island. He faithfully recorded the experience along with some of the islanders' traditions; one of them states that the population consisted of two types of races – the Short Ears and the Long Ears. The Short Ears referred to the typical homo sapiens. As for the Long Ears, Roggeveen and his crew had direct interaction with them: "In truth, I might say that these savages are as tall and broad in proportion, averaging 12 feet in height...the tallest men on board our ship could pass between the legs of these children of Goliath without bending their head..."[ccclxxviii]

Such records it must be admitted are simply overwhelming. That there was Four meter plus high persons in antiquity is mystifying to us today. Yet, as mysterious as this is, reasonable evidence seems to be mounting. People of enormous sizes, exercising incredible skill, knowledge, and strength that exceeded ordinary feats. Characteristics that would in times–past have been considered as 'supernatural', were roaming the globe sometime in pre-history. Glancing through the pages, the author of "When Giants Ruled the World" supplies convincing prose for their existence. Adding evidence to his thesis, Fleischer offers the observations and findings of British archaist Jacob Bryant (1715–1804) who wrote a massive six-volume manuscript titled, A New System, Or an Analysis of Ancient Mythology. In it Bryant touches upon the theme of giants. Most interesting and relevant to this section of our investigation of nephilim giants are the thoughts and comments of Bryant regarding a race of people that many of us would be familiar from Greek Mythology, –the Cyclopes (Cyclopian's - according to Bryant).

> "The giant cyclopean race was very intelligent [he says]. They had astounding knowledge of the sciences, architecture and so on and were founders of cities... They were also known as the serpents because they were said to be serpent worshippers. Despite their immense knowledge...these giants were very fierce...they practiced cannibalism and human sacrifice [and were detested for it.] The Cyclopes of mythology are said to have possessed an eye in the middle of their foreheads... [and] were also fire worshippers [who] also erected great towers, and 'as these buildings were oftentimes light-houses, and had in their upper story one round casement...by which they afforded light in the night season; the Greeks made this a characteristic of the people. They supposed this aperture to have been an eye, which was fiery, and glaring, and placed in their foreheads... Bryant, furthermore, tells us that the cyclopian belonged to the same family as the Cadimines, the Phoenices as well as the Hivites or Ophites 'who came from Egypt' and worshipped the sun under the symbol of a serpent... These giants were so brilliant that the people they taught were said to have been taught by serpents... These giants were known to have lived in Canaan (Palestine) and were the Anakim who lived in the land of Canaan. Although there are a number of reasons for the origin of the name Phoenician, according to Bryant the Phoenicians were so-named because of their gigantic size."[ccclxxix]

DECONSTRUCTING ENDTIME DELUSIONS

Interesting is the 'fear' and dread such 'persons' conjure in the modern mind. Our modern minds are it seems, awash with vivid and elaborate images. Most often the Cyclopes are described as some greatly deformed and fearsome 'creature' that had one massive eye in the center of their foreheads. Symbolically, what does the cyclopes account for? Reports of these beings are most likely portrayed as violent brutes. In Homer, Odysseus expected they were wild men, totally ignorant of civility. Enkidu again anyone? The single-eye aperture most captivatingly, figuratively calls attention to the idea these giants also required realistic acumen, having little, or no depth of insight. According to the compilers of the aforementioned- "The Book of Symbols: Reflections on archetypal Images",

> "... the Cyclopes represent the attunement to fruitful nature as well as the brute instinctual powers that are the biological foundation of human as of animal being. One does well to approach such energies with something other than temerity and contempt. Psychologically they point to the residue in ourselves of "that unconscious wholeness at the beginning of mental development that is full of life and has the potential for consciousness, but is as cruel, as uncivilized (sic), as nature itself... and has a tendency to swallow its own product." (The Book of Symbols, p.698.)

Interestingly also is this singular eye is right where we know the pineal gland –third-eye is situated! What if the Cyclopes are then, akin to persons of great spiritual awakening and consciousness? Those who for all intent and purposes, can operate from their 'awakened Third-eye –pineal gland', more than their physical eyes? Maybe, the Adam and Eve hendiadys (of 'eating some fruit) represent in a sense, also an 'opening of the third eye' of mankind? Opening of the Third-eye allows you to operate on multiple levels of consciousness. Many websites, with confirming science point to the fact that it's a potent source of intuitive wisdom that with meditation. Gives us insight, forewarning, and intelligence to the past, future, and most importantly to and of the present moment. What if the huge cranial remains unearthed with a cavernous hole where it was assumed an eye once sat, were just the heads of a very large exotic animal; like an Elephant/ Mammoth, or of some other now extinct megafauna species. We know that many creatures that we are familiar with today, were once considered extremely exotic and unusual in times-past. For instance, lions/ tigers/ elephants/ the giraffe and many other creatures of particularly the African Continent were thought of as strangely exotic and wondrous. Often, such animals became gifts and the prized possessions of the elite classes of distant regions of their natural habitat. There are numerous theories and documentation that extinct megafauna skeletal remains inspired many creatures we read about in mythic tales; like the Cyclops. All former descriptions surely seem to add some credence to the enochic tales of the 'Watcher' angels. Parallels can surely be easily recognised. With this information, it is easy to draw connections to how and why one of the Bible's most mysterious passages Genesis 6:1-4 be recorded.

As stated in the Introduction, the Bible is a very 'human' book. It has our dna markers written within, and all over it. If you can accept this, no 'supernatural' entity needs then are present. That these individuals are labelled 'supernatural' is purely an inference of the religious elite who has little, or no knowledge of pre-history. Many also show distain for academic fields like, anthropology, which is recognised as showing too much favour for 'evolution.' What is also fascinating about Bryant's recollections above, is the inference to the serpent worships. A practice that was prevalent throughout ancient Egypt, Canaan and Palestine. That Aylmer von Fleischer's, and Patrick Chouinard's books, "When Giants Ruled the World", and "Lost race of the Giants", may be largely verified as factual with its accounts. I however still purposefully do not see any validity in lumping these, or the giants of the Bible texts automatically into a category of persons deriving from a 'supernatural' ilk. Inscrutability abounds. Thus, as with the next topic suitable and satisfying answers to these mysteries may yet continue to be enigmatic and indefinable even to the best investigator. That is, if Collins' and Silva's, Chouinard's, or Fleischer's, or, even this research and that of others research are dismissed as holding any credit. Clearly Christian authors proposing an 'angel/Watcher' hypothesis as a reasonable and 'biblically' sound explanation for nephilim; they have not done a great service to their readers. But have drawn their conclusions from the usual line of persuasive theological, but dated past material. They generally do not and have not considered anything outside the set parameter and so, don't consider sourcing some of the well-grounded materials available outside the usual religious parameters before entering a conclusion. As I have in the least attempted to succinctly advance.

Vesica Piscis:

ADD TO THIS PRESENT discussion, the various guessed theories being proposed by scientists and conspiracy theorists - christians included. Surrounding the abundant discoveries the globe over of cranial deformation remains. Skulls of individuals the world over has been excavated showing the crazy practice of head binding causing elongation. As with gigantism, and double–rowed teeth this malformation can be a congenitally natural phenomenon. A Wikipedia entry that explains Dolichocephaly (the medical term) assists our understanding:

> "Dolichocephaly (derived from the Ancient Greek, meaning "long") is a condition where the head is longer than would be expected, relative to its width. In humans, scaphocephaly is a form of dolichocephaly. ...in humans the anterior–posterior diameter (length) of dolichocephaly head is more than the transverse diameter (width). It has an incidence of 1 in every 4,200 babies. It can present be in cases of Sensenbrenner syndrome, Crouzon syndrome, Sotos syndrome as well as Marfan syndrome." Although dolichocephaly may be associated with some other abnormalities, alone it is just a normal variation; unless symptomatic, it is not a cause for concern. Early diagnosis can be made by X-ray or ultrasonography. Treatment is not essential.●[ccclxxx]

Aside this common description, the practice of 'head-binding' causing this abnormality unnaturally, is understood to have been carried out particularly by the Huns (Attila), and many other ancient peoples; essentially to force the extension/elongation of skulls while still pliable during early growth. It would seem, this practice was performed on normal 'otherwise' skulls/ heads'. Some of the skulls in photos found online, may just be naturally formed dolichocephaly heads. Many

'Cone-Almond head' remains have been dated to ancient Sumerian and Egyptian times. Not only that, but as the mentioned ancient-wisdom website attests, the elongation of skulls was performed 45(ka) thousand years ago.[ccclxxxi] Yet, the reason this practice was popular among various tribes is still very elusive. It could well be that the elongation of the head was seen to imitate the 'gods'. Seeing that in various cultural mythologies the 'gods' are often depicted as possessing such cranial deformations. Or, it could just be simply; this was a sign of great power, wealth, and attractiveness. No one really knows. Whatever the real reason, no doubt such skull discoveries have played into the nephilim/ Alien/ 'Watcher' Angel myth as well. These are after all, very alien to our culture. There is one hypothesis regarding the elongation of these skulls I wish to mention for further consideration. Maybe this practice was introduced as a 'sacred ritual'? Maybe the practice was to imitate a symbol recognised throughout the world; the sacred symbol of the Vesica Piscis. According to Barbara Walker, "The Woman's Dictionary of Symbols..." in her entry on the Vesica Piscis, this emblem was the

> "...worldwide ancient synonym for..the vulva. In religious symbolism, it stood for the feminine creative-force...the mysterious magic inside a woman's body that could actually produce new life."

It was then, a magical religious experience linked with sexual coupling. The vesica piscis is a shape that is the intersection of two circles with the same radius, intersecting so the center of each circle lies on the perimeter of the other. So, the vulva synonym. The name literally means the "bladder of a fish" in Latin. The shape is also called mandorla <"almond"> in Italian. Many elongated skulls are known to belong to Aztec's and others who populated the South America's. But as stated, no conclusive reason has been proposed for this practice.[ccclxxxii] And yet, no doubt a similar ritual practice is still prevalent throughout the world in some cultures. The weird practices and rituals of head and neck, ear, and lip binding, stretching, and piercing was, and still is performed by various tribes and people groups even today, causing their strange disfigurements. Some individuals, it seems though were (are) naturally born with elongated skulls and extra limbs...and so, it would be safe to assume that just as today, in antiquity there were also such persons. At least as much as the dinosaur, Neanderthal, and prehistoric Neolithic persons were roaming the earth in times–past. Were they of such menacing heights as 36ft tall, as large and fearsome as some dinosaur skeletal evidence shows? Who can really say with any surety and absolute conviction. More possibly would be 12ft – 15ft high persons' and their interactions with races of much smaller stature. These would undoubtedly have been referred as giants. Some researchers attest to enormous sizes of some beings. There is still much this world can, and probably will eventually divulge that yet, is unknown.

Giant Nephilim conclusion:

AS STATED AT THE BEGINNING of this Nail; the investigation into Genesis chapter six, nephilim giants. The earliest myth or tale surrounding the creature nephilim is long past and is no longer extant. We can only really grasp at a very fragmentary Genesis idea of what such a tale might have consisted of by using known parallel stories in possible proximity to the ancient author. Those that eventually found its way into the Judaeo-Christian book.[ccclxxxiii] Besides, as also noted above by Steve Jones, modern dna, genetic, and anthropologist and evolutionary scientific evidence all seem to confirm on the one hand, as well as nullify on the other many a religious speculation surrounding this topic. A true perspective of metaphysics – as a study and understanding of reality would also dismiss as speculation and unfounded theorising of any recent 'religious' publications on such matters. A 'spiritualised' rendition of those sacred book passages as discussed throughout this section is therefore greatly weakened by the above scientific and secular evidences and argumentation. Many a religious argument postulated simply does not attempt to broaden the scope of the original believed argument into the many sciences available to pursue today. When seeking viable answers to religious quandaries. Those that have greatly enhanced our working-knowledge base of Hominid prehistory and the prehistory of the Earth. Rather these sciences and their findings are met with skepticism if they are perceived to not align with a religious premise. If the projected benefits of CO2 are correct - in that super levels of this prominent gas, along with higher levels of oxygen in ancient atmosphere's; that these alone promote exceptional growth, health, and nutritional value of crops and body mass of its consumer, – I wonder how much CO2 and Oxygen would it take to sustain 36ft + tall persons? A 36ft individual would amount to someone who was 10.9meters + tall, the height of a double-story house! Levels of Oxygen and CO2 in the atmosphere would undoubtedly need to have been far, far greater in our planet's pre-history, than what current 'climate change scaremongers' nonsensically flaunt as dire and apocalyptic for our current world environment. According to one writer the author confirms, as does the mentioned earlier and cited book, "The many benefits of Atmospheric CO2 Enrichment"; there were massive Carbon Dioxide levels in ancient pre-history; about 3 million years ago.[ccclxxxiv] Also, regards the science of CO2, we all seem to have dementia when it comes to any climate hypothesis; i.e., all climate-changes and weather patterns the globe over is dictated by the very explainable forces of three well-understood fields of academic study; the physics of the earth's rotation, the equator, and atmospheric occurrences; and only very minimally by human intervention. It is complete nonsense to insist we (Homo Sapiens) have an increasingly dire impact on climate that many pundits are hypothesising. Though we do seem to have a very fractional influence. Moreover, climate changes happen daily! The stupidity of many above hypotheses; i.e., that of dire climate-change mirrors attempting to coordinate every human being alive the world over to simultaneously leap into the air, and land at exactly the precise moment of everyone else; in the express hope of causing the earth to wobble even more on its axis and so change its trajectory ever so slightly again. Maybe, someone will devise an experiment and the technology that cause Earth's Magnetic Polarity to change again. How about affectively causing the Sunrise to be in the West, and Sunset in the East; which according to Velikovsky and other more recent researchers, happened in our not too distant past along with other weird celestial, and terrestrial phenomena. Like the

DECONSTRUCTING ENDTIME DELUSIONS

History Channel with its fascinating (2008) t.v. series 'Life After People,' and book The World without Us, by Alan Weisman; What happens to the stuff we leave behind?

Mythology investigator Scott Corrales' probes into the world of mythology and giants, have directed him also to make some interesting observations. He notes below there are numerous tales and mythological world legends about 'giants' on par with many Greek mythologies and the pantheons of God-like entities. These still exist worldwide. Like, the mysterious Yeti, the Bermuda Triangle, the Cyclops and others! Confidently, not all myths are tales and mysteries to only amuse children. Myths, invariably contain various kernels of truth and wisdom. Just as it is often the case; however, when did it become the goal to focus attention on the characters of the tale? Are not many of these 'stories' loaded with numerous morals from which to learn and benefit? To understand something of myth, both ancient and present, is to understand more of human psychology. To say the least the sheer volume of myths still recognisable, believed, practiced, and loved the world over is testament to the fact: they underline both the variety and continuity of human nature. From one of the earliest known recorded tales; the epic poem of Gilgamesh. Such tales have shaped and illumined societal values, countless fears, and attached to the tangled web of ordinary life. To this, Scott Corrales adds:

> "What would the lore of all human cultures be like without the presence of giants? They are a fixture of folk tales and myth from Europe and the Americas to the farthest reaches of Asia. They are mentioned with equal ease in holy books and in fairy tales. Giants fill us with wonder and not inconsiderable envy as we marvel at their strength and feats. Those dwelling in the Middle Ages, caught in the turbulence of their troubled times, ascribed the engineering achievements of the Roman Empire to the work of giants. Giants may have been relegated to the realms of fable and sword-and-sorcery novels, but there is considerable evidence that beings of great size shared our world in primeval times."[ccclxxxv]

Corrales described clearly what human endeavours ascribe. What then if mention of giants/nephilim in our sacred texts had next to nothing to do with size (as I clearly believe truer than many Christian hypotheses); but, were actually presenting to the reader, the astounding intellect, and prowess of the persons that clearly baffled audiences and opponents alike? Do we not still call some perspicacious individuals; Intellectual Giants in their fields? Earlier was mentioned that Rob Skiba made a connection between another Old Testament passage, and his Genesis 6 proposal. So, what about Israel's Prophets and the vast arrays of 'prophetic' writings we read in the Judaeo-Christian book, another twist of more ancient legends? For example, It was suggested that the recorded episodes of nephilim in the Bible should most probably be recognised as a retelling and reshaping of the many certain and famous literary and oral traditions (myths) that must have been in circulation. Cassuto explains parallels of this Genesis six myth and the Canaanite/Ugaritic pre-biblical myths of Baal and various other gods circulating the region. This for sure then was in the minds of the sacred author of this episode. He writes:

> "Various myths were current, as we know, among the peoples of the ancient East, concerning the relations between the gods and the daughters of men, and concerning the children who were born from these unions and were regarded as demigods or were even elevated to the rank of divinities. Also, among the Canaanites there were widespread legends of this kind, as the Ugaritic texts testify. The poem on the pleasant and beautiful gods is, it is true, obscure in detail, yet it is at any rate clear that it speaks of the father of the deities, El, who took to wife two daughters of men and begat by them two sons ... who both became gods."[ccclxxxvi]

Above, was attempted to cover a broad and sweeping array of possible's to assist in explaining one of the bibles' most enigmatic narratives Genesis 6:1-4. Few, if any believers writing on this same episode have considered to postulate what might have led to the inclusion of this story in the sacred text in the first place? Having rather regurgitated what has come beforehand. With the slight adages and personal spin in the attempt to authenticate their reasoning. I have endeavoured not to follow suit. No doubt some, if not every proposal offered above has caused some angst with readers. The above proposals may have even clashed with a readers' preconceived religious understanding, and so

DECONSTRUCTING ENDTIME DELUSIONS

salted the abrasions these proposals caused. But working with reason and logic and the sciences consulted, there was simply no way around the issues that were brought to mind other than the way in which I attempted to approach them. This is a topic scattered with minefields. The issues surrounding nephilim are extensive and long-standing and will not be resolved easily. In the least, my hope is that the above has offered readers some very interesting summations, which a reasonable conclusion might be added. At this juncture, it would be beneficial to remind readers again of the earlier cited dictum from Aesop's Fables: "One story is good; i.e., until another is told!"

The guessing of an angel/alien–hybrid nephilim hypothesis, spruiked by numbers of often prophetic Christian philosophers seems very much erroneous; far–fetched and simply the efforts of an over–indulgent imagination. An imagination that seeks to find reasonable theories and conclusions to enigmatic themes to sacred stories via the usual tightly–bound theological parameters. Which, arrive at the standard, but egregious conclusion. Here then is my current conclusion to the Genesis six episode. The "Metaphysical Bible Dictionary" can assist with a concluding meaning. Giants it says, represent the untrained, undisciplined, undeveloped mind. The myth of the nephilim could easily be recognised as portraying this explanation. Likely, the episode of Genesis 6:1-4 is derived from numerous ancient stories; the memories, and depictions about encounters the early residents; the skhul-quafez (Israel) and later descendants of the Levant had with Neanderthals, Cro-Magnons, the gigantopithicus, or some other pre-history ancestor. Neanderthals and offspring of interbreeding with another sapient species– birthing the Cro–Magnon species may be representative of (1) "the sons of the God's" (Neanderthal), and (2) nephilim = Cro–Magnon species; of the episode of Genesis 6:1-4. Considering these early races often are portrayed as being somewhat dim-witted and undisciplined – a portrayal that is most unfair. In many ways, early hominids were just as intelligent. Convincingly, the back cover to Andrew Collins' title "From the ashes of Angels" confirms the proposal; that what is considered now sacred myth, primarily speaks with flesh-and-blood tales of the ancients:

"Andrew Collins shows that these angels, demons, and fallen-angels were flesh-and-blood members of a race predating our own." Probably originating from Persian tales and stories of their Kings.[ccclxxxvii]

Nephilim is, it seems a word the Genesis 6 author chose as it was the best known that described a remembered mythic tale; a tale that is unfortunately, no longer extant. Nephilim could also, and most probably be an evocative term used by the author of this Bible episode; an imaginative explanatory devise of a tribe and race of incredible warrior-type people. Originating around the regions of modern-day Iraq/ Yemen. The illusiveness in meaning of nephilim, and its occasional transliteration giant, as far is concerned, there is no legitimate reason to assume this word has any specific relation to any supernatural being, as is the usual posturing of countless Christian end-time materials marketed today. As stated, I do not recognise the introduction of this term nephilim in Genesis 6:4 as remotely having any divine attachment. This, despite most scholarship more than likely disagreeing, and the fact the supernatural interpretation comes solely from the readings of the prolific rabbinic para-sacred renderings of ancient times. Genesis 6 begins its narrative describing human and earthly things; i.e., a population explosion, it is extremely confusing for the reading audience to then suddenly be introduced to some otherworldly supernatural entity who, just as quickly arrived on the scene, disappeared in the next instant, and is not spoken of again until much later, and in another unrelated narrative! To read a supernatural entity into the verses of Genesis 6, just doesn't follow the usual cognitive processes when reading the plain text. Any supernatural thought would then be required to be derived from another source. Exactly what we find when we start to delve into sources that have analogous characters; i.e. 1 enoch. So, what could the moral of such tales as described in the Bible be?

To assist let's employ the services of a well-known Greek legend. Take the possibly parallel legendary anecdote of the Greek champion <Achilles>. That this is classed as Greek folklore is not the point. The point is to look beyond the tale, searching for a deeper moral it could be teaching. Thus, can we not draw a similar theme between his celebrated heroism and arrogance and the accounts of nephilim? As the earlier cited "Lexham Bible Dictionary" which clearly stated: "Nephilim places emphasis not on the state of what these individuals had been in their lives, but on the state in which they now were" (i.e., dead fallen warriors..."). 'Shades': those forgetful, imbecilic, 'fallen' individuals who also represent the untrained, undisciplined, undeveloped mind of the dead. Might these two legends, of the nephilim and Achilles be teaching essentially the very same thing? Though one may be known and seen by others as valiant, unbridled intrepidness leads to committing Hubris: a classical Greek term meaning, outrageous arrogance. Thinking you are wise and powerful, when you may not be all that astute or invincible. Committing Hubris turns to contentment, which in turn, destroys a man! Becoming a Shade; one of the dead. Whether the originating author meant nephilim as the physically deceased, or just mind-dead who knows for sure! Either could be probable, fitting within a symbolic framework (see my symbolic rendering in Appendix 1) Recall from the Grecian tale, an arrow pierced ACHILLES' heel; eventually destroying him! Achilles did we are informed in this legend believe he was invincible! All the described attributes and more, are, I believe portrayed in both legends of Achilles, and the accounts of the nephilim of Genesis 6:4, and possibly also numbers 13:33, and definitely used in a similar fashion in other passages we have: like Amos 2:9; the chronicle verses and others!

What we have are two sides of the same moral coin; one side defines Greek mythology, the other of Semitic myth making. Speaking from his own milieu each writer teaches us the same thing; hubris in any form, committed by anyone has fatal consequences. Much the same, be aware of the tendency for your own unbridled pride and solipsism. 'Ego' – here is surely – a dirty word! Further, as stated above there are found several reasonable explanations and possibilities of how the Genesis of this tale began. Maybe similar tales were entrusted to various persons about certain encounters with Neanderthals, the Gigantopithicus Blackii, or some other; and in time these were embellished at every turn. Becoming the story of Genesis 6:1-4. Like a game of Chinese whispers – rarely is the final statement the same as how the game began. Unfortunately, Church-sponsored sacred texts more often than not. Read as they were specifically written from a misogynist's perspective. They subtly paint a picture that women are somehow to blame for the ills of humanity, while increasing the power of the male species. The dominant deity in most religions is male today. But, this was surely not the case in early history and the earliest history of religious theorising. To this writer the above explanations – of Neanderthal, or Yemenite people groups, and my other efforts at sketching this Genesis episode - explain more succinctly how or even why the Genesis 6:1-4 episode found its way into the corpus of scripture. Being the first full-scale and real lesson about the result of unchecked pride in the pages of the sacred book. The mythic episode of the monstrous beings, the nephilim, could just as easily be used also as a frightful 'warning' of dangerous encounters with predators, or male hominid ancestors, particularly directed to the female species. Recall again comments regarding the sacred tree of the previous study of Genesis chapter three (Nail four). It was intimated that such a tale of Genesis three might have served as a warning to the female species to not venture too close to the mysterious/sacred. The realm set aside for male humankind. Despite earlier, it was also noted (Nail one) the female hominid species embodied the role of medicine-man, astrologer, healer, priestess. Further, the sacred book does indicate that these creatures chose (seemingly an indiscriminate act) from whom they desired to breed. In the mentioned earlier fascinating study "Deadly Powers: Animal Predators and the mythic imagination", Paul Trout convincingly argues the point:

> "Whatever the particular form the monster may have taken within a specific geographical area, its essential features would clearly have identified it as a very dangerous creature even to those unfamiliar with local fauna. Monsters were used as a means of imbuing sacred or dangerous geographical areas with taboo...But the basic function of the monster was to give fear a face, to graphically capture the dread that is bred into us by millions of years as a prey species that was stalked...by huge and terrifying carnivores (and or other horrifying acts committed by hominid ancestors)." (Ch. 6. subsection - Animal Predation into Mythic Monsters.)

DECONSTRUCTING ENDTIME DELUSIONS

Hence, the 'Watcher' angel and counterpart - alien theories are both considered void of all lasting importance. These are to this writer stupid, imbecilic, fantasies of the untrained, undisciplined, undeveloped observance of the mind-dead and mind–blind believer. Mythic stories such as this Genesis six account more likely portrays deep seated horrifying memories of encounters with either other proto-hominids or of animal predation. Cassuto and many scholars and laymen today may still however likely disagree; the consensus is after all, that angels committed the deed of 'taking the daughters of men' for themselves. A description defined also by Owens again in his supernatural novel mentioned earlier. Yet, why does every account in any supposed sacred text need to be specifically interpreted through or via a so-called 'spiritual' sense?

Why might this story be here?

A FINAL PRESSING QUESTION to ask; why is the story of Genesis 6:1:4 here? Why is it placed directly after the long string and lineage stretching from Adam to noah? The answer offered is that it counteracts the then folklore. Which was achieved cleverly without polemic! Cassuto speaking with this offers us one final and educational explanation. Bringing to bear the following,

> "This is the way of the Torah (the first five books of the Bible): even when her purpose is to oppose the notions of the gentiles, she does not derogate, by stooping to controversy, from her ingrained majesty and splendour. She states her views, and by inference other ideas are rejected. The same method is also adopted in the passage under consideration. Following her usual procedure, the Torah explains how the giants came into being, and from what is stated we can infer that which is rejected. The giants are not at all related—Heaven forfend! — to the deity, but only to 'the sons of God', that is to say, to the Divine household, to the attendants of God, and actually to the lowest order of them. Every word is carefully weighed. The Torah was deliberately brief, confining the subject to a few verses, as though she wished to say that the episode was entirely uncongenial to her, and was not mentioned for its own sake, but only so as to disabuse the reader's mind of certain concepts. When the sons of God saw—Scripture informs us—that the daughters of men were good, that is to say, that they were beautiful, they

took some of them as wives. There is no allusion here to a revolt of the sons of God against the Lord, nor to any obscene behaviour on their part. The sons of God are not of the same rank as the Ministering Angels, who do not procreate, but resemble in this respect the sons of men."[ccclxxxviii]

The choice of the reader is left open which is or not of more worth. I have attempted to state clearly my position - long and drawn out as it was. Despite disagreeing with the prevailing idea that these creatures were 'Watcher' angel or alien, or, an advanced being just as it is promoted in the book, "Lost race of the Giants", I agree somewhat, with Cassuto in that whatever these creatures ultimately represented, whether 'fallen' mankind (as explained further below), or angel types they resembled sons of men who happened to be of a godly line. Leading to a conclusion that this Genesis episode and the creatures it describes most probably have derived from lost story's regarding Neanderthals and other prehistoric hominids and predators. Is this not a much stronger and more palatable than the explanation of 'angels.' For, this then demands answering what angels mean. Our inclination to hubris, the Bible indisputably seems to sound a stern warning, spanning unimpeded across space, and time to our ears. The Bible's first goal as attested by many is after all to dissuade readers of all generations, not just its initial students from all apparent prevailing polytheistic assumptions and myths and ultimately cause a monotheistic revolution. Despite it (the Bible) itself not exactly is being wholly monotheistic. Though not outwardly condemning 'other' God's we can articulate and sum another way, this is to say the divinity that the Bible presents its readers with "...has communicated an explicit will for human behavior (sic) in this world; and he rewards and castigates because of obedience to that will."[ccclxxxix] With all this in mind, we can now finally review the passage of Amos 2:9. Does the Prophet support Rob Skiba's assumption that the giant Amorites were descended from nephilim. Or, does Amos' accounting and warning to Israel about the Amorite more accurately ring with an equally parallel tone to the treaties just described? Entreating readers to keep a weather eye on not only your own. But, also neighbours' potential to commit transgression through overbearing pride. See

DECONSTRUCTING ENDTIME DELUSIONS

(Matthew 23:12; luke 14:11, 18:14; 2 corinthians 11:7; philemon 2:8; 1 Peter 5:5; deuteronomy 8:2, 3, 16; 2 samuel 22:28) to cite but a few passages that confidently look to press home this very point.

Nail Ten:

Yet it was I who destroyed the Amorite before them, Whose <u>height</u> was like the height of the cedars, And he was as <u>strong</u> as the oaks... (Jewish Prophet, Amos 2:9)[cccxc]

UNFORTUNATELY FOR ROB Skiba and his supporters, no Jewish Prophet could become a legitimate spokesman for the latest christianised end time propaganda. The Prophet Amos does not lend himself at all to the interpretation he assumed as valid. Amos does in actuality carry on in the same fashion as his contemporaries. The Prophet is not transmitting to either his original audience, nor to modern audiences the idea that the Amorite was a race of beings of enormous height –as Cedar trees: persons of huge stature with super-human ability and strength –as an Oak. The first point to convey is the author of this Amos passage has most surely employed hendiadys! Just as we saw in Genesis chapter three; in the garden there are two trees, one of life, and a second, tree of wisdom! So the author of Amos undoubtedly wishes to convey an idea. The original audiences most likely understood using hendiadys. A single message using two expressions. Using the height of Cedars, and strength of Oak trees. Secondly, an emphasis of height and strength could well be a feasible assumption under certain pre-recorded historic conditions. But, unlike the point Rob Skiba assumes and wishes to make, the context of Amos does not allow such a fanciful interpretation. A difficulty lay ahead of us. That is, what was the message in this verse of Amos? Unbeknown to many English readers of the sacred books, the exact same Hebrew words for height, and strong (underline above) have like countless others, been translated differently elsewhere in the Old Testament corpus. The particular Hebrew word translated height in this verse has elsewhere been translated: pride, dignity, and arrogant, haughty, loftiness, tall, towering, and raised. While interestingly, and so, according to the English Standard Version. The only other place where hason (strong) is used –is the alleged work of one of Amos' contemporaries (isaiah 1:31)! The Prophet (isaiah) here speaks of the wickedness of judah, whose evil if not repented, will cause them to become dry and withered; like a garden without water (isaiah 1:30.)

Certainly playing into our moral foray above! The problem: what do we choose as the most applicable or fitting meaning of these words in Amos? How do we decide what is or not correct? Surely, Amos' own context would dictate. Therefore, what Rob's interpretation shows are a strained predilection to the height of the Cedar, and the strength of the Oaks which are now modern well-known facts. He clearly did not understand the use of hendiadys in this passage. Either that, or he completely ignored it. To Rob Skiba facts and, literary devises seem to be irrelevant. Not fitting a predisposed ideology it was glossed over completely. If this is the case, no wonder such an outrageously flawed interpretation ensued! Rob clearly wanted to find a passage that in his mind enhanced and validated the notion of an otherworldly creature/ 'giant' roaming the earth, terrorising the status quo. Seemingly finding it in Amos 2:9 he ran with it uncritically. He has fallaciously used the known enormity of Cedars and strength of Oak trees today, which Amos likens the Amorite to as 'hopefully' what the Prophet was originally conveying. So very wrong again. Hence, Rob's guessed emphasis and link to fallen angelic entities is birthed. However, all readers of prophetic books must take pains to understand first; no prophetic text can legitimately be read or understood from a 'modern' perspective. As with the rest of the corpus, these must also be understood from their own contextual perspective before attempting to integrate a feasible or modern interpretation for a modern audience. A long way to achieving this is to research the Hebrew words in context behind the English. Understanding a little of the conventions of language. In this case, English, as briefly outlined above. The 'dictionary' forms, called lemma's of both Hebrew words that lay behind strong and height in this Amos passage were searched using Logos' powerful electronic algorithms. Above are the concise results of the numerous occurrences where height was translated differently; and the single use of strong, which was found is only used in one other passage (isaiah 1:31). If; therefore, these two words were understood in their rightful context, readers will not be tempted to think the first gloss given in any Bible lexicon or Hebrew/English word reference work is sufficient, or the correct understanding. Let alone what our brain more often than not automatically assumes. Living in the 21st Century, we now have greater education standards and knowledge than any author of any sacred book ever had. Readers must get into the practice of utilising that standard much better. Especially when it comes to reading some message from an outdated parchment! Below is offered two sources that tender not only a brief gloss from which to choose, but also more importantly a contextual discussion that helps determine a correct meaning.

> (gābōah) high, exalted. Strong's 1363.

> The usual nuance behind the words under discussion is pride or haughtiness. Of interest is the negative usage of this word in connection with some part of the human body. For example, pride is linked with the heart... Isaiah 2:11; 5:15 and Ps 101:5 connect pride with the eyes. Proverbs 16:18... tie pride with man's spirit, and Psalms 10:4 with man's "nose"/countenance. On a few occasions individuals are said to be guilty specifically of this sin of pride: Uzziah (II Chr 26:16); Hezekiah (II Chr 32:25-26); the prince of Tyre (Ezk 28:2, 17). Conversely, Isaiah speaks of the suffering servant who will be exalted (rûm), lifted up (nāśa') and be very high (gābah) (52:13).[cccxci]

While strong, (ḥā·sōn) Strong's 2634, according to the "New International Dictionary of Old Testament Theology and Exegesis" (NIDOTTE) makes worthy mention that:

> "The pitiful powerlessness of titans in comparison with God's irresistible destroying energy is highlighted in Amos 2:9 (Fosbroke, 789). The ungrateful and unfaithful people of the northern kingdom are denounced for their transgressions against Yahweh, who had manifested his love for them by graciously bringing them out of Egypt, guiding them in the wilderness, and giving them the land he had promised (v. 10), annihilating in the process (his fruit above and his roots below, i.e., root and branch [cf. 2 Kgs 19:30; Job 18:16; Isa 37:31; Ezek 17:9; Hos 9:16]) the Amorites (Amorite is a broad term for the pre-Israelite inhabitants of Canaan,.. who are described hyperbolically as having been tall as cedars and strong as oaks

DECONSTRUCTING ENDTIME DELUSIONS

(v. 9); the legend of the remarkable physical stature and prowess of the original population of the land is widespread in the OT... The implication is that just as Yahweh destroyed the Amorites, so too he may destroy the Israelites, who themselves are behaving as oppressors."[cccxcii]

Was it noticed? The aforementioned Amorite are stated to have been the pre-Israelite occupant of the lands called Canaan. Disputing the postulating of those Christian authors, and their fanciful publications; of Derek Gilbert, Rob Skiba and others. That the Amorite can be associated with the Nephilim/giant of Genesis chapter six (1-4). Clearly, those authors have not bothered to research using available Bible helps any thing regards these people groups. But, have committed the usual conjecturing; the standard Christian ideology that is based on utter fallacy. The only potential relation to the Genesis six talks about is that the Amorite, represented the now 'fallen- deceased' former mighty tribes of the region. Again, there is no ultra-spiritual, heavenly being. Rather, just another humanoid tribe recognised for their prowess, and other superior feats. Further, "The 'new' English translation of the Septuagint" by Logos Bible Systems offers an even clearer picture of what the text of Amos 2:9 most probably means. All without the use of any high-end lexicon, or Bible dictionary as the two sources cited above. It reads:

"But I lifted up the Amorites from their face, whose height was just as the height of a cedar, and he was mighty like an oak, and I dried his fruit from above, and his roots from below."[cccxciii]

From their faces speaks with their pride; while 'Mighty' speaks on the same level as Genesis 6:1-4: the 'mighty' men of renown. Quite astoundingly this passage of Amos 2:9 confirms again the overall conclusion of what the Genesis 6:1-4 passage was (potentially) inferring; what the originating author/ redactor in these short verses was appealing an audience to decipher. The sacred texts are so very infused with human dna. It is appalling how religious persons with their heads in the clouds, have literally butchered such lessons. Turning them into what most assuredly was likely not in the redactors mind. Despite also, the ideology we looked at earlier; that we saw was offered by ancient interpreters.

If Rob is acquainted even minimally with such resources as these Bible helps. He, and other Christian authors should have taken this passage of Amos and other texts in their rightful contexts. So, should have reassessed his initial conclusion. I doubt therefore, that Amos 2:9 can be legitimately linked to nephilim. Be it the nephilim of Genesis 6, numbers 13, or some other passage mentioning giants! 'Giants' of menacing heights and feats in the Judaeo-Christian books are simply untrue! The only individual remotely described is goliath. It is bad theology and bad research that Rob Skiba, and others seem to employ. Assuming; 'giant/nephilim' are always (1) wicked or evil by nature, (2) does fit into some end time assumption. A corrected parallel. As we discovered earlier, nephilim/giant is somewhat analogous to hubris. Here in theme, relating this time to the Amorite, hubris illumines (or in the least appears) in the passage of Amos also. Amos does not lend itself readily to any such hypothesis Skiba has endeared as –"The Genesis Six Experiment". His eschatological end-time arguments have suffered tremors. If an eschatological nuance is found in the passages he assumes (Amos 2:9; Genesis 6:1:4; numbers 13:33); it does not focus on or support any supernatural/angelic mythical creature being of immense height or strength. No fanciful creature once tumbled down from the heavens. No creature, or human lusted after any daughter. No mystical supernatural entity interbred to produce a progeny that terrorised Mesopotamian regions in antiquity. This is sheer illogical nonsense; a sure abuse of the grandeur of a potential message of this mythological Genesis legend. The message is here again in (Amos 2:9) a warning against hubris! Myths of terrorising entities as we have seen just are not recorded in the pages of scripture. They are though seen in archaic folk legends. The sacred books offer nothing to readers but profound moral truths. In which this case speaks again, quite clearly of the human propensity to fall headlong into effrontery. Continually we are warned of this tendency. Even our own 'spiritual' and natural senses assist us. But, we need fresh eyes to see.

What the Genesis six experiment shows, is Rob's directorial and wild imagination at play. His ideas surrounding nephilim are little else than

DECONSTRUCTING ENDTIME DELUSIONS

a 'straw-man' masquerading under a banner of 'truth.' Rob Skiba, as we all on occasion has allowed his own distortion of logic to reign. That: (1) when giants are mentioned in the scripture (esp., the Septuagint), often, if not most times, it literally implies size. (2) That 'giants' must also equate to supernatural 'fallen' beings who chose to descend to the earth and breed with the daughters of men. Finally, (3) Amos 2:9 can relate (specifically by-word association and meaning) to nephilim and therefore also to The Genesis Six Experiment. Yet, this has been shown to be nothing but guess, madness, manipulation, and adulteration of the text. Without doubt any serious scholar, biblical theologian, or astute Bible reader would unashamedly affirm it! The only things Rob's conclusions reveal is his blatant overemotional, and complete insouciant manner he chose to address his topic. Yet, we have really only begun to scratch at the surface of areas that could be studied in this passage; i.e., what relation could tales and stories of the many 'other' gods of antiquity teach us about this episode? So, what is Amos' over arching context? The passage (Amos 2:9) is about how the deity Yahweh, through the Prophet Amos attempts to arrest the attention of his countrymen! The problem, according to modern scholarship is that Israel had again allowed her spiritual and moral condition to waiver and fallen into disrepute. The danger was effrontery that if not addressed it "would surely lead to their being driven off the land just as the Amorites had been (9:7–8)."[cccxciv] Thus,

> "[t]his prophetic word is not about the Amorites; it is about Israel's covenant with God dating from the Exodus, the act of God par excellence." Regarding the Amorites, [w]hose height was like the height of the cedars, and who was as strong as the oaks, men who were as tall as cedar trees and as strong as oaks. Such full comparisons are usually not hard to translate except for the terms cedar trees and oaks.[cccxcv]

Because of space, time, and subject restrictions we cannot delve into contemporaneous 'prophets' like isaiah in any great length here. Except to say both Amos and he began their 'ministry' in chorus. What Christian 'theologians,' ministers, pastors, and teachers however would declare, on religious grounds about the oracles of these two seers. Both were attuned to announcements of a 'future' Messiah figure. But, consistently reality and scientifically historical evidence flat out disputes all such 'religious' assumptions. Both seers, and dare I suggest, all Hebrew seers, including the john of Revelation are in unison in every pronouncement presumably uttered. Sure, some details and situations differ, yet the macro picture seems to point to their oracles being manifestly regarding celestial oddities and the devastating effects that could arise. In confirmation, opening Part II of "Worlds in Collision" Immanuel Velikovsky interestingly proposes:

> "About seven hundred fifty years passed after the great catastrophe of the days of the Exodus, or seven centuries after the cosmic disturbances in the days of Joshua. During all this time the world was afraid of the recurrence of the catastrophe at the end of every Jubilee period. Then, starting about the middle of the eighth century before the present era, a new series of cosmic upheavals took place at intervals of short duration. It was the time the Hebrew prophets...the period... part of the well authenticated history of the lands of the eastern Mediterranean...The seers who prophesied in Judea were versed in the lore of heavenly motion; they observed the ways of the planetary and cometary bodies and, like the stargazers of Assyria and Babylonia, they were aware of future changes." (Worlds in Collision, Part II, Ch1, p211.)

Thus, the oracles of Hebrew prophets seem to be focused upon the observation of the heavenly bodies, and the calamities these could bring again to the planet and their native regions. If Velikovsky's research efforts and understanding are on the Mark, and is thus, closer to the 'truth' surrounding these, and other 'prophetic' verdicts; then, rationally, logically we'd have to assume 'religionists' and current expositors of sacred texts have 'missed the Mark' quite severely. They have misinterpreted by miles such foreshadowing pronouncements. The scene beginning to emerge is not as many believers in some 'supreme' deity figure assume. That such a supernatural 'being' exists and is somehow distinct and separated from the laws that govern the universe, but is however, still able to 'pull' certain strings to violate and impact those laws at its own discretion. This is illogical reasoning for two simple reasons: (1) it severely blunts Ockham's Razor; i.e., it does not offer the simplest explanation for anything. Rather, it complicates things, as A. C. Grayling asserts by, "...bring[ing] in an unnecessary addition to the framework of explanation..."[cccxcvi] How does one go about a logical, reasonable explanation that is happily able to fit an entity who is apparently outside the realm of all known conventional parameters? But is then also able to impinge at will upon those parameters. From that position, and not disrupt the whole in the process? (2) W. K. Clifford once stated: "It is wrong always, everywhere, and for anyone, to believe anything upon insufficient evidence." Evidence for a religious hypothesis is surely waning, non–existent in all religious accounts yet explored.

As stated the ancients directed their attention to the celestial realm for pretty many all life-cycles. Claiming and believing that the stars, the planets, and other heavenly entities were gods who exhibited certain powers. Over eons then, these 'divine' entities were eventually, anthropomorphised. Becoming the demanding of reverence in appeasement. Thus, maybe, just maybe when mentioned in the sacred book at least; the terms, the Lord, the Lord God, Elohim, or any other cognate, the author is noway meaning and voicing an opinion about some otherworldly, insubstantial, unverifiable being –humanity calls, God –or deity; rather, their pronouncements and predictions are squarely spoken about planetary-deities' common to their milieu and what effect they could wreak upon the population. What if that were a more truthful explanation? Obviously; therefore, a fair amount of alternate material that could be relevant has either been lost to the mind, or purposefully glossed over through the extensive use of the extra-sacred works that Rob Skiba and other religious researchers employ; works remaining within eyesight of the belief system already in use. That is essentially why again it must be stated the work of writers and scholars like Immanuel Velikovsky, as an outsider, and the conclusions he draws are possibly closer to the truth of many sacred books' accounts. Obviously, most expositors of sacred texts have not thought to look too far adrift their particular mindset on what certain texts mean either. Few, if any would mention the materials and sources Velikovsky or any other alternative researcher cites. Rather they most likely have relied on what they themselves were taught during their seminary training. This has filtered through to their professional work. Despite Rob and others often citing various ancient Jewish books; like the troïka books of enoch, Jasher, and Jubilees for the success of their arguments. Not every one of these texts though are wholly extant despite what some would assert. Of those, we possess today are but copies, of copies, of copies. Nonetheless, the use of these copies is systematically squeezed and moulded to fit the projected and wishful thesis of an end time/ apocalyptic scenario. There really is no surprise then that the result is the production of exactly the desired result. Believing readers would be all the wiser though to note carefully the warning against such manipulation. The small letter to titus clearly admonishes:

> "...avoid foolish controversies and genealogies and contentions and quarrels about the law, for they are useless, and fruitless."[cccxcvii]

Countless Christian authors with a bent on exploiting an end time theme, have played right into this. Through their own perfidy, these authors manipulate readers with countless foolish controversies about genealogies and contentious ideologies. One other: The hyperbolic nature of the text of (Amos 2:9) has also not been noticed. If it were noticed, Rob and others have chosen to gloss over and ignored it. Rather, the usual English gloss of certain words; i.e., Cedar and Oak trees, has been shown to take center stage. It is the misrepresentation of such myths and the unrealistic interpretations of certain passages like (Amos 2:9; Genesis 6:4) that have surely kept such end-time scenarios alive and in the forefront of many Christian minds. Such materials have flooded all forms of modern media. Which is all too easily accessible to the searching, yet unwary religious disciple? The moral of this exercise: simply seek out unconventional sources. Do not get locked into one frame of mind and accept blindly what is served as an astounding religious truth. Whether that be from a proposed Christian/ religious viewpoint, or a secular standpoint. Attempt to gain an understanding of any and every statement that seems too good to be true. They most likely will be false and unfounded. Especially those commentaries on certain religious passages from traditional (religious) sources; as well as another, not so well-known source. Alternate, unusual, non-religious sources may just contain more gems than you'd expect! That said, such undesirably persistent and persuasive interpretations of certain passages are not only protruding from the pen and mind of ill-informed lay-believers like Rob Skiba. There are also copious examples from well-respected professionals. From scholars, preachers, and Bible teachers who should themselves know better. Many may not be as overtly questionable, being more refined than the snippet reviewed above; nonetheless their examples and conclusions can be noted. Let us now change gear again and wrestle with the subject of angels: Angelology and several other associated salient themes that are becoming increasingly popular and just as enigmatic these days. Though another rabbit-trail, angels or some other otherworldly beings do figure often in many end-time scenarios as witnessed above in Rob Skiba's Genesis Six Experiment.

Nail Eleven:

An oft-confused world - Angelology:

It was Arthur C. Clark who once stated: "Two possibilities exist. Either we are alone in the universe, or we are not. Both are equally terrifying."[cccxcviii]

TERRIFYING, FOR WE have absolutely no clue which is true. What is equally terrifying is that our Universe is in a state of constant Apocalypse. As knowledge of the Universe has expanded and grown through physics and other sciences. We have become increasingly aware of just how apocalyptic the entire known cosmos is. Any serious study into Black Holes and other strange phenomena informs us so. Further, the question of whether we are the sole life forms is debatable. Our Universe and the undoubted others we don't yet know, because of the immeasurable distances involved, could well be infinitely populated. Thinking about and the asking of the age–old question, are we alone? Has been pondered by countless people throughout the ages. The Drake Equation (first proposed in 1961) for the last fifty years has been attempting to offer an answer to this most profound of questions. But, yet there has been nothing other than silence across the (thus far) scanned Universe and other galaxies. This is a puzzling phenomenon; as according to the Drake Equation, there may be upwards of 50,000 intelligent and productive extraterrestrial civilisations somewhere out there! Aside the silence met by the S.E.T.I. Institute, it seems that Planet Earth isn't, or more to the point wasn't the first Planetary body to sustain a 'life–form' in our solar–system. According to Frank Joseph, John E. Brandenberg Ph.D. proposes that

> "...a nonhuman civilization (sic) flourished on Mars more than a quarter of a billion years before our species evolved on Earth... The terrible truth: Mars was actually Earthlike (sic) for most of its geologic history. Mars held a massive and evolving biosphere, but was wracked by a mysterious and astonishing nuclear catastrophe. The possible archaeology at Cydonia Mensa

DECONSTRUCTING ENDTIME DELUSIONS

and Elysium on Mars looks like a primitive civilization. It appears, from examining several, possibly archaeological locations, that the destroyed culture was roughly equivalent to our Western European Bronze Age that began during the late 4th Millennium BCE, and ended around 600 BCE. But that is only an impression from orbit. We must land there and find out ... If it is correct, Brandenburg's analysis verifies the existence of extraterrestrial civilizations, (sic) at least in the remote past."[cccxcix] Ongoing studies in "The world of quantum physics has taught us that there are possibly infinite numbers of alternate dimensions to what we call reality."[cd]

Our 'reality' may therefore be just one of many realities! One of those unexpected realities that might come to light is that Mars was indeed populated sometime in its ancient history. But, until archaeological exploration occurs, this is but speculation. Aside studies in quantum physics, are frequent studies published today announcing the possible, and probable existence of alternate dimensions; parallel and multi-dimensions to our known Universe. Studies in quantum physics (String Theory) also suggest our Universe is a Simulation or holographic computer program.[cdi] Being potentially multi-dimensional, with vast quantities of parallel Universes, we could assume those dimensions are also littered with any number of 'life-forms.' Space, we now know with absolute surety, is really, really, REALLY BIG! To paraphrase the late Douglas Adams. Some of that 'life', may not be life as we know it on Planet Earth. Some of that 'life' may be analogous to our very animation:

> "As there are those who believe that 'life' here began out there. Far across the universe, with tribes of humans who might have been the ancestors and forefathers of tribes and peoples: the Egyptians, the Aztecs, or the Mayans, or another ancient race. Some yet believe there still may be brothers of men who even now fight to survive. Somewhere beyond the heavens..."

So is narrated the prelude to each of the original episodes to the 1970's Sci-fi drama – "Battlestar Galactica." A wonderfully spectacular futuristic escape for all ages. Unfortunately, there is not the same prelude to the remake series of the early 2000's. Nonetheless the remake does reflect our modern milieu. Graphically the series is upgraded. The agenda and storyline however remain largely intact. That, some yet believe there still may be brothers of men who even now fight to survive. Somewhere beyond the heavens... 'Out there, in Space', and so the Earth was seeded by these ancient peoples. Along these lines, there are emerging some astounding publications available that suggest quite plausibly that:

> "Humanity was created by an offworld (sic) race of beings roughly 200,000 years ago. Our species was created as both a slave work force and as a food supply. Even Egyptian texts, such as the Instruction for Merikare, plainly states: "Well tended is mankind-God's cattle."[cdii]

There are after all in much world mythology similar attestations. There is also the canard that "...the Jewish word goyim, translates directly to mean "cattle". However, there is much dispute regarding this. Goyim surely is a Jewish/ Hebrew term, yet, according to well-regarded etymological Bible helps, goyim essentially are referent to nations. Specifically, nations that are not Israel. Whereas the Hebrew term for 'cattle' is– bakar. The assumptions proposed by the author cited above, going by the name Beall Endall, seem rather farfetched, and misguided. Surely, as was hinted at earlier, humanity through ancient mythology was considered as cattle of the gods. Nonetheless, there is an air surrounding such thoughts reemerging today, due I guess, to the persistent alien/ extraterrestrial/ U.F.O. phenomenon. It is not my place to comment any further upon this subject. Readers are encouraged to review the cited books and decide for themselves. We have digressed. Similar to the idea cited above, suggesting that Mars was in ancient history populated. In the Late 19th century, early 20th century there was an alleged superstition proposed by a Mr. Percival Lowell. He zealously believed and attempted to convince his contemporary scientific community that the canal system we recognise today on the surface of Mars was the "work of intelligent human beings."[cdiii] This story unfolds thusly:

> "A number of prominent scientists, beginning in 1877 with Italian astronomer Giovanni Schiaparelli, were convinced that they saw through their telescopes an intricate system of canals on Mars. These canals were all very geometrical and hence obviously carried water for the great Martian civilization. The certainty of intelligent life on Mars was trumpeted (with

the aid of businessman and amateur astronomer Percival Lowell). Books were published. Major newspapers declared the evident certainty to the astounded (and gullible) public. Helping to whip the public into a frenzy was alien enthusiast H. G. Wells, whose War of the Worlds seared into people's minds the dire fate that awaited Earth once the Martians stopped boating around their canals and launched their inevitable attack. By 1930, this certainty was exploded by another astronomer, E. M. Antoniadi, who pointed out that the "canals" weren't canals; they weren't nice geometrically drawn lines of precision traced on the surface of Mars, but just fuzzy shapes. The lesson is simple enough. Schiaparelli, Lowell, Wells, and a host of other scientists and popularizers (sic) wanted to see life on Mars. The alien enthusiasts just wanted to see what was fuzzy as straight and geometrical because they wanted Mars to be populated with aliens. It is often our desire to have something be true that makes us clearly and distinctly see the false as true, the imagined as real. This is as true in the history of science as it is in our everyday life. In either case, reality is the appropriate test of our everyday beliefs and scientific theories."[cdiv]

Is there any wonder that when, on October 30, 1938. Orson Wells produced the radio drama, "The War of the Worlds"; that this production caused widespread hysteria in America? World War Two was on the horizon, recall. Yet, if the findings and conclusions of well–respected scientists like Brandenberg, and the studies of Quantum and Physics generally prove that incontestably correct, maybe we should rethink the postulations of those like Lowell? Maybe, it isn't all just science–fiction. Considering also that for more than fifty years S.E.T.I. have continued in its quest to contact life from the stars. The whole S.E.T.I. venture I believe has a skewed objective, however. It should not be an objective to contact life from the stars. But to harmonise with, or in the least, understand that life. As stated at the close of the first part to this investigation. There is conclusive evidence that we are the life from the stars. We are made of 'star-stuff.' This I understand could be a tough pill for religionists and the U.F.O. advocate to swallow. Yet, the known evidence does seem to support the conclusions of those that propose its reality. Why then is S.E.T.I.'s objective to peer 'out-there?' Does it truly matter if intelligence of some form exists elsewhere? Then there are questions of distance:

> "...as recently as October 2016, the Christian Science Monitor reported that "a team of international scientists was able to create a 3-D map, and now calculates there are at least two trillion galaxies in the universe."[cdv]

Thus, trillions of galaxies could constitute literally trillions of life–forms. How many have a form of recognisable intelligence? Nonetheless, confirmation abounds stating our universe is filled with life, a truth S.E.T.I. also acknowledge. What kind of life though is a project the likes of S.E.T.I. is searching? It is clear from the S.E.T.I. website that they seek to find answers to where we come from and are we alone in the Universe. Questions intelligent Homo sapiens have been asking for eons. As we are led to believe via the very S.E.T.I. name, it is intelligent life that is sought after. But, how are we to gauge intelligence? Intelligence according to another species might completely call for something differently to the parameters we have set. Besides, the intelligence of any array of terrestrial life does differ greatly to our own. A Honey Bee's intelligence as one example, is completely different from ours. So, whose 'intelligence' is of greater worth? Is the Honey Bee less intelligent because it works from a set of parameters that differ to our own? Do Bees have a kind of 'spiritual' awareness or capability we don't yet consider or understand? How do you gauge, tap-into or comprehend this idea? If they do, are we then the less intelligent species? S.E.T.I. and all its constituent parts and questions is a much broader avenue than we here can traverse. So, how does all this talk about whether the Universe. Specifically our Universe lead into the present topic of this Nail– angels? According to Rabbi's and religious folk, there are two types of denizen in our Universe. One populates the seen (earthly) plane. The other the unseen (heavenly) realm –those above, are 'angels', and those below are the human race. We find this teaching largely in the Talmud.

> The Talmud (Hebrew for "study") is the record of rabbinic teachings that spans a period of more than six hundred years. Beginning in the first century c.e. and continuing through the sixth and seventh centuries c.e.[cdvi] "The general belief was that angels were immortal and did not propagate their species (Genesis. Rabba. 8.11). On occasion, however, God may destroy numbers of them when they withstand His will (Sanhedrin. 38b). They

require no physical nourishment ...being sustained by the lustre of the Shechinah... They are not troubled by the Jetzer Hara, the evil impulse, which means that they are not subject to normal human passions."[cdvii]

Very interesting is the Rabbi's also held an ideology that angels were ignorant of the Aramaic language. The sister Semitic language to biblical Hebrew, considered to be the mother holy tongue. Hence, we read also from "Everyman's Talmud":

> "On the point of language, with the exception of Gabriel, who was acquainted with every mode of speech, the angels were said to be ignorant of Aramaic; and for that reason, one should not offer petitions for his needs in that language, since it was an angelic duty to carry the prayers which were uttered to the Throne of God." (Sota. 33a). (ibid, p.49). Astrophysicist, progressive creationist, and Christian apologist Hugh Ross chimes in with: "Humans are physical beings with spiritual awareness and spiritual capabilities. Angels, however, are spiritual beings who are not bound to Earth but are capable of manifesting themselves—even physically—on Earth within limits established by God."[cdviii]

A fair description for each type; yet, as with what was earlier postulated and argued. How do spiritual beings manifest as something physical? Are the two compatibles then in reverse? Can a physical being (me and you) suddenly break a natural law and become a spiritual being –without dying first, just as religion proposes with their postulations of rapture theory, or as is also advanced about a spiritual realm to be infested? You may elect to call this crackpot reasoning? Why is it though not reasonable? If one dominion can 'break into' the other without disturbing the whole, why would the reverse be untenable; and on what grounds could either be true or false? Interesting, is the Egyptian word neteru. Meaning: representatives of universal principals and functions, – i.e., 'gods,' which were later anthropomorphised. Moustafa Gadalla, "Historical Deception" offers further insight:

> "The neteru who were called 'gods' by some, were endorsed and incorporated into Christianity under a new name, 'angels'...

The term 'angels', according to the "Metaphysical Bible Dictionary", refers to those who "guard and guide and direct the natural forces of mind and body, which have in them the future of the whole man." Angels, or neteru, are living energies. In the wisdom teaching of various cultures, these Causal Powers are called by many names including Agents, Angels, Conscious Thought, Forms, Creative Energies, Gates... and Shining Ones. Edwin C. Steinbrecher, an astrologer, metaphysician, and author of "The Inner Guide Meditation", says that angels are:

> "...living energies that contain ideas and information, specific patterns of instinctual behavior and thought. They, are the energies, which somehow attach themselves, without our conscious awareness to everything we meet in the world we call real. [They] are the life energies that pour out of each of us unceasingly night and day...influencing everyone in our lives and causing us to be influenced in return." [brackets mine.]

Certainly eye opening is that angels are referred as 'energies'. Regarding the study of angels, Abraham Cohen again, "Everyman's Talmud", explicitly states:

> "...angelology, did not originate with (the rabbi's). The picture of a celestial court, with God as King, and a host of ministers surrounding Him, is to be found in the Bible, angels, as servants of the Most High are frequently mentioned in its narratives... Unlike many thoughts today surrounding angels "[t]he underlying motive of Rabbinic angelology was certainly not to invent intermediaries between God and the world, as is sometimes alleged."[cdix]

Rather, an angel's purpose was to glorify God, either by special message, an affirmation, warning, or proclamation (sometimes to his people). This is the report found throughout the Bible. This is still; it is presumed for most readers their existent purpose, unless the scriptures have changed! Witnessed in numerous passages including isaiah 6:3; Revelation 4:8f; luke 1:11ff, 2:8f; acts 12:23. To the contrary, the role of angels has been inverted today. The impression is that many christians and non-religious people alike simply expect these entities are real, or most likely imagined, are presumed to be intermediaries. Our go-betweens who convey

DECONSTRUCTING ENDTIME DELUSIONS

messages of hope and comfort from 'a' benevolent God/deity to humanity. Unfortunately, this is also taught in many houses of delusion, and Christian and secular publications. Have we become so dull in our understanding to believe such is truth (1 Timothy 2:5-7; 2 corinthians 11:14.)? There is definitely an increased reverence for, romance regarding, and a growing interest in these ethereal beings - angels. Officially labeled, Angelology –it is the study of such entities. The phenomenon has exploded over the years - boasting no fewer than 386,000 hits on the Internet in a simple search. The 'new age' movement has also popularised angels. The study of and all manners of other esoteric venturing regarding them. Angel 'clubs', and angel seminars; workshops are offering various 'angel trinkets' are in abundance in major cities. We should be so insolent, because honestly, most published materials on this subject simply is ridiculous and unsustainable. Some devotees and self-proclaimed 'masters' of this subject would even assume to possess the 'power' to offer their blinded adherents "the sealing of the servants of God in their foreheads" and the "third-eye blessing with the emerald matrix." The What?

Numerous small and silver screen programs dedicated to such phenomenon also feed our intrigue and imagination. Popular television programming like Touched by an Angel or the 1998 movie –City of Angels, starring Nicolas Cage and Meg Ryan comes to mind. These programs play into our previous themes of 'fallen' Watcher angels. What such programs prove is that understandably people are apprehensive about the future. Maybe even more so than any previous generation. Twenty-first century government officials and scientific experts who relentlessly drum into the minds of their populations. The idea that drastic measures must be taken on deemed and apparent disasters; even if that means there is a decline in people's general welfare. Sacrifices must be made (mostly by those that can least afford it) to rectify this that, or another looming disaster on the horizon. Currently this focuses on the Climate Change hypothesis. Which plays very much into that which resembles an end–time religion. Where do people often turn for succour, answers or comfort in such times as these? Most likely these days comfort are drawn from the ethereal world of transcendent beings; beings who permeate mostly the Eastern religions, Egyptian cultic magic, Hinduism, Buddhism, Judaism, occultism. All which christianity has heavily 'borrowed' - actually, stolen! On behalf of adherents these practices have become the source of many a mystical knowledge base. Rosemary Ellen Guilley put it best when she wrote:

> "Popular culture portrays angels as anthropomorphic 'best friends,' which is in stark contrast to the awesome, impartial, unknowable beings of Jewish angelology and early Christian lore." (11), Hines, C, gateway of the gods, Part ii - Touched by an Angel.

Copious 'angel' paintings, pictures, figurines, and any amount of other paraphernalia and trinkets, including statues adorning buildings heavily influence us no doubts subconsciously as well. Many of which portray these beings as either 'good', or evil in nature. Angels, and gargoyles (which are not always angelic figures, but often trans-mutated animals) are everywhere. Some titivate the cornices of state and religious buildings. Regarding gargoyles and the Church, a Wikipedia entry revealingly reads:

> "Gargoyles were viewed in two ways by the Church throughout history. Often gargoyles were used to assist the Church in conveying messages to the common people. Since literacy was uncommon, images were the best way to constantly convey ideas. Gargoyles were used as a representation of evil. It is thought that they were used to scare people into coming to Church, reminding them that the end of days is near. It is also thought that their presence assured congregants that evil is kept outside of the Church's walls. However, some medieval clergy viewed gargoyles as a form of idolatry. In the 12th century a Church leader named St. Bernard of Clairvaux was famous for speaking out against gargoyles. "What are these fantastic monsters doing in the cloisters before the eyes of the brothers as they read? What is the meaning of these unclean monkeys, these strange savage lions, and monsters? To what purpose are here placed these creatures, half beast, half man, or these spotted tigers? I see several bodies with one head and several heads with one body. Here is a quadruped with a serpents head, there a fish with a quadruped's head, then again an animal half horse, half goat... Surely if we do not blush for such absurdities, we should at least regret what we have spent on them."

Surely, St. Bernard makes a terrifically truthful point. Should we indeed not blush or at least regret the obscene waste of capital spent on such artefacts and trinkets. Barbara Walker also shares some illuminating insight from a Feminist Theological perspective in both her Angel and Gargoyle entries.

Angel:

ANGELS WERE ORIGINALLY female: they were seen as,

> "dispensers of bliss" who were every man's notion of the perfect reward in heaven, "ever desirable, ever willing mistresses of those blessed souls who are reborn into Indra's heavenly world.".. The association of mortal female sexuality with angels apparently arose from the fact that the angels or "cherubim" (Akkadian karibu, Hebrew kerubh, Sheban karribim) were priestesses who wore artificial wings in token of their affiliation with the heavenly spirits... Christian angelology had a gradual development. It was given a great boost by the spurious writings attributed to Dionysius the Areopagite, who never really existed, but whose book (written about the sixth century A.D.) purported to be the work of the first bishop of Athens, who learned all about the heavenly hierarchy through a personal visit from the spirit of Saint Paul. Pseudo-Dionysius described nine orders of angels: Seraphim, Cherubim, Thrones, Dominions, Virtues, Powers, Principalities, Archangels, and ordinary angels. For centuries the Church accepted this as a factual view of the divine ranks, and even modelled the earthly orders upon it.[cdx]

Such descriptions and 'ranking' as described by Dionysius should immediately sound familiar. Readers familiar with their sacred books should realise similar lists are states in the New Testament. That Angels have the origin in a Female; as a dispenser of bliss is not surprising either. One religion particularly still conveys such thoughts: Islam, – though they have twisted and contorted this idea to prostitute for male suicide-bombers. Visits into the assumed 'heavenly-realm' to learn of various entities are still prevalent also. To have these episodes; however, they are induced through psychedelic (magic) mushrooms and other drug-induced means. In the 'Gargoyle' entry, Barbara writes:

> "Gargoyles were not strictly mythical but were invented late in the Middle Ages, during the great age of cathedral building. Gothic cathedrals were liberally covered with gargoyles to provide Church-goers with demon figures to populate their nightmares and fears of hell. Gargoyles were also used as extensions of the ancient belief that holy buildings should have ugly, threatening stone guardians to keep away evil influences. It was believed that man-made demons could frighten away real demons. Some churches were so heavily ornamented with gargoyles that an objective observer might think the churches were built in honour of the pandemonic (sic) residents of hell instead of the angelic population of heaven..."[cdxi]

Affirming these 'entities' is a creation by the religious cleric to ward off 'demons' and were situated strategically to instil fear of damnation in their congregations. Modern christianity has not been impenetrable to such an onslaught of superstitious insinuation either. Throughout many generations through to the present, such artefacts, trinkets and depictions have been used by countless christians in their homes and cars. Mostly as talisman and amulets providing 'protection' to the barer. To this, Andrew Roth offers this commentary,

> "While they don't pray to these idols, they do give them power by expecting good will come by having them around, which is pure paganism. Some Christians have dreams and visions of Angels and some believe they have met with Angels; but this does not provide license to make or own images, because that is contrary to the Word of YHWH."[cdxii]

Despite the use of such trinkets and depictions of 'angels' most people, are only attentive to what they perceive as the 'good' -most often –male- angels; these 'heavenly' beings often are portrayed as boasting bulging, well sculptured biceps, thighs, and a rippled six-pack torso (like a bodybuilder!) They are decked out in either a 'free-flowing,' blindingly white or brightly coloured full-length one-piece garment, or an ancient Greco-Roman military types attire, typically also brandishing swords and shields, and unforgettably flawlessly stylised free-flowing golden or brunette hair.[cdxiii] The very opposite is depicted for demons or 'fallen angels.' Demons are your average ugly, disfigured, more oft naked, emaciated looking creature with elongated heads and ratted or little hair, drawn-out jaws, protruding discoloured fangs, and claws. They have menacingly piercing jaundiced eyes and sport no Armour or specified armament. Oh, and we cannot forget many in either camp have wings![cdxiv] Why did these beings depicted in similar fashion to humans? Do they need a skeletal system? Why did they die? I have always had the impression that angels and the like (1) are not subject to death formally, and (2) were ethereal; metaphysical, and so would not be in need of a skeletal system. But, there are those who for whatever reason, like Rob Skiba and the late Zachariah Sitchin, seem to insist that mysteriously enormous skeletal remains are somehow linked to either an alien or angelic race. It is also amusing that these remains carry the same bone structure as any human alive today. Maybe dna samples will or have already provided answers to the many questions these dead bodies cause. But for whatever reason, core science has not fully disclosed its findings. Today much of the information offered in all media forms across the board has the stench of cryptic philosophy and sensationalism. So, for this writer, many depictions and publications of either demons or their moral counterpart offer very little actual truth. Even in 'Christian' circles such obscure philosophy has been engaged and is staggeringly common. The subject of angels for many in society conjures any amount of bazaar ideas surrounding who, the what, and the how of these mysterious beings. Those who espouse a modern ideology of angels. It seems, each exhibit the one common flaw; in that it is much simpler to answer the what do I 'feel' or 'think' about it question. Instead of how rational the conclusions are I draw about what I feel and think. Readers when exploring with me Rob Skiba's Genesis six hypotheses above might have recognised this. But, he is only one of many. There is an astonishingly vast array of angel websites, books, and other media sources dedicated to spreading the word, –every word, - via blog posts and stories of people's personal encounters with such beings. It's as if caution has been thrown to the wind, and every whim, or wish is neatly catered for. Relativism I say, rules this post-modern roost! If 'I' like it –it 'must' be true. What if such relativism is again founded upon a false premise, one's prosthetic memory? Though I am noway an expert, angelology and demonology would seem to have suffered the same fate and effects of distorted logic, and prosthetic memory as that which has been earlier described. Being the case with what has been discussed to date one could make the case; such thought is extremely existential - what something means to any given individual is what counts the most. This is the premise from which most people would attack the following subjects. If true, those who speak or write about angels are viewing the subject purely from an Occidental Greek mind-frame. The Christian, and other religious scriptures appear to be plain enough announcing their prominence in the spirit realm. Yet, many Christian's esp., seem to again only speak about and assess this subject from an existential point of reference. Even when approaching it through the sacred text. In the remainder of this Nail is attempted a brief deconstruction of these, and the subtopic of the spiteful entities. Many believers are 'frightened' about and see in their sacred books. This sidestep will eventually lead us back to answering just who, or what angels are, according to the sacred texts. Are any of these of some ethereal realm? Are believers absolutely justified in thinking there are evil as well as benevolent entities surrounding them in some spiritual sense? Or, again is this just all a load of Taurus excretio?

Deconstructing fallen Angels Satan evil spirits (Demons):

deconstruct:

Examining something to show it can (or should) be understood differently

IN A SOCIETY THAT SUFFERS the very real and medically diagnosed condition, Information Overload Syndrome, and, at the risk of adding to this phenomenon. I feel it necessary to dispel some more popular myths. We began above with brief acknowledgement surrounding numerous ideas regarding angels. In the following pages we look at who, how, and the why of these beings. The question most people I presume internally ask most about angels and devils are not whether what is taught are true or logical? Rather, Do I like it - another sure symptom and process of a distorted, prosthetic logic. If we 'like' a result —our internal distortion of logic allows that we believe whatever

DECONSTRUCTING ENDTIME DELUSIONS

it might be to be true and factual. Over time this feeds, the greater mythos and so it enters unobtrusively, full-time into society makeup and lore. There are many, many distortions of logic to be found when reviewing 'angels' and devils. The evidence is to conduct a quick Internet search, which will show multiple hits and a multitude of perspectives. As incredible as it may sound, most ideas, myths, and convictions 'out' there in cyber-land and those published in hard copy regarding angels are wrong! Very few truthful accounts have yet to be found. Especially those accounts that proclaim to be biblically sound. Respectfully, even those written or taught by well-respected religious people with credentials. Christian pastors, teachers, authors, and scholars are often only regurgitating mistakes taught to them in seminary. The topic of angels and devils is also strangely a subject very few in the Church talk about or takes the time to muse and disseminate meaningfully. I wonder if a reason for often a 'Christian' silence on this topic is that deep down people either have no idea. Or, simply don't believe in their existence. Here, is the attempt to redress that. More often than not these beings/entities are taken for granted. Beings believed by thousands to be true and real. But, they are nothing else than a deception and trickery by the brain that feels real at the time. Much like those 'witnesses' claiming to have seen or been in contact with U.F.O.'s and other 'weird,' other-worldly phenomena. If you start with the premise and 'belief' that such things exist, brain studies have shown that your brain will eventually conjure an image and trick your other senses into believing it is real because it cannot be sufficiently explained. So, 'sightings,' 'feeling' the presence of a 'spiteful or benevolent 'entity and the like will automatically become a U.F.O.; a demon, a Devil, glowing eyes, shadow figures, ghosts, gods, angels... Conclusions' however surrounding all these is, as mentioned are often the result of existential myth and confusion. Lawrence Chestnut in one of his publications sums the reality of this thinking in christianity, noting that,

> "Myth means an invented story of an imaginary person, or thing coming down from the past, which many people have believed. And it is this that the fate of the King of Babylon is compared in isaiah 14:12."[cdxv]

To many christians the passage of isaiah 14:12 equates to the creature labelled –Satan/ lucifer or the Devil. This is exactly what many theologians, preachers, and Christian teachers consistently edify. But, even a cursory glance at the text in question, as a whole cannot support such a proposition. It is nonsensical to say the least. What's more, Velikovsky interestingly adds a few comments believers should note well. Even if they consider his proposals are ultimately farfetched. To the closing of chapter three of part II, under the title, lucifer cut down he explains,

> "Venus, which collided with the earth in the fifteenth century before the present era, collided with Mars in the eighth century... The awe of the world for many centuries, Venus became a tame planet. Isaiah, referring figuratively to the King of Babylon who destroyed cities and made the land into wilderness, uttered his remarkable words about Lucifer that fell from heaven and was cut down to the ground... The metaphor regarding the King of Babylon implied that his fate and the fate of the Morning Star were not dissimilar; both of them fell from on high... Significant are the words of Isaiah about the Morning Star, that it "weakened the nations" before it was cut down to the ground. It weakened the nations in two collisions with the earth, and it weakened the nations by keeping them in constant fear for centuries. The Book of Isaiah, in every chapter, provides abundant evidence that with the removal of Venus, so that it no longer crossed the orbit of the earth, danger was not eliminated, but became even more threatening."[cdxvi]

Despite the possibility of disagreement with this hypothesis, the additions of some Bible headings should offer readers more understanding than the oft granted nonsense of such a passage as isaiah 14:12; that it is related somehow to a figure the believing community consistently label –Satan. The reality is this passage is part of a taunt song concerning the fall of a Babylonian king whom, obviously was caught out by his own solipsism. In a sense therefore, yes, there is a hint to a satan. One who is an antagonist (see the brief study on satan below). Thus, technically those espousing these verses speak of a satan are correct. Yet, the satan spoken is the Babylonian King, not some ethereal mystical entity.

DECONSTRUCTING ENDTIME DELUSIONS

More so the passage seems undoubtedly to be related to the history of the planet Venus. Thus, the recordings of the Bible 'prophets' speak more of looming celestial calamities they recognised, than any other assumption proposed by past and present theologians. Just as proposed above. Old Testament prophets do not for instance; hail the arrival or whatever of a supposed Messiah figure, though there possibly were yearnings for the arrival of such an individual. It is doubting worthy that any 'Prophet' was truly enabled with a far future gaze, 700+ years into the future. If modern examples are anything to go by, what is the difference (without the assumption of heavenly guidance), between an Old Testament or New Testament 'Prophet' and modern predictors of the weather, or stock exchange? Chesnut's assessment is only true to an extent. All the same we must also recognise that myth may be simply explained by humanity's relentless struggles against its own depravity. We struggle against the how or why of our existence constantly. The problem he highlights for us about fallen angels however is simply grasped:

> "It has been from the beginning, the plan and work of the Devil, the enemy of God, and man, to distort, confuse, deceive, and lead man away from the divine plan of present and eternal salvation. His work has been very effective, and powerful in many areas by using the Divine inspired Word of God, and in a sly, deceptive, and cunning manner has in such flagrant ways misinterpreted, and misapplied the meaning and message of God's Holy Word, the Bible... The theory that sometime, somewhere, God created certain angelic beings and put them on probation is wholly unscriptural, and false. The only created, creature of God, put on probation was man. Probation means nothing more than during a time of living on earth; man is to live by the rules of God. But during this time there will be periods when he will have temptations, trials, testing his conduct and character. Mankind is the only created creature of God placed in this realm."[cdxvii]

Ample great theological publications explaining numerous Christian doctrines, like the massive six-volume work, "God, Revelation, and authority", by Carl F. H. Henry (1999) only; unfortunately, disseminate their theories and ideological treaties about angels or demons mainly as the ethereal, otherworldly entities also; and so, these too offer little to clear the muddy waters of understanding. More often than not when asked about angels, or demons most people would automatically assume one is always referring to or meaning such beings. Yet, it was only in quite recent history where such ideas became prevalent. We observe an entry in the "Anchor Yale Bible Dictionary" that interestingly offers when the heavenly, as opposed to earthly emissaries (angels) became systematically influential.

> "It was only with the Vulgate that a systematic distinction was made between angelic emissaries (Lat angelus - heavenly) and human ones (Lat nuntius). Nevertheless, there are indications that already in the LXX aggelos was beginning to take on the quasi-technical meaning of heavenly being. In several instances aggelos is used for terms such as běnê (hā) ʾĕlōhîm [the son(s) of God] (Genesis 6:2; Deuteronomy 32:8; Job 1:6; 2:1; 38:7), ʾĕlōhîm (Psalms 8:6; 97:7; 138:1), and śār (Daniel 10:21; 12:1), and in one case malʾāk [Hebrew for angel/messenger] is translated as theos [God] (Qohelet [Ecclesiastes] 5:5—Eng 5:6). There is even one instance in the Hebrew Bible (Judges 13:6) in which a character implies a distinction between a "man of God" (ʾîš ʾĕlōhîm) and a "messenger/angel of Yahweh" (malʾāk yhwh)."[cdxviii]

The simplest and most common meaning has given after all, of both the Greek and the Hebrew words for angel. Are no more, or no less; envoy, messenger, or agent. Either of which could be of earthly or heavenly dominion. Finding or discerning the difference, this is where most modern understanding seems to fall short. Made even more difficult by the fact that 'angel' can also express a meaning of divine status, special sanctification (holy one's), or any other term that refers to their functions. Readers would benefit greatly by scholarly works on these subjects. Like, "Devil of a Job to find Satan in the Bible" by Dr. Ann Nyland.

Nail Twelve:

Sons of God:

TODAY, THE BELIEF IS that Yahweh, the defunct deity of the Judaeo-Christian sacred book created heavenly beings –angels. It is these entities who are the 'sons' of the gods. Some of these beings chose (for whatever reason) to be (come) disobedient, and fornicated with human women resulting in the nephilim, Genesis 6:1-4. Such ideology is widely postulated by countless 'Christian' authors. Authors as mentioned above: Rob Skiba, Scott Roberts, Brian Godawa, Derek Gilbert all advocate for angels as the sons of a deity, or a very similar assumption. Specifically assuming the episode of Genesis 6:1-4 relays a story of some wicked 'fallen' angel type mated with human women and essentially caused the flood episode.[cdxix] But, I think it fair to say scholarship is still out as to their constituting the 'sons of God' (Genesis 6:4). Lay men and women must be wary of falling headlong into that same assumption. Whether angelic or not is still very difficult to conclude in extenso. Many sacred book passages simply do not elaborate. The deity, as believed by the religious did create an angelic occupant in the heavenly abode prior to the earth. Interesting; however, is the fact that often the Bible uses various synonyms such as, Son(s) of God, to refer to this heavenly denizen (as noted below.) A key for those who are persuaded in this understanding is (jób 38:4-7.)[cdxx] If; however, it is to be insisted that 'the sons of God' in this passage and others like it (Genesis 6:4; jób 1:6), must be a referent to the host of angels surrounding the throne, you may shortly I think, be in for a Damascus Road experience. First, the phrase, bênê Elohim (son(s) of God), according to the English Standard Version Bible (ESV), is mentioned a mere 6 times in 6 verses throughout the Old Testament corpus! That is an amazing and 'few' times this phrase is used. Which are somewhat surprising, –recognising the emphasis and importance that modernity seems to place on it. Secondly, the gospels (mathew, john, luke, Mark) account for (24) of the (42) verses scattered throughout the whole of the New Testament; and these (24) refer exclusively to the figure; the deity–man Jesus! Of the final (18x) eighteen times in the New Testament, we find (9) are in pauline missives. John in his three short epistles has (7); and there is only (1x) one time in Revelation. Luke, writing the acts also sees one occurrence of this phrase. Most often, except for (romans 8:19) these refer to the Messiah figure. Which brings us to a grand total of (48x) forty-eight times throughout the whole corpus of scripture. That is, according to (ESV) translators. Interestingly the nrsv (The New Revised Standard Version) has only two occurrences of the phrase, 'sons of God'; both occurring in Genesis 6. Ten times (10x), an equivalent is mentioned and is often translated as, 'heavenly beings,' or another derivative. Nevertheless, one of the prevailing general understandings of this phrase in particularly the Old Testament, offered by another contemporary translation is as follows,

> "The "sons of God" in the Old Testament is generally taken to refer to angels. They are not actually "sons" of Elohim; the idiom is a poetic way of describing their nature and relationship to God. The phrase indicates their supernatural nature, and their submission to God as the sovereign Lord."[cdxxi]

Here, we strike a problem. For finally and the most amazing of all, Son (ben/ or in Aramaic bar), in the Old Testament is never used to Yahweh –the specified supreme deity of the Judaeo-Christian book! Rather, always Elohim which as readers surely know by now, is widely used in the scriptures in a generic sense, meaning any 'deity'! This in and of itself surely offers readers further confirmation of my insistence. When reviewing the Genesis 6:4 passage that the mentioned 'sons of God' do not, and cannot refer to any angelic, or alien types entity! Rather, again is most likely a reference to "other" men who the author worshipped as a different deity, or deities! Recall, the Psalms passage (82:6). "You are sons of god..." Meant to rejuvenate confidence in those who were displaying a weakness, and doubtful attitude. Basically, despite their assumed 'station' as the religious elect, these folk still stumble about. They do not 'get' it that they are the congregation of the elect of the deity. Psalm 82 is an encouragement to the congregant. Who are referred by the psalmist as; "Sons of the Deities." Not in reference to an ethereal entity, for verse seven declares death is still present. Though, mythologically, it was not unusual for a mythic deity/ hero to be subjected to death. As numerously stated however; the bible is a very human book. The subjects are more often not meant to be literal. But, describing the symbolic for the hearer, and reader for them to use as a guide to better their own lives, and the lives of the other. From Genesis 2:4 are we introduced to whom elohim, (translated here in the psalm passages and elsewhere as God). That the text speaks of the Lord God: Yahweh; the supposed supreme deity. To complicate matters further Andrew Collins, in his "Ashes of angels" adds,

> "...the name Elohim is a female noun with an irregular plural, implying not 'gods' at all, but 'sons of the goddesses."[cdxxii]

Yahweh/Elohim the supreme universal deity of the Judaeo-Christian books is undoubtedly an <Androgynous> deity. A deity of both sexes. Yet, christianity to a large degree denies this! Preferring to focus its attention on the sky deity – thought of entirely as male. A whole new example must then be opened and explored. Yet, because of time and space constraints we will not explore the connections or the wealth of information available surrounding the Christian religion and goddess worship. We must reiterate also that the phrase 'sons of God' cannot be used in isolation of the rest of the Genesis 6 tale and other narratives; as I believe Rob Skiba has attempted in his Genesis six experiment. Attempting to call and justify these 'sons' as some type of ethereal otherworldly entity, angels. Ideas trusted that readers are beginning to understand come solely from extra-biblical texts. Specifically, the mentioned earlier books of enoch. "The Dictionary of Deities and Demons in the Bible" contributes:

> "...the 'Israelite concept of divinity included all preternatural [beyond natural or normal] beings, also lower deities (in modern usage called 'spirits', 'angels', 'demons', 'semi-gods', and the like) may [also] be called ʾĕlōhîm."[cdxxiii]

What this means are the Bible authors and audiences often recognised a whole pantheon of deities. William Harwood confirms this idea in his book: "Mythology's Last Gods, Yahweh and Jesus". Thus, Judaism and her two-rival sibling 'religions', cannot be altogether monotheistic! Monotheism is another myth imposed by the elitist of all claimant religions. Need scholarly proof? Just as the rabbinic Talmudists noted above, an entry in Little Kittel reads,

> "The idea is that of a pantheon under the sovereignty of God. Yahweh is Judge in the heavenly council. The heavenly beings are totally subject to God and his will (jób 1:6ff.). There is no strict father-son relationship such as one finds in surrounding cults. If divine beings, including the gods of other nations, exist under the supreme God, they have no independent power and simply constitute a heavenly court."[cdxxiv]

Another nail in the coffin for the proposal by Rob Skiba and those with him; that the mention of sons of God in (Genesis 6:2) and other places in the Old Testament (jób 1:6, 2:1, 38:7); refer to heavenly beings –angels (fallen or not). This is simply untrue and founded solely upon a preconceived hypothesis and haphazard research! Skiba, like so many modern and past christians drag the line that these 'sons' of the deity are the offspring of an 'unholy union'. A union between 'corrupted' otherworldly entities who lusted after certain human females. Mating with them and producing a hybrid that caused havoc and eventually caught the ear of the deity. At that, it destroyed all life. The early presbyters 'Church 'Fathers'' are an indication to the origins of such ideas. Bushby for instance makes mention, 'St Justin Martyr (like all his contemporaries) believed in demons and said they were the offspring of angels who had sex with the daughters of men.'[cdxxv] Sons of God can, and often do quite legitimately refer however, to very human persons. Despite also the objections by several scholars; i.e., Cassuto who has earlier been mentioned. Attested by other reputable theological dictionaries and theologians, the phrase in question: sons of God, is most probably a reference to the 'sons of Israel,' or other earth bound 'peoples' of the deity Yahweh or some other knew regional deity! Why? Simply, because a major objective of the whole corpus of the Old Testament testimony was to force and focus readers' attention upon whom they were, who they are, and their relation to other societies around about. A core emphasis of the Hebrew scriptures was to introduce and convince its readers with the innovative concept of a single God, they endeared - Yahweh, to who all must be held accountable. In short, the Hebrew sacred book conceptualised monotheism, instead of endorsing the dominant pantheistic faith or religion. "The Dictionary to the Old Testament: Pentateuch", interestingly adds this insight:

> "Although it is possible that Hebrew idiom only used the phrase to refer to angels, other meanings would be logically possible. If the sons of God belong to the "'ĕlōhîm" category, they theoretically could be a group of humans who are related to the divine through their office. Such usage of 'ĕlōhîm occurs in the OT in Exodus 22:8–9 (Adam is "son of God"). Regarding the NT evidence, even if one is satisfied that Jude and 2 Peter reflect 1 Enoch's interpretation of Genesis 6, hermeneutical [interpretive] issues need to be discussed similar to those concerning the author of Hebrews' presentation of Melchizedek."[cdxxvi]

Scholars the likes of the late Professor Umberto Cassuto, were acutely aware of different textual variations and traditions of texts. One example would benefit readers. In various ways angles are prevalent to our current discussion is the difference in phrase, regarding (deuteronomy 32:8). First, is given this passage in a Standard English Bible. Secondly, the same passage is offered as found in the (Septuagint – the Greek Bible). Most Standard English bibles render this verse, thus:

> "When the Most High gave the nations their inheritance, when he divided all mankind, he set up boundaries for the peoples according to the number of the sons of Israel"[cdxxvii]

The new international version, as other modern standard bibles base their old testament translations traditionally on what has become the standard Hebrew text, called the Masoretic Text. Which means the standard text by which Rabbis and exegetes (interpreters) of the Hebrew Bible wished to standardise the transmission and copying process of the sacred work to assure as few mistakes as possible were made in transmission.

> "The purpose... in the narrow sense was to preserve the integrity of scripture precisely, so that nothing would be added to the text or taken away."[cdxxviii]

Notice in the NIV translation above that it makes a minor notation that brings to a reader's attention a difference in the text, which any Study Bible should also contain, either again as a superscript or another notation. However, we notice a different variation and translation tradition when; secondly, the Septuagint of the same passage is read. Reading as follows:

> "When the Most High distributed nations as he scattered the descendants of Adam, he set up boundaries for the nations according to the number of the angels of God"

The significance (although minor in some respects) of such differences, and translation tradition in these two texts may not be apparent to many readers. Nonetheless scholars attest that such variants highlight particularly the different traditions in how various ancients, even of the same sect, read and understood a passage. Often leading to a divergence in tradition and theological practice. This would then surely be of assistance when attempting to find out what is meant by such a phrase as 'sons of God'. Bringing to our attention the fact that not all people in antiquity had a complete or even uniform belief. In this respect, the ancients were no different to modern believers. Just as there are several 'christianities', Baptist, Catholic, Pentecostal..., so too were there numerous sects of the Judaic faith. Still prevalent are the Hasidic, and other mystery Judaic sects; the orthodox, and modern messianic Jews. Believers in the christianised deity-man. All holding to a faith that use the same texts. Yet, do also interpret those texts according to their own manner. Just as the Qumran sects of the Dead Sea also did. Thus, it would seem reasonable that if such phrases in the sacred texts were confusing for the 'experts' of the day, as well as the lay reader. Why would they today be any clearer? A problem that I think the translators of our

DECONSTRUCTING ENDTIME DELUSIONS

current English Bible corpus must also have wished to amend. Modern English texts are in the main uniform in the way it transmits the Greek and Hebrew text. But, this was not essentially the case, as noted above in antiquity. The Septuagint was the Bible of the 'Greek' speaking and influenced Jews of Alexander, Egypt. 'Israeli' Jews who resided in the Levant used the masoretic texts. So, which is the most accurate? That is anyone's guess. Squabbling over which 'holy writings' are the most 'accurate' is a stupid obsession by all religionists. Recall the Christian New Testament book of Titus, and parallels that warned about such idiocy. It is not a matter whether one text is more 'accurate' than another. Accuracy is a distraction to the entire point of a religious creed. Believe what you will. Use that belief if you must, and your favoured texts to better your life for that is their objective. It is this simple. To be in constant squabble regards accuracy, has and continues to lead adherents tward the destructive acts against another. Those that shockingly opened the First nail to this investigation. Therefore, to all believers. Regardless of creed. Grow up! Prove the value and worth of your deity, and act accordingly. Each one of the World's major religions; Islamic, Judaic, Christian claim its deity is benevolent, and the supreme. Well, prove it! If unwilling to attempt this, might be best to abandon your creed altogether. There seems to be more empathy, care offered to others by those who do not claim a religion. Religion has not, and does not heighten any individual. Rather, somehow transforms them into a tribal sectarian.

But we have digressed. Undoubtedly and despite the assertion below, both texts above speak of the same people group. Neither is reporting anything about the ethereal being angel. One group refers to their fellow Jews in the ordinary and human sense, as sons of Israel; while the other refers to the same peoples in the sense of their status to Yahweh, as angels of God, messengers of Revelation. Both groups are Jews and are very human. Both are borne about by the specific translation differences between the LXX (Septuagint), and a popular Standard English Bible (NIV). The LXX being the translation used by Greek speaking and living Jews of Alexander (Egypt). Whereas, the standard Masoretic text, from which the n.i.v. translation derived. Carried the description most familiarly to those who spoke Hebrew/Aramaic; the Jewish population living in and around Palestine. A translation note (14) from the NET Bible may clarify further what I mean:

> "Heb "the sons of Israel." The idea, perhaps, is that Israel was central to Yahweh's purposes and all other nations were arranged and distributed according to how they related to Israel. See S. R. Driver, Deuteronomy (ICC), 355–56. For the MT (béney yisra'el, "sons of Israel") a Qumran fragment has "sons of God," while the LXX reads ἀγγέλων θεοῦ (angelōn theou, "angels of God"), presupposing(béney 'el) or (beney 'elim). "Sons of God" is undoubtedly the original reading; the MT and LXX have each interpreted it differently. MT assumes that the expression "sons of God" refers to Israel (cf. Hos. 1:10), while LXX has assumed that the phrase refers to the angelic heavenly assembly... The phrase is also attested in Ugaritic, where it refers to the high God El's divine assembly. According to the latter view, which is reflected in the translation, the Lord delegated jurisdiction over the nations to his angelic host (cf. Dan. 10:13–21), while reserving for himself Israel, over whom he rules directly. For a defense of the view taken here, see M. S. Heiser, "Deuteronomy 32:8 and the Sons of God"..."[cdxxix]

In Genesis 6:4 and other passages mentioning nephilim, as offspring of an unholy union between the sons of God and daughters of men, they do so I submit only to describe and draw an emphasised point of difference between. Those who were, according to the Bible author, apparently obedient to Yahweh, against the disobedient. Or, other sect not necessarily understood as holding essentially the same belief. 'Daughters of men', may be those of another sect different to the sect referred as 'sons of God.' This, either/or my previous summation in the study of nephilim neanderthal et al. Again, there is no reason to always assume a convoluted ultra-religious ethereal entity. Despite complications regarding the passages, grammar and phrase we have not touched upon; and to the phrase 'daughters of men' and what meaning is to be attached to this. Or, to any other grammatical insight missed. Add to this the fact that scholarly consensus seems to still widely favour an angelic interpretation. The (DOT: P) again states,

DECONSTRUCTING ENDTIME DELUSIONS

> "Direct lexical [word] evidence favors (sic) the "angels" view, but that evidence is mitigated by the slim lexical foundation and the plausible logical alternatives presented by the nature of the syntagm [the string of words forming the larger unit]"[cdxxx]

It is, to labor the point a case I believe of the more probably human (obedient) sons of God becoming corrupted in heart and therefore action (psalm 58:2; proverbs 15:28; ecclesiastes 8:11; Matthew 15:18; luke 6:45.) They interbred with the daughters of men; a synonym for those considered corrupt! Not the wild assertion of heavenly (or more biblically accurate, sky) beings caught procreating and marrying daughters of human's – angels. Presuming their 'otherworldly' nature, we are told later in the New Testament, that angels don't procreate (Matthew 22:30; Mark 12:25!) As many a religionist determines still, the disobedient always seem to become the mighty, rich, and powerful 'giants'–nephilim, themselves! Walter Kaiser adds his learned voice writing some way to affirm this understanding. In his book "The Promise-Plan of God", he sees

> "The best view is the sociologically mixed races view. The "sons of God" title was an early but favored titulary [title] (sic) for kings, nobles, and aristocrats in the ancient Near East. Such power-hungry despots were driven to be "men of renown" in their quest for a "name" (Gen 6:4). In this power drive, they despotically usurped control. They perverted the whole concept of God-given government by doing whatever they pleased, with no amelioration of any of earth's injustices or iniquities, for which relief God had given government in the first place (Gen 6:5–6). They also became polygamous (Gen 6:2)."[cdxxxi]

The whole sacred text is a very human composition that speaks with and of very human difficulties, obstacles, attributes, or the like. I stated it before, and now again. The Bible is no more 'spiritual, or consecrated' than any other work of fiction. The consensus may well continue to be in modern scholarship, entertaining an angelic host cohabiting with humans. But, the evidence I have attempted to highlight above simply seems to dispute that interpretation being the only or come il faut meaning. Generally, a very likely reason for entertaining 'sons of gods' as beings of a former divine status who once chose disobedience are directed again to the many mythological tales of the ancient God's and their progeny mating with the daughters of men; which in turn produced an extraordinarily legendary progeny. Ancient civilisations numerously taught such tales which instilled in their hearers unequalled patriotism, and as stated earlier; these fantastic ventures that were originally passed down orally, must have played a role in the shaping and the inclusion of certain myths and legends found in current Bible texts; the texts we have inherited. An interesting mirrored development opened to me months before attempting this project, which also seems to support my above thesis. That was the birth narrative of able, and cain of Genesis 4:1-5a. "The New Contemporary Torah: A Gender-sensitive adaptation of the JPS Translation" interestingly reads:

> "Now the Human knew his wife Eve, and she conceived and bore Cain, saying, "I have created a person with the help of YHWH." She then bore his brother Abel. Abel became a keeper of sheep, and Cain became a tiller of the soil. In the course of time, Cain brought an offering to YHWH from the fruit of the soil; and Abel, for his part, brought the choicest of the firstlings of his flock. YHWH paid heed to Abel and his offering, but to Cain and his offering [God] paid no heed."

What I found fascinating in these verses is that in most other Modern English Translations, Eve says of cain, "I have produced a man with the help of the Lord." But, the NJPS intriguingly has: I have created a person with the help of Yahweh. The notes to this passage render, Person, according to this translation Committee, as,

> "More precisely, a member of the human species. NIPS "male child "; traditionally, "man." and, instead of with the 'help' of Yahweh; rather has the connotation of "as 'did' Yahweh..." (Italics my emphasis)

This establishes mankind in their minds as surely made in the image and by the help of Yahweh! But, it also establishes 'mankind in its fallen' state. Rendering cain as a person "serves as a typology or characteristic example." Thus, the term person embodies the group-oriented thinking found throughout the ancient Near East. However, the JPS Bible (notes on ish) is also inspiring in that the term (ish- man) presumes inseparability from a larger entity. The order in which the brothers are born also causes us to pause. First, cain: in a sense, he is the representative of the typical, characteristic example of the sacred book's presumption of sinful mankind. Born with a 'predisposition' to sinfulness. Being born sometime after the mythic 'fall' into the disobedience of the parents. Abel, in contrast though born also into this atmosphere, is not mentioned as a mere 'ish' - a man! Rather, we are strangely told from the first - his Name, Abel. Meaning, breath, vapour, or vain. After, we are told of his occupation. Thus, mankind is affirmed throughout the Judaeo-Christian book as either being born in the likeness of cain –sinful; or after the likeness of his brother - abel. Further, the teacher (Ecclesiastes) noted numerously all human effort and work/fruit of it; is vain (hebel= abel) (mentioned 38x, thirty-eight times alone) which apparently shows just how futile our endeavours are; if they are not encapsulated with the true breath of Yahweh. This also is a clear projection of other Bible writers. But has not medical science benefited humankind greatly? Hasn't the understanding of the 'laws of physics,' our DNA, microbiology offered us a broader view of our expanding universe? Do we not now grok that if 'new' vaccines are not built; the evolution of viruses poses greater dangers for human health each year? Can anyone insist on the fruits and endeavours of these discoveries have been in vain? Only arrogance it seems would imply such is true. No wonder countless former believers and 'pastors' and religious leaders are finally awakening, becoming enlightened and forsaking everything they once held to be true regarding the Christian theory. Has the religious human left his/her brain on the bus? Such emotional manipulation is clearly false. Furthermore, I have observed over the years the same people week in and week out at a so-called 'healing service' who gets prayer; for exactly the same problem that they went out for the week before. Clearly this is a myth. Clearly, it's bumpkin. Claim it till the cows come home, but that does not change a thing. When the time comes for their milking, cows will not produce flavoured milk, no matter how much you may 'claim' it so! There is however, a science as to why and how this idea of 'prayer' and so-called miracles works sometimes; but there is no intention to explain it here. It appears that much of what could be attached to the religious 'teachers''' understanding just does not add up. His pale is full of holes. According to the Bible, he once applauded,

> "The end of the matter; all has been heard. Fear God, and keep his commandments; for that is the whole duty of everyone. For God will bring every deed into judgment, including every secret thing, whether good or evil."[cdxxxii]

It must be admitted the writer penning the end to the book of ecclesiastes was ignorant on more than a few levels. What kind of suppressive, oppressive deity demands everyone's allegiance and then passes judgment? Judgments upon those traits of humanity mentioned tward the beginning of Nail Four above. Traits, and characteristics believers seem to think will be more expressive the closer a looming end-time approaches (2 Timothy 3:1-5). Why punish anyone for unintentional misdemeanours or some violation (leviticus 4:13)? Surely, such verses show how much churches, and their religious-mythologists rely on fear! Such assumes humanity possess' the thing we like to call 'free will.' Which as stated earlier in this investigation is denied to exist. Consider:

> "If humans had free will they would be able to side step their brain's programming. People's desires, thoughts, actions, and beliefs would be completely independent of one's genes, memories, environment, and conditioning. All humans would be then left to flounder in a chaotic sea of total and complete indecision. 'What should I do next? I can't make up my mind' would rule each of our moment to moment lives... With 'free will' our super intelligent genetic code and personal experiences would now be completely erased, and we would no longer know what we'd prefer doing in any given situation or circumstance." (Enel Vale, Chapter 2, The total, complete, utter insanity and nonsense of Free Will: The Newer TestamentTwo.

Believers today have not physically seen or interacted with the fabled abel figure, attested to be the breath of Yahweh (Jesus). But, they still insist nonsensically that all people can and must come to knowledge of him through the accounts written in their scriptures. Abel for them

DECONSTRUCTING ENDTIME DELUSIONS

obviously is therefore, metaphorically speaking: Jesus; their Messiah, whom we read was only here (physically) for a short time also, and despite being filled with the 'breath' of Yahweh, his life vanished as a vapour. The rest of us are reckoned as cain's of this world, 'wise in our own eyes,' by which such persons are evaluated as useless, and heretical. Here's the thing: Though this Messiah figure's life was but a breath; a vapour, many Bible commentators insist he showed humanity how to counter the perishableness of human endeavour if it were only aligned with Yahweh's regulations! But he died also. The only 'proof' he still lives comes from the inconsistent and often incompatible contradictory testimony of the authors of the New Testament. Authors who wrote their accounts no less than twenty years after the Jesus figure is said to have walked the length and breadth of Israel, and then was committed to crucifixion for insurrection! Accused successfully or not that was the charge of the dogmatic elite of the day. Besides, there are no extant contemporary works, comments, shopping lists, letters, postal notes, or receipts indicating anyone actually spoke with the Jesus figure. Nor witnessed any of the tales told in these letters unfold! Was Jesus' presumed perfection in following the 'commandments' also not up to scratch? He apparently died a horrendous death and so too did many of the apparent disciples? The depiction we see in Genesis 6:1:4 wishes to confirm, if nothing else, how the intermingling of two types of human being ends in tragedy. As stated, the opening statements to Genesis 6 are offered as a warning to highlight the accustomed belief that such things should noway ever occur! Which in itself is a violation of human rights. In our own visible propensity, it often does. Mixed relations are common these days. Then there are the 'in' crowds, and the 'others' who either cannot or will not be 'saved' from their so-called sin nature. An altogether different subject not explored. Returning briefly to the phrase sons of God: if indeed this phrase was to denote angelic, superhuman heavenly beings as Rob and others promote. Did this mean that the same should also apply to the Jesus figure, whenever the New Testament texts speak of him as the 'son of God'? If the Apostles had meant Angels, in the various (42) remaining places they wrote of the son(s) of theos (God), to either Jesus, or the heavenly host. Does that then not change their message? What messages were they announcing? Did they proclaim the message of ethereal angels. Or, were they attempting to announce the apparent, but highly objectionable risen son of God? Is this Jesus fellow to be viewed as an exulted angel, in the ethereal sense? Even when physically walking the earth in human bodily forms. Considering, after his apparent resurrection, and while walking about, a couple of people never twigged that it was their God-man deity speaking with them. How was that? Why didn't they recognise him? Such hyperbole I trust is recognised. Often, particularly with reference to the Old Testament, esp., in the psalms for instance. Mention of the 'host/angels of the heavens' as seen in job 38:4-7; psalm 19; psalm 148ff, is proclaiming the magnificence of the celestial worship, which is exemplified and amplified beyond measure.

This is indeed the case with passages like (psalms 19:1) Declaring that the heavens ring with noise, sound that "...declares the glory of God." Interpreted by the psalmist as worship of the deity. Do we know this actually happens? Well, yes, we do. The music/sounds emitted by the cosmos are immeasurably splendid, as one pastor discovered. He was so impressed he gave a series of sermons about 'the heavens', which are posted on Youtube. Louie Giglio.[cdxxxiii] Although he and his computer geeks transposed an obvious modern spin and Christian anthem to the sounds from deep space. The sounds, aside the usual Christian propaganda, captured from deep space is quite remarkable. The adage, no one can hear you scream in space may be fitting. But, it does not fit well to the reverberation emitted by star systems light years from our ears. The heavens (Space) are awash with music and sound! Paul similarly seems to exhort his believing community in his letter to the romans:

> "...For we know that the whole creation has been groaning together in the pains of childbirth until now. And not only the creation, but we ourselves, who have the first fruits of the Spirit, groan inwardly as we wait eagerly for adoption as sons, the redemption of our bodies. For in this hope we were saved. Now hope that is seen is not hope. For who hopes for what he sees? But if we hope for what we do not see, we wait for it with patience."[cdxxxiv]

DECONSTRUCTING ENDTIME DELUSIONS

The Apocryphal book of Baruch adds: "...the stars shone in their watches, and were glad; he called them, and they said, "Here we are!" They shone with gladness for him who made them. This is our God; no other can be compared to him."[cdxxxv] Back to angels: Malak (Hebrew, angel/messenger) has a number of uses in the Old Testament. One of the more prominent is:

> "...not so much a mere messenger as an instrument of the covenant and personification of divine aid, turning against Israel only in exceptional circumstances (cf. 2 sam. 24:17). Sometimes (e.g., gen. 16:7ff.; ex. 3:2ff.) he is so closely identified with God as to be almost indistinguishable. He is God, as it were, entering human apperception (cf. the alternation in Genesis. 21: 17ff.). 2. With the angel of the Lord are other heavenly beings, though these are seldom called angels. Forming God's entourage, they seem to have no autonomous functions and are in no sense objects of worship."[cdxxxvi]

It would seem then the role most often played by angels/messengers (of Yahweh) in the Old Testament economy at least, is safeguarding, announcing, or ratifying the Covenant. Never do they condone anything that may remotely resemble their own worship. Numerously, both written covenants continually warn against such, and fiercely announce it as idolatry. Human messengers/angels also play a minor role in the New Testament. If it is to be argued that heavenly angelic hosts are numerous. A reason for their appearance at the birth, ascension, and the returning of the Messiah, Jesus, is it is said he, directly presents, and represents Yahweh! Completing the circle in harmony with the Old Testament. Angels recall minister to Yahweh and have no true independence of choice, nor should nor do they command an interest of their own. This, we clearly recognise all through the scriptures. Affirmation is thus sought by the phrase "Angel of the Lord," with angel capitalised. This denotes the superhuman beings of Yahweh, which are found only (68x, sixty-eight times in 64 verses) throughout the nkjv. It would be difficult for English only readers to make an informed judgment, however. 'Angel' may begin a sentence, as here, because our English construction demands we capitalise the words beginning a sentence. But, this is not the case with the Hebrew text (an advantage again of using the power of logos' reverse-interlinear capabilities.) The alleged paul and the other apostles understood all this as they read their ancient texts. Making the applicable comments, and corrections necessary to their audiences. Allowing full well the benefit their original audience may well have understood and known. They felt no need to emphasise what was happening and to whom reference was to be accorded. All educated men understood they were not under the jurisdiction of Angelic beings (galations 1:8) but to their deity Yahweh alone. Neither should any Angel be worshipped. That constituted idolatry. These beings rather have a desire to understand the gospel (1 Peter 1:12), but it wasn't for them, but us humans that the Messiah figure died (hebrews 2:16.) If angels in the Christian Bible are not what we would ordinarily assume, but are more often than not human emissaries where does our modern conception of them derive? The consent of modern scholarship is that such ideologies surrounding angels come essentially from Second Temple literature; i.e. (the Dead Sea Scrolls; the book of enoch...): where a feature of these texts is a frequent appearance of ethereal beings. Such manuscripts have shaped and permeated much of the theology and religion of Israel, so also, much of modern christianity. Angelology is thus, primarily a development of the post-exilic period. The period in Israel's recent history that produced the particular writings we have already referred to on occasion, "...the Apocrypha, Pseudepigrapha, and Dead Sea Scrolls [which in turn] attest a heightened awareness and importance of the role of angels in the worldview of early Judaism."[cdxxxvii] Somewhat disconcerting is that most commentators and theorists, especially those flirting a modern Eschatology and end time assumption use extensively these texts as support for their hypotheses. Seemingly without attempting to find out their own rightful context first. Only after which, can we draw upon their wisdom for our days and struggles. This too we have noticed in various places during this analysis. Evident within these extra-biblical texts is 'good' and 'bad' angels. Such a distinct hierarchy thus comes only from these extra-biblical Second Temple texts. Little, or no evidence despite some mainly modern interpretations of a certain few Old

Testament passages (like isaiah 14:12f) is available in the biblical cannon. They, angels do figure as noted above, in the New Testament. Though playing a very minor role in all except one of the gospel accounts! "The Dictionary of Early Judaism" recounts:

> "Angels are conspicuously absent in the Gospel of Mark. Their absence may owe in part to the lack of a nativity story. Mark makes two references to the existence of angels, but they do not actually appear in the narrative (Mark 8:38; 13:32)." There is also a possible reference to an angel in Mark 16:5 if read alongside Matt. 28:3, although Mark describes the figure as a "young man."[cdxxxviii]

Though somewhat convoluted, the attempt in this Nail was to differentiate the scriptural, and standard Christian perspective regards the phrase: 'sons of God'; finding that most commonly these 'sons' are not an otherworldly entity. Rather, according to scripture are referent of those believers in an ethereal deity. A group of humans whose 'office' was considered of godly standard. Opposed to an ethereal being - angel. Context weighs heavily. The term 'Angels' likewise, is often referring to human emissaries. Some readers may yet again offer an objection. Obsessed with the notion of the 'fallen angels.' If angels in the scriptures normally refer to human emissaries (aside the phrase 'Angel of the Lord') with a capitalised 'A' for angel. Which as seen above does refer to some form of superhuman entity? Who or what are angels written about in the New Testament? Further, what of the Devil or Satan? Surely, the biblical evidence is abundant showing indisputably their existence as 'fallen angels'.

Nail Thirteen:

Fallen Angels:

> Surely 2 Peter 2:4; Jude 6 clearly substantiates their reality

THE WORLD STILL OBSESSES over and holds a deathly fascination with all things 'evil', horrific, and pertaining to the underworld of the dead. For some reason we seem to be built to enjoy the mystery and odd shudder down the spine. The horrific and lands of evil are lands often portrayed as dark, dank, dusty, and inhospitable; they are worlds full of various demons and spiteful spirits that intrigue. While then, also-making us 'feel' alive. Frightened out of our senses is a thrill, a buzz! New testament texts attempts to portray such a thrill, and sense of dread. Where the reader is informed of the fate of the dead in such a place is very much dependent upon earthly lives. How they were conducted. An example insinuating such a scenario is (luke 16:19-31). The story is of two men who died. One a rich fellow, the other as poor as a mouse. The rich man finds himself in Hades, while the poor man is apparently taken to paradise at his das Nichts. This story is obviously meant to play on peoples fears about life and the finality of death. It is essentially used as a manipulative tool to coerce people into treating others with a sense of decency; which as we saw in the very first Nail (One) is not our strongest suit. Fellow humans in other regions; as far as the other side of the world, or as close as the next suburb are not treated by anyone alive with the same care we like to fool ourselves with. Honestly, we cannot state we give a true damn about those who are not of our own kind. Life, according to the passages of luke it seems the persons mentioned did not cease when one died; rather continues. But, as we also studied in earlier Nails, this too is a complete deception of what the sacred texts teach about an abode of a torturous habitat. Hell as is taught by religion, just does not exist! Nonetheless, such ideas are not foreign to the religious. There are many comparable ideas to these descriptions all

DECONSTRUCTING ENDTIME DELUSIONS

through the annals of world mythologies of the ancients also. There are nowadays numerous tomes available that seem to highlight as a fact. Our proto-hominine ancestors' cosmological ideas were in direct relation to a

> "...belief in the transmigration of the soul, of a world beyond the grave, [which] has been a human characteristic for at least 100,000 years. The emergence of spiritual consciousness and its symbolism, is directly linked to the evolution of the temporal and frontal lobes and to the Neanderthal and Cro-Magnon peoples, and the first cosmologies, 20,000 to 30,000 years ago."[cdxxxix]

From the earliest understanding our earliest Homo-Sapien ancestors is thought to have had a belief in the ascendance of souls; for about the last 100,000 years. If a soul transcended to the heavens (where-ever that is) surely there was also the thought and belief in malevolent souls from some other opposing region. Indeed 2 Peter and jude 6, and the luke passages described above are just some such accounts we find in the Christian sacred book. Depicting the apparent reality of wicked/ fallen souls/angels. What we seem to have in such passages, is the author's attempts to portray the reality of an underworld and the fates of persons that are just as horrific as the surrounding Mediterranean mythological beliefs. The ancient understandings of an underworld. Maybe such texts served in a similar vein as a funerary text. Similar to how the Egyptian Book of the Dead is referred? But without the usual incantations and spells; for divination for the Jew is/ was prohibited. Though as has also been noted earlier. Divination practices were a reality for man, especially by those who practice Kabbalah and other Jewish occultist, esoteric forms of worship. There are great misconceptions today surrounding the beings called 'fallen angels,' as readers might have already guessed. The problem is, as stated above and despite popular myth, I do not believe there are such organisms as 'fallen angels.' Simply, such an idea does not seem to fit well within the corpus and overall manifesto of the Judaeo-Christian book. The concept of 'sinful beings'= demons/ or fallen angels someone famous once said; is of our own making. I am inclined to agree. "Everyman's Talmud" again confirms, stating explicitly,

> "The story of the fallen angels, which figures in the Apocalyptic literature, is not found in Talmud or Midrash. In the writings of the Rabbinic period the evil angels are nothing more than an invention to express the divine wrath, and their function is to carry out the decree when God has to punish men for their wickedness. This is clearly stated in several places. For instance: 'What is the meaning of "slow to anger" as ascribed to God? It signifies keeping anger afar off. The matter may be likened to a king who had two legions consisting of cruel soldiers. If, he said, they dwell in the same city with me, should the inhabitants provoke me, my men will stand against them and act cruelly towards them. I will therefore send them on a long journey, so that if the citizens provoke me, before I send to bring my soldiers back, they will seek to appease me and I will accept it of them. Similarly said the Holy One, blessed be He, Aph and Chémah are the angels of destruction. I will send them a long way off, so that if the children of Israel provoke Me, before I can fetch them back, they will repent and I will accept it of them'.. When the Holy One, blessed be He, said to Moses, "Arise, get thee down quickly from hence" (Deut. 9: 12), five angels of destruction heard it and wished to do him harm. They are Aph, Chémah, Kétzeph, Mashchith (destroyer), and Mechalleh (consumer)..."[cdxl]

Did a reader once again notice? Not a single angel mentioned is called explicitly 'fallen, or even 'evil' by nature. Rather, it is the specific task that seems to differentiate each angel type. According to the rabbis, some are simply angels of destruction. Others are said to carry forth important instructions. While others still, have any array of tasks. Specifically in the sacred text such entities, as either a fallen or evil angel, are only known courtesy of the Second Temple period. Such entities feature heavily particularly in the earlier mentioned Book of Watchers in 1 enoch (Chapters 6-16). Which again is recognised as having filtered through to modern ideas and much Christian theology? Thus, these texts have added to the confusing quagmire of the library of Christian dogma. Supposing such entities as evil fallen angels are evidently seen in their sacred texts. Surely, evident from my study of Rob Skiba's Babylon Rising. As further evidence to the 'fallen angel' hypothesis deriving from a second Temple incursion, and thus, filtering into our modern psyche; again the TEDEJ, "The Eerdmans Dictionary of Early Judaism". Interestingly offers us a foundational idea of these entities,

DECONSTRUCTING ENDTIME DELUSIONS

"Beginning in the second century b.c.e., we find efforts to assert human responsibility for sin and to downplay the fallen angels' culpability for the origins of evil. This is achieved, in part, through the suppression or minimization (sic) of traditions about their corrupting teachings. In the Animal Apocalypse (1 Enoch 86–89), angels are represented by stars. One star falls first, followed by others, who transform into "bulls" (i.e., men) that mingle with "cows" (i.e., women), thus causing earthly chaos. Born of this intermingling are destructive offspring. Heavenly angels then intervene and imprison their fallen brethren..."[cdxli]

If we firmly believe (heavenly) angels were created by the express will of the Judaeo-Christian deity Yahweh –for his express service, and therefore possess no 'free will' of their own; it makes perfect sense to insist. They cannot suddenly become disobedient to that deity! According to Chesnut, free will was apparently by divine privilege and is the providence of human beings alone! Despite the dispute offered above. What's more, proponents of a 'fallen angel' theory must consider the fact that if their deity Yahweh is a holy God, and no evil can exist in his presence –how is it to be explained that, particularly to the divine counsel. How can Evil (as either a Satan, – adversary, or, free-willed angels who 'chose' disobedience), be in among this counsel? To accuse any one of any wrongdoing? Does the deity make one exception, suspending its presumed holiness? That would to many be inconceivable and outright illogical! Maybe even blasphemous. If the supreme deity were to do so. It could very well be interpreted that such a deity is a 'lesser' deity than the one it itself affirms, see (Exodus 3:14.) "And God said unto Moses, I will become what I please." See the footnote of this Bible for an explanation.[cdxlii] This Exodus passage in many ways interestingly mirrors the pre-existent creation speech of the ancient Egyptian deity Atum. Surely, a parallel between the Exodus verse and the following is clearly evident. The Egyptian deity Atum was believed to have spoken:

"I am he among the gods who cannot be repulsed." Who is he? He is Atum, who is in his sun disc. Another version says: "He is Re, when he arises on the eastern horizon of heaven.> "I am yesterday, while I know tomorrow." Who is he? As for "yesterday," that is Osiris. As for "tomorrow," that is Re on that day on which the enemies of the All-Lord are annihilated and his son Horus is made ruler."›› [cdxliii]

A patron thought of as a great Hebrew leader, as Moses most probably drew a similar comparison. We are told by the scripture he was well versed and educated in the Egyptian milieu of his day. He was apparently well acquainted with all Egypt's creation myths, and for an extremely good reason! Numerous scholars of history, archaeology, ancient Egyptology and other fields of study affirm what could be a major eye-popping Revelation for readers. That the Moses of the Bible record is the Egyptian Pharaoh, Akhenaten. If so, this would specifically question the Bible's account of a mass Exodus of Hebrews from Egypt just as was seen in the earlier study of Exodus. On this, Tim Wallace-Murphy in his book interestingly states,

> "It was in 1991 that a meticulous scholar from the Islamic tradition, Ahmed Osman, published research proving beyond any reasonable doubt that the biblical figure of Moses was the Egyptian Pharaoh Akhenaten himself. Akhenaten had tried to institute a monotheistic belief in Egypt that nearly provoked civil war; one that had within it, oddly enough, the concept of a Trinity. The God Aten had become a Trinity, consisting of Re, as the father, Aten as the visible form of the father, and Akhenaten - who was both the son of Re, the son of Aten and yet at the same time the father of both; and further he was both Aten and Re."[cdxliv]

Despite ongoing polemical debates as to the veracity of this finding, many scholars are still

> "...in agreement that those who led and took part in the Exodus originated among Akhenaten's entourage and believed in his distinct form of monotheism. The strange desertion of Amarna and the sudden disappearance of all who lived in it impart a high degree of plausibility to this new vision of the Exodus. Not only did the nobility and priesthood vanish but also so did all the artisans, craftsmen, workers and servants. Akhenaten's Egyptian priests, scribes and notables - the national elite - were the first true monotheists in humanity and believed in one God, Aten."[cdxlv]

DECONSTRUCTING ENDTIME DELUSIONS

Who as the Bible has it, the Hebrew scribes adapted to be the Israelite peoples and the one God they came to worship, named: Yahweh. Which possibly drove him (aka, Moses/Akhenaten), as is recorded to question the deity's speech from the bush, and the subsequent charge given him. Namely, to return to Egypt; to Pharaoh's court and request the release of a numerous people so they could 'worship' the deity who had arrested Moses' attention. Such a request makes no logical sense at all! Moses fled, so we are told, for fear of retribution of the new Pharaoh (Exodus 2:15). Only to be asked to return! What is happening in this story?

These sidetrack arguments serves to highlight several things: (1) Again, there are more inferences that clearly show the Judaeo-Christian books were most likely pilfered from Egyptian sources; (2) it is pretty difficult to reconcile a presumed 'holy' deity and some malevolent angels in the same vicinity; and finally (3) sinful, corrupt, evil angelic types 'only' come to us through esoteric, Second Temple sources. Not via the Judaeo-Christian books themselves. There are then, no such ethereal beings as 'fallen nor incorruptible angels' outside imaginary thoughts. The very thoughts that composed the fantastical stories of texts like Legends of the Jews, and certain entries in resources like The Eerdmans Dictionary of Early Judaism. If this is all true: What then of the Devil, Satan, evil spirits, or 'angels bound in chains' that jude 6, 2 Peter 2:4, and Revelation 20:2 mention? Both Jude, and 2 Peter bear similar resemblances. Covering the same materials. Of these New Testament books, Lawrence Chesnut summarises their messages; thus; first of jude he writes,

> "We find packed into one page an amazing abridgment (sic) of Biblical history, and a short summary of the essential, true statements of fact conforming to truth, and genuine reality."[cdxlvi]

In the same work, "This second epistle of II Peter was meant as a sharp rebuke of the unfaithful among the professing disciples of Christ." Although both New Testament authors at some point mention angels, neither passage refers to the 'heavenly', but earthly messengers, the Yahweh's earthly envoys. The messengers in both Peter (2 Peter 2:4) and jude (jude 6) explicitly we are warned. Made foul of their estate/position that was commissioned by Yahweh. The context of 2 Peter confirms this in (2 Peter 2:5)! Also, Peter's earlier composition verifies substantially (1 Peter 4:17). If these are but again earthly messengers (angels) who are they? To learn who these 'messengers' one should be compelled to return to the opening pages of the Judaeo-Christian book: specifically, to the genealogy of Genesis chapter 5. Here, we witness the patriarchs of the antediluvian world, the pre-flood era. The chronology of men from 1-10 = Adam – noah. Of these Chesnut adds, that only three of the first world Patriarchs remained righteous and continued to be followers of God's original plan of living and way of worship. These three were apparently enoch, methuselah, and noah. The other seven fell away from God's original plan (apparently) sinned, died, and was eternally lost in hell. These are the angels. The messengers that both Peter and jude were referring; those who 'fell' and are reserved in everlasting chains of darkness unto the judgment of the great day. Maybe, these are also those who are referred in Genesis 6:1-4?

If readers are unwilling to accept the conclusions at the end of Nail Nine above, where I concluded the nephilim were possibly Neanderthal peoples, and the 'sons of the gods, the Cro-Magnon; well, here is another twist to consider. What if the nephilim; those 'mighty men of renown' were the seven patriarchs of Genesis chapter 5 who forsook the deities original plan? What a terrible thing to 'fall' into the hands of the Living Yahweh wrote paul to his Hebrew brothers in the faith (hebrews 10:26-31.) Bollocks! If this is the truth of the matter. This places another and much greater understanding upon other often-misapplied New Testament passages. For example, ephesians 6:10-19. Favourite's for 'Spiritual Warfare' junkies.[cdxlvii] These verses speak specifically regarding the 'earthen' forces at work among and against men and women of the 'book'. Yet, this does not mean a struggle with physical flesh, – people. But, the adverse 'spirit' by which they operate. Those satans, antagonists to the cause. Our current social and political climate and those attributes and acts earlier attested; in the earlier Nails of this investigation. If not, where do we propose 'the evil intent of a man's

DECONSTRUCTING ENDTIME DELUSIONS

heart 'continually'" lay in relation (Genesis 6:5)? As 'proof' to the bona fide spirit of this assertion, only a tiny sampling of (ephesians 6:12, as recorded in the esv) is briefly explained. Ephesians 6:12reads:

> "For we do not wrestle against flesh and blood, but against the rulers, against the authorities, against the cosmic powers over this present darkness, against the spiritual forces of evil in the heavenly places." (The Holy Bible: English Standard Version. (2016). (Eph 6:12). Wheaton, IL: Crossway Bibles.)

In explanation "Thayer's Greek-English lexicon of The New Testament" interestingly calls attention to:

> "The authorities, in Greek = 'freedom of 'choice'; the cosmic powers, in Greek (only 1x) one time = 'world-power/ruler' or supernatural power. Rabbinic writings used both of human rulers, and the angel of death [according to Thayer, J. H. (1889). A.])."

The battles believers should fight are not with flesh or blood. They never have been! It has rather always been spiritual in nature (2 corinthians 10:4.) Specifically, spiritual forces of evil in 'heavenly places', does not by any definiens; mean a battle fought against literal wraithlike 'demonic' forces either! Rather, I reiterate, it speaks of the spiritual battles that wage within ourselves and the external manifestation of wickedness (heretics) that often oppress. Example, paul spoke candidly of this fight raging within himself (romans 7:4-25.) There is account after account of such a 'battle' being waged against the spirit of antagonism in others who oppose a believers' particular belief. The sacred texts are a very human composition. Symbolically detailing human struggles written in a spiritualised vernacular. Confirmation is offered again in the "Dictionary of Early Judaism" for Chester's and my assertions. That modern thoughts surrounding 'fallen angels' are a fable and myth. It says that

> "...by the Second Century, of the Common Era, rabbinic Judaism had rejected the 'fallen angel' hypothesis as proposed by The Book of Enoch in (The Book of Watchers). Not only that, the interpretation of 'sons of God' in Genesis 6:1-4 as angels, was also rejected. Surprisingly christianity also rejected these assertions in the Fourth and Fifth Centuries and reinterpreted

some materials about Satan and his minions. Unfortunately; however, such fables as described in the Book of Watcher's were kept alive and eventually made a resurgence in the Middle-Ages (Dictionary of Early Judaism, p. 629.)

Obviously, this resurgence has filtered through to our day also. Particularly to proponents like Rob Skiba and Thomas Horn. Regarding Devil - briefly, the "Encyclopaedia of Christianity, Vol 1-3, entry (Devil)", interestingly says that the word is a latecomer to religion. It does however carry the meaning, like its Old Testament predecessor Satan; of accuser, slanderer or is in use to a 'leader in unbelief, and heresy', and a seducer and paramour (lover) of wicked intent. So as expressed below in the brief discussion of Satan; Devil only became prominent from the 10th Century onward. By the 13th Century, 'Satan' had become a fully-fledged personality. These terms and what they have come to mean today is extremely recent to world history, which should cause us to pause to recalibrate and verify our beliefs.

> "In the 10th century the Devil was often understood as a repugnant mixed form, as attributes of ancient mythical monsters were attributed to him, for example, horns, often like the Minotaur (Greek Religion), or ram's feet like Azazel (Demons), or an ass's tail, possibly like the slayer of Osiris, Seth, who was later identified with the Greek monster, Typhon" (Egyptian Religion 1.1).[cdxlviii]

Bamberger again in his book "Fallen Angels", observes:

> "The belief in the reality and power of the Devil is indeed to be found in every age of historical Christianity. Tertullian, for example, was obsessed by the horror and danger of the spirit world. But the violent intensity of his feeling was, for his age, somewhat exceptional. More and more, however, as centuries went by, did this mood become characteristic. Bulky tomes were compiled by monastic writers, setting forth in minutest detail the innumerable activities and stratagems of the Devil and his hosts."[cdxlix]

Thus, the concept of a Devil grew over time to recognition as a personified myth; an amalgamation of various ancient mythological monsters! As difficult and hard this message is for some readers; it can readily be accepted that although the scriptures often speak in a very high 'heavenly' tone. More often than not when it does by using such phrases and words as angels, 'fallen' or otherwise, 'sons of God', Satan, Devil, along with other difficulties. These are most probably directly linked to earthen vessels, our earthen ancestors. The Christian scriptures are either highlighting their waywardness or their piety. Apparently the sacred texts on do on rare occasions see fit to have the deity Yahweh send as a 'special' envoy. A 'Heavenly' messenger, like the archangels michael or gabriel to his servants, the prophets –i.e., Daniel, or another lowly servant of his choosing, joseph, mary, zechariah (announcing the birth of john the immerser), cousin to Jesus! It appears that emissaries are sent on very specific errands, to specific people, at specific times, and for specific reasons. Gabriel, we read announced Jesus, and john's birth. Jesus is said to be the direct representative of the deity Yahweh; hence, an angel had to announce his birth. John; he, was the fulfilment of the promised elijah who was to precede him (malachi 4:5!)

Luke 10:18 – Help me if you can, I'M FALLING DOWN.

BEFORE SUMMARISING this section on 'fallen angels' it might be worth analysing briefly also the meaning behind our English word – 'fallen/fell/fall,' to a Satan; who as the belief goes, apparently 'fell' from the heavens. Again, the result may take the wind out of the sails of some readers. It does noway carry the same import as would be supposed. One of the favoured New Testament texts advocates use to bolster the idea that a 'personified' Satan 'fell' from the heavens is (luke 10:18.) Luke records:

> "And he (Jesus) said to them,*/>w "I saw Satan/>x fall like lightning from heaven..."[cdl]

The immediate context is Jesus had sent the disciples (72) in number out into all the towns he was to go. They returned to him elated that everything 'submitted' to the preaching in his name. Notice; however, the text does not say Satan fell from heaven! Rather, what 'fell' was likened to how 'lightening' flashes across the sky. Which is limited to the aerial heavens, –which are not where Yahweh presides! This is the confusion. Too many readers of this passage assume it clearly states Satan 'fell' and so (he) to them, obviously sinned. Bollocks! A careful reading cannot substantiate this. This is again theory and is based upon shoddy interpretation. Besides, the Greek of the word 'fall' in this verse also confirms my assertion. The Greek word translated as 'fall' here is, pipto; which in the New Testament does not mean - 'sin'. According to Kittel and other theological sources, pipto actually means,

> "In most instances literal falling down is intentional, either in obeisance to a master (Mt. 18:26) or, with proskynéō, in connection with the worship of deity (Mt. 4:9; Acts 10:25; 1 Cor. 14:25; Rom. 4:10), or alone, in face of Jesus, to emphasize (sic) a petition, to express gratitude, or to show respect (Mk. 5:22; Lk. 17:16; Jn. 11:32). Jesus himself adopts this attitude in prayer (Mt. 26:39)."[cdli]

Therefore, it might be of benefit to think; the 'fall' of an antagonist (Satan) was potentially in obeisance, worship, respect, or gratitude. Briefly, if a reader were to take the illogical stance that a Satan did actually sin, when (he) apparently 'fell' (pipto). How then do you reconcile this same idea with the alleged Messiah figure, Jesus in prayer? The above quote clearly states that the Messiah figure adopted the same attitude (pipto) he also 'fell' down: Matthew 26:39. Did the Messiah then sin also? Illogical thinking, true enough. Yet, the same word in a similar context is used for both personalities. The same sense is seen for the equivalent Hebrew term for 'fall' that has been mentioned in the early pages of Nail Nine above. See Dr. Nyland's explanation again for confirmation. Besides, according to the "Oxford Dictionary" confirms. There is absolutely no sinning to the verb form to fall (pipto):

> "fall- verb (past fell; past participle fallen). 1. move from a higher to a lower level, typically rapidly and without control. (fall off) become detached and drop to the ground. hang down. slope downwards. (of a person's face) show dismay or disappointment by appearing to droop. 2. cease to be standing or upright; collapse. 3. decrease in number, amount, intensity, or quality. 4. pass into a specified state: the buildings fell into disrepair. occur or arrive. (fall to doing something) begin to do something. 5. be captured or defeated. Cricket

DECONSTRUCTING ENDTIME DELUSIONS

(of a wicket) be taken by the bowling side. archaic yield to temptation. 6. be classified in the way specified."[cdlii]

There is no attempt at playing semantic games here. Just attempting to make the point that it is utterly ridiculous to assume that an act of 'falling' (verb form), as the luke passage above, means something sinned! Have scales begun to fall from your eyes? Are you beginning to see clearer? Is it not conceivable that the deity–man Jesus, is said to have believed he saw enmity to the rule of Yahweh 'bow the knee'. Just as the disciples would later also announce in affirmation that this would happen. But, somehow on a much wider scale (romans 14:11; philippians 2:10). If so, it was this that the disciples were elated to have apparently witnessed in every town he had sent them to minister. This however, we know is a false assertion. Unless, in reference to the known world of the period. The whole world has not, and will likely not fall foul to this manipulation. I wonder though: if whoever it was that this verse of luke speaks, did they 'know' they were being manipulative and coercive? Or, did they truly 'believe' what they were saying and teaching? It wasn't that demonic entities', in a malevolent 'spiritual fallen angel' sense that bowed the knee...pipto doesn't allow that... (not even in traces that possibly are said in other places; i.e., where Jesus heals the Gerasene demoniac (Matthew 8:28–9:1; Mark 5:1; Luke 8:26–39). The disembodied spirits of wickedness here, that inhabited this man could very well, and just as likely be another reference to those entities apparently banished by Yahweh, on the same level as 2 Peter, or jude spoken of above. Carrying forth the traditions of the Old Testament writers by incorporating mythical legends for the express purpose of highlighting a deeper moral.

In summary: Angels; demonic, or benevolent, and the entity Satan has become of central interest to many modern proponents of an apocalyptic end-time scenario. So much so that it has been completely misread, misinterpreted. At some point in the distant past, these subjects became a 'corrupted' trace of Yahweh's perfectly obedient angelic host and were found to have 'fallen' from grace. Recall Harwood's commentary of

Genesis 6 above. They then became licentious, at which they mixed with and from now on-corrupted mankind through their progeny...and such will inevitably reemerge in the near-future. That in essence is what many apocalyptic doom-sayers assume will happen. Beginning maybe around or not long afterward the beginning of an end–time. Not surprisingly others project the notion of five years into the near future, around the year 2016-17; or sometime in the 2020's are when end-times officially begin. The current fouling of the 'air' about the world seems to lend credence to this. But, in the religious sense as countless believers assume; that a deity will be showing up or causing numerous oddities throughout the Earth and 'save' a certain crowd, and forsake and banish another, less desirable. This is wrong. Whatever must these mythologists mean by 'end-times'? However, an 'ending' as a *transformation* - a new order likely will occur. Such is a fact of history. Empires are birthed, they grow, they decline, and then whither and fade to black. Only to be (re)discovered in the annals of history texts in a future. The Egyptian, Roman, Greek, Mesopotamian, Middle-Eastern, have all risen to great heights of power, influence, dominance. Only to run their courses, fade, and whither and die. It seems now is the time when it is Western cultures turn. But, again we digress.

The Yahweh surely created 'angelic' beings. This, the sacred texts seem to affirm, and as so this is absolutely and undeniably true for believers. Before the earth, they were created. They are the spirit(s) of the deity Yahweh who is predisposed to his 'service'. Being part of this deity means they can neither choose, nor act contrary to his express desires at any stage. If this idea is held to be absolute, it is undoubtedly a fallacious and crazy teaching that allow it to be said that this God would rebel against himself and place a portion of that rebelliousness on probation, outside the realm of the heavens to attempt to corrupt and destroy forever his prize. His apparent crowning achievement –mankind (Genesis 1:26-28f.) This it would also seem true, for every new and Old Testament author must have understood that when speaking of angels, whether of the divine council, or son(s) of God; these were, –most often a reference to celestial bodies (planets/stars...psalms 103:20-21; 148.) Or those angels are either the obedient or disobedient men of earthly office and rank; see (jeremiah 23:18,22; isaiah 6:8f, 40:14)! Of the mentioned angels in the New Testament, of whom it is said they 'sinned,' these are the antediluvian patriarchs, and the later generations of men and women leaders whose original design and providence were to the godly governance of his people. But, this charge they had forsaken. Casting this privilege aside to 'follow' after their own dissolute desires according to (proverb 11:6; matthew 5:28; romans 1:24; 1 Thessalonians 4:5; 2 Peter 2:10.) Such men and women "'fell' from the high plane, to the lowest state of sin, rebellion, and corruption."[cdliii] Such a pattern of 'falling' men and women unfortunately repeats and sadly continues to repeat itself to the present. Therefore, again be forewarned; take great pains to heart (James 4:6, 10; 1 Peter 5:5.)

Satan devils evil spirits:

THERE IS AN APPARENT witness to such forces at work in our day. The sum total of the words marking this section combined is a four-letter-word, – 'evil.' It is however intriguing. Just the pronunciation of any of these concocts in the mind a fear, dread, and any amount of ghoulish imagery. Maybe this also is related to myths personified by years of distorted logical teachings making mirages that have over time, crept into the sanctuary (1 john 4:1.) No doubt the explosion across the media in recent decades has contributed and fuelled greatly how the above words are perceived, and the meaning many population 'attaches' to them. Every year it seems, movie and small screen magnates churn out, almost mechanically, more macabre programming. The more horrific a show the more it would seem to incur interest and greater the cult following. However, there are three truths that remain specifically regarding 'evil' and our perceptions. Bishop Wright generally again hit it on the head in the opening pages of his book on evil. Suggesting our perception of 'evil' is driven and characterised in three ways. He says:

> "First, we ignore evil when it doesn't hit us in the face. Second, we are surprised by evil when it does. Third, we react in immature and dangerous ways as a result."[cdliv]

However, true these statements are; readers are encouraged to source for themselves this resource for further comments. Knowing therefore, these three characterise our perceptions, and if my summations above regarding angel's (fallen, or not) stand true. Much searching of the 'Christian' heart as well as the digesting of the texts needs to be entertained; see (ezekiel 2:8, 3:1; jeremiah 15:16; revelation 10:9-10; psalms 19:10, 119:103). The understanding of the sacred texts must be viewed as allegory; via symbol. Characters, entities, patriarch's etc., should be viewed through the prism of Symbol. To this resolve, the Christian psyche must come from a heart and mind after the legendary, but mythical king David; who we are told pleaded his deity – "Unveil thou my eyes that I may discern Wondrous things out of thy law..." (psalms 119:18. Rotherham. (1959). The Emphasized Bible.) See also (philippians 3:13-21.) As with the subject matter already discussed, here too, the intent is not to offer readers a suppositional something about 'evil;' but to show what the sacred texts teach. Again, no attempt has been entered to cover it in any great depth. For that, there are numerous books already available, some of which may be mentioned in this brief. Evil, and its effects on us all are a most vexing predicament.

> "The bone in the throat of Western theology," Sidney Hook remarks, "is the problem of evil–the ever-recurrent question why an allegedly all-powerful and all-benevolent Supreme Being permits in every age the torture of innocent multitudes" ("On Western Freedom," p.94).[cdlv]

This problem is exemplified with the question of its origin. And is still as the previous discussions surrounding Genesis 6:1-4, considered one of the most perplexing in scholarship. There are again two sides of the coin: the one states it was the invention of the divine (i.e. from a prosthetic memory of passages the likes of isaiah 45:7); the other states it is the cause of humanity. This is further complicated by the fact that several Dead Sea Scrolls are attested to holding the same kind of dualism,

> "...in which humans are believed to be under the influence of two types of superhuman beings, one good and the other evil. The "Treatise on the Two Spirits", found in... some copies of the Rule of the Community, is exemplary in this regard. This text teaches that God has placed in humankind two spirits", the spirits of truth and of deceit," which determine, respectively, humanity's good and evil deeds. This text says that a figure called the "Prince of Lights" has dominion over the righteous and that the "Angel of Darkness" is in charge of the wicked. These opposing angelic leaders appear in a number of other texts from the Dead Sea Scrolls."[cdlvi]

So, humanity is plagued with an irrational fear of some spiteful, malicious entity or entities that are outside the human character. In the studies below, readers I trust will become more aware that such reasoning is again sheer nonsense, and another manipulative tool of the religious elite which dismisses and excuses our very nature.

Satan:

'SATAN'? HERE IS A NEEDLESSLY perplexing 'entity;' one that all too often becomes the personified force of evil the world over. Why though italicise or even capitalise the word Satan and place this assumed entity in quotation marks? Great question. Multiple myths surround such subjects today (see Bamberger.) Despite popular opinion, a personified Satan is nonetheless again pure sensationalised speculation; a fiction! Dr. Ann Nyland, in the introduction to her study, Angels, Archangels, and Angel Categories: What the Ancients said, confirms that modern conceptions of 'Satan' as a personified being, are nothing but a pure imaginary narrative tale!

> "John Milton's 'Paradise Lost,' she says, has given Christianity today their view of "Satan", a view not supported by the Bible itself."

One of the more persistent, particularly rumoured through the halls of christendom is the 'belief' we first see this entity personified as a serpent in the garden of Genesis 3:1. In my study above on Genesis three, in Nail four above. It was discovered that Dr. Nyland is correct. There are other admirable scholars of Hebrew confirming; - there is no devilish entity to be found in any of the Hebrew scriptures. It is rather another illegitimate transfer of (1) Milton's prose, Paradise Lost; and (2) Milton's text has been coupled with numerous New Testament passages that, to the minds of the interpreter/ commentator, are compatible. There are also other Hebrew commentators who so assume and propagate the satanic ideology In the garden episode. The authors of "From God's to God" also assume the serpent in the garden was the mythological evil Demi-God, Satan, in a chapter of Genesis three. Which undoubtedly, does not help to disentangle modern perceptions. Again, it must be asked, where in the text of Genesis 3:1 is this Satan as a personified serpent guess even inferred? It is not. All the text says is that this creature was craftier than any of the other wild creatures the deity had created! Craftier could be read as either a negative, or positive mannerism. As noted in Nail Four of this investigation. the serpent in the garden text should be recognised as positive. Here though as the passage's context seems to dictate, it is negative. Yet, not all references to serpents or snakes in the Bible are pejorative. Indeed, as we also saw, in many world myths, serpents, and snakes have a helpful, positive radiance. They are healers, and representatives of 'regeneration/resurrection;' by 'shedding' their former self (skin) in many cultural myths! Many serpent myths also represent the Goddess and associated themes of worship in antiquity. Tony Bushby: "The Secret in the Bible", sheds some light on the ancient practice of serpent worship. In chapter, twelve he writes,

> "An upraised serpent became the origin of a highly developed and sophisticated religion and was revered in ancient times as an emblem of extreme importance. From that region of unfathomable depth issued forth a powerful tradition of a vertical coiled Serpent, the ancient emblem of Wisdom and Eternity. The earliest initiates or 'The Wise Men' who were initiated into the Mysteries were called 'Serpents of Wisdom' and the curious reference to 'a serpent on two legs' in the Book of the Dead is not a description of an extra-terrestrial being from a spacecraft but simply means a high initiate. The Serpent became the type and symbol of evil later in time, and it subsequently developed into the Devil during the dark Middle Ages. As an image, a serpent standing on its tail obtained a prominent place in ancient initiations and religions and so wide was serpent worship that it was sometimes regarded by ancient writers as the primitive religion of

mankind...Biblical literature is replete with serpents, and when Rabbi Jesus instructed his disciples to be 'as wise as serpents', he meant to be as wise as an initiated person. (p243)."

Over all, this description adds further to Genesis 3. The 'serpent' at the 'tree of the knowledge of wisdom and folly' (good and evil), is one of the Wise Men – Serpents of Wisdom- a High Initiate of the Mysteries. Why the author of this Genesis episode chose to demonise this entity/character, will most likely never be fully resolved. If the garden episode tells of initiation rites being afforded to mankind, clearly early 'Christian' interpreters had no idea. Rather, as thoughts of demons were a prominent fixture of the early Church, the serpent entity was morphed into the archenemy – Satan. Maybe the Genesis chapter is hinting at the initial stages of people seeking guidance or, acceptance into a 'Mystery school'? Because of the themes we are exploring and mainly our preconceived ideas. We are forced to only deal here with the negative aspect to the serpent and the narrative that makes up Genesis 3. For a range of both the positive and negative aspects, readers are encouraged to reexamine entries in reputable Bible dictionaries and other materials in the bibliography, and indeed many world myths. To do so, you would surely be amazed at one idea posited; that the 'evil being'–Satan, as a serpent –some researchers believe has origins in Persian Creation myth and legend (as earlier noted). Most ideas about the reality of Satan, demons, or devils like many other modern mythic doctrines in deceit and certainty; i.e., tongues as a confused babbling of indecipherable consonants 'vocalised' in rapid succession. Only derive from various persistent and stupid myopic conclusions of a vast array of unexplored viewpoints! More often than not, many are the embellishments of an international consortium of myth, legend, and tales of the ancients gathered over many years. Satan as the ultimate force of 'evil' is no exception. Says one researcher in, "A Hitchhikers Guide to Armageddon",

"The God of evil, Set, from which we get our word "Satan," was one of the many gods of Egypt. The religion of Set, like many religions today, was a religion of fear, where, if one gave generously to the temple, then nothing harmful would happen to the person (who was true and faithful)."[cdlvii]

The explanation by David Childress is most interesting. Childress however is, in the tone of his work, again disparaging in a derogatory manner the Egyptian gods. Personifying what was never the original intent? The deity SET to the Egyptians was the deity of evil. But, he was also the God of war, hostility, darkness, hot barren deserts and storms. Why then are these not also personified? Clearly, as was stated tward the beginning of this investigation. The Egyptian deities were intended to fix the attention or ONLY represent the metaphysical ideas represented. Unfortunately for modern believers, is the fact that although 'evil' in and of itself has no personality, but is one of the many hurtful traits born to humankind. We, because of a despising of Egyptian magic (lore/ritual/religion), have allowed a metaphysical birthed ideology, of a full and personable status as the entity Satan. Because of the many 'doctrines' of the three dominant religions, there is in the minds of the 'believer' an outrageous fear of this nonexistent personality which is upheld via preaching of a torturous abode (hell) for the non-compliant. This was beautifully put by "...the founder of the Salvation Army [who succinctly said] 'Nothing moves the People... like the fear of Hell Fire flashed before their eyes.'"[cdlviii] So, people are coerced and manipulated into generous 'gift' donating to the temple/Church...the list of mirrored expectations, and fears are endless. No doubt that the religions of Judaism, and her rival siblings, christianity and Islam very probably have deeper roots in Egyptian mythology and religious cultic practice than most would expect or care to believe. Maybe the story of the rival siblings of jacob and esau in the Judaeo-Christian book reflects such a truth also? Not unbecoming I should imagine! Why could the sacred text author not have welded such several myths and legends, which we know he and later redactors most surely did: only rearranging events and changing names to suit his audiences? Here we have two most probably and palatable ideas to Satan. The one, his name derives from the Egyptian religious cult of Set, the other, adding to it most intriguingly does theological

DECONSTRUCTING ENDTIME DELUSIONS

Anthropologist John Pilch who insightfully states in his "A Cultural Handbook to the Bible" that Satan:

> "...is actually a Persian loanword referring to an undercover agent who tests loyalties for kings." An understandable and most fitting explanation; surely such an individual is constantly referred throughout the text of both testaments. Pilch explains this idea further with this observation: "The classic example in the Bible is Satan in Job 1-2. A modern example is King Abdulla, the young son of King Hussein who succeeded his father as king of Jordan...he travelled the country in disguise seeking opinions from ordinary citizens...He was testing not only the loyalties of the citizens but the behavior (sic) of government employees...Those who test loyalties do so by deception, by pretending to be someone else, or by making leading (or misleading) statements to catch an unsuspecting citizen off guard."[cdlix]

Such behaviour modern believers are most familiar. But again, we all too quickly ascribe this activity to an individual called Satan who is some ethereal entity. Both (jób 1:7f; and 1 Peter 5:8) as well as other new and Old Testament writers however use the interchangeable term Devil, to describe such acts also! Adding somewhat even more to our confusion. That Satan is a loanword, most scholars confer, and thus, I am inclined to think it rings the required veridical bell. Not only does it add to the description below of most reputable Bible lexicons or dictionaries; of carrying the definite article, but interestingly both the Israelites who returned to the promised land, and those that chose to stay put (Cyrus, about, 539B.C. As recorded by ezra and nehemiah), in their allotted Babylonian/Persian territories, most likely were greatly influenced by Babylonian/Persian religious theologies and dogma. Just as much as the Jewish returnees had adopted a Babylonian Calendar. They more than likely had adopted these other rites and folklore teachings and therefore, most likely had integrated those into the religious practices that became the Judaism and then, also christianity of today. Considering also that christians assume to know that the wise men that visited joseph and mary at the birth of Jesus were Babylonian Magi (Astrologers. A practice said to have begun by the young exiled Daniel in Persia- but was really begun in ancient Egypt). Furthermore, Satan, has attached to it the Hebrew article, 'ה, h = the,' as a prefix, more often than not. Thus, technically this means it cannot successfully become, or be a proper noun. Unfortunate for modern believers, as is so often erroneously assumed in Christian circles nobody is taught that the Satan often carries with it the Hebrew article (the), thus, is not a proper noun! Hence , my lower-case, Satan! Returning to serpent and Genesis 3:1 briefly. According to "Louw-Nida Greek lexicon" the word behind our English translations could just as well have been,

> "...several small four-footed animals as well as snakes; for example, rats, mice, frogs, toads, salamanders, lizards..."[cdlx]

Multitudes of people unfortunately are still currently being snookered into the idea this 'entity', - the serpent, is a 'real' ethereal, and sometimes tangible boogieman. A terrifying figure with a nefarious personality. Or, that it represents a talking/walking entity that is some 'fallen angelic' embodiment, called Satan. But, this Satan as any of these descriptions above testify, is simply quite far-fetched and nonsensical. Though the deity Yahweh is said to have created this creature of Genesis 3:1 with the ability to speak, and to converse as humans do with each other. Some animals for sure, are enabled with a very limited vocabulary to speak, i.e., some Parrot species! None of which I am aware however can carry a formal conversation as you, or I am able. They are simply ill equipped physically and anatomically to do so. Chimpanzees, our closest relatives are even ill-equipped with the suitable vocal apparatus for speech. How then is it to be known a serpent spoke. There are also numerous fantastic legends, and myths told, like "Legends of the Jews", which has already been cited that describe this serpent creature as a gifted bipedal – able to converse and walk on two feet. Before being cursed to slither along the ground. Undoubtedly, we have confused many of these stories or unknowingly caused them to have also weighed into contemporary beliefs? What possible roots to this idea can be found? Pilch again in the pages preceding that which is described above, makes a further insightful observation about snakes. Helping us answer the question of roots. He writes in one sub-section, symbolism, and the snake that,

DECONSTRUCTING ENDTIME DELUSIONS

> "...About a thousand years later after the writing of the well-known Genesis 3 <account>, the author of Revelation interprets this animal to be "the great dragon...that ancient serpent, who is called the Devil and Satan, the deceiver of the world...[who] was thrown down to the earth, and his angels were thrown down with him." (Rev 12:9).

Subsequent Christian tradition selectively combined the information from the two passages, applied the insights to Mary the mother of Jesus, and created the statue of Mary with a snake under her feet and,

> "...The Hebrew word for serpent, nahash, is a homonym of the root which means, "to practice divination, to observe signs."[cdlxi]

"This root is observed to occur (51x), fifty-one times in (45) verses throughout the Old Testament, according to the nrsv. And is often-translated snake, or serpent, but not always. Approximately (20x), twenty of those times it stands for literal people. It may therefore be a tricky play or pun on words. Such puns, scholars recognise are noticeable throughout the whole Bible text. If true, this would seem to add further credence to all that which has been stated above regarding the malevolent entities. Pilch again states; "If true to character, the Yahwist is punning or deliberately evoking the homonym in Genesis 3:1..." (Pilch: p.44.), and in other places throughout the scriptures where we read of certain characters learning the art and practices of divination (Genesis 30:27; 44:5, 15.) Confirmation and understanding was sought in other theological works, like the "Theological Wordbook of the Old Testament", again which reads,

> "...divination is outlawed in Lev 19:26 and is spoken of with condemnation in II Kgs 17:17 and 21:6 (cf. II Chr 33:6). It is in the list of forbidden occult practices of Deut 18:10. (naḥaš). Divination, enchantment, omen, sorcery (Berkeley Version) augury (jps). The noun naḥaš is obviously related to the cognate verb nāḥaš II. Numbers 23:23 has the word in the singular, parallel to qesem (q.v.), indicating some variety of the occult. Numbers 24:1, also part of the Balaam passages, has the only other occurrence of naḥaš. Because of the similarity of naḥaš to nāḥāš (q.v.) meaning "snake," some make a connection to snake charming. More contend that there is a similarity of

hissing sounds between enchanters and serpents and hence the similarity of words."[cdlxii]

Concluding Satan:

THROUGHOUT THE HEBREW Bible Satan carries the definite article; i.e., it has the equivalent of our English word 'The,' before it. Literally; therefore, the meaning is no more than 'the adversary, or, the antagonist, the challenger, opponent, enemy, and contender, rival.' It might amaze readers to know that profile portrayals of Alexander the Great on coins, sculptures, and other ancient artefacts are often of him sporting ram's horns (and beard) because of an apparent epiphany he once had at an Egyptian shrine. He came to believe that he was the incarnation of Zeus Ammon; the combined high gods of both the Greek and Egyptian pantheon. Might Alexander's profile then over the centuries have morphed via a continued prosthetic memory. Into the devilish figure where, from such a belief a 'satanic' being the Devil was birthed? Not to mention that the very first mention of Satan in the Bible is (numbers 22:22.) Reviewing the context of this numbers passage readers may be shocked to realise that it is 'the angel of the Lord who stands as 'Satan'', as the adversary in this passage. I would hope therefore, just this may give cause for a more careful understanding brought about by diligent research.

Horny little devil:

THROUGHOUT CHRISTIANITY, there are beliefs and expectations that 'the Devil' and 'his' minions are 'Horned' deity-like entities inhabiting a chthonic realm. In such a place, they hatch plots subscribing to an insatiable bent for the destruction of an unwary humanity. At some point in a future time, according to Christian mythology, an intensely evil character will arise like the Phoenix from the ashes of time and cast the world into chaos. The Apocalypse. These entities seem to be another figment of an over exerted imagination, and again, a reading into texts like the Bible's Revelation chapters describing a multi-horned and multi headed <beast> that ascends from the seas, and chases a pregnant woman, hoping to devour her unborn child. Yet, little do many readers (believers) of Revelation understand such creatures and descriptions are not unique to the Bible. In the Judaeo-Christian sacred books, descriptions of a Satan, Devil, adversary, spiteful person, antagonist is to be understood as Symbolic. Every character and action are symbolic, not literal. The trick is to find the symbolic meaning. Which somewhere in the story will also be stated! If one reads the passage of Genesis 6:4 with open eyes, nephilim are plainly called the mighty men of old. Many such horned beings can be understood through a study of 'horned deities' and their mythologies from around the world.[cdlxiii] Or as Rod Steiger writes,

> "...archaeological digs in the United States that have produced the remains of primitive men and women over seven feet tall; hominids with horns; giants with double rows of teeth; prehistoric people with sharply slanting foreheads and fanged jaws; and pygmy cultures far smaller in height than any known group." (Preface: Worlds before our own.)

The very descriptions of these hominid groups point to the previous comments and those below, regarding angels/demons, nephilim, Satan/devils/ evil angels and the vast majority of weird creatures depicted in the Bible.

Dead Sea Scroll fragments (4Q280 and 4Q286-7):

THOUGH THE DEAD SEA Scrolls are largely fragmented, much could be understood and gained about the religious ancient mindset by a brief study. In the scrolls and parchments that have yet been deciphered, there is a wealth of information. We could also use as a guide to understanding from where certain ideas of a Satan emerged. Two parchments particularly are of relevant interest to this study. In the fragments labelled; (4Q280, and 4Q286-7), is offered something very interesting. Professor Emeritus, of Jewish Studies and Dead Sea Scholar, Geza Vermes writes concerning these fragments:

> "One of these, designated as 4Q286–7, and provisionally entitled 'Blessings (and Curses)', is paralleled by War Rule xiii and Community Rule ii [two

other scroll fragments]. The other (4Q280) depends mainly on Community Rule ii, but reveals Satan's specific name, Melkiresha' (My king is wickedness), the counterpart of Melkizedek (My king is justice), chief of the Army of Light..."[cdlxiv]

Immediately, astute readers of the Christian scripture might recognise a parallel; at least with one of the names. The name particularly new testament readers surely are familiar, Melkizedek. Did the second name strike you as odd, or vaguely intriguing? Notice both names are appointed king? The title 'king - Melek' throughout the Bible is about a monarchy. Which, is only ever attributed to earthbound persons. Recall how the collective of Israel, as an apparently newly established entity had once sought a monarch to rule over them. They wanted a king, just like the nations around them. The collective of Israel felt out-of-sorts; they felt they were being left out of world affairs, so a fellow by the name Saul was chosen (1 samuel 8:1f.) This, despite the system of righteous 'judges' having been already set over them by the Moses figure at the instruction of Yahweh. The ruling Judges were to enact upon, and seek the face of the principle deity- Yahweh on the congregation's behalf (see deuteronomy 16:18f. cf, deuteronomy 1:16; numbers 11:16). Yet apparently, the judges weren't good enough for the population. Israel desired to be governed in a similar fashion to the surrounding nations. They desired a king! This yearning had apparently not abated by the first Century a.d. either; crowds and throngs of people, we are told in New Testament accounts, lined the roadway when the God-man Jesus apparently rode upon an ass up to Jerusalem. From this, we can safely deduce the population was still seeking after the rulership of a king. This deity-man was also pressed about 'restoring the (so-called) kingdom,' see (john 12:12-19 and parallels; acts 1:6). The Jewish deity Yahweh, reluctantly had once offered the Jewish ancestors and anointed their first human king, Saul (1 Samuel 9:1f), then David... and so a pattern followed. Some of these early Israelite 'monarchs' we read governed ancient Israel in the Spirit of Melkizedek, - i.e. with righteousness. Many however did not. To be ruled by the king of wickedness (the 'name' of Satan, – the adversary, - i.e., Melkiresha), is just that. He's what we today refer to as a tyrant, a dictator; an unjust ruler. To the contrary, the saviour/Messiah is typed in the sacred text as the ultimate, and final figure of Melkizedek, – as the ultimate ruler (king) of justice and light. This, according to (hebrews 5:6.) Fitting with the summation of angel and 'sons of God' explanations above. One scholar, Sigmund Mowinckel, had much to say regarding early Israelite kingship. Part of it begins in chapter iv The Future Hope, of his book "He That Cometh". Here he writes,

> "It is important to recognize (sic) that from the very beginning the ideal of kingship in ancient Israel had a certain relation to the future; or, more precisely, it was never fully realized (sic); but there remained always something to be desired. It is of the nature of an ideal that it can never become a present reality, but always belongs to the future. At the very moment when you believe it is already present, it ceases to be ideal; and the ideal itself escapes into the future and so asserts its own nature. It may be associated with something, which is later seen not to correspond to it. Thus, it lives in the borderland between present and future." (Mowinckel, ©2005, p96.)

Thus, the nature of Mowinckel speaks could quite easily be understood as <duality>. There is said to be a dual spiritual nature residing in all humanity. Which survives or dominates our being, the choice is ultimately ours. The sacred text relates there is a kingdom attached to this nature. Said to be gained. A place that is not of this world, it isn't earthly; but comprises the spiritual nature each of us possesses. The deity-man figure Jesus is said to have stated such, conversing with Pilate in john 18:33-37; and in luke 11:14-23 (17-18). When conversing and confronting the believed hypocrisy of the religious establishment. Which was essentially charged to nurture correctly within believers; the figurative nature of Melkizedek, instead of Melkiresha- the 'king of wickedness.' After all, as Mowinckel further writes, "A man's aim (and not least a king's) was to secure the life of his family." (Mowinckel, p 99.) Believers are urged to accept as true such security in 'life,' which is only afforded through the one likened to Melkizedek! To drive this point home; the 'king of wickedness' often reportedly understood today as a most wicked ethereal superhuman spirit being, also described of demons and Devil above. Such a king of wickedness is fallaciously portrayed as sporting horns, a pointed tail, and a three-pronged pitchfork. Reminiscent of numerous other mythological ancient God's and deities. Take for instance the Greeks' Sea God Poseidon ['earth shaker'], or the Runic Norse Sea God, Aegir! Interestingly Frank Joseph in his exposition of the Runes adds to the fallacy of 'Satan' as a creature carrying a triune symbol, enlightening our minds with,

> "Its (the Aegir Rune) triune symbol stands for spiritual synthesis, the reconciliation of matter and spirit with godhood – a meaning also found in the sacred trident of the Greek sea God Poseidon, ruler of the unconscious; the three-pronged scepter of Siva, the Hindu Master of Creation, signifying his omniscient Third Eye; and the three-pronged weapon of the Roman retiarius (gladiator), who, with his net, was the sacred impersonator of Neptune. The sea-God's characteristic fishing net and trident were duplicated in the same objects used by gladiators." (Ch. 6, Aegir – God's of the Runes, Frank Joseph.)

That the symbol Trident throughout antiquity was known and understood to be a representation of reconciliation between matter, spirit, and godhood. It bemuses me why, and at what stage in 'Christian development' did the trident symbol become a weapon attached to the mythological evil figure – Satan? Oh, and never mind that this figure is characterised as also deep Kokkinos (scarlet) in colour. One other truth of this apparent 'most wicked of beings,' however was beautifully captured when Alexander Whyte,

> "...the great Scottish preacher, once stood up in his pulpit in Edinburgh and said: "I have discovered the most wicked man in Edinburgh ..." Then he paused, while the congregation eagerly awaited the name; whereupon the preacher continued— 'Alexander Whyte.'"[cdlxv]

These words should pierce and resonate loudly with many readers today! Alexander, reflecting Pogo, caught in this cited passage what many refuse to acknowledge; that we are the problem; we are our biggest enemy – the big Satan; the greatest adversary![cdlxvi] It is our propensity to the 'malevolence' described in the opening Nail of this book. It is our continued disobedience and a leaning to insecurities, and hatred that hinders and drags us away from receiving the 'fullness' of what is good and decent about humanity. This is often reflected in religious circles as being 'pre-ordained' and 'pre-destined,' that we should partake (acts 4:28; romans 8:29-30; 1 corinthians 2:6-16; ephesians 1:3-14.) Every 'occultist' practice also desires to move its adherents to the same 'enlightenment'. The two mythic figures, of john the baptiser, and the deity–man Jesus made such a reference also; often when confronting the then establishment, or perceived sinful persons in (Matthew 3:1-12; Mark 1:4-8; john 8:44f.) The contrast of this as stated by the book, is the manifestation and acceptance of the inner-self of the figure Jesus – as a type to Melkizedek! To do accordingly for Christian belief, affords living waters to rise from within (john 7:38.) Such a dichotomy is emphasised and brought home by the JPS guide to Jewish Traditions in that, instead of a demonic creature who is the personification of evil and the enemy of God, the biblical word "Satan" is merely a common noun that means "adversary," "accuser," or "hinderer." The role of a Satan is to make things difficult for human beings, so that they can overcome temptations and their evil inclinations and eventually succeed in accomplishing the tasks that God has prepared for them. The venerable scholar James Hastings D.D. ratifies these statements, in the article - Satan, in the "Dictionary of Christ and the Gospels", clearly stating,

> "...suggestions that an evil spirit, a malicious accuser, is described (like the Satan, the accuser of the brethren, διάβολος, κατήγορος of the nt), there is no explicit indication that this is the case..." Even still, Hastings relays the temptation of Messiah, noting his use of Satan in (Matt 4 and other texts), as a proper noun. "...Implying that Satan is the strong man who would enslave mankind, but that Jesus Himself is the Stronger than he, who has appeared for the deliverance of the victims of Satanic power.[cdlxvii]

Satan throughout the Judaeo-Christian book is undoubtedly portrayed as the hostile force in constant opposition to the principle deity Yahweh. The classic 'good' cop – 'bad' cop scenario as it were. But, what then do we do with the passage earlier mentioned (numbers 22:22)? It was only in late Jewish thought that the Satan (adversary) became the impersonal force. An understanding, which the JPS guide also ratifies by announcing it as

> "—strikingly different from the Christian concept of Satan as an autonomous being (Antichrist) who personifies evil."[cdlxviii]

The popular idea of 'Satan' as a presentation, and definite person (I assume by many represents future physical antichrist figure) is still very much inaccurately favoured by many interpreters the world over. The diabolical figure understood as representative of Satan, scholars would attest, only really made headlines in the theology of the Judaeo-Christian book and therefore modern parlance, after the influences of the Greek religions and pantheon. Especially, it would seem when certain passages are encountered in the Old Testament. One such passage is zechariah chapter three. About this chapter, C. Fred Dickason writes,

> "Zechariah 3 could not be understood properly without the reality of Satan opposing and accusing Israel. Here Satan is presented as a definite person who is opposed by the Angel of Jehovah, the pre-incarnate Son of God."[cdlxix]

Unless mistaken in its reading zechariah 3 cannot, as Dickason asserts, be understood without the reality of a personified Satan. But, only if this chapter is read 'with' the prophetic framework, and reference to the accounts of the Messiah figure of the New Testament! Parallels seem to be indeed voluminous. Let us briefly take note of a few. All the alleged prophets of the scripture; ezekiel, zechariah, isaiah and others seem to have one parallel theme. All these writings align with many themes in the Revelation! Or indeed more accurately new testament texts align and mirror some of the materials of the 'prophets' and the old testament corpus. After all, it was from these texts their inspiration was drawn. Parallels between zechariah 3, and the wilderness temptation narratives in the gospels, can be clearly revealed (cf. Matthew 4:1-11; Mark 1:12,13; Luke 4:13-15.) Zechariah, via the spirit of the deity, may have witnessed something that he didn't really understand which was to be enacted by the figure Jesus (=joshua, in Hebrew.) many years into the future. Or so the New Testament would have believers think. The parallels between the charge and mantle laid before joshua in this passage (zechariah 3) is recognised as possibly the very same, or very similar; as offered and exhibited during the earthly life of the deity–man Jesus; which a 'messenger/angel' of the principle deity, Yahweh solemnly also seems to affirm.

> "The Lord who rules overall says, 'If you live and work according to my requirements, you will be able to preside over my temple and attend to my courtyards, and I will allow you to come and go among these others who are standing by you. Listen now, Joshua the high priest, both you and your colleagues who are sitting before you, all of you are a symbol that I am about to introduce my servant, the Branch."[cdlxx]

Recall earlier we guessed that passages such as ephesians 6:10-20, though carrying a 'spiritual warfare' feels for many christians, is but firmly rooted in the earthly dimension. 'Spiritual battles' are earthbound. They begin and end with us here, in this life! There are no 'battles' to be fought in some mystical otherworldly realm – called the heaven (sky – the realm of any mythical deity). That, like the garden of Genesis chapter 2 is a 'shield;' a place of protection and security; the place of harmony and balance.[cdlxxi] The princes, and powers of ephesian 6 refer to the evil inclination, age, as well as the spirit of wickedness working behind or through those operating as antagonists. Many believers believe Yahweh had already spoken a warning of this. First as a plea to the cain figure, by questioning his motives (Genesis 4:6-7f). Then there was the disobedient nature of mankind in (Genesis 6:5-6; see also, proverbs 6:18; matthew 15:19f.) All the prophets of the Old Testament, as well as paul and the other apostles of the New Testament understood this intimately. Which seems to be confirmed by passages like (cf. romans 1:18-26; colossians 3; job 12:7–13; psalms 19:1–6; jeremiah 5:21f). If true, is it not high time the 'Church' realigned itself again to many an 'ancient path', and ceased beating up on those that hold a range of differing views, often labelling them as satanic, evil, or Devil worshippers. The paths their sacred texts also seem to confirm for a reentering into the blessed garden of old (isaiah 35:8, 58:12; jeremiah 6:16). "The Dictionary of the Apostolic Church", article –entitled Devil, adds to these thoughts.

> "It is curious that we never in English use 'Devil' as a proper name without the article, while we always use 'Satan' in this way. Hence the title does not convey to our ears quite the same idea as it conveyed to the Jews. Conversely, we should do well if we did not always treat 'Christ' as a proper name, but sometimes used it as a title or attribute, 'the Christ,' as occasionally in RV (e.g. Lk 24:26). In the OT 'Satan' (from שטן, 'to hate,' 'to be an enemy to,' the root idea being the enmity between the serpent and the seed of the woman, Gn 3:15) is generally used with the article, word השטן, as denoting the adversary: in 1 K 5:4 it is used without the article, as denoting any adversary (ἐπίβουλος, Vulg. Satan). The name 'Satan,' however, had not been transliterated into Greek till shortly before the Christian era, for we never find it so rendered always (ha satatos) ὁ διάβολος. The latter is used as a proper name in the LXX of Job 1:6f., Zec 3:1 (Vulg Satan), and Wis 2:24 (Vulg. Diabolus); and so often in the NT. There we have, as frequently, ὁ Σατανᾶς, [Satanas] almost always with an article, but in 2 Co 12:7 we have Σατᾶν [Satan] or Σατανᾶ [Satana] without the article; some cursives in Rev 20:2 have Σατανᾶς anarthrous. The transliteration 'Satan' is found 34 times in the NT, of which 14 cases are in the Gospels."[cdlxxii]

Conclusion:

CURRENT CONCEPTS AND predictions surrounding malevolence, Satan, or demons must all be relegated to the metaphysical realm. Being derived from mainly an abstract system of reasoning, with 'proof-texts;' those favoured texts of holey books that have been added by adherents as an enhancement to bolster the incomplete, yet complex idealism proposed we notice in not but a few of the latest end-time scenarios. Or the situation is built upon a kind of scare mongering tactic. Which seems to completely ignore the deceptiveness of being human. The motto of many christians: there's a fight to be fought by any whom in one word, abide by the judgment of the ethereal entity or guidance, and therefore, by the judgment of faith, which produces 'good fruits.' Which is a reading of passages like (luke 6:37-49.)

> "Having, therefore, such hope, we use great boldness; and are not as Moses, who put a veil upon his face, so that the children of Israel could not fix

their eyes on the end of that which is annulled. But their thoughts have been darkened; for until this very day, at the reading of the old covenant, the same veil remaineth unremoved, which in Christ is done away. But unto this day, when Moses is read, the veil lieth upon their heart. But whensoever it shall turn to the Lord, the veil shall be taken away. Now the Lord is the Spirit, and where the Spirit of the Lord is, [there is] liberty. But we all, looking on the glory of the Lord with unveiled face, are transformed into the same image from glory to glory, even as by the Lord the Spirit.[cdlxxiii]

However, the opinion, attempting to hold a balanced tension; that although transcendent, the reality beyond what is perceptible to the senses may one day be discovered. In all, it must be reiterated, "The Hebrew Bible does not know an organized (sic) realm of spiritual evil arrayed against the Kingdom of God."[cdlxxiv] Bamberger again in the Epilogue to this volume correctly makes the remark even more clear, stating: "The Hebrew Bible itself, correctly interpreted, leaves no room for belief in a world of evil powers arrayed against the goodness of God."[cdlxxv] It is the 'world' of the old testament that any summation must be derived. Even when seeking answers to the questions that emerge through new testament studies. Better yet, readers are encouraged to source and trace, as much as they are able, the developments of such entities as discussed above. From a position that derives from a time as early as possible before drawing conclusions. It is recognised in the sampling above, there are numerous kinds of materials on offer to assist serious students in arriving at interpretations of the Bible text that is not based upon haphazard conclusions or borne of indiscriminate research or no research at all.

Evil Angels:

ALTHOUGH I HAVE COVERED this subject I think quite extensively already, if believers still insist there are such entities as an 'evil angel', well you'd expect their mention to be numerous. Again brace yourself for an eye-popper! Fact: There is only one occurrence of this phrase in the entire Bible. Found in (psalms 78:49) in modern English translations. This psalm retells the apparent actions the book's God took on behalf of Israel in Egypt, and so this verse obviously related in theory to the Exodus. Which, according to most commentators on the psalm, Israel had suffered amnesia. Two modern translations follow: first, the Septuagint. Second, Logos' "Lexham English Bible" translation. Readers should notice in the lexham translation, the superscripted should literally read 'evil.' It bemuses me then that modern translators place proposed 'literal' renderings as a footnote. Why don't they stop beating around the bush so they and the reader could save time and arrive at a fair understanding by translating these words literally. Why go to the trouble of placing the 'literal' rendering in endnotes? Surely, this just adds to confusion?

> "He sent forth to them the wrath of his anger, anger and wrath and affliction sent through evil angels."[cdlxxvi] "He sent against them his fierce anger, rage and indignation and trouble, a band of [destroying] angels."[cdlxxvii]

Some readers I assume would gleefully presume that this passage is speaking of a demonic entity with some form of 'malicious' intent that was ordered by the deity to wreak havoc upon the Israelites, and thus proving again malevolent angelic beings. No modern commentary has any confirming support for this suggestion. Rather, several older, bygone era commentaries seem to be the only works to have hypothesised and wrestled with this idea. The first: the expository work on the psalm by John Calvin, which in relevant passages states:

> "Some think that devils are here spoken of, because the epithet evil or hurtful is applied to angels. This opinion I do not reject; but the ground upon which they rest it has little solidity. They say that as God dispenses his benefits to us by the ministry of elect angels, so he also executes his wrath by the agency of reprobate angels, as if they were his executioners. This I admit is partly true; but I deny that this distinction is always observed. Many passages of Scripture can be quoted to the contrary. When the army of the Assyrians laid siege to the holy city Jerusalem, who was it that made such havoc among them as compelled them to raise the siege, but the angel who was appointed at that time for the defense (sic) of the Church? (2 Kings 19:35.)" In like manner, the angel who slew the first-born in Egypt (Exod. 11:5) was not

only a minister and an executor of the wrath of God against the Egyptians, but also the agent employed for preserving the Israelites. On the other hand, although the kings of whom Daniel speaks were avaricious and cruel, or rather robbers, and turned all things upside down, yet the Prophet declares, (ch. 10:13,) that holy angels were appointed to take charge of them. It is probable that the Egyptians were given over and subjected to reprobate angels, as they deserved; but we may simply consider the angels here spoken of as termed evil, on account of the work in which they were employed, —because they inflicted upon the enemies of the people of God terrible plagues to repress their tyranny and cruelty. In this way, both the heavenly and elect angels, and the fallen angels, are justly accounted the ministers or executors of calamity; but they are to be regarded as such in different senses. The former yields a prompt and willing obedience to God; but the latter, as they are always eagerly intent upon doing mischief, and would, if they could, turn the whole world upside down, are fit instruments for inflicting calamities upon men."

And secondly, there is the musing of a commentary written 100 years ago: the 'Pulpit Commentary' interestingly reads,

"...By sending evil angels among them. Most modern critics regard this clause as in apposition with the preceding one, and consider the "wrath, indignation, and trouble" to be themselves the "evil angels" spoken about. Some, however, Hengstenberg and Kay, interpret the passage of spiritual beings—not, however, of spirits of evil, who are never said to be ministers of God's wrath, but of good angels, who on this occasion were "ministers of woe."[cdlxxviii]

Clearly early expositors wrestled with the conundrum of whom or what these 'angels' might represent. It would seem however that to interpret evil angels as 'good' angels who are sent on a destructive 'mission', are illogical and beyond any reasonable thought. Either this, or they were somehow angelic entities created by the deity, specifically as troublemakers. Which so is utter nonsensical. As we had discussed and hinted above, how can any 'good' angelic being, whether by divine command or not. Be forced to or voluntarily about face and commit something that it is also said, they cannot do? What kind of deity creates a level of reprobate beings as a violation of a heavenly and natural 'law'? It is intriguing that Calvin quoted a Jewish Rabbi – who so interestingly postulated that the evil messengers coincide with moses and aaron; an explanation that may be closer to the truth.

Evil Angel Hyksos:

IT MAY PERHAPS JUST be another novel conspiracy from author, Ralph Ellis'. He theorises regarding the Hyksos peoples that they were really Egyptians from Lower Egypt.[cdlxxix] Further, as was discussed earlier, re: the Dead Sea Scroll fragments earlier referenced, this verse (psalms 78) stands in further confirmation, I think, of the results and conclusion reached above. How so? In answer, we'd have to give a response to whom the 'evil' destroying angels were. Who represents this evil, destroying band of troublemakers that the supposed benevolent deity, in a fit of rage, afflicted Egypt? Sounds as if this deity is more sadistic than benevolent! It is widely attributed by Bible and other scholars, Immanuel Velikovsky being one early advocate in his "Ages in Chaos", volume one (chapter 2) that the 'destroying angels' are a reference to certain peoples – called the Hyksos. Velikovsky related the Hyksos to the Amalekites of the Bible. Who then were the Hyksos? In its entry on these peoples The International Standard Bible Encyclopaedia" begins,

> "Hyksos hik'sos. A people associated with Bible. The Egyptian priest Manetho, cited by the Jewish historian Josephus... speaks of them as "Shepherd Kings" but the term "Hyksos" is derived from the Egypt. [meaning], "rulers of foreign countries." Manetho (3rd century.)

It is however, very difficult to determine with any lasting confidence, information related to this period of Egypt's history and who the Hyksos actually were. An article from the sacred-texts website offers confirmation and further insight. Stating,

> "In absence of reliable records regarding the Hyksos people, or perhaps we should say peoples, for it is possible that there was more than one invasion, we must cross the frontier of Egypt to obtain some idea of the conditions prevailing in Asia during this obscure but fascinating period. Great changes were passing over the civilized (sic) world. Old kingdoms were being broken

up, and new kingdoms were in process of formation. The immediate cause was the outpourings of pastoral peoples from steppes and plateaus in quest of "fresh woods and pastures new", because herbage had grown scanty during a prolonged "dry cycle" in countries like Arabia, Turkestan, and the Iranian plateau. Once these migrations by propulsion began, they were followed by migrations caused by expulsion." The movements were in some districts accompanied by constant fighting, and a people who displayed the best warlike qualities ultimately became conquerors on a gradually increasing scale. Another cause of migration was the growth of population. When an ancestral district had become crowded, the surplus stock broke away in "waves". But, movements of this kind invariably followed the line of least resistance, and did not necessarily involve marked changes in habits of life, for pastoral peoples moved from upland to upland, as did agriculturists from river valley to river valley and seafarers from coast to coast. When; however, peaceful settlements were effected by nomads in highly civilised areas. An increased impetus must have been given to migration from their native country; where their kindred, hearing of their prosperity began to dream dreams of the land of plenty. Nomads who entered Babylon or Egypt became "the outposts" of those sudden and violent migrations of wholesale character, which occurred during prolonged periods of drought. The Hyksos conquest of Egypt is associated with one of these "dry cycles".[cdlxxx]

The Hyksos people accordingly are said to have moved in and made a vassal state of 'Lower-Egypt', forcing tributes to be paid. The sacred-text article continues,

"The country must have been well governed. Queen Hatshepsut admits as much, for she condemns the Hyksos chiefly on religious grounds; they destroyed the temples—perhaps some were simply allowed to fall into disrepair—and they ruled "not knowing Ra". Had the foreign kings followed the example of some of the most popular Pharaohs, they might have purchased the allegiance of the priests of the various cults; but their desire was to establish the worship of the Hittite Sutekh as a result, it may be inferred, of political influence exercised by the foreign power which received the tribute. One or two of the Hyksos kings affected a preference for Egyptian gods." We must take at a discount the prejudiced Egyptian reference to the hated alien rulers. During the greater part of the Hyksos period peaceful conditions prevailed not only in Egypt but also over a considerable area in Asia. The great trade routes were reopened, and commerce appears to have been in a flourishing condition. Agriculture, therefore, must have been fostered; a surplus yield of corn was required not only to pay tribute but also to offer in exchange for the commodities of other countries. We meet, in Manetho's King Ianias, a ruler who was evidently progressive and enterprising. He is identified with Ian, or Khian, whose name appears on Hyksos relics, which have been found at Knossos, Crete, and Bagdad in Persia. His non-Egyptian title "ank adebu", which signifies "Embracer of Countries", suggests that he was a representative of a great power which controlled more than one conquered kingdom. Breasted, the American Egyptologist, translates Hyksos as "rulers of countries", which means practically the same thing, although other authorities show a preference for Manetho's rendering, "Shepherd Kings", or its equivalent "Princes of Desert Dwellers".

It may be, of course, that "Hyksos" was a term of contempt for a people whom the proud Egyptians made scornful reference to as "the polluted" or "the impure". To this day Europeans are regarded in China as "foreign devils". We regard the Hyksos period as "a dark age" mainly because of the absence of those records, which the Egyptians were at pains to destroy. Perhaps we are also prone to be influenced by their denunciations of the foreigners. We have no justification for assuming, however, that progress was arrested for a prolonged period extending over about two centuries. The arts did not suffer decline, nor did the builders lose their skill. So thoroughly was the kingdom reorganised that the power of the feudal lords was completely shattered. Even the Twelfth-Dynasty kings were unable to accomplish as much. The Hyksos also introduced the domesticated horse into Egypt, but at what period we are unable to ascertain. Manetho makes no reference to it in his brief account of the invasion. If, however, there were charioteers in the foreign army when it swept over the land, they could not have come from Arabia, and Bedouins were not likely to be able to manufacture or repair chariots. Only a rich country could have obtained horses at this early period. They had newly arrived in western Asia and must have been scarce and difficult to Obtain.[cdlxxxi] Of all articles scanned, attempting to explain the Hyksos that logos Bible dictionaries and encyclopaedia's offer, there seems to be confirmation of the many contentious concerns regarding this period in history. Few Bible scholars can come to a consensus surrounding this mysterious point of times past. Debates still rage

DECONSTRUCTING ENDTIME DELUSIONS

between various scholars and the issues associated with the Hyksos peoples, and the relation between their invasion of Egypt and the Exodus. It does though seem reasonable to place their movement into Egyptian lands at, or very near after an Exodus narrative. If so, surely those that departed Egypt was confronted by these peoples (see Velikovsky, chapter 2.) If then as the opinion of several writers and scholars; i.e., Velikovsky, stands true, that a real connection to the Hyksos peoples could be made to Bible passages such as (psalm 78:49) being possibly an informal reference to the Amalekites, or as Ellis' hypothesis, ruling Pharaohs and clans of Lower Egypt. Then, it stands to reason and logic that the reference to destroying or evil angels confirms my assertion of the two dead sea scroll texts above: that the (evil angels) too are human hoarders and pillagers, and not some imaginary malevolent 'other-worldly' creature sent from the deity to cause devastation. Let us now for a time, turn our thoughts to a passage many believers are certain as being a reference to 'end-times.' Large quantities of Christian material. No doubt will be published, especially this year (2014), for it is about a series of blood red moon eclipses.

Nail Fourteen:

A darkened sun, and bloodied moon: 'assumed' in Christian theology, to attest a viewing of a coming Messiah, by Prophet Joel. (Joel 2:28-32):

IN THE BIBLE BOOK ACTS of the Apostles, chapter 2, we have a description and explanation by a bloke 'called' Peter to allay the fears of the growing crowds. Readers familiar with this passage will recall that this chapter is entered around the annual Jewish festival of Shavuot (Pentecost). We read the disciples are apparently camped out, actually hiding from authorities in the upper room of a mate– waiting for instructions. Suddenly, according to the story, strange happenings alight upon those in the room (upon their heads)! Flames of 'fire' begin to appear from thin air and alight upon each one present. So goes the description. Surely, though if while reading this, questions of validity would descend from our minds. Has this ever occurred formerly, let alone since it was recorded in this book? If not, I must say this is again another example of Taurus excretio! If there are no records of something like this occurring formerly, let alone since, how can religious people assert it as justifiably true? As far as can be determined at this present time, no single extant text outside this Bible story, conveys such an occurrence ever taking place! Why are no extant 'official' records surrounding such an event available? Surely, such a momentous event caused a frenzied Paparazzi to follow closely this band of 'newly formed celebrities.'

Leaving aside such questions for you to ponder at leisure, we know from studies of mythology that wind and the presence of 'fire' scholars agree denote a theophany – that is, a manifestation of the God/deity – here, of the deity–man Jesus. Other places in the Old Testament specifically confirm the theophany theory, see for example, deuteronomy 4:32-36. All present in the room are somehow affected by this odd occurrence;

every person in the room suddenly begins to spontaneously combust – (into praises)! Not only that. What each disciple present utters is we are informed, was an unknown, and unlearned regional language! Amazing! We are then informed that such 'babbling' causes quite a bit of commotion. As it should. Such a thing has never in-recorded history amazed a population ever! The story further narrates that many people hear but do not yet believe! Neither should they believe I say. Simply, because men from Galilee who for some reason are now residing in Jerusalem, are apparently singing praises of some recently executed individual! If such a thing occurred who in their right mind extols a criminal, aside us Aussies (we have a particular liking to a ditty that praises the theft of a sheep, 'Waltz sing Matilda'). So, what is going on in this Bible chapter? First, Christian historian A. Wedderburn interestingly poses the statement,

> "Whether an outpouring of the Spirit took place on this occasion, clearly the centre of the reborn Jesus-movement moved to Jerusalem at a fairly early point in its history. Also, at some point of time, though not necessarily on this day, some mass ecstatic experience took place."

Many of those gathered in the city stumble around dumbfounded, but, accepting of what was happening. As an aside, we often do so to this day, with certain people at festivals and sporting venues. So, nothing really astoundingly 'new', or outrageous. I must wonder though, is this the first recording and exhibition of 'new' narcissism? Some of the gathering crowd may surely have thought so, as they mockingly announce them as drunkards (acts 2:1-13.) But, then again, remember the context: throngs of people were in Jerusalem for a festival, and most likely had a big night on the town the night before. It wasn't too long however before a scruffy figure stands and motions for the growing spectator's attention. As the murmuring stills, he began to shout, in a slurring kind of manner:

> "...Men, Jews, and all you that reside at Jerusalem; be this known to you, and hearken to my words. For these are not intoxicated, as you suppose: for lo, it is yet but the third hour. But this is what was spoken by Joel the Prophet: It shall be in the last days, saith God, that I will pour my Spirit upon all flesh: and your sons shall prophesy, and your daughters: and your

young men shall see visions, and your old men shall dream dreams. And upon my servants and my handmaids will I pour my Spirit, in those days, and they shall prophesy. And I will give signs in heaven, and prodigies on earth, blood, and fire, and vapor of smoke. And the sun shall be turned into darkness, and the moon into blood, before that great and fearful day of the Lord come. And it shall be, that whoever will call on the name of the Lord, shall live. Men, sons of Israel, hear these words: Jesus the Nazarene, a man made manifest among you by God, by those deeds of power and prodigies which God wrought among you by his hand, as you yourselves know; him, being hereto appointed by the prescience and the good pleasure of God, —you have delivered into the hands of the wicked; and have crucified and slain. But God hath resuscitated him, and hath loosed the cords of the grave; because it could not be, that he should be held in the grave..."[cdlxxxii]

All astute students of the New Testament would be aware this speech of the bloke called Peter is quoted from the past. Directly pilfered from a passage of the Old Testament; from (probably by now) a very shabby and wine stained portion of a speech one made by another drunkard- the shaman Joel. Of particular interest, and requiring further investigation is verse (20). Now, take a glance at the Old Testament account in Joel, verse 2:31 in Standard English bibles. Joel prophesied long ago that the "sun will be darkened, and the moon will be turned to blood..." So, according to Joel the sun will 'fade to black', i.e. die (and turn supernova), and somehow, maybe because of this even, the moon will dramatically change, from its silvery sheen, to blood red. What does that mean? What stands as an acceptable meaning to these phrases? Despite the numerous assertions by modern commentators peddling a latest end-time scenario, the darkened sun, and bloodied moon does not comply with the modern ideal of a yet future fulfilment at the end-of-the-age. Quick, get a wheel Barrow for that assumption is more Taurus excretio! Let's break it down into chunks.

The phrase, 'the sun shall be turned to darkness' is only found (2x) twice in the entire sixty-six books of the sacred book! Once in the book of Acts, but, as we have seen, originating in Joel 2:31. The phrase, 'the moon turned to blood' so is only found in these two passages. Both occurrences that are in the Old Testament and the New Testament admittedly

DECONSTRUCTING ENDTIME DELUSIONS

describe a solar and lunar <eclipse> and other celestial catastrophes (phenomena). That is according to the whole chapter of Joel, (Joel 2). To grasp a meaning within the context surrounding both phrases let us from a typical Christian perspective, revisit luke's first parallel accounting (luke 21:5-28.) There is undoubtedly much that can and should be commented on these and the many other old and New Testament parallel verses. However for the sake of brevity, I will endeavour to be succinct. The 'clue' maybe to a correct interpretation in understanding the whole of these passages of luke 21, are two verses (vv. 5-6.) The deity–man Jesus is recorded to have pronounced the destruction of the Jewish temple, which history tells us, is historically accurate. Occurring in the year 70 C.E. As was noted earlier in another passage, most unfortunate for believers is the fact many bibles have placed titles with passages. Check your own bibles, most are labelled: Destruction of the Temple Predicted, The Disciple's two questions, followed by Signs of the end of the Age, Jesus foretells the future, or Signs of Christ's Coming (HCSB, NIV, NLT, NKJV.) These are all designations and the summations of modern scholars. Such titles to press home the point, are not part of the original text. But, allow as we have also noted earlier, readers to misconstrue what they read. Precisely, as only the small portion of text directly beneath such titles are read and given judgment and interpretation. A title such as any of the above will, and does lead readers to conclude Jesus is speaking about a far-reaching future event. Maybe an event that stretches into our day or beyond? If this is the case, such preconceptions are dragged into the modern era and reading of many other parallel passages that have similar wording and phraseology. Like, acts 2 and matt 24, and Mark 13. This should never be! Thankfully the translators of the Aramaic, and The Hebrew-English Bible, the (ASV, RSV, YOUNG'S LIT.), or any 'original' Greek text, do not feel the need to add any titles. Rather, these particular translations of the sacred texts allow the reader to view the whole passage without interruption. Meaning they can be read in context. The God-man Jesus, in much of luke's record is recognised as simply 'prophesying' the events and turmoil surrounding the sacking of Jerusalem. But, maybe he was not only speaking with this event. A remarkable feat in the least if indeed, he could do this? Forty years into the future. He was believers might say, also prophetically announcing events of his own crucifixion. Both assumptions cannot be asserted as factual; however, because a difficulty lay in answering the question of whether he (Jesus) could know, with unparalleled certainty, All things, even events of a far-flung future? There is however, also apparently a transition into a yet future event (luke 21:11f) according to scholars mixed into this account. Where his apostles and believers will be scattered (probably represented by the stars falling from the heavens) and systematically; persecuted, rounded up, sought after, even slain. Somewhat confirming my summations here is Gary DeMar in his book titled, "Last Days Madness..." He writes,

> "The language that Jesus uses is typical of Old Testament imagery where stellar phenomena represent people and nations. The people of Israel were represented as stars (Genesis. 22:17; 26:4; Deut. 1:10). The flags of many nations include the use of multiple stars..."[cdlxxxiii] Furthermore, "The first chapter of Genesis gives us a clue as to why the Bible compares the sun, moon, and stars to rulers and their kingdoms: The sun ("greater light") and the moon ("lesser light") are said to "govern the day" and "night" (Gen. 1:16). Can we find examples of the sun and moon being used as symbols of government? In a dream Joseph saw "the sun and the moon and eleven stars ... bowing down" to him (Genesis 37:9). The sun, moon, and stars represented Joseph's father, mother, and brothers. Joseph, being only "seventeen years old" (Genesis 37:2), was under the government of his father, mother, and older brothers. In reality, they ruled over Joseph. Upon hearing about Joseph's dream, Jacob asked him, "What is this dream that you have had? Shall I and your mother and your brothers actually come to bow ourselves down before you to the ground?" (37:10). Joseph's father and brothers immediately understood the significance of the images in his dream. They were not looking for the sun, moon, and stars to bow down before Joseph. Stars are used as symbols of earthly rulers and governments in other places in Scripture. Judges 5:19–20 is a good example. In verse 19 we read that "kings came and fought." In verse 20 we read that "the stars fought from heaven." Both verses are describing the same event in terms of Hebrew parallelism. The stars are symbols of kings and their armies. Stars as we see them in space were not fighting from heaven."[cdlxxxiv]

DECONSTRUCTING ENDTIME DELUSIONS

Eclipsing the mind Darkened Sun and Bloodied Moon

ADDING AN INTERESTING background to the solar and lunar experiences highlighted above. Is comments of such phenomenon by "The IVP Bible Background Commentary: Old Testament." Notes to (Joel 2:31) are first, and then (isaiah 53:4-10), which respectfully state:

> "Joel 2:31. eclipses in the ancient Near East. In Neo-Assyrian times, eclipses represented the most powerful and deadly omens, being considered the "prime revealer." They were the most frequent cause for the substitute king ritual being invoked (see comment on Isa 53:4–10). The nature of the threat they signified was judged by the precise time of their occurrence, the position in the sky at the time of the eclipse and the direction from which the eclipse took place. The combination of signs in heaven and on earth would bring further confirmation of the sign and would suggest a more drastic consequence."[cdlxxxv]

Isaiah 53:4–10. substitutionary rites in the ancient Near East. The rite of the substitute king was used in Assyria when evil omens (especially an eclipse) suggested the life of the king was in danger. It is attested primarily in the reign of Esarhaddon in the early seventh century but had been practiced for over a thousand years. It worked on the principle that evil could be transferred from one individual to another. When the dangerous period was to occur, the king was replaced by a substitute on whom the evil fate could fall. In some cases this substitute was someone considered of no significance and was perhaps even mentally or physically impaired. He was then exalted to high status and office for as long as one hundred days, though often a shorter period. During this time the real king was kept in relative isolation (a virtual exile) and participated in numerous purification rituals. Meanwhile the substitute was going through the motions of being king and sitting on the throne. He was portrayed as the shepherd (a common title for Mesopotamian kings), but one could understand that he was simply a sheep about to be slaughtered. At the end of the period the substitute was put to death so that the evident design of the gods would be accomplished. The omens had suggested that it was the will of the gods to crush him. As one text puts it, he died to save the king and the crown prince. He was given a rich state funeral and an offering was made and exorcism rituals performed (including washings and sprinklings) so that the omens would be cancelled and the days of the king could be prolonged."[cdlxxxvi]

By supplying these comments readers are readily able to notice maybe some mirror effects with the recorded life and execution of the gospel's Jesus figure. It is after all presumed that he became some sort of 'substitute' in like manner as described above. Obviously, the shaman (Joel) witnessed an omen unfold: a lunar eclipse, and a celestial catastrophe. Which he perceived as raining down debris that maybe also was a cause to a violent volcanic eruption. Possibly taking place in one of his asc episodes (Altered State of Consciousness) - dream states. Yet, the omens he witnessed this time differed to the events of a close encounter the earth had with the comet Typhon. Although each caused widespread upheaval and destruction throughout the earth: events witnessed by many peoples of many nations, and which they recorded in some detail. If this is so, maybe Joel, attached such an omen, like other peoples of the ancient world, to the confirmation of a coming messianic figure, provided a form of 'messianism' was prevalent at the time. (see comments regarding 'Eschatology' in Appendix 3). But, we are getting ahead of ourselves.

Now consider: believers today continue to attach 'like' meanings to such Old Testament oracles always. In this sense, modern believers are no different to the unknown authors of the gospels and New Testament, as this is exactly how they treated such texts also. Why else would we read that Peter relates the Joel passage to the mythical figure Jesus, and the events that eventually, caused his demise (if indeed they themselves are factual?) It appears that New Testament readers are lulled into believing that this episode in the book of acts, is truly historical. But again, empirical evidence is difficult to attain. Besides, such an occurrence has never been repeated. Further, more often than not we forget this world is a volatile little speck of dust and rock hurtling through a violent Universe. It is filled with violence and disruption. Not only are we humans a violent bunch, but also the earth herself heaves and groans with earthquakes, lashing storm cells; volcanoes and other natural ferocious phenomena. Some of which are the result of close extraterrestrial encounters; the same described by Velikovsky. Though the earth supports life upon her back, much of that life is flat out malevolent, as bacteria and other catastrophe making phenomena. Add also an interesting parallel: 'the gigantic eruption of Toba. A volcano in Sumatra, 74,000 years ago. It shut out the sun (darkened its rays) for six years. Causing the deaths of all but an estimated 2000 of our human forebears.'[cdlxxxvii] So are believers still willing to hold to a belief and faith in a munificent 'supreme deity' in charge? A deity who cares and 'looks' out for your every need? What explanation could such a deity offer for these and the many other 'natural' spiteful occurrences? Occurrences that kill countless innocent people globally, just as easily as one would snuff out a candle.

Lunar eclipses natural occurrences the world over:

LUNAR ECLIPSES WE NOW know occur regularly the globe over. They are naturally occurring phenomena. Scientific advances give us the reasons and answers now for many strange heavenly phenomena. We now are able to scientifically answer questions like what causes a moon to glow red? At wiki.answers an explanation is given,

> "The orange and red tints that the Sun and Moon sometimes take on are caused by the particles in the Earth's atmosphere. When light (or more specifically, packets of light called photons) from an astronomical object [which] passes through the Earth's atmosphere, it scatters off of particles in the latter. It turns out that these particles like to scatter blue light more than they do red light; so "bluer" photons (those with shorter wavelengths) tend to get scattered, and "redder" photons (those with longer wavelengths) pass through." Astronomical objects look redder from Earth than they would from space, because the redder wavelengths from the objects penetrate the atmosphere better than the bluer ones. Incidentally, this is why the sky is blue: blue light from the Sun is scattered in all directions on its way to the Earth. But how does this explain the occasional redness of the Moon or the Sun? You... may have noticed that they always occur when the Sun or Moon is close to the horizon. If you think about it, sunlight or moonlight must travel through the maximum amount of atmosphere to get to your eyes when the Sun or Moon is on the horizon (remember that that atmosphere is a sphere around the Earth). So, you expect more blue light to be scattered from Sunlight or Moonlight when the Sun or Moon is on the horizon than when it is, say, overhead; this makes the object look redder. In other

words, the Sun or Moon tends to look orange or red when it is rising or setting because that's the time when the light has to travel through the most atmosphere to get to you. The effect is exacerbated when there are thin clouds in front or behind the Sun or Moon: the clouds themselves often glow bright pink as well, because they are so good at scattering blue light."[cdlxxxviii]

With these comments let us cast our minds to some words of Jesus, recorded in (luke 24:13-49). Speaking with those on the road to Emmaus, he (as the 'risen,' although astoundingly veiled christ) says, "That all things written of me, in the Law of Moses and in the prophets and in the psalms, must be fulfilled." Indeed, for many believers the case seems to be affirmed. Has a reader ever asked why the two travellers did not recognise to whom they were speaking? If a truthful account, not only was this man a Jewish shaman peering into a future state and peeking behind its veil regarding the destruction of the (physical, earthly) temple, but also maybe, regarding the destruction of his own person and the supposed fulfilment of Israel's God's, who by then had obviously been transferred from a planetary-deity (as described earlier), to something relegated to the metaphysical realm. The redemptive agenda for all humanity – whether the man Jesus knew that he was to suffer crucifixion or by some other means, as we have noted above, is difficult to attain. This second point; clearly, he (Jesus) and the disciples following believed it so. Further, Fitzmyer writes,

> "Yet there is no reason to question the substantial conviction that he undoubtedly had that he would die violently at the hands of his opponents." (Catechism. p.101.)

Such a violent end to life was, historians attest, only carried out for the insurrectionist and criminal. So, this statement does not paint the man Jesus as a very loving, gentle, man of high status as many believers assume him to have been. Statements regarding the darkened sun, and bloodied moon, metaphorically speaking, could only for the believer. Hold a meaning linked to the demise of the deity–man Jesus and events surrounding that period. Including the demise (or beginning of it) of the established system of authority (religious or otherwise). The (physical) sun indeed was darkened, eclipsed; we are told, in mid-daylight hours, for about three hours (see, matthew 27:45, cf, isaiah 13:10; ezekiel. 32:7; Joel 2:31; 3:15; matthew. 24:29; mark 13:24; luke 21:25.) There were, it is also recorded calamities in the earth. According to (matthew 27:51-4 and parallels). Tombs were opened. Corpses raised...all as recorded in the esteemed gospel accounts. Nonetheless, all these accounts rely solely upon subjective faith-based reasoning. There do not seem to be any other records in history that confirm these events actually happening. We have only the words as recorded in the gospels. So end-time beliefs, and the events of a crucifixion, resurrection etc., and that surrounding a darkened sun and bloodied moon relies also solely on subjective means. Faith – you might cry! Yet this is, as stated numerously already, is nothing else than reliance on the provision of no evidence. The sun as it does in most ancient myth, represents to the Jew, the Word/ the written Torah, "the radiance of the glory of deity/ God" (i.e. the Egyptian God Ra, hebrews 1:3f) on one level. The moon, representing the God-man Jesus (as the lesser light (of hebrews 1-3, cf Genesis 1:14-18.)), and the 'stars falling from the heavens' that the prophets/ shaman of old speak of (isaiah 13:10, ezekiel 32:7) represent the disciples; the followers of the God-man and their actions during the recorded trial and crucifixion. Men and women scattered, denied him and hid themselves away... (matthew 24:29.cf. deuteronomy 1:10, where the Moses figure metaphorically likens the people to stars. See other metaphoric use also: in Daniel 12:3, Revelation 22:16) that believers are also told to believe blindly. The figure Jesus again obviously is recorded as believing

> "...all things written of me, in the Law of Moses and in the prophets and in the psalms, must be fulfilled" (luke 24:44).

The tribulation he (Jesus) is recorded to have spoken about (Matthew 24:29; Mark 13:24) I see in the mind of the gospel writer, as relating directly to his trials and scourging prior to crucifixion. The future lay behind us, completely veiled from our understanding and knowledge. But, past events confront us regularly. We are constantly reminded of these occurrences. The recordings of the Judaeo-Christian sacred texts are no fewer than recordings after the fact! They are not eyewitness accounts. The writers most surely spiritualised certain known past events, attaching them to phenomena they had received and been taught as shamanic oracles. Accordingly, the so-called last-days had begun with the apparent crucifixion, or further back, with the birth of the Jesus figure, thirty-three years prior! The anomalous phrase 'Day of the Lord' would also seem to parallel these thoughts. The (ESV) Bible in its entire corpus uses this phrase no more than (21x), twenty-one times in a mere (20) verses. This may cause a strong remonstrance. At least because of 2 Peter 3:10, which reads "...then the heavens will pass away..." As if this is a yet Literal future state Yet, many reading these verses are blinded to the fact that this verse is part of Peter's word of remembrance. He exhorts his readers,

> "This is now the second letter that I am writing to you, beloved. In both of them I am stirring up your sincere mind by way of reminder, that you should remember the predictions of the holy prophets and the commandment of the Lord and Savior through your apostles..."[cdlxxxix]

The same Greek word in 2 Peter 3:10 translated passed away is found in other New Testament texts also (Matthew 5:18 (x2); Mark 13:20; 2 corinthians 5:17.) These other passages surely do not hint at a far future fulfilment! It is ridiculous to even postulate such a scenario. The day of the Lord was, apparently, and had come with the propitiation the apostles believed that was rendered by their God-man Jesus. This is the notion. The believer currently has and continues to live. So, accordingly, if such a premise that is true to form, we are in 'the last days', and have been so for no less than the past two thousand years. Biblically then, 'last-days/end-times is noway a reference to a far-off, or near future day to come. Such an understanding is insightfully and glaringly confirmed by 18th century scholar Johann A. Bengel, who wrote in (1742) in commentary on acts 2:17-18, "All the days of the New Testament are last days: and these last days have now advanced far forward.[cdxc] It is thus, a believer's 'job', to be compelled to continue to live in and by belief of

DECONSTRUCTING ENDTIME DELUSIONS

that and its fulfilment, and within the blessed expectation of witnessing the Second-Advent. Of (1 thessalonians 1:10.)

Returning to Joel. The Prophet Joel, by the so-called spirit of the deity, we can maybe as also with other Old Testament Prophets recognise, possibly calculated celestial events and related them regarding a Messiah figure – which are the last days. If true for Joel and others recorded as Bible Shaman's, such a prophecy was yet future. But, there is no true way to empirically test such a notion. None of us were there at the time of the oracle, and scientific acumen was not as advanced as today. Might this then open us to questions like; was Messiah common? That Joel and every other contemporary 'prophetic voice' can be legitimately slotted into any New Testament passage as purely based upon again, not fact, but subjective faith. Joel and his contemporaries were more likely recording what they witnessed in a sky vision; what they witnessed as an astronomical phenomenon. A celestial upheaval that ravished, and raped the earth: just as Immanuel Velikovsky had written in his book, "Worlds in Collision". In confirmation Velikovsky writes in the section, Samples from the planets, "Since the planets were God's, stones hurled by them or by the comets created in their encounters, were feared as divine missiles, and when they fell and were found, they were worshipped." (Velikovsky, p289). In another section, Planets worship in Judea in the Seventh Century (b.p. before the present era), we insightfully read that planetary-deities and the stones they hurled to the earth, and the cult worships they inspired was present and very much the culture of Judea and Israel. The Scriptures do not hide the fact that in Judea, as well as in Israel. The planetary cult was the official cult with the priests and with kings, with many prophets and with the people. Thus Jeremiah, contemporary of King Josiah, says:

> "At that time, says the Lord, the bones of the kings of Judah, the bones of its officials, the bones of the priests, the bones of the prophets, and the bones of the inhabitants of Jerusalem shall be brought out of their tombs; and they shall be spread before the sun and the moon and all the host of heaven, which they have loved and served, which they have followed, and which they have inquired of and worshiped; and they shall not be gathered

or buried; they shall be like dung on the surface of the ground."●[cdxci] And again he says, "And the houses of Jerusalem and the houses of the kings of Judah shall be defiled like the place of Topheth—all the houses upon whose roofs offerings have been made to the whole host of heaven, and libations have been poured out to other gods."[cdxcii]

"Thus we see the centuries-long struggle for the Jewish God, Creator and not unanimated planet, itself a creation, being carried on in the closing decades before the exile to Babylon with the help of the book whose authorship was ascribed to Moses." (Worlds in Collision.)

Modern conceptions of 'missiles from the heavens' worship or reverence are numerous. The most recognisable today is the Kaaba – the black stone – of Islam. Though not essentially or officially (according to some sources) worshipped, which would constitute idolatry; this meteorite is however greatly revered by all Muslims. They pray to it, make pilgrimage to view it, and have pictures of it adorning the walls of their houses. Remember Peter of acts chapter 2. He was most probably caught up in the working of a subjective faith when he excitedly announced and made a connection with one of Joel's oracles, along with the others who were, we assume, imbued by the 'power' of the (spirit). They most likely didn't wish to have the name of a recently slaughtered sage wiped from existence, as we saw was the thought process of at least earlier Egyptian records. As happened with Akhenaten. Rather, knowing numerous myths floating around the region they attached their sage and his exploits to them, which subsequently became a new 'religion! If anything, these Jewish men/women believed the end-times/ Last-days had surely begun, and it was therefore not pointing to a yet future event. Let alone a time closer to our day, or beyond. After all the presumed crucified God-man believed as much also, 'reportedly' saying with his final breath, "It is completed!" (john 19:30.)

Armageddon Antichrist. Gog and Magog final conflict:

ARMAGEDDON IS ALSO a much-confused and debated area particularly for today's Christian. Precisely because it is a greatly favoured

DECONSTRUCTING ENDTIME DELUSIONS

subject of those who would wish to promote the latest scenario of the perceived end-times. It involves for advocates several sub-subjects, like gog, and magog, and who, the what, and the when of 'antichrist'. As has been voiced above there are many and often confusing interpretations. And this subject offers no less. Many are not dissimilar to the confusing world of 'rapture' with its pre, post, mid-rapture, corresponding to the pre, post. And mid tribulation hypotheses... The major cause to this confusion is undoubtedly: "We no longer understand how all the pieces fit together. We may attempt to put things together piecemeal, if we even care at all. We puff ourselves up with our knowledge, separate ourselves from one another and fill the gaps in our knowledge with religion, superstition and speculation. Of course, we think that we are right in our knowledge and everyone else is wrong and we twist the truth to fit the agenda we have to fill our egos. This all causes separation between individuals and between man and creation." (Genesis, Zen, and Quantum Physics, p128. elect., (pdf.)) Lawrence Chesnut in the final chapter in his little booklet on "Armageddon" pointedly adds,

> "The great unanswered, and puzzling question with many today is the nature of this "Armageddon" warfare. There is hardly a religious movement of our day, but what is preaching and teaching it as a great physical and literal combat, that is to happen in the future. This great literal combat as advocated by many will never be. The Bible does not teach it that way."[cdxciii]

Such comments may cause more than a few readers to scratch their heads in disbelief. What? But, my sacred texts 'clearly' state there will be such warfare. Of that I am certain. For many, it says so in 'Revelation.' How can most if not everything published today on this subject be erroneous? Surely Lawrence, those already cited, and I am gravely mistaken. Either that, or we are heretical. The question however is not whether such a war and battle shall take place. The more pressing question likely should be; if such a battle were to take place, "What is the nature of it, and where will this great battle be fought, and by whom..." Another author, H. C. Heffren, in one of his booklets, "Who is the Antichrist (including the Great Tribulation)", nailed the current dilemma of our times perfectly:

> "In more modern times there has been a rash of prophetic preaching about so-called antichrists including Mussolini, Hitler, the black pope, and a continual parade of individuals whom some expositors seem to find some biblical reason for calling antichrists. The only thing this confusion proves is that a great deal of speculation surrounds this subject. Since Nemo-deity is apparently not the author of confusion, we have to brand most of these ideas as whims of human conjecture."[cdxciv]

Many authors, particularly at "Prophesy Blog spot.com" continually propagate the summations that these authors seem to oppose. Undoubtedly, most 'bloggers' and religious commentators today are millennialists. Vehemently holding to the well-worn views of a dispensational interpretation method of the scripture. As might be guessed, I am not advocating any of these views. Frankly, I don't care for such claptrap. Every view from whatever particular angle approached by religious authors of such subjects is subjective; from their own heads. But, it is not the intention here to review those hundreds of opposing theories of a future and literal... [antichrist. Nor are we particularly interested in disseminating a]

> "... reign of righteousness upon the earth; for, as one writer states it, no two Millennial teachers "fix it up the same way. Suffice it to say that during the last few years thousands upon thousands of volumes have been printed and circulated over the world, teaching the people to hope for a better age yet future, when Christ will establish his kingdom, and offer superior means of grace to mankind. Thousands are today adhering to such teaching, and are thus being deceived with a vain hope. Our love for the many precious souls thus deceived, and for the many more who may come under the influence of such nefarious doctrines, prompts us to lift up our voice like a trumpet and pen the following lines in the name of Jesus. No matter how fascinating a thing is, how beautiful and pleasing to the taste, there can be no real benefit derived from holding the same if it only be a creation of fancy, or the result of wrong interpretation of scripture; nor is God in any way glorified in us holding an erroneous hope..."[cdxcv]

Though the above comments by Riggle will no doubt be recognised as leaning heavily to an Amillennialist point of view, and even if they do I but see some value in them. The alarm he raises is that to this

DECONSTRUCTING ENDTIME DELUSIONS

day, thousands upon thousands of volumes continue to be published. Books of this sort are lining bookshelves the world over. Most which are undoubtedly misleading. In recent years online sellers, the likes of 'Survivormall.com' and 'superstore.wnd.com', are bulging (if an Internet site is capable of doing so?) with volumes and materials sporting an end-time theme. From the amillennialist, to a post/ pre/ mid-tribulation, and every other apocalyptically inspired theme imaginable. I wonder however, whether sentiments in the Foreword of, "God, Order, and Chaos: René Girard and the Apocalypse", aren't worthy of a reader serious consideration. Here it is stated,

> "In the gospels, the story is told from the perspective of the scapegoated person, asserting his innocence. This, according to Girard, has the effect of unmasking cultures based on violence. Humanity is thereby challenged to initiate a way of renunciation of violence advocated and practised by Jesus, lest they destroy themselves. In contrast with human society's version of the story of the fate of the victims who are regarded as troublemakers and subversives. The words of Caiaphas 'it is fitting for one man to die for the people' (John 11:50) represents the sentiments of the leaders of state security forces down the centuries. Jesus identifies with the victims in his society and as a result sets in train a process of victimization (sic) of him, which leads to a violent reaction as the political elite, plots to rid himself or herself of a troublemaker."[cdxcvi]

The premise of the deity of: "Order and Chaos", seems to be questions surrounding the idea that 'end time' apocalyptic events as described in numerous sacred texts represent little else than what many Eastern religions have averted for eons; that being, a challenge to relinquish and renounce human violence lest we destroy ourselves! Cannot the apocalyptic text of the New Testament and indeed many old testaments stories also read, as the foreword continues:

> "...as the unmasking of the violence of human culture by the gospel of the slain Lamb. The lamb's death and exaltation unmask the violence of the world, which in Rev 6 [Zech 1:8; 6:2, 3, 6.] and following is described in all its horror as the vindication of the lamb provokes a violent reaction in an unjust world." Such a notion would seem to align with the opening statements about the state of the earth recorded in Genesis.

Said to be a very literal rendering, Jeff Benner offers the following interpretation of Genesis 1:2:

> "The land, she existed empty and unfilled. In addition, chaos was over the faces of the deep. And the wind of the Powers brooded over the faces of the waters." (Brenner and Calpino, p32.)

Comments by the authors regarding this verse state that all the raw materials that went into making this world come from a state of 'chaos.' So logically without chaos, the opportunity for 'order' to arise might not be afforded. Thus, despite what christianity believes from the opening verses in Genesis, Chaos is not an enemy but can be quite honestly viewed in the same light as the first law of thermodynamics. This law simply states energy can be neither created nor destroyed (which is a conservation of energy). Thus, power generation processes and energy sources actually involve conversion of energy from one form to another; instead of creation of energy from nothing. We have earlier mentioned it, but maybe this is what the writer meant when it was penned that the anticipation of the 'earth' longs for restoration (see, romans 8:22), and the present suffering which paul seems to offer as a similitude of chaos. Jeff Benner and Michael Calpino further declare,

> "It was as if there were light atoms and dark atoms all mixed together and the Elohim (powers) were both. 1 Kings 8:12 says that Elohim lives in a dark cloud and Isaiah 45:7 tells us that God created the darkness and the light, good and evil. Elohim, 'God,' is associated with both order/light/shalom and chaos/darkness/evil. We often don't like to think of God as being involved with things we consider negative but there is nothing that is outside of God, or outside of Ayn Soph. Without the evil, we would not know the good. Without chaos, we would not know order. Without darkness, we couldn't appreciate the light. In Chinese culture this is the yin/yang, two opposing forces inextricably linked in the world." (Genesis, Zen, and Quantum Physics, p33.)

What then do we make of the final 'book' of our testament, Revelation? Is it depicting some future 'end-time' scenario? Where by the conclusion to the perceived calamitous forecasts in its pages, a Messiah figure finally is exposed/ or returns, and all humanity is once and for-all restored to its original status of innocence. Or, is such a 'world-view' skewed, and frankly, not the overall objective of the announcements of the presumed author and Prophet - john. One of the problems any reader faces when attempting to unpack the final 'book' of Revelation, is it is often viewed as a text 'predicting' a future state. Yet, as with statements and much of the discussion yet explored, the book of 'Revelation' is undoubtedly another of those supposed enigmatic texts that are all too often misconstrued by believers. Having an application that to many reaches far off into the future distance. Reaching into our day, or a not-so-future date? This ideology again is most surely unwarranted. If Heffren, secular scientists, and other theorists are correct, this text could just as well be studied as not only that which lies beyond human knowledge, but more so, as a treaty by the 'energy' labeled God, that sets the heart aflame, showing the majesty of its deity that when understood gives strength to its bondservants. It does after all announce itself as,

> "the 'Revelation' of Jesus, that the deity presented him with so that he should show his servants what must 'soon' take place..." (Revelation 1:1.)

How soon, is soon? How long is this 'soon' time period? How long is a length of string? Knowing there are other ways of understanding this first verse, and despite the controversies surrounding his person, deity, life, death etc., my current confidence is that here, as postulated by the gospel writers also. Revelation describes what this Jesus was attempting to announce throughout his three-year earthly ministry. This he now disclosed as narrated, to a beloved disciple. A bloke we are told who was marooned on the isle of Patmos. A detail that a-matter-of-factly is only mentioned here in the 'book', Revelation, and only this one time. Recall that during the '40-day wilderness proofing,' the supreme deity 'proofed' whether he (the God-man Jesus) was 'fit' for the task. This, the texts state, took place immediately following a baptismal ritual. So, the descriptions and messages one find in the entire text of the 'Revelation' might have been undisclosed to the disciples until such a time. Until such a time that this john had spiritually matured as much as it was fitting he and other 'bondservants,' both present and future, required its transmission;

that they continue in the Great Commission. Surely though, it might be argued that the 'book of Revelation' provides elements surrounding eschatological and future events that are yet to unfold. I do not believe so. If it does, are such events to be perceived as distant or present future events for 'our' day; or were they future events yet to unfold completely while the God-man walked the streets of first-century Jerusalem? Or, were they for the author's immediate contemporaries? Was this a part of the hope to cling, recognised as important knowledge to support and fulfil? That is the conundrum the text of Revelation specifically highlights for modern believers. We just do not know either way with any surety. Eschatological and apocalyptic materials are such that we can often recognise that much of the terminology throughout the book (Revelation), is just as Bishop Wright calls, 'a type of language-game.' Striking parallels can be identified when we view a Dead Sea Scroll - The War Scroll, for instance. The subject of this scroll is Armageddon. Which the authors of "The Dead Sea Scroll: A New Translation" poignantly state is

> "...the ultimate catharsis that ushers in an age of peace. All of these issues come to a head in the War Scroll, a text that describes the 'end-time' last battle in gory detail, as righteousness is fully victorious and evil is forever destroyed. This vivid account gives us insight into how, at about the time of Jesus, some Jews conceived of Armageddon."[cdxcvii]

Doyen of the dead sea scrolls Geza Vermes, also calls our attention to the fact that this scroll draws inspiration from several Old Testament passages. Particularly (Daniel 11:40-12:3.) Of the text of this rule Vermes notes, "Scripture doubtless exercised a definite influence on the author of this Rule, but there is nevertheless a great deal of material completely foreign to it, and he must have possessed, in addition, at least some acquaintance with contemporary warfare... It is a theological writing, and the war of which it treats symbolises the eternal struggle between the spirits of Light and Darkness. The phases of its battle are fixed in advance, its plan established, and its duration predetermined. The opposing forces are equally matched and only by the intervention of 'the mighty hand of God' is the balance between them to be disturbed when he deals an 'everlasting blow' to 'Satan and all the host of his kingdom.'"[cdxcviii] Reminiscent again of the text of the Revelation to 'john.' Maybe Revelation then is meant to produce the same end product; but is specifically directed to an audience who although distinct and distant, faced similar struggles as the audience of the War Scroll. Aside this quaint possibility, what if the text of Revelation is not specifically to be read and understood as either eschatological, or apocalyptic in the modern sense. What if, despite showing elements of both, the text of Revelation is specifically more likened to an astronomical treaty. A guidebook relaying past celestial events? A 'record' of peering into the heavens and foretelling of starry events that the alleged author understood to be present and active at the time of his incarceration? What if Revelation (the book) were a concluding cento incorporating many past prophetic oracles for the then 'believer.' We know that the text draws from many Old Testament prophets and wisdom writers. So this is a most possible assumption I'd assume. Instead of out-rightly believing it has a devastating message of destruction of the world. The text of the Revelation is rather a recording of strange occurrences of the starry night skies. Those mystically disturbing portents the author were shocked to have realised. One of those horrifying portents is said to be a beastly antichrist figure who is full of deceit and ferociousness.

Antichrist:

ONE OF THE MOST PERPLEXING anomalies of modern end-time expectations posed today is the 'importance' countless 'fundamental' believers place upon a figure of antichrist. There are indeed widespread speculations surrounding the identity of this 'person.' Many authors and scholars insist this is an actual 'person' who is to be the reemergence and reincarnation or rebirth of some demonic entity. Many believers think for instance, this figure is either; Osiris/ Apollo/ or Nimrod who apparently was foretold to arise during the 'end-times' by apostle Paul.[cdxcix] Unfortunate for one author espousing this ideal is Peter Goodgame. He assumes his hypothesis is solidly founded upon fact:

that the Bible is historically sound; that the demonic is real; and that Osiris/Apollo/Nimrod were authentic real characters. Nimrod might have been. But, as for Apollo and Osiris and many other characters of mythology from which antichrist is based, I am confident are still better understood as mythic symbols! Symbols have a message; they convey truths. Nothing more, nothing less. As a reminder, in the early stages of my investigations it was intimated that not only the Egyptian; but also the Greek, Roman, and other gods and divine entities; these were never thought of as true somebodies. Thus, gods like Osiris were never seen or known or worshipped as real beings. Real people. Rather, they were intended to fix the attention and epitomise the abstract ideas they were believed to represent. Every Egyptian God/goddess functioned as the personification/attribute of the idea portrayed. The same must apply to such figures in the Bible; and in all mythology. To espouse otherwise is again, sheer nonsense. Nonsensical. Clearly, Goodgame as with those 'Christian' commentators mentioned assumes what is most untenable. I take for granted that because his starting premise is just as faulty as the rest, the whole of his hypotheses follows suit. For instance, Goodgame attempts to give credence to his hypotheses that antichrist is related to the book of revelations' seven 'fallen' kings; (Revelation 17:9-11). Working backward from seven – to one, he links the Egyptian Pharaoh (the so-called despotic king) of the 'Exodus' as the second personification of the kings of Satan –as he calls them (see chapter two: the first and the last). His explanation for this is,

> "I cannot be dogmatic about this choice, but he is the primary villain in the story of Moses and the Hebrew release from Egyptian bondage. Pharaoh is characterized (sic) by pride, blasphemy, violence, and hatred, and he died in a vindictive and reckless act that turned into suicide as he drove his armies into the Red Sea. Surely, he must be considered as one of the seven kings of Satan."

Just because a personality in a text is seen as villainous and blasphemous, or an action they apparently carried out turned disastrous for them, does not make them an automatic candidate for antichrist. Not in a pure physical sense, rather through his actions that were recorded as being

DECONSTRUCTING ENDTIME DELUSIONS

despotic. Pharaoh of the 'Exodus' account was antichrist, - symbolically showing the oppugnant relationship with the Moses figure. Like Rob Skiba and those discussed earlier, to think there is a literal connection without empirical evidence, is nothing less than blindness, and typical Christian stupidity. Showing once again the propensity to view the recorded mythology of the Bible as literal, rather than stepping back. To view or ferret the symbolic wisdom of the tale. It is a reliance on nothing else than one's own perception and earlier drawn conclusions. Those bereft of conclusive supporting evidence, because 'faith' apparently trumps verifiable knowledge. These are instances of what was discussed regarding cognitive bias. By now readers must be aware, there are countless issues to be dealt with if these biases are not acknowledged and dealt with. Not that any other demographic is immune from this effect, but Christian 'theologians' and authors are extremely prone to believing their own cognitive biases. Any thinking person must conclude, even through a cursory glance at Exodus that there is absolutely no evidence to suggest that the author (of the Exodus narrative) perceived any Pharaoh as a type of antichrist. This is a pure Christian addendum that does not stand up to scrutiny. It is not in the text, either anywhere in the old or new testaments. But, is again an error of silence - where a conclusion is based on the absence of evidence. What Goodgame offers his readers in his book, is pure and simple, fallacious guess. There is no foundation which a linking of these passages with any Revelation, or any other Bible passage could be valid. Without exception, every person Goodgame assumed to 'link' to or suggested as one of the seven satanic kings –antichrist, has absolutely no legitimacy other than what he suggests is real. But is, has or will such an antichrist be someone we moderns can immediately identify? Is there an actual person identifiable in the Judaeo-Christian book?

Many are of the opinion 'antichrist' is some ghastly tyrannical figure who will suddenly emerge on the world-stage to deceive all except the 'elect of God,' at, or near the close of history as we perceive it. However, to propose this opens wide a raft of other questions. Who is the elect? Why are 'they' not deceived by this apparent fellow? How has this tyrannical figure succeeded in his deception? Like all subjects and questions of end times commented upon thus far, such ideas of some tyrannical figures terrorising populations are not new to our age alone either. Down through the centuries, men from all walks of life and religious belief have concocted abundant suppositions. Many would be familiar with the teachings of the recent past that have projected the idea that personalities such as Hitler, Mussolini, the papacy, or another personality of common history, like; Alexander the Great, or Nero or some other Roman emperor; that these individuals were the 'predicted' antichrist. What made them to be thought of like this? Simply, their actions against a vast array of people that were seen as tyrannical and autocratic. Nothing more, nothing less. H. C. Heffren offers us some helpful and timely advice that any individual 'labeled' antichrist is sure to be speculative.[d] The (ESV) for instance concurs. Recording that an idea of antichrist appears only (5x) five times in only (4) four verses! We see these in the letters of john. All are in his epistles (that's first and second john). Even more interesting is that according to Murdock, and confirmed by the Aramaic English New Testament, antichrist is only mentioned (1x) one time in the Syriac/ Aramaic of the New Testament. That is a figure labeled antichrist is only seen in (2 john 7).

According to Andrew Roth, antichrist is again a Greek loanword. So, once more we see a pilfering of ideas and words from other cultures by the authors of the Christian sacred books. The underlining theme throughout the passages where antichrist is mentioned; however, is that such persons are liars, deceivers, and deniers of truth in Messiah. Hooray! That's me and all those others who have and deny the sanctity of the Judaeo-Christian books! Sounds eerily close also to many Church folk and their leadership too! For, increasingly there are people of faith who are relinquishing and turning their backs on their former beliefs. Unfortunately, modern myths would have the secular and the Christian world believes or fearfully awaits the arrival of a single individual exhibiting such demonstrably tyrannical characteristics. That he seduces the population, esp., the Jewish nation. After which he sets himself up as a God. Maybe in a third temple to be built in Jerusalem?

DECONSTRUCTING ENDTIME DELUSIONS

This is the consensus of thought surrounding such a personality currently sweeping through modern christendom and some factions of Judaism. Yet upon further inspection, the conclusion must be drawn that these interpretations rely again on a 'prosthetic memory;' a biased, preconceived distortion of logic minus any context. Heffren I feel rightly calls attention and affirms this understanding. John does not identify him [antichrist] with the king in Daniel, nor the Man of Sin in Thessalonians, nor with the beast in Revelation (although a John wrote that book), nor with any individual making a covenant with the Jews during any future tribulation period...Antichrist and the spirit of antichrist are expressly concerned with the denial of Christ's coming in the flesh and of his being one with the father. Take away this fundamental pillar and Christianity immediately crumbles into another man–made philosophy. The person of Christ is the jugular vein of faith and the very heart of Christianity.[di] Another nail in the coffin of many modern speculations surrounding this end-time 'personality.' Particularly to those who like Skywatch tv, Rob Skiba, Peter Goodgame and their advocates who promote such speculative ideas. They are found wanting again. Resembling messages from sycophants that, although often studiously and meticulously researched. Such 'research projects and researchers are nonetheless just as jude allegedly warned, (jude 3-16).

> Those who ...walk according to their lusts; and their mouth speaketh shocking things; and they flatter people, for the sake of gain."[dii]

So,

> "Watch" over your life: "let your lamps" be not quenched "and your loins" be not ungirded, but be "ready," for ye know not "the hour in which our Lord cometh." But be frequently gathered together seeking the things which are profitable for your souls, for the whole time of your faith shall not profit you except ye be found perfect at the last time; for in the last days the false prophets and the corrupters shall be multiplied, and the sheep shall be turned into wolves, and love shall change to hate;

for as lawlessness increaseth (sic) they shall hate one another and persecute and betray, and then shall appear the deceiver of the world as a Son of God, and shall do signs and wonders and the earth shall be given over into his hands and he shall commit iniquities which have never been since the world began. Then shall the creation of mankind come to the fiery trial and "many shall be offended" and be lost, but "they who endure" in their faith "shall be saved" by the curse itself."

"[T]hen shall appear the signs" of the truth. First the sign spread out in Heaven, then the sign of the sound of the trumpet, and thirdly the resurrection of the dead: but not of all the dead, but as it was said, "The Lord shall come and all his saints with him." Then shall the world "see the Lord coming on the clouds of Heaven."[diii]

Any suggestion surrounding a 'monstrous' antichrist figure arising to terrorise the planet before the 'reign' of a Messiah figure is a most fanciful conception. Of antichrist, "The Eerdmans Dictionary of Early Judaism" (2010) poignantly writes,

> "...it is a pure Christian conception founded upon the earlier mentioned passages of john. In his reconstruction of the history of the Antichrist legend, Wilhelm Bousset (1895) argued that the concept originated in an esoteric Jewish oral tradition. This view was taken over by many scholars (e.g., Friedländer 1901; Charles 1920) and was held as communis opinio until the late twentieth century. Today the scholarly consensus has moved away from this position and regards the figure of Antichrist as a Christian development rooted in earlier Jewish traditions. Further, the early Christian period did not have one single concept of an eschatological adversary of Jesus Christ. According to this position, the character of Antichrist was molded on the basis of a christological reinterpretation of a number of traditions found in early Jewish sources (Ernst 1967; Jenks 1991; Lietaert Peerbolte 1996; a more critical position is taken by Horbury 1998; a less than critical exception is Lorein 2003, who speaks about "The Antichrist in the Qumran Writings")." The constitutive Jewish traditions include the climax of evil that was expected to take place preceding God's ultimate intervention in history; the expected appearance of false prophets; the coming of an eschatological tyrant; the final defeat of Belial/Beliar and of the chaos monsters Leviathan and Behemoth; the tradition of the final assault of Gentile nations; and the legend of Nero redivivus. Many early Jewish sources depict the period

immediately preceding God's ultimate intervention in history as a period of general upheaval in which the social, natural, and even cosmic order will be inverted."[div]

In sum Peerbolte's article, Antichrist, in "The Dictionary Deities and Demons in the Bible", helpfully appends:

"The tradition of an evil tyrant as the climax of eschatological evil should be understood as a specification of the tradition of the eschatological enmity of the pagan peoples and Israel (cf. Isa 5:25–30; 8:18–20; 10:5–7; 37:16–20; Nah 3:1–7; Joel 4; Zech 14). This expectation of eschatological hostility between Israel and the peoples is also expressed in extra-biblical sources. Sometimes the hostility is thought to reach a climax in the rise of an eschatological tyrant (1 En.90:9–16; Ass. Mos. 8; 2 Apoc. Bar. 36–40; 70; 4 Ezra 5:1–13; 12:29–33; 13:25–38.)"[dv]

It would seem therefore from the above evidence; antichrist began life like all previous subjects studied. Via a convoluted journey throughout history and is little else today, based firmly on a man-made philosophy. Today's conceptions are primarily supported upon the fraction of verses written by john that advocates have moulded to fit a preconceived idea of their own liking. Heffren again offers a timely reminder: "The importance of a teaching in the Bible is often shown by space. It is given in the Word. On this basis, one would say that the observation of the Antichrist is unimportant, since it is mentioned by only one writer very briefly."[dvi] Thus, in agreement with Heffren, "Not one iota of evidence can be attached to a future Antichrist or a Rapture!"[dvii] Unfortunately for modern antichrist, Armageddon advocates and hunters the world over, neither a figure representative of Antichrist, nor a 'final' eschatological confrontation can be proven from a sacred book, aside some convoluted 'tradition', to exist!

Nail Fifteen:

Armageddon Gog Magog a Final Conflict:

ARMAGEDDON, A NAME and place for many christians that are evocative and synonymous with a final cataclysmic, terrifying conflict between the 'forces' of darkness, and the 'forces' of light. Undoubted, modern believers' perceptions of such a 'conflict' are heightened by the myriads of publications that feed one's imagination. The conflict said and believed by many to occur sometime in the coming future is sequenced rather straightforwardly in the final book of the Christian canon, Revelation. Most still believe this text is eschatological and apocalyptic. Despite the study above showing, it most likely is not. In addition, many insist on believing it to be a trustworthy accounting of the proposed author, but there is no indication that the beloved apostle 'john' penned this final 'Revelation'. Rather, the prophesy is attributed to an otherwise unknown 'Prophet/seer/shaman' who went by the name john in Asia Minor. Who for reasons largely unknown other than his specific notation, was on the Island of Patmos 'because of the Word of Nemo and the testimony of deity–man, Jesus.' (Revelation 1:9.) Was this man there by his own understanding? Or was he incarcerated for some offence? We can really only speculate. These complications aside, assumptions surrounding a final conflict at a place (known also as Megiddo in Hebrew) are based upon projections and the interpretation of a single verse (Revelation 16:16.) Here we find one doctrine whose foundation is a solitary verse. How can such a thing be solid fact? One text surely doesn't or cannot be legitimate cause for a lasting idea. Yet here it clearly is! Despite the place identified by scholars as Armageddon/Megiddo being a known ancient battlefield, there seems to be little evidence supporting a final cataclysmic and final battle that causes a modern 'end-time' advocates proposal. Which then ushers in some form of Utopia. Difficulties lay in the fact that scholars of numerous persuasions over the years have offered various explanations. Most of which readers are encouraged to read carefully and source through Bible dictionaries and encyclopaedia's, the likes of "Anchor Yale", "The International Standard Bible Encyclopaedia", and, or the "Dictionary of the Old and New Testament(s) [InterVarsity Press]", or, "HarperCollins Bible Dictionary". Most reputable Bible dictionaries, those cited in this document, will have entries explaining both terms, Armageddon and Megiddo. A snippet from the "Dictionary of Prophesy and End Times" may prove illuminating:

> "Revelation 16:16 may also draw on the Gog-Magog tradition of the end-time defeat of enemy nations on "the mountains of Israel" (Ezek. 38–39). Regardless of the questions that remain about the specific background of the "mount of Megiddo," this much can be known for certain: Megiddo was connected to warfare. How should Armageddon be interpreted? Some see real armies gathered at the exact geographical location in northern Palestine for a future battle. Satan will deceptively gather the military powers of the world in the Holy Land to combat the armies of heaven. The battle will rage for some time, ending in the defeat of the forces of evil at the return of Christ. Other interpreters see Armageddon as a symbol of the final conflict between the forces of evil and the forces of God that occurs throughout the earth. As a result, "Armageddon" does not refer to a specific geographical location (as with other place names, such as "Babylon" or "Euphrates"), but to the whole world as a battlefield. Regardless of whether Revelation 16:16 is interpreted literally or figuratively, the passage clearly describes a real, final battle in which Christ is victorious simply by his appearance."[dviii]

Question: When or how is this scenario to be played out, if, on the world stage? Considering it has already been proposed that the 'Revelation' most surely is not a recording of a 'future-state.' Rather, is likely a tome describing celestial events that for whatever reason probably were misinterpreted, by the original author, and subsequent believers since? Another enlightening, and more apparent scenario that (Revelation 16:16) could be alluding to is offered by Michael Baigent, in his book "Racing to Armageddon". He wrote,

> "The first recorded battle [in this Megiddo region] was in 1479 b.c.e. when Egyptian Pharaoh Thutmosis III fought [a confederate] Canaanite [/Hittite

army]. Thutmosis, "Son of the God," fought a great army lead by many kings, which leads one to ask, has some dim memory of this disaster for the Canaanites been included in the description in Revelation? Surely, we should be open to the possibility."[dix]

Aside this alluring proposal, a poignant statement by the foremost expert on myth, Joseph Campbell goes a long way to explaining simply what Apocalypse is,

"Apocalypse does [he writes] not point to a fiery Armageddon, but to our ignorance and complacency coming to an end", in A Joseph Campbell Companion: Reflections On The Art Of Living (1991)."[dx]

Distinguished Assistant Professor of archaeology and ancient history, Eric H Cline in a review of his tome,

"The Battles of Armageddon: Megiddo and the Jezreel Valley from the Bronze Age to the Nuclear Age" adds convincingly, "One lesson that can be learned from the history surrounding the area is the importance of maintaining a strategic presence on military and/or mercantile routes. We also see that, while weapons and technology have changed over the millennia, the strategies and tactics frequently have not. Often different commanders and different armies repeat the strategies used in the battles fought at such places in different eras. Finally, we learn that, probably as a result of the necessity of occupying such strategic positions, certain areas of the world have seen consistent fighting for literally millennia."[dxi]

7-year itch tribulation - true or false?

THE TEXT THAT SEEMS to spur most people's imaginations to run uncontrolled regarding a seven-year tribulation period; where antichrist figure emerges, seduces populations and causes defilement of a third temple belongs to three verses of Daniel's prophesy (Daniel 9:24-27.) Unfortunately, for those dispensational believers who espouse this 'teaching,' it is they who have been deceived: being led up the garden path. Below is the text from Daniel. I challenge any reader to read it without the above predispositions:

> "Seventy weeks are decreed for your people and your holy city: to finish the transgression, to put an end to sin, and to atone for iniquity, to bring in everlasting righteousness, to seal both vision and Prophet, and to anoint a most holy place. Know therefore and understand: from the time that the word went out to restore and rebuild Jerusalem until the time of an anointed prince, there shall be seven weeks; and for sixty-two weeks it shall be built again with streets and moat, but in a troubled time. After the sixty-two weeks, an anointed one shall be cut off and shall have nothing, and the troops of the prince who is to come shall destroy the city and the sanctuary. Its end shall come with a flood, and to the end there shall be war. Desolations are decreed. He shall make a strong covenant with many for one week, and for half of the week he shall make sacrifice and offering cease; and in their place shall be an abomination that desolates, until the decreed end is poured out upon the desolator."[dxii]

Gary DeMar confirms my understanding, writing,

> "In order to get a seven-year tribulation period, the dispensationalist must first prove that there is a gap of nearly 2000 years between the 69th and 70th weeks. He must also demonstrate from these verses that the antichrist will make a covenant with the Jews during a post-rapture tribulation. Then there must be proof of another rebuilt temple that skips over the rebuilt temple that stood in Jesus' day. Revelation to make a covenant with the Jews during the so-called seven-year tribulation period since Revelation is an expansion of Daniel's 70th week. There is no mention of the antichrist making a covenant with anyone, either in Daniel 9:27 or in Revelation. In fact, there is not a single example of this unholy covenant in the entire Bible. It's Jesus who makes a covenant with the many: "this is My blood of the covenant, which is to be shed on behalf of the many for the forgiveness of sins" (Matt. 26:28). The Bible couldn't be clearer. You can read from the first verse to the last verse of Revelation and not find any mention of "antichrist" or "seven-years," let alone a seven-year tribulation period."[dxiii]

The scriptures in neither the old covenant, nor the new teach anything remotely resembling a period of tribulation of seven years for either Jew or any other person. Believer or not! This then is yet another false myth founded upon untruths and modern myopic insinuation! It is an arduous task to go through these verses of Daniel with any great depth, and others more qualified than I have done so presently. However, let it be understood by readers that regarding these verses. They relate, quite possibly and specifically, again, as with Joel or other prophets, the time of a Messiah figure; His revealing and three-and one-half year ministry, culminating in the fulfilment of verse (Daniel 9:24) with his crucifixion. This however again is a typically indoctrinated explanation. What if; however, Osman and the other authors earlier cited, contend that famous Bible figures, like David, Joseph, Jesus, and no doubt Daniel, are Egyptian by genealogy? That the stories about these figures, as recorded in the Judaeo-Christian book have been fabricated and reconstructed to fit a new interpretation. For a fitting Christian explanation to the events described by Daniel in these verses, readers are encouraged to source (Jordan, J. B. (2007). "The Handwriting on the Wall: A Commentary on the Book of Daniel". Powder Springs, GA: American Vision.) Specifically, the chapter of most relevance to the above statements is chapter eighteen of that work. Another fact to contend: most scholarship today seems to have revised initial thoughts about the dating and composition of the biblical text of Daniel, contending now for the second of the two outlined below. There are two schools of scholarship on the issues surrounding the book of Daniel; one school adheres to the traditional view, which is where we would expect to find most dispensational writers and scholars that Daniel were composed of the sixth century B.C.E. Placing it within the general time frame of its subject matter. It is therefore recognised as an apocalyptic/eschatological text. Notice also (though a minor point), that Daniel is placed within the Old Testament corpus of modern Protestant bibles, as the final prophetic work, coming after ezekiel.It is therefore presumed to be a 'prophetic' manuscript! However, a great number of other scholars hold an opposing view, which I also adhere. This school has leanings to a much later composition, of around (175-165B.C.E.) placing it squarely within the Maccabean period of Jewish history. This makes some sense and seems to be the more probable for a range of reasons. First, two scholars, Douglas Knight and Amy-Jill Levine in, "The Meaning of the Bible" (p38) state,

> "Daniel 7-12 reflects this period of 167 – 164, veiled as an apocalyptic piece set in the time of the Neo-Babylonian and Perspires."

DECONSTRUCTING ENDTIME DELUSIONS

Secondly, Jewish Tradition, and modern Jewish bibles (The Jewish Study Bible: JPS tanakh translation (2004)), have always placed Daniel squarely among the wisdom literature; which includes ezra, nehemiah, psalms, proverbs. A helpful guide for understanding some of the debates raging about the composition of Daniel, readers should source a reliable commentary and handbook "A handbook on the Book of Daniel". UBS Handbook Series. New York: United Bible Societies, on old testament texts. As a start the reasonable mid to high-end commentary: "The New American Commentary" (nac) briefly notes,

> "Traditionally [i.e. Christian] it has been held that Daniel wrote the book substantially as it exists today, that the prophecy is historically reliable, and that its predictions are supernatural and accurate. Likely there was some modernization of the language as the work was copied throughout the centuries, but otherwise it originated with the Prophet in the sixth century b.c. Daniel would have completed his prophecy as an old man soon after the last dated event recorded in the book (10:1; 536 b.c.). In modern times many scholars have maintained that an anonymous Jew produced the book in its present form during the second century b.c., writing under the pseudonym Daniel, and that it consists of nonhistorical accounts and pseudoprophecies. The purpose of the work was to encourage Jewish believers in their struggle against the tyrant Antiochus IV Epiphanes (175–163 b.c.) during the Maccabean period. This supposition may be called the Maccabean thesis. According to this view the Book of Daniel would be the latest of the Old Testament Scriptures. Often scholars who accept the Maccabean thesis identify the second-century writer as a member of the religious sect known as the Hasidim."[dxiv]

All said and done:

WHAT IS THERE LEFT to say regarding the plethora of subjective 'end-time' notions, 'prophesies' and falsified myths, and theories that have, and no doubts will continue to sprout throughout 'Christian fundamentalism'. (1) In this Second Part of my studies, the attempt was to stay faithfully to the Judaeo–Christian books by showing that many subjects the fundamentalist focus on, i.e., angels/fallen angels, satan, enoch etc., lack credibility and permanency when viewed through the corpus of the written text, without at minimum an understanding of how and where such 'myth' originated, and for what purpose they might have served the intended/original reader. (2) We have found that many subjects that often exist today within a 'rapture', or end time disaster theory is plainly and simply fallacious and are the efforts of an over-reactive, over-active religious mind of those who carry the God Virus. Finally (3) simply the Christian 'holy' texts do not in any way announce a coming conflagration of tremendous force that will literally wipe the planet of all its inhabitants, but a very 'lucky' few. Readers may not agree, but I do not endorse that we are on the verge of an antichrist figure making claims of great piety, but who underneath is seething deceitfulness. Nor is the world-as-we-know-it about to disintegrate. Either by cause of 'climate-change' or some other catastrophe brought about by mankind. Let alone by a presumed ruling deity. That simply is an unreasonable theory. Unless, maybe through war, and the devastations this brings and wreaks on our home. A deity advocating for a certain crow of persons to be 'saved', or not (whatever 'saved' means) is really not worth a look in! What we cannot deny however is the fact that from times eons past, mankind still suffers the collective memory of massive trauma. This traumatic memory has made its way into various religious texts and traditions. There are indeed many ideas spread throughout not only the Judaeo-Christian sacred book. But, also numerous other sacredly held texts that presuppose such calamitous events occurring, but again when analysed, many are found wanting and are little else than the workings of an over-reactive mind. Taught to adherents of any particular religious order, for the prime purpose as with the "Hydra" of Hamburg. Which if recalled, did monks create to instil fear of retribution by the deity if any believer so much as deserted the 'faith'. Of all, the continuing 'prophetic' guesses that unfortunately attract rash Christians and secular folk alike I think Gary DeMar succinctly sums the situation beautifully: "Today's end-time preoccupied Church and those who make millions of dollars off the nonsense of... prophetic novels (Left Behind series) and their supposed non-fiction counterparts are giving aid and comfort to the enemies of the gospel."[dxv] Hosea (4:6): "...people are destroyed for lack of knowledge..." (ESV) must surely strike a sour chord for many readers. Considering the attempt throughout this investigation, to highlight and succinctly disseminate where I believe Christian believers are being duped, and in effect are destroyed for lack of knowledge. I hope to have shown this, specifically in my examination of Rob Skiba's end-time scenario, focussed on his ideology surrounding Genesis 6:1-4 and the proposed nephilim/ giants. It must be noticed by all readers that without at least minimal knowledge of the original intent or something as close to a possible original intent of any passage of a sacred book; coupled with a historical and scientific parallel in explanation could clear for readers much more than they inhibit. We run the grave risk of showing the world our own ignorance, self-aggrandisement and foolhardiness if we run off with our preconceived ideologies. Believers who insist that their studies have lead them to conclude what mainstream christianity asserts as valid understandings and interpretation methods of subjects, was found to continually be only a regurgitation of the very same assertions that can be read from any psychobabble that the oxymoronic 'Christian' bookstore offers. They are deluding themselves and doing not only themselves a great disservice, but also their potential readership. Many believers will be well served by digesting the reasonable explanations of many Bible stories offered by alternate history writers scattered throughout this work. Whether one ultimately views their hypotheses as valid or not afterward, is hardly the point. Rather, I think those that do not attempt to at least source alternate explanations to the usual dogmatic jargon are in effect, forfeiting their own growth and understanding. They are buying into the nonsense of every house of delusion -the Church.

A substantive amount of time was spent attempting to succinctly explain the proposal of Rob Skiba and his study of Genesis 6:1-4. That the mystical and enigmatic entities named 'nephilim' of this story are somehow a supernatural angelic type of massive proportions; that at some time in the ancient past, these entities terrorised human women; which had a dire effect altogether of Planet Earth. Through research, was offered reasonable conclusions as to why Rob's, and other Christian's proposals of a wicked angel type (nephilim) are as far from actual and real, as there being a purple spaghetti monster deity living on the dark side of the moon feasting on a diet of spam and cheese. Even the sub-sections tackled that arose from Rob's guesses were most likely found to have a perfectly scientific and sound explanation. Explanations Christian authors often dismiss or do not think to consider when formulating their specific hypotheses. Elongated skulls, double-rows of teeth, gigantism, all are still prevalent in our day. These therefore also do not require the usual supernatural explanation we assume to come from the sacred books' perspective. The passages cited do not lend themselves to an interpretation of menacing gigantic proportions; rather, depict more often the prowess of those so named giants. Finally, the trust is near-on each of the other subjects studied in this Second Part, were described effectively. These were also found to hold largely and completely different meanings than what Christian authors today propose. Many held to archaic interpretations that had been morphed and twisted to suit a modern audience, and so, were in essence unrecognisable. Unfortunately, there is a modern perspective of myth. That these are somewhat demonic in nature; and therefore, useless for sound teaching. I disagree. See Appendix 3. Numerous Christian authors nowadays have twisted many of these tales and their gods/ demi–gods, monsters to suit the author's own predisposed ideology. Viewing the demonic in all mythic entities of the ancients. Clearly such authors do not understand myth, and its purposes or the meanings they might have held for the original audiences. Books like Babylon Rising, and Clash

DECONSTRUCTING ENDTIME DELUSIONS

of the Titans, by two Christian authors, is packed with the usual christianeze psychobabble, telling their hypotheses in such a way so as to attempt to instil in readers a sense of maximum fear. For instance, Gilbert asserts, of the ancient mythic gods: "So, since all those gods were imaginary, what's the harm of using Thor, Zeus, and Hercules as fodder for entertainment? Well, none, unless the thought of eternity in the Lake of Fire bothers you."[dxvi] If the underline text is not a statement meant to set one's teeth on edge, to instil a sense of fear of the so-called lake of fire into the reader, I truly do not understand the English language! Statements as these are absurd and are made as a 'dire warning'. Where is the evidential proof? One can find such statements of 'fact' without proof in any and every Christian tome on end-times in circulation. No wonder a large portion of the believing community is simply mind–blind. Such statements as Gilbert's are astoundingly lacking in common sense. Such ideology as these authors highlighted has undoubtedly made both men look extremely addeplated. Unfortunately, they are not the only authors projecting doubtful ideologies without so much as a skerrick of empirical evidence. As was earlier stated, Faith, cannot be a reason for a belief. Faith is letting go of something, not clinging to it! So, to believe in such statements because faith, you'd have to let go of it and not believe it. Now there's a quandary for you! How does one let go and still believe in the veracity of something? Unfortunately (for the religious reader at least) what we have witnessed throughout this exercise is the over-imaginative mind and reaction of most of Evangelicalism. Churches, their 'pastors', 'priests', and 'leadership' have lead many malleable souls on a journey that all too often is unwarranted, downright dangerous, and ridiculously nonsensical. While also offering ridiculous protestations that are 'claimed' to be based upon fact, or set as dire warning (hosea 4:6). The focus however is far too often on a very select number of passages. Those that yes I have also cherry-picked; which are objectionably interpreted and over 'spiritualised' and their mythic messages often demonised or over dramatised to enchant the hearer/ reader. Passages that advocates reassemble, twist, and mould to fit one's own liking. Which reeks of ultra-dispensationalist views. A consequence is the fact that this has lead many a good 'believer' astray. Allowing many imagined and so, unacceptable interpretations to persist, and for some, broadly believed. The Heaven's Gate cult mass suicide, and Waco compound destruction are two tragic events of recent history where 'believers' took several apocalyptic end time 'predictions' and beliefs literally. So literally they suicided for their cause! Clear refutations of erroneous religious teachings can be read on Holly Pivec's site, "Spirit of Error".[dxvii] Many an end time proposition bang on about at the 'parousia' of the Messiah figure.[dxviii] But, not just a few have no clue this Greek word is erroneously used by apocalyptic advocates. So, we are forced to acknowledge that what the Judaeo-Christian sacred book portrays and what many preachers, theologians, pastors, religious teachers portray as absolute and factual regarding the stories and derived doctrines from Bible pages; is often completely different, errant, and calculating. The undeniable fact is that what often occurs is a twisting and manipulation of texts and ideas to hold control of those that listen to the religious tripe sprouted on a weekly basis. There is a vast suppression of knowledge and information that every believer would undoubtedly be all the wiser. If only they took a broader view of what they are taught. Instead of mindlessly taking the 'word' of one of – 'God's bouncers', as Bill Bailey jibbed in one of his video releases, on any given sunday sermon or study session. The Judaeo-Christian book is indeed full of misrepresentations, numerous contradictions, misplaced histories and astounding manipulation devises. Some of its stories do seem to echo a much more ancient telling. Some may be based upon actual events witnessed by our distant relatives that many scientists and historical researchers are just now beginning to penetrate. But as these story's are today taught and believed by the religionist; these same stories, without the insight offered by secular fields of study, are shamefully repugnant. The majority are little else than the workings of a myopic delusion. Prosthetic memories handed down through the ages. We have seen from this exercise that there is any amount of helpful information available for an informed analysis and conclusion. Provided the believer is willing to do some hard

DECONSTRUCTING ENDTIME DELUSIONS

explorative work! Religious end-times and many, if not all, associated doctrines and ideas have a very minimal basis in truth. They are all based either on fable that was passed from generation to generation. Hinting at their historicity or the myopic delusions of a wayward prosthetic memory. Though science does not possess all the answers, what it does supply us with is empirical conclusions to many questions and a safeguarded appraisal of findings. In essence, scientific enquiry always questions the validity of its own proposed truths. If the projections about 'end-times' are false, what 'end-time' scenario do we face? That the Bible can be a legitimate source for any 'end-time' cataclysmic event is not viable. There is literally a multitude of texts, and articles - both ancient and modern – now being published to show with reasonable assertion that the Christian faith, its dependence upon archaic writings and associated endeavours - are completely without merit. There is then, very little veracity to any of the Bible's assertions of the proposals surrounding 'end-time' themes. The final text of the canon, Revelation, is an account of astro-theological myth making. This has been shown in the pages above.

What then can be a legitimate end-time scenario? One such scenario has appeared in the September 2014, issue 3 of "Know How" magazine (Australia). In her brief article, *Found in Space*, Rosslyn Beeby outlines the growing threat of 'space debris' on life on the planet, and our dependence on space reliant endeavours. According to reports across the media, space junk poses a very real threat, and if not managed '...this problem, space will become unusable within 20 years.' A further impression, offered by Susan Mendez in her book, "Time of the Quickening", is that despite the numerous 'scare-mongering' of the Church and secular 'academics': "It is a paradigm shift we are looking at. No, it is neither the end of the world nor some huge conflagration or disaster resulting from the sudden shifting of the poles that we are up against. The likeliest scenarios give us social upheavals, with obsolete, even wicked institutions collapsing from within. Imploding. "The old is crumbling from its own activities," says Chet Snow in his book "Mass Dreams of the Future". Isn't this the pattern already established by today's failed states: Russia, Somalia, the Solomon Islands, Haiti, Ruanda, Afghanistan, Yugoslavia, and so on? The World Bank estimates that there are at least twenty-six failing states in the world today." Unbeknown by believers everywhere is the fact that has been, I see, revealed by Tony Bushby's research. That is that yes the contradictions, misappropriations, fudging of facts are all-extant within the Bible text. But, Tony's research has uncovered the very possible fact that what the narratives of the New Testament retell, are the initiation rites of the assumed rabbi Jesus. It is clear in the closing chapters of "The Secret in the Bible" that this is so. Many symbols and acts portrayed in the New Testament were the uninitiated retelling of Jesus' initiation into the Egyptian mysteries. Describing the death and resurrection ritual Tony writes:

> "An initiate could justly say that he had died, ascended and resurrected, awakening to discover a higher understanding of the significance of death. The same rite of 'death' and spiritual 'resurrection' for the neophyte, or the suffering, trial and new birth, was later historicized (sic) by the Gospel writers who were not spiritually advanced enough to understand what really happened to Jesus. The nucleus of their story was built up from an outward interpretation of an inward initiation experience. They were 'simple creatures who understood nothing'... Their exoteric nature provided confusion and their understanding of what had happened became externalized (sic) as an earthly event, and not the esoteric personal experience that it was."[dxix]

THANK YOU for joining me on this journey.

Bibliography:

Logos Bible Software:

ACHTEMEIER, PAUL J., Harper and Row, and Society of Biblical Literature. Harper's Bible Dictionary. 1st ed. San Francisco: Harper and Row, 1985.

Alexander, T. Desmond, and David W. Baker. Dictionary of the Old Testament: Pentateuch. Downers Grove, IL: InterVarsity Press, 2003.

Arnold, Bill T., and H. G. M. Williamson. Dictionary of the Old Testament: Historical Books. Downers Grove, IL: InterVarsity Press, 2005.

Balz, Horst Robert, and Gerhard Schneider. Exegetical Dictionary of the New Testament. Grand Rapids, Mich.: Eerdmans, 1990-.

Bamberger, Bernard J. Fallen Angels: Soldiers of Satan's Realm. Philadelphia, PA: The Jewish Publication Society, 2006.

Barker, Kenneth L., and John R. Kohlenberger, III. Expositor's Bible Commentary (Abridged : Old Testament). Grand Rapids, MI: Zondervan Publishing House, 1994.

Barry, John D., Michael R. Grigoni, Michael S. Heiser et al. Faithlife Study Bible. Bellingham, WA: Logos Bible Software, 2012.

Biblical Studies Press. The NET Bible FirstNotes. Biblical Studies Press, 2006.

Boyce, Edward Jacob. An Etymological Glossary of Nearly 2,500 English Words in Common Use Derived from the Greek. London: George Bell and Sons, 1878.

Brown, Colin. New International Dictionary of New Testament Theology. Grand Rapids, MI: Zondervan Publishing House, 1986.

Brown, Francis, Samuel Rolles Driver, and Charles Augustus Briggs. Enhanced Brown-Driver-Briggs Hebrew and English Lexicon. electronic ed. Oak Harbor, WA: Logos Research Systems, 2000.

Burge, Gary M. Vol. 3, Interpreting the Fourth Gospel. Guides to New Testament Exegesis. Grand Rapids, MI: Baker Book House, 1992.

Burton, Ernest DeWitt. A Harmony of the Synoptic Gospels for Historical and Critical Study. New York; Chicago; Boston: Charles Scribner's Sons, 1917.

Cassuto, U. Biblical and Oriental Studies, Volume I: Bible. Translated by Israel Abrahams. Jerusalem: Magnes Press, 1973.

Cross, F. L., and Elizabeth A. Livingstone. The Oxford Dictionary of the Christian Church. 3rd ed. rev. Oxford; New York: Oxford University Press, 2005.

Day, Colin A. Collins Thesaurus of the Bible. Bellingham, WA: Logos Bible Software, 2009.

DeMar, Gary. 10 Popular Prophecy Myths Exposed: The Last Days Might Not Be as Near as You Think. Powder Springs, GA: American Vision, 2010.

DeMar, Gary, and Francis X. Gumerlock. The Early Church and the End of the World. Powder Springs, GA: American Vision, 2006.

DeMoss, Matthew S. Pocket Dictionary for the Study of New Testament Greek. Downers Grove, IL: InterVarsity Press, 2001.

E. Michael, and Sharon Rusten. The Complete Book of When and Where in the Bible and Throughout History. Wheaton, IL: Tyndale House Publishers, Inc., 2005.

Easton, M. G. Easton's Bible Dictionary. Oak Harbor, WA: Logos Research Systems, Inc., 1996.

Hays, J. Daniel, J. Scott Duvall, and C. Marvin Pate. Dictionary of Biblical Prophecy and End Times. Grand Rapids, MI: Zondervan Publishing House, 2007.

Heiser, Michael S. Glossary of Morpho-Syntactic Database Terminology. Logos Bible Software, 2005.

Jenni, Ernst, and Claus Westermann. Theological Lexicon of the Old Testament. Peabody, MA: Hendrickson Publishers, 1997.

Johnson, Luke Timothy. Reading Romans: A Literary and Theological Commentary. Reading the New Testament Series. Macon, GA: Smyth and Helwys Publishing, 2001.

Johnson, O. L. The Second Coming of Christ. James L. Fleming, 2005.

Jordan, James B. The Handwriting on the Wall: A Commentary on the Book of Daniel. Powder Springs, GA: American Vision, 2007.

Kaiser, Walter C., Jr., Peter H. Davids, F. F. Bruce, and Manfred T. Brauch. Hard Sayings of the Bible. Downers Grove, IL: InterVarsity, 1996.

Kittel, Gerhard, Gerhard Friedrich, and Geoffrey William Bromiley. Theological Dictionary of the New Testament. Grand Rapids, MI: W.B. Eerdmans, 1985.

Martin, Ralph P., and Peter H. Davids. Dictionary of the Later New Testament and Its Developments. electronic ed. Downers Grove, IL: InterVarsity Press, 2000.

Matthews, Victor Harold, Mark W. Chavalas, and John H. Walton. The IVP Bible Background Commentary: Old Testament. electronic ed. Downers Grove, IL: InterVarsity Press, 2000.

Merriam-Webster, Inc. Merriam-Webster's Collegiate Dictionary. Eleventh ed. Springfield, MA: Merriam-Webster, Inc., 2003.

Miller, Stephen R. Vol. 18, Daniel. The New American Commentary. Nashville: Broadman and Holman Publishers, 1994.

Oswalt, John N. The Bible Among the Myths: Unique Revelation or Just Ancient Literature? Grand Rapids, MI: Zondervan, 2009.

Péter-Contesse, René, and John Ellington. A Handbook on the Book of Daniel. UBS Handbook Series. New York: United Bible Societies, 1994.

Porter, Stanley E., and Craig A. Evans. Dictionary of New Testament Background: A Compendium of Contemporary Biblical Scholarship. electronic ed. Downers Grove, IL: InterVarsity Press, 2000.

Porter, Stanley, Matthew Brook O'Donnell, Jeffrey T. Reed et al. The OpenText.org Syntactically Analyzed Greek New Testament Glossary. Logos Bible Software, 2006.

Rotherham, Joseph Bryant. The Emphasized Bible: A Translation Designed to Set Forth the Exact Meaning, the Proper Terminology, and the Graphic Style of the Sacred Original. Bellingham, WA: Logos Research Systems, Inc., 2010.

Runge, Steven E. The Lexham High Definition New Testament: ESV Logos Bible Software, 2008.

Runge, Steven E. Discourse Grammar of the Greek New Testament: A Practical Introduction for Teaching and Exegesis. Bellingham, WA: Logos Bible Software, 2010.

Ryken, Leland, Jim Wilhoit, Tremper Longman et al. Dictionary of Biblical Imagery. electronic ed. Downers Grove, IL: InterVarsity Press, 2000.

Scanlin, Harold P. The Dead Sea Scrolls and Modern Translations of the Old Testament. Wheaton, IL: Tyndale House Publishers, 1993.

Smith, F. G. Prophetic Lectures on Daniel and the Revelation. James L. Fleming, 2005.

Smith, Mark S. The Early History of God: Yahweh and the Other Deities in Ancient Israel. Grand Rapids, MI; Cambridge, U.K.; Dearborn, MI: William B. Eerdmans Publishing Company; Dove Booksellers, 2002.

Smith, Stelman, and Judson Cornwall. The Exhaustive Dictionary of Bible Names. North Brunswick, NJ: Bridge-Logos, 1998.

Spicq, Ceslas, and James D. Ernest. Theological Lexicon of the New Testament. Peabody, MA: Hendrickson Publishers, 1994.

Strong, James. Enhanced Strong's Lexicon. Bellingham, WA: Logos Bible Software, 2001.

Strong, James. A Concise Dictionary of the Words in the Greek Testament and The Hebrew Bible. Bellingham, WA: Logos Bible Software, 2009.

Swanson, James. Dictionary of Biblical Languages With Semantic Domains : Hebrew (Old Testament). electronic ed. Oak Harbor: Logos Research Systems, Inc., 1997.

Swanson, James. Dictionary of Biblical Languages With Semantic Domains: Greek (New Testament). electronic ed. Oak Harbor: Logos Research Systems, Inc., 1997.

Swete, Henry Barclay. The Old Testament in Greek: According to the Septuagint. Cambridge, UK: Cambridge University Press, 1909.

Tan, Paul Lee. Encyclopedia of 7700 Illustrations: Signs of the Times. Garland, TX: Bible Communications, Inc., 1996.

Tasker, George P. The King Is Coming. James L. Fleming, 2005.

Thayer, Joseph Henry. A Greek-English Lexicon of the New Testament: Being Grimm's Wilke's Clavis Novi Testamenti. New York: Harper and Brothers., 1889.

Thomas, Robert L., and The Lockman Foundation. New American Standard Exhaustive Concordance of the Bible: Updated Anaheim: Foundation Publications, Inc., 1998.

Torrey, R. A. Anecdotes and Illustrations. New York: Fleming H. Revell Co., 1907.

Tov, Emanuel. The Parallel Aligned Hebrew-Aramaic and Greek Texts of Jewish Scripture. Bellingham, WA: Logos Bible Software, 2003.

van der Toorn, Karel, Bob Becking, and Pieter Willem van der Horst. Dictionary of Deities and Demons in the Bible. 2nd extensively rev. ed. Leiden; Boston; Köln; Grand Rapids, MI; Cambridge: Brill; Eerdmans, 1999.

Vermes, Geza. The Dead Sea Scrolls in English. Revised and extended 4th ed. Sheffield: Sheffield Academic Press, 1995.

Walton, John H. Ancient Near Eastern Thought and the Old Testament: Introducing the Conceptual World of the Hebrew Bible. Grand Rapids, MI: Baker Academic, 2006.

Whyte, Alexander. Bible Characters: Ahithophel to Nehemiah, Vol. 3. Edinburgh; London: Oliphant Anderson and Ferrier, 1896.

Whyte, Alexander. Bible Characters: Gideon to Absalom, Vol. 2. Edinburgh; London: Willmington, H.L. Willmington's Book of Bible Lists. Wheaton, IL: Tyndale, 1987.

Wilson, Douglas. Knowledge, Foreknowledge and the Gospel. Moscow, ID: Canon Press, 2007.

Wise, Michael O., Martin G. Abegg, Jr., and Edward M. Cook. The Dead Sea Scrolls: A New Translation. New York: HarperOne, 2005.

Witherington, Ben, III. The Jesus Quest: The Third Search for the Jew of Nazareth. 2nd ed. Downers Grove, IL: InterVarsity Press, 1997.

Wood, D. R. W., and I. Howard Marshall. New Bible Dictionary. 3rd ed. Leicester, England; Downers Grove, IL: InterVarsity Press, 1996.

Wright, Tom. The Millennium Myth. Louisville, KY: Westminster John Knox Press, 1999.

20th Century Jewish Religious Thought: Original Essays on Critical Concepts, Movements, and Beliefs. Edited by Arthur A. Cohen and Paul Mendes-Flohr. Philadelphia, PA: The Jewish Publication Society, 2009.

The Anchor Yale Bible Dictionary. Edited by David Noel Freedman, Gary A. Herion, David F. Graf et al. New York: Doubleday, 1992.

Baker Encyclopedia of Psychology and Counseling. Edited by David G. Benner and Peter C. Hill. 2nd ed. Baker reference library. Grand Rapids, MI: Baker Books, 1999.

The Contemporary Torah: A Gender-Sensitive Adaptation of the JPS Translation. Edited by David E. S. Stein, Adele Berlin, Ellen Frankel and Carol L. Meyers. Philadelphia, PA: The Jewish Publication Society, 2006.

Dictionary for Theological Interpretation of the Bible. Edited by Kevin J. Vanhoozer, Craig G. Bartholomew, Daniel J. Treier and N. T. Wright. London; Grand Rapids, MI: SPCK; Baker Academic, 2005.

A Dictionary of Christ and the Gospels: Aaron–Zion. Edited by James Hastings, John A. Selbie and John C. Lambert. Edinburgh; New York: TandT Clark; Charles Scribner's Sons, 1906.

Dictionary of Jesus and the Gospels. Edited by Joel B. Green, Scot McKnight and I. Howard Marshall. Downers Grove, IL: InterVarsity Press, 1992.

Dictionary of the Apostolic Church (2 Vols.). Edited by James Hastings. New York: Charles Scribner's Sons, 1916-1918.

The Eerdmans Dictionary of Early Judaism. Edited by John J. Collins and Daniel C. Harlow. Grand Rapids, MI; Cambridge, U.K.: William B. Eerdmans Publishing Company, 2010.

Eschatology, Messianism, and the Dead Sea Scrolls. Edited by Craig A. Evans and Peter W. Flint. Studies in the Dead Sea Scrolls and Related Literature. Grand Rapids, MI: William B. Eerdmans Publishing Company, 1997.

The HarperCollins Bible Dictionary (Revised and Updated). Edited by Mark Allan Powell. Third New York: HarperCollins, 2011.

The Hebrew Bible: Andersen-Forbes Analyzed Text. Logos Bible Software, 2008.

Holman Illustrated Bible Dictionary. Edited by Chad Brand, Charles Draper, Archie England et al. Nashville, TN: Holman Bible Publishers, 2003.

The Holy Bible: English Standard Version. Wheaton: Standard Bible Society, 2001.

The Holy Bible: New Revised Standard Version. Nashville: Thomas Nelson Publishers, 1989.

The International Standard Bible Encyclopedia, Revised. Edited by Geoffrey W. Bromiley. Wm. B. Eerdmans, 1988.

The Lexham Analytical Lexicon to the Greek New Testament. Logos Bible Software, 2011.

The Lexham Bible Dictionary. Edited by John D. Barry and Lazarus Wentz. Bellingham, WA: Logos Bible Software, 2012.

The Lexham English Septuagint. Edited by Rick Brannan, Ken M. Penner, Israel Loken et al. Bellingham, WA: Logos Bible Software, 2012.

The Lexham English Septuagint: Alternate Texts. Edited by Rick Brannan, Ken M. Penner, Israel Loken et al. Bellingham, WA: Logos Bible Software, 2012.

The Lexham High Definition Old Testament: ESV Edited by Steven E. Runge and Joshua R. Westbury. Logos Bible Software, 2012.

The Lexham High Definition Old Testament: Glossary. Edited by Steven E. Runge and Joshua R. Westbury. Lexham High Definition Old Testament. Bellingham, WA: Logos Bible Software, 2012.

New Dictionary of Biblical Theology. Edited by T. Desmond Alexander and Brian S. Rosner. electronic ed. Downers Grove, IL: InterVarsity Press, 2001.

The New International Version. Grand Rapids, MI: Zondervan, 2011.

The Reformation Study Bible: English Standard Version. Edited by R. C. Sproul. Orlando, FL; Lake Mary, FL: Ligonier Ministries, 2005.

Religion In the Dead Sea Scrolls. Edited by John J. Collins and Robert A. Kugler. Studies in the Dead Sea Scrolls and Related Literature. Grand Rapids, MI; Cambridge, U.K.: William B. Eerdmans Publishing Company, 2000.

Standard Bible Dictionary. Cincinnati: Standard Publishing, 2006.

Zondervan Dictionary of Biblical Imagery. Edited by John A. Beck. Grand Rapids, MI: Zondervan, 2011.

Other materials for further Study:

NOT SUBJECT TO ORDER or preference. Not Alphabetical.

www.thegreatcourses.com

Lectures pertaining to the following subjects:

-The Old Testament, taught by Prof. Amy-Jill Levine

-The Dead sea Scrolls, taught by Prof. Gary A. Rendsberg.

-God and mankind: Comparative Religions, taught by Prof. Robert Oden

-Myth in human history, taught by Prof. Grant L. Voth

* www.torahresource.com[1]

Messianic (Jewish) teachings on various subjects

* www.wikipedia.org/wiki[2]

*www.mashiyach.com/rapture[3]

Messianic/ Aramaic leanings. Producers of the AENT.

*www.dailykos.com/story/2006/08/08234333/-history-of-rapture-doctrine[4]

*www.therefinersfire.org[5]

Favours the Aent. A 'Messianic' teaching site.

*www.michaelheiser.com/thenakedbible/Eschatology-discussion[6] and

---

1. http://www.torahresource.com
2. http://www.wikipedia.org/wiki
3. http://www.mashiyach.com/rapture
4. http://www.dailykos.com/story/2006/08/08234333/-history-of-rapture-doctrine
5. http://www.therefinersfire.org

DECONSTRUCTING ENDTIME DELUSIONS

* www.michaelheiser.com[7]

Dr. Heiser is (at the time of writing) the Academic editor of LOGOS Bible Systems. He has a number of linked websites that are worthy of greater notice. Though academic in content, they are written in plain language.

*www.logos.com[8]

A highly recommended Bible study platform.

Serious students of the Bible should have an electronic Bible Study platform. Or at least access to sites like www.esword.com[9] (free to download and most resources are free also but is limited in power in relation to what logos offers customers.)

*www.biblicalarchaeology.org[10]

for the latest archaeological discussions and finds (toward a Bible perspective).

*www.closertotruth.com[11]

Interesting conversations on a range of subjects with numerous scholars and experts.

*www.imaginnosatan.com[12]

on subjects re: the Satan myth.

*www.virtuequmran.huji.ac.il[13]

---

6. http://www.michaelheiser.com/thenakedbible/eschatology-discussion
7. http://www.michaelheiser.com
8. http://www.logos.com
9. http://www.esword.com
10. http://www.biblicalarchaeology.org
11. http://www.closertotruth.com
12. http://www.imaginnosatan.com
13. http://www.virtuequmran.huji.ac.il

Brilliant virtual world of the dead sea scrolls.

*www.pantheon.com[14]

Encyclopedia Mythica: website dedicated to bring the world myth together. from the welcome page: [an] award-winning internet encyclopaedia of mythology, folklore, and religion.

www.en.wikipedia.org[15]

www.bibleinterp.com[16]

www.skepticink.com[17]

- skeptic magazine, vol 18 no: 4 (2013); vol's 19 no's:1-3 (2014)

www.edfu-books.com[18]

www.sis-group.org.uk[19]

www.freethoughtblogs.com[20]

www.robertmprice.mindvendor.com[21]

www.livescience.com[22]

www.topdocumentarfilms.com/Christian-dilemmas[23]

free documentary films covering various subjects.

---

14. http://www.pantheon.com
15. http://www.en.wikipedia.org
16. http://www.bibleinterp.com
17. http://www.skepticink.com
18. http://www.edfu-books.com
19. http://www.sis-group.org.uk
20. http://www.freethoughtblogs.com
21. http://www.robertmprice.mindvendor.com
22. http://www.livescience.com
23. http://www.topdocumentarfilms.com/christian-dilemmas

DECONSTRUCTING ENDTIME DELUSIONS

www.topdocumentaryfilms.com/michael-shermer-th-believing-brain[24]

www.spiritoferror.org[25]

www.theopedia.com/end_times[26]

www.openlibrary.org[27]

www.ancient-origins.net/videos[28]

www.ancient-origins.net/videos/interview-brian-foerster-unveiloing-genetics-elongated-skulls-001316[29]

www.perankhgroup.com[30]

---

24. http://www.topdocumentaryfilms.com/michael-shermer-th-believing-brain
25. http://www.spiritoferror.org
26. http://www.theopedia.com/end_times
27. http://www.openlibrary.org
28. http://www.ancient-origins.net/videos
29. http://www.ancient-origins.net/videos/interview-brian-foerster-unveiloing-genetics-elongated-skulls-001316
30. http://www.perankhgroup.com

Ebook resources:

(NOT EXTENSIVE. THE following list offers a broad cross-section of the academic/ Christian/ scientific subjects and authors consulted. Some 400+ electronic titles were either liberally consulted/or read entirely during my research for this project):

Albert, J Gun Control USA...

Alford, A GODS of the New Millennium

Alexander, T.D. Ancient Secrets: Astronomy of the Gods

Andrews, S Deconverted: A journey from Religion to Reason

Ashe, G Eden in the Altai

Atran, S In GODS we Trust

Atlantis Rising Anthology: Lost Ancient Wisdom

Library Lost History

Alternative Archaeology

Atwell, J Caesar's Messiah

Aukofer, C and Thomas, A J Why we believe in God(s)

Bane, T Encyclopedia of Imaginary and Mythical Places

Baigent, M The Jesus Papers

Barrett, J. L Cognitive Science, Religion, and Theology

Beatie, W Ancient Etymological Correlatives – The Annunaki Enigma

Becker, E The Denial of Death

Bering, J The God Instinct

DECONSTRUCTING ENDTIME DELUSIONS

Berlinerblau, J The Secular Bible

Benigni, H The Mythology of Venus: Ancient Calendars and Archaeoastronomy

Bellah, R Religion in Human Evolution

Bennett, Bo Logical Fallacies

Black, J The Secret history of the world

Booysen, R, Thera and the Exodus

Breshears, J Shocking Secrets of Antiquity

Brockman, J This will make you smarter

Brown, A F In the days of Giants

Briggs, C V Encyclopedia of the Unseen World

Burrow, J A history of Histories

Butler-Bowden, T 50 Philosophy Classics

Carpenter, E Pagan and Christian creeds: their origin and meaning

Carroll, R A Skeptic's Dictionary

Carroll, J M The Trail of Blood

Carrier, R Proving History

Carver, T The Newer, More English Version

Campion, N Astrology and Cosmology in the world and religion

Cerow, D When dragons wore the crown: putting Starlight back into the myth

Cline, E From Eden to Exile: Unravelling the mysteries of the Bible

Coogan, M D Stories from Ancient Canaan [2nd]

Cohen, A Everymans Talmud

Cohn, N The Pursuit of the Millennium

Charles River Editors - Judgment Day: the historical and religious Evolution ...

The religion of ancient Mesopotamia

Chouinard, P Lost race of the giants

Cosmological Science Pub - NEAR DEATH: After-death dreams, Spirits, Souls...

Curran, B Man-made Monsters

Currie, D. B. Rapture

Cumont, F Astrology and Religion among the Greeks and Romans

Darrel, R The God Virus

Davies, W Nervous States

Dawkins, R The God Delusion

Detering, H The Fabricated Paul

Dever, W G The rise of ancient Israel

Doane, T. W. Bible Myths

Doherty, E Jesus Neither God nor Man: the case for a mythical Jesus

Dunn, C The Giza Power plant

Edgerton, R. B Sick Societies: Challenging the myth of Primitive harmony

Ehrman, B Jesus: Apocalyptic Prophet...

DECONSTRUCTING ENDTIME DELUSIONS

Forged – writing in the name of God

Ellerbe, H The Darker side of Christian History

Ellis, R Jesus, last of the Pharaoh's

Espinoza, J The Biblical God doesn't exist: arguments and evidence

Ezzat, Ashrat Egypt knew no Pharaohs nor Israelites

Feather, R The Secret Initiation of Jesus at Qumran: The Essene mysteries of john Fillmore, C Metaphysical Bible Dictionary

Metaphysical Bible Dictionary: The revealing Word

Ford, B Bible Fallacies: a must read for those with an open mind

Foubister, L Goddess in the Grass

Farrell, J P Genes, Giants, Monsters, and men

Fort, G The book of the damned – collected works of Charles fort

Flem-Ath, R and R Atlantis beneath the ice

Freud, S Moses and monotheism

Freke, T The Laughing Jesus

Fritze, R H Invented Knowledge

Gadalla, M Historical Deception: The untold story of ancient Egypt

Gardiner, M fads and fallacies in the name of science

George, A and E The Mythology of Eden

O'Grady, S And Man Created God

Graham, Llyod M Deceptions and Myths of the Bible.

Gray, J Dead Men's Secrets: tantalising hints of a Lost Super Race

Greer, John Michael Apocalypse: A History of the End of Time

Apocalypse Not: Everything you know about 2012,

Grayling, Prof. A C The Good Book – a secular Bible

Grazier, K, Di Justo, D - The Science of Battlestar Galactica

Greenberg, G 101 Myths of the Bible

Goodwilie, F Miraclescam

Graves, K The Worlds Crucified Saviors

Grimassi, Raven The Wiccan Mysteries

Hart, D. Man the Hunted

Hall. M. P. How to Understand Your Bible

Halaw, A. D. God is Nothingness

Hanson, P The Dawn of the Apocalyptic

Harding, F Nephilim Skeletons Found!

Harrison, G P Think – why you should question everything

Harpur, T The Pagan Christ

Hand-Clow, B Catastrophobia

Heather, L The Sumerian Controversy

HowStuff Works The End of the World

Higgins, G Anacalypsis Volume One

Hines, C Gateway of the gods: an investigation...

Houk, J. T The Illusion of Certainty

Hume, D The David Hume collection: 17 classic work

DECONSTRUCTING ENDTIME DELUSIONS

Pyysiainen, Ilkka Magic, Miracles, and Religion: A scientist's perspective

Kaplan, M The science of monsters

Kenyon, J, D (editor) - Forbidden History

Koester, C. R. Revelation and the End of things

Kragel, C M The grand deception: Fallacies in theology and faith

Kuhn, A B Who is this King of Glory

The Alvin Boyd Kuhn Collection

Knight-Jadczyk, L The secret History of the World: and how to get out alive

Jennings, J Gog Magog, and Armageddon: Origins of End.

Joseph, F. Military Encounters with Extraterrestrials: The Real War of the...

Jones, D. E. An Instinct for Dragons

Jones, S The Serpent's Promise: The Bible retold as science

Julien, N The Mammoth book of Lost Symbols

Laertius; Diogenes The Lives and opinions of Eminent Philosophers

Largo, M God's lunatics

Lataster, R There was no Jesus, there is no God

Lavarda, A The Bioarchaeology of Ritual and Religion

Lee, E From the Bodies of the Gods

Leick, Dr. G A Dictionary of Ancient Near Eastern Mythology

Lewis, B R Dark history of the Popes

Linden, D, J The accidental Mind

Lipton, B H Biology of Belief

Loftus, J W (ed.) Christianity is not great

Long, Dr. J Biblical Nonsense

Lynn, H Anthrotheology: Searching for God in Man

Malley, B How the Bible Works

Maddison, D Ten Tough Problems in Christian thought and Belief

Marsh, E C; Yonge, C D - The works of philo judaeus of Alexandria

Massey, G Ancient Egypt, Light of the World: Vol I and II (complete collection)

The Historical Jesus and mythical Christ:...

Martinez, S. B. PhD. The Mysterious Origins of Hybrid Man

Mathews, V H Old Testament Parallels

McLachlan, T. D. The Saturn Death Cult

Mcliveen, Lloyd E Evaluating Outdated Beliefs

McRoberts, S The Cure for Fundamentalism: Why the Bible cannot be the Word

McNamara P The Neuroscience of Religious Experience

McVeigh, B How Religion Evolved

Mehler, S From Light into Darkness

Merriman, Z The Evolution of Religion

Mills, D Atheist Universe

Mithen, S The Prehistory of the Mind

Montague, C ANGELS: The complete Mythology of angels...

Mott, Wm M Caverns, Cauldrons, and Concealed Creatures – 3rd edition

Murdock, D M (S Archarya) Did Moses Exist: the myth of the Israelite Lawgiver

Suns of God: Krishna, Buddha and Christ unveiled, and others.

Mutton, K Scattered Skeletons in our Closet

Murphy, D (phd) Jesus Potter Harry Christ

Netlancers Inc. Collection of Astrology and Sky Lore

Niles, D Dragons: The Myths, Legends, and Lore

Nyland, Dr. A All written material by this author is recommended.

Newberg, A Born to Believe

Newman, R C Jewish polemic against Christianity in the second Century

Olcott, W T Sun Lore of all ages

Osman, A The lost city of the Exodus, and others.

Owen, J The ninth generation (A 'supernatural' adventure novel)

Oubre, A Instinct and Revelation: Reflections on the Origins...

Parks, W Atlantis: The eyewitnesses (Parts i, ii, iii)

Patai, R Hebrew Myths: The Book of Genesis

Paulkovich, M Beyond the Crusades

Perry, R H The complete idiot's guide: The Last Days

Preston, S Four Armageddon's, and others.

Price, R M The Politically Correct Bible

Pippin, T Apocalyptic Bodies

Proux, D R Lies have ruined the world

Porphyry, ed. (Hoffman, J) - Porphyry's Against Christians

Pye, and Dalley, K Lost secrets of the Gods

Rawlings, P Atlantis: the great flood and the asteroid

Redfern, N The Pyramids and the Pentagon

Remsberg, J E The Christ

Robinson, J M The Nag Hammadi scriptures

Rohl, D The Lords of Avaris

Sand, S The Invention of the Jewish people

Sallustius On the gods and the world

Scranton, L The Velikovsky Heresies

Sacred Texts Sacredtexts.com (Flashdrive 9.0) Various book/subjects

Silva, F Legacy of the God's

Sharpe, S Egyptian Mythology and Egyptian Christianity

Shermer, M How We Believe, and others.

Shorto, R Gospel Truth – on the trail of the historical Jesus

Slone. D. J and Slyke. J (ed.) - The Attraction of Religion: A New Psychology of Religion

Livingstone Smith, D Why we Lie

DECONSTRUCTING ENDTIME DELUSIONS

The Most dangerous Animal

Souza, A, Doomsday chronicles

Sprague de Camp, L Lost Continents

Stefanelli, A, Free Thoughts

Steiger, B Worlds Before Our Own

Tate, JP All God Worshippers are Mad: A little book of sanity

Taylor, Rev. R The Diegesis: a discovery of the origin, evidences...

Taylor, T Arguments of Celsus, Porphyry, and the emperor Julian...

Trzaskoma, S Anthology of Classical Myth: Primary Sources in Translation...

Twain, M The War Prayer

Letters from the Earth

Travis, C and Aronson E - Mistakes were made (but not by me)

Trout. P. A DEADLY POWERS

Velikovsky, I Mankind in Amnesia

Vendramini, D Them+Us

Vintner, J C Ancient Earth Mysteries

Vortex Lost continents: The legend and the myth.

Von Fleischer, A When giants Ruled the world

Warren, S The Bible Naked, the greatest fraud ever told

Wade, N Before the Dawn

Wake, C. Staniland The Origins of Serpent Worship

Watts, A The Wisdom of Insecurity

Wells, S The Skeptic's annotated Bible

Werleman, C J God hates you, Hate him back

West, A The Cycle of Cosmic Catastrophes

West, P The Old ones in the Old book

Wheless, J Is it God's word?

Forgery in Christianity

Wright, R The Evolution of God: The origins of our beliefs

Wong, Ir, J K K The Evolution of the God illusion

Zevit, Z. What really happened in the Garden of Eden

Appendix One:

Signs and Symbols:

AS WITH MANY USEFUL words, symbol comes from Greek. It means to bring together things that had come apart, the way you might glue the bits of a broken plate together. Then a symbol became an object that stood for or represented something else. It still had the idea of joining things up, but it had become more complicated than simply glueing bits of pottery together. Symbolism, is an art not a science. According to Steven Olderr, author of "Symbols: a comprehensive dictionary".

> "The governing factor of any sign or symbol must be the context. But, contexts are often used differently by any people group. Even those within the same ethnicity might use a certain symbol or sign differently and for a different purpose. It is noteworthy that signs and symbols are expressions of, and instruments for man's knowledge. They regard the knowledge about himself and the wider world he inhabits. Symbolism is basic to the human mind; to ignore it is to suffer a serious deficiency; it is fundamental to thinking, and the perfect symbol should satisfy every aspect of man – his spirit, intellect and emotions. All religious rites have a symbolic significance and quality without the understanding of which they become empty and 'superstitious.'"[dxx]

It is fascinating to take the time to study signs, and symbols. This is why I have decided to include as an Appendix a brief number of signs and symbols that anyone reading the sacred texts of the Judaeo-Christian tradition would most likely recognise. Some entries may be unfamiliar as constituting a sign or symbol. But, these only offer further intrigues and value as most likely, a comprehension of these will open instead of occlude the sacred texts possible meaning. I have endeavoured to keep entries as succinct, and relevant as possible. I have utilised for this Appendix several sign and symbol books available (e-book resources). The following abbreviations denote some of the main texts consulted.

Entries for this Appendices were gathered from any of the following sources, but they do not intend to be exhaustive:

- (**Sym.**) Symbolism: A Comprehensive Dictionary, Second Steven Olderr.

- (**B, Sym.**) The Book of Symbols: Reflections on Archetypal Images. Various authors; WWW.ARAS.ORG (hard-copy)

- (**Lit Sym.**) A Dictionary of Literary Symbols: Third Michael Ferber.

- (**DK**.) Signs and Symbols: An Illustrated guide to their Origins and Meanings. (DK: Dorling and Kindersley Ltd.)

- (**CJC**) An Illustrated Encyclopaedia of Traditional Symbols: C. J. Cooper. Thames and Hudson Ltd.

- (**P B Sym**) The Pretty Big Book of Symbols: A Handy Quick Reference Guide with Keyword Meanings for Over 1400 Psychic Symbols, Animals, Plants, Gemstones, Everyday Objects and More! Clare McNaul. Chinwag Press.

- (**Wd S**) The Woman's Dictionary of Symbols and Sacred objects: Barbara G Walker. HarperOne.

- (**DBS**) Dictionary of Biblical Symbolism: Compiled, edited, and with Introduction by Stanislaw Kapuscinski (aka Stan I.S. Law), Stanislaw. INHOUSEPRESS.

- (**Harwood**) William Harwood. Dictionary of Contemporary Mythology (2011) Independent Custom Press.)

These are just a few of the numbers of books on the study of Symbolism. There are many more that could have been noted. Readers interested in Symbolism are encouraged to source for themselves these, or another

DECONSTRUCTING ENDTIME DELUSIONS

Symbol study. It is the hope that by supplying the following entries, readers are better equipped to comprehend and understand that their favoured sacred texts are literally imbued with multiple signs and symbols. A comprehension of these should offer another perspective to a given meaning than what is proposed by Christian authorities. Specifically, the authorities that do not account for the symbolism, mythologies and their meanings are rather prone to follow the present state holding to an opinion of their sacred texts as literal compositions. Just as was seen throughout the studies in this book. If a word, symbol, or sign is felt to be too extensive for this publication, readers are directed to the applicable source(s). Unfortunately, christianity has often pilfered many signs and symbols from around the world, and have attached to these various twisted and contorted meanings far adrift from what is likely the original. For example: in the Introduction of Signs and Symbols, the author interestingly hints at the origin of gargoyles; that, "...the tao t'ieh, or highly stylised face that appears on the bronze vessels of Ancient China, re-emerges in the gargoyles of European cathedrals and in the motifs of cultures around the Pacific Rim." Thus, we can see that according to this resource, gargoyles were 'originally' stylised faces that decorated vessels, and are Chinese in origin. They are not a stylised motif of an often-disfigured animal or mythic creature invented by christianity to titivate Church buildings. As you will shortly see gargoyles have several symbolic meanings today: they could represent any or all the following; forces of the cosmos; evil forces made to serve good; evil spirits; objectified powers of evil; scarecrows for evil spirits; fertility enslaved by superior spirituality. To grasp and understand signs and symbols has the potential of enriching each of our lives, adding a sense of depth, particularly to sacred texts. "Once we see objects as representing truths or deeper issues, we begin to develop a realization (sic) of the dual nature of existence – the inner and outer life – all around us... Seeing objects in this symbolic way allows us to live more "harmoniously" by increasing our awareness, not only of day-to-day living but also of the universal truths of existence."[dxxi]

Signs and Symbols:

- Achilles - (Sym) [of Greek mythology] representing the vulnerable hero; the one prone to hubris.

- Adam - (DBS) Symbolises the consciousness that identifies with the physical self. Both Adam and Eve symbolically are ONE person. (Sym) spirituality made flesh; weak, sinful man. (Harwood) Masculinization (sic) of Adamah, the primeval Hebrew earth mother. (Locations 123-124).

- Adamah - (DBS, (p.78).) [c] red earth, fortress; [the color (sic) red often symbolizes (uncontrolled) emotions]. (Harwood) Hebrew word that in the Yahwist's time meant "clay" and "red," but originally meant Earth as mother of all life. (Location 130).

- Air - (Sym.) creation; masculinity (principal of); represents the mental plane.

- Androgyne - (Sym.) Self-creation; perfection of Oneness/wholeness; integration of opposites. (CJC) Primordial perfection; wholeness; the coincidentia oppositorum; the unconditioned state; autonomy; paradise regained; the reunion of the primordial male-female forces; the union of heaven and earth, king and queen, the two becoming the One, the all-father, all-mother. [Location 170. Italics Original]

- Apple - (DK) In Europe the apple symbolizes (sic) love, fertility, youth, and immortality; its circular shape indicates eternity. It is widely associated with the Tree of Knowledge. To the Celts it was a symbol of the afterlife and fertility. In China it indicates peace. In the Bible the apple is [said to be] the [alleged] forbidden fruit eaten by Eve and symbolizes temptation and sin. (Page 98). [my addition]

DECONSTRUCTING ENDTIME DELUSIONS

• Ararat - (Sym) Jewish the second cradle of humanity; World Navel. (Location 465).

• Armageddon - (DBS) Traditionally a place of (spiritual) battle, between the (good) of christ consciousness, and (evil/bad) sentience. Symbolically, victory over limitation of these two aspects of the nature of humankind. (Sym.) Conflict within the Self.

• Almond - (CJC.) Virginity; the self-productive; the yoni; conjugal happiness. It is also the vesica piscis which, in art, often surrounds virgin Queens of Heaven... As the first flower of the year the blossom is 'the Awakener', hence it depicts watchfulness; it also represents sweetness, charm and delicacy. Chinese: Feminine beauty, fortitude in sorrow, watchfulness. Christian: Divine favour and approval. The purity of the Virgin. Hebrew: 'Skeked' – to waken and watch. Iranian: The Tree of Heaven. Phrygian: The father of all things: Spring. It is associated with the birth of Attis, the almond having sprung from the male genitalia of the androgynous Cybele. (Locations 121-127.) (Wd S) Almonds symbolise fertility and a fruitful union in marriage. See entry: Almond in (Lit Sym); (Sym); (DK).

• Antichrist - (Sym) symbolically the antagonist of the soul. (DBS) In christianity, is against the christ-consciousness. The limited mind; the material mind.

• Atlantis - (Sym) • Greek ancient mysteries, wisdom, enlightenment; the lost Paradise. (Location 548).

• Beast - (Sym) selfishness; self-centredness (sic); the lower instincts • Christian four beasts of the Apocalypse: desires of the four lower chakras (Locations 686-687). (italics original).

- Bone - (CJC) Indestructible life; resurrection; also, mortality and the transitory. (Sym) strength, virtue and resoluteness. See also (B, Sym. p.334–5). Broken: weakness in your plans or an approach to your way of thinking about something - A broken relationship or one that needs attending to may be indicated (P B, Sym. (Locations 3245-3247)). (Wd S) Across the world bones have been seen as being infested and invested with numerous magical/mystical powers– the curse of 'pointing the bone', believed to cause destruction or other mayhem to the pointee. Bone powders are a sought-after cure for some illnesses. By association: Skeleton (P B, Sym) an endeavour past its prime; something hidden, not revealed, a need to 'get to the "bone" of something'– the 'essence' of something.

- Cedar - (CJC) nobility, strength, incorruptibility; majesty and beauty. (Sym) immortality, prosperity, growth, height, vengeance; mystery and longevity. (Lit Sym) often denotes pride, vanity and arrogance (which is, as has been seen in the passage of Amos 2:9 in the study: The Genesis Six Experiment, exactly how it is used by the author of the Amos passage), and does not assume immense height (as would be expected if speaking of giants. The assumption made by Rob Skiba and others). (P B Sym) healing, protection, cleansing.

- Clouds - (see CJC article. Location, 1086.) symbolises the Unseen deity figure; divine protection.

- Cyclopes - (DK) with their single eye in the middle of the forehead, some consider the cyclopes as a subhuman race of brutish folk.

- DNA - (Harwood) Deoxy ribonucleic acid; molecule containing the genetic blueprint of all terrestrial life forms, containing millions of atoms and capable of trillions of permutations. DNA has provided the final proof of the reality of evolution, by revealing similarities far beyond the widest bounds of coincidence, not only between human and bonobo/chimpanzee DNA, but also between human and bacterial DNA... (Locations 2419-2421).

• Dead; Death; dead bodies - (DBS) the dead are said to symbolise those who have not come to realise their heritage of Divinity. Dead bodies, symbolise those things, thoughts, and concepts that have been overcome by our (beastly) nature, the negative nature as opposed to a spiritual nature. Death, (1) change in consciousness, (2) loss of Divine Presence (loss in awareness), (3) an illusory state.

• Devil - (DBS) (Heb. sair): hairy one, kid, goat; spoiler, destroyer; (Gr. daimonion): daimon, demon, shade; (Gr. daimon): a difiled (sic) spirit; (Gr. diablos): accuser, calumniator; [All the above are translated as Devil. The Devil always symbolizes the product of the mind] (p.112). [gramma discrepancies/ mistakes original]

• Devil - (Harwood) From Indo-European devas, "God"; any minor God belonging to the faction opposing the good gods; originally a Devil was distinct from a demon, in that a Devil had never been endowed with a corporeal body. In Essene mythology, which became Christian mythology, a Devil was a member of the band of messenger gods, (Greek: angeloi), that supported the Satan in his rebellion against Yahweh. Devil, the In Judaeo-Christian mythology, the planetary God Azaziel, a masculinized (sic)Venus, who led a rebellion against Yahweh and was thereafter known as ha-Satan , "the enemy." (Locations 2326-2330).

• Demon - (Harwood) minor gods of mythology. Essene mythology, demons became the souls ofdeceased giants.

Christianity reversed this, becoming rebellious angel type entities.

• Dragon - (See CJC article. Location 1688.) (DBS) symbolising the complexities of life that are buried deeply within the conscious. (Harwood) generic names of reptilian creatures common to world mythology.

• Dinosaur - (Sym) [as would be expected] symbolically represents extinction; primitive nature.

• Duality - (Sym) ambivalence; the physical and spiritual nature of all things.

• Eclipse - (Sym) omen of a cataclysmic event, such as war, plague, the death of the kings; the Day of the Lord is at hand.

• Elohim - (DBS.) Many variations in translation, nonetheless, "...is evocative of the Power Within, the El of the human equation." (p.119).

• Enemy - (Sym) symbolises the inner threat.

• Egypt - (DBS) Symbolises shut in, physical detainment, materiality. (Sym) the animal in man; bondage; idolatry; concern with life after death; ancient wisdom; antiquity. (Locations 2024-2025).

• Eschatology - (Harwood) the mythology of prophesy focussed on an end-time.

• Eye - (DBS) Symbolises the ability to focus on, detect and gather knowledge (in religious view, Divine); (Sym) eyesight = mental perception; enlightenment;.one eye divine omniscience; the self-contained; the eye of God; subhumanity (sic); extra human effort devoted to one aim, usually unfavorable (sic); may imply the possession of second-sight... (Locations 2097-2098).

- Excrement - (CJC. Location 1921.) Associated with gold and riches; contains the power of the person...

- Extraterrestrial - (Sym) unknown part of the self; unknown known threats. (Aliens) P B Sym)- Undiscovered parts of yourself - Wild imagination - Wish to escape - Feeling like your space or privacy is being invaded.

- Famine - (DBS) symbolically = a mental/ spiritual yearning. Female (DBS) Symbolises the emotional and subconscious (both sexes).

- Feet - (DK) said to support the soul; The power of mobility and a "solid foundation" is symbolized (sic) by our feet. In Hinduism, feet are seen as a point of divine contact between human beings and Earth. In the Middle East one showed respect for a visitor or friend by washing their feet, while in Asia feet are considered unclean, so it is taboo to point the soles of your feet towards another person. (DK. Signs and Symbols (Page 117).

- Flood - (Sym) represents the inundation of spirit and emotion; most universally floods are representative of punishment, rather than complete obliteration; cyclic ends; purification through regeneration. Most have an apocalyptic element. There are however exceptions to apocalyptic Flood themes. Regions that experience annual flooding, Egypt: the Nile, and the Amazon basin, do not possess an apocalyptic flood narrative, (DK). Flooding is the creator and bringer and sustainer of life. (DBS) a flood also symbolises mental anguish. (CJC) ending of a cycle, beginning of another, causing both death and regeneration.

- Fruit - (Sym) Symbolically = abundance (spiritual); wisdom; immortality; plentifulness.

- False Witness - (DBS) Negativity; negative consciousness.

- Fingers - (See Symbolism: A Comprehensive Dictionary).

- Gargoyle - (Sym) forces of the cosmos; evil forces made to serve good; evil spirits; objectified powers of evil; scarecrows for evil spirits; fertility enslaved by superior spirituality; evil passions • on the outside of a Church evil passions driven out of man by the Gospels. (Locations 2426-2427).

- Giant - the unconscious; the forces of dissatisfaction; everlasting rebellion; despotism; evil; impending evil; the Terrible Father; Universal Man; the father principle; quantitative simplification; man before The Fall; the id; tyranny; the brute force of nature; primordial power and forces; the elemental; innate regressive tendencies; protector of the common people; associated with darkness, cannibalism, Winter... [Steven Older. Symbolism: A Comprehensive Dictionary, 2nd (Location 2464-2466).] (CJC) brute force [nature's]; can be beneficent or malefic/destructive.

- Gog - (DBS) High; extended; (Wikipedia) In Ezekiel 38, Gog is an individual and Magog is his land; in Genesis 10 Magog is a man, but no Gog is mentioned; and centuries later Jewish tradition changed Ezekiel's Gog from Magog into Gog and Magog, which is the form in which they appear in the Book of Revelation, although there they are peoples rather than individuals. Hence, both Gog and Magog reference (groups/ ethnicities) of people.

- Gomorrah - (DBS) symbolically = Oppression; (Sym.) In Jewish symbolism = carnal passions.

- Hand - (DBS) Ability of expression of spiritual ideas on the physical plane. (Sym.) protection; justice; authority. Right (hand) aggressiveness; logic; conscious. Left (hand) weakness, death, irrationality...

- Heart - (DBS) symbolises embedded ideas in the subconscious. (Sym.) seat of intelligence and understanding.

- Heaven - (DBS) The state of contentment (spiritual); (Sym.) spirituality; the masculine principle; spiritual reward; union with God; the higher self; bliss; joy; father of earthly rulers; superhuman power; abode of the blessed • Egyptian matter; the feminine principle • Jewish the godhead Oceanic matter • Teutonic matter. (Locations 2802-2803).

- Hell - (DBS) the state of mind devoid of knowledge of (deity)

- Horses - (DBS. pp.141-142) In the book of Revelation black, red and dun horses symbolize (sic) the intellectual, emotional and physical aspects of human nature. The white horse symbolizes our spiritual aspect. The concept of man's fourfold nature goes back (at least) to the Egyptian God Horus and his 4 sons. It reappears in the story of Noah and his 3 sons and later in the story of Shadrach, Meshach, Abednego and the fourth man. There are ample examples of it in the Revelation of John. It continues in the Christian tradition in the Christ's halo being into four; (Sym.) lust; fertility; selfishness; fidelity; vanity... See, horse article by Steven Older. Symbolism: A Comprehensive Dictionary, 2nd edition (Locations 2910-2911).

- Jericho - (DBS) city of the moon-deity; symbolising intellectual understanding.

- Kingdom - (DBS, p.161) Symbolizes (sic) any established state of consciousness – thus kingdom can refer to a negative as well as positive state of consciousness, depending on the content of thoughts ruling or being preponderant in such a "kingdom". That is why the kingdom can only be: "within you".

- LORD - (DBS) symbolises the I AM conscious; inner divinity (metaphysically)

- Magog - (DBS, p 167.) [Akkadian mat gugu = land of Gog; Sumarian gug = darkness; thus: "the land of darkness?" In the Revelation of Saint John the Divine (20:8), Gog and Magog are recognised as symbols of the enemies of God. Darkness always symbolizes the absence of divine light, i.e. of divine knowledge, i.e. of the Presence of God.

- Male - (DBS) Intellect; conscious - as opposed to feelings (subconscious/female)

- Milky Way - (Sym.Locations 3533-3534) infinitude • Australian aboriginal the river of heaven • Celtic the chain of Lug • Chinese the celestial river • Norse the pathway to Valhalla • North American Indian the pathway of ghost. [Steven Older.]

- Moon - (DBS) symbolises the subconsciousness of the soul. See also extensive article in (CJC).

- Name - (DBS) ...In the Bible the name always describes or symbolises the nature or the principle traits of character of the person [or place] so named... names therefore refer to different states of consciousness the soul or psyche may enter on its path towards Self-Realization (sic). (p.14). ...symbolizes the nature of that which is being named; all that comprises the sum-total of the character of an object and/or person thus designated. (p. 177). (Sym.) The Name is the symbol, the key to power, it is regarded as the soul of the named.

• Naked(ness) - (Sym. Location 3764.) freedom from worldly tainting; renunciation of worldliness; pagan/ demonic shamelessness. (P B Sym. Location 7950.) Honesty; Vulnerability...

• Patmos - (DBS) mortal; (A sterile island in the Ægean sea) Symbolises physical or mortal (state of) consciousness. (p.185).

• Pineal glands - (Sym) associated with self-realised individuals, Mercury (planet) • Christian associated with Christ, the Church at Philadelphia • Hindu associated with light and the higher mind, the 6th chakra... (Locations 4089-4090).

• Pleiades - (Sym.) completeness; order; since there are seven of them, they share in the symbolism of that number [Seven: (CJC)The number 7 is the number of the universe, the macrocosm. Completeness; a totality. With the three of the heavens and the soul and the four of the earth and the body, it is the first number which contains both the spiritual and temporal. It is perfection; security; safety; rest; plenty; reintegration; synthesis, also virginity and the number of the Great Mother. There are seven cosmic stages, heavens, hells, major planets and metals of the planets, circles of the universe, rays of the sun, ages of man, pillars of wisdom, lunar divisions of the rainbow, days of the week, notes of the scale, wonders of the world etc. (Location 3810.)] • rising of the Pleiades = start of the navigation season; the early or Spring harvest; beginning of a new year • setting of the Pleiades = new sowing; Fall. [Steven Older. (Sym)Locations 4123-4125.)]

- Psyche - (Harwood)... The Greek word psyche originated as an undefined life force, and is now interpreted as soul. (Locations 5725-5726).

- Psykhe - (Psyche) Originally, the metaphysical life that was an attribute of all living things. In ACTS 2:41, the psykhai triskhiliai converted by Peter should be translated "three thousand living persons." MARK 8:36, correctly translated, reads, "How much does a human profit if.. he loses his life." As mythology evolved, psykhe came to mean a separate entity incorporated into the physical body, usually translated soul, even though losing one's psykhe continued to mean die. The Greek myth of the mating of Eros and Psykhe symbolised the total union of flesh and mind, or body and soul. (Locations 8491-8495).

- Pyramid - (See article in Lit. Sym.) (CJC) representing the axis Mundi the world Centre and Sacred Mountain. It is said to also represent symbolically fire, the flame as well as the planes of consciousness; symbolises the highest manifestation of spirituality; is also a phallic symbol.

- Rephaim - (DBS) giant; strong. One of the Dead, a deceased warrior.

- Resurrection - (DBS) the metamorphosis/change of the sub/conscious of mankind, from sensual to spiritual.

- River - (a directional flow) symbolizes (sic) a change in consciousness. Crossing the water demonstrates a victory over oneself. (Dictionary of Biblical Symbolism) (p.195). Italics original.

- Serpent/ Snake - (see extensive article in CJC) Recall also the symbolic images of these animals, Nail Four above.

DECONSTRUCTING ENDTIME DELUSIONS

- Six - (DBS) number "6" is symbolic of labour, particularly work without fulfilment... [In the Revelation, "666" symbolizes (sic) ongoing 'abortive' work]. (p.209).

- Sodom, Sodoma - (DBS, p.210.) [c] place of lime; burning; consuming with fire; secret intrigues; covered conspiracies; [Revelation 11:8, equates Sodom with Egypt and with: "where also our Lord was crucified"].

- son - (DBS). p.210.) symbolizes (sic): 1. the outcome of a mental process, e.g. a (new) idea; 2. the result or a consequence of an action; (see children) son of man symbolizes the human personality; [Son of man, with S capitalized symbolizes One in whom the human consciousness is already redeemed]. Son (CJC) The double; the living image; the alter ego.

- Stars - (DBS) Undiscovered truth

- Titans - • Buddhist supermen with the failings of aggression, ambition, and envy which lead to their downfall • Greco-Roman wild and untamable (sic) forces of primeval nature; the force of manifestation; the brute strength of the earth; desire in rebellion against the spirit... [Steven Older. Symbolism: A Comprehensive Dictionary, 2nd edition (Locations 5285-5286).]

- Teeth - (DK) often symbolise animal strength and aggression; can also be a symbol of beauty; ambition; fertility in some cultures; wrathful aspects (of particularly deities); to lack teeth is a sign of a loss of youth; a sign of vulnerability

- Tree - (P B Sym) - Knowledge - Protection - Striving - Achievement - Stability - Self-development and individuation - Cycle of life and the passage of time - Grounding energy may be needed - Concentration on self-growth and development...

- Trojan - (Sym) lower emotions; diligence; endurance; war. (Location 5407).

- Thousand Years - (DBS) Not literal time, but symbolic long period.

- Warrior - (DBS) symbolically represents those who struggle toward 'spiritual' consciousness. [Relate this symbolism to the nephilim of Genesis six, the said 'men of renown'.]

- Zodiac - (DBS. p.227.) is a powerful symbol throughout the Bible. Every approx. 26,000 years the earth traces an orbit called the Procession of the Equinoxes symbolised by the Zodiac. Each of the 12 "signs" (about 2150 years each) stands for a basic quality of human nature, and during each segment (sign) we are to learn our relationship to God through the development of that particular quality.

AS EVIDENCED IN THIS very brief and incomplete overview of some words chosen to highlight in this appendix, there are numerous symbolic meanings offered to the diligent and studious student. This is not only true of the sacred texts, but the same could be applied to much of literature. Indeed, the symbolic nature of words and phrases has been offered by numerous authors of better standing and expertise, than could offer here. It is however, the context in which any number of meanings should be derived. The few books cited in this appendix are available on the market today for interested party's to study at leisure. I have NOT in any way attempted to be comprehensive in this appendix, but have attempted to highlight some of the more relevant words that religionists should maybe be more wary of, instead of initially holding a 'spiritualised' concept. I trust readers, after reading this Appendix, can cast their minds back to some of a few of the Nails and their subject matters. For instance, it is very interesting that son of man, with the capital S clearly denotes hope; this at least may offer readers a glimpse of the symbolic meanings many of our words convey still today. Readers are encouraged to source for themselves. The resources cited esp., those related to Symbolism. All are found in the Bibliography. Most are also e-book resources.If believers chose to view their beloved mythic sacred texts primarily by the prism of symbolism, instead of ultimately literal, I wonder what that might look like? The following is now offered for interested readers' consideration. It was the famed Joseph Campbell who asserted that Symbols are but the vehicle of communication, not its final form. So, it is with this in mind that I offer my own opinion as to a possible, or probable essence to one of the passages that have been investigated already; Genesis 6:1-4. I have endeavoured to consider some of the keys symbolic meanings as noted in the brief gloss offered above. The result has been astoundingly similar to my over all conclusions in Nail Nine; possibly also related to what was concluded in the study of Genesis chapter three.

Genesis 6:1-4 - Symbolic:

(1) When men [consciousness] began to multiply on the face [(was) recognised] on the ground/earth [conscious awareness became widespread], and daughters [birth (of) emotional consciousness], (2) the sons [alter ego's/ living images/ the consequence] of the God's/ Elohim [(those) powers within] saw [bonded (see Symbolism of eyes)] the daughters [emotional consciousness] of men [consciousness] were fair; and they took to wife, any they chose. (3) Then the Lord said, "my Spirit [life essence] shall not abide in man [(shall not abide as) conscious awareness] forever, for he is flesh [a physical entity with all its allegiances]: his days will be 120 years [a continuity; dynasty] (4) The Nephilim [impending evil] were on the earth [(had) conscious awareness] in those days, and also afterward, when the sons [(the) consciousness] of God [(the) powers within] came into the daughters of man and they bore children [(further) emotional consciousness] to them. These were the mighty men who were of old [personification of death], the men of renown [to/ of those with 'higher' consciousness].

Genesis 6:1-4 - A New reading. Incorporating the Symbolic:

(1) When consciousness began to be recognised and was becoming widespread, it birthed emotional consciousness. (2) The consequences of that alter ego and the living image of these powers within was that they bonded. (3) (But) life essence and consciousness will not last, it is physical; (It will however) continually (be a) dynasty. (4) (There was also an) impending consciousness (of) evil, when consciousness bonded with alter ego. (It) brought about death, (to the) consciousness.

IF AN UNDERSTANDING of these few passages in Genesis 6 are Symbolic by nature, we can easily see that unlike most Christian authors today, and those of the past who project Angel/alien (watcher or otherwise) entity that nonsensically mated/ interbred with the human population; that ideology quite emphatically, and simply does not in any way make much sense. Aside viewing these verses and passages as ultra-spiritualised and literal composition. Surely, verse (3) taken in a Symbolic nature, offers a potential reason of WHY the redactor left this verse in the text! The context of the four verses, as was highlighted in my study in Nail Nine above, begins outlining that populations of humankind began to multiply (the plain reading). It therefore makes absolutely NO sense to have verse (3) follow, i.e., unless viewed through the prism of Symbol (as I have attempted to succinctly show above); only to again revert to the previous context (verse 4). Recall Andrew Roth's point, that the Hebrew goes something like this, beginning with (A), moves somewhat to (B), and then back to the original (A).

Appendix Two:

Religion a very brief, brief:

RELIGION: THE PURSUIT of answers to the countless questions we have regarding the How, the What, the Where, the Why, and Who of our existence. Since the human animal became 'aware' of itself (see Nail Four, study of Genesis chapter 3) it has persistently sort to answer some of the most profound questions to existence ever perceived. We have an inquisitive mind. We are never just satisfied with just being. Unlike other animals on the Earth whom as far as we can determine, don't persistently question their existence. The human animal is inquisitive. We want to know things. We persistently question everything. Like; where have we come from? Why are we here? What's the thing we have labelled, the Universe; how did that come to be? Is there a 'special' entity aside (and outside) ourselves that birthed all that we see around us- we consistently label "God". A 'God' is the most profoundly cherished concept. The human animal has ever conceived. So, religion was born! If religion's most important belief is the existence of a reality beyond this world that we call God, what prompted the belief and when did it start? It began ages ago. In fact, there doesn't seem to have been a time when human beings didn't believe in the existence of a supernatural world beyond this one. Wondering about what happened to people after they died may have been what started it off? All animals die, but unlike the others, humans don't leave their dead to decompose where they drop. As far back as we can follow their traces, humans seem to have given their dead funerals, and how they planned them tells us something about their earliest beliefs.[dxxii] It's a lovely idea to think that there is something beyond. Yet, that is all this concept seems to be, an elaborate idea! The most primitive of the human animals that survive in far-flung regions of the Earth no doubt has also conceived of an idea of a deity-entity. The state of religion nowadays is astonishingly all over the shop. Particularly, the three world religions of Judaism, Islam, and christianity are still at odds with the other. In short, I liken all three of these religious institutions to the life-cycles of Sapiens. Let me elaborate: Each of the three major world religions of today; Judaism, christianity and Islam were cut from the same cloth. Evident and known throughout the world. Islam, if you like, is the adolescent of the three. Christianity, could be likened to a close but older sibling. Judaism meanwhile, could be likened to a Grandparent/ guardian. Let it be stated clearly though, 'There are No favourites!' None of these three religious institutions are better, or worse than the other. Opinions, beliefs, doctrines may differ greatly nowadays, but in the whole each was birthed from pretty much the same family-tree. As was hinted in the main body of this study, there is substantial evidence mounting that the grandparent was essentially birthed via a conglomeration of various tribal, and state beliefs that in pre-history most likely had an origin in or around Egypt and its Magical cults and practices. These ancient practices are long-dead. But, thanks to disciplines like archaeology and Egyptology, we are becoming aware again of these fascinating early rites. Meanwhile, Islam and christianity (adolescent/ older sibling) rivalry and bigotry rages on. As the adolescent of the family, Islam continues to throw a hissy-fit. Much like an adolescent today, they are still attempting to find their way in the world. They are essentially the risk-takers, the #MeToo generation of religion. NOT all Islam (the adolescent religion) is thinking or acting in this manner. Just as Not all Sapien adolescents are rebellious to the point of insanity! There are maturing factions - also with Islam. Though it is the adolescent of the major religions of the world, there are countless followers of this religion who have matured or are maturing into adulthood. Please Understand I am NOT stating that the other two world religions are the adults on the block. They, in their turn has and continue to show the same traits of a rebellious adolescent from time to time. I attempted to outline and highlight this in my first Nail above, where I outlined the atrocities the emergent belief system of christianity was prepared to go as it made its way onto the world-stage. No doubt, Judaism did similarly in its pre-history regarding the prehistoric cults and practices it pilfered, and those rites it doctored to fit its own ideas and practices. Recall the words of historian Yuval Harari, - "Tolerance is not a Sapiens trademark." Indeed! We witness continually this trademark of Sapiens being played out through the three major world-religions today. So, why then do we have this thing called religion? Historic annals, and academic studies in Anthropology– i.e., the study in the origins and social relationships of human beings and other respected secular like-disciplines, inform us that some form of spiritual confidence is one of those things that people are always going to be naturally drawn; we call religion. Transcendental religion as a defined concept; evades a simple explanation (like myth, Eschatology and its close cousin, Apocalypse. See Appendix 3). The difficulty lay in the affirmed fact by various academic fields; that ancient languages do not contain a comparative term to what a modern person 'means' by 'religion.' Religion as proposed by European Christian cultures for instance are a recent phenomenon only:[dxxiii]

> "And when the names do derive from ancient words, we find that the early occurrences of those words are best understood as verbal activities rather than conceptual entities... the Arabic Islam was not "the religion of Islam" but "submitting to authority." More generally, it has become clear that the isolation of something called "religion" as a sphere of life... is not a universal feature of human history. In fact, in the broad view of human cultures, it is a strikingly odd way of conceiving the world. In the ancient world, the gods were involved in all aspects of life... [but not all ancients should be recognized as] uniformly religious."[dxxiv]

Neil MacGregor fascinatingly adds:

> "Most faiths of the world for most of history have not had texts that claimed such unique status – if they had texts at all. Even fewer have any notion of a central authority, which, like the Vatican, might define a corpus of doctrine which adherents are required to believe. Hindus and Buddhists of course have many texts, but none that has self-evident primacy, [that Judaism and christianity claim] and so the meanings accorded to them and the practices around them vary enormously from place to place. The Greeks and Romans, rigorous in so much else, had virtually nothing that we would regard as a statement of faith: their notion of religion was essentially something that citizens did."[dxxv]

Moreover, in his extraordinary volume exploring religious thought, "Creation of the Sacred: Tracks of Biology in early Religions", Walter Burkert adds the following commentary for consideration. "The first principal characteristic of religion is negative: that is, religion deals with the nonobvious, (sic) the unseen, that "which cannot be verified empirically." Protagoras the sophist spoke of the adelótes, the "uncleanness" or "nonevidence" (sic) of the gods. Religion is manifest in actions and attitudes that do not fulfil immediate practical functions. What is intended and dealt with cannot be seen, or touched, or worked upon in the usual fashion of everyday life. This is why strangers are usually puzzled by religious practice. Conversely, we are tempted to suppose that anything puzzling and not immediately apparent may be religious– a problem often met in prehistoric archaeology; drastic misunderstandings may of course occur. It is difficult to "get what is meant in religious behavior (sic), but some common basis for empathy, interpretation, and translation evidently does not exist. The criterion of adelótes is insufficient, yet it remains basic."[dxxvi] Humanity does seem to be hardwired to invoke a form of spirituality, despite its ultimate negativity (of not being empirically verifiable). This we equate with 'religion.' Our prehistoric proto-ancestor hominids, including Neolithic, Neanderthal, and Monolithic people/ ancestor hominids undoubtedly practiced various rituals and rites for their dead, and possibly even various spirits and entities they came to know as deities. Practices, which eventually, morphed into the variety of complex religious philosophies we recognise today. This premise does seem to hold some warrant. Though the following may also just as well be an example of Burkert's insertion above; that anything puzzling and not immediately apparent may be religious, a problem often met in prehistoric archaeology; a misunderstanding might have then occurred. Confirming, Yuval Harari again rightly informs readers:

> "Instead of erecting mountains of theory over a molehill of tomb relics, cave paintings and bone statuettes, it is better to be frank and admit that we have only the haziest notions about the religions of ancient foragers. We assume that they were animists, but that's not very informative. We don't know

DECONSTRUCTING ENDTIME DELUSIONS

which spirits they prayed to, which festivals they celebrated, or which taboos they observed. Most importantly, we don't know what stories they told. It's one of the biggest holes in our understanding of human history."[dxxvii]

To the closing remarks of the Preface, Rod Steiger, in Worlds Before our Own records that

> "[I]n November 2006, Sheila Coulson of the University of Oslo announced the discovery of 70,000-year-old artefacts that appeared to indicate the worship of a massive snake, by it revealing the earliest known human religious' ritual."

This artefact may however just simply indicate an idea of the birth-death cycle. There is when one thinks of it not one religious system or religious philosophy today that does not have death and re-birthing (like the snake that sheds its skin) as a central or highly esteemed tenant. Why? Where did such thoughts originate? There is also the fascinating statue, The Lion Man.[dxxviii] Discovered in a cave in southwest Germany in 1939, just preceding the outbreak of World–War Two. It is clearly meticulously carved by a very skilled artisan from Mammoth Tusk; and is dated to approximately 40,000 years. Neil MacGregor again adds his learned voice to this artefact considered to be one of the earliest religious relics uncovered of Ice–age religion. Citing the British Museum's Deep History doyen Jill Cook:

> "...the Lion Man. Why would a community make such a huge investment in order to produce an object which could play no part in its physical survival? Jill Cook gives her view: I think it is probably more about the community's psychological survival, something that strengthens the sense of themselves as a group. We do not know whether the Lion Man was a deity, a spiritual experience, a being from a creation story or an avatar used to negotiate with the forces of nature. But it is an object that makes sense only if it is part of a story, what we might now call a myth. There must have been a narrative or a ritual to accompany the statue that would explain its appearance and its meaning. What that story was, of course, we can now only guess. It was about humans and animals obviously – but presumably it was also about something beyond ourselves, beyond nature, which can somehow help to strengthen a community and enable it to overcome dangers and difficulties.

We know that at this time the people in the area were also making and listening to music. A variety of flutes, for example, have been found, some made of bird bones, which were already hollow, others much more complex and carved from ivory, which would again require a large investment of skill and time. We have also found a little figure who is clearly dancing. All these objects are about shared social activity, but also about transporting you into another realm, and that may well link to the purpose of the Lion Man."[dxxix]

This is fascinating. This object has no known religious identity, yet, as specialist of deep history, Jill Cook postulates, there could be a psychological assurance meaning to such objects. This if correct might have played into the study of Genesis chapter 6, and what christians propose and offer as a meaning to the first four verses of this Genesis chapter. The happiness and future enlightenment of our species do seem to rely on and inculcate a saturation of irrational fears; fear of the unknown, of a tormented death, of death itself, and more recently - of hellfire, damnation, excommunication, and an eternal separation from 'an ethereal' deity, so on - if one does not comply with mainstream religious practice. All which are lacking verifiable, rational credibility. Walter Burkert again to the closing remarks of the same chapter as his previous note, insightfully adds these comments for further consideration.

"There is no denying that anxiety is often evoked to validate religious messages, and that it has its repercussions upon the substance of religion. To transmit religion is to transmit fear. "Fear, first of all, produced gods in the world, primus in orbe deos fecit timor, Statius wrote. While this is a criticism from his standpoint..it shares the self-interpretation of many religions. The main word to characterize gods and religion in Akkadian is puluhtu, fear... Solomon used the Hebrew variant [previously cited: Ps 111:10; Pr 1:7; 4:7.]..The... Greek expression, theoudes, God-fearing, occurs as a Mark of moral distinction... Another Greek word commonly associated with religious rites is, phrike, hair-raising shudder. Moderns came back to the suggestion that awe was the basic religious feeling; Rudolf Otto substituted a neo-Latin term, mysterium tremendum, shivering mystery. Shudders of awe are central for the experience of the sacred. The very means of indelible transmission, threat and terror, are correlated with the contents of the religious part of the mental world: the prerogative of the sacred requires the fear of God. (pp. 30-31." [Brackets] mine.)

DECONSTRUCTING ENDTIME DELUSIONS

It appears that although "shudders of awe are central to the sacred" the brief excursion into some of christianity's early indictable offences to 'the pagan', and any of those it saw as intolerable in action, for they must be violating the sacred; I identified clearly, was attempting to instil a sense of shuddering awe of their deity. But, this idea went much further than to cause mere veneration of a 'new' deity. The Church in a sense used Malthusian reasoning to help justify its oppressive policies. Incredibly there are much blindness and ignorance to the truth of untold and countless bloodstained fields and human suffering that has and continues to be caused by the present three major cosmic-world religions; their constant push for supremacy and, world control. Highlighting the self–aggrandising attitude of the Church, and religion particularly, are the following statements:

> "The vast majority of religions in human history — excepting only those invented extremely recently — tell stories of events that would constitute completely unmistakable evidence if they'd actually happened. The orthogonality of religion and factual questions is a recent and strictly Western concept. The people who wrote the original scriptures didn't even know the difference."[dxxx]

One of America's foremost atheists, Al Stefanelli, in his book, "Free Thoughts" perfectly sums the odd opinions instilled into those inveigled by religion still today.

> "Religious belief [he writes,] impresses upon its followers that the worth of human life is not based upon our existence in the here and now, but in the before and after. They fight for the unborn, stating that abortion is the murder of God's precious creation, but as soon as the child enters the world it is a filthy rag, and does not regain favor (sic) in the sight of God until after death." (. Footnote 24.)

Another author writes: "The vast majority - billions of people on this Earth - hold a superstitious belief that their current life has little or no meaning, and only the next, "eternal" life has any importance: "heaven."[dxxxi] This is purely double-tongued rhetoric. A passionate non-sequitur sprouted by deluded individuals. It is a zealous belief that life meaning and worthiness is based upon the before and after. Based on a 'supernatural' mindset that 'otherworldly better place' can be attained if we listened and conformed to the calling of a super-being; a deity who is ultimately in control. Nonetheless, such an ideology is a negative concept; unverifiable for its non-evidence. Insistence on an ethereal 'outside' manipulator at work (a deity) of some variety, and that it offers Utopia does little but open one to extensive questioning and criticism. Further, how can religious believers see an early term abortion as an affront to their mythical celestial 'spaghetti monster' bastard? Especially when admittedly, by those same religionists' texts this same entity demanded and applauded the slaughter of countless men, women, and children throughout their 'old' texts. Then, it also apparently sanctioned with equally high-praise, the slaughter of innocent children decades before the torturous murder of one 'particularly saintly' man as an apparent atonement for the planet later, in its addendum! Celsus again questions with good reason why the babe-deity should have fled to Egypt,

> "What occasion was there, while you were yet an infant, that you should be brought to Egypt, in order that you might not be slain? For it was not fit that a God should be afraid of death. But an angel came from heaven, ordering you and your associates to fly, lest being taken you should be put to death. For the great God [it seems] could not preserve you, his own son, in your own country, but sent two angels on your account."[dxxxii]

Why are so many people hell-bent on 'getting' to another 'otherworldly' place? This is utter nonsense. It is an abuse of human intelligence and new scientific knowledge and complex functioning of the human brain and mind. It cannot be denied; however, that weekly millions of believers hear, read, fanaticise and study fantastic stories of favourite but greatly narcissistic hero's, mystifying villains and ordinary folk in their 'sacred' texts. Texts from another era and culture; that no doubt cleverly has been stage-managed to offer a form of meaning for a society not its original intent. The honest problem the modern houses of Delusion and their congregants face are undoubtedly the full acknowledgement of the countless and bloodthirsty atrocities; as well as those crimes-against

DECONSTRUCTING ENDTIME DELUSIONS

humanity that the earliest inception of the Christian religion wrought upon humankind. Perfectly summed in the following statement by American writer, historian, and philosopher Will Durant:

> "The Church had begun with the Prince of Peace, who had bidden Peter put his sword back into its sheath; it had become a warrior using swords, pikes, and guns against the Albigensians of France and the Jews of Spain. The lowly carpenter of Nazareth had been replaced by a pope more richly housed than most emperors, and controlling more wealth than most states. In disputes between oppressors and oppressed the hierarchy had almost always supported the oppressors and suppressed the oppressed."

RELIGION: you have been found wanting!

Appendix Three:

Myth:

UNDENIABLY, MYTH IS a fascinating subject to even assume to study, let alone disseminate to readers efficiently. Literally, the Ancient World was covered from head to toe in Myth. The lives of all ancient people were embroiled in myth. Throughout the ancient world myths are evident on temple walls, friezes, and artworks of all kinds. Including statues and painted pottery. Myths were discussed by citizens from all walks of life. They were constantly alluded to and recounted and written about in the engravings on walls and at sites of significance. We have today literally countless engravings of offerings made to the gods, as well as numerous songs to the gods. There are numerous tragedies, sonnets, comedies, philosophical discussions, and countless stories about the constellations of the sky scrawled everywhere, even in ancient classroom exercise books.

> "The poets were not alone in sanctioning allegories, for long before the poets the states and the lawmakers had sanctioned them as a useful expedient. They needed to control the people by superstitious fears, and these cannot be aroused without myths and marvels. Strabo, Geographia, 1.2.8, c.20 BC–AD 23. (Cited in O'Grady, S, and Man Created God." (Ch. 2: Augustus: God and first citizen))

Attempting to explain myth and its role in society is a mammoth task. A task well suited to other writers. Here, I will utilise one worthy study: The Mythology of All the Races. In the opening statements we read:

> "The intrinsic interest of the subject is very great; for better than almost anything else myths reveal men's first notions about their world and the powers at work in it, and the relations between men and those powers. They show what things in their surroundings early engaged men's attention; what things seemed to them to need explanation; and how they explained them. For a myth is commonly an explanation of something, in the form

DECONSTRUCTING ENDTIME DELUSIONS

of a story—what happened once upon a time, or what repeats itself from day to day—and in natural myths, as distinct from the invented myths of philosophers and poets, the story is not the artificial vesture of an idea but its spontaneous expression, not a fiction but a self-evident fact. The student of the mind of man in its uniformity and its variations therefore finds in mythology a great fund of instructive material. A comprehensive collection like the present lends itself also to comparative study of single myths or systems of myth among different and widely remote peoples..."[dxxxiii]

So,

"Mythology is not, then, a thing of mere academic interest; its value is real — real to you and to me. It is the history of the thought of early man, and of primitive man today. In it we may find much to tell us how he lived, and how he had lived in the ages of which his myths recount. As affording us materials for a history of civilization mythology is of inestimable value. We know now that history is something more than a matter of dates and events. "Magma Charts was signed by King John at Runnymede in 1215. What of it, if that be all? The exact words of the document, the particular monarch who signed it, the precise spot, the specific date are of no worth in themselves. The real historical question is—What were the causes which led the English Barons, at a certain point in the development of the British Nation, to compel the King to sanction a document abridging the Royal prerogatives; and what have been the consequences, not merely to the subsequent evolution of the British Constitution, but to all States and Colonies thereby affected? So, too, we read mythology, not only for its specific statements—its legends of gods and of heroes, its theories of the world, and its attempts to solve the mystery of the destiny of each and every individual—but also, with a wider purview, for the light which it sheds upon the infancy and the childhood of the race to which we—you who read and I who write—belong."[dxxxiv]

In relation to religion the author's state:

"The connexion (sic) of mythology with religion is obvious, yet a word of caution is needed here. Mythology is not synonymous with religion, but only a part of it. Religion consists of at least three parts—the attitude of soul, which is religion par excellence; the outward act of worship, which is ritual; and the scientific explanation, which—in the very highest and noblest sense of the term—is myth; and these three—which we may call the attitude of soul, body, and mind—go together to make religion. Throughout our study of mythology we must bear constantly in mind that we are dealing with only one feature of religion—its causal aspect. We must not take the part for the whole, else we shall be one-sided and unjust in our appreciation of religion as a whole. One attitude of mind is absolutely essential in reading mythology—sympathy—and almost as important a requisite is that, while reading it, its premises must be granted. If we approach mythology with the preconception that it is false or nonsensical or trivial, it will be but [a] waste of time to read it; indeed it will be better never to have read it, for reading in such a spirit will only embitter. It is, perhaps, not sufficiently recognized how important a factor one's attitude of sympathy is, not merely in regard to religion or psychology or philosophy, or any other "mental and moral science," but also toward the "exact sciences." If, for example, I make up my mind that spectral analysis is utterly impossible, the discovery of a new element in the gaseous emanation of a distant planet by such analysis will be to me nothing but folly. If, again, I reject the mathematical concept of infinity, which I have never seen, and which cannot be weighed or measured, then I shall of course deny that parallel lines meet in infinity; you cannot give me the precise location of infinity, and, besides, all parallel lines that I have ever seen are equidistant at all points from each other. This is a reduction and absurd notion of an attitude which is far too common in regard to mythology and religion. This does not, of course, mean that we must implicitly believe all that we read; but it does mean that we should approach with kindly hearts. With reverence, then, and with love we take up myths. We may smile, at times, at their naivete (sic); but we shall never sneer at them. Unblushing, sometimes, we shall find them, and cruel; but it is the modesty and the cruelty of the child. Myths may be moral or non-moral; they are not immoral, and only a morbid mind will see uncleanness in them."[dxxxv]

Superstitious fears of christians are still evidently prevalent. Recall the statements earlier made by authors like Rob Skiba and Derek Gilbert above; sounding very much like statements that all 'myths' are immoral, except for those myths of their sacred books, which are wonderful and life-giving. Surely, these authors and countless other Christian authors projecting similar sentiments show only themselves to have a morbid mind, for they see uncleanness in them! Most unfortunate for the modern believer is the projected analysis and meaning of fable common to secularist and Christian alike. That these anecdotes invariably comprise no more than the shallow description analogous to Manser

below, being, stories that are made up and which is contrary to right doctrine or holy living.

[Citing as evidence the following Bible verses from Titus]:

- Some prefer myths to truth: 2 titus 4:3-4.

- Myths are harmful to the body of Christ: 1Ti 1:3-4 See also 1 titus 4:6-8.

- Sound teaching by God's servants dispels myths: titus 1:13-14 See also 1 titus 4:1-6; titus 1:9-11.

This is however utter whitewash! It is extremely religious shortsightedness. Projecting such ideas is very one-dimensional and is undoubtedly based on the modern perceived irrational fear and the false perception in the lack of integrity and aptness of the ancient mind. It is also undoubtedly a corrosive abuse, and cherry picking of certain texts that one assumes is supportive of the popular and modern claim. The contemporary Christian/ religious whim that myths are evil and therefore 'damaging' to someone's welfare, and that 'sound teaching' (particularly now of the Christian doctrine) dispels them and makes it right. A whim as this speaks with people's ignorance and inflated ego and lust for superiority. Their narcissism. Their susceptibility to 'libido dominandi'– a desire to control! Many valuable lessons can be attained if we broke from this mindset – even minimally. Few people today seem to comprehend, let alone accept, that a large portion of their beloved 'scriptures' derive from a long-told allegory! It was myth, allegory, folklore, legend (however one chooses to label them) which imparted life, giving a sense of animation to sacred writings. In essence, myth is to teach valued ideals that its authors considered relevant to the counter then atmosphere that the ancients were steeped in. Seeing the invention of the written word as a means of transmission for future recollection is a recent phenomenon, we tend to view myths/ allegory as shear superstition. How can anyone truly believe that ancient people faced and fought with often terrifying and destructive monsters? The problem lies not in differing intelligence but in differing resources for the storage and transmission of data. Quite simply, "before writing, myths had to serve as transmission systems for information deemed important; but because we— now that we have writing— have forgotten how nonliterate (sic) people stored and transmitted information and why it was done that way, we have lost track of how to decode the information often densely compressed into these stories, and they appear to us as mostly gibberish. And so we often dismiss them as silly or try to reinterpret them with psychobabble. As folklorist Adrienne Mayor points out, classicists in particular "tend to read myth as fictional literature, not as natural history" [Mayor 2000b, 192]— not least because humanists typically don't study sciences like geology, palaeontology, and astronomy, and so don't recognize (sic) the data.[dxxxvi]

We cannot then consistently insist on reading and comprehending any Bible text as I have said all through the above investigation, as purely literal. It is far from a completely literal composition. As earlier stated, all Bible stories are myth; they are the literary devises of their composers to further teach their original audiences' important information. That said, some of the myths of the sacred books may surround an element of facts. The sacred accounts might consist of a minimal amount of history; though I could not verify much of that attested history. Many a Bible allegory are nonetheless closely associated with any classical myth known today; those of the Greeks, Egyptians, Romans and other ancient societies. So, we are faced with numerous dilemmas; how much if any of the sacred myths can be legitimately based on actual history? Unfortunately, nowadays the myths told by other ancient peoples are linked in the modern mind to paganism; which religion condemns. Few would normally admit those objects one associate with pagans; those being trees, stones, and heavenly bodies [that these] were never worshipped in themselves but were revered because they were epiphanies of an unclear force that could be seen powerfully at work in all-natural phenomena, giving people intimations of another more powerful reality.[dxxxvii] Additionally, today; there is also among many christians at least the notion that religious concepts and descriptions of people groups of antiquity can be classed as primarily polytheistic. While Judaism and her offspring are essentially monotheistic. Not so according to Thomas Thompson:

> "...the terms polytheistic and monotheistic [are not, he writes] accurate descriptions of religion in antiquity. Within the ancient Near East, from the early times, all religious thought shared some aspects of both polytheistic and monotheistic metaphors of the divine. Such was the nature of religious thought in this world. This world-view understood gods specifically as reflections of the functions of power as they were perceived within the human world."[dxxxviii]

It is in this world environment that many a sacred myth was produced.

How Myth functions:

THE PREMISE FOR ATTEMPTING to understand how myth operated in times past is vital for understanding how we today should also consider how myth still operates. The two-work hand in glove. Myth in antiquity performed an incredible social service. The legends and stories labeled 'myth' should be described as the storybooks of children and the wider ancient society. Serving in principle as the educational textbooks, which constituted the legacy shared by all: of dreams, of hopes, of hurts, of triumphs, and of failures, and fears. Exactly how the sacred books of Western religion should still be viewed. Though not literal, sacred books and there story's should still be seen as 'educational tools'; as a tool that moderns might utilise to comprehend the hopes, dreams, aspirations, and fears of the ancients. For the sole reason to learn how we could incorporate those lessons. Undoubtedly, myths of the ancients were told as a means to pass on whatever moral the narrator wished to make known. Quite simply "...mythology [is] the child of language."[dxxxix]

> "It [therefore should] constantly be borne in mind that a myth is, ... a process and not a finished product." And so, myths evolve with time. A myth practically then is: "A [progressive] meaning-making story, having significance beyond itself, helping listeners to make sense of their lives."[dxl]

Whether these stories are of the birth and the feats of the gods or other semi-divine persons, it is clear "We must understand [their birth] ...does not relate to their physical or material existence. It is about their functions and roles because their birth is connected to the origins of natural phenomena." In mythology, to understand what (let's say) the Egyptians talk about, you have to see what the Egyptians saw. We had to get into our viewfinder the Egyptian sources of their all-important mortuary supplies to see how Isis might find Osiris inside a tree at Byblos. To understand why Ptah's creation of the universe takes place on a primeval mound of mud that differentiates itself from the waters of chaos, we have to focus on what Egyptians saw when the all-covering Nile floodwaters began to recede each year: the tip of a mound of mud here, then one there, growing in size until the whole land of Egypt gradually reappeared, completely refertilized (sic) and ready to bear new life-giving crops. Life, to the Egyptian, began each year with and on those mounds. Some have suggested that the shape of the pyramids constitutes a geometric analog of the Primeval Mound of Mud [Wilson 1949, 60]. Hilda Davidson posits a camera-angle solution to the origin of Odin's eight-legged horse,

"Sleipnir... Odin included among his duties the receiving of the dead. So Davidson places her camera to watch (Noting the pairs of horses sometimes found in the entryways of Mycenaean Greek tombs, one may wonder if this conception of the eight-legged steed carrying the dead goes back to earlier, Indo-European times.). Odin's eight-legged horse, Sleipnir, that carries off the souls of the dead. Viking period memorial stone; Alskog, Tjangvide, Gotland. ...the bier on which a dead man is carried in the funeral procession by four bearers; borne along thus, he may be described as riding on a steed with eight legs..."[dxli]

As with all myth and mythology:

> "Different peoples divide up the same world differently, as they fasten onto different aspects within the multiplicity. Consider water. We view it simply as H2O. But the Hawaiians distinguish wai "sweet water" from kai "salt water", and kai, the shallow ocean near shore, from moana "deep sea" (the

line between turquoise kai and lapis moana being sharply evident to the eye). The Mesopotamians, for their part, divided water into the sweet waters that spring from the earth (Apsu), the salty sea (Ti'amat), storm waters that pelt us from above (Enlil), and water as a generative agent (Enki) [Jacobsen 1949, 153-61, 184-86]."[dxlii]

NATURAL PHENOMENA GAVE sustenance to many ancient anecdotes for what was perceived as reality, being the retelling of the birth and death cycle witnessed roundabout during daily life. Unfortunately, today we do not have anything that really resembles these vast often-spellbinding anecdotes: stories of the gods, villains, monsters, and the heroes who slew or overcame them by extra ordinary feats. The closest we have to them today are the vast publications about them, and the snippets recorded in religious texts. John Oswalt, "The Bible among the Myths" (p44) agreeably writes it's not whether these mythic stories are false or true. That has never been the point. Alas this is how society as a whole view them still today; they're either right and good, or false, and bad. But, this is as stated above, shallow and restrictive and most likely destructive. Oswalt offers:

> "...myth is a form of expression, whether literary or oral, whereby the continuities among the human, natural, and divine realms are expressed and actualized (sic). By reinforcing these continuities, it seeks to ensure the orderly functioning of both nature and human society."

The truth to these comments does not detract from the fact; if we are honest, myth is notoriously abstract, and difficult to determine. Its difficulty lay in arriving at any substantial and 'working' manner, a definition that completely satisfies the scholar and layperson alike. It comprises many branches and root systems that reach deep into and out of the psyche of populations the world over. Examples highlighting this complexity follow. In a Wikipedia article, we read:

> "Mircea Eliade [one of the greatest 20th Century Romanian historians of Religion, a fiction writer, and a Philosopher] argued that one of the foremost functions of myth is to establish models for behavior and those myths may also provide a religious experience. By telling or reenacting myths, members

of traditional societies detach themselves from the present and return to the mythical age, thereby bringing themselves closer to the divine."

"The Anchor Yale Bible Dictionary" Eliade is said to have admitted further,

"...it would be hard to find a definition of myth that would be acceptable to all scholars and at the same time intelligible to nonspecialists".

Closer still to desperation is J. Rogerson statement that

"finding an adequate and all-purpose definition of myth" remains an "impossible task". This admitted difficulty has not prevented the appearance of many studies, especially recently, attempting to formulate an adequate definition."[dxliii]

In classical religious, and especially Ancient Near East parlance myth simply came to mean, as earlier stated: 'story's about the gods and general life.' Such stories were considered functional, as an explanation of how the world worked. Authors John Walton and Michael Baigent in their books explain this. First Walton,

"The Sumerians seem to have perceived mythological reality as historically actual." The gods were real to the ancients, and their stories gave account of the gods and the world in ways that were important for understanding the world and life in general. Jan Assmann's observation concerning Egypt is true across the board: "The theme of myth was not the essence of the deities, but rather ... the essence of reality." He elaborates: "Myths establish and enclose the area in which human actions and experiences can be oriented. The stories they tell about deities are supposed to bring to light the meaningful structure of reality. Myths are always set in the past, and they always refer to the present. What they relate about the past is supposed to shed light on the present." For the Israelites, the stories in the Old Testament served a similar function. Yahweh was real to them and his deeds were important. Like everyone else in the ancient world, the Israelites believed that everything that happened and everything that existed found its ultimate cause in deity. In this way of thinking, it is irrelevant whether the modern reader believes the gods of the Babylonians or the God of Israel exist."[dxliv]

Michael Baigent,

DECONSTRUCTING ENDTIME DELUSIONS

"From Omens of Babylon: Astrology and Ancient Mesopotamia" adds, "The mythology of a nation can be viewed as its reflection in the mirror of the heavens. For myth mirrors the hidden side of a nation: the tales of the gods are the tales of a nation's unconscious life expressed in symbolic form. Through myth a culture seeks to understand and accept the reality within which it lives. These myths arise out of the very deepest layers of the masses and the individual's psychic make-up; they are a symbolic expression of the psyche's innermost processes. Buried in the unconscious, the individual and collective, are energy patterns which all mankind holds in common: it is these which emerge in myth."[dxlv]

Another author convincingly argues,

"It is humbling, perhaps even worrisome, to think that ancient people, with minimal technical apparatus, might have developed an acuity sharper than ours to sense natural phenomena they sought to express symbolically... They painted their knowledge of the natural world on a far larger canvass than we. The sky myths they created joined a world we regard as inanimate to the animate sphere of their lives, the unfolding of their history, politics, social relations, ideas about creation and life after death. They forged links between the sky and just about every phase and component of human activity – what we call astrology. And they celebrated this knowledge not only in text but also in art, architecture and sculpture, poetry and song. Much of this knowledge was sophisticated and highly organized. We deserve to appreciate it, to be enlightened by the reflection of a very different comprehension of nature."[dxlvi]

The Anchor Bible Dictionary again adds,

"...a myth is "a story, presented as having actually occurred in a previous age, explaining the cosmological and supernatural traditions of a people, their gods, heroes, cultural traits, religious beliefs, etc." (778). Eliade, who admitted the problems inherent in any definition of myth, proposes that "myth narrates a sacred history; it relates an event that took place in primordial Time, the fabled time of 'beginnings' ... The actors in myths are Supernatural Beings" (1963: 5–6). The American biblical scholar T. H. Gaster suggests that a myth "may be defined as any presentation of the actual in terms of the ideal" (1954: 185). For the theologian P. Ricoeur myths are "traditional narratives which tell of events which happened at the origin of time and which furnish the support of language to ritual actions" (1969: 101). And W. Burkert, a prolific German scholar whose analyses of myths have found a wide audience of late, concludes that "myth is a traditional tale with secondary, partial reference to something of collective importance" (1979: 23)..." Meanings and functions of myths are offered in an extensive article by the authors of the Anchor Yale Dictionary.[dxlvii]

Further:

> "The recent progress by biblical scholars in returning openly to the issue of the presence of myths in the Bible is quite remarkable and altogether in keeping with the broader trend toward moving biblical study into the mainstream of academic studies. But equally remarkable is the century-long refusal by OT scholars to pay any great heed to those efforts to redefine myth accomplished by scholars from other disciplines, such as anthropology or folklore study. This refusal is fundamentally grounded in the assumption that all things biblical must be firmly and forever distinguished from the non-biblical and, especially, the mythological world. The forcefulness of this foundational and long unquestioned distinction accounts for the otherwise inexplicable desire to divide the OT from myth."[dxlviii]

Nephilim, 'fallen' angels, Satan and numerous ethereal entities that fill the pages of religious texts; these I hope have been sufficiently called out and shown to be completely mythical. Not to be taken literally as is the custom of Fundamental Evangelicals, as witnessed all through this study. The I.S.B.E. (The International Standard Bible Encyclopedia) interestingly offers what I now choose as what is probably the best definition for my purposes, and therefore is fundamentally my 'working' definition of 'Myth' and "Mythology.' Both words being related to the Greek mythos, and Mythologoi; originally meaning,

> "thought, either unexpressed ("intention," "purpose," "opinion," "idea") or expressed ("word," "saying," "statement," and "speech"). As expressed thought m? Thos can be either an "account of facts," or rumour. They include story's of God's and deities, demons, and devils. A teller of myth was a teller of legends, a romancer.[dxlix]

Relevant to the general discussion of this treaty and the I.S.B.E. statement above another fitting remark is offered by "The Dictionary of Jesus and the Gospels" that: they were told to explain events, beliefs

DECONSTRUCTING ENDTIME DELUSIONS

and ritual. Times before record making. One final theological source helpfully adds and affirms much that I attempted to state clearly throughout the above investigation. Primarily that:

> "...myth [are] a didactic literary genre, a form of exposition, a means of demonstration that expresses reality in a pictorial form—what the rhetor Heraclitus calls a "philosophy in symbols."

It matters little that

> "these things never happened but always are so," and it is a "pious investigation" to discern beneath the material component and the symbolic expression a certain religious truth or moral idea. The heterodox Ephesians and Cretans, trained according to the currently fashionable principles of hermeneutics, must have applied this method of symbolic and allegorical interpretation to the Bible, producing all kinds of intellectual fantasies... myth is the name given all that is ancient, fabulous, or outlandish; while history is the label for the truth, whether the event be ancient or recent, and with rare exceptions does not admit anything fantastic", (philomythia = love of legends)."

Though greatly insufficient still, myth is something that retells an opinion, aim, or purpose, and, narrates the origin of-or a thought that may or not be verifiable. Conceivably a myth could be an exaggeration of either fact or fiction. In that they strive to teach hard-hitting truths. Essentially then, myths in sacred texts are religious storytelling. Precisely how the Bible uses it! But, I do not agree that all myths were fictitious, rather many were true, and are based on true-life experiences. The deities and malevolent entities were however, mythic. They were never to mean to be known as real! These experiences were then couched in a medium known and readily used and understood by the population addressed. Finally,

> "...the results of [this] analysis...: A myth is a statement, or a virtual statement as implied in a symbol, an attribute, or an epithet, accepted as true by its original maker and his hearers, and referring to the eternal nature and past acts of beings greater than man, and frequently to circumstances which are to us improbable or impossible."

Whether substantially right or wrong, and I am aware of stretching the bounds to the accepted meaning earlier articulated by also announcing; myths abound and are ever present still to this day, being recognised in almost every facet of modern life. Our modern world is invaded daily by various myth and legend. Often the wall that separates the fact from legend/fiction is paper-thin. They have however greatly changed in form. No longer, as earlier stated, do they carry entirely the same influence and message of those from antiquity. Today's myth center on external advertising prophets spinning legendary tales of some form of prosperity, if only the population did or acquired (x factor). Right to the shelves of Christian bookstores lined with the latest pop psychology and 'prophetic' mantra. We would be hard-pressed to escape a modern myth in any form it might assume. But, in any form, modern or ancient, myth plays an important role in shaping society. We next turn our attention to two words often used by various scholars in their treaties regarding 'end-times'.

Eschatology:

LET US NOW ATTEND TO the other two equally strange and often perplexing terms that play a role in any 'end-time' themed studies: Eschatology and Apocalypse. Extrapolating Eschatology first.

> "The word Eschatology was coined by Protestant theologians in the seventeenth century. It refers to the last things, which may be either the end of the world or the end of the individual and that which follows it. The range of the word has broadened over time to include any kind of teleology."[dl]

Some scholarly commentators have also remarked that theologically speaking, it would have been better if the term Eschatology were not existing (Longenecker.) Maybe this statement should also be applied to an Apocalypse? They are both problematic. Despite also being somewhat recognised as fair, simple and easily defined, Eschatology, a case in point, doesn't carry any real value in meaning in the world of most people. Most people today only really assume and understand it carrying a basic meaning of – 'last days,' which altogether isn't wrong. Rather, again is shallow, shadowy, and unassuming. It is nonetheless a specialist term. Like its complement, Apocalypse, both are not as simple an expression to give explanation. None can assume to announce in conversation with others either word and expect the other to be on the exact same page as you. Meanings abound! In some scholarly circles, Eschatology has rather an eclectic range of meanings and subjects. Among this eclectic range is personal Eschatology, which essentially derives from Egyptian Cultic religion. New testament scholar John Collins writes:

> "Most peoples in the ancient world believed in the survival of a soul after death, but in many cases, this was a weak, shadowy existence. This was true both of the Hebrew idea of the nepes̆ and of the Homeric idea of the psychē. Egypt was distinctive in the ancient world for its belief in the judgment of the dead (Griffiths). The Book of the Two Ways describes ways that await the deceased, many of them tortuous and fearful. The text was usually inscribed on the inside base of coffins, as a guide for the dead. The deceased must pass through a series of gates, each one defended by a terrifying guardian, which must be overcome by spells. But the main issues that determined the welfare of the person in the hereafter were innocence and purity. In the Book of the Dead (125) the deceased is instructed to say: "See I have come to you without sin, without guilt, without evil, without there being any evil in me, without there being a witness against me."

Other motifs that are characteristic of Egyptian Eschatology are the weighing of the souls of the dead and the association of the right side with salvation and of the left with damnation. Also, characteristic is the role of the God Thoth as impartial recorder in the tribunal after death. Schweitzer was one scholar who offered the scholarship of his day a range of understandings that generally have since been refuted. Nonetheless, many of today's ideas undoubtedly are still comparable with the ancient Stoic. The Stoics—a group founded by the philosopher Zeno (300 B.C.) who believed life's goal was to rise above all things and to show no emotion in either pain or pleasure." Thus, their basic philosophy was

> "... a man's happiness consisted in bringing himself into harmony with the course of the universe. They were trained to bear evils with indifference, and so to be independent of externals. Materialism, pantheism, fatalism, and contentment were the leading features of this philosophy."

New Testament Scholar I. Howard Marshall on Eschatology understands Stoics also:

> "...believed that the world would come to an end with a conflagration in which everything would be destroyed. Probably most ordinary people, however, had little concern about the world coming to an end and were more preoccupied with their own deaths and what would happen to them individually in the hereafter. So, the mystery religions offered immortality to pious individuals who accepted initiation into their rites."

It is not difficult to draw connections and numerous parallels to Stoicism with our modern understanding. Most especially and to end-times and rapture. In many Christian circles, there are simply unmitigated beliefs surrounding much end-time speak saying also that a God-driven inferno will engulf and destroy the earth at some point soon. Additionally, twenty-first Century society thrives on materialism and fatalism, where events have been foretold and are thus, inevitably inescapable. Some would call this –karma. But, karma itself is a misnomer as it is dependent upon randomness! Sadly, society is very much driven by the same independent externals as the mentioned earlier stoic, which is also dependent upon randomness. Maybe christianity should here-for better be thought of as a product of Stoic theory: a random philosophy birthed purely by chance instead of a 'religion'. Interesting in Marshall's statement above is his mention of initiation rites into some state of immortality that seemed to be exclusive to a certain class –the pious. These points are surely worthy of remembrance. Yet, Eschatology is still rather arduous for some other reasons. "Harper's Bible Dictionary" defines it as: a non-biblical term, denoting the end time period or last of history. Here, it is further characterised as:

> "...ambiguous in that it may refer to events during the last days of the present age, events occurring at the Parousia (return of Christ), or conditions of life in the new world or age. The expression 'last day' is used in the nt in at least two of these senses: ...Paul held that those 'in Christ' were already a new creation (2 Cor. 5:17) but cautioned against believing that the day of the Lord had come (1 Cor. 4:5; 2 Thess. 2:1-2). Paul expected to be alive when Jesus came as Lord. Then, the dead in Christ would be raised incorruptible, while those still alive would be given new ('spiritual') bodies in order to

> 'inherit' the Kingdom of God, visualized (sic) as a heavenly community up 'in the air' (1 Cor. 15:35-53; Phil. 3:20-21; 1 Thess. 4:13-18). Like Jesus, Paul believed that the Parousia events might occur at any time (Phil. 4:5; 1 Thess. 5:1-7). As Jesus taught his followers to pray, 'Thy kingdom come!' (Matt. 6:10), Paul prayed, 'Our Lord, come!' (1 Cor. 16:22; cf. Rev. 22:20)."[dli]

It would surely seem that believers assume to be alive at the so-called Parousia. This school of thought is very much alive today. Yet, as attributed earlier in this study, several scholars, and particularly Catholic authorities; i.e., the Catholic Encyclopaedia state the New Testament, the authenticity of which we must, largely, take for granted. It would therefore also appear that the authors of Bible dictionary explanations commit the same fallacy as their readership, believing the texts expounded to speak of the first century. Aside being unclear and non-biblical, Eschatology is, as already stated a more complex expression. Not only does it have a simple and usual 'last days' meaning, such jargon also undoubtedly involves for the 'religious' a 'Messiah' figure. For christians, this individual is God-man Jesus. Regarding the Messiah notion, Old Testament scholar Sigmund Mowinckel (d.1965.) interestingly offered the following consideration. In his impressively comprehensive study of messianism in the Bible (Old Testament) he writes,

> "In later Judaism, the term 'Messiah' denotes an eschatological figure. He belongs 'to the last time'; his advent lies in the future...In Christian Eschatology, too, the Messiah (Christ) became the central figure in the expectation of the last time..."[dlii] But, the 'expectations' of theologians today, those placed upon 'Messianic prophecies' or 'Messianic hopes' as synonyms for 'eschatological expectations' are incorrect, he also writes; explaining there was no specific messianic figure in the Old Testament.[dliii] Such a figure emerged more predominantly in the New Testament. "Nevertheless, it was most important to the Old Testament that the early Church turned for evidence in support for their belief that Jesus was the Messiah." (Ibid. Mowinckel.)

Nicolas Wright (Millennium Myth) seems to confer discussing briefly the well-known synonymous term, christ. Christ, he writes

"...was not of itself a 'divine' title; however, much it has been used in Christian circles, and been not in earliest Christianity reducible to a mere proper name."[dliv]

Both authors make mention that the question of Jesus' 'Messiah-ship' was truly one relevant question that demanded an adequate answer throughout the gospels. This is often why polemical debates are encountered when reading these texts and the other literary works of the alleged apostles. For modern christians, such an answer obviously came through the epistles and gospels. Interestingly Joseph Fitzmyer argues that by the close of the second century B.C., 'Messiah' as a title at least, was a positive development within the Qumran Scrolls (the Dead Sea texts), showing this Jewish sect possessed a clear belief in such an individual or individuals. He writes,

> "The titular use of "Messiah" for the risen Christ is another instance of how the Scrolls have aided our understanding of a christological title. For the Qumran material reveals that Judaism had, indeed, developed at least by the end of the second century b.c. a clear belief in a coming Messiah or Messiahs. Jewish scholars sometimes ascribe the emergence of messianism among Jews to the Roman period. The only place in the Old Testament where Hebrew mašîăḥ has the connotation of an expected or awaited anointed figure of Davidic descent is found in Dan 9:25: ʿad māšîăḥ nāgîd, "to the coming of an anointed one, a prince". There in the book of Daniel one may debate whether one should translate the Hebrew word māšîăḥ as "anointed one" or as "Messiah," but Qumran texts that date from only a short time after the final redaction [revision] of the book of Daniel (165 b.c) now make it clear, as they build on that Danielic passage, that Palestinian Jews had developed a belief in the coming of a "Messiah" (with a capital M) or even "Messiahs" (in the plural)."[dlv]

In another of his titles, Fitzmyer paints an idea that when paul came to write, "christ/Messiah" had somewhat become a proper name, "save in Romans 9:5...It was most likely Pilate's inscription on the cross, "King of the Jews" (Mark 15:26) that served as the catalyst for the use of 'Messiah' for a crucified anointed agent of Yahweh." See also, the Lucan expression (acts 2:36). Closely connected to Eschatology at least for the Qumran sect so it would seem, was 'the' suggestion and expectation of

DECONSTRUCTING ENDTIME DELUSIONS

a 'Messiah' figure. This is possibly exemplified in one Qumran fragment (4Q521: entitled: 'messianic Apocalypse' by its original editor); which (DSS) scholars say offers a clear expectancy of what 'the Messiah' will accomplish when he arrives. Part of the fragmented interpretation reads:

Frg. 2, Col. ii

1 [the hea]vens and the earth will listen to His Messiah,

2 [and all th]at is in them will not swerve from the commandments of holy ones.

3 Be strengthened in His service, all you who seek the Lord!

4 Shall you not find the Lord in this, all those (= you) who hope in their hearts?

5 For the Lord will visit pious ones, and righteous ones He will call by name.

6 Over afflicted ones will His Spirit hover, and faithful ones He will renew with His power.

7 He will honor (the) pious ones on a throne of eternal kingship,

8 freeing prisoners, giving sight to the blind, straightening up those be[nt over].

9 For[ev]er shall I cling [to tho]se who hope, and in His steadfast love He will recompense;

10 and the frui[t of a] good [dee]d will be delayed for no one.

11 Wondrous things, such as have never been (before), the Lord will do, as He s[aid].

12 For He will heal (the) wounded, revive the dead, (and) proclaim good news to the afflicted;

13 (the) [po]or He will satiate, (the) uprooted He will guide, and on (the) hungry He will bestow riches;

14 and (the) intel[ligent], and all of them (will be) like hol[y ones]

Here is a historic Jewish text; a clear description of what Jews of Palestine expected God would accomplish when His expected Messiah would arrive on the scene.[dlvi] Fitzmyer among other scholars does admit it is difficult to determine whom 'The Lord' or 'His Messiah' spoken of here is, caused by the fragmentary nature of the text. Yet, a first Century understanding of 'Eschatology' is we see replete with numerous subjects and concerns and are not just to be simply understood (albeit normally is) as carrying a simplistic meaning of, 'last days;' besides, the 'Last Days' of what exactly? As will be seen later, the last days continue to unfold through our days. They have been for the past two thousand years! Possibly longer, pending from which angle it is viewed. Further, it might be suitable to here also add regarding a Messiah figure and his subsequent death; burial, and apparent resurrection as believed and recorded in Christian texts that these derive also from much earlier mythical traditions. Strong connections between the Christian ideal of Jesus' death and resurrection, and that of the Egyptian deity Osiris for instance are revealed in alternative research works such as, "Forbidden History: Suppressed Heresies of the West", edited by J. Douglas Kenyon. The above is the most often thought of understanding and meaning (of an end-time) added to Eschatology by the majority. But, what is to be said of both began and realised Eschatology? Without spending too much time on these terms, let me quote their meanings as offered by Theopedia and other sources:

> "Inaugurated Eschatology is a term used to describe the belief that the end times (or latter days) were inaugurated at the life, death and resurrection of Jesus. In other words, Jesus' bringing of the Kingdom of God has both a present and future aspects. Sometimes called already and not yet, it argues that the end is already here, but it has yet to be consummated. For example, Christians await the final resurrection where they will receive new bodies, yet in a sense, believers are already "raised with Christ" (Col. 3:1). Or, as believers await the final judgment, in a sense they have already passed through it, for "there is now no condemnation for those who are in Christ Jesus" (Rom. 8:1) for believers that are justified by faith in Christ (cf. Rom. 3:21-36).

DECONSTRUCTING ENDTIME DELUSIONS

Overall, there is a tension between this age and the age to come. (theopedia) According to inaugurated Eschatology, all the promises of the kingdom can be fulfilled in the Church today. For example, Isaiah 35:5 makes the promise that, in the kingdom, "the eyes of the blind [will] be opened and the ears of the deaf unstopped." This promise can be claimed today, say promoters of the "already but not yet" concept, if we have faith to make the kingdom "break through" into our world. The reasoning is thus: Jesus is the King on the throne in heaven, and His kingdom has already been established, so the blind should see and the deaf should hear. Inaugurated Eschatology is popular in the Charismatic movement, for it provides a basis for claiming miracles today. Scripturally, there is a sense in which we are living in the end times, because the return of Christ is imminent. And there is a sense in which the kingdom is already in force. Colossians 3:1 says that believers "have been raised with Christ," although, of course, this cannot be speaking of a physical, bodily resurrection yet. Paul must be speaking spiritually. One of the problems with inaugurated Eschatology is that it tends to look for a present physical fulfilment of the kingdom promises made to Israel, when Jesus clearly said, "My kingdom is not of this world" (john 18:36). Earlier in Jesus' ministry, He did say that the kingdom of God was "near" (matthew 4:17). But Israel rejected their King and, in so doing, rejected the kingdom. The kingdom years are now "on hold" as God works through the Church, made of both Jew and Gentile. Once the Church age has ended, God will again make Israel the focus of His work in the world. Jesus will return, Israel will receive their Messiah, and then the kingdom of God will come."

Wikipedia offers,

> lyrical (rather than transhistorical) phenomenon. Those holding this view generally dismiss "end times" theories, believing them to be irrelevant. They hold that what Jesus said and did, and told his disciples to do likewise, are of greater significance than any messianic expectations. This view is attractive to many people, especially liberal Christians, since it reverses the notion of Jesus' second coming as an apocalyptic event, something which they interpret as being hardly in keeping with the overall theme of Jesus' teachings

in the canonical gospels. Instead, Eschatology should be about being engaged in the process of becoming, rather than waiting for external and unknown forces to bring about destruction."

Most skeptics I assume to align near the position of realised Eschatology. Although dismissing the whole Eschatology 'end-time' theory as significant, we go one step further, and dismiss as fable the whole gospel 'story.' The prime figure – Jesus is proved mythological, by numerous authors, there is then no need to postulate the veracity of the gospel, or any doctrine that should arise from it. We can now attend to the analogous subject that often causes much fearfulness within the christianised population - Apocalypse.

Apocalypse. Now, later, never - or something completely different?

CLOSELY ASSOCIATED today with biblical Eschatology is the other equally confounding and slippery term, Apocalypse. As with the former there are basic modern, understandings and dictionary definitions offered. An Apocalypse as one will find in most Bible dictionaries for instance carries the understanding of being a: "Revelation" or "unveiling." An Apocalypse is a work that features a heavenly figure (usually God or an angel) using apocalyptic language to reveal a "secret" message, often having an eschatological focus (e.g., relating to heaven or the kingdom of God or the end of the world). The book of Revelation is described as "the Revelation [apokalypsis] of Jesus Christ" (Rev. 1:1), meaning either that the book reveals something about Jesus or that Jesus reveals something about God's plan in the book (or perhaps both). In either case, a message is being revealed or disclosed. Many interpreters refer to Revelation as "the Apocalypse."[dlvii] In another source we read,

> "Apocalypse is a genre of revelatory literature with a narrative framework, in which a Revelation is mediated by an otherworldly being to a human recipient, disclosing a transcendent reality which is both temporal, insofar as it envisages eschatological salvation, and spatial insofar as it involves another supernatural world;" it is "intended to interpret present earthly circumstances in the light of the supernatural world and of the future, and to

influence both the understanding and the behavior of the audience by means of divine authority."[dlviii]

In his article in the experimental journal, Semeia, John J. Collins (DePaul University) further identifies a number of important problems to be mindful of with the identification and classification of 'Apocalyptic' material stating,

> "It is important to note that the classification "apocalyptic" or "Apocalypse" is a modern one. Some ancient Jewish, Christian and Gnostic works are entitled Apokalypsis in the manuscripts (e.g. 3 Baruch, the Apocalypse of the Holy Mother of God, the Apocalypse of Adam). However, the title is not a reliable guide to the genre. The so-called Apocalypse of Moses (a variant of the Life of Adam and Eve) is quite different from the main bulk of apocalypses. On the other hand, several works, which are not, called "apocalypses" in the mss. must be included in any discussion of the genre. It is obvious then that the identification of a genre "Apocalypse" is not a simple matter of collecting texts, which bear this label or have already been otherwise clearly identified. An "Apocalypse" is simply that which scholars can agree to call an Apocalypse."[dlix]

Similarly, and agreeably, Thomas Thompson (The Messiah Myth) offers an understanding worthy of more of our recognition, stating,

> "Whether a saying (or literary composition; i.e., Bible book) is understood as Apocalypse depends entirely on the setting the author gives it."[dlx]

We can deduce, there are also numerous and varied accents to apocalyptic materials, broadly spanning from the second Century B.C.E, to the second Century C.E. (common era.) The same should be applied to eschatological materials. 'Apocalyptic/Apocalypse,' and Eschatology is therefore, as Bishop Wright informs,

> "...a type of language-game. [They] regularly involve vivid metaphors which enable the writer to say, and the reader to understand (Mark 13:14, in the middle of a passage most would see as "apocalyptic", coaxed "let the reader understand", though most still don't), the significance, within God's dimension of reality, of events that happen within our dimension, within the world of space, time and matter. To take Isaiah's stars [isaiah 13:10],

sun and moon–to suppose that are, that he thought they would really be darkened or <falling> out of the sky–is as silly a mistake as it would be to take paul's metaphor [colossians 2:15] and to suggest that the gospels have gotten it wrong, and that actually Jesus was not crucified, but won a military victory over Pilate, Herod and the Chief Priests. And, whichever city is called "Babylon" in Revelation 18, the one place it surely isn't is–Babylon."[dlxi]

It is proper to add, scholars are also aware that the very earliest inception of Apocalypse has been traced back to Iran, between 1,500, and 1200B.C.E. 'Apocalypse' is recognised as the disputed invention of the oldest known religion, Zoroastrianism. Social science Anthropologist and theologian Bruce Milna insightfully appends to our discussion from one of his commentaries,

> "While the terms "Apocalypse" or "eschatological Apocalypse" sound duly esoteric and learned, the terms shed little light on the sort of book this last document of the New Testament really is. Perhaps some scholars believe that such labels appropriately categorise the work both in the history of scholarship and in terms of appropriate categorical distinctions; however, it seems, rather, that "Apocalypse" and "Eschatology" are simply part and parcel of the theological jargon of the past century [terms coined first in the early 19th Century by German Theologians] that fossilise perception and misdirect interpretation. Thus, while the Greek word "Apocalypse" ...originally meant the process of revealing or making known something secret about persons, the word is inadequate to describe the book of Revelation."[dlxii]

Dr. Ben Witherington aptly weighs in with what many seem to always forget:

> "What is completely lost in the shuffle in much of the popular discussion of such material is not merely literary sensitivity to the sort of material one is dealing with, but the recognition that these prophesies were the word of God for the Jews and Christians many centuries ago and that they also had meaning for those audiences. Indeed, they were written for those audiences in the first place, not for us. What the text meant then, is still what the text means today. And what it could not possibly have meant in the first Century

DECONSTRUCTING ENDTIME DELUSIONS

A.D. or before, it does not mean now. These texts were not written to scare the living daylight out of us..."[dlxiii]

The descriptions and specified meanings of these rather arcane words as well as the insight offered by these scholars and websites then beg the question. Is history linear? Our modern Western culture tends to assume so by the assertion of the religious regarding rapture and the constant bold referral to these cognates. Yet, can we for certain today perceive a foreseeable end game, or eschaton and Apocalypse scenario of modern civilisation; one understood as absolute final, marking it with a definitive phase and, or event as the ancient Stoic also believed. The leading features as attributed above, of the twenty-first Century are after-all also materialism, pantheism, fatalism, and pride. If an end game is noteworthy and definitive, will that encompass hope for relief or renewal: a global 'golden age' of Jewish, Islamic, or Christian/Jew hybrid hegemony initiated by their Messiah's return? I wouldn't assume to dream so. If it should, and I be proved wrong, I wonder if an overall result would be any different to the demonic and tragic histories of persecution and bloodshed of countless millions of other freethinkers, and skeptics for their proposals and non-compliance to what these three 'power' religions deem as good and right. Where then did the initial idea of an end-game type scenario begin to meet with common interest? Collins confirms what was hinted above, offering the maxim it was rather late in history, being recognised in the specified earlier. Apocalyptic literature, which flourished in Judaism during the Hellenistic and Roman periods [is where] an elaborate end-oriented view of history was developed. Apocalyptic literature was not uniform; it embraced different modalities of this view of history. So by all reasonable accounts the notion of Apocalypse, and subsequent topics is no more than an adolescent. Such ideas are not ancient. Rather are a conglomeration of many past ideas and conceptions. The material referred above is the "Dead Sea Scrolls", and those other ancient Jewish (extra-biblical) manuscripts found at Qumran in the late 1940's, early 1950's. In many of these ancient manuscript writings, it is attested, as noticed in the fragment (4q521 above) there was an expectation of an intervention of some deity. Such an intervention it was hoped would ultimately put an end to the current dislocated civil situation and ultimately usher in a Utopia of the 'Dictum of the Kingdom,' particularly of Israel's God. Justice and peace were expected to then forever be in governance, for disobedience, and opposition to the 'Kingdom' was finally, and completely destroyed. Thus, when speaking of 'the last days,' it wasn't signalling at all "the end of God being or activity. Rather, they would constitute the eternal last phase that would be introduced by the end of the present world-order. It was not uncommon for people to believe that this transitional crisis was not far distant in time. There were, therefore, numerous cases of disappointed hope and numerous fresh formulations of the people's expectations." Such disappointments, expectations, and formulations obviously continue to this day. We have already toyed with the idea, but what influences might ancient texts and expectations have had on the early and our modern Christian musings surrounding end-time events? Today more than ever it seems astoundingly strange modalities thrive. We witness a gluttony of confusing and highly subjective interpretive methods and the conclusions they often draw, touted as fact surrounding events close to 'a' second advent. Whether there is a central Messiah figure or not, these themes are obvious. From the fanciful and imminent disclosure of an alien 'mother' race that caused the evolution of humankind, to the U.F.O. phenomenon; or the advent of a 'new' breed of human, that science has termed Transhumanism, which is (the intermingling of human, animal, and technological synthetic genomes, forming a superhuman –Human 2.0 (advanced humans.) This is currently a tried, tested, and real science); to the more vivid and known recent scenarios portrayed on the small and silver screens: –Mad Max movies, Hellboy, M.I.B. Battleship, Dark Shadows, Contact, Hunger Games, Apollo, to name but a few. Any amount of printed material has hit bookstore shelves in recent decades. One newly released (April 2012) 'Christian' publication claimed knowledge of "The Final Pope -Petrus Romanus" (who is said to be the predicted false Prophet of The scroll of 'Revelation'). Articles surrounding the book can be read (with much skepticism), Easily recognised all the same is that every prediction offered on the

DECONSTRUCTING ENDTIME DELUSIONS

apocalyptic smorgasbord today, at some point, carries a dire end-time theme; where the proverb - 'survival of the fittest' loudly resounds! Chiefly, most doomsday events for the modern 'Christian theorist' are slightly different from the silver screen; the focus is what happens to those few 'lucky' illusory 'believers' who are alive at their messiahs expected and most 'Glorious' return. Most of these predictions and hypotheses surrounding not only Eschatology, but also the Millennium and some type of apocalyptic scenario are predictably spewing forth at a great rate of knots from The Land of the Free, –America. There are numerous websites like Raiders News Update offering not only numerous end-times materials, and the 'latest' research into this that, and another guess it is truly mesmerising. But what's more, these sites go so far to offer 'essential' survival wares for the 'discerning;' for when the global disaster (Apocalypse/World-wide Tribulation) eventually does rear its ugly head.[dlxiv] Bishop Wright is one sensible, levelheaded theologian. He confirms these sentiments as awash with hype. Likening much of it to essentially the same fervour that saw the tragic events of Waco Texas, and I'd add, 'Heaven's Gate' suicide pact that unfurled late last century (1990's.) Early in his book, Millennium Myth, Wright posed an insightful statement to be considered still as relevant for concerned patrons of the many theories on offer today:

> "Few such groups will stop to ask, I guess, why God should be bound by the decision of a sixth-century [or twelfth-century] ...monk, [or any such mortal] rather than by the exact chronology... [maybe] the anniversary of the crucifixion or resurrection, which might perhaps be (in terms of Jewish months) 14 Nisan (sometime in April) 2026 or thereabouts. Even a little historical information, even a few moments of reflection, might go some way towards defusing millennial [and end-time] hysteria."[dlxv]

Aside what is currently assumed, approximately two millennia or more have passed; and the 'Christian' Messiah tarries still! Every 'prediction' of either Messiah's return or an end event disaster, or such since at least the first-century has fallen way short of its Mark, having come and gone and failed to deliver on any utopian or calamitous promise. Rather the only delivery has been pain, sorrow, and the tragically stupid loss of life. An interesting compilation of such spectacularly failed predictions can be accessed via Wikipedia. There, one can read a periodically updated List of dates predicted for apocalyptic events; events which are now added the date, 21st December 2012![dlxvi] Contemporary theories abound and not surprisingly are widespread inside, and outside evangelical and charismatic Christian circles. Few Christian ideologies do not however assume to hang all bets upon a widely believed notion that millions of people (they call, the 'true' Church), will suddenly disappear! Why? Why do millions seem to wish to bail, and opt for the 'cheap' and vacate? Why do many of these people today not only think, but also attempt to 'justify' the absurd notion that the last generation of christians will somehow escape trials and tribulations when none of their predecessors ever did? Who says that this is the final generation of Christian or any other people group anyway? Generations have lived, have worked, and have loved, hated, waged war and slander before us. All those same generations have died ahead of us. Including the figures by which the mythic Jesus, and his apostles (are based) and all subsequent believers through the ages who have bought into the lie that is the Church! Again, this is the course set for humanity, which is until 'a' deity (if there be one) says otherwise! So who can announce with surety that this, or any other generation is final? Consider the powerfully analogous passage (Genesis 3:24) carefully: the passage of our forefathers being booted from paradise for whatever speculative reason that might be individually assumed by readers. A passage, which the recently published Lexham English Septuagint translation of the Greek old testament interestingly reads,

> "So, he threw out Adam and settled him opposite the paradise of luxuriousness and stationed the cherubim's and the flaming sword, which turns, to guard the way of the tree of life."

Not remarkably different to most Standard Bible texts. But, the idea is greatly asserted by the author that the deity of the Bible placed a certain and definite hindrance, a curtain obstructing humanity's return to the paradise of luxuriousness; that is, without at least one prerequisite. There is, because of the flaming sword, no way back to the immortality once enjoyed –not without the sting of death! Which altogether is contrary to modern rapture theories, proposing that there is somehow some escape of this bane to being human, –death! But, we can learn from this episode and a classic myth referred to earlier, that escaping death is not the point. Death is forever peering over our shoulder. Life's aphrodisiac is Death. Death's aphrodisiac is so, Life! The two labour feverishly together. Without the chaos of death, there cannot be life or ordered. The above commentaries regarding myth, Eschatology and especially, 'Apocalypse' were all offered from the distinctively Christian perspective. The 'standard' thinking of many will be analogous when confronted by the question – what is the 'Apocalypse?' However, there is one other perspective I wish to convey. In a fascinating article authored by occult scholar Donald Tyson, titled, "Enochian Apocalypse". 'Apocalypse' is understood as:

"...a mental transformation that will occur, or is presently occurring, within the collective unconsciousness of the human race."[dlxvii]

Furthermore, Donald sums his article, writing:

"Fundamentalist Christians commonly believe that the end of the world will be a completely physical event, sparked by some horrifying material agent – global thermonuclear war, or the impact of a large asteroid, or a deadly plague... [this] is in keeping with the materialistic worldview ... But nobody stops to consider that this destruction is described by angels, or that angels are spiritual, not physical, beings. In my opinion, the Apocalypse... must be primarily an internal, spiritual event, and only in a secondary way an external, physical catastrophe... [Therefore 'when' this 'event' occurs]..the demons of Coronzon, [will enter] not into the physical world, but into our subconscious minds.[dlxviii] Spirits are mental, not material. They dwell in the depths of mind and communicate with us through our dreams, unconscious impulses, and more rarely in waking visions. They affect our feelings and our thoughts... through us, and only through us, are they able to influence physical things... To allow a foul wind to blow through the common mind of the human race.This would explain the senseless slaughter of the First World War and the unspeakable horror of the Nazi Holocaust during the Second World War....If this chilling scenario [of the battle of the 'predicted' Apocalypse, as being a spiritual event first and foremost, that is sparked in the mind, and only secondarily a physical act] ever comes to pass, the wars of the twentieth century will seem bucolic to those who survive the slaughter."[dlxix]

This amazing explanation of 'Apocalypse' offered by Donald Tyson seems a more fitting and real account. It is after all, I think, a correct summation of what could befall, or has befallen numerous ethnic groups in the last couple of centuries. Listen to or view any media broadcast and most of the information could be undoubtedly locked into 'happening' just as Donald describes. Precisely because, a foul wind seems to have been blowing through the common mind of many regions and cultures around the globe. Widespread indignation through a clash of cultures is most obvious today throughout the Mid-East. It is however, also undeniable and often confusing. Many passages in the sacred book seem to indicate to the reader that an end-game motif and disappearance act are present, one analogous to what Professor John Collins described earlier. We often read passages containing several puzzling phrases like: 'day of the Lord', "end of days," and 'judgment day.' What are these referents to aside the brief explanation above and, - what effect did apocalypticism and Eschatology have on paul and early christianity? If an answer is found, what would that mean for christianity today, and how would today's assumptions fair against it? Such questions can be sufficiently answered along the way. Apocalypse, Eschatology and rapture are all combined when any discussion of end–time topic or scenario arises. I trust in the above commentaries, I have been somewhat successful in illuminating these for readers. Now let us move a critical eye briefly over millennium the meaning of Rapture and the main theory contending for its validation.

Millennium - Millenarianism:

A MILLENNIUM (PLURAL millennia) is time approximating 1,000 years. It derives from the Latin mille, thousand, and annus, year (Wikipedia). Aside this usual giving, Millennium is a complex idea to consider, for the simple reason; nobody with absolute surety, or accuracy can pinpoint exactly when this time begins. In history, it was somewhat a 'hit and miss affair'. Basic to the conundrum faced: Does or do the calculations of years begin with years: x99 –y00; or, x00 - y01? Our modern calculations typically attest to the presumed dating of the birth of the mythical personage, christ. Yet, this too cannot be established as fact. Besides, it appears that all our modern calculations are wrong if just as it is also a common thought that the figure –christ –was born around the years 4-6B.C.E. Apparently, our current dating system is up the creek, being anywhere from 4-6years miscalculated if these presumed dates are remotely correct. Did the year 2,000 –the 'new millennium' as we nowadays suppose it, for instance, begin in the year's 1994, 1996, 1999, 2000, or 2001? Modern calendars it would seem are somewhat inaccurate, for there was no year 0.[dlxx] As if to further complicate matters, there is a very analogous term used by many Christian theologians and authors –Millenarianism. Millenarianism is specifically again derived from the Latin - "containing a thousand," is the belief by a religious, social, or political group or movement in an advent major transformation of society, after which all things will be changed – primarily because of some God-awful Apocalypse/end-time saga being played out on the world-stage. Millenarianism is a concept or theme that exists in many cultures and religions.[dlxxi] Now, that millennium has been briefly explained, we must also recognise that the Bible does refer to a Second Advent of the Messiah figure. Jesus himself is said to have spoken numerously of such a time. All the saying attributed to a Second Advent, people not dying beforehand, millennial reign etc. however have never been fulfilled. Interestingly enough,

> "...in the first century of the Church, millenarianism was a whispered belief, whereto the book of Daniel, and more particularly the predictions of the Apocalypse bestowed an apostolic authority, but, when the Church imbibed Paganism, their belief on this subject lent it a more vivid coloring [sic] and imagery... According to the general opinion, the millennium was to be preceded by great calamities, after which the Messiah... would appear... bind Satan... annihilate the godless heathen... [making] his religion... supreme. This is the "Golden Age" of the future, which all nations of antiquity believed in and eagerly awaited." (Doane, Ch. 24. The Second Coming...)

The Indians, Buddhists, Chinese, Inca's, ancient Persians... and ancient Scandinavians, to name but a few ancient people groups who had a "Last Days, or Latter days" scenario analogous to the Christian, where great calamities would befall mankind. The earth would tremble, and the stars fall from heaven. After which, the great serpent would be chained...and their supreme deity would reign unopposed for One Thousand years or more. There is then, nothing truly amazing, or sacred about any Bible text that bolster these concepts. Every religion on earth promotes the same, differing only in the detail. Again, we can say in confidence, christianity filched and absorbed these ideas from Pagan religions. Before moving through to an excursion of rapture, one other word needs to be explained. Belief.

Belief:

IN A FEW WORDS: WHAT is it? How does it shape our perspectives and world? As attributed in the opening pages, the Dictionary definition of belief is: an acceptance that something exists or is true, especially one without proof... [its] the trust, faith, or confidence in (someone or something). This perspective is only partly correct. Partly correct, because humans tend to be rather short-sighted. It's a popular thought that we do not 'believe' something unless we can visually catch sight of it; however, more correctly we 'see' what we believe. It is our beliefs that mould and give shape, and life to everything we encounter. An ancient Egyptian mystic, Kalika said of belief,

> "A belief is just an idea about reality, not a part of reality itself, so once identified it can be changed or replaced as you like."

And so,

> "Altering the conscious aspects of your inner self automatically alters the exterior circumstances."[dlxxii]

Everything that human's encounter, were given life by someone's 'belief.' In 1837 Charles Babbage 'believed' he could invent the first general

DECONSTRUCTING ENDTIME DELUSIONS

mechanical computer, the Analytical Engine. The Analytical Engine contained an Arithmetic Logic Unit (ALU), basic flow control, and integrated memory, and is the first general-purpose computer concept. Today's computers are far more sophisticated, but the basic point is the idea/belief began in the mind. Believing became a reality! A belief in e.t. encounters, U.F.O. sightings, and other strange oddities will inevitably lead to experiencing those beliefs. Wholehearted 'belief' in something lures whatever is believed upon. It is not 'seeing' that leads to your believing rather the 'believing' enables seeing. The 'belief' manifests what is expected! Everything encountered in this life; the good, the bad, and the indifferent is a direct result of your beliefs! Yet, as hinted our believing can contain very subtle lies, some of which are undoubtedly imbued with intent to circumvent. Hence, earlier statements regarding cognitive bias. Be forewarned, not everything one believes should be. At the very heart of some beliefs are lies. Allan Watts, Wisdom of Insecurity sums belief succinctly stating,

> "Belief... is the insistence that what one would wish it to be. The believer will open his mind to the truth on condition that it fits in with his preconceived ideas and wishes."[dlxxiii]

[i] Butler-Bowdon, T. 50 Philosophical Classics: Thinking, Being, Acting, Seeing - profound insights and powerful thinking from 50 key books (50 classics) p.3. Hodder and Stoughton.

[ii] Buckingham, Will. The Philosophy Book (big ideas). Dorling Kindersley Ltd.edition. (locations 148; 155.)

[iii] Taussig, Hal. A New New Testament: A Bible for the Twenty-First Century Combining Traditional and Newly Discovered Texts. Houghton Mifflin Harcourt. (Location beginning 605)

[iv] Humanology® The science of understanding Human Nature. According to author, Don Magyar. The Essence Of Man: Discover The Theory That Explains Human Nature (Humanology® Book 1) (Locations 112-113). Permanent Publications.

[v] Purcell, Carl. Your Artist's Brain (p.17). F+W Media.

[vi] All <Underline> Words are found in a small dictionary in the Appendixes, in Appendix 1: Symbolism.

[vii] Jones, Marie D. and Flaxman, L. Demons, The Devil, and Fallen Angels (Location 168). Visible Ink Press.

[viii] Conner, Jonah David. All that's wrong with the Bible: Contradictions, Absurdities, and More (p.16).

[ix] Poole, Cecil A. In Search of Reality (Rosicrucian Order AmorcEditions) (Locations 447-451; 452-455). Rosicrucian Order, Amorc. See http://www.amorc.org.au/

[x] Halaw, andre Doshim. God Is Nothingness: Awakening to Absolute Non-Being (p.8). No-Mind Zen Publications.

[xi] Walker, Barbara G. Man Made God: A Collection of Essays. Stellar House Publishing. (Location 632.)

[xii] Schopenhauer, A. The Horrors and Absurdities Of Religion (Penguin Great Ideas) (p.5-6). Penguin Books Ltd.

[xiii] Green, Ivan. The Anti-Bible: For Atheists, Freethinkers, and Christians Who Know Better. (Location 67.)

DECONSTRUCTING ENDTIME DELUSIONS

[xiv] Delingpole, James. Watermelons: How Environmentalists Are Killing The Planet, Destroying The Economy and Stealing Your Children's Future. Biteback Publishing. (Location 168.)

[xv] Price, R.G. Deciphering The Gospels: Proves Jesus Never Existed (Locations 61-62). Lulu Publishing Services.

[xvi] Quote By S. Sharpe, Egyptian Mythology and Egyptian Christianity, Ch. - The Religion Of Upper Egypt.

[xvii] Christians must reconcile these questions because their own 'testimonies' – esp. their Old Testament. in the work attributed to a fellow claimed as a great Prophet who strolled around naked for three years. Are these words of the deity: "Before me no God was formed nor shall there be any after me." (Isa 43:10) The New Testament Jesus claimed by christians to have been 'prophesied' as 'coming' by isaiah cannot be true. According to this verse!

[xviii] Classicist Arthur J. Droge has written that it is incorrect to refer to Celsus' perspective as polytheism. Instead, he's an "inclusive" or "qualitative" monotheist. As opposed to the Jewish "exclusive" or "quantitative" monotheism; historian Wouter Hanegraaff explains that "The former has room for a hierarchy of lower deities which do not detract from the ultimate unity of the one." Celsus shows himself familiar with the story of Jewish origins. [Clarification Needed] ...Celsus wants [christians] to be good citizens, to retain their own belief...it is an earnest and striking appeal on behalf of unity and mutual toleration... Celsus attacks the christians as feeding off faction and disunity, and accuses them of converting the vulgar and ignorant, while refusing to debate wise men. As for their opinions regarding their sacred mission and exclusive holiness, Celsus responds by deriding their insignificance, comparing them to a swarm of bats, or ants creeping out of their nests, or frogs holding a symposium round a swamp, or worms in conventicle in a corner of the mud. It is not known how many were christians at the time of Celsus (the Jewish population of the empire might have been about 6.6-10% in a population of 60 million to quote one. reference. wikipedia: https:// en.wikipedia.org[1]/wiki/celsuscite_note-ha-4

[xix] Celsus (Platonic Philosopher), active 180. Arguments of Celsus, Porphyry, and The Emperor Julian, against The Christians. Also extracts from Diodorus Siculus, Josephus, and Tacitus, Relating to the Jews, Together with an Appendix (locations 233-234).

[xx] Ibid, (locations 262-266; 345-350).edition.

---

1. http://en.wikipedia.org

[xxi] Location 505.

[xxii] Halaw, Andre Doshim. God Is Nothingness: Awakening to absolute non-being (pp. 10-11). No-mind Zen Publications.edition.

[xxiii] A concept coined by Cambridge psychologist Simon Baron-Cohen. Cited in Bering. (Location 1235.)

[xxiv] Halaw, Andre Doshim. God Is Nothingness: Awakening to absolute non-being (p.2). No-Mind Zen Publications.edition.

[xxv] Such a concept has been misused by religion, and the men caught by its grip. Man being mankind, has misunderstood that 'creative' force too is 'symbolic'. Biological males can and do create, but not in the sense of literally, biologically creating other humankind. The concept of such was 'birthed' in ancient times when womenkind were the 'lesser' species. No wonder Feminism rails against any patriarchy!

[xxvi] Ashe, Geoffrey. Eden in the Altai: The prehistoric golden age and the mythic origins of humanity. Inner Traditions/Bear and Company.edition. Introduction to the second edition. (loc. 136)

[xxvii] Lynn, Heather. Anthrotheology (p.58). Midnight Crescent Publishing.edition. Brackets mine. [] my inclusion.

[xxviii] Feldman, Dr. Stanely. Global Warming and Other Bollocks (pp.25-26). John Blake Publishing.edition.

[xxix] Yudkowsky, Eliezer. Rationality: From Ai To Zombies (Locations 410-414). Machine Intelligence Research Institute.

[xxx] Slone, Jason. Theological Incorrectness: Why Religious People Believe What They Shouldn't (p. Vii). Oxford University Press. Quoting David Hume: The Natural History Of Religion. The author is by no means advocating another end time proposal offered by christianity. That of a 'One world religion, and One world Religion. This is a massive topic not commented upon in these pages, as such likely require a separate tome themselves.

[xxxi] Bacevich, Andrew J. The Essence Of Conservatism (Locations 90-91). The American Conservative.

[xxxii] Berlinerblau, Jacques. The Secular Bible: Why Nonbelievers Must Take Religion Seriously (p.80). Cambridge University Press.edition.

DECONSTRUCTING ENDTIME DELUSIONS

[xxxiii] Pippin, Tina. Apocalyptic Bodies: The Biblical End Of The World In Text and Image. Taylor and Francis.edition.Location 74.

[xxxiv] William Robertson Smith. Lectures On: The Religion Of The Semites: The Fundamental Institutions (Locations 558-559). The Macmillan Company.

[xxxv] See, Matthew 28:18-20; Mark 13:10;16:15; Acts 1:8; Romans 10:18.

[xxxvi] Michelet, Jules. Satanism and Witchcraft (p.9). @Annierosebooks.edition.

[xxxvii] Gaiman, Neil. The End of The World: Stories of The Apocalypse (pp. 2-4). Skyhorse Publishing.edition.

[xxxviii] [A] burden of proof lay with those who believe that every word, deed, action recorded in their sacred books is factually sound, and comes down to us generally unadulterated. One who starts from the premise that the text is meaningful, coherent, and true who starts from the premise that the text is meaningful, coherent, and true to the words of an ancient Israelite, or Jew is practicing theology. One who rejects these assumptions is called a secular hermeneut. –Berlinerblau, Jacques. The Secular Bible (p. 51). Cambridge University Press.

[xxxix] Locations 48; 52-54; 105-106.

[xl] Gilbert has I assume used extensively the ideologies offered by the Greek poet Hesiod. The Golden Age derives particularly from the work, Works and Days. How did Gilbert arrive at the conclusion that myths like 'The Golden Age' is comparable with his ideology? During the 'Golden Age', none were present; people lived extraordinarily long lives, and had no hang-ups with death. Obviously, Gilbert seems to have pilfered and twisted more than a few ideas. Using them alongside his predisposed thoughts regards Genesis 6:1-4, in a desperate hope of supporting his theory.

[xli] Langdon, Robert John. Giant Skeletons: - Found By French Archaeologists Now Dismissed By Anthropologists (13 Ancient Things That Don't Make Sense In History) (Locations 58-64). Abc Publishing Group.

[xlii] Bering, Jesse. The God Instinct: The Psychology Of Souls, Destiny and The Meaning Of Life (Locations 967-973). Hodder and Stoughton. Theory of Mind is explained later in [Nail Four] of this investigation.

[xliii] Harari, Yuval Noah. Sapiens: A Brief History of Humankind (pp.147-148). Random House.

[xliv] Bering, Jesse. The God Instinct: The Psychology of Souls, Destiny and The Meaning Of Life (Locations 1864-1867; 1891-1892; 1910-1913). Hodder and Stoughton.

[xlv] Nyland, A. Fallen Angels, Watchers, Giants, Nephilim and Evil (Angelology Demonology) (pp.10-11).edition.

[xlvi] The Future Of 'God' and Organized (sic) Religion, Chapter 6. p4 of 9.electronic edition.

[xlvii] Slone, Jason. Theological Incorrectness: Why religious people believe what they should not (p.4). Oxford University Press.

[xlviii] Completing a Symbolic comprehension of these passages of Genesis 6, it was noticed afterward that a symbolic interpretation conformed to personal thoughts regarding this Bible chapter as it might relate to Genesis chapter three. I am fully cognisant to the fact that my interpretation is based on a symbolic meaning of the English, not Hebrew of these verses.

[xlix] Wright, T. (1999). The Millennium Myth (pp.20–22). Louisville, Ky: Westminster John Knox Press.

[l] See, Atlantis Rising Magazine: May/ June 2018, ; Australian Rationalist: Journal Of The Rationalist Society Of Australia, Vol 109. June 2018.

[li] Though often recognised as a perplexing narrative, Genesis 6:4 and analogous passages as mentioned are discussed at some length in Part Two, Nail Nine of this investigation.

[lii] Without doubt all religious people, particularly, display the phenomenon. Esp., when attempting to argue their religious view at confronting an alternative perspective.

[liii] Icke, D. Phantom Self (and how to find the real one), page 24.

[liv] Macrae, P., False Alarm: Global Warming, Facts Verses Fears.(Ch. 1).

[lv] Deceptions and Myth in The Bible; The Bible Fraud; The Christ Scandal. Also, texts by Hugh Schonfield, and William Harwood.

[lvi] Cited by Bushby, The Bible Fraud, Ch. 16, p168. Bushby offers many examples in this chapter.

[lvii] Bushby, T. The Christ Scandal. 'A Frank Priesthood Confession.' p.17.

DECONSTRUCTING ENDTIME DELUSIONS

[lviii] Berlinerblau, Jacques. The Secular Bible: Why Nonbelievers Must Take Religion Seriously (pp.30-31). Cambridge University Press.

[lix] Smith, David Livingstone. The Most Dangerous Animal: Human nature and the origins of war (pp.25-26). St. Martin's Press.

[lx] Becker. The Denial Of Death (Locations 172-174). Souvenir Press.edition.

[lxi] Floyd, W. The Mistakes Of Jesus. Gutenberg. [Openers. p11 of 24.]

[lxii] Rohl, David. The Lords Of Avaris. Introduction. p66 of 79.

[lxiii] Breshears, J. Shocking Secrets Of Antiquity:... That Buried History, Ch. 1, p7. [Brackets mine] See Also his: Giants On The Earth: An In-Depth Study On The Nephilim. •This word is likely a typo. There is no such word as Infeigned. Likely, should be **Unfeigned**. Which does not change the sentence or original author's intended meaning. Jason also uses various questionable authorities, like Zachariah Sitchin who was not a reputable Scholar. Much of the information in the book, Shocking Secrets... it would be pertinent, and diligent to be versed in critical thinking skills.

[lxiv] Delingpole, James. Watermelons: How Environmentalists Are Killing The Planet, Destroying The Economy and Stealing Your Children's Future. Biteback Publishing. (Location 176.)

[lxv] Smith, David Livingstone. The Most Dangerous Animal: Human Nature and The Origins Of War (p.60-61). St. Martin's Press.

[lxvi] Pippin, T. Apocalyptic Bodies. Quote By Fiction Writer, Flannery O'Connor. p28.

[lxvii] Ibid. Smith, David Livingstone. p.109

[lxviii] Holloway, Richard. A Little History Of Religion (Little Histories). Yale University Press.(Location 616.)

[lxix] Harari, Yuval Noah. Sapiens: A Brief History Of Humankind (p.18). Random House.

[lxx] For an accurate assessment of 'Religious Violence' See Religious Hostility: A Global Assessment Of Hatred and Terror, By Rodney Stark and Katie E. Corcoran., 2014.

[lxxi] Nixey, Catherine. The Darkening Age (Locations 1705-1714; 1629-1636; 1766-1773). Pan Macmillan Uk. [Is modern 21st century mankind reliving these descriptions?]

[lxxii] Ibid, p.37

[lxxiii] 'Holy Mass' was in the earliest days of christianity, conducted in Latin. No congregant truely knew, understood what was said by the priest. Let alone what a meaning was. Rather, the officiating cleric was viewed as the personification of the deity. An acclamation they relished. Though it would be denied today, christians still revere their clergy as being 'God-like.'

[lxxiv] Ellerbe, Helen. The Dark Side Of Christian History (Locations 99-110). Bookbaby.

[lxxv] Nixey, Catherine. The Darkening Age (Locations 1820-1824). Pan Macmillan Uk.

[lxxvi] Ibid. Bushby, T. The Papal Billions. p96.

[lxxvii] Smith, David Livingstone. The Most Dangerous Animal: Human Nature and The Origins of War (p.29). St. Martin's Press. [Brackets mine.]

[lxxviii] Ibid. (p108).

[lxxix] Shermer, Michael. The Moral Arc: How Science Makes Us Better People (Locations 158-161). Henry Holt and Co.

[lxxx] Readers are especially encouraged to study the book: Dangerous Illusions, how religion deprives us of happiness, by Vitaly Malkin.

[lxxxi] The Holy Bible: New Revised Standard Version. (1989). (Dan 5:26–27). Nashville: Thomas Nelson Publishers.

[lxxxii] Carroll, J. M. The Trail Of Blood (pp.4-5). Challenge Press.

[lxxxiii] Hall, Manly P. How To Understand Your Bible: A Philosopher's Interpretation of Obscure and Puzzling Passages (pp. 149-150). White Crow Productions Ltd.

[lxxxiv] Floyd, E. Randall. The Dark Side Of History: 5000 Years Of Bizarre Beliefs, Mysteries and Wondrous Events From Around The World (Locations 166-183; 223-231). Batwing Press.

DECONSTRUCTING ENDTIME DELUSIONS

[lxxxv] Shermer, Michael. The Moral Arc: How Science Makes Us Better People (Locations 3711-3717; 3722-3723). Henry Holt and Co.

[lxxxvi] Ibid. (Locations 3742-3750).

[lxxxvii] Conner, Jonah David. All That's Wrong With The Bible: Contradictions, Absurdities, and More (p.63).

[lxxxviii] Shermer, Michael. The Moral Arc: How Science Makes Us Better People (Locations 3825-3838). Henry Holt and Co.

[lxxxix] See J Loftus, T Freke's, Paulkovich's as well as those cited. See Bibliography.

[xc] The Most Dangerous Animal. p.54.

[xci] Livington-Smith, D. The Most Dangerous Animal... Ch. 3: Our Own Worst Enemy. [Brackets mine]

[xcii] *To 'tergiversate' is to be deliberately unclear, or unclear to mislead or withhold information. As it is to apostatise.

[xciii] Acharya S. The Christ Conspiracy: The Greatest Story Ever Sold (Locations 99-104; 104-112; 112-118).

[xciv] Becker: Denial Of Death. Ch. 1, Human nature and the heroic.

[xcv] Smith, David Livingstone. The Most Dangerous Animal (pp.136-137). St. Martin's Press.[bracket my addition]

[xcvi] Ibid. (p.138).

[xcvii] Harari, Yuval Noah. Sapiens: A Brief History Of Humankind (p.157). Random House.

[xcviii] Ibid. Ch. 4 'The Origins Of Human Nature', p86.

[xcix] Babones, Salvatore. The New Authoritarianism: Trump, Populism, and The Tyranny of Experts (p4; 6). Wiley.

[c] Example: fierce debate on both sides raged a number of years ago that women could not become ordained Tekel: Religion– You Are Found Wanting!

[ci] Example: fierce debate on both sides raged a number of years ago that women could not become ordained Tekel: Religion– You Are Found Wanting!

[cii] Zubrin, Robert. Merchants Of Despair: Radical Environmentalists, Criminal Pseudo-Scientists, and the fatal cult of Antihumanism (New Atlantis Books) (pp.5-6). Encounter Books.

[ciii] See Albert Jack's Wonderfully Concise Booklet, Gun Control USA: The NRA: Why Mass Shootings In America 'Won't Stop.'

[civ] Davies, William. Nervous States: How Feeling Took Over The World (Locations 89-91; 93-94). Random House.

[cv] Macgregor, Neil. Living With The Gods: On Beliefs and Peoples (Locations 530-541). Penguin Books Ltd.

[cvi] Celsus. Locations 228–230.

[cvii] Ibid. Locations 190-192.

[cviii] Loftus – Ch. Two, The Failure Of The Church and The Triumph Of Reason.

[cix] Michelet, Jules. Satanism and Witchcraft. Introduction.

[cx] Harris, W. H., Iii, Ritzema, E., Brannan, R., Mangum, D., Dunham, J., Reimer, J. A., and Wierenga, M. (Eds.). (2012). The Lexham English Bible (Mt 5:29-30). Bellingham, Wa: Lexham Press. An undoubted absurdity.

[cxi] Zubrin, Robert. Merchants Of Despair: Radical Environmentalists, Criminal Pseudo-Scientists, and the Fatal Cult of Antihumanism (New Atlantis Books) (p.16). Encounter Books.

[cxii] See the various writings of Ahmed Osman, Ralf Elis, Riaan Booysen. As with the balance archaeological title: The Bible Unearthed.

[cxiii] A race of men who were hateful to the God's. Obviously this has to refer to the Egyptian pantheon of God's.

[cxiv] Sitchin's. (pp42 (35), 44 (37) Of 318). Pdf Version.

[cxv] Though in the main, modern scholarship no longer really supports this hypothesis. It is still popular so, to draw such comparisons.

DECONSTRUCTING ENDTIME DELUSIONS

[cxvi] Such an idea is truth. Today, for instance, Egypt is an Islamic nation, over run, and controlled by numerous Islamic factions, with minority groups of christians, and Jews.

[cxvii] Preface, p12.

[cxviii] Booysen, R Thera and the Exodus...Chapter 2, (2.2 Josephus' account)edition. Confirming Velikovsky's comments below, also.

[cxix] See, Pdf Article By Gerald Wheeler, http://www.auss.info/auss_publication_file.php?pub_Id=1041 Accessed 23/6/2014.

[cxx] For an insightful summary of the issues of the Exodus account, see Eric H. Cline: "From Eden to Exile", ch.4.

[cxxi] The Exodus events from Egypt most likely, if the thesis of Ashraf Ezzat is accepted, happened. Yet, on a very small scale. See, also Kamal Salibi.

[cxxii] Mcneal, T. R. (2003). Miracles, Signs, Wonders. In (C. Brand, C. Draper, A. England, S. Bond, E. R. Clendenen, and T. C. Butler, Eds.) Holman Illustrated Bible Dictionary. Nashville, Tn: Holman Bible Publishers. Apparently, as with Faith, no exemplary evidence need be offered. How is a mechanistic perspective, 'limiting'? Considering every believer and nonbeliever lives u der the same unutterable laws governing the Universe.

[cxxiii] http://Maverickphilosopher.Typepad.Com/Maverick_Philosopher/2009/11/Kant-On-Miracles.Html Ontology: is about what there is. Epistemology: is about how and how much we can know about what is there.

[cxxiv] Great Thinkers, Baruch Spinoza- Philosophy. pp.64-65.

[cxxv] Livingstone-Smith, Ch. 3.

[cxxvi] The demise of these towns was caused by a volcanic eruption. According to W. Harwood in his 'Dictionary of Contemporary Mythology', "Yahweh: originally, an active volcano in Anatolia [Asian part of Turkey]... Last erupted in The Third Millennium Bce, and buried Sodom and gomorrah..."

[cxxvii] Brancazio, p144. There is still considerable scholarly argument surrounding the destruction of the town. Some say that the archaeological evidence vindicates the accuracy of the Bible record. Others disapprove. Clear however is, from a Christian point of view, all evidence used vindicates Bible accuracy; the Exodus happened, The ancient Israelites sojourned the desert regions for 40yrs. Clear is that much of the evidence is supplied with a predetermined bias.

[cxxviii] Collins, S. (2012). Sodom and the Cities of the Plain. In (J. D. Barry and L. Wentz, Eds.) The Lexham Bible Dictionary. Bellingham, WA: Lexham Press.

[cxxix] http://www.skepticink.com http://www.skepticink.com/dangeroustalk/2013/11/19/is-God-a-metaphor-too/respond

[cxxx] See Jessica Cecil's article, The Destruction Of Sodom and Gomorrah posted online at: http://Www.Bbc.Co.Uk/History/Ancient/Cultures/Sodom_Gomorrah_01.Shtml and Links

[cxxxi] Ancient Mysteries: Discover the latest intriguing, scientifically sound explanations...by Peter James and Nick Thorpe. Copyright©1999 by Peter James and Nick Thorpe. The Random House Publishing Group, Inc. New York.

[cxxxii] The fateful disappearance of the Malaysian Airline MH370 that vanished without a trace is one very recent example. In less, than a year there were books being published about this incident.

[cxxxiii] Where was the 'protection' of the deity of those recently murdered by a 21yr old at a 'Church Bible-study'? Charleston shooting suspect Dylann Roof appeared by closed-circuit television at his bond hearing in Charleston, South Carolina U.S.A.

[cxxxiv] Little known, is that 'Pope' John Paul II before becoming pope was a chemist; a cyanide salesman!. He sold the deadly gas to the Nazis for their 'Death camps" Maybe, it was this fact that prompted him to use as his 'official' transport, a Bullet-proof vehicle? See, The Christ Scandal, pp319-320.

[cxxxv] Levavi, Ben-Ami, Garden Of Secrets... Ch. 2: Enuma Elish/ Epic Of Creation, p. 13 Of 167. () Unfortunately, Levavi's entire hypotheses throughout the book come from the writings of the late Zecharia Sitchin. See Also Hebrew Myths: The Book Of Genesis, Robert Graves, and Raphael Patai.

[cxxxvi] Davis, Erik. Techgnosis: Myth, Magic, and Mysticism In The Age Of Information (p. 3). North Atlantic Books. (Footnote 1) Bruno Latour, We Have Never Been Modern, Trans. Catherine Porter (Cambridge, Ma: Harvard University Press, 1993). It is most interesting: according to scientific contributors of [Howstuffwords] in their book, "The End of the World" is the earth is technically still in a ICE AGE.

[cxxxvii] Slone, Jason. Theological Incorrectness: Why Religious People Believe What They Shouldn't (p.7-9). Oxford University Press.

DECONSTRUCTING ENDTIME DELUSIONS

[cxxxviii] McKnight, S. (1989). Vol. 1: Introducing New Testament interpretation. Guides to New Testament exegesis (14–16). Grand Rapids, Mich.: Baker Book House.

[cxxxix] Acharya S. The Christ Conspiracy: The Greatest Story Ever Sold (Locations 58-61).

[cxl] Koenig. J. 'Ludiosis' entry: 'Dictionary of Obscure sorrows'.

[cxli] The actual meaning of rapture is expounded later in this document.

[cxlii] See, Dr. Manjir samanta-laughton's chapter (4) A Cosmological Journey: How Modern Scientific Data is Taking us back to the wisdom of the Ancients, in, Mysteries of the Ancient Past: A Graham Hancock Reader.Ed. See also, www.spacetelescope.org[2]/news/heci0211/ * See also the Netflix program: BlackHole Apocalypse.

[cxliii] See, 1 Thessalonians 4:13-27; Matthew 9:24; 2 Corinthians 5:15.

[cxliv] Paul Lee Tan, Encyclopaedia of 7700 Illustrations: A Treasury of Illustrations, Anecdotes, Facts and Quotations for Pastors, Teachers and Christian Workers (Garland TX: Bible Communications) 1996. says, "This is not a period just prior to the Second Coming of christ.

[cxlv] 2 Timothy 3:1-5. The Compact Fully Translated Bible, Edited and Translated by William Harwood, (p.212.)

[cxlvi] Conner, Jonah David. All That's Wrong With The Bible: Contradictions, Absurdities, and More (p.66).

[cxlvii] Wetherill, R. Dictionary Of Typical Command Phrases, (3). Copyright@ 1961, 1978, 1992 By Humanetics Fellowship. http://www.alphapub.com/our-books.html See parallel thoughts in (Isaiah 5:20; Amos 5:7; Luke 11:34-35).

[cxlviii] Beall, Endall. Gutting Mysticism: Explaining The Roots Of All Supernatural Beliefs (Beyond Second Cognition Book 1) (Locations 666-669). Unknown.

[cxlix] Acharya S. The Christ Conspiracy: The Greatest Story Ever Sold (Locations 2630-2639).

[cl] Graves, Robert. Hebrew Myths: The Book Of Genesis (p.12). Rosettabooks.

[cli] Ibid. Hebrew Myth. p.12.

---

2. http://www.spacetelescope.org

[clii] Ibid. (pp.14-15).

[cliii] Ibid. (p.12-13).

[cliv] Zevit. 2013. Location 71.

[clv] Nyland, A. Fallen Angels, Watchers, Giants, Nephilim and Evil (Angelology Demonology) (p.86).

[clvi] Zevit, Ziony. What Really Happened In The Garden Of Eden? Yale University Press.

[clvii] Ibid. (pp.20-21)

[clviii] Price, Robert M. Holy Fable: The Old Testament Undistorted By Faith (p.16; 18). Tellectual Press.

[clix] Zevit, Ziony. What Really Happened In The Garden Of Eden? (p.25; 27). Yale University Press.

[clx] Is there a single tree? Or, are there two trees in the garden? Some scholars are of the opinion that the tree of knowledge, and evil are only one tree.

[clxi] The Revised Standard Version. (1971). (Ge 1:29). Oak Harbor, Wa: Logos Research Systems, Inc.

[clxii] Price, Robert M. Holy Fable: The Old Testament Undistorted By Faith (p. 16-17). Tellectual Press. For a satirical telling of the Genesis 3 account, readers might consider the author's other publication; "A Standard Religiously Irrelevant Version (S.R.I.V.) - Twist of Fate" (2023). Available in both ebook, and print format.

[clxiii] Earl Lee, From The Bodies Of The Gods: Psychoactive Plants and The Cults Of The Dead, Ch. 20, Prometheus. Loc 2829 – 2842.

[clxiv] But, for one virtue, hope. Which she did eventually release. But, only after every vice had filled the Earth. The moral is that despite the evils and heartaches each of us face, even the deepest, darkest periods. "Hope springs eternal in the human breast." Alexander Pope.

[clxv] Graves, K. The World's Crucified Saviors, p9 of 9, Chapter Three: 'Prophesies By The Figure Of A Serpent.

DECONSTRUCTING ENDTIME DELUSIONS

[clxvi] Greenberg, Gary, 101 Myths of the Bible: How Ancient Scribes Invented Biblical History. (40[9/341]), Copyright © 2000 By Gary Greenberg cover design ©2000 by Sourcebooks, Inc. Adobe Digital Editions. Egyptian Gods, Geb = Earth, Nut = Heaven. See Also Korpel and De Moor's book below.

[clxvii] Such assumptions are misplaced. See, "The Serpent In The Garden Of Eden and its Background" at www.bibleinterp.com³. The Serpent as the personification of the Devil of this Genesis narrative, scholars assert was not original.

[clxviii] Expanded(p.11). Taylor and Francis.

[clxix] Zevit, Ziony. What Really Happened In The Garden Of Eden? (pp.161-163; 164-165; 166; 167-168). Yale University Press.

[clxx] Cooper, J. C. An Illustrated Encyclopaedia of Traditional Symbols (Locations 4860-4862; 4867-4872; 4879-4881; 4881-4887). Thames and Hudson Ltd.

[clxxi] Price, Robert M. Holy Fable: The Old Testament Undistorted By Faith (p.16). Tellectual Press. (Brackets Mine) Enuma Elish: The Babylonian Creation Myth.

[clxxii] See for further confirmation to Gardiner's assertion at: http://Www.Hiddenmysteries.Org/Mysteries/Whatsthis/33.Html Footnotes paragraph 12. Gardiner may have gleaned this information from this source.

[clxxiii] See, http://Thenazareneway.Com/Book_Of_Wisdom.Htm (2:24), and "The Serpent in The Garden of Eden and its background" at, www.Bibleinterp.Com. Accessed 1/11/2016.

[clxxiv] Harwood, William, Ph.D. The Compact Fully Translated Bible, (p.298.) The same has very close parallel mythic stories from other ancient cultures. I refer readers to: "Hebrew Myth".

[clxxv] Korpel, De Moor. Adam, Eve and The Devil: A New Beginning (Second Enlarged). back-cover. Copyright © 2015 Sheffield Phoenix Press.

[clxxvi] See The Book Hebrew Myths. Here, is the 'Origin' To The 'Fallen Angel' Legend From Which The Ideology Of A 'Fallen' Satan Most Certainly Derives. See The Specific Chapters: 8 (The Fall Of Lucifer); 12 (The Fall Of Man); 18 (The Sons Of God and The Daughters Of Men).

[clxxvii] Velikovsky, I., Worlds In Collision, (p.110)

---

3. http://www.bibleinterp.Com

[clxxviii] Carver, T. The Newer, More English Version, Genesis 3. p.10-12 Of 149.Electronic

[clxxix] Ch. 1: Once Bitten. "The 'Pulvinar' is considered as a key structure for visual attention function. As opposed to static often non-threatening stimuli. Our vision will be attuned to a writhing 'snake' that could be considered a threat and will most likely not be ignored. The pulvinar is suspected to play an important role in visual attention. However, there remain many hypotheses on the pulvinar's specific function. One hypothesis is that the pulvinar may play a role in filtering distracting stimuli when they are actively ignored." http://Www.Visionsciences.Org/2012-1-Symposia/

[clxxx] Despite knowing full well this summation is the opposite to what Robert Price believes. Even so, why cannot Price's hendiadys stand also alongside?

[clxxxi] History, Captivating. Gilgamesh: A Captivating Guide To Gilgamesh The King and The Epic Of Gilgamesh. (Location 177.)

[clxxxii] Grazier, K, and Justo Di, P. The Science Of Battlestar Galactica, Ch. 4: Cylon Intelligence and The Society Of Mind.

[clxxxiii] Wake, C. Staniland. The Origin Of Serpent Worship. (Location 25.)

[clxxxiv] Burnett, Dean. The Idiot Brain: A Neuroscientist Explains What Your Head Is Really Up To (p.29). Guardian Faber Publishing.

[clxxxv] Joseph, R. Ph.D. Ch. 1, Near Death: After Death Dreams, Spirits...

[clxxxvi] Harari, Yuval Noah. Sapiens: A Brief History Of Humankind (pp. 21-22; 24). Random House. Israel adopted the Lion among others, as its Totem.

[clxxxvii] Thomson, J. Anderson. Why We Believe In God(S))...(p.1-2.)

[clxxxviii] See Tarih Shar, The Legacy Of Arab Science.

[clxxxix] "Tree of Life", such expressions and figures are also present in other cultures and their 'myths' and stories. See LloydGraham and Greenberg's, and other books cited. See bibliography.

[cxc] History, Captivating. Gilgamesh: A Captivating Guide To Gilgamesh The King and The Epic Of Gilgamesh. (Locations 68.)

[cxci] Davis, Gerald J. Gilgamesh: The New Translation (pp.92, 93-94). Insignia Publishing.

DECONSTRUCTING ENDTIME DELUSIONS

[cxcii] Ibid.(p.17-18). Insignia Publishing.

[cxciii] Before this point, the tale tells of Gilgamesh's quest to regain what was once lost, searching for purpose, meaning of life, and a way to regain immortality. He is after all said to be partly Divine - might that not have been enough? In this sense the person Gilgamesh very much parallels in numerous ways what the early chapters of Genesis recount about the creation of humankind (Gen 1:26-28); not surprisingly. This Epic tale was written and well known and understood in Sumer many centuries before Genesis.

[cxciv] Audio Series: Lecture 3, Religious Hero's 1 – Gilgamesh and The Dawn Of History. See The Great Courses[4] Website In The Bibliography. The Great Courses. Course No. 2332 ©1991, 1998. The Teaching Company.

[cxcv] Becker, E. Forward: The Denial Of Death.

[cxcvi] Garland, Prof. R. The Other Side of History: Daily Life in the Ancient World, (Dvd, Vol 1, Lecture 4) The Great Courses. Course No. 3810 ©2012 The Teaching Company.

[cxcvii] Baigent, M, Ancient Traces: mysteries in ancient and early history, Penguin Publishers (Adobe Digital Ed.). xii-xiii. Copyright © Michael Baigent, 1998.

[cxcviii] Runge, S. E. (2008–2014). The Lexham High Definition New Testament: ESV(1 Th 4:17). Bellingham, Wa: Lexham Press. Italics mine.

[cxcix] Runge, S. (2008). The Lexham High Definition New Testament: ESV Logos Bible Software. (1 Thess 4:17). High Definition markers in this NT text are derived from Dr. Runge's and other Gk scholars' understanding of the grammatical constructions and discourse relationships of the Greek, in context, instead of the English of the translation.

[cc] Introduction to Biblical Hermeneutics: The Search for Meaning. 2007 (W. C. Kaiser, Jr.M. Silva, Ed.) (39). Grand Rapids, MI: Zondervan. Chapter two: The Meaning of Meaning.

[cci] Chilton, B., and Good, D. (2009). Starting New Testament Study: Learning and Doing (6). London: Society for Promoting Christian Knowledge.

[ccii] O'loughlin, T. (2010). The Didache: A Window On The Earliest Christians (Xiv). London; Grand Rapids, Mi: Society For Promoting Christian Knowledge; Baker Academic.

[cciii] James, J. G. (1916–1918). <u>Rapture, Ecstasy</u>. In J. Hastings (Ed.), Dictionary of the Apostolic Church (2 Vols.) (Vol. 2, p. 299). New York: Charles Scribner's Sons. Logos Bible Systems. Underline my emphasis.

[cciv] Harwood, William. The Protestant Bible Correctly Translated. World Audience Publishers.

[ccv] See Appendix 1: symbolism of clouds and other words.

[ccvi] Aramaic English New Testament appendix notes, Rapture, p 933, Andrew Gabriel Roth

[ccvii] Snide comments by John Hagee in, Racing Toward Armageddon, by Michael Baigent. (p56.) HarperOne™, Copyright ©2009 by Michael Baigent.

[ccviii] Andrew Gabriel Roth, Appendix Article: Rapture (The Catching Up), p 934-5 Aent, Fourth Ed., ©2008 By Netzari Press Llc. See Also Selected Rapture Articles At (http://Therefinersfire.Org/Rapture.Htm)

[ccix] Carmen. Welker, and there was War in Heaven: Surviving The End-Times, (89) ©2009, Carmen Welker. Netzari Press Llc.

[ccx] Welker - footnote #210. The Holy Bible: New Revised Standard Version, 1 Co 15:51–53 (Nashville: Thomas Nelson Publishers, 1989). See The Foretaste Of This Process Already Shown To Us. We Call It The Transfiguration, (Matt 17:1-13; Mk 9: 1-12; Luke 9:27 - 36. See Also 2 Peter 1:1-11).

[ccxi] See Appendix 1: The Study On Symbols.

[ccxii] See The Parable of the Unclean Spirits: Matt 12:43-45; Luke 11: 24-26.

[ccxiii] Jeffrey, Armageddon, 136

[ccxiv] See Hal Lindsey, The Rapture (New York: Bantam Books, 1983), 88–91. Demar, G. (1999). Last Days Madness: Obsession Of The Modern Church (Fourth Revised) (217). Powder Springs, Ga: American Vision.

[ccxv] Harwood, William. The Protestant Bible Correctly Translated. World Audience Publishers. Titus 3:9-10.

[ccxvi] See Malina, On The Genre and Message Of Revelation. Other Non-Religious Authors Confer That The Bible Is Essentially An Astrological Handbook: Recording The Events, Beliefs, and Warnings Of Wise Astrologers Who Understood How To Access Celestial Information.

[ccxvii] 2 Timothy 4:3-4

[ccxviii] Andrew Gabriel Roth, Appendix Article: Rapture (Rapture Not The Goal), (935) Aent, Third Ed., ©2008 By Netzari Press Llc.

[ccxix] Hengel, M. (1977). Crucifixion: In The Ancient World and The Folly of The Message of The Cross (J. Bowden, Trans.) (5). Philadelphia: Fortress Press.

[ccxx] The Syriac New Testament: Translated Into English From The Syriac Peshitto Version. 2001 (J. Murdock, Trans.) (49). Piscataway, Nj: Gorgias Press. Matt 24:36.

[ccxxi] Skeptic Magazine, Volume 18 Number 4. 2013. (Pg8)

[ccxxii] Swanson, J. (1997). Dictionary Of Biblical Languages With Semantic Domain: Hebrew (Old Testament). Oak Harbor: Logos Research Systems, Inc.

[ccxxiii] Strong, J. (2009). A Concise Dictionary Of The Words In The Greek Testament and The Hebrew Bible. Bellingham, Wa: Logos Bible Software.

[ccxxiv] p142: 153/284.

[ccxxv] Louw, J. P., and Nida, E. A. (1996). Greek-English Lexicon of The New Testament: Based on Semantic Domains (Electronic ed. of The 2nd). New York: United Bible Societies. 12.28 Ἄγγελος (Angels)

[ccxxvi] Neece, W. C. (2005; 2005). Various Views Of Prophecy. James L. Fleming.

[ccxxvii] Soanes, C., and Stevenson, A. (2004). Concise Oxford English Dictionary (11^Th Ed.). Oxford: Oxford University Press.

[ccxxviii] Chilton, B. (1996). Pure Kingdom: Jesus' Vision Of God (2). Grand Ra Pids, Mi: William B. Eerdmans Publishing Company.

[ccxxix] Ibid

[ccxxx] Dr. Michael Heiser, Why Obsessing Over Eschatology Is A Waste Of Time, Part 13, At His Website, (http://michaelsheiser.com/Thenakedbible/Eschatology-Dicussion/)

[ccxxxi] Dictionary of the Apostolic Church (2 Vols.). 1916-1918 (J. Hastings, Ed.). New York: Charles Scribner's Sons. Volume 2, Page 299.

[ccxxxii] Campion, Nicholas. Astrology and Cosmology In The World's Religions (p.24-25). NYU Press.

[ccxxxiii] Penprase, Bryan E. The Power Of Stars: How Celestial Observations Have Shaped Civilization, © Springer Science+Business Media, Llc 2011. Adobe Digital Ed. E-Isbn9781441968036 (p3 [13/353])

[ccxxxiv] Dvd, Lecture 17: The Qumran Biblical Canon

[ccxxxv] Wise, M. O., Abegg, M. G., Jr., and Cook, E. M. (2005). The Dead Sea Scrolls: A New Translation (p.279). New York: Harperone.

[ccxxxvi] Ibid. (p.278)

[ccxxxvii] Bushby, The Christ Scandal, p247.

[ccxxxviii] Theological Dictionary of The New Testament. 1964- (G. Kittel, G. W. Bromiley and G. Friedrich, Ed.) (Electronic Ed.). Grand Rapids, Mi: Eerdmans.

[ccxxxix] Ibid. Theological Dictionary of The New Testament

[ccxl] Bamberger, B. J. (2006). Fallen Angels: Soldiers of Satan's Realm (17). Philadelphia, Pa: The Jewish Publication Society.

[ccxli] The Holy Bible: English Standard Version. (2016). (Ge 5:24). Wheaton, Il: Crossway Bibles. The word not in this verse has two additional footers: (1) that the Septuagint reads, *was not found,* (2) while linking Hebrews 11:5 and 2 Kings 2:11. Both are suspected misleading.

[ccxlii] (Kittel...(1985). Theological Dictionary Of The New Testament. Abridged Enóch [Enoch]).

[ccxliii] The Lexham English Bible. 2012 (W. H. Harris, Iii, E. Ritzema, R. Brannan, D. Mangum, J. Dunham, J. A. Reimer, M. Wierenga, Ed.) (Jud 10–11). Bellingham, Wa: Logos Bible Software.

[ccxliv] Ibid, (Jude 16)

[ccxlv] The Holy Bible: New Revised Standard Version. 1989 (Sirach 44:16). Nashville: Thomas Nelson Publishers. My Emphasis. Not The (Messianic) Jesus Of The

Scriptures. Jesus – A Common Name In Judaism. Sadducees, a ruling sect of Judaism who opposed the Pharisaism of the day.

[ccxlvi] Apocrypha: the collection of Jewish writings that were in the Septuagint. Trans., by the early Church, but excluded from the official Protestant canon.

[ccxlvii] Technically the Septuagint of this text is literally: 'Enoch Pleased...Lord and... 'Taken'...Example...'

[ccxlviii] Kittel, G., Friedrich, G., and Bromiley, G. W. (1985). Theological Dictionary Of The New Testament (1179). Grand Rapids, Mi: W.B. Eerdmans.

[ccxlix] The Revised Standard Version. (1971). (Sir 44:1). Oak Harbor, Wa: Logos Research Systems, Inc.

[ccl] ●The Only (Relative) Exception Would Be 2 Cor 7:9–10: "You Were Grieved To The Point That You Repented (Ἐλυπήθητε Εἰς Μετάνοιαν) ...Grief (Λύπη) According To God Works Unto Salvation A Repentance That Is Not Regrettable (Μετάνοιαν Εἰς Σωτηρίαν Ἀμεταμέλητον)."

[ccli] ♦Preaching The Gospel of Christ in the Manner Of The Early Church.

[cclii] Spicq, C., and Ernest, J. D. (1994). Vol. 2: Theological Lexicon Of The New Testament (475). Peabody, Ma: Hendrickson Publishers. I Am Aware This Is The Explanation Of Nt Use.

[ccliii] Ginzberg, L., Szold, H., Radin, P. (2003). Legends Of The Jews (2nd Ed.) (123). Philadelphia: Jewish Publication Society. A work in which, Myth, Tale, and Magic co-exist in stories and the moral re=telling of the lives of the patriarchs and other revered personalities.

[ccliv] Wikipedia: Mythic Winged Horses.

[cclv] Lightfoot, J. B., Harmer, J. R. (1891). The Apostolic Fathers (61). London: Macmillan and Co. 1 Clement 9:2-3

[cclvi] Charles, R. H., Oesterley, W. O. E. (1917). The Book Of Enoch. (1:1-9) London: Society For Promoting Christian Knowledge.

[cclvii] The Holy Bible: New Revised Standard Version. 1989. (Rev 7:3). Nashville: Thomas Nelson Publishers. Also, What is to be made of: Mark 13:19, 24; Dan 12:1-4

[cclviii] Whyte, A. (1902). Bible Characters: Adam to Achan, Vol. 1 (51-56). Edinburgh; London: Oliphant Anderson and Ferrier.

[cclix] Casey, P.M. 1991. From Jewish Prophet To Gentile God: The Origins and Development Of New Testament Christology. (p88)

[cclx] Ibid. Whyte (54–56). Peace that passes all understanding (Jn 14:27-31) *Skirt of God* announces a recollection of the woman with a haemorrhage (Matt 9:20-22)

[cclxi] Received email, 11th January, 2014. http://www.grahamhancock.com

[cclxii] Devastating 'Flood' epics abound throughout the globe. Often using the same language.

[cclxiii] Clow, Barbara Hand, Catasrophobia, Chapter Three: The Holocene Epoch. The Holocene Epoch Refers To Our Currant Epoch In Geological Time.

[cclxiv] Ibid.

[cclxv] Atlantis, The Deluge and The End Of The Ice Age, (Midpoint p 36 Of 91) By Zarin, Published by Metamystics, Llc. Copyright ©2011, Metamystics, LLC.

[cclxvi] Graves, Robert. Hebrew Myths: The Book Of Genesis.

[cclxvii] Search internet for Assyrian Cuneiform tablets - flood narrative.

[cclxviii] Vos, H. F. (1979–1988). Flood (Genesis). In G. W. Bromiley (Ed.), The International Standard Bible Encyclopedia, Revised (Vol. 2, p.319–320). Wm. B. Eerdmans.

[cclxix] T. D Alexander, Ancient Secrets, Chapter Three.

[cclxx] Any christianised depiction of such a vessel is flawed. Looking more like an oversized dingy.

[cclxxi] See Dr Finkel's fascinating book, 'The Ark Before Noah'. The principal figure Atrahasis, of the Tablet is Not the same hero as the above described in the Gilgamesh Epic, but he is a figure of an earlier mythological composition concerning the flood epic.

[cclxxii] Redfern, N, The Pyramids And The Pentagon: Chapter 4, Ararat And The Agency.

DECONSTRUCTING ENDTIME DELUSIONS

[cclxxiii] This foray into the book "Babylon Rising" by Rob Skiba is by no means a personal attack directed to Rob in any manner. There is no malice directed toward Rob, or a questioning of his sincerity, or intelligence. This study only scrutinises some of the content that I thought to be grave mistakes from a feckless research methodology. Especially that noticed and highlighted from the first chapter of his book. It appeared that Rob employed a similar methodology as that employed by any cryptozoologist: Beginning with a belief that a mythical, but undiscovered something exists. Whereby he searches for 'evidence' in support of the premise.

[cclxxiv] Kuhn, Alvin Boyd. *Shadow of the Third Century*: A Revaluation of Christianity. Papamoa Press. (Location 1618.)

[cclxxv] Skiba, Rob. Babylon Rising: And The First Shall Be Last (Updated And Expanded) (p.18). King's Gate Media, Llc.

[cclxxvi] http://Www.Babylonrisingblog.Com/Faq.Html

[cclxxvii] Page (xxx), Babylon Rising, Copyright © 2011 By Rob Skiba II.

[cclxxviii] [4]. Fritze, Invented Knowledge, 12. Colavito, Jason. Foundations Of Atlantis, Ancient Astronauts and other alternative pasts: 148 Documents cited by authors of Fringe History, Translated with Annotations (p.1). Mcfarland and Company, Inc., Publishers.

[cclxxix] For References, See passages: Genesis 9:29; Isaiah 54:9; Matthew 24:37; Luke 17:26; 1 Peter 3:20.

[cclxxx] Skiba, Rob. Babylon Rising: And The First Shall Be Last (Updated And Expanded) (p. 25). King's Gate Media, Llc.

[cclxxxi] Amos 2:9 Is Studied Later In This Section. Rob Most Probably Has Gained This Understanding From A Mystical Jewish Interpretation Highlighted Below.

[cclxxxii] Massey, Gerald. *Ancient Egypt: Light of the World Vol. 1 and 2* Complete with Biography and Poems by Gerald Massey (pp.11;16). ZuuBooks.

[cclxxxiii] Babrius was a poet who made these fables into short poems. Though these fables are closer to folktales than mythic lore. Several are quite revealing of popular attitudes toward religious, and mythic mattersSee, Anthology Of Classical Myth (p. 61). Hackett Publishing Company, Inc..

[cclxxxiv] Ibid. Skiba. (p.25-26)

[cclxxxv] See a Symbolic meaning of DNA in the Appendix- Symbolism section.

[cclxxxvi] Gregor Mendel, A Scientist and Augustinian friar, discovered genetics in the late 19th century. Mendel studied "Trait inheritance" patterns in the way traits are handed down from parent to offspring. He observed that organisms inherit traits by way of discrete "units of inheritance". Modern: called Genes.

[cclxxxvii] There are today numerous books that assume to cover the DNA/ end time scenario. e.g., author known as - Minister Dante Fortson - "As the Days of Noah Were - as others. See also, Douglas Hamp - Corrupting the Image.

[cclxxxviii] "There is a book called "The Book Of Jasher" Today, Although it is not the same as that mentioned in the Judaeo-Christian Old Testament. It is an eighteenth-century forgery. Alleging to be a 'translation' of the lost book of Jasher. See, http://Www.gotquestions.org/book-of-jasher.html. "The Only Complete Version Of The Book Of Jubilees is written in Ethiopian, Though most scholars believe that it was originally written in Hebrew. There are some fragments existing today in Greek and Latin, But not near a complete book in either language..." Also, at http://www.gotquestions.org/book-of-jubilees.⁵html. See quotes of Dr. A. Nyland below. She has offered a translation of this ancient text.

[cclxxxix] Nyland, Dr. A. Nephilim And Giants (Discover The Truth Series, Book 2) (p. 24). Angel Publishing. Watchers Are A Class Of Angel Often Seen In Esoteric/ Mystical Jewish Writings.

[ccxc] The Book Of Jubilees (The Little Genesis, The Apocalypse Of Moses) Old Testament / Apocrypha / Pseudepigrapha (p. 6). Angel Publishing.

[ccxci] Skiba, Rob. Babylon Rising: And The First Shall Be Last (Updated And Expanded) (p. 8. (2008)). King's Gate Media, LLC. according to Logos Bible Systems source, Jasher was written by a Pharisee sometime during the accession to the High-Priesthood power of John Hycranus around 134BC. It is one book often referred by numerous scholars as if it were a familiar source. Primarily, it seems because there are apparently two testament sources that mention it. **Jasher** nonetheless essentially a collection of songs of praise, and poems of early Israelite battles. **Jubilees**, has a theme not mentioned by those wishing to use it as an end time tale. However, the book Jubilees by various scholars is attested to be concerned with the Calendar, and proper observance of Feasts, and Sabbaths.

[ccxcii] Ibid. Skiba. (p.33-34).

---

5. http://www.gotquestions.org/bbok-of-jubilees

DECONSTRUCTING ENDTIME DELUSIONS

[ccxciii] Graves, Robert. Hebrew Myths: The Book Of Genesis (p.121;124). Rosettabooks.

[ccxciv] Ibid. (p.36). See: http://Www.In2Greece.Com/English/Historymyth/Mythology/Names/Minos. And http://Www.Mythweb.Com/Encyc/Entries/Crete.

[ccxcv] Nyland, Dr. A. Nephilim and Giants (Discover The Truth Series, Book 2) (p. 6-7; 12; 13). Angel Publishing.

[ccxcvi] Dr. Heiser has written a number of alluring documents that interested readers are encouraged to browse, www.michaelsheiser.com (Dr. Heiser is at the time of writing, the academic editor for logos Bible systems) see also various books by Jason Colavito, faking history; Foundations of Atlantis, Ancient Astronauts and other alternative pasts.

[ccxcvii] Godawa, Brian. When Giants Were Upon The Earth: The Watchers, The Nephilim, and The Biblical Cosmic War of The Seed (p.320). Embedded Pictures Publishing.

[ccxcviii] Ibid. (p.3-4)

[ccxcix] Nyland, Dr. A. Nephilim and Giants (Discover The Truth Series, Book 2) (p.29-30). Angel Publishing.

[ccc] Skiba, Rob. Babylon Rising: And The First Shall Be Last (Updated And Expanded) (p.22). King's Gate Media, Llc.

[ccci] See Chapter One: Did Adam Exist? In Secrets of the Bible People.

[cccii] The Holy Bible: English Standard Version. (2016). (Ge 6:1–4). Wheaton: Standard Bible Society. Interested readers are directed to Appendices 1.

[ccciii] The age of the French woman is disputed. See, Australian News Paper article 1 January, 2019: www.Theaustralian.Com.Au/News/World/The-Times/Old-Fraud-Worlds-Oldestever-Person-May-Have-Been-A-Supercentenarian-Scammer/News-Story/Bdc94C369Ddc63Df72Cad1E19378393A[6]

[ccciv] Harwood, W. The Pre-Pentateuch Torah's: Before They Were Interwoven. (p.16-17) Edited and translated by William Harwood. Copyright 2008, By William Harwood. 1935– [Bold Original]

[cccv] Graves, Robert. Hebrew Myths: The Book of Genesis (p.104). Rosettabooks.

---

6. https://Www.Theaustralian.Com.Au/News/World/The-Times/Old-Fraud-Worlds-Oldestever-Person-May-Have-Been-A-Supercentenarian-Scammer/News-Story/Bdc94C369Ddc63Df72Cad1E19378393A

[cccvi] See The Encyclopaedia of Jewish Myth, Magic and Mysticism Second© 2016 By Geoffrey W. Dennis. Articles: Nefilim; Giants; Fallen Angels and Related Topics.

[cccvii] See also, John 1:12, 3:16; Luke 3:38; Job 1:6, 2:1, 38:7. All related to Sons of God.

[cccviii] ./>9 Enoch 9–10. Comp., further 67-69 for the exact description of the sins of the angels. See, Legends of the Jews (2nd ed. p.135.)

[cccix] Ibid. Ginzberg, (136).

[cccx] Grudem, W. A. (1988). 1 Peter: An Introduction and Commentary (Vol. 17, p.225–226). Downers Grove, Il: Intervarsity Press.

[cccxi] •Igigu, is a group of celestial deities. Likely, the Babylonian equivalent of the Jewish term Elohim.

[cccxii] Franke, Sabine. An Anthology of Ancient Mesopotamian Texts: When The Gods Were Human (Locations 98-123). Pen And Sword.

[cccxiii] S. Baring-Gould. Legends Of The Patriarchs and Prophets.

[cccxiv] For its mythic connection and other interests read Pleiades entry: https://En.Wikipedia.Org and see the Symbolic explanations offered in Appendix 1.

[cccxv] Graves, Robert. Hebrew Myths: The Book Of Genesis (p.119). Rosettabooks.

[cccxvi] Nyland, A. Fallen Angels, Watchers, Giants, Nephilim And Evil (Angelology Demonology) (p.68).

[cccxvii] See Briggs, K. Gods And Heroes: Mythology From Around The World. A book that succinctly explains various gods, and hero's from all over the world.

[cccxviii] See Dr. Bob Curran's Man-Made Monsters: A Field Guide To Golems, Patchwork Soldiers, Homunucli, and other created creatures. (Introduction).

[cccxix] Strong's Lexicon: 5303.

[cccxx] Fisher, M. C. (1999). 1393 נפל. R. L. Harris, G. L. Archer Jr., and B. K. Waltke (Eds.), Theological Wordbook of the Old Testament (electronic ed., p.587). Chicago: Moody Press.

DECONSTRUCTING ENDTIME DELUSIONS

[cccxxi] Thomas, R. L. (1998). New American Standard Hebrew-Aramaic And Greek Dictionaries : Updated Anaheim: Foundation Publications, Inc.

[cccxxii] A meaning of 'grotesque' according to Barbara Walker literally is: "a creature from the grotto" the sacred cave where deities were worshipped by proto-Christian europeans. Similarities between a Grotesque and Gargoyles are evident. A 'Grotesque' was incorporated into the fabric of the Church liturgy. Gargoyles adorn Gothic cathedrals as demonic influences to ward off the influence of evil. See Giant, Gargoyle, and Grotesque entries: The Women's Dictionary Of Symbols and Sacred Objects.

[cccxxiii] Williams, Sarah B. Stories About Human History (Extended): Travels On The History Of Mankind (Locations 6799-6808). [Brackets mine].

[cccxxiv] Ibid. (Locations 6815-6822; 6828-6829; 6837-6842).

[cccxxv] Who Were The Nephilim? The Nephilim: Human, Or Supernatural? (p3) Pshat = Plain and Simple meaning. http://Www.Therefinersfire.Org/Nephilim.Htm

[cccxxvi] Cassuto, U. (1973). Biblical and Oriental Studies: Bible. (I. Abrahams, Trans.) (Vol. 1, p.17). Jerusalem: Magnes Press. Logos Bible Systems Copy.

[cccxxvii] See, http://www.stevequayle.com

[cccxxviii] Bamberger, B. J. (2006). Fallen Angels: Soldiers Of Satan's Realm (12). Philadelphia, Pa: The Jewish Publication Society.

[cccxxix] Colavito, Jason. Faking History (Locations 2901-2919; 2921-2923; 2923-2928). www.Jasoncolavito.com[7] Books.

[cccxxx] Mcghee Jr., George. Carboniferous Giants and Mass Extinction: The Late Paleozoic Ice Age World (Locations 2754-2761). Columbia University Press. See also, Rake, M. Prehistoric Giants, and Prehistoric Ancestors of modern animals.

[cccxxxi] http://www.valeslake.com/bookmart.htm

[cccxxxii] Preston, Steve. Incredible Titans (Locations 70-74; 79; 101-102; 221-222; 223-227; 227-230).

[cccxxxiii] 'without dying...' and our immortality, is pure conjecture.

[cccxxxiv] Lindsay, D. G. (1999). The Canopied Earth: World That Was. Dallas, Tx: Christ For The Nations. See also http://Www.Sciencedaily.Com/Videos/2007/0603-

---

7. http://www.Jasoncolavito.com

Can_Carbon_Dioxide_Be_A_Good_Thing.Htm; Http://Wattsupwiththat.Com/2011/02/11/The-Benefits-Of-Carbon-Dioxide/Or several programs by searching, 'Benefits of Co2.' i.e., http://Www.Youtube.Com/Watch?V=Oia7L48Jqkafeature=Related

[cccxxxv] Ibid. Chapter 20: Food For Giants, Carbon Dioxide.

[cccxxxvi] •Hyperoxic: An atmosphere containing more than 21% Oxygen.

[cccxxxvii] Pickrell, John. Weird Dinosaurs: The Strange New Fossils Challenging Everything We Thought We Knew (Locations 150-151). Newsouth.

[cccxxxviii] Ibid. (Locations157-159; 190-193; 194-199). Sauropod's Were The Largest Animal On Earth.

[cccxxxix] The Bible does report at least six 'giant' races, pre, and post-flood. The Egyptian book of the dead calls them 'guardians', as do other ancient sources. More often than not these were normal, yet much taller in stature than the majority. See Bushby's The Secret In The Bible.

[cccxl] 'Knickers' — Knickers the Giant steer really is abnormally large. (Abc News: Anthony Pancia) https://Www.Abc.Net.Au/News/2018-11-29/A-Defence-Of-Knickers-The-Giant-Steer/10567066

[cccxli] The Skhul-Quafez Peoples of the Levant, or possibly ancestors to the Kurgan. See, http://Www.Disclose.Tv/Forum/The-Giants-Lost-In-History-T59036-20.Html (Accessed 6/7/2014). Anthropologists have determined many interesting findings regarding proto-hominids.

[cccxlii] Mithen, Steven. The Prehistory of the Mind: A search for the origins of art, Religion and Science (Locations 2395-2402; 2406-241; 2421-2428; 2459-2463; 2482-2495). Thames And Hudson Ltd.

[cccxliii] Langdon, Robert John. Giant Skeletons: - Found by French archaeologists now dismissed by anthropologists (13 Ancient Things That Don't Make Sense In History) (Locations 98-100; 115-117; 156-159; 177-178; 179-180; 184-189; 196-198; 202-209; 213-220; 224-233; 255-263; 263-275; 370-372). Abc Publishing Group.

[cccxliv] Langdon, Robert John. Giant Skeletons: - Found By French Archaeologists Now Dismissed By Anthropologists (13 Ancient Things That Don't Make Sense In History) (Locations 308-311). Abc Publishing Group.

DECONSTRUCTING ENDTIME DELUSIONS

[cccxlv] Stern, D. H. (1998). Complete Jewish Bible: An English Version Of The Tanakh (Old Testament) And B'rit Hadashah (New Testament) (1St Ed., Ge 6:2). Clarksville, Md: Jewish New Testament Publications. (Brackets my addition.)

[cccxlvi] Description Courtesy: www.themandus.Org[8].

[cccxlvii] See http://Australianmuseum.Net.Au/Homo-Neanderthalensis For a fuller accepted picture. All Quotes Chapter 3, Them+Us: The Perfect Predator. See http://Australianmuseum.Net.Au/Homo-Neanderthalensis For a fuller accepted picture. All Quotes Chapter 3 Of Them+Us: The Perfect Predator.

[cccxlviii] Owens, John, "The Ninth Generation: Surviving The Giants Of Pre-Flood Earth" Smashwords, Copyright©2008, By John Owens

[cccxlix] Bering, Jesse. The God Instinct: The Psychology of Souls, Destiny and the Meaning of Life (Locations 2083-2087; 2090-2091; 2093-2101). Hodder and Stoughton.

[cccl] Mendez, S. B. Phd. The Mysterious Origins Of Hybrid Man,Ed.

[cccli] Langdon, Robert John. The Cro-Magnons: Dawn Of The Lost Civilisation (page 25). Abc Publishing Group.

[ccclii] Ibid. Pages 96; 98.

[cccliii] Secrets Of The Bible People, Chapter One: Did Adam Exist? p33-34.

[cccliv] See, Collins, Andrew, From The Ashes of Angels. Ch. 8.

[ccclv] Mcghee Jr., George. Carboniferous Giants and Mass Extinction: The Late Paleozoic Ice Age World (Locations 2637-2638; 2754-2761). Columbia University Press.

[ccclvi] Floyd, E. Randall. The Dark Side Of History: 5000 Years of Bizarre Beliefs, Mysteries and Wondrous Events From Around The World (Locations 3012-3018-3025). Batwing Press.

[ccclvii] Ibid. (Locations 3035-3039).

[ccclviii] Ibid. (Locations 3041-3045; 3045-3049; 3122-3125).

---

8. http://www.themandus.Org

[ccclix] •See, https://Www.Medicinenet.Com/Script/Main/Art.Asp?Articlekey=7756 Definition Of Six Fingers Or Toes.

[ccclx] Langdon, Robert John. The Cro-Magnons: Dawn Of The Lost Civilisation (Page 87). Abc Publishing Group.

[ccclxi] Source: http://Massufosightings.Blogspot.Com.Au/2013/02/Ancient-Advanced-Civilizations-Giant.Html

[ccclxii] Lents, Nathan. Human Errors: A Panorama Of Our Glitches, From Pointless Bones To Broken Genes (Locations 525-530; 530-532). Orion.

[ccclxiii] https://Www.Healthline.Com/Health/Hyperdontiacauses.

[ccclxiv] Harris, R. L., Harris, R. L., Archer, G. L., and Waltke, B. K. (1999). Theological Wordbook Of The Old Testament (Electronic ed.) (752). Chicago: Moody Press. Fingers and Toes in this verse essentially have been translated using the same Heb., word. See, Ps 8:3; (Heb 8:4); Ex 8:19; 31:18; Lk 11:20; Isa 2:8; 17:8; 59:3.

[ccclxv] Powell, M. A. (2011). Rephaim. In M. A. Powell (Ed.), The Harpercollins Bible Dictionary (Revised and Updated) (M. A. Powell, Ed.) (Third) (874). New York: Harpercollins. Emphasis Mine. Logos Bible Systems. See, Job 26:5; Psalms 88:10; Proverbs 2:18; 9:18; 21:16; Isaiah 14:9; 26:19.

[ccclxvi] Ibid, (2011). Sheol, (950).

[ccclxvii] Ugarit = Language Of Ugarit, In Ancient Sumer, which flourished in the late Bronze era. Ugaritic interestingly provides the only archaeological records of social, economic and political conditions of Late Bronze Age Canaan.

[ccclxviii] Schmidt, B. B. (2000). Rephaim. In D. N. Freedman, A. C. Myers And A. B. Beck (Eds.), Eerdmans Dictionary of The Bible (D. N. Freedman, A. C. Myers and A. B. Beck, Ed.) (1119). Grand Rapids, Mi: W.B. Eerdmans.

[ccclxix] Smith, M. S. (1992). Rephaim. In D. N. Freedman (Ed.), The Anchor Yale Bible Dictionary (Vol. 5, p.674). New York: Doubleday.

[ccclxx] See www.Atrueott.Wordpress.Com/Forbidden-Archeology[9]/_____; http://News.Nationalgeographic.Com.Au/News/2012/11/121102-Gigantism-Ancient-Skeleton-Archaeology-History-Science-Rome/_____; http://Www.Ancient-Wisdom.Co.Uk/Giants.Htm

---

9. http://www.Atrueott.Wordpress.Com/Forbidden-Archeology

DECONSTRUCTING ENDTIME DELUSIONS

[ccclxxi] Www.Snopes.Com/Fact-Check/Giant-Human-Skeleton-Photographs/[10]

[ccclxxii] Zimmerman, Fritz. The Nephilim Chronicles: Fallen Angels In The Ohio Valley (Locations 121-126–129). Unknown.

[ccclxxiii] Cremo, M. Human Devolution: A Verdic Alternative To Darwin's Theory, (p12: Ch 2, Forbidden Archeology...). Copyright ©2003 By Bhaktivedanta Book Publishing, Inc.

[ccclxxiv] See http://Www.Prehistoric-Wildlife.Com/Species/G/Gigantopithecus.Html.[11] It I also intriguing that photo's attach many strange theories to them. See Skeptic Magazine Volume 18 Number 4 2013 Article Bigfoot Or Baloney, By Jonathan Blais.

[ccclxxv] Hall, Mark A. True Giants: Is Gigantopithecus Still Alive? (Pp.22-24). Anomalist Books.

[ccclxxvi] His Website www.invisibletemple.com[12]

[ccclxxvii] 9 Cubits = A Staggering, 4.165092 Meters Tall. Calculation Made at: http://Www.Unitconversion.Org/Length/Cubits-Greek-To-Meters-Conversion.Html [13]The earlier shown chart of presumed sizing of giants range from the standard 6ft, through 36ft high. That is a 10.97mtr individual!

[ccclxxviii] Atlantis Rising Anthology Library: Lost Ancient Wisdom: Places Of The Builder Gods: Understanding The Ancient Science Of Temple Creation, By Freddy Silva.

[ccclxxix] As Quoted By Fleischer, When Giants Ruled The World.

[ccclxxx] •See, https://En.Wikipedia.Org/Wiki/Dolichocephalycite_Note-Urldolichocephalic_-_Definition_From_Merriam-Websters_Medica

[ccclxxxi] http://Www.Ancient-Wisdom.Co.Uk/Cranialdeformation.Htm[14]

[ccclxxxii] See Karen Mutton's Scattered Skeletons In Our Closet. In this text she explains various skeletal remains assumed to have been giants.

---

10. http://Www.Snopes.Com/Fact-Check/Giant-Human-Skeleton-Photographs/
11. http://www.prehistoric-wildlife.com
12. http://www.invisibletemple.com
13. http://www.unitconversion.org
14. http://www.ancient-wisdom

[ccclxxxiii] See, 'From Gods To God', Chapter Two: When God's Seduced Women.

[ccclxxxiv] See a new Publication "Carboniferous Giants And Mass Extinction: The Late Paleozoic Ice Age World", By George, R., Jr. Mcghee.

[ccclxxxv] Scott Corrales as a frequent contributor to FATE magazine and editor of Inexplicate, the journal of Hispanic Ufology. http://Fatemag.Com/Issues/2000S/2006-05Article2A. Html See Also, http://Www.Mysteriousworld.Com/Journal/2003/Spring/Giants/

[ccclxxxvi] Cassuto, U. (1973). Biblical And Oriental Studies, Volume I: Bible (I. Abrahams, Trans.) (23). Jerusalem: Magnes Press.

[ccclxxxvii] See, Firdausi, The Epics Of Kings: Hero Tales Of Ancient Persia, (Unknown Author.)

[ccclxxxviii] Ibid. Cassuto, U. (1973). (24). Jerusalem: Magnes Press.

[ccclxxxix] Oswalt, J. N. (2009). The Bible Among The Myths: Unique Revelation Or Just Ancient Literature? (23). Grand Rapids, Mi: Zondervan.

[cccxc] Amos 2:9 The New King James Version. 1982 (Am 2:9). Nashville: Thomas Nelson.

[cccxci] Harris, R. L., Harris, R. L., Archer, G. L., and Waltke, B. K. (1999). Theological Wordbook of the Old Testament (Electronic Ed.) (146). Chicago: Moody Press.

[cccxcii] Vangemeren, W. (1998). New International Dictionary Of Old Testament Theology and Exegesis. Grand Rapids, Mi: Zondervan Publishing House.

[cccxciii] The Lexham English Septuagint. 2012 (R. Brannan, K. M. Penner, I. Loken, M. Aubrey and I. Hoogendyk, Ed.) (Am 2:9). Bellingham, Wa: Logos Bible Software.

[cccxciv] Smith, B. K., and Page, F. S. (2001). Vol. 19B: Amos, Obadiah, and Jonah (Electronic Ed.). Logos Library System; The New American Commentary (65). Nashville: Broadman and Holman Publishers.

[cccxcv] The Hebrew Word Translated Cedar Trees probably indicates one particular species of the genus 'conifer'. A Tree which could reach heights of Ten to Twenty-Five meters.

DECONSTRUCTING ENDTIME DELUSIONS

Waard, J. D., Smalley, W. A., and Smalley, W. A. (1979). A Translator's Handbook On The Book Of Amos. Helps For Translators (51). Stuttgart: United Bible Societies. See Also The Charge Brought By The Prophet Ezekiel, (Ezek 31:3.)

[cccxcvi] Grayling, A. C. The God Argument... Ch 9. 'Arguing By Definition'

[cccxcvii] Harris, W. H., Iii, Ritzema, E., Brannan, R., Mangum, D., Dunham, J., Reimer, J. A., and Wierenga, M. (Eds.). (2012). The Lexham English Bible (Tt 3:9). Bellingham, Wa: Lexham Press.

[cccxcviii] Joseph, Frank. Military Encounters With Extraterrestrials: The Real War Of The Worlds. Inner Traditions/Bear and Company. Forward.

[cccxcix] Ibid. Military Encounters with Extraterrestrials (p.4;5-6).

[cd] Jones, Marie D. Demons, The Devil, and Fallen Angels (Locations 1649-1650). Visible Ink Press.

[cdi] See https://Www.Youtube.Com/Watch?V=Lmbt_Yfgkpu The "Holographic Universe" Series.

[cdii] Beall, Endall. Gutting Mysticism: Explaining The Roots Of All Supernatural Beliefs (Beyond Second Cognition Book 1) (Locations 219-221; 222). Unknown.

[cdiii] See Velikovsky, Worlds In Collision, (p358.)

[cdiv] Wiker, Benjamin. 10 Books That Screwed Up The World: And 5 Others That Didn't Help (p.25-26). Regnery Publishing.

[cdv] Joseph, Frank. Military Encounters With Extraterrestrials: The Real War Of The Worlds (p.7). Inner Traditions/Bear and Company.

[cdvi] Katz, M., and Schwartz, G. (1998). Swimming In The Sea Of The Talmud: Lessons For Everyday Living (9). Philadelphia, Pa: The Jewish Publication Society.

[cdvii] Cohen, A. Everymans Talmud (p.49). Orion.

[cdviii] Ross, H., Samples, K., Clark, M. (2002). Lights In The Sky and Little Green Men: A Rational Christian Look At Ufos And Extraterrestrials (113). Colorado Springs, Co: Navpress. All Conjecture!

[cdix] Cohen, Abraham. Everyman's Talmud: The Major Teachings Of The Rabbinic Sages. (p47 - § iii. Angelology). Schocken Books. Copyright ©1949 By E. P. Dutton. See, 1 Kings 22:19; Isaiah 6:1; Job 1:6.

[cdx] Barbara G. Walker. The Woman's Dictionary of Symbols and Sacred Objects (More Crystals and New Age) Harpercollins. (Locations 5443-5444; 5457-5459; 5471-5476).

[cdxi] Ibid. (Locations 5835-5840).

[cdxii] Aent 4Th , June 2011, Appendix Article, 'Messengers (Angels)' By Andrewth (p911).).

[cdxiii] Philosopher, Plato once wrote: "White is the colour of the gods." A statement that seems to have influenced early christianity. The vestments of clergy, baptismal garb... See F. Viola and G. Barna, Pagan Christianity, p150-151.

[cdxiv] According to scripture, 'wings' are not the hallmark, rather an exception. The only class of angel sporting them are either cherubim, seraphim. Gen 3:24; Eze 1:1, 10:1F; Isa 6:5; 2 Kings 6:11; Matt 28:3.

[cdxv] Chesnut, L. J. (2005; 2005). Was The Devil One Time an Angel in Heaven. (Preface) James L. Fleming.

[cdxvi] Velikovsky, I. Worlds In Collision, (p258-259).

[cdxvii] Ibid. An Effect of a Long-Standing Hypothetical Coupled with a Distorted Logical View of Yahweh's Heavenly Beings – Angels.

[cdxviii] The Anchor Yale Bible Dictionary. 1996 (D. N. Freedman, G. A. Herion, D. F. Graf, J. D. Pleins and A. B. Beck, ed.). New York: Doubleday.

[cdxix] I refer readers once again to the previous Nail.

[cdxx] The Anchor Yale Bible Dictionary. 1996 (D. N. Freedman, G. A. Herion, D. F. Graf, J. D. Pleins and A. B. Beck, Ed.). New York: Doubleday.

[cdxxi] Biblical Studies Press. (2006; 2006). The Net Bible First ; Bible. English. Net Bible.; The Net Bible. Biblical Studies Press. Study Note (33), Sons Of God Of Job 1:6.

[cdxxii] Collins, A, From The Ashes Of Angels, (p62), Ch Six. Pending Context. See, http://Ftp.Gnosticteachings.Org/Glossary/E/2328-Elohim.Html

[cdxxiii] Van Der Toorn, K., Becking, B., Van Der Horst, P. W. (1999). Dictionary Of Deities And Demons In The Bible (2nd Extensively Rev. Ed.) (353). Leiden; Boston; Köln; Grand Rapids, Mi; Cambridge: Brill; Eerdmans.

[cdxxiv] Kittel, G., Friedrich, G., and Bromiley, G. W. (1995). Theological Dictionary Of The New Testament (1208). Grand Rapids, Mi: W.B. Eerdmans.

[cdxxv] The Bible Fraud, p174. Brackets Mine. Mt Masoretic Text [The Now Standardised Hebrew textthat the majority of English bibles are translated]

[cdxxvi] Alexander, T. D., and Baker, D. W. (2003). Dictionary of The Old Testament: Pentateuch (796). Downers Grove, Il: Intervarsity Press.

[cdxxvii] The New International Version. 2011 (Dt 32:8). Grand Rapids, Mi: Zondervan.

[cdxxviii] Kelley, P. H., Mynatt, D. S., and Crawford, T. G. (1998). The Masorah Of Biblia Hebraica Stuttgartensia: Introduction and Annotated Glossary (2). Grand Rapids, Mi: William B. Eerdmans Publishing Company.

[cdxxix] Biblical Studies Press. (2005). The Net Bible First ; Bible. English. Net Bible.; The Net Bible. Biblical Studies Press.

[cdxxx] Dictionary of Old Testament: Pentateuch. Article: "son's of God, daughters of man". Conclusion. p797.

[cdxxxi] Kaiser, W. C., Jr. (2008). The Promise-Plan of God: A Biblical Theology of The Old and New Testaments (50). Grand Rapids, Mi: Zondervan.

[cdxxxii] The Holy Bible: New Revised Standard Version. (1989). (Ec 12:13–14). Nashville: Thomas Nelson Publishers.

[cdxxxiii] See http://Www.Youtube.Com/Watch?V=7Zwkm-Lzwm4Feature=Share

[cdxxxiv] The Holy Bible: English Standard Version. 2001 (Ro 8:22–25). Wheaton: Standard Bible Society

[cdxxxv] Ibid. (Baruch 3:34–35). Nashville: Thomas Nelson Publishers.

[cdxxxvi] Kittel, G., Friedrich, G., Bromiley, G. W. (1995). Theological Dictionary of The New Testament (13). Grand Rapids, Mi: W.B. Eerdmans.

[cdxxxvii] The Eerdmans Dictionary of Early Judaism. 2010 (J. J. Collins, D. C. Harlow, Ed.) (329). Grand Rapids, Mi; Cambridge, U.K.: William B. Eerdmans Publishing Company.

[cdxxxviii] Op.Cit. Opus Citandum (Previously cited. (330).

[cdxxxix] See, Alper, M. And 9 More, Near Death: After Death, Out-of-Body, Dreams, Hallucinations, Neuroscience and Evolution of Spirituality. Cosmology Science Publishers, Cambridge, 2015.

[cdxl] Cohen, A. Everymans Talmud (p.54). Orion.

[cdxli] Op.Cit. Opus Citandum. (629). Reminiscent to Modern Assertions Surrounding Such Bible Texts as Jude 6, and 2 Peter 2:4.

[cdxlii] Rotherham, J. B. (1959). The Emphasized Bible: A Translation Designed to set forth the exact meaning, the proper terminology, and the graphic style of the sacred original (Ex 3:14). Grand Rapids, Mi: Kregel Publications.

[cdxliii] > The Eternally Rising Sun Cannot Be Destroyed. >> See, The Ancient Near East An Anthology of Texts and Pictures. 1969 (J. B. Pritchard, ed.) (3rd ed. With Supplement) (4). Princeton: Princeton University Press.

[cdxliv] Ibid. Can Anyone Answer, What a 'Monotheistic' Trinity is? The Two Cannot Be Compatible.

[cdxlv] Ibid.

[cdxlvi] Chesnut, L. J. (2005; 2005). Was The Devil One Time An Angel In Heaven. James L. Fleming.

[cdxlvii] See also, (2 Cor 10:1-6).

[cdxlviii] Fahlbusch, E., and Bromiley, G. W. (1999-2003). Vol. 1: The Encyclopaedia Of Christianity (824). Grand Rapids, Mich.; Leiden, Netherlands: Wm. B. Eerdmans; Brill.

[cdxlix] Bamberger, B. J. (2006). Fallen Angels: Soldiers of Satan's Realm (208–209). Philadelphia, Pa: The Jewish Publication Society.

[cdl] The Holy Bible: English Standard Version. 2001 (Luke 10:18). Wheaton: Standard Bible Society. />W [John 12:31; 16:11; Colossians. 2:15; Revelation. 12:8, 9]

[cdli] Kittel, G., Friedrich, G., Bromiley, G. W. (1995). Theological Dictionary of The New Testament (847). Grand Rapids, Mi: W.B. Eerdmans.

[cdlii] Soanes, C., and Stevenson, A. (eds.). (2004). Concise Oxford English Dictionary (11Th Ed.). Oxford: Oxford University Press.

[cdliii] Chesnut, L. J. (2005; 2005). Was The Devil One Time An Angel In Heaven. (Preface) James L. Fleming.

[cdliv] Wright, N. T. (2006). Evil and The Justice of God (8). London: Society for Promoting Christian Knowledge.

[cdlv] Henry, C. F. H. (1999). Vol. 6: God, Revelation, and Authority (283). Wheaton, Ill.: Crossway Books.

[cdlvi] The Eerdmans Dictionary of Early Judaism. 2010 (J. J. Collins D. C. Harlow, Ed.) (615). Grand Rapids, Mi; Cambridge, U.K.: William B. Eerdmans Publishing Company.

[cdlvii] Childress Hatcher, D., A Hitchhikers Guide to Armageddon, (Ch 1, Pros and Cons Of Hitchhiking- Previous Armageddon's (p35 of 71)) ©Copyright 2000, Published by adventures unlimited press.

[cdlviii] Hughes-Wilson, John. The Puppet Masters: Spies, Traitors and The Real Forces Behind World Events. Endeavour Media. (Location 1085.)

[cdlix] Pilch, J, John, A Cultural Handbook to The Bible, (49). Copyright ©2012 John J Pilch. Eerdmans Publishing Co.

[cdlx] Louw, J. P., and Nida, E. A. (1996). Greek-English Lexicon of The New Testament: Based on Semantic Domains (Electronic ed. of The 2nd). New York: United Bible Societies.

[cdlxi] Pilch J. John, A Cultural Handbook to The Bible, (43) ©2012 John J Pilch. Wm B. Eerdmans Publishing Co. <My Inclusion> i.e. Astrology!

[cdlxii] Alden, R. (1999). 1348. In R. L. Harris, G. L. Archer, Jr. and B. K. Waltke (eds.), Theological Wordbook of The Old Testament (Electronic ed.) (572). Chicago: Moody Press.

[cdlxiii] See Horns of Power: Manifestations of the Horned God, edited by, Sorita D' Este.

[cdlxiv] In one other Qumran text this Melkiresha is also named: Chief Angel of Darkness. See p311, (Vermes Below) Vermes, G. (1995). The Dead Sea Scrolls in English (Revised and Extended 4th ed.) (185). Sheffield: Sheffield Academic Press. A. Rules – 16. Curses of Satan and his lot (4Q286-7)

[cdlxv] Tan, P. L. (1996). Encyclopaedia of 7700 Illustrations: Signs of The Times. Garland, Tx: Bible Communications, Inc. '2093. The Most Wicked Man in Edinburgh' - Eugene A. Hessel

[cdlxvi] The Central Character of a Long-Running Daily American Comic Strip, Created by Cartoonist Walt Kelly (1913–1973).

[cdlxvii] Vol. 2: A Dictionary of Christ and The Gospels: Aaron–Zion. 1906 (J. Hastings, J. A. Selbie, J. C. Lambert, Ed.) (569). Edinburgh; New York: Tt Clark; Charles Scribner's Sons.

[cdlxviii] Ibid, (570).

[cdlxix] Dickason, C. F. (1995). Angels: Elect and Evil (122). Chicago, Il: Moody Press.

[cdlxx] Biblical Studies Press. (2006; 2006). The Net Bible First ; Bible. English. Net Bible.; The Net Bible (Zechariah 3:7–8). Biblical Studies Press.

[cdlxxi] The Word *Gan* is the root of the Hebrew word Magen, Meaning 'Shield.' [J. Benner, Genesis, Zen, Quantum Physics, p122]

[cdlxxii] Dictionary of the Apostolic Church (2 Vols.). 1916-1918 (J. Hastings, Ed.). New York: Charles Scribner's Sons. Vol. 1, p293.

[cdlxxiii] Grant, F. W. (1901). The Numerical Bible; being a revised Translation Of The Holy Scriptures With Expository Notes: Arranged, Divided, and Briefly Characterized according to the principles of their numerical structure: Acts to 2 Corinthians (547). Neptune, Nj: Loizeaux Brothers, Inc.

[cdlxxiv] Bamberger, B. J. (2006). Fallen Angels: Soldiers of Satan's Realm (13). Philadelphia, Pa: The Jewish Publication Society.

[cdlxxv] Ibid, (240).

[cdlxxvi] Brannan, R., Penner, K. M., Loken, I., Aubrey, M., and Hoogendyk, I. (Eds.). (2012). The Lexham English Septuagint (Ps 77:49). Bellingham, Wa: Lexham Press.

DECONSTRUCTING ENDTIME DELUSIONS

[cdlxxvii] Harris, W. H., Iii, Ritzema, E., Brannan, R., Mangum, D., Dunham, J., Reimer, J. A., and Wierenga, M. (Eds.). (2012). The Lexham English Bible (Psalms 78:49). Bellingham, Wa: Lexham Press.

[cdlxxviii] Spence-Jones, H. D. M. (Ed.). (1909). Psalms (Vol. 2, P. 127). London; New York: Funk and Wagnalls Company.

[cdlxxix] See Ralph Ellis', Jesus, The Last of the Pharaohs.

[cdlxxx] Www.Sacred-texts.com[15]-Texts.Com/Egy/Eml/Eml31.Htm

[cdlxxxi] Ibid.

[cdlxxxii] The Syriac New Testament: Translated Into English From The Syriac Peshitto Version. 2001 (J. Murdock, Trans.) (Acts 2:14–24). Piscataway, Nj: Gorgias Press.

[cdlxxxiii] Demar, G. (1999). Last Days Madness: Obsession of The Modern Church (Fourth Revised) (143). Powder Springs, Ga: American Vision.

[cdlxxxiv] Ibid. (145).

[cdlxxxv] Matthews, V. H., Chavalas, M. W., and Walton, J. H. (2000). The IVP Bible Background Commentary: Old Testament (Electronic Ed.) (Joe 2:31). Downers Grove, Il: Intervarsity Press.

[cdlxxxvi] Ibid. (Is 53:10).

[cdlxxxvii] Williams, R., Unintelligent Design: Why God Isn't as Smart as She Thinks She Is,Ed. (Pt 1: Proud Ignorance)

[cdlxxxviii] www.wiki.answers.com[16]/Q/What_causes_a_red_moon

[cdlxxxix] The Holy Bible: English Standard Version. 2001 (2 Pe 3:1–2). Wheaton: Standard Bible Society.

[cdxc] Bengel, J. A. (1860). Vol. 2: Gnomon Of The New Testament (M. E. BengelJ. C. F. Steudel, Ed.) (A. R. Fausset, Trans.) (527). Edinburgh: Tt Clark. (Acts 2:17-18). Bengel originally wrote The Gnomon Nt Commentary In 1742 After Twenty Years Labor. It is Today still a treasured New Testament Commentary for New Testament expositors.

---

15. http://www.sacred-texts.com

16. http://www.wiki.answers.com

[cdxci] •The Holy Bible: New Revised Standard Version.

[cdxcii] ÝIbid. (1989). (Je 19:13).

[cdxciii] Chesnut, L. J. (2005; 2005). The Battle of Armageddon. James L. Fleming.

[cdxciv] Heffren, H. C. (2005; 2005). Who is the Antichrist? James L. Fleming.

[cdxcv] Riggle, H. M. (2005; 2005). The Kingdom of God. James L. Fleming.

[cdxcvi] Finamore, S. (2009). God, Order, and Chaos: René Girard and The Apocalypse (xiii). Milton Keynes: Paternoster.

[cdxcvii] Wise, M. O., Abegg, M. G., Jr., and Cook, E. M. (2005). The Dead Sea Scrolls: A New Translation (146). New York: Harperone.

[cdxcviii] Vermes, G. (1995). The Dead Sea Scrolls In English (Revised and Extended 4Th Ed.) (124). Sheffield: Sheffield Academic Press.

[cdxcix] According To Peter D. Goodgame, Author of The Second Coming of The Antichrist. Published By Defence. Copyright © 2012 By Peter Goodgame. www.Redmoonrising.Com[17]

[d] See Ch, xxvii. Who is The Antichrist? – What The Bible Says About Antichrist, In, Heffren, H. C. (2005; 2005). Thine Is The Kingdom. James L. Fleming.

[di] Ibid.

[dii] The Syriac New Testament: Translated Into English From The Syriac Peshitto Version. 2001 (J. Murdock, Trans.) (441). Piscataway, Nj: Gorgias Press. (Jude 16.)

[diii] Clement I, P., Clement I, P., Ignatius, S., Bishop Of Antioch, Polycarp, S., Bishop Of Smyrna, and Lake, K. (1912-13). Vol. 1: The Apostolic Fathers (P. Clement I, S. Ignatius, Bishop Of Antioch, S. Polycarp, Bishop Of Smyrna and K. Lake, Ed.). The Loeb Classical Library (333–335). London; New York: Heinemann; Macmillan.

[div] Peerbolte, B. J. L. (2010). Antichrist. In J. J. Collins and D. C. Harlow (Eds.), The Eerdmans Dictionary Of Early Judaism (J. J. Collins and D. C. Harlow, Ed.) (333). Grand Rapids, Mi; Cambridge, U.K.: William B. Eerdmans Publishing Company.

[dv] Peerbolte, L. J. L. (1999). Antichrist. In K. Van Der Toorn, B. Becking and P. W. Van Der Horst (Eds.), Dictionary Of Deities and Demons In The Bible (K. Van Der

---

17. http://www.Redmoonrising.Com

DECONSTRUCTING ENDTIME DELUSIONS

Toorn, B. Becking and P. W. Van Der Horst, Ed.) (2nd Extensively Rev. Ed.) (62). Leiden; Boston; Köln; Grand Rapids, Mi; Cambridge: Brill; Eerdmans.

[dvi] Heffren, H. C. (2005; 2005). Thine Is The Kingdom. James L. Fleming. Chapter xxvii –Who Is The Antichrist?

[dvii] Ibid.

[dviii] Hays, J. D., Duvall, J. S., and Pate, C. M. (2007). Dictionary Of Biblical Prophecy and End Times (44). Grand Rapids, Mi: Zondervan Publishing House.

[dix] Baigent, M, Racing Toward Armageddon, (48). Harperone Publishers, 2009. Copyright ©2009 By Michael Baigent.

[dx] Cited In, The Myth of The Great Ending, Copyright © 2011 By Joseph M. Felser, Ph.D

[dxi] See Cline, E, Bible and Interpretation At: http://Www.Bibleinterp.Com/Articles/Armageddon. Shtml © 2000-2014 The Bible and Interpretation. All Rights Reserved.

[dxii] The Holy Bible: New Revised Standard Version. 1989 (Da 9:24–27). Nashville: Thomas Nelson Publishers.

[dxiii] Demar, G. (2010). 10 Popular Prophecy Myths Exposed: The Last Days Might Not Be As Near As You Think (93). Powder Springs, Ga: American Vision. 4 Cf. B. S. Childs, Introduction to The Old Testament as Scripture (Philadelphia: Fortress, 1979), 611; D. R. G. Beattie, First Steps in Biblical Criticism (Lanham, Md.: University Press of America, 1988), 90–91.5 Cf. Pfeiffer, Introduction, 773; Montgomery, Daniel, 87. For a further discussion of the identity of the supposed author of author's see, J. E. Goldingay, Daniel, Wbc (Dallas: Word, 1989), 326–29; A. Lacocque, The Book of Daniel (Atlanta: John Knox, 1979), 10–11; W. S. Towner, Daniel, Int (Atlanta: John Knox, 1984), 6–8. J. C. Trever sets forth the unusual hypothesis that the founder of the Qumran community, the 'teacher of righteousness' was the book's author and compiler ("The Book Of Daniel and The Origin of the Qumran Community," Ba 48 [1985]: 89–102).

[dxiv] Miller, S. R. (1994). Vol. 18: Daniel. The New American Commentary (23). Nashville: Broadman and Holman Publishers.

[dxv] Demar, G. (2010). Myths, Lies, and Half-Truths: How Misreading the Bible Neutralizes Christians and Empowers Liberals, Secularists, and Atheists (280–281). Powder Springs, Ga: American Vision.

[dxvi] Gilbert, Derek P. Last Clash of the Titans: The Second Coming of Hercules, Leviathan, and Prophetic War Between Jesus Christ and The Gods of Antiquity (Locations 155-156). Defender Publishing.

[dxvii] www.spiritoferror.org[18]

[dxviii] Parousia is an Ancient Greek word meaning Presence, Arrival, or Official visit.

[dxix] Bushby, T. Chapter Fourteen, p289-90.

[dxx] Cooper, J. C. An Illustrated Encyclopaedia of Traditional Symbols (Locations 70-72). Thames and Hudson Ltd.

[dxxi] Ibid. (p 8-9). Dorling Kindersley Ltd.

[dxxii] Holloway, Richard. A Little History of Religion (Little Histories). Yale University Press. (Location 82.)

[dxxiii] Nongbri, Brent, Before Religion: A History of Modern Concept. Introduction.

[dxxiv] Ibid.

[dxxv] Macgregor, Neil. Living With The Gods: On Beliefs and Peoples (Locations 639-643). Penguin Books Ltd.

[dxxvi] Burkert, W. Ch. 1 p5-6.

[dxxvii] Harari, Yuval Noah. Sapiens: A brief history of Humankind. (p.55) Random House.

[dxxviii] "Lion Man" with Internet search.

[dxxix] MacGregor, Neil. Living with the Gods: On beliefs and peoples (. Loc., 768-779) Penguin books Ltd.

[dxxx] Yudkosky, Eliezer. Rationality:From AI to Zombies. (ed. Loc., 1429-1432) Machine intelligence research institute.

[dxxxi] Paulkovich, M. Beyond the Crusades...

[dxxxii] Celsus (Platonic philosopher), active 180. Arguments of Celsus, Porphyry, and Emperor Julian against the Christians... (ed. Loc 184-186).

---

18. http://www.spiritoferror.org

DECONSTRUCTING ENDTIME DELUSIONS

[dxxxiii] Louis Herbert Gray, George Foot Moore, John Arnott Macculloch. The Mythology of all Races (Locations 66-74). Marshall Jones Company.

[dxxxiv] Ibid. (Locations 94-105)

[dxxxv] Ibid. (Locations 116-135)

[dxxxvi] Barber, Elizabeth Wayland; Barber, Paul T. When They Severed Earth From Sky: How The Human Mind Shapes Myth (Locations 178-184). Princeton University Press.

[dxxxvii] Armstrong, K., A Short History of Myth. (Ch. 2)

[dxxxviii] Thomas L. Thompson, The Mythic Past, (p174)

[dxxxix] Barber, Elizabeth Wayland; Barber, Paul T. When They Severed Earth From Sky: How The Human Mind Shapes Myth (Location 713). Princeton University Press.

[dxl] Dr. Kathryn Mccymond, Ph.D. Chair and Professor In The Dept. of Religious Studies – Georgia State University. See, The Teaching Company, 'Great Mythologies of The World,' Lecture 13: The World's Oldest Myth of Gilgamesh.

[dxli] Barber, Elizabeth Wayland; Barber, Paul T. When They Severed Earth From Sky: How The Human Mind Shapes Myth (Locations 1067-1082). Princeton University Press.

[dxlii] Ibid. (Locations 1138-1144).

[dxliii] Oden, R. A. J. (1992). Myth and Mythology: Mythology. In D. N. Freedman (Ed.), Vol. 4: The Anchor Yale Bible Dictionary (D. N. Freedman, Ed.) (948). New York: Doubleday.

[dxliv] Walton, J. H. (2006). Ancient Near Eastern Thought and The Old Testament: Introducing The Conceptual World Of The Hebrew Bible (43–44). Grand Rapids, Mi: Baker Academic.

[dxlv] Baigent, M, From The Omens Of Babylon: Astrology and Ancient Mesopotamia, (p78). Published by The Penguin Group. Copyright © Michael Baigent, 1994.

[dxlvi] Aveni, A., 'Conversing With The Planets: How Science and Myth Invented The Cosmos', (22-23,24). Copyright © 1992 Anthony Aveni. [Digital Edition]

[dxlvii] Oden, R. A. J. (1992). Myth and Mythology: Mythology. In D. N. Freedman (Ed.), The Anchor Yale Bible Dictionary (Vol. 4, pp.948–949). New York: Doubleday.

[dxlviii] Ibid. Myth and Mythology: Myth in the Old Testament. (Vol. 4, p.960).

[dxlix] Vol. 3: The International Standard Bible Encyclopedia, Revised. 1988 (G. W. Bromiley, Ed.) (455). Wm. B. Eerdmans.

[dl] Collins, J. J. (2000). Eschatologies of Late Antiquity. In (C. A. Evans and S. E. Porter, Eds.) Dictionary of New Testament Background: A Compendium of Contemporary Biblical Scholarship. Downers Grove, Il: Intervarsity Press.

[dli] Achtemeier, P. J., Harper and Row, P., and Society of Biblical Literature. (1985). Harper's Bible Dictionary (1St Ed.) (277). San Francisco: Harper and Row.

[dlii] °Mowinckel, S. He That Cometh, (3-4) ©2005 Wm. B. Eerdmans Pub. Co.

[dliii] •Other Scholars confirm as much. In Messianism Among Jews and Christians, Horbury (Below), Congruently cautions that care should be taken when surveying 'Messianic Passages against over-interpretation. (p8).

[dliv] Wright, N. T. (1992). The New Testament and The People of God (xiv). London: Society For Promoting Christian Knowledge.

[dlv] Fitzmyer, J. A. (2000). The Dead Sea Scrolls and Christian Origins. Studies In The Dead Sea Scrolls and Related Literature (33–34). Grand Rapids, Mi; Cambridge, U.K.: William B. Eerdmans Publishing Company.

[dlvi] Dead Sea Scrolls. 36–37. See also Pfeiffer, C. F. (1969). The Dead Sea Scrolls and The Bible. (p127, Paragraph Vii) Grand Rapids, Mi: Baker Book House; Schiffman, L. H.

[dlvii] Hays, J. D., Duvall, J. S., and Pate, C. M. (2007). Dictionary of Biblical Prophecy and End Times (34). Grand Rapids, Mi: Zondervan Publishing House.

[dlviii] Religion In The Dead Sea Scrolls. 2000 (J. J. Collins and R. A. Kugler, Ed.). Studies in The Dead Sea Scrolls and Related Literature. Grand Rapids, Mi; Cambridge, U.K.: William B. Eerdmans Publishing Company. (Footnote 12, pg115)

[dlix] John Joseph Collins, Ed., John Joseph Collins, Ed., Society of Biblical Literature. (1979). Vol. 14: Semeia. Semeia 14. Apocalypse: The Morphology of a Genre (2). Missoula, Mt: Society Of Biblical Literature. [Mss = Manuscripts]

DECONSTRUCTING ENDTIME DELUSIONS

[dlx] Thompson, T. (2007). The Messiah Myth: The Near Eastern Roots of Jesus and David. (p19) Published by Pimlico. Copyright ©Thomas L Thompson 2005.

[dlxi] Wright, T. (1999). The Millennium Myth (29–30). Louisville, Ky: Westminster John Knox Press.

[dlxii] Malina, B, On The Genre and Message of Revelation: Star Visions and Sky Journeys, (12) Copyright ©1995 By Hendrickson Publishers, Inc.

[dlxiii] Revelation and The End-Times, Dr. Ben Witherington iii. Adobe Digital , (p19.) Copyright 2010 Abingdon Press.

[dlxiv] Titus 2:13.

[dlxv] Wright, T. (1999). The Millennium Myth (18). Louisville, Ky: Westminster John Knox Press.

[dlxvi] Http://En.Wikipedia.Org/Wiki/List_Of_Dates_Predicted_For_Apocalyptic_

[dlxvii] See, New Dawn Magazine – 'Special ', Vol. 10 No.3. Article Enochian Apocalypse, by Donald Tyson, p49.

[dlxviii] The 'Real,' Heavenly name of Satan, according to The Enochian Angels of whom this article speaks.

[dlxix] Ibid, pp49-50.

[dlxx] See Wikipedia Article For Year 0. Http://En.Wikipedia.Org/Wiki/0_(Year)

[dlxxi] Wikipedia: Http://En.Wikipedia.Org/Wiki/Millenarianism

[dlxxii] Hawking, M.G.. Egyptian Mysticism, Ancient Keys to the Paranormal: From the Age of Pharaoh Amenhotep IV (Akhenaten) . Unknown. Kindle Edition.

[dlxxiii] Chapter 1: The Age of Anxiety, p24 of 153.

Don't miss out!

Visit the website below and you can sign up to receive emails whenever Steve Morgan publishes a new book. There's no charge and no obligation.

https://books2read.com/r/B-A-TAKAB-CSZOC

BOOKS 2 READ

Connecting independent readers to independent writers.

Did you love *Deconstructing Endtime Delusions (A study of Christian Endtimes)*? Then you should read *A Standard Religiously Irrelevant Version (S.R.I.V) Twist of Fate Edition*[19] by Steve Morgan!

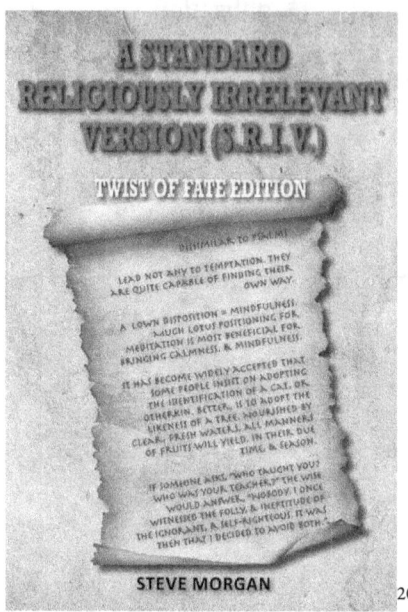

[20]

Satire, hyperbole, lampooning, mockery, taunting, comical, ridiculous. Call the scriptures what you will, just don't call it a holy adytum. A sanctuary of the soul, unless that soul wish to be amused to the point of 'holy' risibility. A gelastic disposition, this should be a mandated staple of all who read, study, or swoon over the scriptures. If one observes the plain translated English text as it has been offered by scholars. Time & again numerously places, & occasions read in the Judaeo-Christian Bible transmogrify, causing a scratching of the head, & quizzical thoughts. This book records several of those thoughts in recognition that much of the world today has forsaken, & forgotten how to laugh at itself. Let alone some praised notional religious anecdotes. This is a storybook offering readers a harmless, & jocose account of several Standard Bible anecdotes

---

19. https://books2read.com/u/bpYkaz
20. https://books2read.com/u/bpYkaz

to help remedy this. Those that are too often read, & believed as only topics of homiletics. Including parodied episodes from Genesis, Exodus, Leviticus, Numbers, Proverbs, Psalms, the book of Esther; the gospel of Matthew, Acts, several epistles, & a reevaluation of Revelation. A Glossary (an A-Z) of unusual English terms, & phrases to assist a reader, & bring to an audience a facetious account of several Bible tales. Also, are parodied versions of several Apocryphal texts, from Apostles Paul, Peter... The Bible, nobody should be able to evade upon observation the root & branch of its ventriloquism, its quisquous bumfuzzling antics.

This Standard Religiously Irrelevant Version is an aniconic motley collection of Judaeo-Christian Bible folktales highlighting several extraordinary modern oddities, beliefs homogenised with the folklore of the Christian religion. Tales that are entertaining & easily relatable to modern people. In celebration of the weirdness of the stories, humanity, & Promethean human ingenuity.

Enjoy this facetious edition of the Bible!

Also by Steve Morgan

A Standard Religiously Irrelevant Version (S.R.I.V) Twist of Fate Edition
Wokeless Dictionary (A Wicked Wordbook)
Deconstructing Endtime Delusions (A study of Christian Endtimes)

About the Author

Born into a Christian family, in 1971, Steve applied himself to an extensive study of Christianity through the 1990's. Leading to a departure from the faith in the mid 2000's. In 2012 Steve was forced into retirement with a disability. Since, his life has grown with several interests emerging. An amateur parrot breeder, amateur Colour Pencil artist, writer, reader & avid lawn Bowler. Is a fan of quality film, documentaries, & intelligent comedy: "Fluffy", & Bill Bailey. He has an ever widening assortment of interests; Current affairs, quirky history, Stoicism, philosophy, & Egyptian History. Never married, he lives alone in regional Victoria, Australia, with his beloved parrots. Interest in paronomasia, & neologisms began in earnest during the worlds longest lockdown in Victoria, Australia during the recent Covid-19 pandemic, 2021. Producing The Standard Religiously Irrelevant Version, a parodied edition of several Christian folklore.

www.ingramcontent.com/pod-product-compliance
Lightning Source LLC
Chambersburg PA
CBHW071933220426
43662CB00009B/896